The University in Your Life

About the Author

Jeffrey Gordon was educated at Northwestern University (B.A. 1969), where he studied philosophy with William Earle, and the University of Colorado (M.A. 1976, Ph.D. 1979), where he continued his studies of existentialism under Hazel Barnes. Since 1978 he has been teaching in the Philosophy Department at Southwest Texas State University, a comprehensive university with 21,000 students set in the Texas hill country. There he has offered courses in existentialism, philosophy of literature, philosophical explorations in film, philosophy of human experience, and metaphysics. His lifelong preoccupation has been with problems relevant to the question of the meaning of life, and his many essays on aspects of this question have appeared in journals throughout the world. Since its inception at SWT in 1986, he has been director of Freshman Seminar.

The University in Your Life

Jeffrey Gordon
Southwest Texas State University

Boston, Massachusetts   Burr Ridge, Illinios   Dubuque, Iowa
Madison, Wisconsin   New York, New York   San Francisco, California   St. Louis, Missouri

McGraw·Hill
A Division of The McGraw·Hill Companies

Book Team

Publisher *L. Bevan O'Callaghan*
Acquisitions Editor *Michael Llwyd Alread*
Managing Editor *John S. L. Holland*
Production Manager *Brenda S. Filley*
Managing Art Editor *Pamela Carley*
Development Coordinator *Alan M. Sturmer*
Editor *Ava Suntoke*
Designer *Charles Vitelli*
Art Editor *Elizabeth L. Hansen*
Permissions Coordinator *Janice M. Ward*
Typesetting Supervisor *Libra Ann Cusack*
Typesetter *Juliana Arbo*
Proofreaders *Diane Barker, Jan Jamilkowski*
Graphics *Shawn Callahan, Lara M. Johnson, Laura Levine*
Marketing Manager *Katie Rose*

President and Chief Executive Officer *Thomas E. Doran*
Vice President of Production and Business Development *Vickie Putman*
Vice President of Sales and Marketing *Bob McLaughlin*
Director of Marketing *John Finn*

The acknowledgment section for this book begins on page vii
and is considered an extension of the copyright page.

Cover Giorgio de Chirico, *The Double Dream of Spring,* 1915
Oil on canvas, 22⅛ × 21⅜″ (56.2 × 54.3 cm)
The Museum of Modern Art, New York. Gift of James Thrall Soby
Photograph © 1995 The Museum of Modern Art, New York.
Cover design *Charles Vitelli*
Research by *Elizabeth L. Hansen*

Library of Congress Catalog Card Number: 94-062138

ISBN 1-56134-237-8

Printed in the United States of America

10 9 8 7 6 5 4 3 2

Sources

HOUSTON A. BAKER. "What Charles Knew," in AN APPLE FOR MY TEACHER, ed. by Louis D. Rubin Jr. Copyright © 1990 by Algonquin Books of Chapel Hill. Reprinted by permission of Algonquin Books of Chapel Hill, a division of Workman Publishing, New York, NY.

IMAMU AMIRI BARAKA. "Poem for Half White College Students," in THE BLACK POETS. Copyright © 1969 by Imamu Amiri Baraka. Reprinted by permission of Sterling Lord Literistic, Inc.

WENDELL BERRY. "The Loss of the University," in HOME ECONOMICS (Berkeley: North Point Press, 1987). Copyright © 1987 by Wendell Berry. Reprinted by permission of North Point Press, a division of Farrar, Straus & Giroux, Inc.

ALLAN BLOOM. "Music and the Soul of Youth," in THE CLOSING OF THE AMERICAN MIND (New York: Simon & Schuster, 1987). Copyright © 1987 by Allan Bloom. Reprinted by permission of Simon & Schuster, Inc.

BLYTHE MCVICKER CLINCHY. "The Development of Thoughtfulness in College Women," in *American Behavioral Sciences.* Copyright © 1989 by Sage Publications, Inc. Reprinted by permission of Sage Publications, Inc.

FRANK CONROY. "Think About It," in *Harper's Magazine,* November 1988. Copyright © 1988 by *Harper's Magazine.* Reprinted by permission of *Harper's Magazine.* All rights reserved.

SUSAN BLAND DAY. "In Defense of Today's Students." Reprinted by permission of the author.

JOAN DIDION. "On Self-Respect," in SLOUCHING TOWARDS BETHLEHEM (New York: Farrar, Straus & Giroux, Inc., 1990). Copyright © 1961, 1968 by Joan Didion. Reprinted by permission of Farrar, Straus & Giroux, Inc.

LOREN EISELEY. "The Badlands and the School," in ALL THE STRANGE HOURS (New York: Charles Scribner's Sons, 1975). Copyright © 1975 by Loren Eiseley. Reprinted by permission of Scribner, an imprint of Simon & Schuster.

RICHARD FEYNMAN. "The Dignified Professor," in SURELY YOU'RE JOKING, MR. FEYNMAN! ADVENTURES OF A CURIOUS CHARACTER (New York: W. W. Norton & Company, Inc., 1984). Copyright © 1985 by Richard P. Feynman and Ralph Leighton. Reprinted by permission of W. W. Norton & Company, Inc.

CHARLES FRANKEL. "A Promise of Lifelong Discontent," in *Swarthmore College Bulletin.* Copyright © 1978 by Charles Frankel. Reprinted by permission of the *Swarthmore College Bulletin.*

MARITA GOLDEN. "Migrations of the Heart," in BEARING WITNESS. Copyright © 1991 by Carol Mann Agency. Reprinted by permission of Carol Mann Agency.

REBECCA GOLDSTEIN. "The Legacy of Raizel Kaidish: A Story," in *New Traditions,* Vol.2. (Spring 1985). Copyright © 1985 by Rebecca Goldstein. Reprinted by permission of the author's agent, HWLA, Inc.

PATRICIA HAMPL. "A Romantic Education," in A ROMANTIC EDUCATION (Boston: Houghton Mifflin Co., 1981). Copyright © 1981 by Patricia Hampl. Reprinted by permission of the Rhonda Weyr Agency, New York.

HARPER'S. "Harper's Index." Copyright © by *Harper's Magazine.* Reprinted by permission of *Harper's Magazine.* All rights reserved.

BELL HOOKS. "Loving Blackness as Political Resistance," in BLACK LOOKS: RACE AND REPRESENTATION (Boston: South End Press, 1992). Copyright © 1992 by South End Press. Reprinted by permission of South End Press.

ROBERT MAYNARD HUTCHINS. "The Autobiography of an Uneducated Man," in EDUCATION FOR FREEDOM (Baton Rouge: Louisiana State University Press, 1943). Copyright © 1943 by Louisiana State University Press. Reprinted by permission of Louisiana State University Press.

JEAN KILBOURNE. "Killing Us Softly: Gender Roles in Advertising," in *Adolescent Medicine: State of the Art Reviews,* October 1993, (Philadelphia: Hanley & Belfus, Inc.). Reprinted by permission of Jean Kilbourne and Hanley & Belfus, Inc.

STANLEY KOBER. "Revolutions Gone Bad," in *Foreign Policy* #91. Copyright © 1993 by Carnegie Endowment for International Peace. Reprinted by permission of Foreign Policy #91.

DAVID LEAVITT. "The Lost Cottage," in FAMILY DANCING (New York: Alfred A. Knopf, Inc., 1984). Copyright © 1983, 1984 by David Leavitt. Reprinted by permission of Alfred A. Knopf, Inc.

DAVID LEAVITT. "The New Lost Generation," in *Esquire,* May 1985. Copyright © 1985 by David Leavitt. Reprinted by permission of Wylie, Aitken & Stone, Inc.

URSULA K. LE GUIN. "The Ones Who Walk Away from Omelas," in THE NORTON ANTHOLOGY OF AMERICAN LITERATURE (New York: W. W. Norton & Company, 1973). Copyright © 1973 by Ursula K. Le Guin; first appeared in *New Dimensions 3.* Reprinted by permission of the author and the author's agent, Virginia Kidd.

MARCUS MABRY. "Living in Two Worlds," in *Newsweek on Campus, Newsweek,* April 1988. Copyright © 1988 by Newsweek, Inc. All rights reserved. Reprinted by permission.

JESSICA TUCHMAN MATHEWS. "Man and Nature: The Future of the Global Environment," in REPRESENTATIVE AMERICAN SPEECHES (New York: H. W. Wilson,

Sources

1990). Reprinted by permission of Jessica Mathews, currently Senior Fellow, Council on Foreign Relations.

JAY MCINERNEY. "Story of My Life," in *Esquire*, July 1, 1987. Copyright © 1987 by Jay McInerney. Reprinted by permission of International Creative Management, Inc.

SUE MILLER. "The Lover of Women," in INVENTING THE ABBOTTS AND OTHER STORIES (New York: HarperCollins Publishers, 1987). Copyright © 1987 by Sue Miller. Reprinted by permission of HarperCollins Publishers, Inc.

EDMUND S. MORGAN. "What Every Yale Freshman Should Know," in *The Saturday Evening Post*. Copyright © 1960 by *The Saturday Evening Post*. Reprinted by permission of *The Saturday Evening Post*.

CHARLES MORRIS. "Ways to Live," in VARIETIES OF HUMAN VALUE. Copyright © 1956 by Charles Morris. Reprinted by permission of the University of Chicago Press.

JACOB NEUSNER. "Grading Your Professors" and "Learning and Growing Up," in HOW TO GRADE YOUR PROFESSORS AND OTHER UNEXPECTED ADVICE (Boston: Beacon Press, 1984). Copyright © 1984 by Jacob Neusner. Reprinted by permission of Jacob Neusner.

ROBERT NOZICK. "The Experience Machine," in ANARCHY, STATE, AND UTOPIA (New York: Basic Books, Inc., 1974). Copyright © 1974 by Basic Books, Inc. Reprinted by permission of Basic Books, Inc., a division of HarperCollins Publishers, Inc.

SHARON OLDS. "Sex Without Love," in THE DEAD AND THE LIVING (New York: Alfred A. Knopf, Inc., 1987). Copyright © 1983 by Sharon Olds. Reprinted by permission of Alfred A. Knopf, Inc.

SHARON OLDS. "On the Subway," in THE GOLD CELL (New York: Alfred A. Knopf, Inc., 1987). Copyright © 1987 by Sharon Olds. Reprinted by permission of Alfred A. Knopf, Inc.

CYNTHIA OZICK. "The Seam of the Snail," in METAPHOR AND MEMORY (New York: Alfred A. Knopf, Inc., 1989). Copyright © 1989 by Cynthia Ozick. Reprinted by permission of Alfred A. Knopf, Inc.

NORMAN PETERSON. "The Training of the Third Pig." Copyright © 1989 by Norman Peterson. Reprinted by permission of Kathryn Peterson.

MARGE PIERCY. "Unlearning to Not Speak," in CIRCLES ON THE WATER (New York: Alfred A. Knopf, Inc., 1982). Copyright © 1982 by Marge Piercy. Reprinted by permission of Alfred A. Knopf, Inc.

PLATO. "The Republic," in THE DIALOGUES OF PLATO, 2nd ed. (Oxford: Clarendon Press, 1875). Translated by Benjamin Jowett.

ADRIENNE RICH. "Claiming an Education," in ON LIES, SECRETS, AND SILENCE: SELECTED PROSE 1966–1978 (New York: W. W. Norton & Company, Inc., 1979). Copyright © 1979 by W. W. Norton & Company, Inc. Reprinted by permission of the author and W. W. Norton & Company, Inc.

RICHARD RODRIGUEZ. "Going Home Again: The New Scholarship Boy." Copyright © 1975 by Richard Rodriguez. Reprinted by permission of Georges Borchardt, Inc. for the author.

RICHARD RORTY. Adapted from "The Opening of American Minds," a speech given in 1989.

BERTRAND RUSSELL. "Impersonal Interests," in THE CONQUEST OF HAPPINESS (New York: Liveright Publishing Corporation, 1930). Copyright © 1930 by Horace Liveright, Inc., renewed 1958 by Bertrand Russell. Reprinted by permission of Liveright Publishing Corporation.

BERTRAND RUSSELL. "What Really Matters," in THE PROBLEMS OF PHILOSOPHY (New York: Oxford University Press, 1912). Reprinted by permission of Oxford University Press.

WILLIAM SAROYAN. "And Man," in DARING YOUNG MAN ON THE FLYING TRAPEZE (London: Faber & Faber, 1958). Copyright © by William Saroyan Foundation. Reprinted by permission of the William Saroyan Foundation.

RICHARD SCHMITT. "Becoming Myself," in PHILOSOPHY NOW (1979). Reprinted by permission of the author.

PEPPER SCHWARTZ. "The Family as a Changed Institution," in *Journal of Family Issues*. Copyright © 1987 by Sage Publications, Inc. Reprinted by permission of Sage Publications, Inc.

DE SELLERS. "Center Stage: Performing on College Tests," "College Thinking," "How to Learn in Class," "How to Study," "The Time of Your Life," "Thoughtfulness and Sexuality," "Walking the Tightrope." Reprinted by permission of the author.

ARLENE SKOLNICK. "The Paradox of Perfection," in *Wilson Quarterly* (Summer 1980). Reprinted by permission of the author.

DANIEL SMITH-ROWSEY. "The Terrible Twenties," in *Newsweek*, June 1991. Copyright © 1991 by Daniel Smith-Rowsey. Reprinted by permission of the author.

SHELBY STEELE. "The Recoloring of Campus Life," in THE CONTENTS OF OUR CHARACTER (New York: St. Martin's Press, Inc., 1990). Copyright © 1990 by Shelby Steele. Reprinted by permission of St. Martin's Press, Inc.

RABINDRANATH TAGORE. "Fruit Gathering," in COLLECTED POEMS AND PLAYS OF RABINDRANATH TAGORE (New York: Collier Books, 1993). Reprinted with permission of Simon & Schuster, Inc.

JORGE VALADEZ. "The Metaphysics of Oppression." Reprinted by permission of the author.

WALT WHITMAN. "Song of Myself," in LEAVES OF GRASS, ed. Emory Holloway (Garden City, NY: Doubleday & Company, Inc., 1926). Copyright © 1926 by Doubleday & Company, Inc.

Photo Credits

ROBERT ARNESON. *Eye on Mrak (Fatal Laff)* from the EGGHEAD SERIES, (1991–1992). Acrylic on bronze. Mrak Hall Mall, UC Davis Campus. Richard L. Nelson Gallery & The Fine Arts Collection; Commissioned by the Campus Art in Public Places Work Group with private funds [94.3] © UC Regents and Nelson Gallery; all rights reserved. Photo credits: Pam Maddock/Todd Hammond.

Imagine for a moment that each one of us takes only a little more care for each hour of his days, that he demands in it a little more of elegance and intensity; then, multiplying all these minute pressures toward the perfecting and deepening of each life by all the others, calculate for yourselves the gigantic enrichment, the fabulous ennobling which this process would create for human society.

—José Ortega y Gasset

Preface

If we cannot relate the encounter with learning in college to the student's experiment in defining an identity, we ignore what is truly essential. If I can show that what we do—that is, learning a subject in a particular way—is critical to what the students want to become, mature and independent women and men, then I will realize the ideal of the college experience.

—Jacob Neusner

I think a liberal education is an education which is designed to raise an individual to the highest level of civic responsibility and personal culture of which he or she is capable. And if you ask, "Yes, but what is a liberal education for?" that's what it's for—that's its end in itself.

—Charles Frankel

Most colleges and universities have some sort of course for first-year students intended to ease the passage from high school (or work world) to postsecondary education. The designers of these programs take an inventory of freshman needs and structure their own courses accordingly. Since the average new student's under- preparation for the rigors of college work (and life) has been a constant of faculty experience for several decades, it is no wonder that most of these "first-year experience" courses focus on the strengthening of study skills, training in time management, instruction in financial budgeting, and so on. The aim of these courses is to help the freshmen become successful students, success being measured by persistence to graduation and maintenance of a respectable grade point average.

We who are responsible for the present text do not sneer at these ambitions. A course that could bring all our incoming students up to speed academically would certainly be accomplishing an important mission. But our text concentrates on a need we believe to be more fundamental than the need for academic savvy. And it is a need which nothing in the student's four or five years' collegiate experience—with the possible exception of the commencement keynote—will acknowledge or address. That is the need for some understanding of the purposes and promise of a college education, the ultimate reasons a student might have for persisting so doggedly and racking up that impressive grade point. This text is designed to help students arrive at clear, informed, and motivating ideas as to why they are in college. It focuses on the question, What in the best case can I hope to achieve as a university student?

If we want real students to populate our classes—which is to say, seekers and not mere grade-hounds—then we'd better try to give them some idea of the nature and value of the quest. How can we be so eager to teach our students the laws of prosody, Kant's twelve categories, and the periodic table without once breaching the primary question, Why should you care to know any of this?

At Southwest Texas State University, a comprehensive school with an undergraduate enrollment of 21,000, we have been experimenting with this text in our Freshman Seminar course for the last nine years. A required course for every incoming freshman, it is taught by faculty from every college of our university (and a number of staff people and administrators). What we've learned is that we can motivate students to become involved in the pursuit of a general education by exploring the connection between university study and these three projects: establishing an identity, navigating effectively amid the challenges of the twenty-first century, and living a fulfilled and humane life. This book is a collection of readings intended to provoke reflection on those three relationships.

The organization of the text parallels these three strategies. Hence, Part One contains essays, reminiscences, short stories, and poems intended to provoke thinking about the questions, "Who am I? Who is my generation? Who do I want to become?" Part Two focuses on the nature of a university and the value of broad learning. The symposium in this section of the text, "The Challenges of the Twenty-first Century," contains contributions by thinkers and artists in six core disciplines. The point of the symposium is to demonstrate to students the value to their future effectiveness of being conversant in these several disciplines. Finally, Part Three is a collection of essays and reminiscences intended to help students connect their reflections on themselves and their goals (Part One) with what they have learned about a university and its disciplines (Part Two). The issue in this section of the text is, "What is the relation between university education and a fulfilled human life?"

Thoughtfulness about what it means to be a college student is not the only requirement for a meaningful university career. In fact, of all such prerequisites, this one is probably the most frequently ignored. But the conviction that underlies this text is that if our primary aim as university educators is to foster critical awareness in our students, then no prerequisite is more fundamental and more important. What better place to begin our students' career in thoughtfulness than through guided meditation on the very meaning of being a student?

Acknowledgments

Putting together a book of this kind is a lot harder than it looks. Selecting material is by far the hardest part of it. Given our parameters, this was, to put it immodestly, extremely difficult. Since the questions at the center of this course cut across disciplines, the book had necessarily to do the same. Sometimes in the process of preparing this text, I wished I were one of those supremely erudite Renaissance men I admire so deeply. The options confronting me were either to become one very quickly or to call on many people for help. The call was responded to promptly and thoughtfully by a good many old and new friends. With much gratitude, I want to acknowledge the research, suggestions, and advice of the following colleagues at Southwest Texas, whom I list in alphabetical order: Woody Anderson of History, Jim Bell of the School of Business, Rebecca Bell-Metereau of English, Ann Blakely of the Reference Library, Ron Brown of History and Honors, Vicki Bynum of History, Francine Carraro of Art, Roger Colombik of Art, Jack Corbett of Political Science, Susan Day of Sociology, Pat Deduck of English, Dennis Dunn of History, Mike Farris of Media Services, Chris Frost of Psychology, Mike Hennessy of English, Elvin Holt of English, Audrey McKinney of Philosophy, Mike Nowicki of Health Professions, Karen Ostlund of Curriculum and Instruction, De Sellers of General Studies, David Watts of Sociology, Tom Williams of Art, Miles Wilson of English, David Ziegler of Biology. Each of these people and many others sent me material to review. The essays and stories collected here were culled from over five hundred that were carefully reviewed. Although I have had much help, complaints about the selections made ought rightfully to be sent to me at the philosophy department.

I am likewise responsible for all the editorial material: introductions to each selection, study questions, suggestions for writing assignments, and so forth. Again, commentary and criticism, friendly and unfriendly, are very welcome.

I am indebted to many people whose efforts helped shape this book. My reviewers Neal A. Hartman of Boston College, Katherine Haley Arneson of Augustana College, and Richard Lawhon of the University of South Carolina made helpful comments and suggestions. The professionals at Brown & Benchmark Publishers, Guilford, listed on the copyright page saw the book through the stages of production.

To all these good people, my heartiest thanks, gratitude that will go stronger still if this text proves to be the mind- and eye-opener I hope it will be.

Jeffrey Gordon

Contents

Contents

▼ PART TWO

What Is a University? 129

What Is the Case for Broad Learning? 187
A Symposium: The Challenges of the
Twenty-First Century

▼ PART THREE

University Education: For What   273
Reasons? To What Ends?

Contents

▼ PART FOUR

Everyday Matters   353

Now I Will You to Be a Bold Swimmer

Walt Whitman

I tramp a perpetual journey, (come listen all!)

My signs are a rain-proof coat, good shoes, and a staff cut from the woods,

No friend of mine takes his ease in my chair,

I have no chair, no church, no philosophy,

I lead no man to a dinner-table, library, exchange,

But each man and each woman of you I lead upon a knoll,

My left hand hooking you round the waist,

My right hand pointing to landscapes of continents and the public road.

Not I, not any one else can travel that road for you,

You must travel it for yourself.

It is not far, it is within reach,

Perhaps you have been on it since you were born and did not know,

Perhaps it is everywhere on water and on land.

Shoulder your duds dear son, and I will mine, and let us hasten forth,

Wonderful cities and free nations we shall fetch as we go.

If you tire, give me both burdens, and rest the chuff of your hand on my hip,

And in due time you shall repay the same service to me,

For after we start we never lie by again.

This day before dawn I ascended a hill and look'd at the crowded heaven,

And I said to my spirit *When we become the enfolders of those orbs, and the pleasure and knowledge of every thing in them, shall we be fill'd and satisfied then?*

And my spirit said *No, we but level that lift to pass and continue beyond.*

You are also asking me questions and I hear you,

I answer that I cannot answer, you must find out for yourself.

Sit a while dear son,

Here are biscuits to eat and here is milk to drink,

But as soon as you sleep and renew yourself in sweet clothes, I kiss you with a good-by kiss and open the gate for your egress hence.

Long enough have you dream'd contemptible dreams,

Now I wash the gum from your eyes,

You must habit yourself to the dazzle of the light and of every moment of your life.

Long have you timidly waded holding a plank by the shore,

Now I will you to be a bold swimmer,

To jump off in the midst of the sea, rise again, nod to me, shout, and laughingly dash with your hair.

Song of Myself

How to Use This Book

Jeffrey Gordon

The purpose of this book is to introduce the university and to invite you to reflect on your reasons for being here. Our hope is that by the end of the term you will have a much fuller understanding of the opportunities that await you and a much firmer sense of bearings than seems possible now.

Perhaps the most important thing you will do here is a lot of growing up. This text is designed to stimulate thinking about the relation between your university education and growing up; that is, coming into your own as a thoughtful, independent person, molding a self, and assuming a share of the task of creating the new world.

The key to this maturation is the development of a strong, critical, independent mind: the ability to release yourself from the grip of this present moment, with all its excitements, confusions, and pressing demands, in order to view it within a larger context. If the most significant aspect of this process is learning to expand your vision, the university ought to be a prime agent in your maturation, for the expansion of awareness is its primary reason for being.

Since the two points of focus of this course are *you* and *the university,* a key aim of the text is to encourage you to step back and take a critical view of each. How can you think deeply about why you are here without some clarification about both *who you are* and *where this is?* The organization of the text is determined by the logic of this question. The articles and stories in Part 1 are intended to provoke reflection on yourself, your values, the generation with whom you have grown up, the process of becoming a self, and the goals you should now set. The pieces in Part 2 direct your thinking toward the kind of place a university is, what is studied here, and why. Having thought about yourself and the nature of a university, you are in a position to consider more deeply *the relation between the two:* what meaning a university education can have in your life; and this is the focus of the essays in Part 3.

The text aims at raising issues very important to your present and future life. But how does one get people to think hard, deeply, searchingly about something? Sometimes with a fresh and daring perspective, sometimes with a jolting piece of information, sometimes with a starkly realistic portrait, sometimes with a direct assault on what they hold dear: in other words, by disturbing their peace. For when people are perfectly content, they have no motive to think. This is why so many readings of this collection are contentious in tone and sharply critical in content. Many of the authors will speak with a candor and honesty almost nonexistent in heavily monitored high school readings, and this may seem remarkable—even perhaps offensive—to you. But note well that this forthright approach reflects an important characteristic of the world you have entered: our principal agenda is truth. If you react with anger to some of these writings, let your emotion serve a worthwhile end: go further and deeper than the author; try to show where he or she has erred.

A word ought to be said about the level of difficulty of these selections, for many will be more complex than what you are used to. As a new college student, you probably expected this. But not being surprised differs from being prepared for the problem. We have tried to help by providing a good deal of auxiliary material: brief introductions at the beginning of each reading, and two kinds of questions at the end. The Questions to Focus Reading are intended to help you identify the key points and central arguments of the selection. Questions for Reflection encourage you to try to get a view of the whole, and to reflect critically on the key themes of the piece. Both are the kinds of queries that occur to very good readers as they read. Our hope is that you will find yourself asking such questions; that you will pick up the habit of active, interrogative reading, which goes after the meaning of the text. Suggestions for writing assignments and journal entries follow almost all the selections, because we believe that the more you engage the themes of these pieces—that is, the more you relate them to your own experience and interweave these ideas with your own—the clearer and more meaningful they will become for you. We believe this process of engagement of new ideas is a necessary ingredient in all significant personal change.

All the pieces were chosen, or expressly written, for your pleasure as well as for your provocation; in some cases more for the first, in others more for the second. But, as with most life projects, many will require some work on your part before you can appreciate the pleasure they bring. If you enjoy browsing through this book, reading much of it that your instructor does not assign, you will be enhancing a talent that marks the best of college students: the talent for *embracing*—for delightedly taking to your heart—*ideas*.

Introduction: The University in Your Life

Jeffrey Gordon

As you have undoubtedly been feeling continuously for some days now, your arrival at college marks a significant passage. Everything in your recent experience has been heralding this fact. If this is your first extended time away from the watchful eyes of your parents, you are probably already tasting the dizzying bounty of your freedom. If you arrived here after many years of work, the passage is no less emphatic, probably exhilarating, perhaps a bit intimidating. Some classes already seem formidable. Like an assault of unwelcome guests, doubts keep rising: Will you be equal to the challenge? If you are living on campus, you've been wrenched from the setting and props upon which, until recently, your firm sense of bearings was based. There is a whole new geography to traverse, new people everywhere. Surrounded by the new, you feel perhaps the stirrings of a new self aborning. And many questions are swarming: Will I be comfortable here? Will I find people I can relate to? Will the workload be overwhelming? Will I be able to manage my money? Am I ready to direct my own life?

In the tumult of these many stresses, one issue is likely to be all but eclipsed. Like all the big questions in our lives, it will seem remote, even abstract in face of the press of immediate demands. That is the question, Why am I here? Why have I chosen this direction for my life rather than another? Why am I a university student?

The purpose of this text is to give you the opportunity to explore in depth precisely that question.

An Overview of This Book

The key objectives of the course for which this text has been designed are to introduce the idea of a university, to ensure that you take time at the point of your embarkment to reflect upon the nature of the institution you are now a part of, and to encourage you to investigate the highest possibilities of a university education, and the ways you can avail yourself of them. We hope you will leave this course with a much clearer sense of what a university has to offer, of what you wish to achieve here, and of what kind of life you want to make.

Some of the questions you will explore in this course are as follows: What is involved in becoming a self, establishing an identity? What are the things in life of the highest value? What is worth pursuing in life? Who is the person you want to become? What is a university education? What are the disciplines of which this university is composed? What is their nature and what is the value of studying them? What are the aims of a university education? What function does a university serve in society? What is the connection between the process of becoming the person you want to be and a university education? What is the relation between education and happiness?

The book you are holding contains essays, stories, and poems intended to provoke reflection on these, and related, questions. Some are daring and audacious, some are passionate, some are wise. I think I can say with confidence (and a little audacity of my own, since I am the author of one of them) that all are thoughtful and worth reading. Most were not written expressly for a readership of freshmen, but even those that were do not patronize freshmen, do not bend over backwards to speak to them on exactly their level. In my view, this is all to the good. An essay that is too easy to understand is probably covering ground already well traveled; it is not advancing your thinking beyond its present comfortable place. And so, many of the articles in this text will seem hard to you on first reading; many will require second and even third readings if you are to get from them whatever insight or original idea the author intended. And almost every one will contain words unfamiliar to you, although in common use among the educated. You at the beginning of your college career need not feel ashamed that you do not know their meaning. But let me extend my personal invitation to you to feel deeply ashamed if you have no interest in *learning* what they mean, or worse, if you are inclined to *complain* of the difficulty of the vocabulary. The reason educated people use "big words" is that the scope of their thought demands it. For the thinker, speaker, and writer, words serve the same role that stroke and color serve for the painter; they are the keys to the **variegations** of reality. The person who refuses to expand his or her vocabulary is like the painter who confines his or her palette to only three colors. He cripples the range of his thought, limits his vision of the panorama. No complaints, then. The works in this book will be failing their aim if they do not expand your reality.

What Does It Mean to Be Educated?

Try to imagine yourself in four or five years. You have received your confirmation of graduation. Letter in hand, you fall back into your favorite chair. Completion of your undergraduate education is another important passage. But what, you begin to ponder, does it signify? What is the measure of your achievement?

There is, of course, a wonderfully straightforward answer, so readily available that even your best-intentioned mentors will often fall prey to its seductive simplicity. That simple answer is the grade-point average you have garnered. Two instances from my recent experience should illustrate its seductive appeal.

Last spring semester, I attended an awards ceremony for graduating seniors. In an effort to personalize the event for award recipients, the organizers of the ceremony chose to announce, with the reading of each name, the grade-point averages achieved by the student, both in their major field and overall. Instead of the monotony of a **litany** of mere names, we had another, more **pernicious**, kind of monotony: Jylvan O'Faolain, 3.7 in her major, 3.65 overall; Raul Valadez, 3.9 in his major, 3.57 overall; John Dickerson, 3.68 in his major, and so forth. After a half hour of this, it was difficult to escape the implication, doubtless unintended, that the most informative statement about the academic careers of each of these honor students (or any students, for that matter) was expressed in those all-important three digits, rounded to the nearest hundredth. How can we faculty complain of the narrow, grade-grubbing focus of our students when we seem to be adopting precisely that criterion ourselves?

Only a few days after this event, I ran into a student I hadn't seen for over a year. After an exchange of greetings, I heard this issue from my mouth: "Well, how have you been doing in school?" He immediately grasped my meaning. "3.32 overall," he said. "Might just have a chance at law school." This was *me*, for God's sake, **tacitly** sending the very message that had so repelled me in the ceremony: All I want to know about you as a student is what grade-point fruit your efforts have borne!

"Well," you might ask, "if not this, what *should* you have been interested in knowing about your former student?" And how happy I am that you have asked this. For in doing so, you go to the heart of this text and give me an opportunity

variegations: diversifications
litany: incantatory recital
pernicious: insidiously harmful
tacitly: in a manner that is not spoken but implied

to wax philosophical on the question at its crux: Just what are the features, the characteristics, the indelible telltale marks of the educated person? What does it mean to be educated?

Let me say at once that I don't think this is the kind of question to which there is one and only one right answer. (A personal bias: all the most interesting questions are like this.) My purpose in addressing this theme is not, therefore, to deliver myself of the one **unassailable** Truth on the matter. My purpose is rather to lose no time in getting to the heart of this course, to offer my own thinking on the matter in order to generate reflection in you, reflection that, with the help of your instructor and the readings in this text, you will develop, deepen, and amplify throughout the term. My purpose is to open the questioning. Once again, then, what does it mean to be educated? If you emerge from this school in four or five years with the highest benefits of a university education, just what will you be like?

A Personal Standpoint

First, you will have a passion to arrive at your own standpoint in the world. You will have had enough experience seeing past your own prejudices and the prejudices of your social class to realize what an obstacle they are to seeing the world with your own fresh and unprotected eyes. You will insist that your own original experience of the world, and not some rote **catechism**, shape your standpoint in it. You will be an independent thinker. And this will not be so easy an attainment as it may sound. The big questions of a human life are difficult and often terrifying; they make us feel most deeply the solitariness of our human condition. For this very reason, there are voices all around us, from the moment of our birth—in our family, our social class, the media—eager to provide ready-made answers, answers intended to save us the trouble of having to live our own life. What is the good life? What activities are most worth pursuing? What is human excellence? Having a limited amount of time on this earth, hence confronted constantly with the necessity of choosing, of determining priorities, all of us deal with these issues, whether explicitly or implicitly. But solutions are on the eager tongue of every adult, who has already made many of his or her most important life decisions and must now persuade him- or herself that they were the right ones. And even more **ubiquitously**, answers are on bright display in the advertisements of any magazine. Long before most of us have any experience of the death of a loved one (for a further example), we have been taught what to think of this and how one is supposed to deal with it. We are protected from the immediacy of this confrontation with death by ritualized attitudes and beliefs that steal from us the originality of our experience. The educated person values his experience too highly to have its significance thus co-opted. He insists on thinking through the superficial answer, on arriving at the one that is *his*.

The Capacity for Disinterested Reflection

Most human thinking is focused on the task, the project immediately at hand. For this reason, the habits of thought and sensibility of most people are determined by their work. It would be foolish to complain about this practical orientation of human thinking, but while recognizing its value, we should also realize that this can be a profoundly limited perspective. So many modern lives have the frantic quality of the ant or the rat, remarkably energetic creatures in desperate thrall to their survival, the scope of their thought constricted to the tiny orbit of the present task. Educated persons, as I see it, are those with a talent for detaching themselves from the strut and fret of our daily agitation, persons capable of viewing their life, man, woman, and world, as sources of interest irrespective of the impact their thinking

unassailable: undeniable

catechism: belief system forced on you by your environment

ubiquitously: in an omnipresent way

6

about them may have on their own personal destinies. Educated persons are capable of *disinterested* reflection; they do not weigh the worth of their thinking in the small scales of practical utility. Moreover, these persons take deep pleasure in the exercise of this capacity.

The demands of our careers and the pace and publicness of modern life make this contemplative attitude more and more difficult to assume. As the poet Wordsworth said of a much less frenzied generation, "The world is too much with us." We are preoccupied with getting on with things, whose numbers and complexity are always increasing. In such a climate, thinking that is not wholly **pragmatic**, that has not an immediate payoff in action, may be felt as an indulgence in irrelevance. But our higher instincts cannot endure a life lived in thrall to worldly pressure. Detached contemplation brings an escape from the constrictions of one's singular history. And so the man condemned to death can sit in his cramped cell and ruminate on the scheme of things and, in doing this, experience a part of himself that is absolutely free of the executioner's chains. Education in the true sense is the cultivation and expansion of that part of ourselves. It is an apprenticeship in meditative thinking, and so it should develop that center of tranquillity that is the source of genuine happiness.

Thoughtfulness

Educated persons should be recognizable by their heightened vitality, their determination to seize hold of life and claim the raw stimuli of experience for the domain of awareness. They have come to realize that the quality of a human life is not determined by the quality of the products with which that life is stuffed, whatever contrary wisdom our consumer economy spends billions to **promulgate**. *The quality of a human life is determined by the quality of mind of the person living it.* A human being is continually transforming the raw chaotic stimuli of perceptions into meaningful episodes, and this transformation is accomplished in thought. This yields a simple equation: the richer the thinking, the richer the life. Of all the wastes we can speak of, surely none is greater than the waste of a human life unlived. There are two ways not to live one's life—to reject new experiences, insisting on the comforts of small routines, and to refuse to *reflect* on one's experiences, discarding each moment with its secret intact. The educated person seizes the moment, examines its nuances, puts it together, uncovers its inner sense. He or she *tracks* their experiences like a person in a fire holding fast to the only thing he owns.

A Mastery of Language

A familiar parody of the educated person has him or her assuming airs, flashing his vocabulary, dropping names, talking in impossibly complex sentences. No doubt there are people who like to show off their intellectual attainments. I doubt any of them is truly educated (in my understanding of the word). But we should very definitely expect the learned to sound different from the unlearned, and this not because they want to impress us, but because they take great care with their words. Having seen the power of ideas to transfigure lives both in history and in their own case, they have a deep respect for the vehicle of their expression: language. Ask a complex question of an educated person. Note the thoughtful pause, the smile of appreciation for the opportunity for reflection; note especially the art and precision in the reply. The mastery of language reminds you of the dancer whose every muscle is within his or her control.

pragmatic: practical
promulgate: set forth publicly

Solicitude toward Humankind

The educated person thinks of him- or herself as a member of the human community and strives to have some positive impact on its condition. The study of history has imbued him or her with a keen sense of the present historical moment, an awareness of the fact that our present lives are part of an ongoing enterprise, the enterprise of human destiny. And a study of literature has taught them to see loneliness, dashed hopes, injustice, cruelty through the eyes of the oppressed and hence to feel a profound sympathy for the human struggle. The combination of these learnings—the sense of **historicity** and the compassion for human suffering—is what implants in the truly educated a deep **solicitude** for the well-being of all people. At this moment in the history of humankind, for better or worse, he or she reasons, the chalice falls to me.

Life as an Adventure of the Spirit

The person in whom higher education has really taken hold should be a very exciting type to be around, and this primarily because he or she regards life as an adventure of the spirit, an endeavor with the highest stakes. Exposure to the finest of human achievements should fill one with a sense of life's possibilities. And once one feels the excitement of this recognition, it is hard for him or her to let loose the question, What is the best life for a human being? Of all the possibilities, what is most worthy of achievement? The educated person will not be happy in endless small talk. If ever he speaks of a need to "kill time," he will be referring to his desire to overcome his hated mortality, not to his having time he cannot fill.

In her very use of time and in the enthusiasm with which she speaks of her plans, the educated person will demonstrate a commitment to excellence in living. But what has such a commitment to do with being educated? It is not that education is a prerequisite for it. Uneducated people can certainly have this degree of commitment. But it seems to me that a meaningful education should have this effect. For it is a question of a person's view of just how worthwhile a business this is, this business of a human life. If our highest conception of human possibilities is drawn from television and popular film, there is, I think, little hope that we will develop this kind of intensity: life will simply not seem sufficiently important. But the educated person has read great literature, has studied world religions, has seen in great art and heard in great music a depth of spiritual striving of which there is no trace in popular culture. He or she has been awakened to human possibilities of a wholly different order, and so life becomes for him or her an adventure, a quest, the drama of the soul in search of a proper object for its infinite passion.

There you have it, one man's view of what higher education should "do" to and for its charges. In this book and in your classroom discussions, you will be introduced to many others. There will be, I'll hazard, at least one element all these views will have in common. All will agree that the best thing we in higher education have to offer our students is neither a body of knowledge, nor a set of skills, nor improved prospects for a successful career. What we have to offer when we don't lose sight of our highest beacons is the promise of a transformation in students, of the quality of their being.

Welcome, dear reader, to your university, to your freshman year, to this humble course. I wish you the talent to use wisely and well this radiant opportunity.

historicity: being situated in history
solicitude: concern

▼ **Vocabulary**

catechism	pernicious	solicitude	unassailable
historicity	pragmatic	tacitly	variegations
litany	promulgate	ubiquitously	

PART ONE

▼

Who Am I?
Who Is My Generation?
Who Shall I Become?

You have made an important decision. You have chosen to go to college. Maybe it doesn't feel as though you *decided* to do this at all. Maybe it was just a matter of taking the next expected step. That doesn't make it any the less a decision. But it may take a while before you really *own* it, before you commit yourself to it. In this course, we hope to help you with that process by examining the connection between a university education and the kind of life you want to live. In this first phase of the course, you will be encouraged to reflect on who you are, what is important to you, who it is you want to become. Later in the term, we will turn to the question of how a university education can connect with your larger life goals.

A word about the format of this text is in order. You will note that there are definitions for glossary words in the margin and questions at the end of each reading. The question to focus the reading are the sorts of questions a very good reader would ask of him- or herself, in order to be assured that he or she was following the key ideas and arguments in the article. If you are already a very attentive, disciplined, and self-demanding reader with a strong vocabulary, you may have little need of these aids. Most entering freshmen in American colleges and universities unfortunately have only a ninth-grade reading proficiency. The aids, especially the questions on the substance of the text, are provided in the hope that they will help you to develop better reading skills. If you are unable to answer a question, you should re-read the text until you can. And, of course, if there are any unfamiliar words that are not defined in the glossary, you must look them up.

1

Becoming Myself

Richard Schmitt

Personal identity is something we must achieve, *asserts Richard Schmitt, philosophy professor at Brown University; it does not come automatically. Here he explains what it means to attain a "genuine self."*

When I was growing up, adult speech was often confusing to me. Particularly, when people said that someone "had not found" him- or herself, I was unsure of what they meant. When I was in my teens, I was sometimes told to "be myself," usually in a critical tone of voice—but I had only the very vaguest idea of what that meant. As an adolescent I faced, so I was told, the task of becoming myself. I was very troubled by being expected to do something that I could not understand. I remember asking a few **tentative** questions but getting little satisfaction.

I never did make any headway with these questions of what is meant to be myself until much later, because I got stuck in the initial logical problems of how anybody could possibly be anything other than him- or herself. If I was not myself, I must be somebody else. But that somebody else would have the same problem that I do, and adults would still scold him and tell him to be himself.

These were the years when change—physical, emotional, and intellectual—was the dominant experience. New emotions went hand in hand with new relationships, with new responsibilities, and hence, with successes and failures of new dimensions. I was changing, but it was *me* that was changing. Somewhere amid all this change, there was an "I," which remained the same, which I always was, however much I was different in other respects. I understood this simple, logical truth that whatever changes in certain respects must, at the same time, remain identical with itself.

Persons, of course, also have a legal identity that is unalterably theirs, whatever else they may do. As soon as they begin to work, young Americans acquire a Social Security number, which remains theirs as long as they live and survives with them, in government records, long after they have died. Legal identities are an embarrassment to some. In detective thrillers, we read about criminals who have undergone painful surgery to alter their fingertips, because fingerprints can identify them without chance of error. But this only serves to conceal their legal identity; it does not change it. Their legal identity remains the same.

There is also an accompanying moral identity that all people have. Everyone is legally—within the statute of limitations—and morally responsible for their past actions. You can't act really badly at one time, and then, ten years later, say that you are a changed person and that, therefore, you can no longer be held responsible for what you did ten years ago.

Even the sinner who has seen the error of his or her ways and has reformed—even to the point of becoming a saint—may be sure that he or she will not repeat past errors; but he or she cannot shed responsibility—and even guilt—for past misdeeds.

As an adolescent, I had difficulties understanding the advice to be myself, because I could not distinguish my logical, legal, and moral identity—with which we are all born and that survives us beyond the grave—from that other self, which

tentative: provisional

12

I shall call the "personal self"—which some persons have and most do not. In fact, at least logically, someone can lack a personal self only if they are self-identical in these other ways. Thus, the first step in solving my childish confusion was to draw a distinction between myself as logically, legally, and morally self-identical, and myself as a person. The personal self is a much richer concept than these others. To have such a self, much more is required than logical, legal, or moral self-identity, and hence, there are many ways in which one can fall short of attaining such a personal self.

Are there examples of persons who are genuinely themselves? Let us not talk about Jesus, Buddha, or Albert Schweitzer; we do not know them, and they are too exceptional. But, on the other hand, **alienation** is a problem faced by everyone, not only by the exceptional. Everyone is, in their own way, struggling to become a person in the fullest sense. What does it mean to be a genuine person for ordinary people like you and me? Everyone has some image of what full self-identity is like. Who do you think of as being as close to being fully themselves as anybody you have ever met? I can recall two people like that.

The first was Levi, a woodsman in the Adirondacks. One summer I watched him build a monumental entrance arch to a summer camp out of the huge pines growing all around. The only tool he used was a two-headed axe, with which he felled, trimmed, and shaped the trees just as he wanted them. He handled that axe with almost magical precision. We talked some, but he was not much given to conversation; mostly, I just stood and watched him. He was a master at his craft and was at home in the woods, not only because he knew them but also because he was safe in them; he had the skills necessary to live well under those tall pines and by the sides of those many lakes. In short, he had mastered his world. Mastery is not domination, not the use of force, and not violation to get what one wants; but rather, mastery rests on the creation of a harmony with the world that is mastered—a harmony that flows from and that breeds a harmony of the soul.

The other person, a woman named Ann, whom I met in Maine a few summers later, had the same sort of mastery, but unlike Levi, she liked to talk and was not alone. I was young then, and married, but not happily. One day, my wife and I went canoeing, which I had never done before, and Ann drove us to the banks of the Penobscot River. She had lived her life with her eyes open, and she had learned a good deal. She could see, and she saw that my wife and I had launched our marriage as clumsily as we were launching our canoe. She gave us some hints about stashing the gear in the canoe and told us about her own life and marriage, without intruding upon or crowding us. She talked, without any anxiety, about reaching us, because she wanted to help, and she was not trying to meet any needs of her own in doing so. She was the master of her own life, and she knew what had made a good marriage for her. She also understood how little one person can learn from another, and she knew how to talk to others in such a way as to be helpful to them. She radiated a quiet assurance. In her own world, she knew what she was doing, and she was therefore completely at home in it. If she had felt exiled in her younger years, she was now at home. She was strong, and she knew it.

From those two people I learned much of what it means to be oneself. Both had chosen a way of life that seemed particularly suited to them. I don't know whether, at any time, they felt it necessary to make an explicit choice to become a woodsman or to live in a small town in Maine. But both had chosen to acquire the many skills it took to live well in their respective worlds. Ann had chosen to be married, and she was very serious about it and had given much thought to its difficulties and to their solutions. No doubt, she had fought about many of them. Thus, in becoming themselves, they had learned to face the dangers the world presented and had gained the calm confidence that so impressed me: little could occur for which they could not find remedies. They were free from the anxieties

alienation: estrangement

13

that torment the alienated; from the indecisiveness; from the sudden, panic-stricken question "What if . . . ?" and from the constant reexamination of decisions, once they have been made, the ever-repeated "Perhaps I should have . . ." They saw their environment with clear eyes, their vision unclouded by such anxieties or by their own unmet needs. Ann could, therefore, see the causes of my difficulties and address them helpfully.

To have a self, then, is to be someone in a world for which one has taken some degree of responsibility, by learning to master it, if not create it. It is to be a person who knows his or her strengths and who can stand calmly by his or her decisions, once they have been made. The lives of such people have content and meaning, because they stand for something. Typically, the alienated lack conviction and complain that the world no longer holds causes to which they can dedicate themselves. But the world, alone, is not at fault. Those who have a firm self-identity take firm stands, although more often than not, they do so **unobtrusively** and become demonstrative only when forced to do so.

While we are all born with logical, legal, and moral identities, our personal selves are only slowly developed. Every child must grow up to be an adult; every young person must grow into middle age; and every adult must ultimately confront declining powers and, eventually, death. This is, once again, universal human destiny that no one can escape. But the common experience we all share in the present age, which is expressed frequently in contemporary novels, plays, and books on sociology and psychology, attests to this fact: the attainment of a genuine self is virtually impossible in our society, and that of full selfhood is extremely rare. This is the insight we express by saying that we are alienated.

A few years ago, I was teaching a course on existentialism, in which the meaning of human life was one of the major topics. One of the students, Tom, came around occasionally to talk, **ostensibly** about the course, but really about the questions it raised about his own life. His life, he declared, was without meaning. Nothing he did or might do made the least bit of difference to him.

We began to talk. I asked some questions. What was it like for him to be in school? He was a freshman, and he was bored. A good deal of his talk about the meaninglessness of life was, more precisely, a reflection of his **disenchantment** with college. He had come, expecting to be excited, to find new worlds opening up to him, and instead, he was lonely and could barely get himself out of bed in the morning, or more accurately, around lunchtime. We talked some more. Why not quit school? His father would not hear of it, and that was that.

It seemed to me that, with that revelation, we had arrived at the center of his complaint: he did not particularly want to be in school; it had not really been his idea to begin with, and it certainly was not his decision to stay there. On the other hand, it also became clear that, regardless of his father's wishes, he had no clear idea of what he would like to do if he were not a student.

In this example, we see many of the symptoms of alienation from the self, and meaninglessness is by no means the most important among them. Central to Tom's experience was his sense that his life was not his own. This means that he did not like what he was doing; that he felt that he had no choice about whether or not to continue being where he was; and finally, that, if he had more freedom, he would not really know what to do with it. His immediate conflict pitted him against his father, who wanted him to go to college and then on to law school and into a successful career in law. He did not know whether or not that should be his course.

Lack of self presents itself here as a lack of a settled social role. His sense of insecurity sprang from his inability to decide who he wanted to be—a college graduate and lawyer, or someone else. Once that choice had been made, he would have found himself and would have been well on his way toward becoming a person in his own right.

unobtrusively: in a nonaggressive way

ostensibly: appearing to be such

disenchantment: loss of an illusion about something

14

Without doubt, the making of such occupational choices, as well as the corresponding decisions many young adults make about marriage and children, do provide a greatly strengthened sense of self. I can well remember the great sense of relief I felt when I finally emerged from graduate school—by that time almost thirty years old and having spent most of my life as a student. For the first time, I had some money of my own that was not earmarked for further education. Most important, I had, for the first time, a clear identity of my own: I was a teacher; I had some authority by virtue of both my position and my expertise; and I even had some power over students, who were still in the condition I had labored under for so many years, that of being dependent on others—parents and school for money and teachers for instruction, help, and grades. While being a student is an identity of sorts, it lacks the central ingredient of a self, a certain degree of self-determination.

The decision to adopt a certain career, the first job, marriage, moving into one's first house—all of these are powerful experiences that help provide gains in self-identity. They are important stages in the process of becoming somebody, a person in one's own right who has a recognized position in the world and who is known by more than his or her legal identity. It is, therefore, not surprising that someone is said to have "found him or herself," or is said to have finally "discovered who he or she wants to be" when they have made career choices, taken a job, or settled in a nuclear relationship intended to last a long time. Self-identity is here defined implicitly as occupation, marital status, or social position.

But a definite identity requires more than just the creation of a settled way of life. Everything depends on how the person came to be settled, whether his or her permanence flowed from well-considered choices or from unthinking imitation. Was the present way of life embraced with open eyes, or was it a refuge from a threatening world or [was it embraced] because of the anxiety of making independent life choices for which he or she must take responsibility?

Persons must, in time, decide many things about themselves if they are to have a genuine identity. But not all ways of settling these matters will succeed in creating a genuine self. Conformists create a sham identity, stuck together more or less **haphazardly**. Character and personality are not really theirs; it is something that they have put on, the way one puts on a suit of clothes, and that they can shed just as easily. Putting on a monkey suit does not make one a monkey. It takes more than a facade to make an identity. Social roles are important ingredients in one's identity, but only if they have been genuinely **assimilated**, not merely adopted as a front.

Without a settled character, a person has no identity. To be someone is to be a public person, in some respects, because one does certain things, and does them in certain ways. One can be counted on to take certain stands and to be visible in a variety of roles: identities exist in public space. Identity is one's own only to the extent that one has developed it oneself. My identity is genuine to the extent that it is mine, because I made it what it is.

Identities are therefore made, not found. One is not alienated because one has failed to find an identity. People never just fail to find themselves: they are prevented or prevent themselves from creating an identity for themselves. Identities do not lie around to be picked up as dimes off the sidewalk if you are looking for them and it is your lucky day; one makes oneself be a definite person only if conditions allow one that much space and creativity.

haphazardly: without plan or order

assimilated: to take in and make part of oneself

▼ Questions to Focus Reading

1. When he was in his teens, adults sometimes told him to "be yourself." What was young Schmitt's problem with this directive?

15

2. Schmitt begins his examination of the concept of becoming a self by setting out several different senses of self. He begins with a minimal or "logical" sense of self-identity. What does he have in mind by each of these senses?

3. What was Schmitt's first step in resolving his confusion over the idea of becoming a self? What do you think Schmitt had in mind by the "personal self"?

4. What does Schmitt mean when he writes of "mastery of one's world"?

5. In what respects is the woodsman, Levi, a "genuine person," in Schmitt's view?

6. Which of Ann's qualities convince Schmitt that she has achieved a genuine self? To what does Schmitt attribute Ann's ability to see so clearly the nature of his situation and to address his problem so helpfully?

7. What does it mean, in Schmitt's view, to have a genuine self? What do you think Schmitt means when he says that the lives of genuine persons have "content and meaning"?

8. In what respects does Schmitt's student, Tom, exemplify alienation from self?

9. Settling down, according to Schmitt, is not enough to give one a definite identity. Why not?

10. "Identities exist in public space," Schmitt writes. What does he mean?

11. "Identities are made, not found." Explain what Schmitt means by this.

▼ Questions for Reflection

1. What is Schmitt's conception of a genuine self? In what respects do Levi and Ann illustrate what he has in mind?

2. Schmitt contrasts the genuine self with an alienated self. What does he have in mind in the latter case?

3. Schmitt writes that choice of career, marriage, and social position are important aspects of self-identity. But none of these assures a genuine identity. Why not, in Schmitt's view? Do you think he is right?

4. What is your conception of a genuine self?

▼ Discussion

1. What is Schmitt's conception of a genuine self? In what respects do Levi and Ann illustrate what he has in mind?

2. Schmitt contrasts the genuine self with an alienated self. What does he have in mind in the latter case?

3. Schmitt writes that choice of career, marriage, and social position are important aspects of self-identity. But none of these assures a genuine identity. Why not, in Schmitt's view? Do you think he is right?

4. What is your conception of a genuine self?

5. "The attainment of a genuine self is virtually impossible in our society, and that of full selfhood is extremely rare." What features of our society do you suppose Schmitt has in mind? Do you agree with him? Why or why not?

6. Do you think there are ways in which your university experience will help you to create a "genuine self"? If so, specify these ways.

▼ Writing Assignments

1. Write an essay about a person in your experience who struck you as having attained a genuine self. Be sure to specify the characteristics of this person that lead you to think of him or her in this way.

2. Do you agree with Schmitt about the difficulty of creating a genuine self in our society? If so, write an essay in which you try to reach some understanding of the obstacles to genuine selfhood that our society presents.

3. Write about how your university experience can help you to create a genuine self.

4. Write a description of a person whom you have known, who seems to you to be alienated from him- or herself. Be sure to specify the characteristics of this person that lead you to believe this.

▼ Journal Entry

1. Are you a genuine self according to Schmitt's criteria? Explain why you answer as you do.

▼ Vocabulary

alienation	disenchantment	ostensibly	unobtrusively
assimilated	haphazardly	tentative	

2

▼

On Self-Respect

Joan Didion

"However long we postpone it, we eventually lie down alone in that notoriously uncomfortable bed, the one we make ourselves. Whether or not we sleep in it depends, of course, on whether or not we respect ourselves." Joan Didion is a novelist, essayist, and screenwriter.

Once, in a dry season, I wrote in large letters across two pages of a notebook that innocence ends when one is stripped of the delusion that one likes oneself. Although now, some years later, I marvel that a mind on the outs with itself should have nonetheless made painstaking record of its every tremor, I recall with embarrassing clarity the flavor of those particular ashes. It was a matter of misplaced self-respect.

I had not been elected to Phi Beta Kappa.[1] This failure could scarcely have been more predictable or less **ambiguous** (I simply did not have the grades), but I was unnerved by it; I had somehow thought myself a kind of academic Raskolnikov, curiously exempt from the cause-effect relationships which hampered others.[2] Although even the humorless nineteen-year-old that I was must have recognized that the situation lacked real tragic stature, the day that I did not make Phi Beta Kappa nonetheless marked the end of something, and innocence may well be the word for it. I lost the conviction that lights would always turn green for me, the pleasant certainty that those rather passive virtues which had won me approval as a child automatically guaranteed me not only Phi Beta Kappa keys but happiness, honor, and the love of a good man; lost a certain touching faith in the totem power of good manners, clean hair, and proven competence on the Stanford-Binet scale.[3] To such doubtful **amulets** had my self-respect been pinned, and I faced myself that day with the nonplussed apprehension of someone who has come across a vampire and has no crucifix at hand.

Although to be driven back upon oneself is an uneasy affair at best, rather like trying to cross a border with borrowed credentials, it seems to me now the one condition necessary to the beginnings of real self-respect. Most of our **platitudes** notwithstanding, self-deception remains the most difficult deception. The tricks that work on others count for nothing in that very well-lit back alley where one keeps **assignations** with oneself: no winning smiles will do here, no prettily drawn lists of good intentions. One shuffles flashily but in vain through one's marked cards—the kindness done for the wrong reason, the apparent triumph which involved no real effort, the seemingly heroic act into which one had been shamed. The dismal fact is that self-respect has nothing to do with the approval of others— who are, after all, deceived easily enough; has nothing to do with reputation, which, as Rhett Butler told Scarlett O'Hara, is something people with courage can do without.[4]

To do without self-respect, on the other hand, is to be an unwilling audience of one to an **interminable** documentary that details one's failings, both real and imagined, with fresh footage spliced in for every screening. *There's the glass you broke in anger, there's the hurt on X's face; watch now, this next scene, the night Y came back from Houston, see how you muff this one.* To live without self-respect is to lie awake some night, beyond the reach of warm milk, phenobarbital, and

ambiguous: uncertain; vague

amulets: a charm or talisman used to ward off evil spirits

platitudes: cliché

assignations: appointment

interminable: having no end in sight

the sleeping hand on the coverlet, counting up the sins of commission and omission, the trusts betrayed, the promises subtly broken, the gifts **irrevocably** wasted through sloth or cowardice or carelessness. However long we postpone it, we eventually lie down alone in that notoriously uncomfortable bed, the one we make ourselves. Whether or not we sleep in it depends, of course, on whether or not we respect ourselves.

To protest that some fairly improbable people, some people who *could not possibly respect themselves,* seem to sleep easily enough is to miss the point entirely, as surely as those people miss it who think that self-respect has necessarily to do with not having safety pins in one's underwear. There is a common superstition that "self-respect" is a kind of charm against snakes, something that keeps those who have it locked in some unblighted Eden, out of strange beds, **ambivalent** conversations, and trouble in general. It does not at all. It has nothing to do with the face of things, but concerns instead a separate peace, a private reconciliation. Although the careless, suicidal Julian English in *Appointment in Samarra* and the careless, incurably dishonest Jordan Baker in *The Great Gatsby* seem equally improbable candidates for self-respect, Jordan Baker had it, Julian English did not.[5] With that genius for accommodation more often seen in women than in men, Jordan took her own measure, made her own peace, avoided threats to that peace: "I hate careless people," she told Nick Carraway. "It takes two to make an accident."

Like Jordan Baker, people with self-respect have the courage of their mistakes. They know the price of things. If they choose to commit adultery, they do not then go running, in an access of bad conscience, to receive **absolution** from the wronged parties; nor do they complain unduly of the unfairness, the underserved embarrassment, of being named co-respondent. In brief, people with self-respect exhibit a certain toughness, a kind of moral nerve; they display what was once called *character,* a quality which, although approved in the abstract, sometimes loses ground to other, more instantly negotiable virtues. The measure of its slipping prestige is that one tends to think of it only in connection with homely children and United States senators who have been defeated, preferably in the primary, for reelection. Nonetheless, character—the willingness to accept responsibility for one's own life—is the source from which self-respect springs.

Self-respect is something that our grandparents, whether or not they had it, knew all about. They had instilled in them, young, a certain discipline, the sense that one lives by doing things one does not particularly want to do, by putting fears and doubts to one side, by weighing immediate comforts against the possibility of larger, even **intangible**, comforts. It seemed to the nineteenth century admirable, but not remarkable, that Chinese Gordon put on a clean white suit and held Khartoum against the Mahdi;[6] it did not seem unjust that the way to free land in California involved death and difficulty and dirt. In a diary kept during the winter of 1846, an emigrating twelve-year-old named Narcissa Cornwall noted coolly: "Father was busy reading and did not notice that the house was being filled with strange Indians until Mother spoke about it." Even lacking any clue as to what Mother said, one can scarcely fail to be impressed by the entire incident: the father reading, the Indians filing in, the mother choosing the words that would not alarm, the child duly recording the event and noting further that those particular Indians were not, "fortunately for us," hostile. Indians were simply part of the *donnée.*[7]

In one guise or another, Indians always are. Again, it is a question of recognizing that anything worth having has its price. People who respect themselves are willing to accept the risk that the Indians will be hostile, that the venture will go bankrupt, that the **liaison** may not turn out to be one in which *every day is a holiday because you're married to me.* They are willing to invest something of themselves; they may not play at all, but when they do play, they know the odds.

That kind of self-respect is a discipline, a habit of mind that can never be faked but can be developed, trained, coaxed forth. It was once suggested to me

irrevocably: impossible to alter
ambivalent: conflicting
absolution: forgiveness
intangible: insubstantial or immaterial
liaison: relationship

that, as an antidote to crying, I put my head in a paper bag. As it happens, there is a sound physiological reason, something to do with oxygen, for doing exactly that, but the psychological effect alone is incalculable: it is difficult in the extreme to continue fancying oneself Cathy in *Wuthering Heights* with one's head in a Food Fair bag.[8] There is a similar case for all the small disciplines, unimportant in themselves; imagine maintaining any kind of swoon, **commiserative** or carnal, in a cold shower.

But those small disciplines are valuable only insofar as they represent larger ones. To say that Waterloo was won on the playing fields of Eton is not to say that Napoleon might have been saved by a crash program in cricket;[9] to give formal dinners in the rain forest would be pointless did not the candlelight flickering on the liana call forth deeper, stronger disciplines, values instilled long before. It is a kind of ritual, helping us to remember who and what we are. In order to remember it, one must have known it.

To have that sense of one's **intrinsic** worth which constitutes self-respect is potentially to have everything: the ability to discriminate, to love and to remain indifferent. To lack it is to be locked within oneself, **paradoxically** incapable of either love or indifference. If we do not respect ourselves, we are on the one hand forced to despise those who have so few resources as to consort with us, so little perception as to remain blind to our fatal weaknesses. On the other, we are peculiarly in thrall to everyone we see, curiously determined to live out—since our self-image is **untenable**—their false notions of us. We flatter ourselves by thinking this compulsion to please others an attractive trait: a gist for imaginative empathy, evidence of our willingness to give. *Of course* I will play Francesca to your Paolo, Helen Keller to anyone's Annie Sullivan: no expectation is too misplaced, no role too **ludicrous**.[10] At the mercy of those we cannot but hold in contempt, we play roles doomed to failure before they are begun, each defeat generating fresh despair at the urgency of divining and meeting the next demand made upon us.

It is the phenomenon sometimes called "alienation from self." In its advanced stages, we no longer answer the telephone, because someone might want something; that we could say *no* without drowning in self-reproach is an idea alien to this game. Every encounter demands too much, tears the nerves, drains the will, and the **specter** of something as small as an unanswered letter arouses such disproportionate guilt that answering it becomes out of the question. To assign unanswered letters their proper weight, to free us from expectations of others, to give us back to ourselves—there lies the great, the singular power of self-respect. Without it, one eventually discovers the final turn of the screw: one runs away to find oneself, and finds no one at home.

commiserative: sympathetic or sorrowful

intrinsic: inmost, inherent

paradoxically: in a seemingly contradictory way

untenable: undefendable

ludicrous: laughable

specter: ghost

▼ Endnotes

1. Phi Beta Kappa is an honorary society of scholars in the arts and humanities.
2. Raskolnikov is the rebel against morality in *Crime and Punishment,* by Russian novelist Fyodor Dostoevsky (1821–1881).
3. The Stanford-Binet is an IQ test.
4. Rhett Butler and Scarlett O'Hara are characters in Margaret Mitchell's novel, *Gone with the Wind,* which was made into an immensely successful film in 1939.
5. *Appointment in Samarra* is a novel by American author John O'Hara (1905–1970); *The Great Gatsby,* a novel by American writer F. Scott Fitzgerald (1896–1940).
6. Charles George Gordon (1833–1885) was the British general who led the defense of the Sudanese city of Khartoum against a siege of Muslim forces under the leadership of Mohammed Ahmed, the self-proclaimed "Mahdi"

(messiah). Despite the absence of military support from his superiors, Gordon held Khartoum for ten months before the city fell and he was killed.

7. *donnée:* the given
8. Cathy is the beautiful romantic heroine in *Wuthering Heights* by English novelist Emily Brontë (1818–1848).
9. Napoleon was defeated at Waterloo, Belgium, in 1815 by British armies led by officers educated at Eton, a boarding school for the upper class. Cricket and other sports were part of a curriculum aimed at building character.
10. Francesca and Paolo are the lustful lovers punished in *The Inferno,* an allegorical poem by Italian poet Dante (1265–1321); Annie Sullivan was the devoted teacher of the deaf and blind American lecturer Helen Keller (1880–1968).

▼ Questions to Focus Reading

1. Why does Didion call her reaction to not having been elected to Phi Beta Kappa a case of "misplaced self-respect"?
2. In what respect did this experience mark the "end of innocence" for Didion?
3. "Self-respect has nothing to do with the face of things, but concerns instead a separate peace, a private reconciliation." What does Didion mean by this?
4. How does Didion explain what it means to have "the courage of one's mistakes"?
5. In what ways does the diary entry about the Indians illustrate what Didion has in mind by "self-respect"?
6. Didion suggests that one can be trained to have self-respect, that it can be "coaxed forth." How?
7. "To assign unanswered letters their proper weight, to free us from the expectations of others, to give us back to ourselves—there lies the great, the singular power of self-respect." What does she mean by this?
8. What is the ultimate price for the lack of self-respect, as Didion sees it?

▼ Questions for Reflection

1. Didion doesn't define the concept of self-respect in any one place, but develops her conception of it throughout her essay. What are some of the key characteristics of self-respect as she presents it?
2. Being "driven back upon oneself" is, Didion writes, the necessary condition to the beginning of self-respect. What do you think she means by this? Do you think she is right?
3. How does Didion define "character"? How would you define it? Do you agree that character has suffered "slipping prestige"?
4. To lack self-respect is to be "locked within oneself," Didion writes. What do you think she means?
5. The person without self-respect is alienated, Didion tells us. In what sense? Do you think she is right about this?

▼ Discussion

1. What is self-respect, according to Didion? Why is it, in her view, so essential to living? What is it like, according to Didion, to live without it?
2. What does Didion mean by the concept of "character"? What do you mean by it?
3. What opportunities does your life at the university offer for the development of self-respect?

4. Do you think Didion and Schmitt (Reading 1) have the same thing in mind in their respective conceptions of "self-alienation"?

▼ Writing Assignments

1. Didion opens her essay with an account of her reaction to her failure to be elected to Phi Beta Kappa. She calls this a case of "misplaced self-respect." Why does she think of it that way? If you have experienced similar instances of misplaced self-respect, describe one or two in detail and explain why you are calling them this.
2. Have you ever experienced a serious decline in self-respect? In order to get a focus on the importance of self-respect to living a human life, describe in detail the circumstances that led to this decline and the feelings of the decline itself.
3. Didion thinks we can adopt small disciplines to develop self-respect. If you agree with this, present a plan of action for training in self-respect, one that you have already put into action successfully or think you can adopt.
4. Describe an experience that helped you to develop self-respect.

▼ Journal Entry

1. What aspects of your character provide the bulwarks of your self-respect? What aspects present the gravest challenges to your self-respect?

▼ Vocabulary

absolution	assignation	intrinsic	paradoxically
ambiguous	commiserative	irrevocably	platitude
ambivalent	intangible	liaison	specter
amulets	interminable	ludicrous	untenable

3

On Excellence

Cynthia Ozick

Cynthia Ozick is the author of many novels, essays, and short stories. Here she reflects on her own identity in relation to her mother, on the strong contrast between her mother and herself, and on an equally striking similarity.

In my Depression childhood, whenever I had a new dress, my cousin Sarah would get suspicious. The nicer the dress was, and especially the more expensive it looked, the more suspicious she would get. Finally she would lift the hem and check the seams. This was to see if the dress had been bought or if my mother had sewed it. Sarah could always tell. My mother's sewing had elegant outsides, but there was something catch-as-catch-can about the insides. Sarah's sewing, by contrast, was as **impeccably** finished inside as out; not one stray thread dangled.

My uncle Jake built **meticulous** grandfather clocks out of rosewood; he was a perfectionist, and sent to England for the clockworks. My mother built serviceable radiator covers and a serviceable cabinet, with hinged doors, for the pantry. She built a pair of bookcases for the living room. Once, after I was grown and in a house of my own, she fixed the sewer pipe. She painted ceilings, and also landscapes; she reupholstered chairs. One summer she planted a whole yard of tall corn. She thought herself capable of doing anything, and did everything she imagined. But nothing was perfect. There was always some clear flaw, never visible head-on. You had to look underneath where the seams were. The corn thrived, though not in rows. The stalks elbowed one another like gossips in a dense little village.

"Miss Brrrrooobaker," my mother used to mock, rolling her Russian *r*s, whenever I crossed a *t* she had left uncrossed, or corrected a word she had misspelled, or became impatient with a *v* that had tangled itself up with a *w* in her speech. ("Vvventriloquist," I would say. "Vvventriloquist," she would obediently repeat. And the next time it would come out "wiolinist.") Miss Brubaker was my high school English teacher, and my mother invoked her name as an emblem of raging **finical** obsession. "Miss Brrrrooobaker," my mother's voice hoots at me down the years, as I go on casting and recasting sentences in a tiny handwriting on **monomaniacally** uniform paper. The loops of my mother's handwriting—it was the Palmer Method—were as big as hoops, spilling generous splashy **ebullience**. She could pull off, at five minutes' notice, a satisfying dinner for 10 concocted out of nothing more than originality and **panache**. But the napkin would be folded a little off-center, and the spoon might be on the wrong side of the knife. She was an optimist who ignored **trifles**; for her, God was not in the details but in the intent. And all these **culinary** and agricultural **efflorescences** were extracurricular, accomplished in the crevices and niches of a 14-hour business day. When she scribbled out her family memoirs, in heaps of dog-eared notebooks, or on the backs of old bills, or on the margins of last year's calendar, I would resist typing them; in the speed of the chase she often omitted words like "the," "and," "will." The same flashing and bountiful hand fashioned and fired ceramic pots, and painted brilliant autumn views and vases of imaginary flowers and ferns, and decorated

impeccably: flawlessly

meticulous: done with extreme care

finical: extremely accurate or exact

monomaniacally: with excessive care given to a single object

ebullience: enthusiasm and liveliness

panache: flamboyant style

trifles: items of little value

culinary: referring to cookery

efflorescences: development; blossoming

23

ordinary Woolworth platters with lavish enameled gardens. But bits of the painted petals would chip away.

Lavish: my mother was as lavish as nature. She woke early and saturated the hours with work and inventiveness, and read late into the night. She was all **profusion**, abundance, fabrication. Angry at her children, she would run after us whirling the cord of the electric iron, like a lasso or a whip; but she never caught us. When, in the seventh grade, I was afraid of failing the Music Appreciation final exam because I could not tell the difference between "To a Wild Rose" and "Barcarolle," she got the idea of sending me to school with a gauze sling rigged up on my writing arm, and an explanatory note that was purest fiction. But the sling kept slipping off. My mother gave advice like mad—she boiled over with so much passion for the predicaments of strangers that they turned into permanent cronies. She told intimate stories about people I had never heard of.

Despite the gargantuan Palmer loops (or possibly because of them), I have always known that my mother's was a life of—intricately **abashing** word!—excellence: insofar as excellence means ripe generosity. She **burgeoned**; she was endlessly leafy and flowering. She wore red hats, and called herself a gypsy. In her girlhood she marched with the **suffragettes** and for Margaret Sanger and called herself a Red. She made me laugh, she was so varied: like a tree on which lemons, pomegranates, and prickly pears absurdly all hang together. She had the comedy of **prodigality**.

My own way is a thousand times more confined. I am a pinched perfectionist, the ultimate **fruition** of Miss Brubaker; I attend to **crabbed minutiae** and am **self-trammeled** through taking pains. I am a kind of human snail, locked in and condemned by my own nature. The ancients believed that the moist track left by the snail as it crept was the snail's own essence, depleting its body little by little; the farther the snail toiled, the smaller it became, until it finally rubbed itself out. That is how perfectionists are. Say to us Excellence, and we will show you how we use up our substance and wear ourselves away, while making scarcely any progress at all. The fact that I am an exacting perfectionist in a narrow strait only, and nowhere else, is hardly to the point, since nothing matters to me so much as a **comely** and muscular sentence. It is my narrow strait this snail's road: the track of the sentence I am writing now; and when I have eked out the wet substance, ink or blood, that is its mark, I will begin the next sentence. Only in treading out sentences am I perfectionist; but then there is nothing else I know how to do, or take much interest in. I **miter** every pair of **abutting** sentences as **scrupulously** as Uncle Jake fitted one strip of rosewood against another. My mother's worldly and bountiful hand has escaped me. The sentence I am writing is my cabin and my shell, compact, self-sufficient. It is the **burnished** horizon—a merciless planet where flawlessness is the single standard, where even the inmost seams, however hidden from a laxer eye, must meet perfection. Here "excellence" is not strewn casually from a tipped **cornucopia**, here disorder does not account for charm, here trifles rule like tyrants.

I measure my life in sentences, and my sentences are superior to my mother's, pressed out, line by line, like the lustrous ooze on the underside of the snail, the snail's secret open seam, its wound, leaking **attar**. My mother was too **mettlesome** to feel the force of a comma. She scorned the minutiae. She measured her life according to what poured from the horn of plenty, which was her ample, cascading, elastic, susceptible, inexact heart. My narrower heart rides between the tiny twin horns of the snail, dwindling as it goes.

And out of this thinnest thread, this ink-wet line of words, must rise a visionary fog, a mist, a smoke, forging cities, histories, sorrows, **quagmires**, entanglements, lives of sinners, even the life of my furnace-hearted mother: so much wilderness, waywardness, plenitude on the head of the precise and impeccable snail, between the horns.

profusion: abundance

abashing: disconcerting

burgeoned: bloomed

suffragettes: women who advocated extending the right to vote to all women

prodigality: extravagance

fruition: completion

crabbed minutiae: minor details

self-trammeled: self-restricting

comely: attractive

miter: match or pair up

abutting: touching

scrupulously: painstakingly

burnished: lustrous; polished

cornucopia: a curved receptacle shaped like a horn of a goat that is usually overstuffed with fruit to symbolize abundance

attar: fragrance

mettlesome: thrusting oneself into the affairs of others

quagmires: predicaments

▼ Questions to Focus Reading

1. Ozick writes of her mother, "She thought herself capable of doing anything, and did everything she imagined." What evidence does Ozick offer for this?
2. Ozick describes her mother as an optimist who ignored trifles: "for her, God was not in the details but in the intent." What are some examples that illustrate this philosophy of her mother's?
3. "She was all profusion, abundance, fabrication." What concrete details about her mother support this claim?
4. Ozick describes herself as "self-trammeled through taking pains." "I am a kind of human snail," she writes, "locked in and condemned by my own nature." What do you think she means by these descriptions?
5. She and her mother "measured their lives" in very different scales. What do you think it means to "measure" a life? What measure does Cynthia Ozick use? What measure did her mother use?

▼ Questions for Reflection

1. What is the key point Cynthia Ozick makes in this essay?
2. "I have always known that my mother's was a life of—intricately abashing word!—excellence." What criteria for the excellence of a life was Ozick using here? Why does she call "excellence" an "intricately abashing word"?
3. Do you think she judges her own life to be excellent? Give reasons for your answer.
4. Ozick develops in depth and detail the contrasts between herself and her mother. But there are important similarities, too. One of these is suggested in her final paragraph. What are the similarities?
5. What are your own criteria for excellence in life? Is yours a life of excellence according to these criteria? If not, what action would you have to take to make it so?

▼ Discussion

1. What are Ozick's criteria for calling her mother's life a life of excellence? What criteria would you use for judging a life to be excellent?

▼ Writing Assignments

1. Most of us shape ourselves, at least initially, by reference to a family member. We pattern ourselves after that person in some important respects, or by trying hard not to do this, still make that person a key determiner of our identity. A third alternative is the one illustrated in this essay: a combination of emulation and avoidance. Think about a person in your family who has played an important role in the shaping of your identity, and try to write an essay like this one, in which you compare and contrast that person to yourself.
2. Note how much of Ozick's characterizations of her mother and herself are conveyed in concrete images: the dress in the opening paragraph, the corn her mother grew, her mother's handwriting, the sling, the snail. Strive to give life to the generalizations you make in your essay by punctuating them as often as possible with similarly memorable concrete images.

▼ Journal Entries

1. What form or forms of excellence does your life now embody? What forms are open to you in your life?

2. Consider how Ozick develops the image of the snail as a metaphor for herself. Create a metaphor that expresses your essential self.

▼ **Vocabulary**

abashing	crabbed minutiae	meticulous	proliferate
abut	culinary	mettlesome	quagmire
attar	ebullience	miter	scrupulously
burgeon	efflorescence	monomaniacally	self-trammeled
burnish	finical	panache	suffragettes
comely	fruition	prodigality	trifles
cornucopia	impeccably	profusion	

4

▼

And Man

William Saroyan

*This is the story of a boy's awakening to the promise of life and of his discovery
of a life-altering, if barely articulable, truth.*

One morning, when I was fifteen, I got up before daybreak, because all night I
hadn't been able to sleep, tossing in bed with the thought of the earth and the
strangeness of being alive, suddenly feeling myself a part of it, definitely, solidly.
Merely to be standing again, I had thought all night. Merely to be in the light
again, standing, breathing, being alive. I left my bed quietly in the darkness of
early morning and put on my clothing, a blue cotton shirt, a pair of corduroy pants,
stockings and shoes. It was November and it was beginning to turn cold, but I did
not wish to put on more clothes. I felt warm enough. I felt almost feverish, and
with more clothes I knew it would not happen. Something was going to happen,
and I felt that if I put on too much clothing it would dwindle away and all that I
would have would be the remembrance of something expected, then lost.

All through the sleeplessness of the night I could feel turning in me like a
multitude of small and large wheels, some swift and wordless thought, on the verge
of **articulation**, some vast remembrance out of time, a fresh fullness, a new solidity,
a more graceful rhythm of motion emerging from the hurried growth that had taken
place in me during the summer.

With the beginning of spring that year came the faint and fragmentary beginning of this thought, burning in my mind with the sound of fire eating substance,
sweeping through my blood with the impatience and **impetuosity** of a **deluge**.
Before the beginning of this thought I had been nothing more than a small and
sullen boy, moving through the moments of my life with anger and fear and bitterness and doubt, wanting desperately to know the meaning and never quite being
able to do so. But now in November I was as large physically as a man, larger,
for that matter, than most men. It was as if I had leaped suddenly from the form
of myself as a boy to the vaster form of myself as a man, and to the vaster meaning
of myself as something specific and alive. Look at him, my relatives were saying,
every part of his body is growing, especially his nose. And they made sly jokes
about my private organs, driving me out of my head with shame. How about it?
they asked, even the ladies. Is it growing? Do you dream of big women, hundreds
of them?

I don't know what you're talking about, I used to say. But I did know. Only
I was ashamed. Look at that nose, they used to say. Just look at that enormous
nose on his face.

During the summer I sometimes stopped suddenly before a mirror to look
at myself, and after a moment I would turn away, feeling disgusted with my ugliness, worrying about it. I couldn't understand how it was that I looked utterly
unlike what I imagined myself to be. In my mind I had another face, a finer, a
more subtle and dignified expression, but in the mirror I could see the real reflection
of myself, and I could see that it was ugly, thick, bony, and coarse. I thought it
was something finer, I used to say to myself. I hadn't bothered before about looking
at myself. I had thought that I knew precisely how I looked, and the truth distressed

articulation: the act of expressing interrelated thoughts in a
clear and understandable manner

impetuosity: impulsive vehemence

deluge: an overwhelming flood

sullen: dismal; gloomy

27

me, making me ashamed. Afterwards I stopped caring. I am ugly, I said. I know I am ugly. But it is only my face.

And I could believe that my face was not the whole of it. It was simply a part of myself that was growing with the rest, an outward part, and therefore not as important as the inward part. The real growth was going on inside not simply within the boundaries of my physical form, but outward through the mind and through the imagination of the real largeness of being, the limitless largeness of consciousness, of knowing and feeling and remembering.

I began to forget the ugliness of my face, turning again to the simplicity and kindliness of the face I believed to be my own, the face of myself in the secrecy of my heart, in the night light of sleep, in the truth of thought.

It is true that my face seems ugly, I said, but it is also true that it is not ugly. I know it is not, because I have seen it with my own eyes and shaped it with my own thought, and my vision has been clear and my thought has been clean. It cannot be ugly.

But how was anyone to understand the real truth, how was anyone to see the face I saw, and know that it was the real reflection of my being? This worried me a lot. There was a girl in my class at high school whom I worshipped, and I wanted this girl to see that my face, the face she saw, was not the truthful one, that it was merely a part of the growth that was going on. And I wanted her to be able to see with me the truthful face, because I felt that if she did see it, she would understand my love for her, and she would love me.

All through the night I had tossed with the thought of myself somehow alive on the earth, somehow specific and at the same time a substance that was changing and would always change, from moment to moment, imperceptibly, myself entering one moment thus, and emerging thus, over and over again. I wanted to know what it was in me that belonged not to myself alone but to the body of man, to his legend, to the truth of his motion over the earth, moment after moment, century after century. All through the night it seemed that I would soon learn, and in the morning I left my bed, standing in the darkness and the stillness, feeling the splendour of having form and weight and motion, having, I hoped, meaning.

I walked quietly through the darkness of the house and emerged, standing for a moment in the street, acknowledging the magnificence of our earth, the large beauty of limitless space about our insignificant forms, the remoteness of the great **celestial** bodies of our universe, our oceans, our mountains, our valleys, the great cities we had made, the strong and clean and fearless things we had done. The small boats we had made and sent over the wild waters, the slow growth of railroads, the slow accumulation of knowledge, the slow but everlasting seeking after God, in the vastness of the universe, in the solidity of our own earth, in the glory of our own small beings, the simplicity of our own hearts.

Merely to be standing, merely to be breathing that day was a truth in the nature of an **inexplicable** miracle. After all these years, I thought . . . I myself standing here in the darkness, breathing, knowing that I live. I wanted to say something in language, with the words I had been taught in school, something solemn and dignified and joyous . . . to express the gratitude I felt to God. But it was impossible. There were no words with which to say it. I could feel the magnificence coming through the cold clean air, touching my blood, racing through it, dancing, but there were no words with which to say it.

There was a fire hydrant in our street, and I had always wanted to hurdle it, but I had always been afraid to try. The hydrant was made of metal and my substance was of flesh and bone and blood, and if I did not clear the hydrant, leaping swiftly, my flesh would smash against it, paining me, perhaps breaking a bone in one of my legs.

Suddenly I was leaping over the hydrant, and, clearing it, I was thinking, I can do it now, I can do anything now.

celestial: relating to the heavens or sky

inexplicable: unexplainable

28

I hurdled the fire hydrant six or seven times, leaping away over it, hearing myself landing solidly on the earth, feeling tremendous.

Then I began to walk, not slowly, not casually, but vigorously, leaping now and then because I couldn't help it. Each time I came to a tree, I leaped and caught a limb, making it bend with my weight, pulling myself up and letting myself down. I walked into the town, into the streets where we had put up our buildings, and suddenly I saw them for the first time, suddenly I was really *seeing* them, and they were splendid. The city was almost deserted, and I alone in it, its only inhabitant, seeing it as it really was, in all its fineness, with all its meaning, giving it its real truth, like the truth of my hidden face, the inward splendour. The winter sun came up while I walked and its light fell over the city, making a cool warmth. I touched the buildings, feeling them with the palms of my hands, feeling the meaning of the solidity and the precision. I touched the plate-glass windows, the brick, the wood and the cement.

When I got home, everyone was awake, at the breakfast table. Where have you been? they asked. Why did you get up so early?

I sat in my chair at the table, feeling great hunger. Shall I tell them? I thought. Shall I try to tell them what is happening? Will they understand? Or will they laugh at me?

Suddenly I knew I was a stranger among them, my own people, and I knew that while I loved them, I could not go out to them, revealing the truth of my being. Each of us is alone, I thought. Each is a stranger to the other. My mother thinks of me as a pain she once suffered, a babe at her breast, a small child in the house, a boy walking to school, and now a young man with an ugly face, a restless and half-mad fellow who moves about strangely.

We ate mush in those days. It was cheap and we were poor, and the mush filled a lot of space. We used to buy it in bulk, by the pound, and we had it for breakfast every morning. There was a big bowl of it before me, about a pound and a half of it, steaming, and I began to swallow the food, feeling it sinking to my hunger, entering my blood, becoming myself and the change that was going on in me.

No, I thought. I cannot tell them. I cannot tell anyone. Everyone must see for himself. Everyone must seek the truth for himself. It is here, and each man must seek it for himself. But the girl, I thought. I should be able to tell her. She was of me. I had taken her name, her form, the outward one and the inward one, and I had breathed her being into my being, joining her meaning to my meaning, and she was of my thought, of my motion in walking over the earth, and of my sleep. I would tell her. After I had revealed my hidden face to her, I would speak to the girl about ourselves, about our being alive together, on the same earth, in the same moment of eternity. I had never spoken to the girl. I had loved her secretly, worshipping her, worshipping the very things she touched, her books, her desk, the earth over which she moved, the air about her, but I had never had the courage to speak to her. I wanted my speaking to mean so much, to be so important to each of us, that I was afraid even to think of breaking the silence between us.

I went for a little walk, I replied.

Everyone began to laugh at me, even my mother. What's the matter with you? they asked. Why can't you sleep? Are you in love again? Is that it? Are you dreaming of some girl?

I sat at the table, swallowing the hot food, hearing their laughter. I cannot tell them, I thought. They are laughing at me. They think it is something to laugh about. They think it is a little joke?

I began to blush, thinking of the girl and worrying about something to say that would satisfy and silence them, stopping their laughter. Then they began to laugh louder than ever, and I couldn't help it, I began to laugh too.

Yes, they laughed. It must be some girl. Look how handsome he is getting to be. Dreaming about a girl always does that.

I ate all the mush in the bowl and got up from the table. If I try to tell them the truth, I thought, they will laugh more than ever.

I'm going to school, I said, and left the house. But I knew I would not go to school that day. I had decided not to go in the middle of the night, when I had been unable to sleep. In school, in that atmosphere, it would never happen. I would never be able to understand what it was that turned in me, circling toward truth, and it would be lost, maybe forever. I decided to walk into the country and be alone with the thought, helping it to emerge from the bewilderment and confusion of my mind, and the fever of my blood, carrying it to silence and simplicity, giving it a chance to reach its fullness and be whole.

Walking through the country, moving quietly among the leafless grapevines and fig trees, the thought became whole, and I knew the truth about myself and man and the earth and God.

At the proper hour I returned home, as if I were coming home from school, and the following day I went to school. I knew I would be asked for an excuse and an explanation for my absence, and I knew I would not lie about it. I could tell them I had been at home, sick with a cold, but I didn't want to do it. There would be a punishment, but I didn't care about that. Let them punish me if they liked. Let old man Brunton give me a strapping. I had walked into the country, into the silence, and I had found the truth. It was more than anything they would ever be able to teach. It was something that wasn't in any of their books. Let them punish me. I wanted also to impress the girl. I wanted her to understand that I had strength, that I could tell the truth and be punished for it, that I would not make up a cheap lie just to get out of a strapping. My telling the truth ought to mean something to her, I thought. Being so much a part of myself, she would be able to see beneath the surface and understand what I had done, and why.

After the roll was taken, my name was called and our teacher said: You were not at school yesterday. Have you brought an excuse?

No, I said, I have not.

Suddenly I felt myself to be the object of the laughter of everyone in the classroom, and I could imagine everyone thinking: What a stupid fellow! I looked at this girl whom I loved so much and I saw that she too was laughing, but I would not believe it. This sometimes happens. It happens when a man has given another person his own dignity and meaning, and the other person has not acquired that dignity and meaning. I saw and heard the girl laughing at me, but I would not believe it. I hadn't intended to entertain her. I hadn't intended to entertain anyone, and the laughter made me angry.

Why were you away from school? said the teacher. Where were you?

I was in the country, I said, walking.

Now the laughter was greater than ever, and I saw the girl I secretly loved laughing with the others, as if I meant nothing to her, as if I hadn't made her a part of myself. I began to feel ill and defiant, and there was warm perspiration on the palms of my hands.

The teacher stood over me, trembling. One must, perhaps, be a teacher to be able to appreciate precisely how angry she felt. For years she had been asking boys why they had been absent from school, and for years the boys had replied that they had been at home, ill. She had known that in most cases they had not told the truth, but the tradition had been maintained and everything had remained solid in her world. Now everything was being shattered, and she was standing over me, trembling with rage. I think she tried to shake me, and I would not let her do it, holding myself solidly. For a moment she budged at me, hating me, and then she said, You Armenians, you, you . . . and I thought she would burst into tears. I felt sorry for her, for the stupidity she had preserved in herself after so many years of trying to teach school, a woman almost fifty years of age.

And I hadn't meant to hurt her. That hadn't been my object at all. I had meant simply to tell the truth. I had meant to reveal to the girl my true face, the face which had been shaped by the dignity and simplicity of man and which she had helped to shape, and I had meant to reveal to her the truth of my presence on earth. And then her laughter, just like the laughter of the others . . . it mangled something in me, and I stood in the midst of the noise, embarrassed and bewildered, bleeding, and breaking to pieces. God damn it, I thought. This is not true. God damn it, this is a lie.

But I knew I was deceiving myself. And I knew I would never be able to speak to the girl about my love for her, and the meaning of that love to me, and to the earth and the universe, and to man.

I was sent to the principal of the school, and he stood over me, grumbling in a deep voice. You, he said, you are a disgrace to this school. You are a disgrace to your own race. You break rules. Then you come to school flaunting your crime. What have you to say for yourself?

Nothing, I said.

Why did you do it? he asked.

I wanted to walk, I said.

You could have waited till Saturday, he said.

No, I said, I had to walk yesterday.

Can you think of any reason why I shouldn't strap you? he asked.

That's up to you, I said.

I was angry. I felt bitter about the girl, and I wasn't afraid of the principal, or of the strapping I knew he would give me. It was all over. I would have to walk alone with the secret. I would have to accept the sickness in me that the girl had made by laughing, but the truth would remain whole and I would have it to keep forever, walking alone, in the secrecy of my heart.

The strapping made me cry, big as I was, strong as I was. While I cried, though, I knew it wasn't the strapping that was hurting me . . . it was this other thing, this incredible blindness everywhere. I cried bitterly, and when I returned to class my eyes were red and I was ashamed, and the whole class was laughing at me, even the girl.

After school, walking alone, I tried to heal the wound in my heart, and I began to think again of the swift and bright truth of being, the truth I had earned for myself by walking alone through the silence of the earth, and walking, thinking of it, I could feel myself becoming whole again, and I could hear myself laughing through the vastness of the secret space I had discovered.

The truth was the secret, God first, the word, the word God, out of all things and beyond, spaceless and timeless, then the void, the silent emptiness, vaster than any mortal mind could conceive, abstract and precise and real and lost, the substance in the emptiness, again precise and with weight and solidity and form, fire and fluid, and then, walking through the vineyards, I had seen it thus, the whole universe, quietly there in the mind of man, motionless and dark and lost, waiting for man, for the thought of man, and I felt the stirring of inanimate substance in the earth and in myself like the swift growth of the summer, life emerging from time, the germ of man springing from the rock and the fire and the fluid to the face of man, and to the form, to the motion and the thought, suddenly in the emptiness, the thought of man, stirring there. And I was man, and this was the truth I had brought out of the emptiness, walking alone through the vineyards.

I had seen the universe, quietly in the emptiness, secret, and I had revealed it to itself, giving it meaning and grace and the truth that could come only from the thought and energy of man, and the truth was man, myself, moment after moment, and man, century after century, and man, and the face of God in man, and the sound of the laughter of man in the vastness of the secret, and the sound of his weeping in the darkness of it, and the truth was myself and I was man.

▼ Questions about the Story

1. "All night I hadn't been able to sleep, tossing in bed with the thought of the earth and the strangeness of being alive, suddenly feeling myself part of it, definitely, solidly." How would you describe in your own words the kinds of thoughts that are keeping the boy awake?

2. "I wanted to know what it was in me that belonged not to myself alone but to the body of man, to his legend, to the truth of his motion over the earth, moment after moment, century after century." What can the boy have in mind by what belonged not to himself alone but to the "body of man, to his legend"?

3. There is such a dramatic discrepancy between the power and depth and sublimity of the truth he has seen and the shabbiness of his interaction with all the other people in this story—his family, his classmates, the girl, his teacher, the principal. What effect would you expect this discrepancy to have on the path he chooses in life?

4. "I had seen the universe, quietly in the emptiness, secret, and I had revealed it to itself." In what sense do you think he revealed the universe to itself?

5. "The truth was man, myself, moment after moment, and man, century after century . . . and the truth was myself and I was man." What do you think he means by this?

6. This is the story of a young man experiencing a call to a quest. What kind of knowledge or understanding is he seeking? How does he make himself receptive to this truth? (How does he go after it?) What in your understanding is the truth he finds? How would you expect this truth to influence his life choices?

▼ Relating the Story to Yourself

1. The story begins with the boy's sense of keen anticipation. Something of great importance was going to be revealed to him, he sensed. Have you ever had this kind of experience? Was something revealed to you? If so, what was it?

2. The boy feels a painful contradiction between the ugliness of his face and the face he senses from the inside, "the face of myself in the secrecy of my heart." Have you experienced this kind of contradiction between the inner and the outer? How did the boy deal with this? How did you deal with it?

3. The boy is very much aware of growing from a "small and sullen boy" into a man. Have you had a similar experience of coming into your own?

4. "I walked into the town, into the streets where we had put up our buildings, and suddenly I was really *seeing* them, and they were splendid." What do you think he means when he says he was suddenly "really *seeing* them"? Can you recall a similar experience, the sudden seeing of a place or a person?

5. In stark contrast to the quality of the boy's inner life is the quality of his interaction with people in this story. Have you experienced this sense of not being understood, of not being able to share a profound feeling or truth, of this kind of discrepancy between inner and outer worlds?

6. The boy decides not to go to school, because he needs to try to understand what "turned in me, circling toward truth." He walks in the country to help his thoughts emerge. Have you ever had to create conditions that would allow for some deep truth to emerge?

7. In his highly charged state of mind, he is filled with appreciation for the miracle of his simply being. Have you had a similar experience?

8. The boy is filled with a desire to know his connection with the scheme of things, "what it was in me that belonged not to myself alone, but to the body of man." Can you recall a similar desire in yourself?

▼ Discussion

1. "I had walked into the country, into the silence, and I had found the truth. It was more than anything they would ever be able to teach. It was something that wasn't in any of their books." Have you learned things in life that no one could have taught you? What were these things?

2. What truth do you think the boy had found?

▼ Writing Assignments

1. Recall a time of great intensity in your life when thoughts were stirring so uncontrollably that you could not find words for them. Describe this time, and try now to make sense of these then-inarticulable thoughts.

2. "Coming into My Own" Describe an experience in which it became clear to you that you were coming into your own.

3. "Suddenly Seeing" Describe an experience in which you really see for the first time some place or situation or person that you had long taken for granted.

4. If you have had the experience of a profound discrepancy between inner and outer worlds, write about this experience.

5. Have you ever had an experience similar to the boy's of the promise, mystery, and depth of life? Describe it.

▼ Vocabulary

articulation	deluge	inexplicable
celestial	impetuosity	sullen

5

▼

The Lover of Women

Sue Miller

Sue Miller's story depicts a kind of obsession, a young man's obsession with a certain family, especially with the daughters of the family and the place in the world they represent. It is, in part, a study of the effect of class consciousness on a young man's values and goals.

Lloyd Abbott wasn't the richest man in our town, but he had, in his daughters, a vehicle for displaying his wealth that some of the richest men didn't have. And, more unusual in our midwestern community, he had the inclination to do so. And so, at least twice a year, passing by the Abbotts' house on the way to school, we boys would see the striped fabric of a tent stretched out over their grand backyard, and we'd know there was going to be another occasion for social anxiety. One of the Abbott girls was having a birthday, or graduating, or coming out, or going away to college. "Or getting her period," I said once to my brother, but he didn't like that. He didn't much like *me* at that time either.

By the time we'd return home at the end of the day, the tent would be up and workmen would be moving under the cheerful colors, setting up tables and chairs, arranging big pots of seasonal flowers. The Abbotts' house was on the main street in town, down four or five blocks from where the commercial section began, in an area of wide lawns and overarching elms. Now all those trees have been cut down because of Dutch elm disease and the area has an exposed, befuddled air. But then it was a grand promenade, nothing like our part of town where the houses huddled close as if for company; and there probably weren't many people in town who didn't pass by the Abbotts' house once a day or so, on their way to the library for a book, or to Woolworth's for a ball of twine, or to the grocery store or the hardware store. And so everyone knew and would openly discuss the parties, having to confess whether they'd been invited or not.

My brother Jacey usually had been, and for that reason was made particularly miserable on those rare occasions when he wasn't. I was the age of the youngest daughter, Pamela, and so I was later to be added to the list. By the time I began to be invited to the events under the big top, I had witnessed enough of the agony, which the **whimsicality** of the list cost my brother, to resolve never to let it be that important to me. Often I just didn't go to something I'd been invited to, more than once without bothering to RSVP. And when I did go, I refused to take it seriously. Sometimes I didn't dress as the occasion required, for instance. At one of the earliest parties I attended, when I was about thirteen, I inked sideburns on my cheeks, imagining I looked like my hero of the moment, Elvis Presley. When Jacey saw me, he tried to get my mother not to let me go unless I washed my face.

"It'll look worse if I wash it," I said maliciously. "It's india ink. It'll turn gray. It'll look like dirt."

My mother had been reading when we came in to ask her to **adjudicate**. She kept her finger in the book to mark her place the whole time we talked, and so I knew Jacey didn't have much of a chance. She was really just waiting for us to leave.

whimsicality: unpredictable playfulness

adjudicate: settle judicially

"What I don't understand, John," my mother said to Jacey—she was the only one who called him by his real name—"is why it should bother you if Doug wants to wear sideburns."

"*Mother,*" Jacey said. He was forever explaining life to her, and as far as he was concerned, she never got it.

"This isn't a costume party. No one else is going to be *pretending* to be someone else. He's supposed to just come in a jacket and tie and dance. And he isn't even wearing a tie."

"And that bothers you?" she asked in her gentle, high-pitched voice.

"Of course," he said.

She thought for a moment. "Is it that you're ashamed of him?"

This was hard for Jacey to answer. He knew by my mother's tone that he ought to be above such pettiness. Finally, he said, "It's *not* that I'm ashamed. I'm just trying to protect him. He's going to be sorry. He looks like such a *jerk* and he doesn't even know it. He doesn't understand the *implications.*"

There was a moment of silence while we all took this in. Then my mother turned to me. She said, "Do you understand, Doug, that you may be the only person at this party with artificial sideburns?"

"Yeah," I answered. Jacey stirred restlessly, desperately. He could see where this was heading.

"Do you understand, honey, that your sideburns don't look real?" her voice was unwaveringly gentle, kind.

Well, I had thought they might almost look real, and this news from someone as impartial as my mother was hard to take. But the stakes were high. I nodded. "Yeah," I said.

She pressed it. "That they look, really, as though you'd drawn them on?"

I swallowed and shrugged. "Yeah," I said again.

She looked hard at me a moment. Then she turned to Jacey. "Well, darling," she said. "It appears he does understand. So you've really done all you can, and you'd better just go along and try to ignore him." She smiled, as though to try to get him to share a joke. "Just pretend you never saw him before in your life."

Jacey was enraged. I could see he was trembling, but he had boxed himself in with his **putative** concern for my social welfare. I felt the thrill of knowing I was causing him deep pain.

"Mother," he said, as though the word were a threat. "You don't understand *anything.*" He left the room, slamming the door behind him.

My mother, who never discussed the behavior of one of us with the other, didn't even look at me. She bowed her head in the circle of lamplight and continued to read her book. I left her, too, after a moment, and was in my room when I heard Jacey hurtling past my door and down the stairs again. His rage had been feeding on itself and he was yelling even before he got anywhere near her. "Let me tell you something, Mom. If you let him go to the party like that, I'm not going. Do you hear me? I'm not going." His breathing was audible to me from the top of the stairs—he was near tears—but my mother's answer, which was long, was just a murmur, a gentle flow of her voice for a while. And though he ran out of the house afterward, slamming the front door this time, he was at the party when I got there later. He was dancing and following my mother's advice to pretend he didn't know me.

The reason my entry into his social world, particularly the Abbott part of it, was so painful, so important to my brother, was that he had already fallen in love with their family, with everything they stood for. In an immediate sense, he was in love with the middle Abbott girl, Eleanor. She wasn't the prettiest of the three, but she seemed it. She was outgoing and sarcastic and very popular; and Jacey wasn't the only boy at Bret Harte High trying to close in on her. He spent a long time on the phone each evening talking either *to* her or *about* her to girlfriends of hers who seemed to manage her social life through messages they would or

putative: supposed

35

wouldn't take for her. He was with her whenever he could be after school and on weekends. But here he was at a disadvantage because he, like me, had a part-time job all through high school, which the other boys in our circle of friends didn't. In this difference between us and the others we knew socially lay, I think, a tremendous portion of the appeal Eleanor Abbott had for my brother.

My father was one of the few in Haley who had died in the Second World War, killed by American bombs, actually, while being held prisoner by the Germans. Most of the fathers of our friends had had large enough families by the time America got involved that they didn't go. But my father enlisted when Jacey was two and I was on the way. He died only a few months before my birth, and my mother brought us back to live with her parents here in Haley, the small town in Illinois where she'd grown up.

I can't remember my Grandfather Vetter well—he had a heart attack when I was still quite small—but Grandma Vetter was as important as a second parent throughout my childhood. She died when I was ten. We had just sat down to dinner one night when she said, "I think I'll just lie down for a little while," as though that were what everyone did at the beginning of a meal. My mother watched her walk down the hallway to her room on the first floor, and then went directly to the telephone and called the doctor. Grandma Vetter was dead by the time he arrived, stretched out on the bed with her dress neatly covering her bony knees. I remember thinking that there was some link between the way she looked, as though she *were* just resting and would get up any minute, and the way the table looked, every place neatly set, every plate heaped with food, as though we would sit down any minute. I was very hungry, and looking at the table made me want to have my dinner, but I knew I shouldn't care about the food at a time like this—my mother and brother were crying—and I was ashamed of myself.

Throughout my childhood my grandmother preferred Jacey to me—he was a more polite, conscientious boy—and this left my mother and me with a special bond. She was, as I've indicated, incapable of **overt** favoritism, but she told me later that my infancy provided her with a special physical comfort after my father's death, and I often felt a charge of warmth and protectiveness from her when my grandmother was critical of me in one way or another, as she often was.

My mother was the only woman in our circle who worked. She taught second grade at the Haley Elementary School, moving to third grade the years Jacey and I would have been her pupils. And, as I've said, we boys worked, too, starting in seventh and eighth grade mowing lawns and delivering papers. By our senior years of high school, each of us had a salaried part-time job, Jacey at the county hospital, I at a restaurant in town. It wasn't that others in our world led lives of great luxury—few besides the Abbott girls did. Our home, the things we did, the kinds of summer trips we took were much like those of our friends. But my brother and I provided ourselves with many of the things our friends' parents provided them with, eventually even paying most of our way through college. We were "nice" boys, ambitious boys, but there was a price for our ambition. Somehow we must have understood, too, and yet didn't question, that although our lives were relatively open—we could number among our friends the richest kids, the most popular kids—our mother's mobility in Haley was over. She was single, she needed to work. These facts constituted an insurmountable social barrier for her. Yet it seems to me I barely noticed her solitude, her isolation from the sociable couples who were the parents of my friends. And even if I had noticed it, I wouldn't have believed it could have a connection to the glorious possibilities I assumed for my own life.

Because of our relative poverty, our lives were full of events that were beyond contemplation for our friends, but which then seemed only adventurous and exciting to me. I remember one summer coming back from a trip to California by car, we ran out of money. My mother stopped in Las Vegas with a nearly empty gas tank and about three dollars' worth of change in her purse, and won over two hundred

overt: open

36

dollars—more than enough to get home on—with her second quarter in the slot machine. That kind of thing didn't happen to friends of ours, and somehow, as a result, their mothers seemed more childlike to me, less grown-up, less strong. I thought there was no one else like my mother.

But Jacey yearned for everything she, he, we, were not; and in his senior year of high school, he particularly yearned for Eleanor Abbott.

Now I'm finally able to see that at least a part of my passionate embrace of the role of rebel in high school had to do with a need to deny the embarrassment I could not, out of loyalty to my mother, let myself feel about all those aspects of our lives that I was slowly beginning to perceive as difficult or marginal. I *did* think the Abbott girls and their endless parties **ostentatious**, ridiculous; but in addition, some private part of me angrily yearned for the ease and gracefulness of their kind of life, their sure sense of who they were and how they fit in, as much as Jacey yearned overtly for it.

At the time, though, I thought his yearning, particularly his yearning for Eleanor, was shallow and **contemptible**. She was a year ahead of me in high school, but even I knew she wasn't smart. In fact, she was in biology with me because she'd flunked it the first time around. I couldn't understand what attracted him to her, especially since I knew she hung around at least as much with three or four other senior boys.

One summer afternoon, though, the last summer before Jacey went off to college, the drive-in where I worked closed early because the air-conditioning was out of order. I came straight home, hot but **elated** to have an unexpected day off. My mother had gone up to Chicago to visit a college friend, and I expected Jacey might still be sleeping, since he was working the night shift as an orderly at the county hospital. I was hot, as I've said, and I felt like celebrating my release from routine, so I charged down the basement stairs two at a time to raid the big freezer. My mother kept it stocked with four or five half gallons of various flavors of ice cream. As I opened the case and leaned into the cool sweet darkness, the freezer seemed to exhale up at me. I heard a rustling noise from the front part of the basement, a whisper. I shut the freezer slowly, my heart thudding, and moved silently toward the doorway. I don't know what I expected—thieves perhaps—but it wasn't what I saw in the few seconds before my brother shouted "No!" and I turned away. He and Eleanor Abbott were naked on the daybed set up near the wall of the coal bin, and Eleanor Abbott was sitting on him. He was in the process of reaching up with his body to cover hers from view when I looked at them. The light in the basement was dim, and they were in the far corner—it was like looking at silvery fish in an unlighted aquarium—but the vision lingered with me a long time, clear and indelible.

I left the house immediately—got my bike out of the garage and rode around aimlessly in the heat all afternoon. By the time I came home, it was twilight and my brother was gone. I went down to the basement again. I went into the front room and I lay down on the daybed. I turned my face into its mildew-smelling cover, and imagined that I was breathing in also the rich, mysterious odor of sex.

I remember being less surprised at my brother than I was at Eleanor Abbott. I thought about the three or four other boys she went out with—some of them more seriously than my brother, I knew from the gossip at school. The possibility arose that Eleanor Abbott was having sex, not just having normal sex as I'd been able to imagine it with girls I knew, but actually *sitting* on all of the boys she went out with. The possibility arose that Eleanor Abbott, whom I'd seen as utterly **vacuous**, utterly the conventional rich girl, was a bigger rebel even than I, in my blue jeans and secret cigarettes, in the haircut I now modeled on James Dean's.

My brother never mentioned what I'd seen, and the silence seemed to increase the distance between us, although I felt a respect for him I'd never entertained before. I saw that even his life could contain mysteries unguessed at by me.

ostentatious: showy
contemptible: despicable
elated: overjoyed
vacuous: empty

He went away to college that fall on a partial scholarship. I saw Eleanor Abbott around school. Sometimes she'd smile at me in the halls or say hello, especially when she was with friends. I felt that I was somehow comical or amusing to her, and I felt, at those moments, genuinely exposed, as though what she seemed to think of me was all I really was—a joker, a poser. I discovered, too, that she dominated my fantasy life completely, as she perhaps knew when she'd laugh and throw her head back and say "Hello, Doug" when we met. Once I actually walked into a door as she passed.

She went to college the next year, to a women's college in the East. My brother mentioned her several times in letters to my mother, letters she read aloud to me. He said that he'd gone to visit her, or had her to Amherst for the weekend. I don't know what visions this conjured up for my mother—she never offered her opinion of any of the Abbotts except to say once that Lloyd Abbott had been "kind of a dud" as a young man—but for me, images of absolute **debauchery** opened up. I could hardly wait to be alone in my room. I found these images nearly impossible, though, to connect with my actual living brother when he came home at Christmas or Easter, ever more **trig**, ever more polished.

Eleanor didn't come home at Easter break, I remember, and Jacey seemed to have no trouble finding other women to hang around with. This shocked me, his betrayal of her, in a way that her early possible wildness did not. It seemed cynical. Her wildness I had romanticized as hunger, pure appetite.

Sometime in early May, I was sitting at the dining room table doing some homework when the phone rang. My mother was in the kitchen, and she called out, "I'll get it." She came out to the telephone stand in the hall. Her voice, after the initial hello, was cool and polite, so I assumed it was some social acquaintance of hers and went back to my chemistry. She was silent on the phone a long time, and then she said, sharply and angrily, "No, that's impossible." Her tone made me look up. She had turned her back to me, as though to shield me from whatever was going on. After another, shorter silence, she said, "No, I'm sorry. I can't do that. If you have something to say to my son, you'd better talk to him yourself." I started to stand, my heart thudding, thinking of the various misdeeds of the last weeks, the last months. I ran around at the time with a small gang of misfits, and we specialized in anonymous and, we thought, harmless acts of vandalism—setting a car upside down on its owner's front lawn, breaking into the school cafeteria and urinating into the little cartons of orange juice.

"That's right," my mother said stiffly. "I'm very sorry." And she hung up.

After a moment, she turned and saw me standing there, looking, I'm sure, terrified and puzzled. Her worried face relaxed. She laughed. "Sit down, darling," she said. "You look as though you're about to meet your maker."

She came into the dining room and put her hands along the back of the chair opposite me. "That wasn't even about you. It was Joan Abbott, about John." The vertical line between her eyebrows returned. "I'm going to ask you one question, Doug, and if you have no idea, or don't want to answer, just tell me."

I nodded.

She looked down at her hands, as though she was ashamed to be doing what she was about to do. "Is there any sense, you think, in which John has . . . oh, I don't know, it sounds ridiculous . . . *corrupted* Eleanor Abbott? Led her astray?"

My mind was working in several directions at once, trying to reconstruct the phone call, trying to figure out what the answer to her question might really be, trying to figure out how much I wanted to tell her and if I told her anything, how to put it.

"Well, I know he's made love to her," I blurted finally. She looked startled only for a second. I could feel a deep flush rise to my face. "But not because he's *talked* about it." She nodded, I think, approvingly. "But I would have said that Eleanor was pretty much in charge of her own life. I mean, she had lots of boy-

debauchery: sensual indulgence
trig: extremely precise

38

friends. That she slept with, I think. Even in high school." By now I was talking down to my chemistry book. "I mean, I think he liked her more than she liked him. Not that she didn't like him. I mean, I don't know."

"I see," my mother said. I looked up at her. Suddenly she grinned at me and I felt the pinch of love for her that came only occasionally at this stage of my life. "Well, that was clear as a bell, Doug."

That June, Pamela Abbott, who was in my class, had a tent party to celebrate our graduation. I had been eagerly anticipating seeing Eleanor there, telling her I was going to Harvard in the fall, trying, as I see now, the appeal of my conventional success where the romance of my rebel stance had failed. My brother had been home for a week but he hadn't mentioned her, and some secret, competitive part of me hoped she was done with him and would find in my embrace the intensity she had sought in vain in his.

There was no sign of Eleanor. I danced with her sister and asked about her; she simply said that Eleanor couldn't make it. But what I heard from the others in the course of the evening, in little knotted whispers, was that Eleanor had, in some sense, broken with her family. Run away somehow. She'd flunked or dropped out of school (something no boy in our world, much less a girl, would ever do), and had taken a job as a waitress or a dancer or an airline stewardess, depending on who told the story.

When I got home that night, I saw the light on in my brother's room. I went and stood awkwardly in his doorway. He was reading in bed, the lower part of his body covered with a sheet, the upper part naked. I remember looking at the filled-in grown-up shape of his upper body and momentarily hating him.

"Thought I'd report on the Abbott party," I said.

He set his book down. "I've been to the Abbott party," he said, and smiled.

"Well, everyone was there, except *you.*"

"I'm surprised you still go," he said.

"I'm surprised you don't," I said.

"I'm **persona non grata** there," he said flatly.

After a pause, I said, "Eleanor wasn't there either."

"Mmm," he said. "Well, I'm not surprised."

"I heard she'd left school," I said.

"I heard that, too," he answered.

"What's she doing now?" I asked

"She hasn't told me," he said.

"So you're not in touch with her?" I asked.

"No, I've outlived my usefulness to Eleanor." I was surprised to hear the bitterness in his voice.

"How were you *useful* to her?"

"I should think that would be easy enough to imagine."

I didn't know what to say.

"I mean," he said, "even aside from the little scene in the basement."

I shook my head, confused and embarrassed at the reference.

"Look," he said. "Eleanor was looking for a way not to be an Abbott, to get away from that whole world. And it turns out that it takes a lot to get away. It's not enough that you sleep around with boys from your world. But when you start fucking boys from across the *tracks,*" he said. He was agitated. He sat up, throwing back the covers, and got out of bed. He walked to the dresser, lighted a cigarette and turned to face me.

"You mean she was sleeping with guys we didn't know—from Fountain Park or something?" I was nervous as I tried not to look at his nakedness.

He stood leaning on the dresser. He inhaled sharply on the cigarette and then smiled at me. "No, I mean she was sleeping with *me.* And she made sure her parents found out about it."

persona non grata: not welcome

39

I was silent for a moment, unable to understand. "But *we're* not from across the tracks," I said.

He cocked his head. "No?" he asked. "Well, maybe I'm not talking about literal tracks."

"I don't believe that," I said after a pause. "I don't believe in what you're talking about."

He shrugged. "So don't believe in it," he said. He carried the cigarette and ashtray back to bed with him, covered himself again.

I persisted. "I mean, we're just the same as them. We're just as good as they are."

He smiled. "Ask the Abbotts about that."

"The *Abbotts*," I said, with what I hoped was grand contempt in my voice, forgetting for the moment my eagerness to attend Pamela's party.

"Okay, ask Mom. Ask her about how well *she's* lived in Haley all these years. Ask her whether she's as good as anyone else around here." Then, as though something in my face stopped him, his expression changed.

He shrugged. "Maybe I'm all wet," he said. "Maybe you're right." He tapped an ash into the ashtray. "I mean, this is America after all, right?"

I stood in the doorway a minute more. "So what do you think Eleanor is doing?" I finally asked.

"Look, I don't care what she's doing," he said. He picked up his book, and after a few minutes, I left.

I went to Harvard in the fall, as did Pamela Abbott—though in those days we still called her part of it Radcliffe. The year after that my brother moved to Cambridge to study architecture at Harvard. Gingerly, we began to draw closer together. We still occupied entirely different worlds, mine sloppy and disorganized, his orderly and productive. I thought it **emblematic** of this that I was so utterly unattracted to the women he preferred. They were neat, wealthy, Waspy, and to me they seemed asexual. I was drawn to ethnic types, women with dark skin, liquid black eyes, wild hair. But I had none. My wild women were abstracts, whereas Jacey had a regular string of real women in and out of his apartment; and I could never look at them, with their tiny pained smiles, without thinking of Eleanor perched on top of my brother in the basement the day I wanted ice cream.

We both continued to go home each summer to be with my mother, and it was the summer following his first year in Cambridge, the summer before my junior year, that Jacey fell in love with the oldest Abbott sister, Alice.

Alice had been a year ahead of him in high school, had gone to a two-year college somewhere and then married. She was arguably the prettiest of the sisters, the most conventional, and if she hadn't been older than he was at a time when that constituted a major barrier, she was probably the one my brother would have been attracted to in the first place. If he had fallen in love with her back in high school, I think their courtship might have proceeded at a pace slow enough, tender enough, that her parents might ultimately have been reconciled to it; the issue of our marginal social status might have been overcome if it hadn't been combined with Eleanor's sexual **precocity**, if Alice had come first.

But Alice had married someone else, someone acceptable, and had had two children. And now she was back home, something unmentioned having happened to her marriage. The children were preschoolers, and I was startled once that summer to walk past the Abbotts' house and see a tent set up in the backyard with balloons and streamers floating in the protected air beneath it. I heard children's shouts, someone crying loudly, and I realized that the cycle had begun again for the Abbotts.

I don't know where Jacey met Alice—there certainly were enough people in whose homes they might have bumped into each other—and I can't imagine how he explained himself to her in the context of what her family thought had gone

emblematic: symbolic
precocity: unusually early development

40

on between him and Eleanor, but he began to see her secretly that summer, arranging to go to the same parties, to meet accidentally. I went out with Pamela every now and then without having any romantic interest in her; we mostly **commiserated** on how dull Haley was, talked about places in Boston we missed, and she told me about Jacey and Alice.

I said I didn't believe her.

"Alice told me," she said.

"But *secretly?*" I asked.

"She's afraid of my parents," Pamela said.

"But she's a grown woman, with children. I mean, she's been married, for God's sake."

"Oh, that," Pamela said, waving her hand contemptuously.

"What do you mean, 'Oh that'?" I asked.

"That was practically an arranged marriage," she said. "They think that Alice has peanut shells for brains or something, so they sort of suggested after she graduated that maybe it was time to tie the old knot, and they sort of suggested that Peter was the one to do it with."

"I don't believe it," I said. "No one could be that **malleable**."

She shrugged. "Look, Alice is the good one, and Eleanor was the bad one, and I'm the one who sort of gets off the hook. That's just the way it works."

We sat in silence for a minute. "What do you hear from Eleanor?" I asked.

She looked at me sternly. "I don't," she said.

I'm not sure that Jacey even slept with Alice that first summer, and from what I knew via Pamela, Alice was feeling fragile about the end of the marriage, and tentative about getting involved with someone seemingly as dangerous as Jacey. To me, who saw myself as the truly dangerous potential in our family, that was amusing. But it was striking to me back in Cambridge that year that he stopped seeing other women. The seemingly endless parade in and out of his apartment stopped; and I was the one, finally, who had women.

I only had two, but it was enough to perplex me thoroughly. I was very involved with theater groups at Harvard; I'd been in one production or another practically nonstop since midway through my freshman year. Now, as a junior, I was getting lead roles; and the exotic women I'd dreamed of having, theatrical women who ringed their eyes with black pencil, were interested in me. But somehow, both my romances fell flat; they didn't seem as gripping as the roles I played, or even as exciting as the tense, delicate relationship Jacey was now maintaining by mail with Alice. Though he wouldn't really talk about Alice with me, about what she was like or what they did together, I knew he was determined to have her, to rescue her the following summer, and I watched it all with intense interest.

The summer started and then progressed somewhat as the first one had. There were frequent phone calls, the arranged meetings. But then Jacey brought Alice to our house.

I suppose they had problems finding places to go together privately, and they finally decided they had no alternative. At first it was when my mother was away, off on her annual trip to a college classmate's in Chicago. I was sitting in the living room, watching television, and I heard them come in. I looked up to see Alice, then Jacey, going upstairs. I could hear the murmur of their voices off and on through the night after I went to bed, and the sounds of their lovemaking, but it didn't bother me as it might have if it had been Eleanor. They left sometime in the dead of the night.

He brought her to the house every night my mother was gone, and we never spoke of it. I don't know what they did in the weeks after my mother's return, but in mid-August, he brought Alice to the house when my mother was home. She didn't hear them come in. She was in the backyard watering the plants. And then for a while I could hear her moving around the kitchen. At about ten o'clock,

commiserated: expressed sorrow or compassion

malleable: adaptable

though, she crossed to the bottom of the stairs and stopped, hearing their voices. Then she came into the dining room where I was.

"Who's upstairs with John?" she asked.

"I think it's Alice Abbott," I said.

"Oh," she said. "How long is she likely to stay?"

"I don't know," I said. "But I wouldn't stay up and wait for her to leave."

The next morning when I woke, I could hear Jacey and my mother talking in the kitchen, their voices floating out the open windows in the still summer air, hers steady and his impassioned, occasionally quite clearly audible. From what he said, I could tell she felt he needed to make his courtship of Alice open. It even seemed she was trying to get him to move out if he wanted to sleep with Alice, perhaps rent a room somewhere. "But it's because I *do* love her, Mother. It couldn't be more different from Eleanor. Eleanor was just an *idea* I had."

I don't know what my brother and mother agreed on, but he didn't move out and he didn't, to my knowledge, ever bring Alice to the house again. And then, just before he was to go back to Cambridge and reclaim his apartment from a subletter who was leaving early, it was over. Her parents had found out and simply said no, and apparently Alice didn't have the strength or the financial independence to defy them.

There were several days of phone calls, when my mother and I sat shut into the kitchen or our respective rooms trying not to listen to Jacey's desperate voice rising and falling, attempting to persuade Alice that it could work if she would just make the break.

And then even the calls stopped, and he just stayed in his room until his job ended and he could leave. And that's literally how he did it. He came home from his last day of work, took a shower, and started loading up his car. My mother tried to persuade him to stay overnight and start the trip the following morning, but he argued that he'd have to drive through at least part of one night anyway, and it might as well be at the beginning of the trip. "Besides," he said, "the sooner I get out of this fucking town the better." That he would use such language in front of my mother made it clear to me, finally, how deeply lost in misery my brother was.

When he left, my mother stood looking after his car for a long time. I went up onto the front porch, but she didn't follow. Finally I called to her, "Are you coming in, Mom?" And she turned and began to climb the stairs. I had a sudden revelation then of my mother's age. She had always looked the same age to me, but at that moment she looked as tired as Grandma Vetter had when she told us that she was just going to lie down for a bit.

We had a fairly silent dinner, and afterward, over coffee, she said to me, "Do you think your brother will be all right?"

"Well, he's not going to do anything stupid to himself, if that's what you mean."

"That's not what I mean," she said, her quickly raised hand dismissing even that possibility.

"I know," I said. I felt ashamed. Then, impulsively, I said, "I just wish he'd never met the Abbott family."

She sighed. "If John hadn't met the Abbotts, he'd have had to invent them, one way or another. There are no ends of Abbotts in the world, if that's what you need. And he just needs that somehow." She picked up the chipped yellow cup and sipped her coffee. "Well, really, I know how."

I was startled. "What do you mean, you know how?"

She sat back in her chair wearily and looked at me. She shook her head slowly. "I think John had a hard time, a terrible time, with the way you both grew up, and it made him want—oh, I don't know. Not money, exactly, but kind of the sense of place, of knowing where you belong, that money can give you. At least in a town like Haley." She shrugged. "And the way he grew up—that was my fault."

I answered quickly. "No it wasn't, Mom. If he feels that way, it's his responsibility. I mean, I grew up however he did, and that's not the way I feel."

"Yes, but you're different from John."

I started to protest again, but she lifted her hand to silence me. "No, listen. I can explain it." Then she sighed again, as if coming around to some central, hard truth. "You know that after Charlie—your father's—death, I was just . . . I was just a mess. I hurt so badly that some mornings, I'd be crying before I even woke up. And then I had you." She looked up at me. "And poor old John, well, he just got lost in there. I just didn't have anything for him."

She shook her head. "He was such a sad-sack kind of kid anyway. He'd always been jumpy and intense, even as a baby. I just couldn't settle in and be loving to him. He was too nervous. Whereas *you,*" she smiled at me, "you just slept and smiled and nursed. Even when you were a toddler I had to pin a sign on the back of your shirt saying 'Don't feed this child' because you'd go around the neighborhood and everyone would just *give* you things.

"And I swear, as I remember it, I spent weeks just sleeping with you in bed after you were born. I got dressed for meals, but that was about it. Otherwise I'd just sleep and sleep and sort of come alive just to nurse you or change you. I just couldn't believe Charlie wasn't coming back. I was twenty-four years old." Her face was blank, remembering things I couldn't possibly understand.

She cleared her throat. "And John just floated away from me. My mother was right there, you know, and terribly concerned about me, and she sort of took him over. That was what she felt she could do for me. I can remember early on, sometimes I'd hear him crying or calling for me, and then I'd hear her, and after a while he'd stop, and I'd be *glad.* I'd just hold you and go back to sleep. Or more like a trance, it really was. I'll never forgive myself."

I wanted to comfort her. "But he loved Grandma Vetter," I said. "I mean, he ended up getting a lot *out* of that."

"Well, yes, I think he did, but in the meantime, making that shift from me to her was terrible for him. And also, I'm not so sure having my mother as a substitute was so good for him. I mean, she was born in another century. All her values and rules, while they're perfectly good ones, were ones that sort of . . . stiffened John, fed *that* side of who he was. And I, I knew that he, much more than you, needed to learn to relax, to be playful. But I just didn't, couldn't help him." She twirled her cup slowly in its saucer. "And then I was working and he was so good and reliable, and *you* were the one always in scrapes."

I felt a pang of something like guilt. "But he turned out fine, Mom. He turned out great."

"Oh, I know he did, darling, but I'm talking about something else. I'm talking about why John struggles so hard to have certain things in his life. Or even certain people."

I frowned at her, not sure I understood.

"I let him go, Doug, don't you see?"

I shook my head, resolute on her behalf.

She looked at me for a moment, then suddenly she said, "All right, I know. I'll tell you. It's like one time I remember, I was driving you boys back from some trip somewhere, and we were coming home through Sandusky. We were going to stop at my great-aunt's for the night. Viola. She's dead a long time now. And I just couldn't find it. I tried for about an hour and a half, but nothing was where it was supposed to be by my directions. And I finally just pulled over—I was so aggravated—and I said out loud, 'Well, that's it. We're lost.' And I was so busy looking at these directions and maps and things that I didn't notice John for a few minutes. But when I finally looked at him . . . well, I've never seen a child so terrified. I asked him what the matter was and he said, 'You said we were *lost*!' And suddenly, by the way he said it, I knew he thought I'd meant *lost,* in a sort of fairy-tale sense—like Hansel and Gretel, or someone being lost in a forest. *Never* getting home. Starving to death."

She shook her head. "You know, most kids his age—he was five or six, I think—don't think they're *lost* as long as they've got their mother with them. But he had so little faith in me, in my ability to protect him. I knew right then that I'd lost John. Just lost him." She shook her head again, sadly.

After a moment I said softly, "I think he'll be all right, Mom."

"Oh, I know he'll be all right, honey," she said, "I know it! That's what breaks my heart." And for the first time in my memory since Grandma's death, I saw my mother cry.

I went over to Jacey's apartment more frequently that fall than I had in the past. I had a sense of him as a trust that my mother had placed in me. I'm not sure what made for my conviction that she had never spoken about him to me, but I felt secure in it. And I felt she'd somehow asked me to help her pay a debt to Jacey that she, and therefore perhaps I, too, owed him.

It didn't make much difference to our relationship, because Jacey simply wouldn't speak to me about anything intimate; but in fact, I liked the order and the quiet in his carefully furnished apartment. On Sundays, I almost always bought English muffins and the *Times* and walked over there. We'd sit quietly all morning, eating and going through the paper, occasionally reading aloud or commenting on some story.

But as the fall wore on, I found more and more, when I dropped over un-expectedly, that he'd come to the door in a bathrobe or towel and tell me that it wasn't a good time. He never smiled or suggested in any of the ways some of my friends might have that it was because there was a woman inside. But I knew that's what it was, and I was happy for him, though a little surprised after the intensity of his feeling for Alice. But it was clear to me, by now, that Jacey was a lover of women, that he needed and enjoyed their company in a way that some men don't—perhaps, I remember speculating then, because of my mother's painful turning away from him as a young child. That he was again able to be interested in them seemed to me a sign of health, and I wrote my mother that Jacey was, as I put it, "beginning to go out a bit," though he hadn't actually spoken to me about it.

He invited me to early dinner one Friday in late October. He said it had to be early because he was doing something later on. It was a cold, rainy night, and I remember a sense of nostalgia swept over me as I walked the short distance to his apartment, stumbling occasionally over the bumps in the rain-slicked brick sidewalks. I was in the throes of another dying romance, powerfully disappointed because the woman I thought I had loved was so much more **mundane** than I had originally conceived of her as being. Jacey had made a fine meal—scallops and salad and a very good wine. We had several cups of coffee afterward, and I re-member thinking how thoroughly in charge he was of his own life. He went into his study to get some slides to show me, and the doorbell rang.

"Shall I get it?" I asked.

"Sure," he called back.

A woman stood under the porch light, wearing a poncho, her head bent down, her face lost in the shadow of her hood. As I opened the glass door, she raised her head. It was Pamela Abbott. She looked startled, but her voice was smooth. "Hello, Doug," she said.

I said hello. For a few confused moments, I thought that she'd somehow come to my brother's apartment to see me, but as I followed her in, I realized this couldn't be, that it was, of course, John she had come for. Even then I couldn't make my mind work to understand it.

Jacey greeted her coolly and took her wet poncho, shaking it away from him several times before he hung it up. She sat down at the table and I joined her. He was standing. He asked her if she wanted some coffee. She shrugged. "Sure, if you're having some."

mundane: commonplace

44

While he was in the kitchen, I felt compelled to make small talk. "So, Pamela," I said. "What's up?" She shrugged again.

"I mean, God," I said, feeling more and more like an idiot, "I'm really sweating out this *facing life* business. Trying to decide what in hell I'm going to do next year, you know?" She looked steadily at me and didn't respond. "Do you have any idea what you're going to do?" I asked.

"I don't know," she said. "I'll probably go to New York and get a job in publishing, I think."

"God, that sounds exciting. But it's rough, isn't it? I mean, to get a job?"

"I don't know. My father has a couple of connections. I don't think it'll be too hard to get some shit lower-level thing."

Jacey was standing in the doorway now, a cup of coffee in his hand. "And then climb the ladder, using his connections all the way," he said sharply. I looked at him, but his face was blank. He walked over to her and set the coffee in front of her. She shrugged again. She looked at him as he went back to his seat. I watched her watching my brother and saw that she was frightened of him. I realized that I should have left as soon as she arrived, that she was what he was "doing" later. We sat in silence for a minute. Jacey lighted a cigarette and the smell of sulphur and burning tobacco hung in the little room.

"Well," he said suddenly to Pamela. His voice was still sharp. "Do you want to go to bed?"

She looked quickly at me and then away. After a moment she raised her shoulders. "Sure," she said without emotion, as though accepting some punishment. He stood up. She stood up. I stood up. I was trying to meet my brother's eye, and it seemed to me for a second I did, but his gaze slid quickly sideways. He walked out of the room first, and she followed him, without looking at me again.

I left the apartment immediately. My heart was pounding in my ears. I walked along the black river in the rain, across the Western Avenue Bridge and all the way up to the boathouse on the other side, trying to understand what my brother was doing to himself, to Pamela, to me. He who was so private, who kept his life and emotions so masked, had exposed himself and Pamela to me, had shown me how contemptuously he could treat her, how **despicable** he could be. He who had felt used, I know, by Eleanor, and who, I could guess, had felt abused by Alice, was now doing both to Pamela. It seemed to me like a violation of everything I would have said he believed in. And I felt slapped that he had asked me to witness it all, as though he were exposing also my pretensions to understand anything about life.

I was cold and drenched by the time I got home. I took a long shower, grateful that both of my roommates were out, and went to bed early. I lay awake for a long time, thinking about Jacey, about myself, about how we grew up.

I didn't get in touch with my brother or go to his apartment again for several weeks. Finally he called. It was a Sunday. He said he'd gotten the *Times* and made breakfast and he wondered if I wanted to come over. I said okay, not enthusiastically, and then I said, "Will there be just the two of us?"

"Yes," he said. "That won't happen again."

It was cold outside, gray. The trees were nearly stripped of leaves and I had the sense of winter coming on. John had a fire going in the fireplace and had set breakfast out on the coffee table. I was, for once, repelled by the orderliness. I wondered if I'd ever again see my brother in a spontaneous moment. I swallowed some of his good coffee.

"I wanted to apologize," he said.

"Oh," I said.

"What I did was wrong."

"Did you tell that to Pamela?" I asked.

"What business is that of yours?" he said, flaring suddenly.

despicable: worthless; contemptible

Then he looked away, into the fire for a moment. We were sitting side by side on the couch. "Yes," he said tiredly. "You're right. And I did say it to her. I'm not seeing her anymore. I wanted you to know that." Then he slouched lower in the couch and started to talk. He told me that Pamela had come over unexpectedly almost as soon as school started. It upset him to see her, and he had a lot to drink while she was there, as she did. He said she did most of the talking, about her family, about Alice, about Eleanor. She seemed eager to align herself with him against her parents. She told him that they were stupid, rigid. Worse, they were cruel. She said that they had destroyed Eleanor and were destroying Alice, that she was the only daughter smart enough to see the process, the pitfalls on the one hand of resisting too hard or, on the other hand, of caving in. She called her father a tyrant, a bastard. She said that Jacey couldn't imagine the kinds of things said about him, about our family, in their house.

And then, drunk, she said how wonderful she'd always thought he was, how much she admired him, how much she wanted him. She thought they ought to sleep together.

Drunk, too, and angry, he had done it. Then he had passed out, and in the morning she was gone. He said he had thought that that was probably it, that she'd seen herself as fulfilling some part of what he called her "Abbott destiny" by having him as a lover.

But she kept coming over, and he kept sleeping with her. He said he knew it was wrong, that he didn't even like her really. But that in some ways it was like having Alice again, and it was like getting back at her too. And so he just kept doing it.

He got up and poked the fire. He sat down again, this time on the floor. "And then I began to feel *used* again," he said. "It was crazy; I was using her, too. But I began to feel that somehow I was just . . . some bit *actor* in some part of their family drama. She kept telling me she *loved* me; and I just kept getting more and more cruel to her. More angry." He looked at me suddenly. "I guess inviting you over was a way of seeing how much she'd take, how low she'd go." He turned away again. "I was pretty far gone, too, in some kind of rage I'd lost control over. But finally I just said I wouldn't see her anymore. I was trying to be kind, but it ended up being a pretty ugly scene. Lots of tears and yelling."

I thought of Pamela, so flip, so sure of herself. "Did she not want to stop?"

He shrugged. "She claims she's in love with me. She threatened to tell Alice we were lovers if I wouldn't see her anymore."

"God!" I said. "Think she will?"

He shook his head. "I don't know. She may. I'm hoping that it'll seem so uselessly cruel that she'll decide not to. But it's her family. And I took that risk when I slept with her. And there won't be anything more between me and Alice anyway, so maybe it'd be for the best. Maybe it'd confirm all the terrible things her father has to say about me and make things easier for Alice."

"That's pretty **magnanimous** of you," I said.

He looked at me and smiled. "Not entirely. I'd like to be able to let go of Alice. It's been hard, I mean. I've been in love with her for a year and a half and I've slept with her maybe ten times. And I never will again. She still writes to me all the time, even though I can't answer. That kind of stuff. I mean, maybe it's part of the whole thing. Why I slept with Pamela in the first place. To push that possibility away forever."

That was the end of my brother's involvement with the Abbott girls. He told me a few Sundays later that he thought Pamela must have said something to Alice or to her family, because the letters abruptly stopped, but otherwise we didn't speak of them again. I went home the following summer and he stayed in Cambridge. He had a drafting job with a little design company. Alice was still living at home and I saw her a few times during the summer. At first I didn't recognize her. She'd

magnanimous: possessing a generous spirit

46

put on at least twenty-five pounds. She didn't say hello to me, but I didn't really expect her to. In fact, as by some unspoken agreement, we each pretended not to know the other when our paths crossed.

In the fall I moved to New York. I saw Pamela there, occasionally, for a few years. We still had friends from college in common. She was an assistant editor at a good publishing house, and I was trying to get any kind of acting job. We'd talk when we met, a little edgily. She'd ask about Jacey, and I'd ask about Alice and Eleanor, as if they were vague acquaintances and not a part of who we both were. She was in touch with Eleanor again, but Eleanor refused to see the family at all. She was a stewardess, and she loved it, loved to travel, Pamela said. Alice lived at home and let her parents run her children, her life. Pamela went home every now and then for a few days, which was about as long as she could stand it, she said.

Our only really difficult conversation was our last one, when I had to tell her that Jacey had gotten married. She looked pained for the smallest fraction of a second, and then the tough smile reemerged. "Well, I assume that whoever it is is rich."

"Why do you assume that?" I asked. In fact, Jacey's wife, an architect too, did have some money, perhaps even as much as the Abbotts had. But I knew enough now to know that that really wasn't rich. And Jacey seemed happy no matter what.

"Isn't that the only kind of girl he's ever been interested in?" she asked jauntily. "Hasn't he been trying to marry up since about the day he had his first erection?"

There were so many levels on which her remark offended me—the insult about Jacey's intentions, the implied insult about his, and therefore my, social class—that I wasn't able to choose at which level I wanted to respond. I answered quickly, almost without thinking. "Why do you assume that for him to have married one of you would be to marry up?"

She looked at me for a moment with her mouth open, and then she turned away.

I didn't see her again before I moved to Chicago. I wanted to be nearer my mother, who wasn't well, and I'd gotten a good job with a repertory company there.

My mother got worse over the next three years—she had cancer—and I often went down and spent two or three weeks in the old house with her when there were breaks in my work. One summer night we were driving past the Abbott's and the tent was up again. Dance music swelled out in the summer air. The band was playing "Blowin' in the Wind" to a bouncy foxtrot rhythm. My mother looked over at the soft yellow lights, the moving figures. "Imagine a child of Alice's being old enough to dance," she said. And I recalled abruptly that she had known all the Abbotts, all the children in town, as second graders. That in some sense we remained always young, always vulnerable in her vision. She didn't think of the pain we'd all caused each other.

She died in the early winter of that year. I went down frequently in the fall. We sat around at home in the evenings, often drinking a fair amount. She'd lost so much weight by then that she was, as she called herself, a cheap drunk, and we seemed to float back easily into the comfortable, **desultory** intimacy we'd had when I was home alone with her in high school. Once she asked me what came next for me in life. I asked her what she meant. "Oh, I don't know, darling," she said. "You just seem so content, I wonder if this is really . . . *it* for you."

"I don't know," I said honestly. I felt, at the moment, so peaceful that it wouldn't have bothered me if it was. "It seems to me I've chosen the right profession, certainly. I'm really much better at pretending than at being. You know, I used to have such contempt for Jacey, for what he wanted out of life, for the kinds

desultory: random

47

of women he went after. But in fact he always really went after things. And he suffered with it, but he's all right in the end. I like him. Whereas I haven't done that. I'm happy, but . . . Well, that's all that really counts, I guess. I am happy. I'm actually very happy."

"I know what you mean," she said. "I've been happy, too, and glad I didn't have the messes that some of my friends made of their lives. But sometimes I've worried that I lived a little like a nun, you know. Sort of a *pinched* life, in the end."

We sat. The only sound was the occasional faint noise of the old house shifting somewhere in the cold fall air.

Then I said, "Why didn't you ever remarry, Mother? Surely there were possibilities."

"Fewer than you'd think," she said. "Everyone always thinks things are more possible than they are. I mean, single men don't stay in Haley if they've got any starch. Who was there my age who was eligible? Drew Carter was always around, but he's a washout. And now there's a few old widowers who smell like their dogs." She laughed. "I'm getting mean," she said. "And then I was a schoolteacher for all those years. You don't meet men in a job like that. No, the only time I ever met anyone was in Chicago, a friend of Beatrice Goulding's. I used to go up and visit him every summer, stay with him for five or six days. Surely you remember that. I always told you I was staying with Beatrice." I nodded. I remembered those visits. "He was a wonderful man. Wonderful." And then, with that deft way my mother had of casting the entire story she was telling in a new light, she said, "A little boring, but really, very wonderful."

"Well, why didn't you marry him? Move us all up there?"

"Oh, I couldn't have done that to John," she said instantly. "He'd had such a terrible early childhood, and he was so happy at that stage. Remember? He was playing ball and had a good job and was chasing around after that middle Abbott girl. No." She shook her head. "All this life in Haley had gotten to be too important to him then. I can't imagine having asked him to give it up. I never would have forgiven myself. No, it was better for me to go on as I had been. And besides, I was still really in love with Charlie. With my memory of him. And I've enjoyed my life. I have," she said **wistfully**.

"Well, it's not over yet," I said.

But it nearly was. Jacey came out for the eight or ten days before she died. We took care of her at home, as she'd wanted, with a visiting nurse to help us out. She was very uncomfortable the last few days, though not in actual pain, and I think we were both relieved when her struggle stopped, when we didn't have to listen to her trying to breathe anymore at night.

There wasn't really a funeral, because she'd been cremated and because she didn't want a service. She had requested that we have a hymn to sing, and she had written down three or four of her favorites she wanted us to be sure to do. Jacey and I discussed the plans the morning after she'd died. We were washing the last of her dishes, putting things away in the kitchen. "Isn't it like her," he said, tears sitting in his eyes, "to take charge even of the way we let her go." He shook his head in proud amazement, and I thought how differently we knew her, understood her.

So we gathered, around twenty or so of her friends, mostly women, and Jacey and I, and some young people who were former students, and sang "Guide Me, Oh Thou Great Jehovah" and "Fight the Good Fight" and "Amazing Grace" and "For All the Saints." It seemed so insufficient, as any service does, I suppose, that we went on singing too long, to compensate, and Jacey and I were both hoarse the next day.

But there were still things to pack up, and so we went to the old center of town to get some boxes. It was a cold, bright day, and the town looked small and

wistfully: with yearning desire

48

shabby in the raw light, as though nothing important could ever have happened there. We were loading the trunk and the back seat of the car in front of the liquor store when I saw a woman walking toward us down the street whom I recognized instantly as Mrs. Abbott. She didn't look very different from the way she had at all those parties. Her hair, dyed now, I supposed, was still a pale arranged blonde; her lipstick was a girlish pink. She saw Jacey, and I could tell that for a moment she was thinking of walking past us without acknowledging us. Her step wavered marginally, but then she straightened up. We both assumed, I think, that she would speak to us of our mother's death, which is what every conversation we'd had in the last few days had started with.

But whether she didn't know what we were both in town for or whether her own emotions of the moment drove it out of her mind, that's not what she spoke of. A brilliant social smile flickered quickly across her face and was gone. Then, standing an uncomfortable distance from us on the sidewalk, she made for a minute or two the kind of small talk she'd made all those years ago under the tents in her backyard—a comment on the weather, on how we'd changed, on how busy young people's lives were, they could hardly ever get home anymore. As she spoke she nodded repeatedly, an odd birdlike motion of her head. There was an awkward silence when she finished—I know I couldn't imagine what an appropriate response would be—and then she said with brittle cheer to Jacey alone, "Well, I've no more daughters for you." And though she'd been talking about his loss rather than her own, she smiled again, and walked on.

For a moment we stood motionless on the sidewalk, watching her diminishing figure. Then I turned to Jacey, expecting, I suppose, some comment, and ready to be angry along with him, on his behalf. But he didn't even look at me. Instead, he bent down and started to load the empty boxes that would hold my mother's belongings into the car, as though what Mrs. Abbott had said and done had all happened with the rest of it, years before, when he was a child.

▼ Questions about the Story

1. Consider the opening scene of the story, the scene involving the false sideburns. What does it tell us about the two boys, the mother, and the relationship among them?

2. How do Doug and Jacey react to their less than privileged circumstances? Why are their reactions so different?

3. Describe Doug, Jacey, their mother.

4. What role does Jacey play in the Abbott family drama?

5. In her heart-to-heart talk with Doug about Jacey, the mother says Jacey would have had to invent the Abbotts had they not existed. What does she mean?

6. "Oh, I know he'll be all right, honey. I know it!" the mother says to Doug about Jacey. "That's what breaks my heart." What do you make of this?

7. Why does Jacey treat Pamela with such contempt?

8. Late in the story, Doug speaks somewhat regretfully about the choices he has made. He contrasts his own life with his brother's. "I'm happy," he says, "but . . ." How do you suppose he might have completed this thought?

9. Is "The Lover of Women" a good title for this story? Why or why not?

▼ Relating the Story to Yourself

1. In discussing Jacey, the mother comments on how having money can give to a young person a sense of place, of knowing where you belong. Do you think this is true? Are there other psychological benefits conferred by wealth? Can the sense of place be derived from other sources?

2. Near the end of the story, reacting to a comment of Jacey's about their mother, Doug remarks to us how differently the two of them knew her, understood her. If you have brothers and sisters, can the same be said of your family's knowledge and understanding of your parents? If so, what are some of the possible explanations of the differences?

3. How important is the goal of having a lot of money for you? If it is important, why is it so? What is the value of money for you? In your opinion, how important ought wealth to be as a life goal? Why do you answer as you do? If there is a discrepancy between the importance you accord to money in your actual life goals and the importance you think it ought to have, how do you account for this discrepancy?

4. The Abbott family was a kind of myth for Jacey, an icon embodying for him all the promise of life, and it was a myth into which he would enter. Is there a comparable myth or symbol in your life? What is it?

5. We in America pride ourselves on the relative insignificance of social class distinction. And yet, as this story attests, these distinctions are far from absent in American life. How strong a sense of social class do you have? Are you aware, as Jacey so acutely was, of being a member of a certain social class? If so, what experiences may have forged this awareness in you? What influence has this awareness had on your sense of self and on your life goals?

▼ Discussion

1. For yourself, how important is the goal of having a lot of money? If it is important, why is it so?

2. What are the advantages of wealth? What are its disadvantages? What do you think is the relation between wealth and happiness?

▼ Writing Assignments

1. "The Psychological Advantages of Wealth"
2. Write an essay in which you describe incidents and events that made clear to you the place of money in your personal value system.
3. "Inventing Mother (or Father): The Discrepancies in My Family's Conceptions of Our Mother"
4. "The Importance (or Unimportance) of Having Money"
5. "How Social Class Awareness Has Figured in My Life"

▼ Journal Entry

1. With which of the characters in this story was it easiest for you to identify? Why?

▼ Vocabulary

adjudicate	desultory	mundane	putative
commiserated	elated	ostentatious	trig
contemptible	emblematic	overt	vacuous
debauchery	magnanimous	persona non grata	whimsicality
despicable	malleable	precocity	wistfully

6

▼

Story of My Life

Jay McInerney

Jay McInerney is the author of Bright Lights, Big City. *In this story, published in* Esquire *in the summer of 1987, he introduces us to a young woman of 21 whose life is going very fast and very badly.*

I'M LIKE—I DON'T BELIEVE THIS SHIT.

I'm totally pissed at my old man, who's somewhere in the Virgin Islands, I don't know where. The check was not in the mailbox today, which means I can't go to school Monday morning. I'm on the monthly payment program because my Dad says wanting to be an actress is a flaky whim and I never stick to anything—this from a guy who's been married five times—and this way if I drop out in the middle of the semester, he won't get burned for the full tuition. Meanwhile, he buys his new bimbo, Tanya, who is a year younger than me, a 450 SL convertible—always liked the young kids, haven't we, Dad?—plus her own condo so she can have some privacy to do her writing. Like she can even *read*. He actually believes her when she says she's writing a novel, but when I want to spend eight hours a day busting ass at Lee Strasberg, it's like, *another one of Alison's crazy ideas.* Story of my life. My old man is fifty-two going on twelve. And then there's Skip Pendleton, which is another reason I'm pissed.

So I'm on the phone screaming at my father's secretary when there's a call on my other line. I go hello and this guy goes, hi I'm whatever-his-name-is, I'm a friend of Skip's, and I say yeah and he says I thought maybe we could go out sometime. And I say what am I, dial-a-date?

Skip Pendleton is a jerk I was in lust with once for about three minutes. He hasn't called me in like three weeks, which is fine, okay, I can deal with that, but suddenly I'm like a baseball card that he trades with his friends? Give me a break. So I go to this guy, what makes you think I'd want to go out with you, I don't even know you, and he goes Skip told me about you. Right. So I'm like, what did he tell you? and the guy goes—Skip said you were hot. I say great, I'm totally honored that the great Skip Pendleton thinks I'm hot. I'm just a jalapeno pepper waiting for some strange burrito, honey. I mean, *really.*

And this guy says to me, we were sitting around at Skip's place about 5:00 in the morning the other night wired out of our minds, and I say—this is the guy talking—I wish we had some women, and Skip is like, I could always call Alison, she'd be over like a shot, she loves it.

He said that? I say. I can hear his voice exactly, it's not like I'm totally amazed, but still I can't believe even *he* would be such a pig, and suddenly I feel like a cheap slut and I want to scream at this asshole, but instead I say, where are you? He's on West Eighty-ninth, so I give him an address on Avenue C, a rathole where a friend of mine lived last year until her place was broken into for the seventeenth time, and which is about as far away from the Upper West Side as you can get without crossing water, and I tell him to meet me there in an hour, and at least I have the satisfaction of thinking of him spending about twenty bucks for a cab and then hanging around the doorway of a tenement and maybe getting

51

51

beat up by some drug dealers. But the one I'm really pissed at is Skip Pendleton. Nothing my father does surprises me anymore. I'm twenty-one going on gray.

Skip is thirty-one, and he's so smart and so educated—just ask him, he'll tell you. Did I forget to mention he's *so* mature? Unlike me. He was always telling me I don't know anything. I don't know what I saw in him. He seemed older and sophisticated, and we had great sex, so why not? I met him in a club, naturally. I never thought he was very good-looking, but you could tell *he* thought he was. He believed it so much that he actually sold the idea to other people. He had that confidence everybody wants a piece of. This blond hair that looks like he has it trimmed about three times a day. Nice clothes, shirts custom-made on Jermyn Street, which he might just casually tell you some night in case you didn't know is in London, England. (That's in Europe, which is across the Atlantic Ocean—oh, really, Skip, is that where it is? Wow!) Went to the right schools. And he's rich, of course, owns his own company. Commodities trader. Story of Skip's life. Trading commodities.

So basically, he had it all. Should have been a Dewar's Profile. I'm like amazed they haven't asked him yet. But when the sun hit him in the morning, he was a shivering wreck.

From the first night, bending over the silver picture frame in his apartment with a rolled fifty up his nose, all he can talk about is his ex, who dumped him, and how if he could only get her back he would give up all this forever, coke, staying out partying all night, young bimbos like me. And I'm thinking, poor guy, just lost his main squeeze, feeling real sympathetic, and so like, I go, when did this happen Skip, and it turns out it was ten years ago! He lived with this chick for four years at Harvard, and then after they come to New York together she dumps him for some Rockefeller. And I'm like, give me a break, Skip. Give yourself a break. This is ten years after. This is nineteen eighty whatever.

Skip's so smart, right? My parents never gave a shit whether I went to school or not, they were off chasing lovers and bottles and rails of blow, leaving us kids with the cars and the credit cards, and I never did get much of an education. Is that my fault? I mean, if someone had told you back then that you could either go to school or not, what do you think you would have done? Pass the trigonometry, please. Right. So I'm not as educated as the great Skip Pendleton, but let me tell you. I know that when you're hitting on someone you don't spend the whole night whining about your ex, especially after ten years. And you don't need a Ph.D. in psychology to figure out why Skip can't go out with anybody his own age. He keeps trying to find Diana, the beautiful, perfect Diana, who was twenty-one when she dumped him. And he wants us, the young stuff, because we're like Diana was ten years ago. And he hates us because we're not Diana. And he thinks it will make him feel better if he fucks us over and makes us hurt the way he was hurt, because that's what it's all about if you ask me—we're all sitting around here on earth working through our hurts, trying to pass them along to other people and make things even. Chain of pain.

Old Skip kept telling me how dumb I was. You wish, Jack. Funny thing is, dumb is his type. He doesn't want to go out with anybody who might see through him, so he picks up kids like me. Girls he thinks will believe everything he says and fuck him the first night and not be real surprised when he never calls again.

If you're so smart, Skip, how come you don't know these things? If you're so mature, what were you doing with me?

Men. I've never met any. They're all boys. I wish I didn't want them so much. I've had a few dreams about making it with girls, but it's kind of like—sure, I'd love to visit Norway sometime. My roommate Jeannie and I sleep in the same bed and it's great. We've got a one bedroom and this way the living room is free for partying and whatever. I hate being alone, but when I wake up in some guy's bed with dry come on the sheets underneath me and he's snoring like a garbage truck, I go—Let me out of here. I slip out and crawl around the floor groping for my clothes, trying to untangle his blue jeans from mine, my bra from his Jockeys—Skip wears boxers, of course—trying to be quiet at the same time, slide out the door laughing like a seal escaping from the zoo, and home to where Jeannie has been warming the bed all night. Jumping in between the sheets and she wakes up and goes, I want details, Alison: length and width.

I love Jeannie. She cracks me up. She's an assistant editor at a fashion magazine, but what she really wants to do is get married. It might work for her, but I don't believe in it. My parents have seven marriages between them, and anytime I've been with a guy for more than a few weeks, I find myself looking out the window during sex.

I call up my friend Didi to see if she can lend me the money. Didi's father is rich, and he gives her this huge allowance, but she spends it all on blow. She used to buy clothes, but now she wears the same outfit for four or five days in a row, and it's pretty gross, let me tell you. Sometimes we have to send the health department over to her apartment to open the windows and burn the sheets.

I get Didi's machine, which means she's not home. If she's home she unplugs the phone, and if she's not home she turns on the answering machine. Either way it's pretty impossible to talk to her. I don't know why I bother. She sleeps from about noon till like 9:00 p.m. or so. If Didi made a list of her favorite things, I guess cocaine would be at the top, and sunlight wouldn't even make the cut. So she can be hard to get hold of.

My friends and I spend half of our lives leaving messages for one another. Luckily I know Didi's message access code, so I dial again and listen to her messages to see if I can figure out from the messages where she is.

Okay, maybe I'm just nosy.

The first message is from Brian, and from his voice I can tell that he's doing Didi, which really blows me away, since Brian is Jeannie's old boyfriend. Except that Didi is less interested in sex than any of my friends, so I'm not really sure. Maybe Brian is just starting to make his move. A message from her mom—Call me, sweetie, I'm in Aspen. Then Phillip, saying he wants his $350 or else. Which is when I go, what am I, crazy? I'm never going to get a cent out of Didi. And if I do find her, she's going to try and talk me into getting wired with her, and I'm trying to stay away from that. I'm about to hang up when I get a call on the other line. It's my school telling me that my tuition hasn't been received and that I won't be able to come back to class until it is. Like, what do you think I've been frantic about for the last twenty-four hours. It's Saturday afternoon. Jeannie will be home soon and then it's all over.

By this time I'm getting pretty bitter. You could say I am not a happy unit. Acting is the first thing I've ever really wanted to do. Except for riding. When I was a kid I spent most of my time on horseback. I went around the country, showing my horses and jumping, until Dick Diver got poisoned. Then I got into drugs. But acting, I don't know, I just love it, getting up there and turning myself inside out. Being somebody else for a change. It's also the first thing that's made me get up in the morning. The first year I was in New York I did nothing but guys and blow. Staying out all night at the Surf Club and Zulu, waking up at five in the afternoon with plugged sinuses and sticky hair. Some kind of white stuff in every hole. Story of my life. My friends are still pretty much that way, which is why I'm so desperate to get this check, because if I don't then there's no reason to wake up early Monday morning, and Jeannie will get home, and somebody will call up, and the next thing I know it'll be three days from now with no sleep in between, brain in orbit, nose in traction. I call my father's secretary again, and she says she's still trying to reach him.

I decide to do some of my homework before Jeannie gets home—my sense-memory exercise. Don't ask me why, since I won't be able to go to school. But it chills me out. I sit down in the folding chair and relax, empty out my mind of all the crap. Then I begin to imagine an orange. I try to see it in front of me. I take it in my hand.

A big old round one veined with rust, like the ones we get down in Florida straight from the tree. (Those Clearasil spotless ones you buy in the Safeway are dusted with cyanide or some such shit, so you can imagine how good they are for you.) So I start to peel it real slow, smelling the little geysers of spray that break from the squeezed peel, feeling the juice stinging around the edges of my finger-nails where I've bitten them. . . .

So of course the phone rings. Guy's voice, Barry something. I'm a friend of Skip's, he says. I go, if this is some kind of joke I'm really not amused. Hey, no joke, he goes. I'm just, you know, Skip told me you guys weren't going out anymore, and I saw you once at Indochine, and I thought maybe we could do some dinner sometime.

I'm like—I don't believe this. What am I?—the York Avenue Escort Service?

I don't know where I get these ideas, but sometimes I'm pretty quick. I go, did Skip also tell you about the disease he gave me? That shrinks this Barry's equipment pretty quick. Suddenly he's got a call on the other line. Sure you do.

That son of a bitch Skip. I'm so mad I think about really fixing his ass. First I think I'll call him up and tell him he did give me a disease. Make him go to the doctor, shut down his love life for a few days.

The phone rings and it's Didi. Unbelievable! Live—in person, practically. And it's daylight outside.

I just went to my nose doctor, she goes. He was horrified. He told me if I had to keep doing blow that I should start shooting up. Then the damage would be some other doctor's responsibility.

What's with you and Brian? I say.

She says, I went home with him a couple of weeks ago, I don't know. I woke up in his bed. I'm not even sure we did anything. But he's definitely in lust with me. Meanwhile, my period's late. So maybe we did.

She has another call. While she takes it, I'm thinking. Didi comes back on and tells me it's her mom, who's having a major breakdown, she'll call me back. I tell her no problem. She's already been a big help.

I get Skip at his office. He doesn't sound too thrilled to hear from me. He says he's in a meeting, can he call me back? I say no, I have to talk now.

What? he says.

I'm pregnant, I say.

Total silence.

Before he can ask I say, I haven't slept with anybody else in six weeks. Which is totally true, almost. Close off that little escape hatch in his mind. Slam, bam.

He goes, You're sure? He sounds like he's just swallowed a bunch of sand.

I'm sure.

He's like, What do you want to do?

The thing about Skip is that, even though he's an asshole, he's also a gentleman. Actually a lot of the assholes I know are gentlemen. Or vice versa. Dickheads with a family crest and a prep-school code of honor.

I go, I need money.

How much?

A thousand. I can't believe I ask him for that much. I was thinking five hundred just a minute ago, but hearing his voice pissed me off.

He asks if I want him to go with me, and I say no, definitely not. Then he tries to do this number about making out the check directly to the clinic, and I say, Skip, don't give me that shit. I need five hundred in cash to make the appointment, I tell him, and I don't want to wait six business days for the stupid check to clear, okay? Acting my ass off. My teacher would be proud.

Two hours later a messenger arrives with the money. Cash. I give him a ten-dollar tip.

Saturday night Jeannie and Didi go out. Didi comes over, wearing this same horrible surfer shirt she's been wearing all week and her slept-on unwashed Rastafarian hair. Really gross. But she's still incredibly beautiful, even after four days without sleep, and guys make total asses of themselves trying to pick her up. Her mother was this really big model in the fifties, Swedish. Didi was supposed to be the Revlon girl or something, but she couldn't be bothered to wake up for the shoot. Jeannie's wearing my black cashmere sweater, her grandmother's pearls, jeans, and Maud Frizon pumps.

How do I look, she says, checking herself out in the mirror.

Terrific, I say, You'll be lucky if you make it through cocktails without getting raped.

Can't rape the willing, Jeannie says, which is what we always say.

They try to get me to come along, but I'm doing my scene for class Monday morning. They can't believe it. They say it won't last. I say, this is my life. I'm like, trying to do something constructive with it, you know? Jeannie and Didi think this is hilarious. They do this choirgirl thing where they both fold their hands like they're praying and hum "Amazing Grace," which is what we do when somebody starts to get religious on us. Then just to be complete assholes they sing, *Alison, we know this world is killing you . . . ,* et cetera, which is kind of like my theme song when I'm being a drag.

So I go:

They say you're nothing but party girls! Just like a million more all over the world.

They crack up. We all love that first Costello album.

After they *finally* leave, I open up my script but I'm having trouble concentrating, so I call up my little sister at home. Of course the line is busy and they don't have call waiting, so I call the operator and request an emergency breakthrough on the line. I listen while the operator cuts in. I hear Carol's voice, and then the operator says there's an emergency call from Vanna White in New York. Carol immediately says *Alison,* in this moaning, grown-up voice, even though she's three years younger than me.

What's new? I go when she gets rid of the other call.

Same old stuff, she says. Mom's drunk. My car's in the shop. Mickey's out on bail. He's drunk, too.

Listen, do you know where Dad is? I go, and she says last she heard Virgin Islands, but she doesn't have a number either. So I tell her about my school thing, and then maybe because I'm feeling a little weird about it, I tell her about Skip, except I say $500 instead of $1,000 and she says it sounds like he totally deserved it. He's such a prick, I go, and Carol says, yeah, he sounds just like Dad. And I go, yeah, just like.

Jeannie comes back Sunday morning at 9:00 a.m. She's a shivering wreck. I give her a Valium and put her to bed.

She lies in bed stiff as a mannequin and says, I'm so afraid, Alison. She is not a happy unit.

We're all afraid, I go.

In half an hour she's making these horrible chain-saw sleep noises.

Thanks to Skip, Monday morning I'm at school doing aerobics and voice. I'm feeling great. Really good. Then sense-memory work. I sit down in class, and my teacher tells me I'm at a beach. She wants me to see the sand and the water and feel the sun on my bare skin. No problem. First I have to clear myself out. That's part of the process. All around me people are making strange noises, stretching, getting their ya-yas out, preparing for their own exercises. I don't know—I'm just letting myself go limp in the head, then I'm laughing hysterically, and next thing I'm bawling like a baby, really out of control, falling out of my chair and thrashing all over the floor . . . a real basket case . . . epileptic **apocalypse**, sobbing and flailing around, trying to take a bite out of the linoleum . . . they're used to some pretty radical emoting in here, but this is way over the top, apparently. I don't really remember . . . they take me to the doctor, who says I'm overtired and tells me to go home and rest . . .

That night my old man finally calls. I'm like, I must be dreaming.

Pissed at you, I go, when he asks me how I am.

I'm sorry, honey, he says about the tuition. I screwed up.

You're goddamn right you did, I say.

Oh, baby, I'm a mess.

You're telling me, I go.

She left me.

Don't come crying to me.

I'm so sad.

When are you going to grow up, for Christ's sake.

I bitch him out for a while, and then I tell him I'm sorry, it's okay, he's well rid of her, there are lots of women who would love a sweet man like him. And his money. Story of his life. But I don't say that, of course. He's fifty-two years old, and it's a little late to try to tell him the facts of life. From what I've seen, nobody changes much after a certain age. Like, about four years old, maybe. Anyway, I hold his hand, not literally, you know, and cool him out and almost forget to hit him up for money.

He promises to send me the tuition and the rent and something extra.

He sends me a check, but then he completely forgets my birthday. Not even a phone call. His secretary claims he's in Europe on business. My sister tells me he's in Cancun with a new bimbo. At this point my period is already three weeks late. And if that's not, like, ironic enough, I see Skip Pendleton one night. He's with some anorectic Click model and pretends he doesn't know me. And I'm trying to work out dates and guys, and I figure if I am pregnant it could actually be his.

Of course with my luck it turns out I'm actually pregnant. The rabbit dies, so I have to visit the clinic for real. I can't believe it. I use the check Dad sends for the month's tuition. They give me some Demerol—not nearly enough. I try to tell them I have this monster tolerance but they say this is the dosage for your height and weight—and afterward it hurts like hell. While I'm getting my insides Hoovered out, I swear off the so-called withdrawal method forever.

After it's over, we have a party to celebrate. Me and Didi and Jeannie and a bunch of other people. We start at our place, but it gets too small, so we go over to Didi's place on Fifty-seventh, this zillion-dollar duplex that looks and smells like the city dump, but after a while nobody can smell anything anyway. No problem. The party goes on for three days. Some of the people go to sleep eventually, but not me. On the fourth day they call my father and a doctor comes over to the apartment, and now I'm in a place in Minnesota under sedation dreaming the white dreams about snow falling endlessly in the North Country, making the landscape disappear, dreaming about long white rails of cocaine that disappear over the horizon like railroad tracks to the stars. Like when I used to ride and was **anorectic** and I would starve myself and all I would ever dream about was food. There are horses at the far end of the pasture outside my window. I watch them through the bars.

Toward the end of the endless party that landed me here I am telling somebody the story of Dick Diver. I had eight horses at one point, but Dick Diver was the best. I traveled all over the country jumping and showing, and when I first saw Dick, I knew he was like no other horse. He was like a human being—so spirited and nasty he'd jump twenty feet in the air to avoid the bamboo of the trainer, then stop dead or hang a leg up on a jump he could easily make, just for

apocalypse: cosmic upheaval
anorectic: marked by prolonged loss of appetite

spite. He had perfect **conformation**, like a statue of a horse dreamed by Michelangelo. My father bought him for me; he cost a fortune. Back then my father bought anything for me. I was his sweet thing.

I loved that horse. No one else could get near him, he'd try to kill them, but I used to sleep in his stall, spend hours with him every day. When he was poisoned, I went into shock. They kept me on tranquilizers for a week. There was an investigation, but nothing came of it. The insurance company paid off in full, but I quit riding. A few months later, Dad came into my bedroom one night. I was like, uh oh, not this again. He buried his face in my shoulder. His cheek was wet, and he smelled of booze. I'm sorry about Dick Diver, he said. Tell me you forgive me. He goes, the business was in trouble. Then he passed out on top of me, and I had to go and get Mom.

After a week in the hatch they let me use the phone. I call my Dad. How are you? he says.

I don't know why, it's probably bullshit, but I've been trapped in this place with a bunch of shrink types for a week. So just for the hell of it I go, Dad, sometimes I think it would have been cheaper if you'd let me keep that horse.

He goes, I don't know what you're talking about.

I go, Dick Diver, you remember that night you told me. He goes, I didn't tell you anything.

So, okay, maybe I dreamed it. I was in bed after all, and he woke me up. Not for the first time. But just now, with these tranqs they've got me on, I feel like I'm sleepwalking anyway, and I can almost believe it never actually happened. Maybe I dreamed a lot of stuff. Stuff that I thought happened in my life. Stuff I thought I did. Stuff that was done to me. Wouldn't that be great. I'd love to think that 90 percent of it was just dreaming.

conformation: physical structure

▼ Questions about the Story

1. Describe Alison's relationship with Skip Pendleton.
2. Describe her relationship with her father.
3. Describe an incident in the story that you think best illustrates Alison's values.
4. What do you think Alison wants out of life?

▼ Relating the Story to Yourself

1. Think of a romantic relationship in which you have been involved. Describe an incident that captures what was best in that relationship. Describe an incident that captures what was worst in it.
2. What, in your view, are the key characteristics of an ideal relationship?
3. Describe an incident that seems to capture what is best in your relationship with your father or mother. Describe an incident that captures what is worst in that relationship.
4. What, in your view, are the key characteristics of an ideal relationship between parent and son or daughter?
5. The use of illicit drugs was almost unheard of among college students before the sixties. Since then, despite a torrent of admonition from teachers, counselors, church leaders, celebrities, and government officials, drug use has become something of a staple on American college campuses. Why do you think this is?
6. In the forties and fifties in America, young women from "decent homes" were expected to maintain their virginity until marriage, although young men of the same class were expected to "sow their wild oats" before settling down. During this time, the English philosopher Bertrand Russell proposed that young people who felt a deep emotional attachment for

each other need not restrain themselves from sexual intercourse. This advocacy of free love was among the grounds cited by the administration of City College of New York for denying him an appointment to a professorship there. In the sixties this double standard, among many others, was challenged by the feminist movement, the result being the much liberalized sexual climate in which you have grown up, a climate in which free love and more dominates so completely that there is no longer any need for the term. Where young women before the sixties felt strong social pressure to repel the sexual advances of their suitors, today's young women, even in the age of AIDS, feel equally strong pressure to accede to them. All things considered, which do you think was a better situation—the sexual innocence of the fifties or the sexual permissiveness that replaced it? Why do you answer as you do?

7. What do you want out of life?

▼ Discussion

1. If you could advise Alison, what advice would you give her?
2. The use of illicit drugs was almost unheard of among college students before the sixties. Since then, despite a torrent of admonition from teachers, counselors, church leaders, celebrities, and government officials, drug use has become something of a staple on American college campuses. Why do you think this is?
3. In the forties and fifties in America, young women from "decent homes" were expected to maintain their virginity until marriage, although young men of the same class were expected to "sow their wild oats" before settling down. During this time, the English philosopher Bertrand Russell proposed that young people who felt a deep emotional attachment for each other need not restrain themselves from sexual intercourse. This advocacy of free love was among the grounds cited by the administration of City College of New York for denying him an appointment to a professorship there. In the sixties this double standard, among many others, was challenged by the feminist movement, the result being the much liberalized sexual climate in which you have grown up, a climate in which free love and more dominates so completely that there is no longer any need for the term. Where young women before the sixties felt strong social pressure to repel the sexual advances of their suitors, today's young women, even in the age of AIDS, feel equally strong pressure to accede to them. All things considered, which do you think was a better situation—the sexual innocence of the fifties or the sexual permissiveness that replaced it? Why do you answer as you do?
4. What do you want out of life?

▼ Writing Assignments

1. Think of a romantic relationship in which you have been involved. Describe an incident that captures what was best in that relationship. Describe an incident that captures what was worst in it.
2. Describe an incident that seems to capture what is best in your relationship with your father or mother. Describe an incident that captures what is worst in that relationship.
3. The use of illicit drugs was almost unheard of among college students before the sixties. Since then, despite a torrent of admonition from teachers, counselors, church leaders, celebrities, and government officials, drug use has become something of a staple on American college campuses. Why do you think this is?

4. See Question 6 of Relating the Story to Yourself. Make an in-depth case for the point of view *opposite* your own. If you like, you can refute this case.

5. Write an essay on what you want out of life and how your college education will help to advance these aims.

▼ Journal Entry

1. What are your feelings about Alison? Why do you feel this way about her?

▼ Vocabulary

anorectic   apocalypse   conformation

7

▼

Sex without Love

Sharon Olds

The author of three books of poetry, San Francisco poet Sharon Olds (born 1942)
reflects here on a phenomenon she finds deeply troubling.

How do they do it, the ones who make love
without love? Beautiful as dancers,
gliding over each other like ice-skaters
over the ice, fingers hooked
inside each other's bodies, faces   5
red as steak, wine, wet as the
children at birth whose mothers are going to
give them away. How do they come to the
come to the come to the God come to the
still waters, and not love   10
the one who came there with them, light
rising slowly as steam off their joined
skin? These are the true religious,
the purists, the pros, the ones who will not
accept a false Messiah, love the   15
priest instead of the God. They do not mistake
the lover for their own pleasure,
they are like great runners: they know they are alone
with the road surface, the cold, the wind,
the fit of their shoes, their over-all cardio-   20
vascular health—just factors, like the partner
in the bed, and not the truth, which is the
single body alone in the universe
against its own best time.

▼ Questions for Reflection

1. In the sixth line, the poet describes the partners as "wet as the/children at birth whose mothers are going to/give them away." What do you think she means to convey with this image (simile)?
2. Starting in the eighth line, Olds asks a question in a mood of great puzzlement. At what is she expressing puzzlement here?
3. "These are the true religious, the purists," she says (lines 13, 14). Why?
4. What is the point of her comparison to the runner (lines 18–24)?

▼ Journal Entry

1. What metaphors express your attitude toward sex without love?

8

▼

A Romantic Education

Patricia Hampl

Patricia Hampl explores her own identity in relation to two contexts: her family, with whom she feels acute frustration for being "simply without interest," and her nation, from which, in her years of coming-of-age, she feels painfully alienated.

I was five and was sitting on the floor of the **vestibule** hallway of my grandmother's house where the one bookcase had been pushed. The bookcase wasn't in the house itself—ours wasn't a reading family. I was holding in my lap a book of **sepia** photographs bound in a soft brown cover, stamped in flaking gold with the title *Zlatá Praha*. Golden Prague, views of the nineteenth century.

The album felt good, soft. First, the Hradcany Castle and its gardens, then a close-up of the astronomical clock, a view of the baroque jumble of Malá Stream. Then a whole series of photographs of the Vltava River, each showing a different bridge, photograph after pale photograph like a wild rose that opens petal by petal, exposing itself effortlessly, as if there were no such thing as regret. All the buildings in the pictures were hazy, making it seem that the air, not the stone, held the contour of the **baroque** villas intact.

I didn't know how to read yet, and the Czech captions under the pictures were no more incomprehensible to me than English would have been. I liked the soft, fleshlike pliancy of the book. I knew the pictures were of Europe, and that Europe was far away, unreachable. Still, it had something to do with me, with my family. I sat in the cold vestibule, turning the pages of the Prague album. I was flying; I was somewhere else. I was not in St. Paul, Minnesota, and I was happy.

My grandmother appeared at the doorway. Her hands were on her stout hips, and she wanted me to come out of the unheated hallway. She wanted me to eat coffee cake in the kitchen with everybody else, and I had been hard to find. She said, "Come eat," as if this were the family motto.

As she turned to go, she noticed the album. In a second she was down on the floor with me, taking the album carefully in her hands, turning the soft, felt pages. "Oh," she said, "Praha." She looked a long time at one picture, I don't remember which one, and then she took a white handkerchief out of her **pinafore** apron pocket, and dabbed at the tears under her glasses. She took off the wire-rim glasses and made a full swipe.

Her glasses had made deep hollows on either side of her nose, two small caves. They looked as if, with a poke, the skin would give way like a ripe peach, and an entrance would be exposed into her head, into the skull, a passageway to the core of her brain. I didn't want her head to have such wounds. Yet I liked them, these unexpected dips in a familiar landscape.

"So beautiful," she was crying melodramatically over the album. "So beautiful." I had never seen an adult cry before. I was relieved, in some odd way, that there was crying in adulthood, that crying would not be taken away.

My grandmother hunched down next to me in the hallway; she held the album, reciting the gold-stamped captions as she turned the pages and dabbed at her eyes. She was having a good cry. I wanted to put my small finger into the two little caves of puckered skin, the eyeless sockets on either side of her large,

vestibule: a small passage, hall, or room within a building

sepia: brownish

baroque: a period of art, from 1550 to 1700, characterized by extravagant, flamboyant, and sometimes grotesque forms and shapes

pinafore: a sleeveless apron

61

drooping nose. Strange wounds, I wanted to touch them. I wanted to touch her, my father's mother. She was so *foreign.*

* * *

Looking repeatedly into the past, you do not necessarily become fascinated with your own life, but rather with the phenomenon of memory. The act of remembering becomes less autobiographical; it begins to feel **tentative**, aloof. It becomes blessedly impersonal.

The self-absorption that seems to be the **impetus** and embarrassment of autobiography turns into (or perhaps always was) a hunger for the world. Actually, it begins as hunger for *a* world, one gone or lost, **effaced** by time or a more sudden brutality. But in the act of remembering, the personal environment expands, **resonates** beyond itself, beyond its "subject," into the endless and tragic recollection that is history.

We look at old family photographs in which we stand next to black, boxy Fords and are wearing period costumes, and we do not gaze fascinated because there we are young again, or there we are standing, as we never will again in life, next to our mother. We stare and drift because there we are . . . historical. It is the dress, the black car that dazzle us now and draw us beyond our mother's bright arms which once caught us. We reach into the attractive impersonality of something more significant than ourselves.

We embrace the deathliness and yet we are not dead. We are impersonal and yet ourselves. The astonishing power and authority of memory derive from this **paradox**. Here, in memory, we live *and* die. We do "live again" in memory, but differently: in history as well as in biography. And when these two come together, forming a narrative, they approach fiction. The imprecision of memory causes us to create, to extend remembrance into narrative. It sometimes seems, therefore, that what we remember is not—could not be—true. And yet it is *accurate.* The imagination, triggered by memory, is satisfied that this is so.

We trust memory against all the evidence: it is selective, subjective, **cannily** defensive, unreliable as fact. But a single red detail remembered—a hat worn in 1952, the nail polish applied one summer day by an aunt to her toes, separated by balls of cotton, as we watched—has more real blood than the creatures around us on a bus as, for some reason, we think of that day, that hat, those bright feet. That world. This power of memory probably comes from its kinship with the imagination. In memory each of us is an artist: each of us creates. The Kingdom of God, the nuns used to tell us in school, is within you. We may not have made a religion of memory, but it is our passion, and along with (sometimes in opposition to) science, our authority. It is a kingdom of its own.

Psychology, which is somehow *our* science, the claustrophobic discipline of the century, has made us acknowledge the value of remembering—even at the peril of shame. But it is especially difficult to reach back into the merely insignificant, into a family life where, it seemed, nothing happened, where there wasn't the ghost of a **pretension**. That is a steelier resistance because to break through what is unimportant and as anonymous as dirt a greater sense of worthlessness must be overcome. At least shame is interesting; at least it is hidden, the sign of anything valuable. But for a past to be overlooked, discarded because it was not only useless but simply without interest—that is a harsher heritage. In fact, is it a heritage?

* * *

It seems as if I spent most of my twenties holding a lukewarm cup of coffee, hunched over a table, talking. Innumerable cups of coffee, countless tables: the booths of the Gopher Grill at the University of Minnesota where, probably around

tentative: not worked out; provisional

impetus: stimulus

effaced: worn away

resonates: echoes

paradox: an apparent contradiction

cannily: slyly

pretension: a claim of importance or worth

1965, I first heard myself use the word *relationship;* a little later, the orange formica table of a federal prison where "the man I live with" (there still is no other term) was serving a sentence for draft resistance; and the second-hand tables of a dozen apartments, the wooden farmhouse table of a short-lived commune—table after table, friend after friend, rehashing our hardly ended (or not ended) childhoods. I may have the tables wrong; maybe the formica one was in the farmhouse, the oak one in the prison, maybe the chairs in the prison were orange and the table gray. But they are fixtures, nailed down, not to be moved: memories.

This generation has written its memoirs early; we squeezed every childhood lemon for all it was worth: my mother this, my father that. Our self-absorption was appalling. But I won't go back—not yet—on that decade. It was also the time when my generation, as "a generation," was most political, most involved. The people I sat with, picking at our individual pasts, wearing nightgowns till noon as we analyzed within a millimeter our dreams and their meanings (that is, how they proved this or that about our parents), finally put on our clothes, went outside and, in various ways that are too easily forgotten, tried to end a war which we were the first, as a group, to recognize was disastrous. In fact, our protest against the war is what made us a generation, even to ourselves.

Perhaps no American generation—certainly not our parents who were young during the Depression—had a childhood as long as ours. The war kept us young. We stayed in school, endlessly, it seemed, and our protest kept us in the child's position: we alternately "rebelled" against and pestered the grownups for what we wanted—an end to the war. Those who fought the war had no such long, self-reflective youths. Childhood belonged to us, who stayed at home. And we became the "sixties generation."

Our certainty that the war was wrong became entangled with our analysis of our families and our psyches not only because we were given to self-reflection and had a lot of time on our hands. We combed through our dreams and our childhoods with Jung's *Man and His Symbols* at the ready, and were looking for something, I now think, that was neither personal nor familial and perhaps not even psychological. We had lost the national connection and were heartsick in a cultural way. I don't think we knew that; I didn't, anyway. But at home I didn't talk psychology, I talked politics, arguing with a kind of angry misery whose depths confused me and made my family frightened for me, and probably of me. But there was no real argument—I did all the talking; my family, gathered for Sunday dinner, looked glumly at the gravy on their plates as if at liquid Rorschach blots that might suggest why I, the adored child, had come to this strange pass. They weren't "for the war," but the **belligerent** way I was against it **dismayed** them and caused them to fall silent, waiting for me to stop. I had opinions, I spoke of my "position" on things.

One night my uncle, trying to meet me halfway, said, "Well, when I was in Italy during the War . . ."

"How do you defend that analogy?" I snapped at him, perhaps partly because for them "the War" was still the Second World War. My family couldn't seem, for a long time, to *focus* on Vietnam. But my uncle retreated in the face of the big guns of my new English-major lingo.

On Thanksgiving one year I left the table to find *I. F. Stone's Weekly* and read parts of it to the assembled family in a ringing, triumphantly angry voice. "But," my father said when I finished, as if I. F. Stone had been compiling evidence about me and not the Johnson administration, "you used to be so *happy*—the happiest person I ever met."

"What does that have to do with anything?" I said.

Yet he was right. My unhappiness (but I didn't think of myself as unhappy) was a confusion of personal and public matters, and it was made more intense by the fact that I had been happy ("the happiest person!") and now I couldn't remember

belligerent: hostile
dismayed: astonished

63

what that happiness had been—just childhood? But many childhoods are miserable. And I couldn't remember exactly how the happiness stopped. I carry from that time the feeling that private memory is not just private and not just memory. Yet the resistances not against memory but against the significance of memory remain strong.

I come from people who have always been polite enough to feel that nothing has ever happened to them. They have worked, raised families, played cards, gone on fishing trips together, risen to grief and admirable bitterness and, then, taken patiently the early death that robbed them of a brother, a son. They have not dwelt on things. To dwell, that appropriate word, as if the past were a residence, faintly morbid and barbaric: the dwellings of prehistoric men. Or, the language of the Bible: "The Word was made flesh, and dwelt amongst us."

I have dwelt, though. To make a metaphor is to make a fuss, and I am a poet, though it seems that is something one cannot claim for oneself; anyway, I write poetry. I am enough of them, my kind family, to be repelled by the significance of things, to find poetry, with its tendency to make connections and break the barriers between past and present, slightly embarrassing.

It would be impossible to look into the past, even a happy one (especially a happy one), were it not for the impersonality that dwells in the most intimate fragments, the **integuments** that bind even obscure lives to history and, eventually, history to fiction, to myth.

I will hold up negative after family negative to the light. I will dwell. Dwell in the house of the dead and in the living house of my relatives. I'm after junk. I want to make something out of what my family says is nothing. I suppose that is what I was up to when my grandmother called me out of the vestibule, away from the bookcase and the views of Prague, to eat my dinner with everybody else.

integuments: links

▼ Questions to Focus Reading

1. As the five-year-old Patricia Hampl turns the pages of the photograph album, she feels happy. Why?

2. She is relieved when her grandmother weeps. Why?

3. What is Hampl's explanation for our fascination at looking at old photographs of ourselves, our family?

4. "It sometimes seems . . . that what we remember is not—could not be— true. And yet it is *accurate*." What do you think this means?

5. Memory, she writes, "is a kingdom of its own." What does this mean? How does her recollection of talks over coffee illustrate this?

6. Hampl tells us that she will not "go back—not yet—" on the sixties. Why not?

7. What is Hampl trying to get across in her description of family dinners when she was an activist college student?

8. To help explain her usage of the word "dwell," she quotes the Bible: "The Word was made flesh, and dwelt amongst us." How does this quotation cast light on her use of the word when, for example, she says of her family, "they have not dwelt on things"?

9. Why does she find poetry "slightly embarrassing"?

10. "It would be impossible to look into the past, even a happy one (especially a happy one), were it not for the impersonality that dwells in the most intimate fragments, the integuments that bind even obscure lives to history and, eventually, history to fiction, to myth." What does this mean?

11. At the end of this reminiscence, Patricia Hampl has defined herself in contrast to her family. How?

▼ Questions for Reflection

1. "In the act of remembering," Hampl writes, "the personal environment expands, resonates beyond itself, beyond its 'subject,' into the endless and tragic recollection that is history." She describes the experience of looking at old family photographs and claims that this is one occasion of the expansion of the personal into the historical. When you think of your own experience of viewing old family photos, can you see what she is getting at? What do you think she means by this shift from a personal to an impersonal interest in one's own past?

2. In the opening scene of the five-year-old with the family album, what do we learn about Patricia Hampl? In a Sunday dinner scene she describes, what do we learn about her as a young woman, about her family?

3. "But a single red detail remembered . . . has more real blood than the creatures around us on a bus," Hampl writes. How does she mean this? Can you remember similar single details that have a similar power for you?

4. Examining her generation in their college years, Hampl says, "We had lost the national connection and were heartsick in a cultural way." What do you think she means by this? Do you feel a "national connection"? If so, how would you describe that connection? If not, is its absence the source of heartsickness for you?

5. Hampl states that her generation's stand against the war in Vietnam "is what made us a generation, even to ourselves." Do you feel yourself to be a member of a generation? Does this form any part of your identity? If so, how would you characterize the generation with which you identify?

▼ Discussion

1. Examining her generation in their college years, Hampl says, "We had lost the national connection and were heartsick in a cultural way." What do you think she means by this? Do you feel a "national connection"? If so, how would you describe that connection? If not, is its absence the source of heartsickness for you?

2. Hampl states that her generation's stand against the war in Vietnam "is what made us a generation, even to ourselves." Do you feel yourself to be a member of a generation? Does this form any part of your identity? If so, how would you characterize the generation with which you identify?

▼ Writing Assignments

1. Hampl's family's and her attitude toward "dwelling on things" is a key point of contrast between them. What is a key point of contrast between yourself and your family? Describe in detail an incident involving yourself and your family in which this key point of difference is clearly expressed.

▼ Journal Entries

1. In what respects do you identify with your generation?
2. How would you characterize the values of your family? Which of these values are also your own? Which do you reject?
3. Write about a single vivid detail from the past that brings back a world for you.

▼ Vocabulary

baroque	effaced	pinafore	tentative
belligerent	impetus	pretension	vestibule
cannily	integuments	resonates	
dismayed	paradox	sepia	

9

▼

For Idealism in Youth

Jeffrey Gordon

A philosophy professor at Southwest Texas State University and director of the Freshman Seminar Program, Jeffrey Gordon contrasts his own freshman generation of the sixties with the present freshman generation in "a ritual of mourning" intended to awaken unnamed dreams.

I'm going to engage in some personal reminiscence here, but I am doing so in order to make an important point about your freshman year (and beyond), and so I ask your indulgence.

In the summer of 1963, I had just completed my freshman year. I was at Northwestern University in Illinois, about three miles from my parents' home, and a most remarkable year it had been. When I got my letter admitting me to Northwestern the year before, I rode my ten-speed to the campus one evening to take a careful look. The campus, built on the shores of Lake Michigan, was lush with the colors and fragrances of spring. The walkways, dimly lit with soft, old-fashioned streetlamps, were lined with gracious lawns and large imposing **Gothic** buildings; and with the soft push and pull of the lake always within hearing, the atmosphere **exuded** for my youthful heart a **heady** mix of academic excellence, stern demands, and the unmistakable promise of romance.

Motivation for my first year would be no problem. College was the **crucible**, I'd been told for four highly competitive but academically **tedious** high school years, and this was never so true as in the first year, the legend had it, when college professors, charged with reducing the booming freshman class to manageable size, seized upon the lazy, the undisciplined, the unintelligent like fierce birds. Fear would be a sufficient motivation. But beyond fear there was something else. With each breath I drew of the fine spring air, standing now bestride my ten-speed on the evening sand, watching the gentle waves, the stately buildings still within view, my resolve to do whatever I had to do to stay in this enchanted environment grew stronger.

Academically, that first year was a stunning success, the first and last of a kind, as it turned out, but that is another story. I made Dean's List all three quarters, and in the third of these, just weeks before the summer break, I was given a highly coveted full-tuition prize for creative writing. I had been a lifeguard the summer before, but now that I regarded myself as a recognized writer, I was looking this summer for much more serious employment.

While I was still contemplating just what this more appropriate employment might be, my brother, then 25 and more worldly than I am now at 43, suggested that I join the great **confluence** of people headed for Washington, D.C., to demonstrate their support for the civil rights movement. The chief organizer for the march was the young black leader Martin Luther King, one of the greatest **orators** alive, my brother said, who would probably give a strong and memorable speech. He would go himself, he said, but business required that he stay in Chicago. But if I'd go, well, he'd pay for my airfare, just because he thought it was that important that our family be represented. Hell, I wanted to be a writer didn't I? Well, I'd better live the kind of life that would give me something to say. I'd better live in

Gothic: pertaining to a style of architecture popular in Western Europe between the twelfth and sixteenth centuries

exuded: oozed

heady: intoxicating

crucible: a test of great magnitude

tedious: tiresome or boring

confluence: gathering

orators: speakers

my time, learn to feel personally its particular strains and tensions, its particular advances. And this event promised to be a landmark in one of the most important social movements in this American century.

My brother was a very persuasive man, but for all my literary ambition, for all my passionate desire to become the conscience of my race, I was a terrible homebody; and the civil rights movement had simply not caught my imagination. Oh, I thought it was great that the blacks were standing up for themselves, but despite what I'd read of **strident** James Baldwin, I just didn't see that any of this had much to do with me. In the end, he shamed me into it. Maybe I was still too young to distinguish the really significant from the trivial. Maybe people assumed a maturity in me that my years and inexperience and actual attitudes really didn't warrant. Maybe I was too much in love with small routines and familiar comforts ever to—I began packing: two changes of clothes and a writer's accessories—a portable typewriter and shampoo.

I didn't see Martin Luther King once during the "I Have a Dream" speech he gave that day. I spent the time moving through the crowd, taking in the sights and sounds, allowing my eye to follow out a fine curve or a cute face. The greatness of that speech didn't come home to me until I saw it that night on television with some newly met Washington friends. The trip had not seemed worth my brother's investment, for all I had gotten out of it. But the following morning something happened.

I was walking through a park where buses were parking, their drivers waiting for people to assemble so they could take them back to New York, Philadelphia, Chicago, Los Angeles, Dallas, for people, white and black, and young people especially, had come from everywhere. I was still largely unmoved by the event. What had I been, after all, but one body in a crowd? Why had it been so important that I be there? And what could I possibly write about it? People who watched it on TV had a much better perspective.

And then it started. "Oh-oh freedom, oh-oh freedom!" some black girls had started to sing with strong, vibrant voices. Gathering beside the buses, others joined these girls. "Oh-oh freedom over me." Soon about a hundred people had joined in. They were black and white, mostly in their twenties or younger; they were blond-haired and blue-eyed. They all seemed to know the words of this song I'd never heard before. "Well, before I'd be a slave, I'd be buried in my grave . . ." they sang. Here they were, not the **malcontents**, not the prematurely **disenchanted**, not the **disinherited**, but the flower of American youth, a yearning nation's blue-eyed pride, come hundreds of miles from the **bastions** of Waspitude to lend their body and their support, their witness and their presence to something quite new in American experience: the **univocal** insistence that this nation face down the shame of its bigotry, that it rededicate itself sincerely and without delay to the fulfillment of the ideals set down in its gallant charters. Here were these glorious American youth—blond-haired, for the love of Christ!—who had everything to gain by lying low, by letting the Martin Luther Kings and the Malcolm Xs stir the waters briefly in a sea of **benign** indifference, who had more important things to attend to than the perpetual complaints of the wretched, who had their brilliant careers to consider, the taking of the reins of this golden nation and **imbibing** its rich rewards, if only they'd lie low, for God's sake, play the game as it's always been played—here were these splendid youth, golden-haired and eyes like crystal, who had absolutely nothing to lose by simply staying comfortably put and watching this brief agitation on the tube that renders all things of equal insignificance, nothing at all to lose but their communal and national pride and their sense of personal integrity, nothing to lose but their opportunity for struggling with like-minded friends of their noble generation to affect permanent change for the Good that transcends the suffocation of self-interest—here were these youth, I say (and thank God, I now thought, that I stood among them), clutching the Preamble to the

strident: grating

malcontents: bitterly dissatisfied people

disenchanted: unenthralled

disinherited: deprived of rights and privileges

bastions: strongholds

univocal: unambiguous

benign: kind and gracious

imbibing: drinking in

Constitution and the Declaration of Independence, insisting that the words ring out and **exhorting** us with the powerful energies of hope and **resoluteness** that we live up to them now!

Until that moment, my being an American had been for me an accident of my birth. But in that **amalgam** of youth, black and white, from elegant suburb and inner city, singing out for freedom, I had found the America that was mine.

I dwell on these details at such length as a ritual of mourning. Twenty-three years later, I see in the new generation of American youth nothing whatsoever of this fervor. It's not that your generation is without the hunger for **idealism**. The hunger is there, but it is **latent, repressed** and unnamed, that wild secret longing having no idea what it is about. The great thing about going to college and coming of age in the sixties was that the times provided so many avenues for the expression of youth's larger natural ambitions, the ambitions that go well beyond the pluming of one's personal feathers: the comfortable house, the sporting car, the bulging bank account. In those 23 years, we have grown very cynical about the basic needs of man. Man is essentially selfish, we say, happiest when all his selfish appetites are fulfilled. But youth knows instinctively the poverty of this conception, whatever it may say with its unconvinced voice. For youth feels in its blood the fever of higher dreams, the profound need for a project, a principle, an ideal of such scope and magnitude as to absorb its infinite passion. Where these idealistic fevers are not served, they turn to something else. "Sex, drugs, rock 'n' roll!" the slogan rang defiantly. It was the anguished cry of a generation whose youthful idealism found no communal outlet. The tendency to cast our dreams in purely personal terms has deep roots in our culture. Ours is a country, after all, made by rugged individualists, people who prized above all the liberty to live their own way. But we shouldn't forget that these people were conscious of forging a nation, of acting not for themselves alone, but for history, and we can't overestimate the power this sense of mission must have had in their veins.

Freshman year is a time when you will start thinking with a new energy and seriousness about your goals in life. To do this well, you will need to gather some data. You will need to know yourself, your **dispositions** and talents, your strengths and shortcomings, and the means of personal change. You will have to be able to identify what is important to you. When you are taking this inventory of your basic needs, you will be inclined to ignore the need I've been talking about, the need for idealistic commitment, the need to devote yourself to the world and not merely to take from it. You will tend to ignore this need because for more than a decade now, it has been out of fashion to acknowledge it, having been replaced in the collective mythology by an increasingly cynical materialism. Ignore this need at your peril. For here is a truth everyone learns at some time in life, some in middle age sitting by the pool and staring into their drink, others later still, all their opportunities lost, desperate for redeeming glory: *The measure of a human being is the scope of his or her dream and the* **ardency** *with which he or she pursues it.* Confine your dream to the boundaries of your purely private life and condemn yourself thereby to triviality. Live for yourself alone and discover by the poolside between **cursory** glances at the day's Dow-Jones that your self is nothing.

I will look forward to meeting you and your peers. I will stand by the curbside as the cars and buses bring you. I will watch your vibrant smiles, your colorful **regalia.** I will listen in my heart for your song.

exhorting: urging strongly

resoluteness: strong determination

amalgam: combination

idealism: commitment to an ideal beyond self-interest

latent: undeveloped

repressed: restrained

dispositions: usual temperaments

ardency: passion

cursory: hasty; superficial

regalia: special dress characterized by bright colors, emblems, or symbols

▼ Questions to Focus Reading

1. In the first paragraph, Gordon promises to make "an important point about your freshman year (and beyond)." What is that point?
2. "Motivation for my first year would be no problem." Why not?
3. How does Gordon's brother persuade him to make the trip to Washington?

4. Gordon had just about decided that the trip was not worth his brother's investment when, the morning after Martin Luther King's "I Have a Dream" speech, "something happened" to change his mind. What happened?

5. In the long paragraph beginning "And then it started," why the repeated image of blond hair and blue eyes? Most of this paragraph consists of one very long sentence. Why do you suppose the author didn't express these thoughts in several sentences?

6. What do you think the author has in mind by "the Good that transcends the suffocation of self-interest"?

7. "I had found the America that was mine." What America was this? With what "America" was the author identifying?

8. In the paragraph beginning "I dwell on these details at such length . . . ," Gordon puts forward a theory about the needs, the "larger natural ambitions" of youth (page 69). What is his theory? Someone might object to Gordon that nothing is more traditionally American than casting one's dreams in purely personal, even selfish terms. He seems to have anticipated this objection in the last three sentences of this paragraph. How does he reply to it?

9. How does Gordon define "idealistic commitment"? He says that the need for idealistic commitment has been "replaced in the popular mythology by an increasingly cynical materialism." What does he mean by this?

10. "*The measure of a human being is the scope of his or her dream and the ardency with which he or she pursues it.*" What do you think Gordon means by this statement? What would it mean to "confine your dream to the boundaries of your purely private life," to "live for yourself alone"?

11. What is the meaning of the last sentence in this essay?

▼ Questions for Reflection

1. The author is relating an experience that helped him to define his relation to his country. ("I had found the America that was mine," he says on page 69.) Is being an American an important part of your sense of identity? Just what does it mean for you? Have you had certain experiences that clarified this for you?

2. The author calls his essay "a ritual of mourning." Why? Do you think the contrast he draws between your generation and the college-age generation of the sixties is accurate? Why do you say so?

3. The author believes that idealism is a natural characteristic of youth. What does he mean by idealism? Do you agree with him that it is a natural characteristic of youth? Is it a characteristic of yours? If so, do you have a channel for it?

▼ Discussion

1. What does Gordon mean by idealism? Do you think your generation is more idealistic than he thinks it is? If so, what evidences do you see of its idealism?

2. Is being an American an important aspect of your identity? If so, what does it mean for you? Are there certain experiences that clarified this meaning for you?

3. "*The measure of a human being is the scope of his or her dream and the ardency with which he or she pursues it.*" What does this mean? Is it true? With what does he contrast it?

▼ Writing Assignments

1. The author puts forward a view here of "the measure" of a human being. Write an essay in which you defend or take issue with his conception of

what establishes the worth of a particular human being. If you choose to defend his view, consider how someone might attack it, and show how the attack can be refuted. If you choose to dispute his view, explain exactly where he goes wrong and try to present an alternative criterion of worth that does not fall prey to your criticism of his "measure."

2. Write an essay in which you discuss how the fact of your being an American informs your sense of who you are. If there was some experience that clarified for you the meaning of your being an American, describe that experience and explain that meaning.

▼ Journal Entry

1. What was your predominant *emotional* reaction to this essay? What in the essay provoked that reaction?

▼ Vocabulary

amalgam	disenchanted	idealism	resoluteness
ardency	disinherited	imbibing	strident
bastions	dispositions	latent	tedious
benign	exhorting	malcontents	univocal
confluence	exuded	orators	
crucible	Gothic	regalia	
cursory	heady	repressed	

Music and the Soul of Youth

Allan Bloom

Allan Bloom was a University of Chicago philosopher whose thoughtful and sting-ing critique of the American university, The Closing of the American Mind, *was on the best-seller list for a year (1987–88) and generated a continuing controversy about the present state and proper direction of the American university. Here Bloom discusses American youth's absorption with rock music and theorizes about its contribution to what he regards as the impoverishment of their capacity for liberal education.*

Though students do not have books, they most emphatically do have music. Noth-ing is more singular about this generation than its addiction to music. This is the age of music and the states of soul that accompany it. To find a rival to this enthusiasm, one would have to go back at least a century to Germany and the passion for Wagner's operas. They had the religious sense that Wagner was creating the meaning of life and that they were not merely listening to his works but ex-periencing that meaning. Today, a very large proportion of young people between the ages of ten and twenty live for music. It is their passion; nothing else excites them as it does; they cannot take seriously anything alien to music. When they are in school and with their families, they are longing to plug themselves back into their music. Nothing surrounding them—school, family, church—has anything to do with their musical world. At best that ordinary life is neutral, but mostly it is an **impediment**, drained of vital content, even a thing to be rebelled against. Of course, the enthusiasm for Wagner was limited to a small class, could be in-dulged only rarely and only in a few places, and had to wait on the composer's slow output. The music of the new **votaries**, on the other hand, knows neither class nor nation. It is available twenty-four hours a day everywhere. There is the stereo in the home, in the car, there are concerts; there are music videos, with special channels exclusively devoted to them, on the air nonstop; there are the Walkmans so that no place—not public transportation, not the library—prevents students from communing with the Muse, even while studying. And, above all, the musical soil has become tropically rich. No need to wait for one unpredictable genius. Now there are many geniuses, producing all the time, two new ones rising to take the place of every fallen hero. There is no **dearth** of the new and the startling.

The power of music in the soul—described to Jessica marvelously by Lorenzo in the *Merchant of Venice*—has been recovered after a long period of **desuetude**. And it is rock music alone that has effected this restoration. Classical music is dead among the young. This assertion will, I know, be hotly disputed by many who, unwilling to admit tidal changes, can point to the proliferation on campuses of classes in classical music appreciation and practice, as well as performance groups of all kinds. Their presence is undeniable, but they involve not more than five to ten percent of the students. Classical music is now a special taste, like Greek language or pre-Columbian archeology, not a common culture of reciprocal communication and psychological shorthand. Thirty years ago, most middle-class families made some of the old European music a part of the home, partly because

impediment: hindrance
votaries: devoted admirers
dearth: inadequate supply
desuetude: discontinued use

they liked it, partly because they thought it was good for the kids. University students usually had some early **emotive** association with Beethoven, Chopin and Brahms, which was a permanent part of their makeup and to which they were likely to respond throughout their lives. This was probably the only regularly recognizable class distinction between educated and uneducated in America. Many, or even most, of the young people of that generation also swung with Benny Goodman, but with an element of self-consciousness—to be hip, to prove they weren't snobs, to show **solidarity** with the democratic ideal of a pop culture out of which would grow a new high culture. So there remained a class distinction between high and low, although private taste was beginning to create doubts about whether one really liked the high very much. But all that has changed. Rock music is as unquestioned and unproblematic as the air the students breathe, and very few have any acquaintance at all with classical music. This is a constant surprise to me. And one of the strange aspects of my relations with good students I come to know well is that I frequently introduce them to Mozart. This is a pleasure for me, inasmuch as it is always pleasant to give people gifts that please them. It is interesting to see whether and in what ways their studies are complemented by such music. But this is something utterly new to me as a teacher; formerly my students usually knew much more classical music than I did.

Music was not all that important for the generations of students preceding the current one. The romanticism that had dominated serious music since Beethoven appealed to refinements—perhaps overrefinements—of sentiments that are hardly to be found in the contemporary world. The lives people lead or wish to lead and their prevailing passions are of a different sort than those of the highly educated German and French **bourgeoisie**, who were **avidly** reading Rousseau and Baudelaire, Goethe and Heine, for their spiritual satisfaction. The music that had been designed to produce, as well as to please, such exquisite sensibilities had a very tenuous relation to American lives of any kind. So romantic musical culture in America had had for a long time the character of a veneer, as easily susceptible to ridicule as were Margaret Dumont's displays of **coquettish chasteness**, so aptly exploited by Groucho Marx in *A Night at the Opera.* I noticed this when I first started teaching and lived in a house for gifted students. The "good" ones studied their physics and then listened to classical music. The students who did not fit so easily into the groove, some of them just vulgar and **restive** under the cultural tyranny, but some of them also serious, were looking for things that really responded to their needs. Almost always they responded to the beat of the newly emerging rock music. They were a bit ashamed of their taste, for it was not respectable. But I instinctively sided with this second group, with real, if coarse, feelings as opposed to artificial and dead ones. Then their musical **sansculottism** won the revolution and reigns **unabashed** today. No classical music has been produced that can speak to this generation. Symptomatic of this change is how seriously students now take the famous passages on musical education in Plato's *Republic.* In the past, students, good liberals that they always are, were indignant at the censorship of poetry, as a threat to free inquiry. But they were really thinking of science and politics. They hardly paid attention to the discussion of music itself and, to the extent that they even thought about it, were really puzzled by Plato's devoting time to rhythm and melody in a serious treatise on political philosophy. Their experience of music was as an entertainment, a matter of indifference to political and moral life. Students today, on the contrary, know exactly why Plato takes music so seriously. They know it affects life very profoundly and are indignant because Plato seems to want to rob them of their most intimate pleasure. They are drawn into argument with Plato about the experience of music, and the dispute centers on how to evaluate it and deal with it. This encounter not only helps to illuminate the phenomenon of contemporary music, but also provides a model of how contemporary students can profitably engage with a classic text. The very fact

emotive: emotional
solidarity: unity
bourgeoisie: middle class
avidly: fervently
coquettish: flirting
chasteness: virtuousness
restive: restless
sansculottism: radical or violent extremism
unabashed: not embarrassed

of their fury shows how much Plato threatens what is dear and intimate to them. They are little able to defend their experience, which had seemed unquestionable until questioned, and it is most resistant to cool analysis. Yet if a student can—and this is most difficult and unusual—draw back, get a critical distance on what he clings to, come to doubt the ultimate value of what he loves, he has taken the first and most difficult step toward the philosophic conversion. Indignation is the soul's defense against the wound of doubt about its own; it reorders the cosmos to support the justice of its cause. It justifies putting Socrates to death. Recognizing indignation for what it is constitutes knowledge of the soul, and is thus an experience more philosophic than the study of mathematics. It is Plato's teaching that music, by its nature, encompasses all that is today most resistant to philosophy. So it may well be that through the thicket of our greatest corruption runs the path to awareness of the oldest truths.

Plato's teaching about music is, put simply, that rhythm and melody, accompanied by dance, are the barbarous expression of the soul. Barbarous, not animal. Music is the medium of the *human* soul in its most ecstatic condition of wonder and terror. Nietzsche, who in large measure agrees with Plato's analysis, says in *The Birth of Tragedy* (not to be forgotten is the rest of the title, *Out of the Spirit of Music*) that a mixture of cruelty and coarse sensuality characterized this state, which of course was religious, in the service of gods. Music is the soul's primitive and primary speech and it is *alogon,* without articulate speech or reason. It is not only not reasonable, it is hostile to reason. Even when articulate speech is added, it is utterly subordinate to and determined by the music and the passions it expresses.

Civilization or, to say the same thing, education is the taming or domestication of the soul's raw passion—not suppressing or excising them, which would deprive the soul of its energy—but forming and informing them as art. The goal of harmonizing the enthusiastic part of the soul with what develops later, the rational part, is perhaps impossible to attain. But without it, man can never be whole. Music, or poetry, which is what music becomes as reason emerges, always involves a delicate balance between passion and reason, and, even in its highest and most developed forms—religious, warlike and erotic—that balance is always tipped, if ever so slightly, toward the passionate. Music, as everyone experiences, provides an unquestionable justification and a fulfilling pleasure for the activities it accompanies: the soldier who hears the marching band is enthralled and reassured; the religious man is exalted in his prayer by the sound of the organ in the church; and the lover is carried away and his conscience stilled by the romantic guitar. Armed with music, man can damn rational doubt. Out of the music emerge the gods that suit it, and they educate men by their example and their commandments.

Plato's Socrates disciplines the ecstasies and thereby provides little consolation or hope to men. According to the Socratic formula, the lyrics—speech and, hence, reason—must determine the music—harmony and rhythm. Pure music can never endure this constraint. Students are not in a position to know the pleasures of reason; they can only see it as a disciplinary and repressive parent. But they do see, in the case of Plato, that that parent has figured out what they are up to. Plato teaches that, in order to take the spiritual temperature of an individual or a society, one must "mark the music." To Plato and Nietzsche, the history of music is a series of attempts to give form and beauty to the dark, chaotic, **premonitory** forces in the soul—to make them serve a higher purpose, an ideal, to give man's duties a fullness. Bach's religious intentions and Beethoven's revolutionary and humane ones are clear enough examples. Such cultivation of the soul uses the passions and satisfies them while sublimating them and giving them an artistic unity. A man whose noblest activities are accompanied by a music that expresses them while providing a pleasure extending from the lowest bodily to the highest spiritual, is whole, and there is no tension in him between the pleasant and the

premonitory: warning

good. By contrast a man whose business life is **prosaic** and unmusical and whose leisure is made up of coarse, intense entertainments, is divided, and each side of his existence is undermined by the other.

Hence, for those who are interested in psychological health, music is at the center of education, both for giving the passions their due and for preparing the soul for the unhampered use of reason. The centrality of such education was recognized by all the ancient educators. It is hardly noticed today that in Aristotle's *Politics* the most important passages about the best regime concern musical education, or that the *Poetics* is an appendix to the *Politics*. Classical philosophy did not censor the singers. It persuaded them. And it gave them a goal, one that was understood by them, until only yesterday. But those who do not notice the role of music in Aristotle and despise it in Plato went to school with Hobbes, Locke and Smith, where such considerations have become unnecessary. The triumphant Enlightenment rationalism thought that it had discovered other ways to deal with the irrational part of the soul, and that reason needed less support from it. Only in those great critics of Enlightenment and rationalism, Rousseau and Nietzsche, does music return, and they were the most musical of philosophers. Both thought that the passions—and along with them their **ministerial** arts—had become thin under the rule of reason and that, therefore, man himself and what he sees in the world have become correspondingly thin. They wanted to cultivate the enthusiastic states of the soul and to re-experience the **Corybantic** possession deemed a pathology by Plato. Nietzsche, particularly, sought to tap again the irrational sources of vitality, to replenish our dried-up stream from barbaric sources, and thus encouraged the Dionysian and the music derivative from it.

This is the significance of rock music. I do not suggest that it has any high intellectual sources. But it has risen to its current heights in the education of the young on the ashes of classical music, and in an atmosphere in which there is no intellectual resistance to attempts to tap the rawest passions. Modern-day rationalists, such as economists, are indifferent to it and what it represents. The irrationalists are all for it. There is no need to fear that "the blond beasts" are going to come forth from the bland souls of our adolescents. But rock music has one appeal only, a barbaric appeal, to sexual desire—not love, not *eros,* but sexual desire undeveloped and untutored. It acknowledges the first **emanations** of children's emerging sensuality and addresses them seriously, **eliciting** them and legitimating them, not as little sprouts that must be carefully tended in order to grow into gorgeous flowers, but as the real thing. Rock gives children, on a silver platter, with all the public authority of the entertainment industry, everything their parents always used to tell them they had to wait for until they grew up and would understand later.

Young people know that rock has the beat of sexual intercourse. That is why Ravel's *Bolero* is the one piece of classical music that is commonly known and liked by them. In alliance with some real art and a lot of pseudo-art, an enormous industry cultivates the taste for the orgiastic state of feeling connected with sex, providing a constant flood of fresh material for **voracious** appetites. Never was there an art form directed so exclusively to children.

Ministering to and according with the arousing and **cathartic** music, the lyrics celebrate puppy love as well as **polymorphous** attractions, and fortify them against traditional ridicule and shame. The words implicitly and explicitly describe bodily acts that satisfy sexual desire and treat them as its only natural and routine **culmination** for children who do not yet have the slightest imagination of love, marriage or family. This has a much more powerful effect than does pornography on youngsters, who have no need to watch others do grossly what they can so easily do themselves. **Voyeurism** is for old perverts; active sexual relations are for the young. All they need is encouragement.

The inevitable **corollary** of such sexual interest is rebellion against the parental authority that represses it. Selfishness thus becomes indignation and then

prosaic: dull; ordinary

ministerial: serving as a means or instrument

Corybantic: resembling attendants of the Greek nature goddess Cybele, known for their orgiastic processions and rituals.

emanations: emissions

eliciting: bringing out

voracious: insatiable or huge

cathartic: purging

polymorphous: occurring in various forms

culmination: climax

voyeurism: sexual gratification from visual experience

corollary: natural consequence

transforms itself into morality. The sexual revolution must overthrow all the forces of domination, the enemies of nature and happiness. From love comes hate, masquerading as social reform. A worldview is balanced on the sexual **fulcrum**. What were once unconscious or half-conscious childish resentments become the new Scripture. And then comes the longing for the classless, prejudice-free, conflictless, universal society that necessarily results from liberated consciousness—"We Are the World," a **pubescent** version of *Alle Menschen werden Brüder,* the fulfillment of which has been inhibited by the political equivalents of Mom and Dad. These are the three great lyrical themes: sex, hate and a **smarmy**, hypocritical version of brotherly love. Such polluted sources issue in a muddy stream where only monsters can swim. A glance at the videos that project images on the wall of Plato's cave since MTV took it over suffices to prove this. Hitler's image recurs frequently enough in exciting contexts to give one pause. Nothing noble, sublime, profound, delicate, tasteful or even decent can find a place in such **tableaux**. There is room only for the intense, changing, crude and immediate, which Tocqueville warned us would be the character of democratic art, combined with a pervasiveness, importance and content beyond Tocqueville's wildest imagination.

Picture a thirteen-year-old boy sitting in the living room of his family home doing his math assignment while wearing his Walkman headphones or watching MTV. He enjoys the liberties hard won over centuries by the alliance of philosophic genius and political heroism, consecrated by the blood of martyrs; he is provided with comfort and leisure by the most productive economy ever known to mankind; science has penetrated the secrets of nature in order to provide him with the marvelous, lifelike electronic sound and image reproduction he is enjoying. And in what does progress culminate? A pubescent child whose body throbs with orgasmic rhythms; whose feelings are made articulate in hymns to the joys of **onanism** or the killing of parents; whose ambition is to win fame and wealth in imitating the drag-queen who makes the music. In short, life is made into a nonstop, commercially prepackaged masturbational fantasy.

This description may seem exaggerated, but only because some would prefer to regard it as such. The continuing exposure to rock music is a reality, not one confined to a particular class or type of child. One need only ask first-year university students what music they listen to, how much of it and what it means to them, in order to discover that the phenomenon is universal in America, that it begins in adolescence or a bit before and continues through the college years. It is the youth culture and, as I have so often insisted, there is now no other **countervailing** nourishment for the spirit. Some of this culture's power comes from the fact that it is so loud. It makes conversation impossible, so that much of friendship must be without the shared speech that Aristotle asserts is the essence of friendship and the only true common ground. With rock, illusions of shared feelings, bodily contact and grunted formulas, which are supposed to contain so much meaning beyond speech, are the basis of association. None of this contradicts going about the business of life, attending classes and doing the assignments for them. But the meaningful inner life is with the music.

This phenomenon is both astounding and indigestible, and is hardly noticed, routine and habitual. But it is of historic proportions that a society's best young and their best energies should be so occupied. People of future civilizations will wonder at this and find it as incomprehensible as we do the **caste system**, witch-burning, harems, cannibalism and **gladiatorial** combats. It may well be that a society's greatest madness seems normal to itself. The child I described has parents who have sacrificed to provide him with a good life and who have a great stake in his future happiness. They cannot believe that the musical vocation will contribute very much to that happiness. But there is nothing they can do about it. The family spiritual void has left the field open to rock music, and they cannot possibly forbid their children to listen to it. It is everywhere; all children listen to it;

fulcrum: support

pubescent: relating to puberty

smarmy: marked by an ingratiating and false earnestness

tableaux: pictures or representations of a scene

onanism: masturbation

countervailing: counteracting

caste system: a social system characterized by a highly ordered class structure

gladiatorial: pertaining to gladiators; characterized by a fight to the death

76

forbidding it would simply cause them to lose their children's affection and obedience. When they turn on the television, they will see President Reagan warmly grasping the daintily **proffered** gloved hand of Michael Jackson and praising him enthusiastically. Better to set the faculty of denial in motion—avoid noticing what the words say, assume the kid will get over it. If he has early sex, that won't get in the way of his having stable relationships later. His drug use will certainly stop at pot. School is providing real values. And popular historicism provides the final salvation: there are new life-styles for new situations, and the older generation is there not to impose its values but to help the younger one find its own. TV, which compared to music plays a comparatively small role in the formation of young people's character and taste, is a consensus monster—the Right monitors its content for sex, the Left for violence, and many other interested sects for many other things. But the music has hardly been touched, and what efforts have been made are both ineffectual and misguided about the nature and extent of the problem.

The result is nothing less than parents' loss of control over their children's moral education at a time when no one else is seriously concerned with it. This has been achieved by an alliance between the strange young males who have the gift of divining the mob's emergent wishes—our versions of Thrasymachus, Socrates' rhetorical adversary—and the record-company executives, the new robber barons, who mine gold out of rock. They discovered a few years back that children are one of the few groups in the country with considerable disposable income, in the form of allowances. Their parents spend all they have providing for the kids. Appealing to them over their parents' heads, creating a world of delight for them, constitutes one of the richest markets in the postwar world. The rock business is perfect capitalism, supplying to demand and helping to create it. It has all the moral dignity of drug trafficking, but it was so totally new and unexpected that nobody thought to control it, and now it is too late. Progress may be made against cigarette smoking because our absence of standards or our **relativism** does not extend to matters of bodily health. In all other things the market determines the value. (Yoko Ono is among America's small group of billionaires, along with oil and computer magnates, her late husband having produced and sold a commodity of worth comparable to theirs.) Rock is very big business, bigger than the movies, bigger than professional sports, bigger than television, and this accounts for much of the respectability of the music business. It is difficult to adjust our vision to the changes in the economy and to see what is really important. McDonald's now has more employees than U.S. Steel, and likewise the purveyors of junk food for the soul have supplanted what still seem to be more basic callings.

This change has been happening for some time. In the late fifties, de Gaulle gave Brigitte Bardot one of France's highest honors. I could not understand this, but it turned out that she, along with Peugeot, was France's biggest export item. As Western nations became more prosperous, leisure, which had been put off for several centuries in favor of the pursuit of property, the means to leisure, finally began to be of primary concern. But, in the meantime, any notion of the serious life of leisure, as well as men's taste and capacity to live it, had disappeared. Leisure became entertainment. The end for which they had labored for so long has turned out to be amusement, a justified conclusion if the means justify the ends. The music business is peculiar only in that it caters almost exclusively to children, treating legally and naturally imperfect human beings as though they were ready to enjoy the final or complete satisfaction. It perhaps thus reveals the nature of all our entertainment and our loss of a clear view of what adulthood or maturity is, and our incapacity to conceive ends. The emptiness *of values* results in the acceptance of the natural *facts* as the ends. In this case infantile sexuality is the end, and I suspect that, in the absence of other ends, many adults have come to agree that it is.

proffered: presented for acceptance

relativism: a view that ethical truths are dependent on the individuals or groups that hold them: what is true is what is believed to be true

It is interesting to note that the Left, which prides itself on its critical approach to "late capitalism" and is unrelenting and unsparing in its analysis of our other cultural phenomena, has in general given rock music a free ride. Abstracting from the capitalist element in which it flourishes, they regard it as a people's art, coming from beneath the bourgeoisie's layers of cultural repression. Its **antinomianism** and its longing for a world without constraint might seem to be the **clarion** of the **proletarian** revolution, and Marxists certainly do see that rock music dissolves the beliefs and morals necessary for liberal society and would approve of it for that alone. But the harmony between the young intellectual Left and rock is probably profounder than that. Herbert Marcuse appealed to university students in the sixties with a combination of Marx and Freud. In *Eros and Civilization* and *One Dimensional Man* he promised that the overcoming of capitalism and its false consciousness will result in a society where the greatest satisfactions are sexual, of a sort that the bourgeois moralist Freud called polymorphous and infantile. Rock music touches the same chord in the young. Free sexual expression, **anarchism**, mining of the irrational unconscious and giving it free rein are what they have in common. The high intellectual life I shall describe in Part Two and the low rock world are partners in the same entertainment enterprise. They must both be interpreted as parts of the cultural fabric of late capitalism. Their success comes from the bourgeois' need to feel that he is not bourgeois, to have undangerous experiments with the unlimited. He is willing to pay dearly for them. The Left is better interpreted by Nietzsche than by Marx. The critical theory of late capitalism is at once late capitalism's subtlest and crudest expression. Anti-bourgeois **ire** is the **opiate** of the Last Man.

This strong stimulant, which Nietzsche called Nihiline, was for a very long time, almost fifteen years, **epitomized** in a single figure, Mick Jagger. A shrewd, middle-class boy, he played the possessed lower-class demon and teen-aged **satyr** up until he was forty, with one eye on the mobs of children of both sexes whom he stimulated to a sensual frenzy and the other eye winking at the unerotic, commercially motivated adults who handled the money. In his act he was male and female, heterosexual and homosexual; **unencumbered** by modesty, he could enter everyone's dreams, promising to do everything with everyone; and, above all, he legitimated drugs, which were the real thrill that parents and policemen conspired to deny his youthful audience. He was beyond the law, moral and political, and thumbed his nose at it. Along with all this, there were nasty little appeals to the suppressed inclinations toward sexism, racism and violence, indulgence in which is not now publicly respectable. Nevertheless, he managed not to appear to contradict the rock ideal of a universal classless society founded on love, with the distinction between brotherly and bodily blurred. He was the hero and the model for countless young persons in universities, as well as elsewhere. I discovered that students who boasted of having no heroes secretly had a passion to be like Mick Jagger, to live his life, have his fame. They were ashamed to admit this in a university, although I am not certain that the reason has anything to do with a higher standard of taste. It is probably that they are not supposed to have heroes. Rock music itself and talking about it with infinite seriousness are perfectly respectable. It has proved to be the ultimate leveler of intellectual snobbism. But it is not respectable to think of it as providing weak and ordinary persons with a fashionable behavior, the imitation of which will make others esteem them and boost their own self-esteem. Unaware and unwillingly, however, Mick Jagger played the role in their lives that Napoleon played in the lives of ordinary young Frenchmen throughout the nineteenth century. Everyone else was so boring and unable to charm youthful passions. Jagger caught on.

In the last couple of years, Jagger has begun to fade. Whether Michael Jackson, Prince or Boy George can take his place is uncertain. They are even weirder than he is, and one wonders what new strata of taste they have discovered. Although

antinomianism: refusal to accept a social moral system

clarion: a call to action

proletarian: a member of the lowest economic and social class of a community

anarchism: disorder and confusion

ire: intense anger

opiate: narcotic causing sleep or inaction

epitomized: exemplified

satyr: a Greek mythological figure that was a cross between a horse or goat and a man with excessive, uncontrollable sexual desire

unencumbered: unburdened

each differs from the others, the essential character of musical entertainment is not changing. There is only a constant search for variations on the theme. And this gutter phenomenon is apparently the fulfillment of the promise made by so much psychology and literature that our weak and exhausted Western civilization would find refreshment in the true source, the unconscious, which appeared to the late romantic imagination to be identical to Africa, the dark and unexplored continent. Now all has been explored; light has been cast everywhere; the unconscious has been made conscious, the repressed expressed. And what have we found? Not creative devils, but show business glitz. Mick Jagger tarting it up on the stage is all that we brought back from the voyage to the underworld.

My concern here is not with the moral effects of this music—whether it leads to sex, violence or drugs. The issue here is its effect on education, and I believe it ruins the imagination of young people and makes it very difficult for them to have a passionate relationship to the art and thought that are the substance of liberal education. The first sensuous experiences are decisive in determining the taste for the whole of life, and they are the link between the animal and spiritual in us. The period of **nascent** sensuality has always been used for sublimation, in the sense of making sublime, for attaching youthful inclinations and longings to music, pictures and stories that provide the transition to the fulfillment of the human duties and the enjoyment of the human pleasures. Lessing, speaking of Greek sculpture, said "beautiful men made beautiful statues, and the city had beautiful statues in part to thank for beautiful citizens." This formula **encapsulates** the fundamental principle of the **aesthetic** education of man. Young men and women were attracted by the beauty of heroes whose very bodies expressed their nobility. The deeper understanding of the meaning of nobility comes later, but is prepared for by the sensuous experience and is actually contained in it. What the senses long for as well as what reason later sees as good are thereby not at tension with one another. Education is not sermonizing to children against their instincts and pleasures, but providing a natural continuity between what they feel and what they can and should be. But this is a lost art. Now we have come to exactly the opposite point. Rock music encourages passions and provides models that have no relation to any life the young people who go to universities can possibly lead, or to the kinds of admiration encouraged by liberal studies. Without the cooperation of the sentiments, anything other than technical education is a dead letter.

Rock music provides premature ecstasy and, in this respect, is like the drugs with which it is allied. It artificially induces the exultation naturally attached to the completion of the greatest endeavors—victory in a just war, consummated love, artistic creation, religious devotion and discovery of the truth. Without effort, without talent, without virtue, without exercise of the faculties, anyone and everyone is accorded the equal right to the enjoyment of their fruits. In my experience, students who have had a serious fling with drugs—and gotten over it—find it difficult to have enthusiasms or great expectations. It is as though the color has been drained out of their lives and they see everything in black and white. The pleasure they experienced in the beginning was so intense that they no longer look for it at the end, or as the end. They may function perfectly well, but dryly, routinely. Their energy has been sapped, and they do not expect their life's activity to produce anything but a living, whereas liberal education is supposed to encourage the belief that the good life is the pleasant life and that the best life is the most pleasant life. I suspect that the rock addiction, particularly in the absence of strong counterattractions, has an effect similar to that of drugs. The students will get over this music, or at least the exclusive passion for it. But they will do so in the same way Freud says that men accept the reality principle—as something harsh, grim and essentially unattractive, a mere necessity. These students will **assiduously** study economics or the professions and the Michael Jackson costume will slip off to reveal a Brooks Brothers suit beneath. They will want to get ahead and live

nascent: coming into existence recently

encapsulates: epitomizes; puts in capsule form

aesthetic: dealing with the beautiful

assiduously: diligently

comfortably. But this life is as empty and false as the one they left behind. The choice is not between quick fixes and dull calculation. This is what liberal education is meant to show them. But as long as they have the Walkman on, they cannot hear what the great tradition has to say. And, after its prolonged use, when they take it off, they find they are deaf.

▼ Questions to Focus Reading

1. In his opening paragraph, what comparison is Bloom making between today's students' passion for rock and nineteenth-century Germans' passion for Wagner?

2. What is the role of rock music in the life of today's students as Bloom sees it?

3. What was Plato's teaching about music? How does Bloom explain the indignation students feel toward Plato when discussing the great Greek philosopher's proposals in *The Republic* about musical education? Bloom contrasts the attitudes of his past and present students toward Plato's views of music. What is the contrast?

4. "This is the significance of rock music," Bloom begins one of his paragraphs (page 75). *What* is the significance?

5. "A worldview is balanced on the sexual fulcrum," Bloom writes. What does he mean?

6. Bloom develops at length the theme of the relation between rock music and sexual desire. What is that connection according to Bloom?

7. In the paragraph that begins "This phenomenon is both astounding and indigestible" (page 76), Bloom tries to view the phenomenon of rock from a broad historical perspective. What does he see from this perspective?

8. The result of the power of rock music is, according to Bloom, "parents' loss of control over their children's moral education." What does this mean? How has it come to pass, according to Bloom?

9. When Bloom views the phenomenon of rock as an aspect of the history of leisure in Western culture, what does he see?

10. What is Bloom's explanation for the fact that the Left, which is generally unsparing in its criticism of "late capitalist" cultural phenomena, has been uncritical of rock?

11. "Mick Jagger tarting it up on the stage is all that we brought back from the voyage to the underworld." What "voyage" is Bloom referring to here?

12. Toward the end of the essay, Bloom sketches a theory of the proper use of sensory experience in the aesthetic education of youth. What is that theory? Why in his view have we now come "to exactly the opposite point"?

13. In his final paragraph, Bloom compares infatuation with rock to drug addiction. What is the parallel here as he sees it?

14. In the last two paragraphs of this essay, Bloom tries to explain the connection between students' infatuation with rock and their lack of receptivity to liberal education. What is the connection, as he understands it?

▼ Questions for Reflection

1. Why do you suppose Bloom is willing to spend so much time with his students discussing the importance of music in their lives?

2. Has Bloom accurately characterized the role rock music has played in your life? "The meaningful inner life is with the music" (page 76). Has that been true for you? Has he characterized the consequences accurately?

3. "The first sensuous experiences are decisive in determining the taste for the whole of life, and they are the link between the animal and the spiritual in us" (page 79). What do you think Bloom means by this? Do

you think it is true of your own case? How does this idea relate to Bloom's critique of rock?

4. "Education is not sermonizing to children against their instincts and pleasures, but providing a natural continuity between what they feel and what they can and should be. But this is a lost art" (page 79). What does this mean? In what sense, according to Bloom, have we come to "exactly the opposite point"?

5. In the last paragraph, Bloom compares the deleterious effects of rock music with those of drug addiction. What is the comparison? Why, in his view, would this be particularly destructive of the aims of liberal education?

6. If Bloom could control the exposure of American youth to music, what kind of music would they hear? Why do you say so?

▼ Discussion

1. Has Bloom accurately characterized the role rock music has played in your life? "The meaningful inner life is with the music" (page 76). Has that been true for you? Has he characterized the consequences accurately?

2. "The first sensuous experiences are decisive in determining the taste for the whole of life, and they are the link between the animal and the spiritual in us" (page 79). What do you think Bloom means by this? Do you think it is true of your own case? How does this idea relate to Bloom's critique of rock music?

3. "Education is not sermonizing to children against their instincts and pleasures, but providing a natural continuity between what they feel and what they can and should be. But this is a lost art" (page 79). What does this mean? In what sense, according to Bloom, have we come to "exactly the opposite point"?

4. In the last paragraph, Bloom compares the deleterious effects of rock music with those of drug addiction. What is the comparison? Why, in his view, would this be particularly destructive of the aims of liberal education?

5. If Bloom could control the exposure of American youth to music, what kind of music would they hear? Why do you say so?

6. Bloom sees rock music as destructive of today's students' capacity for liberal education. In exactly what ways? Do you think he is right?

7. What conception of rock music emerges in this essay? Is that conception accurate?

▼ Writing Assignments

1. "Rock Music and Liberal Education: A Defense of Allan Bloom" or "Rock Music and Liberal Education: Bloom's Folly" Write an essay in which you defend or attack Bloom's ideas about the effect of youth's attachment to rock music on their educability.

2. Bloom writes, "The choice is not between quick fixes and dull calculation" (page 80). Make sure you understand what Bloom means by this, then write an essay in which you present an alternative.

3. Write an essay in which you depict your own experience with rock music and its effect on the development of your soul. ("My Life in Rock," or some such.)

▼ Journal Entry

1. How important is rock music in your life? Is it a mere diversion, like television, or is it more meaningful to you than that? If so, in what ways?

▼ Vocabulary

aesthetic	clarion	emotive	opiate	satyr
anarchism	coquettish	encapsulate	polymorphous	smarmy
antinomiani	Corybantic	epitomized	premonitory	solidarity
sm	corollary	fulcrum	proffered	tableaux
assiduously	countervailing	gladiatorial	proletarian	unabashed
avidly	culmination	impediment	prosaic	unencumber
bourgeoisie	dearth	ire	pubescent	ed
caste system	desuetude	ministerial	relativism	voracious
cathartic	elicit	nascent	restive	votaries
chasteness	emanations	onanism	sansculottism	voyeurism

11

▼

The New Lost Generation

David Leavitt

David Leavitt, novelist, essayist, short-story writer, and AIDS activist, tries here to capture the key values and concerns—the identity—of his generation, the older brothers and sisters of today's "Generation X."

Like our older brothers and sisters, my generation belongs to gyms. We find Nautilus equipment consoling. Nothing gets in your way when you're bench pressing, or swimming, or running, not even the interfering subconscious that tended to muck up all those Seventies efforts at psychological self-improvement. Muscles appear as a **manifestation** of pure will.

In contrast to our older brothers and sisters, however, the fact that we believe in health does not necessarily mean that we believe in the future. The same bright young person who strives for physical immortality also takes for granted the imminence of his destruction. At Brown University, students voted last October on a referendum to stock poison tablets in the school infirmary, so that in the event of a nuclear catastrophe, they could commit suicide rather than die of fallout. As if nuclear disaster, rather than being a distant threat, were a harsh reality, an immediacy, something to prepare for. I am reminded of Grace Paley's description of an eighteen-year-old in her story "Friends." "His friends have a book that says a person should, if properly nutritioned, live forever. . . . He also believes that the human race, its brains and good looks, will end in his time."

Brains and good looks. Last year I went dancing at Area for the first time, arguably the choicest dance club in New York. (A friend of mine who is more of an expert than I in these matters insists that the club called Save the Robots is choicer, since it is frequented by the people who work at the Area and does not open until after Area has closed.) At this point Area was dressed in its nuclear holocaust garb. On our way in, we passed **tableaux vivants** of people in Karen Silkwood suits, peeling **lurid** green candy off sheets on a conveyor belt. Women danced inside fantastic, menacing pseudo-reactors. Signs reading DANGER—RADIOACTIVE MATERIAL glowed above the dance floor. Later, at the bar, I was introduced to an artist who had been asked to create a work of art in support of the nuclear freeze, and was thinking of carving a mushroom cloud out of a block of ice. It was hard for me to keep from wondering about the famed holocaust anxiety of my postnuclear generation. The world after the bomb, it seemed to me, had become a cliché, incorporated into our dialogue and our culture with an alarming thoughtlessness. Do most of us dream, like Eddie Albert as the President in the movie *Dreamscape*, of a parched postholocaust landscape, peopled by weird half-human monsters and scared children wailing, "It hurts! It hurts!" I doubt it. I think we purport to worry about the world ending much more than we actually do.

Because the terror of knowing the world could end at any moment haunts them so vividly, older people seem to believe that it must be ten times worse for the young. The realization that nuclear disaster is not only possible, but possibly **imminent**, writes the noted essayist Lewis Thomas, "is bad enough for the people in my generation. We can put up with it, I suppose, since we must. We are moving along anyway. . . . What I cannot imagine, what I cannot put up with . . . is what

manifestation: evidence

tableaux vivants: photographs in which people are in costume as if they are acting

lurid: ghastly pale; gruesome

imminent: impending

83

it would be like to be young. How do the young stand it? How can they keep their sanity?"

Well, I want to say, we do. Indeed, I think we are more sane and less hysterical about the issue of nuclear holocaust than are the generations ahead of us. We do not go crazy, because for us the thought of a world with no future—so terrifying to Dr. Thomas—is completely familiar; is taken for granted; is nothing new.

I have tried time and again to explain this to people who are older than I. I tell them that no matter how hard I try—and I have closed my eyes tightly; concentrated, tried to will my mind to do it—I simply cannot muster an image of myself fifty, or twenty, or even ten years in the future. I go blank. I have no idea where or what or even if I'll be. Whereas my parents, when they were young, assumed vast and lengthy futures for themselves, a series of houses, each larger than the one before, and finally the "golden years" of retirement, knitting by fires, bungalows in Florida. I think we have inserted into our minds the commercialized image of the mushroom cloud and the world in flames in order to justify a blind spot in us—an inability to think beyond the moment, or conceive of any future at all, which makes us immune to the true horror felt by older people. This blind spot has more to do with our attitude toward the nuclear family than with nuclear disaster—with the fact that our parents, as they now reach the golden years they once looked forward to, are finding themselves trapped in unhappy marriages or divorced, are too bitter to ever consider loving again, or are desperate to find a new mate with whom they can share those last happy years that they were promised, that they worked so hard for, that they were so unfairly cheated out of.

And we—well, we aren't going to make the same mistakes they did. Alone at least, we're safe—from pain, from dependency, from sexually transmitted disease. Those who belong to no one but themselves can never be abandoned. . . .

The voice of my generation is the voice of David Letterman, whose late-night humor—upbeat, deadpan, more than a little contemptuous—we imitate because, above all else, we are determined to make sure everyone knows that what we say might not be what we mean. Consider these words from Brett Duval Fromson, in an op-ed piece for *The New York Times:* "Yuppies, if we do anything at all, respect those who deliver the goods. How else are we going to afford our Ferragamo pumps, Brooks Brothers suits, country houses, European cars, and California chardonnays?" The balance of the irony is perfect—between self-mockery and straightfaced seriousness, between criticism and comfy self-approval. "If we do anything at all," Fromson writes, leaving open the possibility that we don't. Certainly, he acknowledges, during the recession we "didn't give much thought to those who wouldn't make it." And now I am thinking about a headline I read recently in *The Village Voice,* above one of a series of articles analyzing Reagan's victory last November. It read DON'T TRUST ANYONE UNDER THIRTY.

Mine is a generation perfectly willing to admit its contemptible qualities. But our self-contempt is self-congratulatory. The buzz in the background, every minute of our lives, is that detached, ironic voice telling us: At least you're not faking it, as they did, at least you're not pretending as they did. It's okay to be selfish as long as you're up-front about it. Go ahead. "Exercise your right to exercise." Other people are dying to defend other people's right to speak, to vote, and to live, but at least you don't pretend you're not wearing a costume.

What is behind this bitterness, this skepticism? A need, I think, for settledness, for security, for home. Our parents imagined they could satisfy this urge by marrying and raising children; our older brothers and sisters through community and revolution. We have seen how far those alternatives go. We trust ourselves, and money. Period.

Fifteen years ago you weren't supposed to trust anyone over thirty. For people in my generation, the goal seems to be to get to thirty as fast as possible, and stay there. Starting out, we are eager, above all else, to be finished. If we truly are a generation without character, as is claimed, it is because we have seen what has happened to generations with character. If we are without passion or affect, it is because we have decided that passion and affect are simply not worth the trouble. If we stand crouched in the shadows of a history in which we refuse to take part, it is because that's exactly where we've chosen to stand.

Characterlessness takes work. It is defiance and defense all at once.

▼ Questions to Focus Reading

1. How does Leavitt explain his generation's devotion to working out?
2. Essayist Lewis Thomas wonders how young people can keep their sanity, living their entire lives in a world threatened with nuclear destruction. Leavitt tries to answer him. How?
3. Leavitt thinks his generation has a "blind spot" toward the future, but he thinks this has less to do with nuclear war than with the nuclear family. Explain what he has in mind.
4. He writes that his generation speaks with the voice of David Letterman. How so? What are the characteristics of his generation's "voice"?
5. Leavitt says that his generation readily admits its "contemptible qualities," but these admissions are a form of self-congratulation. In what sense?
6. What in Leavitt's view does his generation really want, and why do they want it?
7. "Characterlessness takes work." What does this mean?

▼ Questions for Reflection

1. How much of what Leavitt observes of his generation do you think is true of yours? In what respects is your generation different from his?
2. Does the threat of nuclear catastrophe affect your thinking about the future? If it does not, does Leavitt's explanation of his generation's immunity from these fears apply to you?
3. Do you have Leavitt's difficulty in imagining yourself twenty or even ten years in the future? If so, why do you think this is?
4. "We trust ourselves, and money. Period." Is this true of you? If so, is it for the reasons Leavitt attributes to his generation?

▼ Discussion

1. How would you characterize the key values of your generation? What do you think are the reasons your generation has placed such high value on these things?
2. The generation Leavitt is describing is that of the older brothers and sisters of most of the people in this year's freshman class. Do you think his portrait is accurate?
3. Working out, the dance club called the Area, and David Letterman symbolize aspects of his generation, as Leavitt sees it. Are there comparable symbols of yours? If so, what are they, and what do they symbolize about your generation?

▼ Writing Assignments

1. Describe an incident that captures key characteristics of your generation as you conceive them.
2. Create two or three vignettes that reflect your generation's values as you understand them.

▼ **Journal Entry**

1. Leavitt describes his generation with a certain distance but leaves no doubt that he counts himself as one among them, that the characteristics he ascribes to his generation are true of him as well. To what extent are you one among your generation?

▼ **Vocabulary**

imminent   lurid   manifestation   tableaux vivants

12

▼

You Did This to Us

Daniel Smith-Rowsey

Daniel Smith-Rowsey, a senior in politics and film at the University of California–Santa Cruz, sends this letter of condemnation to his parents' generation.

Sometimes I wonder what it would be like to have been twenty, my age, in the 1960s. Back when you could grow up, count on a career and maybe think about buying a house. When one person could expect to be the wage earner for a household.

In the space of one generation those dreams have died. The cost of living has skyrocketed, unemployment has gone up, going to college doesn't guarantee you can get a good job. And no one seems to care. Maybe it's because the only people my age you older people have heard from are those who *do* make a lot of money: investment bankers, athletes, musicians, actors. But more and more of us twentysomethings are underachievers who loaf around the house until we pass our college years.

This is an open letter to the baby boomers from the *next* generation. I think it's time we did a little hitting back. Aside from the wealthy, none of you ever told your children, "Someday this will all be yours," and you're the first middle class to fail that way. Did you think we wouldn't care? Thanks a lot. But the real danger lies in the way we've been taught to deal with failure: gloss over and pretend the problem doesn't exist. It's evidence you never taught us to be smart—you only taught us to be young.

We are the stupidest generation in American history, we 20-year-olds. You already know that. We really do get lower SAT scores than our parents. Our knowledge of geography is pathetic, as is our ability with foreign languages and even basic math. We don't read books like you did. We care only about image. We love fads. Talk to college professors, and they'll tell you they don't get intelligent responses like they used to, when you were in school. We're perfectly mush-headed.

You did this to us. You prized your youth so much you made sure ours would be carefree. It's not that you didn't love us; you loved us so much you pushed us to follow your idea of what you were—or would like to have been—instead of teaching us to be responsible. After legitimizing youthful rebellion you never let us have our own innocence—perhaps because Vietnam and Watergate shattered yours. That's why we're already mature enough to understand and worry about racism, the environment, abortion, the homeless, nuclear policy. But we also were fed on the video culture you created to idealize your own irresponsible days of youth. Your slim-and-trim MTV bimbos, fleshy beer commercials and racy TV shows presented adolescence as a time only for fun and sex. Why should we be expected to work at learning anything?

Not that we're not smart—in some ways. We're street smart, David Letterman clever, whizzes at Nintendo. We can name more beers than presidents. Pop culture is, to us, more attractive than education.

I really don't think we can do this dance much longer. Not a single industrialized country has survived since 1945 without a major re-evaluation of its identity except ours. That's what you thought you were doing in the 1960s, but soon you gave way to chasing the dreams of the Donald Trump–Michael Milken get-rich-quick **ethos**—and all you had left for us was a bankrupt economy. The latchkey lifestyle you gave us in the name of your own "freedom" has made us a generation with missing parents and broken homes. And what about the gays and blacks and Hispanics and Asians and women who you pretended to care so much about, and then forgot? It's not that I'm angry at you for selling out to the system. It's that there won't be a system for *me* to sell out to, if I want to. The money isn't there anymore because you spent it all.

To be honest, I can't blame you for all that's happened. The pre-eminence of new technologies and the turn toward cutthroat capitalism over the past two decades would have happened with or without the peculiarities of your generation. If I had been born in the 1950s, I too would have been angry at racism and the war in Vietnam. But that's not the same thing as allowing the system to unravel out of my own greed. Don't say you didn't start the fire of selfishness and indulgence, building it up until every need or desire was immediately appeased. Cable TV, BMWs, cellular phones, the whole mall culture has reduced us all to twelve-year-olds who want everything *now*. I'm not in love with everything your parents did, but at least they gave you a chance. As Billy Joel said, "Every child had a pretty good shot to get at least as far as their old man got." For most of us, all we've been left with are the erotic fantasies, aggressive tendencies and **evanescent** funds of youth. Pretty soon we won't have youth *or* money, and that's when we may get a little angry.

Or maybe we won't. Perhaps you really have created a nation of mush-heads who will always prefer style over substance, conservative politics and reading lessons. If that's so, the culture can survive, as it seems to be doing with the bright smile of optimism breaking through the clouds of decaying American institutions. And then you really will be the last modern smart generation because our kids will be even dumber, poorer, and more violent than us. You guys will be like the old mule at the end of Orwell's *Animal Farm,* thinking about how great things used to be when you were kids. You will differ from your own parents in that you will have missed your chance to change the world and robbed us of the skills and money to do it ourselves. If there's any part of you left that still loves us enough to help us, we could really use it. And it's not just your last chance. It's our only one.

ethos: fundamental value
evanescent: fleeting

▼ Questions to Focus Reading

1. Smith-Rowsey makes several strong criticisms of your (his own) generation. What are some of them?
2. He places the blame for the deficiencies of his generation on the generation of baby boomers who raised them. What aspects of the boomers' approach to child rearing does he criticize?

▼ Questions for Reflection and Discussion

1. What is the overall picture of your generation that emerges in this essay? Do you think it is accurate?
2. Do you agree with him that your generation has not been allowed to "have our own innocence"?
3. "The money isn't there anymore because you spent it all," Smith-Rowsey charges against the boomers. Do you think he is right about this?
4. Do you think he has correctly characterized the "mall culture" of your generation as eternal "twelve-year-olds who want everything *now*"?
5. In what respects is Smith-Rowsey's view of your generation similar to Bloom's (Reading 10)?
6. Do you share his resentment toward your parents' generation? Explain.

▼ Writing Assignments

1. Write your own open letter to your parents' generation.
2. Write a reply to Smith-Rowsey in which you attack or defend (or both) his assessment of your generation and his analysis of the causes of its condition.

▼ Journal Entry

1. To what extent does Smith-Rowsey's description apply to you?

▼ Vocabulary

ethos   evanescent

13

▼

In Defense of Today's Students

Susan Day

"Are students so awful, so wretched, so morally insufficient as to eliminate hope for life as we know it?" Susan Day, professor of sociology at Southwest Texas State University, thinks it's high time we put today's students in perspective.

The Charges

A common refrain on the campuses where I have taught and among faculty with whom I have been associated is the moral insufficiency of the latest generation (and all the previous generations, save, of course, our own). This is no doubt a common refrain on most campuses throughout the United States, perhaps even throughout the world, since it is a frequent characterization of newer generations by older generations.

This hypothesized moral insufficiency takes many forms: students simply don't care about learning (unlike me and my colleagues who loved to learn no matter whether we were required to learn about apical meristems in botany or quadratic equations in mathematics or *Beowulf* in English—three of my favorite activities in the entire world); students simply don't care about social issues (unlike me and my colleagues who participated in every protest march and every demonstration as students, and even now spend most of our weekends demonstrating, writing letters to our congresspersons, or at least seeing meaningful cinema about the world, to wit, anything directed by Kurosawa, Bresson, or De Sica); students simply don't keep up with current events (unlike me and my colleagues who watch CNN and C-Span all day every day, while reading several newspapers including the *Washington Post,* the *New York Times,* the *Christian Science Monitor,* and the *Texas Observer*—and never, ever, ever *USA Today*—while keeping up in our disciplines); students simply won't do any of the following: study, read assignments, ask questions, attend class, complete assignments on time, or be responsible in a variety of ways. In fact, students lack self-discipline, ideals, and heroes; worse, they do not defer gratification, do not value competence, and do not think of others. They are, in a word, wretched.

As a professor-friend of mine says, "Give it a number."

But are students so awful, so wretched, so morally insufficient as to eliminate hope for life as we know it? Or are professors' standards too high, our memories too short, our visions too narrow to accurately evaluate the student body? Probably, as is so often the case, there is some truth in both possibilities: students have limitations; professors are biased. Perhaps it is time to put students in some perspective in order to produce a clearer evaluation of them, their behavior, and their future.

Some Facts of the Case[1]

To understand the students of the nineties we should understand what they have been up against. They were the first generation of children whose mothers could work outside the home without **stigma**. In fact, many of their mothers had to work outside the home to feed and clothe their children.[2] This means that many of these

stigma: a sign of shame

students spent more time with baby sitters and day-care workers than with their parents.

They were the first generation of children in the United States whose parents could divorce without stigma. In fact, so many of them did end their marriages that the divorce rate spiraled higher than ever.[3] And what of the pain to their offspring, powerless to stop them?

They were the first generation of children whose schools had to hire many teachers who were no longer the best of the female college graduates. Prior to the modern women's movement, women seeking careers had three meaningful choices: teaching, nursing, and child care of some kind. But by 1975, the brightest, most determined female college graduates could aspire to become C.P.A.'s, M.D.'s, J.D.'s and Ph.D.'s, and thus succeed in professions previously denied them which had more status and higher **remuneration** than public school teaching—and they did. More of this generation's teachers went into education for "something to fall back on," and fall back they did.[4]

They were the first generation of children since the twenties whose political and business leaders abandoned the ideals of leadership, sacrifice, and labor to tout the merit of avaricious acquisition and conspicuous consumption. It is no surprise if the nineties generation believes, in the words of Gordon Gecko, "Greed is good." Role models abound in their experience.[5]

They were the first generation of children whose parents were promised lower taxes and a balanced budget only to find themselves, twelve years later, facing higher taxes and the greatest budget deficit of all time. This generation now knows that budget balancing is popular campaign rhetoric, but unpopular political policy—and that taxes lowered somewhere will be made up by raising taxes somewhere else. How can they help but be cynical about the motives of those in power and distrustful to **exhortations** to become one of a thousand points of light?

And finally, they were the first generation of children ever, in America, who grew up being told that most of them would never be able to live as well as their parents had. They have heard since the early eighties that their standard of living might not include home ownership, leisure time, or the luxury of being at home to care for their own children. In fact, they are the first generation whose college degree does not guarantee a career and a standard of living superior to those of their parents or their working class compatriots.

We cannot, must not, forget that this generation of nineties college students— born in the seventies and coming of age in the eighties—has matured during a time of great turmoil: the environment of the world is under attack by pollutants and ignorance; the economic prosperity of the United States is threatened from the European Economic Community and Japan; the country's social organization is **beleaguered** by disease and poverty; its physical infrastructure, collapsing under local debt and apathy; and students' own standard of living—not to mention their psychological well being—is assailed by all this turmoil as they move into their third decade and out of their parents' homes. Surely these events can be seen as discouraging and sobering reminders of a generation's apparent powerlessness in the face of external forces.

Despite their beleaguered coming-of-age, this generation has held its own. As we shall see, though they are not a **consortium** of superstars, neither are they an assemblage of dolts. Rather they are precisely what should be expected: unremarkable students and uneasy citizens.

How They Respond: As Students

Students graduating today in the United States are widely regarded as inferior to previous generations of students. The data for such assertions inevitably come from comparisons of SAT and ACT scores for different years. Such comparisons are

remuneration: payment; salary

exhortations: language that is intended to encourage and excite

beleaguered: troubled

consortium: association

replete with problems: national tests have, at best, a comparability life of ten years; and the population of students taking the tests has changed dramatically over the past thirty years. Thus, comparisons of 1970 exam scores to 1990 exam scores, common in the popular press, are, at best, suspect. Nevertheless, there are suggestions that this nineties generation is comprised of students with equal or superior potential to those in the eighties generation.

National SAT scores have begun to rise in the last few years. In fact, national math scores were higher in 1992 than they were in 1974; verbal scores are three points lower in 1992 than in 1982. Dramatic increases were demonstrated by African-American students (from 686 combined verbal and math in 1978 to 737 in 1992), and by Mexican-American students (from 772 combined verbal and math in 1978 to 797 in 1992). And total scores, combined verbal and math scores, were higher in 1992 than in 1976.[6]

What may be more important than average scores—especially if the populations taking the tests are not comparable[7]—is the proportion scoring above 600 on the math exam which has increased from 15.6 percent in 1975 to 18.0 percent in 1992.[8] The proportion scoring below 400 has declined from 28.5 percent in 1975 to 27 percent in 1992.[9] Similar ratios hold for the ACT exam.[10] While these are not dramatic demonstrations of student proficiency, neither are they dramatic demonstrations of student decline.

Educational attainment continues to increase as well. In 1950, only 34.3 percent of the population had completed four years of high school or more; only 6.2 percent of the population had completed four years of college or more. By 1970, those numbers were 55.2 percent and 11.0 percent; in 1980 they were 68.6 percent and 17 percent. In March, 1988, 76.5 percent of the population had four years of high school or more; 78.4 percent of those between 18 and 24 had four years of high school or more.[11] In addition, 28.1 percent of the population had four years of college or more.[12] Almost twice as many bachelor's degrees were awarded in 1989–90 (984,000) as were awarded in 1965–66 (524,117); the same relationship holds for all degrees: 1,382,000 in 1989–90 to 714,624 in 1965–66.[13]

It is tempting to dismiss such data as indicative of rank careerism, but to do so is to put students in a no-win situation. If they do not seek education, we consider them ignorant and anti-intellectual; if they do seek education, we deem them careerists in pursuit of credentials. Demeaning motives is unproductive. The real issue for those of us in the university—students and faculty alike—is to create the kind of collegiate environment that makes worthwhile those four or more years at the university.

How They Respond: As Activists

So this generation of students has had a rocky time and faces an uncertain future. What generation hasn't had its share of problems? Look at the children of the Great Depression; they had their problems too, right? Life is rough for everyone, isn't it? And what about those of us who grew up during the Cold War with the threat of atomic death just over every horizon? Despite our hardships, we sixties people were idealistic and involved, traits not commonly attributed to this latest generation, isn't that true?

But wait a minute. Is this nineties generation of college students as **pragmatic** and passive as they are often pictured? To get one perspective on students, it seems relevant to consider what they report when asked their attitudes about various subjects. First of all, student opinions have become more "middle-of-the-road," where, in 1989, more than half of freshmen reporting political views said theirs were located. Although the percentage of freshmen reporting themselves to be liberal declined from a third of students in 1960 to only a fifth (21.7 percent) in 1990, approximately the same proportion (21.3 percent) report themselves to be

pragmatic: practical

92

conservative[14]—only slightly higher than the 18 percent who reported conservative leanings in 1970.[15]

But student claims to middle-of-the-road political positions are **enfeebled** by their reported attitudes—which appear not to be middle-of-the-road—on specific traditionally conservative and liberal issues as shown in the following chart:[16]

Political Positions of Surveyed Students

Statements of Survey	Percentage of students who "strongly agree" or "somewhat agree"		
	Men	Women	Total
Government is not doing enough to protect the consumer	64.7	71.5	68.4
Government is not doing enough to promote disarmament	58.8	76.2	68.1
Government is not doing enough to control pollution	84.8	87.6	86.3
Military spending should be increased	30.2	19.6	24.5
The government should do more to control the sale of handguns	67.2	87.6	78.2
A national health care plan is needed to cover everybody's medical costs	72.1	79.0	75.8
Employers should be allowed to require employees or job applicants to take drug tests	76.7	78.9	77.8
Marijuana should be legalized	20.1	13.7	16.7
The death penalty should be abolished	18.4	23.8	21.3

Attitudes are, however, not actions. What students do is more important than what they say. So what have they done, if anything, to demonstrate idealism and involvement? More than one-third of freshmen surveyed in 1989 reported that they had participated in a protest or demonstration the year prior to entering college. This figure was higher than any reported by college freshmen in the late sixties. Nevertheless, there does not seem to be a national student movement, as there was during the sixties and early seventies. Students are not regularly making the nightly news with sit-ins, marches, and other demonstrations. But there are issues which produced coordinated national action at specific times during the eighties: apartheid in South Africa and pollution in the United States. The marches and demonstrations—and a riot at Berkeley—against apartheid, organized nationally in the mid-eighties, produced some meaningful success in insisting that universities divest themselves of stock in corporations doing business in South Africa.[17]

Though not publicized as widely as previous protests, students have responded to local issues with energy and success. A sit-in by Gallaudet students led to the withdrawal of the Trustees' nominee for president and the subsequent selection of the first deaf president for that university.[18] Students in New York's CUNY system protested proposed tuition increases by occupying buildings on the various campuses; other students worked to eject the protesters from the buildings.[19] African-American students have responded to incidents of racism on campuses and in towns throughout the country with protests, demonstrations, and legal actions.[20] Students have marched and organized protests against abortion rights, women's rights, gay rights, acquaintance rape, local campus policies, pollution, and, of course, cafeteria food. Students have marched and organized protests in support of abortion rights, women's rights, gay rights, famine relief, and, of course, Desert Storm soldiers.

Notice that these activities are not exclusively liberal endeavors. In contrast to the sixties, conservative students have a voice on today's campuses. A group of

enfeebled: weakened

93

students at Dartmouth continue to make themselves known through conservative political action, publishing their own newspaper (the *Dartmouth Review*) and challenging university administrators over various university policies. Challenges to "politically correct" thinking or quotas of one kind or another are gaining national attention, if not momentum, through the efforts of conservatives—Dinesh D'Souza is the most famous—who began their activist careers as students. Support of the war in the Gulf was frequently demonstrated on college campuses, sometimes in response to war protestors, but often simply in support of soldiers and their victory in the Gulf.

What the Past Contained

Finally it seems fair to respond to one final question: Was the sixties generation as idealistic and involved as we are commonly portrayed, that is, as we commonly portray ourselves? There was, of course, a national student movement. While it encompassed a number of movements—the free speech movement, the black civil rights movement, the women's liberation movement, and the gay pride movement—its overriding focus was opposition to the Vietnam War. And, of course, the student movement ended when the Vietnam War ended, despite the continued persistence of racism and sexism. Why? Because the student movement was essentially a self-interested movement clothed in idealistic phrases. It was "manned" by middle class students—going to college during an era in which a college degree insured a secure job, if not success—whose interests were achieved by avoiding the draft and its potential for death in Vietnam. The end of the draft was announced on January 27, 1973. The Vietnam peace pacts were signed on the same day. For all intents and purposes, the national student movement ended on January 27, 1973, as well.

Nevertheless the impression remains that most, if not all, students were involved in the student movement while it lasted. Such is not the case. Estimates are that only two percent of students belonged to the student left and another 10 percent were sympathetic to leftist issues. Even when the movement held campuses in its grip, most students simply went to class and avoided demonstrations.[21] Thus, the sixties' student movement may be likened to the concert at Woodstock, New York, an event which, if attended by all the people who now claim to have been there, would have swelled to several million.

What the Future Holds

Are we likely to see the dramatic mass social movements and nationally organized social protests of the sixties reinstated on the campuses of the nineties? I think not, and the reasons have little to do with the *students* of today. The differences, I believe, between campuses of then and campuses of now have to do with both economic forces and political leadership. The sixties were a time of plenty, with all social classes seeing a rise in their standard of living as a result of a political agenda which attempted to supply guns and butter at the same time, thereby stimulating the economy with increased capital, an expanding work force, and a rise in personal income.[22] Students went to school believing that a college degree meant a comfortable life. Indeed, that belief, however unconscious, coupled with the ideology of the times that social change could be effected,[23] freed students to pay greater attention to social issues, particularly those that affected their lives—the war in Vietnam and the draft that provided soldiers for the war.

Such is not the case today.[24] The economy has, for the last decade, been especially brutal on all but the top 10 percent, and to most of us, a better standard of living does not seem easily attained nor maintained, if achieved.[25] Worse, prior to the election of Bill Clinton, there was no ideology, no message, no leadership, no program, no agenda to give hope for solutions to any of the problems facing the United States. A "thousand points of light" seemed not to have the inspirational value of "Ask not what your country can do for you; ask what you can do for your country." And however we expect students to rise above these limiting external forces, the fact is that we—those of us who claim to be among the idealists of the sixties generation—did not have to rise above such forces. Indeed, we were probably driven by their very absence.

So if the mass social protests and movements are unlikely to return to college campuses, what shall we say about students? We can say that they are a great deal like the noncollegiate adults in the country: they have little faith in Washington,[26] and they tend to focus on and respond to smaller, more local issues. Whether they *should* be that way is another issue, but they *will* be that way until the economy provides some sense of optimism or until some charismatic leader suggests once again that *together* we can make a difference in this society.[27]

In Conclusion

So is this nineties generation of college students ignorant or worse, morally insufficient? Probably no more so or any less than preceding generations. With reference to their ignorance and their education, we don't really know if their scores on national exams are lower than, equal to, or superior to those of generations before 1980. And we know that their scores are roughly equal to those of the eighties generation, the only group of students with whom they can legitimately be compared. So whether they care about learning—whether they study, read assignments, ask questions, attend class, complete assignments on time, or are responsible—seems to have only one kind of **empirical** answer: they seem to be learning at about the same rate as other generations. Any other answer is made suspect by **aggrandized** memories of our own behaviors.

With reference to their idealism, their commitment to causes greater than themselves, are they deficient? For me the answer to that question begins with another question: Compared to what? If we compare them to the students of the sixties generation—that small percentage of students genuinely active in the student movement—they may seem to be lacking in that they have not created a national student movement. But they have been active at the local level, and there is every reason to believe that will continue.[28]

Finally, how are we to evaluate this nineties generation? Better asked: What right have we earned to evaluate them? My guess is that we ought to be as generous and encouraging as we are able to be. And rather than continue a meaningless act of **castigating** their morality and belittling their idealism, we had better be at the job of educating them. After all, they will have to solve problems—economic, environmental, and social—bestowed on them by my idealistic, caring, involved, educated, **altruistic** sixties generation.

empirical: based on observation

aggrandized: made to appear greater

castigating: criticizing

altruistic: unselfishly devoted to the welfare of others

Endnotes

1. This section is intended to offer an explanation for the behavior of this generation of college students. Many people believe that explanation is somehow justification. *It is not.* Explanation is simply a way—especially though not exclusively common to scientific disciplines—of creating a story about why things are the way they are. Justification is different; it is a way of arguing that things *should* be the way they are. Explanation involves a causal statement, or a series of causal statements, about the way things are or can be (or are not or cannot be). Justification involves a moral judgment, or a series of moral judgments, about how things should be (or should not be). This section explains; it does not justify.

2. In 1988, 57.1 percent of all married women with children under 6 years of age were in the labor force, compared to only 18.6 percent in 1960. 81 percent of all black married women with children under 6 worked. Wright, John W., 1989. ed., *The Universal Almanac 1990*. Kansas City: Andrews and McMeel, p. 296.

3. U.S. Bureau of the Census as quoted in John W. Wright, ed., *The Universal Almanac 1990* (Kansas City: Andrews and McMeel, 1989), 239. At its peak, the divorce rate was 5.3 per 1,000 people in 1981 (up from 2.5 in 1965, 3.5 in 1970, and 4.8 in 1975). Compare that to the marriage rate, 10.6 per 1,000 in 1981, and you understand how the press can claim—somewhat erroneously—that one in two marriages fails. Such a statement is erroneous in that it compares the number of marriages in a specific year with the number of that year's divorces which came from marriages most of which occurred in years previous to the one being considered. A more accurate statistic is the divorce ratio: the number of divorces in a year divided by the number of existing marriages. In 1988 the divorce ratio was 21 divorces per 1,000 existing marriages compared to 23 in 1980, 15 in 1970, 7 in 1960, and 10 in 1950. (For further discussion of this divorce ratio, see Maxine Baca Zinn and D. Stanley Eitzen, 1990. *Diversity in Families*. New York: Harper & Row, p. 354.) The divorce rate was between 4.8 and 5.0 per 1,000 people from 1982 to 1988, in comparison to a marriage rate of between 10.6 to 10.0 per 1,000 people. U.S. Bureau of the Census as quoted in Wright, John W., ed., 1989. *The Universal Almanac 1990*. Kansas City: Andrews and McMeel, p. 239.

4. High school seniors indicating education as their intended area of study produced lower SAT scores in Mathematics from 1977 to 1991 than *students intending any other area of study*. Their SAT verbal scores were lower than students intending other areas from 1977 to 1988. That year, their verbal scores surpassed those of students intending to study computer and information sciences as reported in *The Digest of Education Statistics, 1992*. National Center for Educational Statistics, p. 127.

5. Where to start? Donald Trump is one icon here. Danny Faulkner, Charles Keating, and Neil Bush are symbols of the S&L debacle for which only a few culprits will ever be penalized. Then there are the stock market scandals for which only a few, though highly publicized, "perps" have been penalized. Even they have impressed the public with an ability to pay unimaginable fines: Ivan Boesky's $100 million fine and Michael Milkin's $600 million fine somehow demonstrate success rather than failure. Add to the list the collapse of the health care industry as physicians' incomes rise and health care costs surpass the ability of many Americans to pay; and the proliferation of insolvent and fraudulent insurance firms, leaving policy holders without medical insurance. Remember the Iran-Contra arms-for-hostages scandal and note the behaviors of President Reagan's subordinates—Ed Meese, Robert McFarlane, Samuel R. Pierce, Jr., Oliver North, and others. Finally, if we were to include elected politicians alleged to have participated in unethical or illegal behavior (like Mario Biaggi, Patrick Swindall, Tony Coehlo, Jim Wright, Ted Kennedy, Alan Cranston, Dennis DeConcini, Donald "Buzz" Luekins) the list could become endless.

6. *College Bound Seniors: 1992 Profile of SAT and Achievement Test Scores*. Educational Testing Service, 1992: p. iii–vi.

7. SAT scores are significantly and positively correlated with parents' income. Fewer disadvantaged or poor high school students were college

bound before the expansion of the student loan program in the mid-sixties; thus students likely to score lowest were less likely to take the exams. As a result, they were excluded from the testing population. With the expansion of the student loan program throughout the seventies and into the eighties, poor students who would not have previously considered entering college at age 18 began to take the SAT or ACT exams and attempt college. Thus, more students who would be expected to have lower SAT scores as a consequence of life in the lower classes took the national exams during the seventies and eighties.

8. The percent above 600 on the verbal test for 1975 was 7.9; for 1980 it was 7.2. For 1992 it was 7.3.

9. The percent below 400 on the verbal test for 1975 was 37.8; for 1980 it was 41.8. For 1992 it was 41.3.

10. For all scores, see *College Bound Seniors: 1992 Profile of SAT and Achievement Test Scores.* Educational Testing Service, 1992: p. iii–9 or Hoffman, Mark, ed., 1991. *The World Almanac and Book of Facts 1991.* New York: Pharos Books, p. 213.

11. Computed from data contained in Hoffman, Mark, ed., 1991. *The World Almanac and Book of Facts 1991.* New York: Pharos Books, p. 207.

12. Computed from data contained in Hoffman, Mark, ed., 1991. *The World Almanac and Book of Facts 1991.* New York: Pharos Books, p. 207.

13. Wright, John W., ed., 1989. *The Universal Almanac 1990.* Kansas City: Andrews and McMeel, p. 206.

14. Astin, Alexander W. "The American Freshman: National Norms for Fall 1989." The American Council of Education and the University of California at Los Angeles as cited in *The Chronicle of Higher Education,* September 5, p. 14.

15. Landers, Robert K., "Student Politics 1980's Style." 1986. *Editorial Research Reports,* August 22, pp. 611–628.

16. Astin, Alexander W., "The American Freshman: National Norms for Fall 1989." The American Council of Education and the University of California at Los Angeles as cited in *The Chronicle of Higher Education,* September 5, p. 14. Astin, Alexander. 1991. "The Changing American College Student: Implications for Educational Policy and Practice." *Higher Education* 22, pp. 129–143. Flanagan, Thomas J. and Kathleen Maguire, eds. 1992. *Sourcebook of Criminal Justice Statistics: 1991.* Washington DC: USGPO, pp. 233–234.

17. By the mid-eighties more than fifty colleges had sold part of their holdings in such companies and another fifty had completely divested themselves of such stocks. Landers, Robert K. "Student Politics 1980's Style." *Editorial Research Reports,* August 22, p. 615.

18. Numerous articles covered this event. For the collegiate perspective, see Orlans, Harold. 1989. "The Revolution at Gallaudet: Students Provoke Break with the Past." *Change.* Jan/Feb, pp. 8, 11.

19. See a series of articles in the *New York Times,* April 18, 1991 to April 26, 1991.

20. Kantrowitz, Barbara. "Blacks Protest Campus Racism; A Rash of Incidents" 1987. *Newsweek,* April 6, p. 30; Davis, Ray. "Anti-Racist Organizing, Then and Now." *Socialist Review 1990.* Vol. 20, p. 29.

21. Peterson, Richard E. "The Scope of Student Protest," in Julian Foster and Durward Long, eds., 1970. *Protest! Student Activism in America.* New York: Morrow, p. 78.

22. Remember, this explanation of the consequences of LBJ's policies is not justification!

23. In large part this belief was a result of the success of the black civil rights movement.

24. The article is being finished in the early days of the Clinton administration. Without doubt, President Clinton is attempting to provide leadership, vision, a program, and an agenda. Whether he can inspire sufficient change in the economy to empower youth is unclear at this time.

25. Phillips, Kevin. *The Politics of Rich and Poor: Wealth and the American Electorate in the Reagan Aftermath.* 1990. New York: Random House. See especially the chart on page 17.

26. See Flanagan, Thomas J. and Kathleen Maguire, eds., 1990. *Sourcebook of Criminal Justice Statistics: 1989.* Washington, D.C.: USGPO, pp. 131, 132. It is also interesting to note that universities in general and professors in particular are generally held in high esteem; see Flanagan, Thomas J. and Kathleen Maguire, eds., 1990. *Sourcebook of Criminal Justice Statistics: 1989.* Washington, D.C.: USGPO, pp. 132, 138.

27. If both of these conditions develop, perhaps under President Clinton, we can expect American youth to once again become galvanized around one or more social issues in some kind of national movement, especially if the issues have a direct impact on their lives.

28. As a reminder, "The share of freshmen who participated in organized demonstrations during the year prior to entering college reached a high of 36.7 percent which is greater than the percentages observed during the late 1960s. At the same time, the percentage of freshman who said that there is a "very good chance" that they will participate in student protests or demonstrations reached an all-time high of 6.3 percent, up from 5.4 percent in 1988 and 4.7 percent in 1967." From Astin, Alexander, 1990. "The American Freshman: National Norms for Fall 1989." The American Council of Education and the University of California at Los Angeles as cited in Hoffman, Mark, ed., 1991. *The World Almanac and Book of Facts 1991.* New York: Pharos Books, p. 239.

▼ Questions to Focus Reading

1. What are some of the criticisms of your generation that Day recounts in her opening section?

2. Day believes there are important facts about your generation that help us understand what it is up against. What are some of these facts?

3. The record of educational attainment for recent generations of Americans is encouraging, according to Day. What facts does she cite?

4. This generation of college students is not as pragmatic and passive as they are often portrayed, Day writes. What evidence does she cite to the contrary?

5. "For all intents and purposes, the national student movement ended on January 27, 1973." What significance does Day see in this?

6. Day doubts we will see in the nineties the dramatic social movements and protests on campus that marked the sixties. But the reasons have to do not with the differences between students then and now, but differences in economic forces and political leadership. What does she have in mind?

▼ Questions for Reflection

1. Day pursues several distinct strategies in making her case in defense of today's college students. What are her strategies?

2. Contrast the overall picture of your generation that emerges in Day's essay with the picture that emerges in the Gordon, Bloom, and Smith-Rowsey

essays. Which of these in your view brings your generation into clearest focus?

3. Do you think of the circumstances surrounding your coming of age as "beleaguered"? If so, what specific circumstances marking your generation make you feel this way?

▼ Discussion

1. Day presents several facts that she believes to be important in trying to understand what your generation is "up against." Which of these do you believe to be most important? Are there other facts, unmentioned by Day, that you believe to be of equal importance in this respect?

2. How would you describe the outlook, values, and attitudes of your generation? What do you think are the most important realities affecting these?

3. What in your own view are the strengths of your generation in comparison, say, to your parents' generation at your age? What are its weaknesses?

4. Are there any social causes that you take seriously? Have you taken any action in regard to any of these?

5. Which of the writers in this text who comment on your generation seem to you to be presenting accurate insights?

▼ Writing Assignments

1. What charges against your generation do you find especially irksome, short-sighted, or unfair? Present your reasons for believing these charges to be inaccurate.

2. Present a portrait of your generation—its values, attitudes, and overall outlook on life. What social realities do you think are most important in having shaped it?

▼ Journal Entry

1. To what extent does Day's description of your generation apply to you?

▼ Vocabulary

aggrandized	castigating	enfeebled	remuneration
altruistic	consortium	exhortations	stigma
beleaguered	empirical	pragmatic	

14

▼

Killing Us Softly: Gender Roles in Advertising

Jean Kilbourne

Jean Kilbourne is a filmmaker who has devoted much of her career to the examination of images of women in advertising. She alerts us here to the "profound seriousness" of the impact of advertising on our values and attitudes, and especially on women's conceptions of themselves.

Role of Advertising in Contemporary Culture

Advertising campaigns no longer simply interrupt the news; in recent years, they have become the news. Community groups successfully halted the marketing of Uptown, a new cigarette that targeted inner-city African Americans. People were and still are outraged by a cartoon camel called "Old Joe," who successfully sells Camel cigarettes to children. The Surgeon General and other public health activists called for restrictions on alcohol and cigarette advertising. The Swedish Bikini Team, featured in beer commercials, was also featured in a sexual harassment suit brought by female workers in the beer company.

More and more people are taking advertising seriously. They realize that the $130 billion advertising industry is a powerful educational force in the United States. The average American is exposed to over 1,500 ads a day and will spend 1½ years of his or her life watching television commercials. The ads sell a great deal more than products. They sell values—images and concepts of success and worth, love and sexuality, popularity and normalcy. They tell us who we are and who we should be. Although individual ads are often stupid and trivial, their cumulative impact is serious.[7,18,30]

Advertising is the foundation and economic lifeblood of the mass media. The primary purpose of the mass media is to sell audiences to advertisers; the primary purpose of television programs is to deliver an audience for the commercials. Advertising is partially a reflection of the culture that created it. Because of its power, however, it does a great deal more than simply reflect cultural attitudes and values; it plays an important role in shaping them. Far from a passive mirror of society, it is an effective medium of influence and persuasion, both a creator and perpetuator of the dominant attitudes, values, and ideology of the culture, the social norms, and the myths by which most people govern their behavior. Advertising performs much the same function in industrial society as myth performed in ancient and primitive societies—and with a similarly conservative effect.[19]

Advertising affects almost all of us throughout our lives. Adolescents are particularly vulnerable, however, because they are new and inexperienced consumers—and the prime targets of many advertisements. They are in the process of learning values and roles and developing self-concepts. Most teenagers are sensitive to peer pressure and find it difficult to resist or even to question the dominant cultural messages perpetuated and reinforced by the media. Mass communication has made possible a kind of national peer pressure that erodes private and individual values and standards as well as community values and standards. Margaret Mead once said that the children of today are brought up by the mass media rather than by parents.[21]

Advertisers are aware of their role and do not hesitate to take advantage of the insecurities and anxieties of young people, usually in the guise of offering solutions: a cigarette provides a symbol of independence; designer jeans or sneakers convey status; the right perfume or beer resolves doubts about femininity or masculinity. Because so many anxieties center on sexuality and intimacy and because advertising so often offers products as the answers, gender roles may be the most deeply affected cultural concept.

Stereotypes

What do teenagers learn about gender roles from advertising? On the most obvious level, they learn the stereotypes that have existed for a long time and certainly have not been created or perpetuated solely by advertising. From birth we receive messages about sexism and gender stereotypes from every aspect of society. No messenger is more pervasive or persuasive, however, than advertising.

The stereotypes in television commercials have changed very little. Advertising creates a mythic, white, middle-class world in which people are rarely ugly, overweight, poor, elderly, struggling, or disabled, either physically or mentally (unless one counts the housewives who talk to little men in toilet bowls).[13] Women are shown almost exclusively as sex objects or as housewives pathologically obsessed with cleanliness. These days, however, they are likely to announce that they also have a career: "I'm a brain surgeon, but right now my trickiest problem is how to get the grease off this stove." Men are generally rugged authority figures, dominant and invulnerable. Men who are married or engaged in "women's work" are often portrayed as idiots and buffoons: "Honey, can you wash these dirty work clothes in cold water?" These stereotypes, and to some extent their effects, have been well documented.[3,6] The stereotyping of children in the media has perhaps never been worse. Television programs for children are filled with active boys and passive girls and sponsored by action products for boys and beauty products and dolls for girls.

Young people are also affected by advertising in more subtle, indirect ways that are perhaps more powerful than stereotypes (which increasingly are recognized and sometimes ridiculed). Advertising could be considered the propaganda of American society. It teaches us to be consumers, to value material possessions above all else, to feel that happiness can be bought, to believe in instant solution to complex problems, and to turn to products for fulfillment of our deepest human needs. In the world of advertising, we are encouraged to have relationships with products. "The best relationships are lasting ones," a Toyota ad announces. Although a couple is featured, the ad certainly implies that the lasting relationship will be with the car. As a result, objects are given great importance and value, and people are often **reified**. This is particularly true for women, who are depicted primarily as sex objects, and increasingly true for men, who are depicted as success objects. In both cases, the person becomes a thing, and his or her value depends on the products used.

Tyranny of the Ideal Image

The sex object is a mannequin whose only attribute is conventional beauty. She has no lines or wrinkles (which are, after all, signs of maturity, expression, and experience), no scars or blemishes; indeed, she has no pores. This perfection used to be achieved through cosmetics, camera tricks, and airbrushing; today it is achieved primarily through computer retouching, which can completely alter a photograph.

The sex object is thin, generally tall, and long-legged; above all, she is young. All so-called beautiful women in the mass media, regardless of product or audience,

reified: regarded as material or concrete things

101

conform to this norm. Women are constantly exhorted to emulate this ideal, to feel ashamed and guilty if they fail, and to equate desirability and the capacity for being loved with physical perfection.

The image is artificial and can be achieved only artificially. As a Bonne Bell cosmetics ad tells us, "Natural beauty is rarely achieved naturally." Desperate to conform to an impossible ideal, many women go to great lengths to manipulate their faces and bodies. Over two million American women have had silicone implanted in their breasts.[11] More than a million dollars are spent on cosmetics every hour in the United States.[5] A woman is conditioned to view her face as a mask and her body as an object, both separate from and more important than her real self, constantly in need of alteration, improvement, and disguise. She is made to feel dissatisfied with and ashamed of herself, whether or not she tries to achieve the ideal. **Objectified** constantly by others, she learns to objectify herself.

It is difficult not to internalize this objectification. Women are told in many ways throughout their lives that they are not quite right. As Wendy Chapkis said, "We are like foreigners attempting to assimilate into a hostile culture."[4] Women will never be accepted as they are, not even the most stereotypically beautiful (for example, the uproar when Madonna revealed her unshaven armpits in *Playboy*). The ridicule of fat women, old women, and bag ladies is a reminder that women must be ever vigilant; they are just one razor blade—or one more year or several more pounds—away from contempt.

Women are also supposed to keep their beauty rituals secret and never expose the artifice. Everything must be taken care of in private. Even in the ads, we see only the results, not the process. Men shave their bristly beards, but women shave legs that are already smooth. We never see a woman tweezing her chin. Women in curlers and cold cream are objects of ridicule. The process is supposed to be magical and must never be questioned.

The essence of "feminine beauty" is vigilance and artificiality. Men may be expected to enhance their appearance (at times by appearing unshaven and completely cavalier), but women are supposed to transform themselves. Vanity is encouraged in women but judged harshly in men. In a print ad, headlined "Simply beautiful," a little girl sits at a vanity table, looking into the mirror. An ad headlined "Simply handsome," with a little boy at a mirror, would be viewed as perverse. Women learn early that their natural state is basically ugly and that beauty depends on how well they learn to disguise themselves.

Even worse, beauty is often virtue in American culture. In the media, only the beautiful deserve love and romance, only the beautiful experience sex. Research confirms that the physically "ugly" are often judged as inwardly ugly. People who are considered unattractive or obese are harshly discriminated against from childhood onward.

Most women learn a sense of inferiority and insecurity that leads to hostile competition with other women. Even the rare teenager who approximates the ideal suffers. She may experience stunted development in other areas of life and damaged relationships with other women. A shampoo campaign in the late 1980s featured a series of conventionally beautiful women, each saying, "Don't hate me because I'm beautiful." Constant objectification can lead to callous disregard for others or to fear that a woman's entire value depends on her appearance. The cultural worship of the adolescent female can lead to unrealistic expectations for the future and can contribute to lifelong rage against women by rejected men. The ideal image harms all women, whether or not they approximate it briefly (there is no other way to do so) in their own lives. It makes most genuine women at best invisible, at worst the targets of contempt and hostility.

Although beauty is generally equated with virtue, sometimes beautiful women are seen as inherently dangerous or untrustworthy. In recent films, such as *Fatal Attraction* and *Final Analysis,* the unmarried beautiful woman is ultimately evil or

objectified: made into or treated as an object

unbalanced. In real life, the beautiful woman is also judged especially harshly as she ages or loses her beauty (for example, the hostility directed against Elizabeth Taylor whenever she gains weight). The beautiful woman is like a rich person doomed to eventual bankruptcy. Even as the "baby boom" generation reaches midlife, the ideal for women remains fixed at about 25 years of age; thus older women turn to cosmetic surgery and elaborate, time-consuming fitness programs in an attempt to maintain the ideal.

Dismemberment

Women are **dismembered** in advertisements, their bodies separated into parts that need change or improvement. If a woman has acceptable breasts, then she must also be sure that her legs are worth watching, her hips slim, her feet sexy, and her panty lines invisible. The mannequin has no depth, no totality. She is an aggregate of parts that have been made acceptable.

Often the woman in a television commercial is a literal aggregate of parts. She seems to be one woman but in reality is four or five—one woman's face, another woman's hands, another woman's legs, another woman's hair. In films, body doubles are increasingly common, not only to protect the star's modesty but also to give the illusion that she has a perfect body.

Women's bodies are not only dismembered but often **gratuitously** insulted. A recent ad for Dep hair-styling products in many women's and teen magazines had the following copy:

> Your breasts may be too big, too saggy, too pert, too full, too far apart, too close together, too A-cup, too lopsided, too jiggly, too pale, too padded, too pointy, too pendulous, or just two mosquito bites. But with Dep styling products, at least you can have your hair the way you want it. Make the most of what you've got.

At about the same time, a Calvin Klein ad made national news by featuring a nude man in a shower, holding a pair of jeans over his crotch. Some reporters claimed that men are now treated as sex objects exactly as women are. But the difference becomes obvious when we try to imagine the ad with the following copy:

> Your penis may be too small, too droopy, too limp, too lopsided, too narrow, too fat, too jiggly, too hairy, too pale, too red, too pointy, too blunt, or just two inches. But at least you can have a great pair of jeans. Make the most of what you've got.

Such treatment of men is unthinkable, but it is routine for women and girls. No wonder recent research indicates that the self-esteem of girls plummets as they reach adolescence, whereas the self-esteem of boys remains intact.[2]

Body Language

As Goffman pointed out in his seminal book, *Gender Advertisements,* we learn a great deal about the disparate power of men and women simply through the body language and poses of advertising.[9] Women are generally subservient to men in ads, both in size and position. Women are often shown as playful clowns, perpetuating the attitude that women are childish and cannot be taken seriously, whereas men are generally portrayed as secure, powerful, and serious.

Goffman also discusses what he calls "canting." People in control of their lives stand upright, alert, and ready to meet the world. In contrast, women often

dismembered: having had one's body taken apart

gratuitously: in a manner that is not called for by the circumstances

103

appear off-balance, insecure, and weak. Often their body parts are bent, conveying unpreparedness, submissiveness, and appeasement. Women often cover their faces with their hair or hands, conveying shame or embarrassment.

Worship of Youth

"You're a Halston woman from the very beginning," the advertisement proclaims. The model stares provocatively at the viewer, her long blond hair waving around her face, her bare chest partially covered by two curved bottles that give the illusion of breasts and cleavage. The average American is accustomed to blue-eyed blondes seductively touting a variety of products. In this case, however, the blonde is about 5 years old.

Young women are discouraged from growing up and becoming adult. Growing older is the great taboo. The traits considered most feminine are also considered most childlike, for example, passivity, submission, and dependence. (Of importance, however, is the far greater relevance of this equation to white women than to women of color.) Advertising slogans such as "because innocence is sexier than you think" and "sensual, but not too far from innocence" place women in a double bind. Somehow women are supposed to be both sexy and virginal, experienced and naive, seductive and chaste. Pressure has increased on women of all ages to be sophisticated and accomplished yet feminine, (that is, fragile and childlike. The **disparagement** of maturity is insulting and frustrating to adult women, and the implication that little girls are seductive is dangerous to children.

We have been surrounded for years by images of grown women who act like little girls, often playing with dolls and wearing bows in their hair. Only within the past decade or so, however, has the little girl been presented as a grown woman, the sex object, the ideal. Today little girls are sexually exploited by everyone from Calvin Klein to the multibillion dollar pornography industry. Sexual abuse of children seems to be increasing dramatically (or perhaps it is just more often reported). Recent research indicates that in America 1 in 3 girls and 1 in 5 boys are sexually abused during childhood.[29] Is there a connection?

It would be foolish to suggest that advertising is the cause of sexual abuse of children. The problem is complex, with many causal and contributing factors. Although flagrant sexism and gender stereotyping abound in all forms of the media, it is difficult to document their effects on individuals and institutions, primarily because it is difficult to separate media effects from other aspects of the socialization process. It is also almost impossible to find a comparison group, because almost everyone has been exposed to massive doses of advertising. Research shows, however, that media users, especially children, are directly affected and influenced by media content.[27]

Health Effects of the Ideal Image

Ironically, the heavily advertised products, such as cosmetics, cigarettes, alcohol, and soft drinks, are in fact detrimental to physical attractiveness. The media place little emphasis on good nutrition, exercise, or other important aspects of health and vitality.

The current emphasis on excessive thinness for women is one of the clearest examples of advertising's power to influence cultural standards and individual behavior. The ideal body type is unattainable by most women, even if they starve themselves. Only the thinnest 5 percent of women in a normal weight distribution approximate the ideal; 95 percent of American women are excluded. Television and the other media thus reflect the visual minority rather than the general population. In fact, the majority of women on television today are much thinner than in previous decades.[10]

disparagement: belittlement

104

As a result, more than half of the adult women in the United States are currently dieting, and over three-fourths of normal-weight American women think that they are "too fat."[25] This mass delusion sells a wide variety of products and supports a $33 billion diet industry.[1] It also causes enormous suffering for women, involving them in false quests for power and control, while deflecting attention and energy from goals that in fact might empower them.

The preoccupation with weight is beginning at increasingly younger ages for women. A 1986 study by Mellin and Irwin showed that nearly 80 percent of fourth-grade girls in the San Francisco Bay Area were watching their weight.[26] In a study of 3,000 adolescents, Rosen and Gross found that most of the boys were trying to gain weight, whereas at any given time two-thirds of girls aged 13–18 years were trying to lose weight.[24] Boys, of course, are encouraged to be bigger and stronger (to the point of using dangerous steroids), whereas girls are supposed to be thin and fragile.

Eating disorders have increased dramatically in recent years.[14] Given the research on the biologic, familial, and psychological contributions to eating disorders, it would be simplistic to hold advertising solely accountable for this increase. However, it is certainly a factor. At least one study of female college students suggests that the impact of advertising is indeed substantial. Brief exposure to several ads showing highly attractive models resulted in decreased satisfaction with personal appearance in comparison with the satisfaction of a control group who saw ads without models.[23]

An emphasis on dieting has been accompanied in the media by an increasing emphasis on fitness, which is often misguided and misleading. An obsession with exercise can be as damaging as an obsession with dieting; indeed, women with anorexia often suffer from both obsessions. The current ideal is especially unattainable for women with limited time or money.

Even more insidiously, the fitness craze displaces the concept of power for women, reducing it to narcissism. A fit body may give the illusion of power and change, but an underpaid and undervalued woman who is physically fit is still underpaid and undervalued.

Women's limited sense of power was strikingly revealed in a survey of middle-aged women who were asked what they would most like to change about their lives. One thinks immediately of low salaries, ill health, poverty, or the environment. Over half of the women, however, said that they would most like to change their weight.[22] In another survey, 30 girls aged 11–17 years were given three magic wishes. The number-one wish of the majority was "to lose weight and keep it off."[28]

In fact, ads and television programs rarely portray women with the same control as men. In the 1987–88 television season, only 3 of 22 new prime-time dramas featured female leads, and 66 percent of the prime-time speaking characters were male.[8] According to a 1993 study by the Screen Actors Guild and the American Federation of Television and Radio Artists, men under the age of 40 years received 43 percent of the roles in films, whereas women under 40 received 23 percent and women 40 years of age and older received only 8 percent. Over 80 percent of voice-overs in television commercials are male.[12]

American culture still has a tremendous fear of feminine power, as if it would be inherently destructive. Some argue that men's awareness of how powerful women can be has created the attempts to keep women small; hence the pressure on women to be thin, to be like little girls, not to take up too much space, literally or figuratively.[17] At the same time, there is pressure to succeed, to "have it all." In other words, women can be successful as long as they stay "feminine" (that is, powerless enough not to be truly threatening). An image of fragility demonstrates that a woman is both in control and still very feminine.[16]

Effects on Sexual Attitudes

Young people learn a great deal about sexual attitudes from the mass media and from advertising in particular. Advertising's approach to sex is pornographic: it reduces people to objects and deemphasizes genuine human contact and individuality. It often directly targets young people. This reduction of sexuality to a dirty joke and of people to objects is the true obscenity of American culture. Although the sexual sell, overt and subliminal, is at fever pitch in most advertising, depictions of sex as an important and profound human activity are notably absent. A sense of joy is also notably absent; the models generally look either hostile or bored.

Sex in advertising is narcissistic, autoerotic, and divorced from relationships. Identical models parade alone through the commercials, caressing their own soft skin, stroking and hugging their bodies, shaking their long silky manes, sensually bathing and applying powders and lotions, and then admiring themselves at length in the mirror. Advertising depicts a world of pervasive sexual innuendo but no love; passion is reserved solely for products.

The curious sterility is due mainly to the stereotypes, which reduce variation and individuality, mock the process of self-realization, and make empathy impossible. When the goal is to embody the stereotype (which by definition is shallow and uniform), depth, passion, and uniqueness are inevitably lost. Men lose, of course, as well as women. Although not as directly subjected to the tyranny of the esthetic ideal, men are made to feel inadequate if their women—that is, their property—do not measure up. Women are portrayed as sexually desirable only if they are young, thin, carefully made-up and groomed, depilated, sprayed, and scented— rendered quite unerotic, in fact. Men are conditioned to seek such partners and to feel disappointed if they fail.

Most advertising places a tremendous emphasis on impulsivity, on being overpowered by a product (such as a perfume or pair of jeans). Advertisements rarely contain accurate information about sex or emphasize relationships or intimacy (30 seconds is hardly enough time for the sexual encounter, let alone development of character). Thus advertising probably contributes to the damaging concepts of the "good girl" who is swept away, unprepared for sex, and the "bad girl," who plans for sex, uses contraception, and is generally responsible. The "sensual but not too far from innocence" phenomenon discussed above undoubtedly contributes to this irrational thinking. A young girl or woman can manage to have sex and yet in some sense maintain her virginity by being out of control or deep in denial of the entire experience.

The main goal of sex in advertising, as in pornography, is power over another, either by the physical dominance or preferred status of men or the perceived exploitative power of female beauty and sexuality. Men conquer, and women ensnare, always with the essential aid of a product. The woman is rewarded for her sexuality by the man's wealth, as in the Cigarette boat ad, in which the woman asks, clearly after sex, "Does this mean I get a ride in your Cigarette?"

Sexual Aggression and Violence

Sometimes the dominance of men escalates to sexual violence. Often hostility to women is openly expressed in the ads, sometimes in the form of outright sexual aggression. This hostility often starts at a very early age.

Advertising does not cause violence. However, as discussed above, it often creates a climate in which certain attitudes and values flourish, such as the attitudes that a woman's physical appearance is her most important and valuable attribute, that aging makes women unattractive and therefore less valuable, and that victims of sexual assault "asked for it." This attitude now applies to females of all ages, as evidenced by the remark of a Wisconsin judge that a 5-year-old rape victim was "an unusually sexually permissive young lady."[15] Although the media do not cause this highly dangerous attitude, they contribute to it with pervasive images of women and girls as passive, decorative, and seductive—and often as enjoying aggression and violence.

The myths of any culture are deep, powerful, and difficult to change. The myth that women love and deserve to be beaten has made it difficult for the millions of women victimized by violence to get help and for the whole issue of domestic violence to be taken seriously. The myth that women ask to be raped and enjoy forcible sex has been perhaps the major factor in encouraging cultural tolerance, if not actual acceptance, of rape. The myth of Lolita, the seductive and manipulative child-woman, undoubtedly contributes to the abuse of children and the readiness of society to blame the victim.

The deeply held belief that all women, regardless of age, are temptresses in disguise, sexually insatiable and seductive, conveniently transfers all blame and responsibility onto women. Recent research indicates that the media reinforce this belief and thus affect people's attitudes and behavior.[20]

Images of Men

Although men are allowed and encouraged to become adults, the acceptable images for men are also limited and rigid. Men are generally conditioned to be obsessed by status and success, as measured in material terms, and to view women as objects to be acquired as further evidence of status. The portrayals of single men and married men are strikingly different in the mass media. Single men are generally independent and powerful, whereas married men are often presented as idiots, as if contaminated by their intimacy with women. This is particularly true of the few male characters who do domestic chores or relate to children. The stereotypes of men have changed very little.

New Stereotypes

Some changes have occurred in the images of women. Indeed, a "new woman" has emerged in commercials in recent years. She is often presented as a super-woman who manages to do all the work at home and on the job (with the aid of a product, such as Hamburger Helper, but not of her husband, let alone an enlightened national child-care policy) or as the liberated woman who owes her independence and self-esteem to the products she uses. The new images do not represent progress; instead, they create a myth of progress, an illusion that reduces complex sociopolitical problems to mundane personal dilemmas, thereby trivializing the issues and diverting energy and attention from a search for genuine solutions.

Superwoman is perhaps the most damaging stereotype of all. Many young women now seem to feel that they can effortlessly combine marriage and career. The myth of progress obscures the fact that the overwhelming majority of women are in low-status, low-paying jobs and are as far removed from superwoman's elite executive status as the majority of men from her male counterpart. The definition of success is still entirely male. The successful woman is presented as climbing up the corporate ladder, seeking money and power. The working woman is expected to get ahead in a man's world, adhering strictly to male values but always giving first priority to her role as wife and mother. In addition, the myth of superwoman places total responsibility for change on the individual woman and exempts men from the responsibilities and rewards of domestic life and child care. It also diverts attention from the political policies that would truly change our lives.

Advertising often reduces the political to the personal. We are told that if we use the right products and get our personal acts together, everything will be fine. There is never the slightest hint that people often suffer because of a socioeconomic and political situation that could be changed. If we are unhappy, something is wrong with us, and buying the right product will solve it. We can smoke a cigarette or have a drink or try a new eyeshadow.

The models of adulthood that advertising offers to adolescents are extremely limited and contradictory. Women are supposed to be little girls or superwomen or both. Men are rigidly socialized to repress all feelings of vulnerability, thereby virtually guaranteeing that intimate relationships will be impossible. Motherhood is presented as essential for women and fatherhood as irrelevant for men. Sexuality becomes a commodity.

Resources for Change

The greatest tragedy is that many people internalize the limitations of stereotypes, which thus become a self-fulfilling prophecy. If one accepts such mythical and degrading images, to some extent one actualizes them. By remaining unaware of the profound seriousness of the **ubiquitous** influence, the redundant message, and the subliminal impact of advertisements, we ignore one of the most powerful educational forces in the culture. Advertising greatly affects our self-images as well as our ability to relate to each other and effectively destroys any awareness or action that may help to change the cultural climate.

Far from trivial, such stereotypes and images are global and economic issues. The Western model of beauty has become an international fantasy, spread by advertising, the media, and multinational corporate power. American television programs are shown worldwide. Strategies of global advertising lead to uniformity of desires as well as of images.

Solutions range from writing letters to advertisers and boycotting products to more powerful strategies such as teaching media literacy in all of our schools, beginning in kindergarten. Parents should be educated to control their children's television viewing and to watch television with their children to counter its effects.

We should also encourage the government to restrict certain kinds of advertising, to ban all cigarette advertising (as Canada recently did), and to put health messages on ads for alcohol and diet products. Physicians, including the Surgeon General, could play an important role by stressing such measures as a major public health issue and by encouraging further research.

We must also work to eradicate sexism, to abolish damaging stereotypes of women and men, and to create avenues to real power for all people. In the short term, it helps to protest the images in advertising, but it is unrealistic to expect radical change. Change can take place in the society, however. An essential step in creating that change is understanding and challenging the cultural myths and stereotypes. Above all, as always, we must break the silence.

ubiquitous: widespread

Endnotes

1. Black, C. "Diet Fad Fattens Firms." *Boston Globe,* April 21, 1990, p. 1.
2. Brown, L. M. and Gilligan, C. *Meeting at the Crossroads.* Cambridge, MA: Harvard University Press, 1992.
3. Butler, M. and Paisley, W. *Women and the Mass Media.* New York: Human Sciences Press, 1980.
4. Chapkis, W. *Beauty Secrets.* Boston: South End Press, 1986.
5. "Cosmetics: Kiss and Sell." *Time,* December 11, 1978, p. 86.
6. Courtney, A. and Whipple, T. *Sex Stereotyping in Advertising.* Lexington, MA: D. C. Heath, 1983.
7. Ewen, S. *Captains of Consciousness: Advertising and the Social Roots of the Consumer Culture.* New York: McGraw-Hill, 1976.

8. Faludi, S. *Backlash: The Undeclared War Against American Women.* New York: Crown Publishers, 1991.

9. Goffman, E. *Gender Advertisements.* New York: Harper & Row, 1979.

10. Gordon, R. *Anorexia and Bulimia: Anatomy of a Social Epidemic.* Cambridge, MA: Basil Blackwell, 1990.

11. Henig, R. M. "Are Breast Implants Too Risky?" *Vogue,* July 1989, p. 108.

12. Hersh, A. "Women, Minorities Still Lagging in Film and TV Roles." *Back Stage: The Performing Arts Weekly,* June 18–24, 1993, pp. 1, 28.

13. Hickey, N. "Many Groups Underrepresented on TV, Study Declares." *TV Guide,* July 3, 1993, p. 33.

14. Johnson, C. and Connors, M. *The Etiology and Treatment of Bulimia Nervosa.* New York: Basic Books, 1987.

15. "Judge Blames Sex Assault on 5-Year-Old Victim." *National Now Times,* January 2, 1982, p. 2.

16. Kaye, E. "So Weak, So Powerful." *New York Times,* June 6, 1993, Section 9, pp. 1, 10.

17. Kilbourne, J. "The Child as Sex Object: Images of Children in the Media." In Nelson, M. and Clark, K. (eds), *The Educator's Guide to Preventing Child Sexual Abuse.* Santa Cruz, CA: Network Publications, 1986, pp. 40–46.

18. Kilbourne, J. "Images of Women in TV Commercials." In Fireman, J. (ed), *TV Book.* New York: Workman Publishing, 1977, pp. 293–296.

19. Leymore, V. *Hidden Myth: Structure and Symbolism in Advertising.* New York: Basic Books, 1975.

20. Malamuth, N. and Donnerstein, E. *Pornography and Sexual Aggression.* Chicago: Academy Press, 1984.

21. Mead, M. Lecture given at Richland Community College, Dallas, Texas: December 6, 1977.

22. Pollitt, K. "The Politically Correct Body." *Mother Jones,* May, 1982, p. 66.

23. Richins, M. "Social Comparison and the Idealized Images of Advertising." *J Consumer Res* 18:71–83, 19xx.

24. Rosen, J. C. and Gross, J. "Prevalence of Weight Reducing and Weight Gaining in Adolescent Girls and Boys." *Health Psychol* 26:131–147, 19xx.

25. Sims, S. "Diet Madness." *Vogue,* May 1986, p. 73.

26. Stein, J. "Why Girls as Young as 9 Fear Fat and Go on Diets to Lose Weight." *Los Angeles Times,* October 29, 1986, pp. 1, 10.

27. Strasburger, V. "Television and Adolescents: Sex, Drugs, Rock 'n' Roll." *Adolesc Med State Art Rev* 4:161–194, 1990.

28. Surrey, J. "Eating Patterns as a Reflection of Women's Development." Wellesley, MA: Stone Center Working Paper, Wellesley College, no. 83–06.

29. Vanderbilt, H. "Incest: A Chilling Report." *Lears,* February 1992, pp. 49–77.

30. Williamson, J. *Decoding Advertisements: Ideology and Meaning in Advertising.* London: Marion Boyars, 1978.

▼ Questions to Focus Reading

1. Kilbourne believes the advertising industry to be perhaps the most powerful educational force in society, "both a creator and perpetuator of the dominant attitudes, values, and ideology of culture, the social norms and

the myths by which most people govern their behavior." What does she think it has been teaching us?

2. She suggests that gender roles may be the cultural concepts most deeply influenced by advertising. What reasons does she give for its especially strong influence in this regard?

3. The stereotypes in television commercials have remained fairly constant, according to Kilbourne. What are they?

4. She argues that a double standard prevails in ads: women's bodies are demeaned and insulted in ways that are unthinkable for men. How does she try to convince us of this?

5. What connection does Kilbourne see between advertising and health?

6. Kilbourne thinks advertising has a seriously harmful effect on attitudes toward sexuality, that it is largely responsible for what she calls "the true obscenity of American culture." How, according to Kilbourne, is sexuality depicted?

7. While recognizing that the causes of violence in our society are complex, she insists that advertising plays a role in this. What role?

8. What images of masculinity are typically presented in ads, according to Kilbourne?

9. Although Kilbourne concedes that a "new woman" has emerged in the ads of recent years, she argues that the new images "do not represent progress." Why not?

10. "Advertising often reduces the political to the personal." How?

11. The models of adulthood that are presented by advertisements to adolescents are "extremely limited and contradictory." Why does she say so?

12. What recommendations does she make for combating the deleterious power of advertising?

▼ Questions for Reflection

1. Kilbourne thinks most teenagers have great difficulty resisting the cultural messages propounded and reinforced by advertising. Was this true in your case? Which of the dominant cultural messages broadcast in your teen years had an impact on you, and what was the nature of that impact? What advertising images and messages, if any, influence your thinking now? In what ways?

2. When you consider your own case, do you agree with Kilbourne that advertising performs the same function in industrial society as myth performed in ancient society?

3. Do you think Kilbourne's generalizations about how women and men are portrayed in ads are accurate?

4. "A woman is conditioned to view her face as a mask and her body as an object, both separate from and more important than her real self, constantly in need of alteration, improvement, and disguise. She is made to feel dissatisfied with and ashamed of herself, whether or not she tries to achieve the ideal. Objectified constantly by others, she learns to objectify herself." If you are a woman, judging from your own experience, do you think these statements are true? Do you agree that these are effects of the power of advertising?

5. "Advertising slogans such as 'because innocence is sexier than you think' and 'sensual, but not too far from innocence' places women in a double bind. Somehow women are supposed to be both sexy and virginal, experienced and naive, seductive and chaste." If you are a woman, do you experience this contradictory pressure? If so, how do you deal with it? If you are a heterosexual man, do you find yourself desiring such contradictory qualities in a woman?

6. Among her suggestions for change, Kilbourne urges that we destroy damaging stereotypes of women and men, that we "create avenues to real power for all people." How can these goals be accomplished?

▼ Discussion

1. Kilbourne argues that ads sell us much more than products. They sell values, concepts of success and worth, love and sexuality, normalcy. They tell us who we are and who we should be. In preparation for class, browse through the ads in a magazine or pay careful attention to certain particularly striking ads on television and reflect on what values, concepts of worth, and so on these ads may be advancing. Bring the magazine ads with you to show the class.

2. Examine some ads involving women to determine what image of femaleness is being projected, and be prepared to describe and discuss these ads in class. Do the same for ads projecting an image of maleness.

3. Is there a fear of feminine power in American culture? What evidences could be adduced for this claim?

4. Kilbourne holds advertising's approach to sex largely responsible for "the true obscenity of American culture": the reducing of sexuality to a dirty joke and of people to objects. She also claims that the usual characterization of sex in advertising is narcissistic. Examine ads to see if she is right about the way sexuality is depicted in ads, and be prepared to discuss your findings in class.

5. Is Kilbourne right in her insistence that a double standard still exists in ads in regard to how men and women are objectified?

6. Models of adulthood offered to adolescents in ads are "extremely limited and contradictory." Examine some television and magazine ads with this claim in mind. What images of adulthood are you finding?

▼ Writing Assignments

1. Describe or attach an ad you find particularly striking, and examine it for the cultural messages—the values, concepts of success, sexuality, adulthood—it is conveying.

2. Describe or attach an ad that you then examine for the image of women (or men or both) it projects.

▼ Journal Entries

1. Describe an ad that has influenced your values, attitudes, concepts of worth, maleness, or femaleness. How has that ad influenced your thinking?

2. Has the objectification of women in advertising influenced your attitudes and/or sense of yourself? In what respects?

3. Has the image of the "superwoman" Kilbourne describes influenced your self-concept, goals?

▼ Vocabulary

dismembered	gratuitously	reified
disparagement	objectified	ubiquitous

111

15

Poem for Half White College Students

IMAMU AMIRI BARAKA

*Poet, playwright, essayist, novelist, and short story writer, Imamu Amiri Baraka
(born LeRoi Jones, in 1934) has often used his harsh poetic talent to stir people—
black and white—to examine the roots of their identity.*

Who are you, listening to me, who are you
listening to yourself? Are you white or
black, or does that have anything to do
with it? Can you pop your fingers to no
music, except those wild monkies go on   5
in your head, can you jerk, to no melody,
except finger poppers get it together
when you turn from starchecking to checking
yourself. How do you sound, your words, are they
yours? The ghost you see in the mirror, is it really   10
you, can you swear you are not an imitation greyboy,
can you look right next to you in that chair, and swear,
that the sister you have your hand on is not really
so full of Elizabeth Taylor, Richard Burton is
coming out of her ears. You may even have to be Richard   15
with a white shirt and face, and four million negroes
think you cute, you may have to be Elizabeth Taylor, old lady,
if you want to sit up in your crazy spot dreaming about dresses,
and the sway of certain porters' hips. Check yourself, learn who it is
speaking, when you make some ultrasophisticated point, check yourself,   20
when you find yourself gesturing like Steve McQueen, check it out, ask
in your black heart who it is you are, and is that image black or white,

you might be surprised right out the window, whistling dixie on the way in.

▼ Questions for Reflection

1. Who is the poet talking to here?
2. The poem consists largely of a series of questions and ends with a kind of command. What is the gist of the questions? What is the command?
3. What do you make of the last line?
4. Is there anything in your situation that is analogous to that of the "half white college student" Baraka is addressing? If the poet were speaking to you on the same themes, what questions and commands might he put to you?

▼ Journal Entry

1. Write a poem to yourself in which you ask certain penetrating questions about your identity and the way you are living your present life.

16

▼

Ways to Live

Charles Morris

Here is an exercise that you can use to help you clarify your overall picture of what is important to you. University of Chicago philosopher Charles Morris (1901–1979) was a member of the pragmatist movement.

Instructions   Below are described 14 ways to live which various persons at various times have advocated and followed. Indicate by numbers which you are to write in the margin in the blank marked *Rating*—how much you yourself like or dislike each of them. Do them in order. Do not read ahead. Do not mark the *Rank Order* blank.

Remember that it is not a question of what kind of life you now lead, or the kind of life you think it **prudent** to live in our society, or the kind of life you think good for other persons, *but simply the kind of life you personally would like to live.*

Use the following scale of numbers, placing one of them in the margin alongside each of the ways to live in the "Rating" slot:

> 7   I like it *very much*
> 6   I like it *quite a lot*
> 5   I like it *slightly*
> 4   I am *indifferent* to it
> 3   I dislike it *slightly*
> 2   I dislike it *quite a lot*
> 1   I dislike it *very much*

Rating _____

Rank Order

_____

Way 1   In this "design for living" the individual actively participates in the social life of his or her community, not to change it primarily, but to understand, appreciate, and preserve the best that humankind has **attained**. Excessive desires should be avoided and moderation sought. One wants the good things of life but in an orderly way. Life is to have clarity, balance, refinement, control. Vulgarity, great enthusiasm, irrational behavior, impatience, indulgence are to be avoided. Friendship is to be esteemed but not easy intimacy with many people. Life is to have discipline, intelligibility, good manners, predictability. Social changes are to be made slowly and carefully, so that what has been achieved in human culture is not lost. The individual should be active physically and socially, but not in a hectic or radical way. Restraint and intelligence should give order to an active life.

Rating _____

Rank Order

Way 2   The individual should for the most part "go it alone," assuring himself or herself of privacy in living quarters, having much time to himself or herself, attempting to control his or her own life. One should stress self-sufficiency, reflection and **meditation**, knowledge of self. The direction of interest should be away from intimate associations with social groups, and away from the physical manipulation of objects or attempts at control of the physical environment. One should

114

aim to simplify one's external life, to moderate those desires whose satisfaction is dependent upon physical and social forces outside of oneself, and to concentrate attention upon the refinement, clarification, and direction of oneself. Not much can be done or is to be gained by "living outwardly." One must avoid dependence upon persons or things; the center of life should be found within oneself.

Rating _____

Rank Order

_____

Way 3 This way of life makes central the sympathetic concern for other persons. Affection should be the main thing in life, affection that is free from all traces of the imposition of oneself upon others or of using others for one's own purposes. Greed in possessions, emphasis on sexual passion, the search for power over persons and things, excessive emphasis upon intellect, and undue concern for oneself are to be avoided. For these things hinder the sympathetic love among persons which alone gives significance to life. If we are aggressive we block our receptivity to the personal forces upon which we are dependent for genuine personal growth. One should accordingly purify oneself, restrain one's self-assertiveness, and become receptive, appreciative, and helpful with respect to other persons.

Rating _____

Rank Order

_____

Way 4 Life is something to be enjoyed—sensuously enjoyed, enjoyed with relish and abandonment. The aim in life should not be to control the course of the world or society or the lives of others, but to be open and receptive to things and persons, and to delight in them. Life is more a festival than a workshop or a school for moral discipline. To let oneself go, to let things and persons affect oneself, is more important than to do—or to do good. Such enjoyment, however, requires that one be self-centered enough to be keenly aware of what is happening and free for new happenings. So one should avoid entanglements, should not be too dependent on particular people or things, should not be self-sacrificing; one should be alone a lot, should have time for meditation and awareness of oneself. Solitude and sociality together are both necessary in the good life.

Rating _____

Rank Order

_____

Way 5 A person should not hold on to himself or herself, withdraw from people, keep aloof and self-centered. Rather merge oneself with a social group, enjoy cooperation and companionship, join with others in **resolute** activity for the realization of common goals. Persons are social and persons are active; life should merge energetic group activity and cooperative group enjoyment. Meditation, restraint, concern for one's self-sufficiency, abstract intellectuality, solitude, stress on one's possessions all cut the roots which bind persons together. One should live outwardly with gusto, enjoying the good things of life, working with others to secure the things which make possible a pleasant and energetic social life. Those who oppose this ideal are not to be dealt with too tenderly. Life can't be too fastidious.

Rating _____

Rank Order

_____

Way 6 Life continuously tends to **stagnate**, to become "comfortable," to become **sicklied** o'er with the pale cast of thought. Against these tendencies, a person must stress the need for constant activity—physical action, adventure, the realistic solution of specific problems as they appear, the improvement of techniques for controlling the world and society. The future of [hu]mankind depends primarily on what we do, not on what we feel or on our speculations. New problems constantly arise and always will arise. Improvements must always be made if man is to progress. We can't just follow the past or dream of what the future might be. We have to work resolutely and continually if control is to be gained over the forces which threaten us. Humankind should rely on technical advances made possible by scientific knowledge. We should find our goal in the solution of our problems. The good is the enemy of the better.

Rating _____

Rank Order

_____

Way 7 We should at various times and in various ways accept something from all other paths of life, but give no one our exclusive **allegiance**. At one moment one of them is the more appropriate; at another moment another is the most appropriate. Life should contain enjoyment and action and contemplation in about equal amounts. When either is carried to extremes we lose something important for our life. So we must **cultivate** flexibility, admit **diversity** in ourselves, accept the tension which this diversity produces, find a place for detachment in the midst of enjoyment and activity. The goal of life is found in the dynamic integration of enjoyment, action, and contemplation, and so in the dynamic interaction of the various paths of life. One should use all of them in building a life, and no one alone.

Rating _____

Rank Order

_____

Way 8 Enjoyment should be the keynote of life. Not the hectic search for intense and exciting pleasures, but the enjoyment of the simple and easily obtainable pleasures: the pleasures of just existing, of savory food, of comfortable surroundings, of talking with friends, of rest and relaxation. A home that is warm and comfortable, chairs and a bed that are soft, a kitchen well stocked with food, a door open to the entrance of friends—this is the place to live. Body at ease, relaxed, calm in its movements, not hurried, breath slow, willing to nod and to rest, grateful to the world that is its food—so should the body be. Driving ambition and the **fanaticism** of **ascetic** ideals are the signs of discontented people who have lost the capacity to float in the stream of simple, carefree, wholesome enjoyment.

Rating _____

Rank Order

_____

Way 9 Receptivity should be the keynote of life. The good things of life come of their own accord, and come unsought. They cannot be found by resolute action. They cannot be found in the indulgence of the sensuous desires of the body. They cannot be gathered by participation in the turmoil of social life. They cannot be given to others by attempts to be helpful. They cannot be garnered by hard thinking. Rather do they come unsought when the bars of the self are down. When the self has ceased to make demands and waits in quiet receptivity, it becomes open to the powers which nourish it and work through it; and sustained by these powers it knows joy and peace. To sit alone under the trees and the sky, open to nature's voices, calm and receptive, then can the wisdom from without come within.

Rating _____

Rank Order

_____

Way 10 Self-control should be the keynote of life. Not the easy self-control which retreats from the world, but the **vigilant**, stern, stoic control of a self which lives in the world, and knows the strength of the world and the limits of human power. The good life is rationally directed and holds firm to high ideals. It is not bent by the seductive voices of comfort and desire. It does not expect social utopias. It is distrustful of final victories. Too much cannot be expected. Yet one can with vigilance hold firm the reins to his or her self, control his or her unruly impulses, understand his or her place in the world, guide his or her actions by reason, maintain his or her self-reliant independence. And in this way, though we finally perish, we can keep our human dignity and respect, and die with cosmic good manners.

Rating _____

Rank Order

_____

Way 11 The contemplative life is the good life. The external world is no fit habitat for humankind. It is too big, too cold, too pressing. Rather it is the life turned inward that is rewarding. The rich internal world of ideals, of sensitive feelings, of reverie, of self-knowledge is our true home. By the cultivation of the self within, a person becomes human. Only then does there arise deep sympathy with all that lives, an understanding of the suffering **inherent** in life, a realization of the futility of aggressive action, the attainment of contemplative joy. Conceit then falls away and austerity is dissolved. In giving up the world one finds the larger and finer sea of the inner self.

Rating _____

Rank Order

_____

Way 12   The use of the body's energy is the secret of a rewarding life. The hands need material to make into something; lumber and stone for building, food to harvest, clay to mold. The muscles are alive to joy only in action, in climbing, running, skiing and the like. Life finds its zest in overcoming, dominating, conquering some obstacle. It is the active deed which is satisfying, the deed adequate to the present, the daring and adventuresome deed. Not in cautious foresight, not in relaxed ease does life attain completion. Outward energetic action, the excitement of power in the **tangible** present—this is the way to live.

Rating _____

Rank Order

_____

Way 13   A person should let himself or herself be used. Used by other persons in their growth, used by the great objective purposes in the universe which silently and irresistibly achieve their goal. For persons and the world's purposes are dependable at heart, and can be trusted. One should be humble, constant, faithful, uninsistent. Grateful for the affection and protection which one needs, but undemanding. Close to persons and to nature, and secure because close. Nourishing the good by devotion and sustained by the good because of devotion. One should be a serene, confident, quiet vessel and instrument of the great dependable powers which move to their fulfillment.

Rating _____

Rank Order

_____

Way 14   The goal of life should be to understand it, and the good life is devoted primarily to the quest for truth, not only about oneself, but about the world. The mind directed to the truths of the world will be free of narrow self-interest and the blindness which that engenders. It will view its purposes and desires as parts of the whole, with the absence of anxiety that results from seeing them as **infinitesimal** fragments in a world largely unaffected by any one person's deeds. The impartiality which, in contemplation, is the unalloyed desire for truth, is the very same quality of mind which, in action, is justice, and in emotion is that universal love which can be given to all, and not only to those who are judged useful or admirable. Thus contemplation enlarges not only the objects of our actions and our affections; it makes us citizens of the universe, not only of one walled city at war with all the rest. In this citizenship of the universe consists our true freedom, and our liberation from the **thraldom** of narrow hopes and fears.[1]

Final Instructions   Now go back through the list and rank the 14 ways to live in the order you prefer them, putting a "1" in the "Rank Order" slot beside the way to live you like the best, then the number "2" beside the way you like next best, and so on down to the number "14" beside the way to live you like the least.

▼ Vocabulary

allegiance: loyalty; obligation
ascetic: self-disciplined
attained: achieved
cultivate: promote
diversity: variety
fanaticism: excessive, uncritical devotion
infinitesimal: incalculably minute
inherent: intrinsic

meditation: reflection
prudent: wise
resolute: unwavering; committed
sicklied: sickened
stagnate: fail to progress
tangible: real; concrete
thraldom: bondage
vigilant: alert; watchful

[1]Way 14 was adapted from Bertrand Russell, *The Problems of Philosophy* (Oxford University Press, 1974), pp. 160–61.—J. G.

▼ A Way of One's Own Making

1. It is quite common to feel that none of the 14 "Ways to Live" fits perfectly. Therefore, in the space below, write a one-paragraph summary of a "way to live" of your own making. You can draw upon the other 14 ways if you wish, or you may choose to design a new way from scratch.

2. What role do you see for education in consciously creating a style of life, as opposed to unconsciously following some beaten path? Again, confine your answer to the space below.

17

▼

What Really Matters?

Plato, Bertrand Russell, Robert Nozick

Three philosophers find imaginative ways to prompt us to ask, What is really important in life?

Introduction

The point of the three excerpts in this selection is to provoke some hard thought on the question, What really matters? For this large issue is one that we should confront when we are trying to work out our life goals. How can we decide what specific directions to pursue in life unless we have faced the ultimate question, What is really important?

The three writers who will help us think about this question are philosophers: Plato (ca. 427–347 B.C.), the great **seminal** thinker of the Greek golden age; Bertrand Russell (1872–1970), the Nobel Prize–winning twentieth-century English philosopher; and Robert Nozick (born 1938), a distinguished contemporary American professor at Harvard.

In *The Republic,* Plato's design for the ideal state, a character named Glaucon argues that what really matters to any of us is that we take for ourselves the material goods of life without regard for anyone else, that it is the true nature of human beings to want only this, and that all claims to nobler ambitions are shams. He tries to prove this with two ingenious thought-experiments.

The excerpt from Russell is drawn from his *Autobiography* (1967). In this brief passage, he is not arguing for anything, but merely telling us what three passions have governed his long life. Reading his simple, **eloquent** words, we can't help but raise the same question of our own lives: What are our own governing passions?

Nozick's piece, from his *Anarchy, State, and Utopia* (1974), asks if anything else can matter to us except the kind of experiences we have; that is, the way our lives feel to us from the inside. He thinks there are several other things that matter a great deal and, like Plato's Glaucon, tries to prove his point by inviting us to perform some intriguing thought-experiments.

My hope is that you will find these readings so interesting in themselves that the great issues they broach will be irresistible; you will be provoked to interrogate your own life, and your own thinking on the matter of your goals will be brought to a new depth.

seminal: germinative; original
eloquent: vivid; expressive

—J. G.

119

Plato: The Ring of Gyges

[Glaucon, speaking to Socrates:]

According to the tradition, Gyges was a shepherd in the service of the reigning king of Lydia; there was a great storm, and an earthquake made an opening in the earth at the place where he was feeding his flock. Amazed at the sight, he descended into the opening, where, among other marvels which form part of the story, he beheld a hollow brazen horse, having doors, at which he, stooping and looking in, saw a dead body of stature, as appeared to him, more than human; he took from the corpse a gold ring that was on the hand, but nothing else, and so **reascended**. Now the shepherds met together, according to custom, that they might send their monthly report about the flocks to the king; into their assembly he came having the ring on his finger, and as he was sitting among them he chanced to turn the collet of the ring to the inside of his hand, when instantly he became invisible to the rest of the company and they began to speak of him as if he were no longer present. He was astonished at this, and again touching the ring he turned the collet outwards and reappeared; when he perceived this, he made several trials of the ring, and always with the same result—when he turned the collet inwards he became invisible, when outwards he was visible. Whereupon he **contrived** to be chosen one of the messengers who were sent to the court; where as soon as he arrived he seduced the queen, and with her help conspired against the king and slew him, and took the kingdom. Suppose now that there were two such magic rings, and the just put on one of them and the unjust the other; no man can be imagined to be of such an iron nature that he would stand fast in justice. No man would keep his hands off what was not his own when he could safely take what he liked out of the market, or go into houses and lie with any one at his pleasure, or kill or release from prison whom he would, and in all respects be like a god among men. Then the actions of the just would be as the actions of the unjust; they would both tend to the same goal. And this we may truly affirm to be a great proof that a man is just, not willingly or because he thinks that justice is any good to him individually, but of necessity; for wherever anyone thinks that he can safely be unjust, there he is unjust. For all men believe in their hearts that injustice is far more profitable to the individual than justice and he who argues as I have been supposing will say that they are right. If you could imagine anyone obtaining this power of becoming invisible, and never doing any wrong or touching what was another's, he would be thought by the lookers-on to be an unhappy man and a fool, although they would praise him to one another's faces, and keep up appearances with one another from a fear that they too might suffer injustice. Enough of this.

Now, if we are to form a real judgement of the two lives in these respects, we must set apart the extremes of justice and injustice; there is no other way; and how is the contrast to be effected? I answer: Let the unjust man be entirely unjust, and the just man entirely just; nothing is to be taken away from either of them, and both are to be perfectly furnished for the work of their **respective** lives. First, let the unjust be like other distinguished masters of craft; like the skillful pilot or physician, who knows **intuitively** what is possible or impossible in his art and keeps within those limits, and who, if he fails at any point, is able to recover himself. So let the unjust man attempt to do the right sort of wrongs, and let him escape detection if he is to be pronounced a master of injustice. To be found out is a sign of **incompetence**; for the height of injustice is to be deemed just when you are not. Therefore I say that in the perfectly unjust man we must assume the most perfect injustice; there is to be no deduction, but we must allow him while doing the most unjust acts, to have acquired the greatest reputation for justice. If he has taken a false step he must be able to recover himself; he must be one who can speak with effect, if any of his deeds come to light, and who can force his

reascended: climbed up again
contrived: devised
respective: individual
intuitively: with keen insight
incompetence: being unqualified

120

way where force is required, by his courage and strength and command of wealth and friends. And at his side let us place the just man in his nobleness and simplicity, wishing, as Aeschylus says, to be and not to seem good. There must be no seeming, for if he seems to be just he will be honoured and rewarded, and then we shall not know whether he is just for the sake of justice or for the sake of honours and rewards; therefore, let him be clothed in justice only, and have no other covering; and he must be imagined in a state of life the opposite of the former. Let him be the best of men, and let him be **reputed** the worst; then he will have been put to the test and we shall see whether his justice is proof against evil reputation and its consequences. And let him continue thus to the hour of death; being just and seeming to be unjust. When both have reached the uttermost extreme, the one of justice and the other of injustice, let judgement be given which of them is the happier of the two.

Bertrand Russell: Love, Knowledge, and Pity

Three passions, simple but overwhelmingly strong, have governed my life: the longing for love, the search for knowledge, and unbearable pity for the suffering of mankind. These passions, like great winds, have blown me **hither** and **thither**, in a wayward course, over a deep ocean of anguish, reaching to the very verge of despair.

I have sought love, first, because it brings ecstasy—ecstasy so great that I would often have sacrificed all the rest of life for a few hours of this joy. I have sought it, next, because it relieves loneliness—that terrible loneliness in which one shivering consciousness looks over the rim of the world into the cold **unfathomable** lifeless abyss. I have sought it, finally, because in the union of love I have seen, in a **mystic** miniature, the **prefiguring** vision of the heaven that saints and poets have imagined. This is what I sought, and though it might seem too good for human life, this is what—at last—I have found.

With equal passion I have sought knowledge. I have wished to understand the hearts of men. I have wished to know why the stars shine. And I have tried to apprehend the **Pythagorean** power by which number holds sway above the flux. A little of this, but not much, I have achieved.

Love and knowledge, so far as they were possible, led upward toward the heavens. But always pity brought me back to earth. Echoes of cries of pain **reverberate** in my heart. Children in famine, victims tortured by **oppressors**, helpless old people a hated burden to their sons, and the whole world of loneliness, poverty, and pain make a mockery of what human life should be. I long to **alleviate** the evil, but I cannot, and I too suffer.

This has been my life. I have found it worth living, and would gladly live it again if the chance were offered me.

Robert Nozick: The Experience Machine

Suppose there were an experience machine that would give you any experience you desired. Superduper neuropsychologists could stimulate your brain so that you would think and feel you were writing a great novel, or making a friend, or reading an interesting book. All the time you would be floating in a tank, with electrodes attached to your brain. Should you plug into this machine for life, preprogramming your life's experiences? If you are worried about missing out on desirable experiences, we can suppose that business enterprises have researched thoroughly the lives of many others. You can pick and choose from their large library or **smorgasbord** of such experiences, selecting your life's experiences for, say, the next two years. After two years have passed, you will have ten minutes or ten hours out of the tank, to select the experiences of your *next* two years. Of course, while

reputed: considered

hither: toward; to

thither: away; from

unfathomable: deeply puzzling; incomprehensible

mystic: pertaining to an immediate intuition that produces spiritual ecstasy

prefiguring: foreshadowing

Pythagorean: referring to the Greek philosopher and mathematician Pythagoras

reverberate: echo

oppressors: tyrants

alleviate: take away

smorgasbord: variety

in the tank you won't know that you're there; you'll think it's all actually happening. Others can also plug in to have the experiences they want, so there's no need to stay unplugged to serve them. (Ignore problems such as who will service the machines if everyone plugs in.) Would you plug in? *What else can matter to us, other than how our lives feel from the inside?* Nor should you refrain because of the few moments of distress between the moment you've decided and the moment you're plugged. What's a few minutes of distress compared to a lifetime of bliss (if that's what you choose), and why feel any distress at all if your decision is the best one?

What does matter to us in addition to our experiences? First, we want to *do* certain things, and not just have the experience of doing them. In the case of certain experiences, it is only because first we want to do the actions that we want the experiences of doing them or thinking we've done them. (But *why* do we want to do the activities rather than merely to experience them?) A second reason for not plugging in is that we want to *be* a certain way, to be a certain sort of person. Someone floating in a tank is an **indeterminate** blob. There is no answer to the question of what a person is like who has long been in the tank. Is he courageous, kind, intelligent, witty, loving? It's not merely that it's difficult to tell; there's no way he is. Plugging into the machine is a kind of suicide. It will seem to some, trapped by a picture, that nothing about what we are like can matter except as it gets reflected in our experiences. But should it be surprising that what *we are* is important to us? Why should we be concerned only with how our time is filled, but not with what we are?

Thirdly, plugging into an experience machine limits us to a man-made reality, to a world no deeper or more important than that which people can construct. There is no *actual* contact with any deeper reality, though the experience of it can be simulated. Many persons desire to leave themselves open to such contact and to a plumbing of deeper significance. This clarifies the intensity of the conflict over psychoactive drugs, which some view as mere local experience machines, and others view as avenues to a deeper reality; what some view as equivalent to surrender to the experience machine, others view as following one of the reasons *not* to surrender!

We learn that something matters to us in addition to experience by imagining an experience machine and then realizing that we would not use it. We can continue to imagine a sequence of machines each designed to fill lacks suggested for the earlier machines. For example, since the experience machine doesn't meet our desire to *be* a certain way, imagine a transformation machine which transforms us into whatever sort of person we'd like to be (compatible with our staying us). Surely one would not use the transformation machine to become as one would wish, and thereupon plug into the experience machine! So something matters in addition to one's experiences *and* what one is like. Nor is the reason merely that one's experiences are unconnected with what one is like. For the experience machine might be limited to provide only experiences possible to the sort of person plugged in. Is it that we want to make a difference in the world? Consider then the result machine, which produces in the world any result you would produce and injects your vector input into any joint activity. We shall not pursue here the fascinating details of these or other machines. What is most disturbing about them is their living of our lives for us. Is it misguided to search for *particular* additional functions beyond the competence of machines to do for us? Perhaps what we desire is to live (an active verb) ourselves, in contact with reality. (And this, machines cannot do *for* us.)

indeterminate: not determined

122

▼ Questions for Reflection and Discussion

Plato

1. The point Glaucon is trying to make in this excerpt from Plato's *Republic* is that the unbridled pursuit of self-interest is the ultimate good in life and that all of us secretly subscribe to this view. He tries to convince us of these conclusions with two thought-experiments. Describe the thought-experiments and explain how they are supposed to make Glaucon's points.
2. How would you live if, starting now, you could live the rest of your life with Gyges's magic ring?

Russell

3. Why has Russell sought love?
4. "I have tried to apprehend the Pythagorean power by which number holds sway above the flux." What do you think this means?
5. What are the passions that now rule your life? How do you expect that you would answer this question at the *end* of your life?

Nozick

6. What is the point of Nozick's thought-experiment involving the experience machine? What is he trying to learn from this thought-experiment?
7. What is the point of the thought-experiments involving other kinds of machines (the last paragraph)?
8. Nozick gives us three reasons why plugging into the experience machine may not be such a good idea. What are his three reasons? What do you think of his reasons? Why should it be so important to us that we *do* certain things other than to have the experience of doing them? Why should what we *are* be important to us? What would be so bad about being limited to a man-made reality?
9. Would you plug into the experience machine? Explain your answer. Can you imagine a comparable machine you would plug into? Explain.

▼ Writing Assignments

1. "What I Would Do with the Ring of Gyges"
2. "The Case for Selfishness" or "The Case against Selfishness"
3. "The Passions That Have Governed My Life" Write this essay as though you are an old man or woman nearing the end of a fulfilled life.
4. "Why I Would Plug into the Experience Machine" or "Why I Would Not Plug into the Experience Machine"
5. "An Irresistible Machine" Describe an imaginary machine (comparable to Nozick's experience machine) that you would be strongly tempted to plug into, and explain why you would be tempted, and what considerations would argue against your plugging in.

▼ Vocabulary

alleviate	incompetence	oppressors	reputed	smorgasbord
contrived	indeterminate	prefiguring	respective	thither
eloquent	intuitively	Pythagorean	reverberate	unfathomable
hither	mystic	reascended	seminal	

18

▼

Fruit Gathering

Rabindranath Tagore

Described by one critic as "a waterfall, flowing out in a hundred streams, a hundred rhythms, incessantly," Rabindranath Tagore, who was born in India in 1861 and died in 1941, was an immensely prolific writer in virtually every form. He won the Nobel Prize for literature in 1913.

Let me not pray to be sheltered from
dangers but to be fearless in facing
them.

Let me not beg for the stilling of
my pain but for the heart to conquer it.   5

Let me not look for allies in life's
battlefield but to my own strength.

Let me not crave in anxious fear to
be saved but hope for the patience to
win my freedom.   10

Grant me that I may not be a
coward, feeling your mercy in my
success alone; but let me find the grasp
of your hand in my failure.

▼ Questions for Reflection

1. How would you restate the two conditions the poet is contrasting in lines 8 to 10? What do you think he means by "freedom"? Why should "winning" this require patience?
2. What is the poet's concept of cowardice in lines 11 to 14? Who is a coward in his conception?
3. What part of this prayer could you make? What commends that part, or those parts, to you? Why do you endorse it/them? Are there parts that you could not endorse? Why?
4. If you were to make a prayer for the qualities most valuable to you, what would you pray for?

▼ Journal Entry

1. Write a short poem in the form of a prayer asking for the qualities of character you most value.

19

▼

Backpack Almanac

Money

___

Percentage of Americans earning less than $15,000 a year who say they have achieved the American Dream: 5;
Percentage of Americans earning more than $50,000 a year who say this: 6
[Roper Organization (New York City), 1988]

Portion of U.S. federal revenues supplied annually by corporate income taxes: 1/10; portion in Japan: 1/3
[Citizens for Tax Justice (Washington, D.C.), 1988]

Chances that a homeless American holds a full- or part-time job: 1 in 5
[U.S. Conference of Mayors (Washington, D.C.), 1988]

Rank of finances, among the things couples say they worry about most on their wedding night: 1
[*What Are the Chances?* by Bernard Siskin and Jerome Staller, with David Rorvik
(Crown, New York City), 1990]

Number of soup kitchens in New York City in 1980: 30; In 1989: 600
[New York City Coalition Against Hunger, 1989]

Increase, since 1980, in the median income of an American, in constant dollars: $64
[U.S. Census Bureau, 1989]

Net foreign debt owed to U.S. government, businesses, and citizens in 1981, per American family: $2,500
Net foreign debt owed by U.S. government, businesses, and citizens in 1989, per American family: $11,000
[Benjamin M. Friedman, Harvard University (Cambridge, Mass.), 1989]

Percentage of two-income families whose income would drop below the poverty line if the wife did not work:
50
[Sheldon Danzinger, University of Michigan (Ann Arbor), 1990]

Average ratio of a CEO's salary to that of a blue-collar worker at major Japanese automobile manufacturers:
20:1
[Yoshi Tsurumi, Baruch College, City University of New York, 1990]

Average ratio at major U.S. automobile manufacturers: 192:1
[United Auto Workers (Detroit), 1990]

125

Who Am I? Who Is My Generation?

Ratio of the average salary of an American CEO to that of an American public school teacher in 1960: 38:1; in 1988: 72:1
[*Business Week* (New York City)/National Education Association (Washington, D.C.), 1989]

Average portion of their tax dollars Americans estimate are wasted: 1/2
[*Washington Post*-ABC News Poll, 1990]

Number of U.S. life insurance companies that have gone bankrupt since 1985: 68
[IDS Financial Services (Minneapolis), 1990]

Percentage of all savings and loan associations that failed during the Depression: 5
[George Bentson, Emory University (Atlanta), 1990]

Percentage that government expects will fail through 1995: 25
[U.S. Dept. of the Treasury/U.S. Office of Thrift Supervision, 1990]

Percentage change, since 1989, in the U.S. investment in foreign stocks and bonds: +68
Percentage change, since 1989, in foreign investment in U.S. stocks, bonds, and Treasury securities: −80
[U.S. Dept. of Commerce, 1990]

Percentage change, since 1989, in the amount of U.S. credit card debt that is at least 30 days past due: +24
[American Bankers Association (Washington, D.C.), 1991]

Ratio of the average CEO's salary to that of a blue-collar worker in 1980: 25:1
Ratio in 1991: 91:1
[Forbes (New York City)/U.S. Bureau of Labor Statistics, 1991]

Percentage increase, since 1988, in the number of American college students who have their own credit card: 37
[College Track (New York City), 1991]

Amount the federal government spent in 1990 on the savings and loan bailout, per hour: $7,420,000
[U.S. Congressional Budget Office, 1991]

Percentage change, since 1989, in the profits earned abroad by American-owned companies: +15
Percentage change, since 1989, in the profits earned in the United States by American-owned companies: −21.
[Robert Reich, Harvard University (Cambridge, Mass.), 1991]

Percentage change, since 1980, in the average amount of tax an American pays to the federal government: 0
[Citizens for Tax Justice (Washington, D.C.), 1991]

Change, since 1979, in the average annual earnings of a black woman with only a high school diploma: +$279
Change, since 1979, in the average annual earnings of a black woman with a college diploma: −$744
[Randy Albelda, University of Massachusetts (Boston), 1991]

Portion of health care spending by U.S. businesses that goes to treat mental illness or chemical dependency: 1/10
[Employee Benefit Research Institute (Washington, D.C.), 1992]

Ratio of the average productivity of a U.S. automotive engine plant to that of a Mexican plant: 5:4
Ratio of the average wages at a U.S. plant to those at a Mexican plant: 17:1.
[Harley Shaiken, University of California (San Diego), 1992]

Change, since 1969, in U.S. median household income, adjusted for inflation: 0
[U.S. Census Bureau, 1992]

Estimated number of people worldwide who live on less than $1 per day: 1,000,000,000
[World Bank (Washington, D.C.), 1994]

Robert Arneson, *Yin & Yang,* from the Egghead Series, UC Davis Campus, © UC Regents and Nelson Gallery, all rights reserved.

PART TWO

▼

What Is a University?

In this phase of the course, we will discuss the nature of a university and the value of university study. You have now met and worked with several professors. If useful generalizations can be made about them, what strange manner of beast is this? What motivates them to spend so much of their time with cowlicked and beribboned youth who have little knowledge of their life's passion? And what, aside from a grade and a bit of information, can the student hope to gain from the professor? Is there a contrast in the ways men and women learn and think, a contrast that university educators have typically not taken into account? The essays by Neusner and Clinchy deal with these questions.

As you know, many universities require students to take a substantial number of courses in the humanities and sciences. Why? If you are hoping to be a district buyer for a major national department store chain, why should you have to take a year of natural sciences? Why do you need art and history or philosophy? These are large questions to which you will probably not have a truly satisfactory answer until you have examined these collegiate disciplines in greater depth. But the "symposium" in this section of the text is intended to provide at least an initial answer. Here you will find a theme of great importance addressed by thinkers from all of the disciplines you may be required to take. The theme is the challenges of the twenty-first century, and a wide range of topics will be treated under that head. Jessica Tuchman Mathews will present the threats to the global environment. Jorge Valadez will examine the philosophical underpinnings of Third World oppression. Stanley Kober will discuss the disappointing turn in the recent revolutions in Eastern Europe. And several of these writers will propose solutions to the problems they depict. In addition, three artistic perspectives will be presented—a haunting story by science fiction writer Ursula Le Guin, a troubling poem by Sharon Olds, and an apocalyptic artwork of monumental scale by Robert Longo. Our hope is that in studying the several perspectives offered here on the theme of the future, you will see for yourself the value to your thinking and to your life in being conversant with the disciplines represented.

20

▼

What Faculty Expect of Students

Edmund S. Morgan

Edmund S. Morgan, professor emeritus of history at Yale, characterizes the ruling passions of faculty so that students will have a better idea of what professors expect of them.

The world does not much like curiosity. The world says that curiosity killed the cat. The world dismisses curiosity by calling it idle, or mere idle, curiosity—even though curious persons are seldom idle. Parents do their best to extinguish curiosity in their children, because it makes life difficult to be faced every day with a string of unanswerable questions about what makes fire hot or why grass grows, or to have to halt junior's investigations before they end in explosion and sudden death. Children whose curiosity survives parental discipline and who manage to grow up before they blow up are invited to join the Yale faculty. Within the university they go on asking their questions and trying to find the answers. In the eyes of a scholar, that is mainly what a university is for. It is a place where the world's hostility to curiosity can be defied.

Some of the questions that scholars ask seem to the world to be scarcely worth asking, let alone answering. They ask about the behavior of protons, the dating of a Roman coin, the structure of a poem. They ask questions too minute and specialized for you and me to understand without years of explanation.

If the world inquires of one of them why he wants to know the answer to a particular question, he may say, especially if he is a scientist, that the answer will in some obscure way make possible a new machine or weapon or gadget. He talks that way because he knows that the world understands and respects utility and that it does not understand much else. But to his colleagues and to you he will probably not speak this language. You are now part of the university, and he will expect you to understand that he wants to know the answer simply because he does not know it, the way a mountain climber wants to climb a mountain simply because it is there.

Similarly a historian, when asked by outsiders why he studies history, may come out with a line of talk that he has learned to repeat on such occasions, something about knowledge of the past making it possible to understand the present and mold the future. I am sure you have all heard it at one time or another. But if you really want to know why a historian studies the past, the answer is much simpler; he wants to know about it because it is there. Something happened, and he would like to know what.

All this does not mean that the answers which scholars find to their questions have no consequences. They may have enormous consequences; they may completely alter the character of human life. But the consequences seldom form the reason for asking the questions or pursuing the answers. It is true that scholars can be put to work answering questions for the sake of the consequences, as thousands are working now, for example, in search of a cure for cancer. But this is not the primary function of the scholar. For the scholar the consequences are usually incidental to the satisfaction of curiosity. Even for the medical scholar the desire to stamp out a dreaded disease may be a less powerful motive than the desire to find out about the nature of living matter. Similarly, Einstein did not wish to create an atomic bomb or to harness atomic energy. He simply wanted to find out about energy and matter.

I said that curiosity was a dangerous quality. It is dangerous not only because of incidental effects like the atomic bomb but also because it is really nothing more or less than a desire for truth. For some reason this phrase sounds rather respectable. Since so many respectable people assure us that they have found the truth, it does not sound like a dangerous thing to look for. But it is. The search for it has again and again overturned institutions and beliefs of long standing, in science, in religion, in politics. It is easy enough to see today that these past revolutions brought great benefits to mankind. It was less easy to see the benefits while the revolutions were taking place, especially if you happened to be quite satisfied with the way things were before. Similarly it is not always easy to see that the satisfaction of a scholar's curiosity is worth the disruption of society that may result from it. The search for truth is, and always has been, a **subversive** activity. And scholars have learned that they cannot engage in it without an occasional fight.

You may therefore find them rather **belligerent** toward any threat to the free pursuit of curiosity. They are wary of committing themselves to institutions or beliefs that might impose limitations on them or deliver ready-made answers to their questions. You will find them suspicious of loyalty oaths, religious creeds, or affiliations with political parties. In particular they will try to preserve their university as a sanctuary within whose walls any question can be asked.

This wariness of commitment can sometimes degenerate into a scholarly vice, a vice that paralyzes curiosity instead of preserving it. A scholar at his worst sometimes seems to be simply a man who cannot make up his mind. Every classroom from here to Melbourne has echoed with the feeble phrases of academic indecision: "There are two schools of thought on this question, and the truth probably lies halfway between them." When you hear this sentence repeated, or when you are tempted to repeat it yourself, remember that the truth may lie between two extremes, but it assuredly does not lie halfway between right and wrong. Don't short-circuit your curiosity by assuming you have found the answer when you have only made a tidy list of possible answers.

Dedication to curiosity should not end in indecision. It should, in fact, mean willingness to follow the mind into difficult decisions.

A second quality that makes a scholar has no apparent relation to the first and yet it is inseparably connected to it. It is a compulsion to communicate. A scholar is driven by a force as strong as his curiosity, that compels him to tell the world the things he has learned. He cannot rest with learning something: he has to tell about it. Scholarship begins in curiosity, but it ends in communication. And though scholars may in a university take refuge from the world, they also acknowledge responsibility to communicate freely and fully everything that they discover within the walls of their sanctuary. The search for truth needs no justification, and when a man thinks he has found any part of it, he cannot and ought not to be silent. The world may sometimes not care to listen, but the scholar must keep telling it until he has succeeded in communicating.

Now there are only two methods of communication for scholars, writing and speaking. The scholar publishes his discoveries in books and articles and he teaches them in the classroom. Sometimes one or the other method will satisfy him, but most of us feel the need for both. The scholar who merely writes books falls into the habit of speaking only to the experts. If he works at his subject long enough, he reaches the position where there is no one else quite expert enough to understand him, and he winds up writing to himself. On the other hand, if he writes not at all, he may become so **enamored** of his own voice that he ceases to be a scholar and becomes a mere showman.

subversive: disorderly
belligerent: hostile
enamored: captivated by

131

Communication is not merely the desire and the responsibility of the scholar; it is his discipline, the proving ground where he tests his findings against criticism. Without communication his pursuit of truth withers into **eccentricity**. He necessarily spends much of his time alone, in the library or the laboratory, looking for answers to his questions. But he needs to be rubbing constantly against other minds. He needs to be tested, probed, and pushed around. He needs to be made to explain himself. Only when he has expressed himself, only when he has communicated his thoughts, can he be sure that he is thinking clearly.

The scholar, in other words, needs company to keep making sense. And in particular he needs the company of fresh minds to whom he must explain things from the beginning. He needs people who will challenge him at every step, who will take nothing for granted. He needs, in short, you.

You may have other purposes in coming here, and you may fulfill them: you may play football or tennis or the trombone, you may sing in the glee club, act in plays, and act up on college weekends. But what the faculty expects of you is four years of scholarship, and they will be satisfied with nothing less. For four years we expect you to join us in the pursuit of truth, and we will demand of you the same things we demand of ourselves: curiosity and communication.

Curiosity, of course, is not something you get simply by wishing for it. But it is surprisingly contagious. The curiosity we expect is more than a passing interest. We will not be satisfied by your ability to ask an occasional bright question, nor yet by your **assimilation** of a lot of predigested information. The accumulation of information is a necessary part of scholarship, and unfortunately the part most likely to be tested on examinations, especially those wretched ones called "objective examinations" where the truth is always supposed to lie in answer space A, B, C, D, or E but never apparently in X, Y, or Z. But the curiosity we expect of you cannot be satisfied by passing examinations or by memorizing other people's answers to other people's questions. We do not wish to put you through a mere course of mental gymnastics. We want you to be content with nothing less than the whole truth about the subject that interests you. Which means that we want you to be forever discontent with how little you know about it and how little we know about it. We want you to back us into corners, show us up, make us confess we don't know. Does this sound **formidable**? It is not. We may tell you what we know with great assurance, but push us and you will find the gaps.

Follow your own minds into the gaps. Follow your minds where curiosity takes them. You will not get the whole truth, not about protons, not about a Roman coin. Nobody does. But if you learn anything, it ought to change your minds, and hopefully it will change ours too. It will be a sign that we have both wasted four years if you leave here thinking pretty much the same way that you do now or if you leave us thinking the same way we do now.

We expect of you, then, that you will be curious for the truth. We also expect that you communicate whatever truth you find, and that you do it both in speech and in writing. Many people suppose that they know something if they can stammer out an approximation of what they mean in speech. They are mistaken. It is extremely unlikely that you have thought clearly if you cannot express yourself clearly, especially in writing. Writing is more than an instrument of communication. It is an instrument of thought. You should have acquired some competence in its use by now. But even if you have, you have a great deal more to learn about it. And if you do not know much more about it four years from now, it will again be a sign that we have failed in part of our job, the job of making you communicate clearly.

Communication is a two-way process, and a university is a community of scholars, where questions are asked and answers communicated, your answers to us, ours to you. For the next four years we will be engaged as scholars together in this community. After the four years are over, most of you will leave Yale, but

eccentricity: oddity; peculiarity

assimilation: absorption; the process of incorporating as one's own

formidable: of discouraging difficulty

if our community is a successful one, if we really do communicate with each other, I believe that you will continue to be in some sense scholars, asking new questions, looking for new answers and communicating them to the world.

▼ Questions to Focus Reading

1. To the scholar, Morgan tells us, a university is where "the world's hostility to curiosity can be defied." What does he mean by this? Why should we believe the world is hostile to curiosity?

2. Morgan says the scientist, the historian, and other university scholars will present bogus practical arguments for their pursuits. What is the true motive of the scientist? the historian?

3. Why is curiosity a "dangerous quality" as much of the world sees it?

4. The second quality that makes a scholar, Morgan asserts, is the "compulsion to communicate." Why do most scholars feel the need to communicate by means of both publication and classroom teaching? Why not one or the other?

5. The scholar "needs company to keep making sense." What does Morgan mean by this? Why the company of students in particular?

6. What are the chief expectations faculty have of students?

7. "The curiosity we expect of you cannot be satisfied by passing examinations or by memorizing other people's answers to other people's questions." Why isn't this enough? What degree of curiosity is expected?

8. Morgan presents two criteria for the failure of a college education. What are they?

9. Morgan closes his essay with one further expectation faculty have of students. What is it?

▼ Questions for Reflection

1. Is the world hostile to curiosity? What are some evidences for your answer?

2. Morgan points out how the pursuit of curiosity has led to enormous transformations in history, whose benefits were not immediately obvious. Can you think of instances in your own life when the discovery of a truth seemed at first to produce quite unwelcome change, but later showed itself to be immensely beneficial to you?

3. Judging from your experience this semester, what would you say are your professors' expectations of you? Does Morgan's characterization of their expectations seem accurate? Explain.

4. What would be Morgan's measures of the success of a university education? What personal characteristics would the successful graduate have? What abilities? What attitudes? What would be your own measures of success in terms of these same categories: personal characteristics, abilities, attitudes?

▼ Discussion

1. Judging from your experience this semester, what would you say are your professors' expectations of you? Does Morgan's characterization of their expectations seem accurate? Explain.

2. What would be Morgan's measures of the success of a university education? What personal characteristics would the successful graduate have? What abilities? What attitudes? What would be your own measures of success in terms of these same categories: personal characteristics, abilities, attitudes?

▼ Writing Assignments

1. Think about your conception of what your professors expected of you when you entered the university. Has your conception changed in light of your experience? If so, how? Have your expectations of your professors changed? If either of these conceptions has changed, what specific experiences inside or outside the classroom have led to this change?

2. Communication, Morgan argues, is the scholar's guard against eccentricity. Have there been times in your life when communication corrected a wholly misguided conception of yourself, your accomplishments, some other aspects of reality? If so, describe the misconception and the communication that freed you from it.

▼ Vocabulary

assimilation	eccentricity	formidable
belligerent	enamored	subversive

21

▼

The Development of Thoughtfulness in College Women

Blythe McVicker Clinchy

Blythe McVicker Clinchy is a psychologist at Wellesley College. She is interested here in understanding the relative silence of women in the coeducational classroom. Her exploration of this phenomenon uncovers two very different ways of knowing, one predominantly associated with men, one with women. A key problem with our colleges, she says, is that they emphasize only one.

Last year there appeared in the *New York Times* an article by Michael Gorra (1988), an assistant professor of English at Smith College. The title of Gorra's piece was "Learning to Hear the Small, Soft Voices," and it began this way:

> "You at a women's college?" a friend said just after I'd been hired to teach English at Smith. "That's a scandal waiting to happen." He never made it clear if I was to be the **debaucher** or the **debauchee**. Another friend, a Smith alumna, told me its students saw the young male faculty, married or not, as "fair game." My mother told me to get a heavy doorstop for my office and to keep my wife's picture on the desk.

The Silence of Women Students

Gorra does not tell us whether he took his mother's advice or not. If he did, it seems to have worked. He has been at Smith for several years now, and the **lurid** fantasies of his friends and relations so far have not been fulfilled. The difficulties that Gorra has encountered in teaching women students have to do not with their sexuality but with their silence. Gorra has trouble getting a class discussion off the ground, because the students refuse to argue. They will not argue with him, even when he tries to lure them into it by taking a **devil's advocate** position. They will not even argue with each other. Gorra tells about a recent incident in which two students, one speaking right after the other, offered **diametrically** opposed readings of a W. H. Auden poem. The second student, Gorra says,

> [D]idn't define her interpretation against her **predecessor's**, as I think a man would have. She didn't begin by saying, "I don't agree with that." She betrayed no awareness that she [had] disagreed with her classmate, and seemed surprised when I pointed it out.

Gorra has found the feminist poet Adrienne Rich's (1979) essay, "Taking Women Students Seriously," helpful in trying to understand this phenomenon. Rich says women have been taught since early childhood to speak in "small, soft voices" (p. 243). And Gorra says,

> Our students still suffer, even at a women's college, from the lessons Rich says women are taught about unfemininity of assertiveness. They are uneasy with the prospect of having to defend their opinions, not

debaucher: a corrupter; one who indulges in unrestrained sensuality

debauchee: the person corrupted by a debaucher

lurid: gruesome

devil's advocate: a person arguing against a position for the sake of argument

diametrically: in a manner exactly opposed to

predecessor: someone who came before

only against my own devil's advocacy, but against each other. They would rather not speak if speaking means breaking with their class-mates' **consensus**. Yet that consensus is usually more emotional, a mat-ter of tone, than it is intellectual.

I have been teaching at a women's college much longer than Gorra has and have had experiences similar to his. A few years ago, I might have described and analyzed the experiences in the same way he does, but in the course of research over the last 10 years I have interviewed a great many women students, both at my own college and at a broad range of other institutions, and as a result of that research, I have come to interpret the phenomenon of silence among women stu-dents differently. As my colleagues (Mary Belenky, Nancy Goldberger, and Jill Tarule) and I pored over the interviews with 135 women, which we had collected in preparation for writing our book, *Women's Ways of Knowing* (Belenky et al., 1986), we were astonished to see how often the women referred to matters of voice: "speaking out," "speaking up," "being silenced," "not being heard," "really listening," "really talking," "words as weapons," "feeling deaf and dumb," "saying what you mean," and so on. We subtitled the book *The Development of Self, Voice and Mind* because issues of voice seemed so intricately intertwined with the de-velopment of women's minds and selves.

Our interviews confirm Gorra's sense that many young women are reluctant to engage in argument, and I agree—and so would many of the women inter-viewed—that this is a limitation. But argument is not the only form of dialogue, and if asked to engage in other types of conversation—"in a different voice," to borrow Carol Gilligan's (1982) phrase—we found that women could speak with **eloquence** and strength. Gorra may not know about this different voice, as I did not, because, like most of us professors, he does not invite it to speak in his classroom. In Gorra's classroom, as in most classrooms run by teachers who pride themselves on encouraging discussion, discussion means disagreement, and the student has two choices: to disagree or to remain silent.

To get a somewhat different slant on the problem, Gorra might take a look at another of Adrienne Rich's essays (1979). It is called "Toward a Woman-Cen-tered University," and in it she says that our educational practice is founded upon a "masculine, adversarial form of **discourse**" (p. 138). Here, Rich defines the prob-lem of silence not as a deficiency in women, but as a limitation in our educational institutions. Argument is not the only style of discourse that exists, but it is the only kind that has found much favor in the groves of academe.

Now, I do not mean to imply that women are incapable of argument. We interviewed a good many students, especially from the more traditional elite col-leges, who, Gorra would be pleased to know, had become skilled in argument and valued their skill. For some, adversarial thinking had become automatic. For ex-ample, one young woman told us, "As soon as someone tells me his point of view, I immediately start arguing in my head the opposite point of view. When someone is saying something, I can't help turning it upside down." And another said,

I never take anything someone says for granted. I just tend to see the contrary. I like playing the devil's advocate, arguing the opposite of what somebody's saying, thinking of exceptions to what the person has said or thinking of a different train of logic.

Separate Knowing

consensus: general opinion

eloquence: graceful power in verbal expression

discourse: speech

These young women are playing what the writer Peter Elbow (1973) calls the "doubting game." They look for what is wrong with whatever it is they are exam-ining. They think up opposing positions. The doubting, argumentative, adversarial mode of discourse is the voice that is appropriate to a way of knowing we call separate knowing. I will not dwell upon separate knowing here, because we all know what it is. It is the way we are supposed to think, according to most of our professors. Separate knowing includes activities like critical thinking, scientific method, and textual analysis. The heart of separate knowing is detachment. The separate knower keeps her distance from the object she is trying to analyze. She takes an impersonal stance. She follows certain rules or procedures that will ensure that her judgments are unbiased. All our various disciplines and vocations have these impersonal procedures for analyzing things. All of the various fields have impersonal standards for evaluating things, criteria that allow one to decide whether a novel is well constructed or an experiment has been properly conducted or a person should be diagnosed as schizophrenic.

Separate knowing is obviously of great importance. It allows us to criticize our own and other people's thinking. Without it, we could not write second drafts of our papers; the first draft would look just fine. Without it, we would be at the mercy of all of the authorities who try to tell us what to believe. Separate knowing is a powerful way of knowing.

But it is not the only way of knowing.

Connected Knowing

In the research that my colleague, Claire Zimmerman, and I did at Wellesley, we interviewed undergraduate women each year and asked them to respond to comments made by other undergraduates, including the one I quoted earlier to illustrate separate knowing made by the woman who says she automatically starts "arguing the opposite point of view." Most of the students said that they did not like the quotation much; they said they were not into that kind of thing.

They could recognize disagreement all right, but they did not deal with disagreement by arguing. For instance, a woman we call Grace[1] said that when she disagreed with someone she did not start arguing in her head. She started trying to imagine herself in that person's situation. She said, "I sort of fit myself into it in my mind and then say, 'I see what you mean.' " She said, "There's this initial point where I kind of go into the story, you know? And become like Alice in Wonderland falling down the well."

It took Claire and me a long time to hear what Grace was saying. We thought at the time that she was just revealing her inability to engage in critical thinking. To us, her comment indicated not the presence of a different way of thinking but the absence of any kind of thinking—not a difference but a deficiency. Now we see it as an instance of what we call connected knowing, and, as we go back over the interviews we have done with women over the years, we see it everywhere. It is clear to us that many women have a **proclivity** for connected knowing.

Here is an especially clear illustration of connected knowing from a student we call Priscilla:

> When I have an idea about something, and it differs from the way another person's thinking about it, I'll usually try to look at it from that person's point of view, see how they could say that, why they think they're right, why it makes sense.

Now, contrast this quotation with the ones illustrating separate knowing. When you play devil's advocate, you take a position contrary to the other person's, even when you agree with it, even when it seems intuitively right. Priscilla turns this upside down. She allies herself with the other person's position even when she disagrees with it. Another student, Leonora, said she seldom played devil's advocate. She said, "I'm usually a little bit of a **chameleon**. I really try to look

proclivity: predisposition

chameleon: inconsistent person

137

for pieces of truth in what the person says, instead of going contrary to them. Sort of **collaborate** with them." These women are playing what Elbow (1973) calls the "believing game." Instead of looking for what is wrong with the other person's idea, they look for why it makes sense, how it might be right.

Connected knowers are not dispassionate, unbiased observers. They deliberately bias themselves in favor of the thing they are examining. They try to get right inside it, to form an intimate attachment to it. The heart of connected knowing is imaginative attachment. Priscilla tries to get behind the other person's eyes, to "look at it from that person's point of view." This is what Elbow means by "believe." You must suspend your disbelief, put your own views aside, and try to see the logic in the idea. Ultimately, you need not agree with it, but while you are entertaining it you must, as Elbow says, "say yes to it"; you must **empathize** with it, feel with and think with the person who created it.

The connected knower believes that in order to understand what a person is saying, one must adopt the person's own terms. One must refrain from judgment. In this sense, connected knowing is uncritical. But it is not unthinking. It is a personal way of thinking, and it involves feeling. The connected knower takes a personal approach even to an impersonal thing like a philosophical **treatise**; she treats the text, as one Wellesley student put it, "as if it were a friend." In Martin Buber's (1970) terms, the text is a "thou," a subject, rather than an "it," an object, of analysis.

So, while the separate knower takes nothing at face value, the connected knower, in a sense, takes everything at face value. She does not try to evaluate the perspective she is examining. She tries to understand it. She does not ask, "Is it right?"; she asks, "What does it mean?" When she says, "Why do you think that?" she does not mean, "What evidence do you have to support that belief, how can you back it up?" She means, "What in your experience led you to that position?" She is looking for the story behind the idea. The voice of separate knowing is argument; the voice of connected knowing is a narrative voice.

Women spend a lot of time sharing stories of their experience. It sometimes seemed to us that first-year students spent most of their time this way. This may help to account for the fact that most studies of intellectual development among college students show the major growth occurring during the first year. The students worry that they waste time chatting with their friends when they should be in the library reading books. But we came to believe that, at least for women, the sharing of stories is a major avenue of growth. When a student who has known many Jews but has never before laid eyes on an Arab listens to her Arab roommate tell her life story, she can stretch beyond the boundaries of her own limited experience. As a separate knower might say, she expands her database or, to paraphrase the philosopher Nel Noddings (1984), the other person's reality becomes a possibility for her. Connected knowing, then, is not only a way of knowing but a way of growing. It opens up new ways of being.

We call these conversations "connected conversations." In connected conversations each participant tries to draw the other one out. These conversations may begin rather like clinical interviews. In interviewing, a still soft voice is an asset. The skilled interviewer says little; mainly, she listens. But the listening is active, although it may appear passive: The skilled interviewer offers support and invites elaboration at the appropriate moments. She is thoughtful: She thinks along with her informant, and offers her careful consideration.

This kind of dialogue can be one-sided. One risks being always the interviewer and never the interviewee, always the listener and never the primary speaker. There is a risk of losing one's self in the other person's story, rather than using the story to expand the self. The psychologist Robert Hogan (1973) identified a group of people who scored relatively high on a measure of empathy and relatively low on a measure of **autonomy**. The behavior of these "overempathizers" suggests,

collaborate: work together

empathize: identify with; understand

treatise: systematic account in writing

autonomy: the condition of being independent; self-ruling

138

Hogan says, that "unleavened role taking can produce an equivocating jellyfish as well as a compassionate person with a broad moral perspective" (p. 224). Connected knowers sometimes look like equivocating jellyfish, "clones" or "chameleons," even to themselves. For example, Adrienne, in her first year at college, laments,

> It's easy for me to take other people's points of view. It's hard for me to argue, sometimes, because I feel like I can understand the other person's argument. It's easy for me to see a whole lot of different points of view on things and to understand why people think those things. The hard thing is sitting down and saying, "Okay, what do *I* think, and why do I think it?"

This may be what is going on behind the apparent "consensus" in Gorra's classroom. His silent students may find it easy to think *with* their classmates and their teacher, hard to think against them, and hard to think for themselves; but connected knowing need not end in static consensus. If we cultivate our students' skills in connected knowing and nourish their development, connected knowing can attain a higher form. In this form, connected conversations involve a *community* of students and teachers engaged in the collaborative construction of knowledge. When we asked women to describe a "good class" they had had, many told of classes that had taken this form, with students and teachers drawing out each other's ideas, elaborating upon them, and building together a truth none could have constructed alone. In *Women's Ways of Knowing,* we quoted one such student:

> We were all raising our hands and talking about I forget what book, and some of the students brought up things that [the teacher] hadn't thought about that made him see it in a whole different way, and he was really excited, and we all came to a conclusion that none of us had started out with. We came up with an answer to a question we thought was unanswerable in the beginning, and it just made you all feel really good when you walked out of class. You felt you had accomplished something and that you understood the book.

This sort of discussion moves well beyond bland agreement. In fact, many women see this sort of discussion as dynamic, while they see arguments as **static**. Arguments, they say, leave the participants in the same place they began, while collaborative conversations can lead the speakers into territory none has ventured into before.

The Question of Gender

Recently, my students and colleagues and I have been interviewing both men and women, asking them to respond to the sorts of comments I have quoted here, illustrating argument and connected conversation. This is highly exploratory research, and I do not want to make too much of it, but so far, typically, the men we have interviewed describe arguments as useful in clarifying their own thinking and helping others to think more clearly. Unlike many women, who see argument as a zero-sum game in which only one side could win, men see arguments as useful for both participants. Men reported that arguments had stimulated their intellectual growth, whereas women—not always, but often—described them as crippling. They told about men in their lives—teachers, lovers, husbands, and, most often, fathers—who had used devil's advocacy against them, reducing them to silence and frequently to tears.

static: going nowhere

139

However, many of these women were **ambivalent**. Although arguments made them uncomfortable, they were ashamed of their discomfort and of their ineptitude. They wished that they could argue better.

Typically, the men's responses to our questions about connected knowing reflected an ambivalence similar to the women's attitudes toward argument. These men said that they knew they ought to try harder to enter the other person's perspective, but it made them uncomfortable, and they found it difficult to do, so they did not do it much.

It is possible that men like this might feel as constricted in the kind of connected class discussion I **envisage** as the women seem to feel in Gorra's classroom. In a connected class, men might sit in silence, and the teacher would worry about what it was in their upbringing that had retarded their intellectual development.

Ideally, we would encourage our men and women students to speak in both voices, and we would help them to integrate the voices. But that is not the way it is. In classrooms that sanction only separate knowing, men can speak up more easily than women, but they may never learn to speak in a connected voice.

Given the present situation, what about the women? Here, we need not imagine the outcomes, because women have told us about them. Some women, unable to acquire the skills of separate knowing, will graduate from college convinced that they are stupid. Others will learn the skills, but often at the cost of alienation and repression. The kind of connected thinking for which they have a **predilection** is disallowed, and the utterly objective, impersonal, detached reasoning that they think they are asked to use in academic life comes to seem increasingly empty and pointless. In playing the doubting game, Elbow (1973) says, you try to "**extricate** yourself," "weed out the self," "make your thinking more like using a computer.... The less involvement of the self the better" (p. 171).

Some students use mechanical metaphors like this to describe their production of essays. They speak of "cranking out" papers. Others, like Simone, use biological metaphors: They call their papers "bullshit." Simone says she can write "good papers" when she tries. By "good papers," she means papers that teachers like. Simone, herself, does not like them much. She says,

> I can write a good paper, and someday I may learn to write one that
> I like, that is not just bullshit, but I still feel that it's somewhat pointless.
> I do it, and I get my grade, but it hasn't proved anything to me.

Simone calls her papers bullshit because she does not care about what she is writing about, and reason, in the absence of feeling, is bullshit. The problem, she says,

> is that I don't feel terribly strongly about one point of view, but that
> point of view seems to make more sense. It's easier to write the paper,
> supporting that point of view than the other one, because there's more
> to support it. And it's not one of my deep-founded beliefs, but it writes
> the paper.

ambivalent: exhibiting conflicting feelings

envisage: conceive a certain picture

predilection: preference

extricate: disengage

insidious: operating inconspicuously but with gravely harmful effect

Simone does not write the paper. "It" writes the paper.

This, to me, is the really **insidious** effect of an education that emphasizes separate knowing to the virtual exclusion of connected knowing: The student removes herself from her work and dissociates thinking and feeling. She learns to think only about things she does not care about and she cares only about things she does not think about. The contemporary philosopher Sara Ruddick (1977) tells us that in college she became, in our terms, an ultraseparate knower. She writes, "In college I learned to avoid work done out of love. My intellectual life became

140

increasingly critical, detached, and dispensable" (p. 135). Think of that word: *dispensable.*

Simone seemed to have dispensed with intellectual life. Nominated by the science faculty at her college as the most outstanding student of her year, Simone in her senior year aborted her thesis, withdrew her applications to the most prestigious graduate schools in the country, and, after graduating without honors, returned to her hometown, married her high school boyfriend, and settled into an undemanding job. Simone's professors were horrified, of course, and I, interviewing her, was worried. Simone seemed to feel that she had to choose between her mind and her heart. Her work had become heartless. I worried that the decision to marry was mindless. Will Simone ever achieve some sort of integration between heart and mind?

Sara Ruddick did, but not until years after she had graduated from college and earned a Ph.D. in philosophy. In rearing her two children Ruddick developed what we call connected knowing. She watched her children closely, attentively, in detail, her attention sharpened rather than clouded by her feeling for them. As a sort of hobby, she began to study Virginia Woolf, and she found that the way of thinking she developed in reading Woolf was closer to the way of thinking she used in rearing children than the way she had been taught in college and graduate school. She writes,

> I seemed to learn new ways of attending. . . . This kind of attending was intimately connected with caring; because I cared I reread slowly, then found myself watching more carefully, listening with patience. . . . The more I attended, the more deeply I cared. The domination of feeling by thought, which I had worked so hard to achieve, was breaking down. Instead of developing arguments that could bring my feelings to heel, I allowed feeling to inform my most abstract thinking. . . . I now care about my thinking and think about what I care about.

Surely we can find ways to help our students achieve this sort of integration while they are still in college. As philosopher Janice Raymond (1986) reminds us, the word *thoughtfulness* contains two meanings: the use of reason and the practice of consideration and care. We are awash these days in rhetoric setting forth the proper aims of higher education. I will settle for thoughtfulness.

Endnote

1. All students' names are pseudonyms.

References

Belenky, M. B., B. M. Clinchy, N. R. Goldberger, and J. M. Tarule. (1986). *Women's Ways of Knowing.* New York: Basic Books.

Buber, M. (1970). *I and Thou.* New York: Scribner's.

Elbow, P. (1973). *Writing Without Teachers.* London: Oxford Univ. Press.

Gilligan, C. (1982). *In a Different Voice: Psychological Theory and Women's Development.* Cambridge, MA: Harvard Univ. Press.

Gorra, M. (1988). "Learning to hear the small, soft voices." *New York Times Sunday Magazine* (May 1): 32, 34.

Hogan, R. (1973). "Moral conduct and moral character: a psychological perspective." *Psych. Bull.* 70: 217–232.

Noddings, N. (1984). *Caring.* Berkeley: Univ. of California Press.

Raymond, J. B. (1986). *A Passion for Friends.* Boston: Beacon.

Rich, A. (1979). *On Lies, Secrets, and Silence: Selected Prose—1966–1978.* New York: Norton.

Ruddick, S. (1977). "A work of one's own," pp. 128–143 in S. Ruddick and P. Daniels (eds.), *Working It Out.* New York: Pantheon.

Ruddick, S. (1984). "New combinations: Learning from Virginia Woolf," pp. 137–159 in C. Asher, L. DeSalvo, and S. Ruddick (eds.), *Between Women.* Boston: Beacon.

▼ Questions to Focus Reading

1. What is Michael Gorra's explanation for the silence of women in the classroom?
2. What is Blythe Clinchy's explanation? What evidence does she give for the correctness of her view?
3. What are the key characteristics of "separate knowing," as Clinchy depicts them?
4. What are the virtues of this kind of knowing, as Clinchy sees them?
5. What are the key points of contrast between separate knowing and connected knowing?
6. In what sense, according to Clinchy, is connected knowing a way of growing?
7. How is connected knowing conducive to a "collaborative construction of knowledge"?
8. Clinchy believes that there is a serious danger in an education with an almost exclusive emphasis on separate knowing. What is the danger?

▼ Questions for Reflection

1. Try to recall recent instances in your own discussions (in class or outside with friends) of the two kinds of thinking that Clinchy is discussing. Describe those instances. Which kind—separate or connected—do you feel more comfortable with? Do her generalizations about gender preferences in this regard apply to you?
2. Clinchy reports that most studies of intellectual development among college students show the greatest growth during the freshman year. Are you seeing such growth in yourself? What are the evidences of it?
3. Clinchy writes of an "insidious effect" of an almost exclusive emphasis in higher education on separate knowing. What is that effect? Do you think she is right about this?
4. Do you think that there are reasons other than those Clinchy proposes that many students feel so little emotional investment in the thinking they do for classes? If this condition is true of you, what do you think are the reasons for it?
5. Clinchy offers the philosopher Sara Ruddick as a model for the sort of integrated education Clinchy believes to be the ideal. How would you describe this ideal?
6. Clinchy's candidate for the proper aim of higher education is the cultivation of thoughtfulness in students. Explain what she means by this. What do you think university education should aim for?

▼ Discussion

1. Does Gorra or Clinchy, or does neither, have the right explanation for the relative silence of women in the classroom? If neither, what in your opinion is the right explanation?

142

2. Do your college classrooms emphasize "separate knowing" to the virtual exclusion of "connected knowing"? What are some examples of both kinds of knowing in recent class sessions?

3. Do you think she is right that people know primarily in one or the other of these modes? Is she right in associating separate knowing mainly with men and connected knowing mainly with women? What evidence does she offer for these claims? What evidence, if any, can you add?

4. What in your opinion are the advantages and disadvantages of the mastery of connected thinking (say, to the virtual exclusion of separate thinking)? What are the advantages and disadvantages of mastery of separate thinking (to the exclusion of connected thinking)?

5. Are there ways of knowing other than the two ways Clinchy describes? How would you describe your own primary way of knowing?

▼ Writing Assignments

1. Clinchy reports that most studies show that the major portion of intellectual growth occurs during the first year. Think about your own intellectual development in college so far. How is your thinking changing? What are some evidences of these changes? Are there problems or situations, for example, that you are dealing with in ways that are new for you? Are you more receptive to ideas that challenge your present framework? If so present some examples of these problems, situations, ideas, and explain your new ways of approaching them.

2. Women's general reluctance to speak in the (coeducational) classroom remains a widely reported phenomenon. How do you think this can be explained? If you are a woman, describe situations in which you've felt this reluctance and explain why you felt this way.

3. It is often the case, as Clinchy points out, that students feel no emotional investment in their college work. What is Clinchy's explanation for this? Do you think she is right? At those times when you find yourself uninvolved in college work, what are the reasons for that lack of involvement? Would there be ways to get yourself involved in what may seem to you at first sight a boring assignment? What would be some possible ways you could do this?

▼ Journal Entry

1. Clinchy proposes that the proper aim of higher education is the development of thoughtfulness. Is your college education having this effect on you? Why do you answer as you do?

▼ Vocabulary

ambivalent	debaucher	envisage	proclivity
autonomy	devil's advocate	extricate	static
chameleon	diametrically	insidious	treatise
collaborate	discourse	lurid	
consensus	eloquence	predecessor	
debauchee	empathize	predilection	

Originally printed in <u>On Lies, Secrets and Silence</u> <u>Selected Prose</u> 1966-1978. Norton and Company 1979.

Reprint Permission Granted via Copyright Clearance Center.

Claiming an Education

Adrienne Rich

Adrienne Rich is a poet and essayist. Although she is addressing women, she has a critical message in this convocation address for all *students: Take control of your education. Take command of your life.*

For this convocation, I planned to separate my remarks into parts: some thoughts about you, the women students here, and some thoughts about us who teach in a women's college. But ultimately, those two parts are indivisible. If university education means anything beyond the processing of human beings into expected roles, through credit hours, tests, and grades (and I believe that in a women's college especially it might mean much more), it implies an ethical and intellectual contract between teacher and student. This contract must remain intuitive, dynamic, unwritten; but we must turn to it again and again if learning is to be reclaimed from the depersonalizing and cheapening pressures of the present-day academic scene.

The first thing I want to say to you who are students, is that you cannot afford to think of being here to *receive* an education; you will do much better to think of yourselves as being here to *claim* one. One of the dictionary definitions of the verb "to claim" is: *to take as the rightful owner; to assert in the face of possible contradiction.* "To receive" is *to come into possession of; to act as receptacle or container for; to accept as authoritative or true.* The difference is that between acting and being acted-upon, and for women it can literally mean the difference between life and death.

One of the devastating weaknesses of university learning, of the store of knowledge and opinion that has been handed down through academic training, has been its almost total erasure of women's experience and thought from the curriculum, and its exclusion of women as members of the academic community. Today, with increasing numbers of women students in nearly every branch of higher learning, we still see very few women in the upper levels of faculty and administration in most institutions. Douglass College itself is a women's college in a university administered overwhelmingly by men, who in turn are answerable to the state legislature, again composed predominantly of men. But the most significant fact for you is that what you learn here, the very texts you read, the lectures you hear, the way your studies are divided into categories and fragmented one from the other—all this reflects, to a very large degree, neither objective reality, nor an accurate picture of the past, nor a group of rigorously tested observations about human behavior. What you can learn here (and I mean not only at Douglass but any college in any university) is how *men* have perceived and organized their experience, their history, their ideas of social relationships, good and evil, sickness and health, etc. When you read or hear about "great issues," "major texts," "the mainstream of Western thought," you are hearing about what men, above all white men, in their male subjectivity, have decided is important.

Black and other minority peoples have for some time recognized that their racial and ethnic experience was not accounted for in the studies broadly labeled human; and that even the sciences can be racist. For many reasons, it has been more difficult for women to comprehend our exclusion, and to realize that even the sciences can be sexist. For one thing, it is only within the last hundred years that higher education has grudgingly been opened up to women at all, even to white, middle-class women. And many of us have found ourselves poring eagerly over books with titles like: *The Descent of Man; Man and His Symbols; Irrational Man; The Phenomenon of Man; The Future of Man; Man and the Machine; From Man to Man; May Man Prevail?; Man, Science and Society;* or *One-Dimensional Man*—books pretending to describe a "human" reality that does not include over one-half the human species.

Less than a decade ago, with the rebirth of a feminist movement in this country, women students and teachers in a number of universities began to demand and set up women's studies courses—to *claim* a woman-directed education. And, despite the inevitable accusations of "unscholarly," "group therapy," "faddism," etc., despite backlash and budget cuts, women's studies are still growing, offering to more and more women a new intellectual grasp on their lives, new understanding of our history, a fresh vision of the human experience, and also a critical basis for evaluating what they hear and read in other courses, and in the society at large.

But my talk is not really about women's studies, much as I believe in their scholarly, scientific, and human necessity. While I think that any Douglass student has everything to gain by investigating and enrolling in women's studies courses, I want to suggest that there is a more essential experience that you owe yourselves, one which courses in women's studies can greatly enrich, but which finally depends on you, in all your interactions with yourself and your world. This is the experience of *taking responsibility toward yourselves.* Our upbringing as women has so often told us that this should come second to our relationships and responsibilities to other people. We have been offered ethical models of the self-denying wife and mother; intellectual models of the brilliant but slapdash **dilettante** who never commits herself to anything the whole way, or the intelligent woman who denies her intelligence in order to seem more "feminine," or who sits in passive silence even when she disagrees inwardly with everything that is being said around her.

Responsibility to yourself means refusing to let others do your thinking, talking, and naming for you; it means learning to respect and use your own brains and instincts; hence, grappling with hard work. It means that you do not treat your body as a commodity with which to purchase superficial intimacy or economic security; for our bodies and minds are inseparable in this life, and when we allow our bodies to be treated as objects, our minds are in mortal danger. It means insisting that those to whom you give your friendship and love are able to respect your mind. It means being able to say, with Charlotte Bronte's *Jane Eyre:* "I have an inward treasure born with me, which can keep me alive if all the **extraneous** delights should be withheld or offered only at a price I cannot afford to give."

Responsibility to yourself means that you don't fall for shallow and easy solutions—predigested books and ideas, weekend encounters guaranteed to change your life, taking "gut" courses instead of ones you know will challenge you, bluffing at school and life instead of doing solid work, marrying early as an escape from real decisions, getting pregnant as an evasion of already existing problems. It means that you refuse to sell your talents and **aspirations** short, simply to avoid conflict and confrontation. And this, in turn, means resisting the forces in society which say that women should be nice, play safe, have low professional expectations, drown in love and forget about work, live through others, and stay in the places assigned to us. It means that we insist on a life of meaningful work, insist that work be as meaningful as love and friendship in our lives. It means, therefore, the courage to be "different"; not to be continuously available to others when we need time for ourselves and our work; to be able to demand of others—parents, friends, roommates, teachers, lovers, husbands, children—that they respect our sense of purpose and our integrity as persons. Women everywhere are finding the courage to do this, more and more, and we are finding that courage both in our

dilettante: one who toys with a variety of interests
extraneous: nonessential
aspirations: goals

145

study of women in the past who possessed it, and in each other as we look to other women for comradeship, community, and challenge. The difference between a life lived actively, and a life of passive drifting and **dispersal** of energies, is an immense difference. Once we begin to feel committed to our lives, responsible to ourselves, we can never again be satisfied with the old, passive way.

Now comes the second part of the contract. I believe that in a women's college you have the right to expect your faculty to take you seriously. The education of women has been a matter of debate for centuries, and old, negative attitudes about women's role, women's ability to think and take leadership, are still **rife** both in and outside the university. Many male professors (and I don't mean only at Douglass) still feel that teaching in a women's college is a second-rate career. Many tend to eroticize their women students—to treat them as sexual objects—instead of demanding the best of their minds. (At Yale a legal suit [*Alexander v. Yale*] has been brought against the university by a group of women students demanding a stated policy against sexual advances toward female students by male professors.) Many teachers, both men and women, trained in the male-centered tradition, are still handing the ideas and texts of that tradition on to students without teaching them to criticize its antiwoman attitudes, its omission of women as part of the species. Too often, all of us fail to teach the most important thing, which is that clear thinking, active discussion, and excellent writing are all necessary for intellectual freedom, and that these require *hard work*. Sometimes, perhaps in discouragement with a culture which is both anti-intellectual and antiwoman, we may resign ourselves to low expectations for our students before we have given them half a chance to become more thoughtful, expressive human beings. We need to take to heart the words of Elizabeth Barrett Browning, a poet, a thinking woman, and a feminist, who wrote in 1845 of her impatience with studies which cultivate a "passive recipiency" in the mind, and asserted that "women want to be made to *think actively:* their apprehension is quicker than that of men, but their defect lies for the most part in the logical faculty and in the higher mental activities." Note that she implies a defect which can be remedied by intellectual training, *not* an inborn lack of ability.

I have said that the contract on the student's part involves that you demand to be taken seriously so that you can also go on taking yourself seriously. This means seeking out criticism, recognizing that the most affirming thing anyone can do for you is demand that you push yourself further, show you the range of what you can do. It means rejecting attitudes of "take-it-easy," "why-be-so-serious," "why-worry-you'll-probably-get-married-anyway." It means assuming your share of responsibility for what happens in the classroom, because that affects the quality of your daily life here. It means that the student sees herself engaged *with* her teachers in an active, ongoing struggle for a real education. But for her to do this, her teachers must be committed to the belief that women's minds and experience are **intrinsically** valuable and indispensable to any civilization worthy the name; that there is no more **exhilarating** and intellectually fertile place in the academic world today than a women's college—*if* both students and teachers in large enough numbers are trying to fulfill this contract. The contract is really a pledge of mutual seriousness about women, about language, ideas, methods, and values. It is our shared commitment toward a world in which the inborn potentialities of so many women's minds will no longer be wasted, raveled-away, paralyzed, or denied.

dispersal: breaking up and scattering

rife: common; frequent

intrinsically: by its very nature

exhilarating: invigorating

▼ Questions to Focus Reading

1. Adrienne Rich believes university education in any meaningful sense implies an "ethical and intellectual contract" between teacher and student. What is the student's part of the contract? And what is the teacher's part of the contract?

2. "You cannot afford to think of being here to *receive* an education," Rich writes. Why can't you afford this, in her view? If you are not to receive an education, what *are* you to do?

3. Early in the essay, Rich explains what she takes to be a "devastating weakness" of university education as it is presently structured. What is that weakness? Why does she think it is "devastating"?

4. As important as she believes women's studies to be, there is "a more essential experience" that Rich urges upon her female student audience; it is the experience of "taking responsibility toward yourselves." She develops this idea in some depth. What does she mean by it? Why does she think it is especially important for women to do this?

5. What actions are entailed in taking yourself seriously as a student?

6. What does Rich believe to be the "most affirming thing anyone can do for you"?

▼ Questions for Reflection

1. The author offers her idea of a contract between students and professor as a contrast to the mere "processing of human beings into expected roles." What do you think she means by such "processing"? What would be the characteristics of a university education that was no more than such processing? What would the students be like?

2. Rich refers to the "depersonalizing and cheapening pressures of the present-day academic scene." Judging from your own experience of a university campus, what do you think she has in mind?

3. Rich charges the academic community with "the almost total erasure of women's experience and thought from the curriculum." Does this accord with your experience?

4. What do you take to be the most important message Rich has to deliver?

5. What, in your own view, does it mean to take responsibility toward yourself? In what respects is your view similar to Rich's? How is it different from hers?

▼ Discussion

1. What in Rich's essay struck you as especially pertinent to your personal situation?

2. What is your own concept of taking responsibility toward yourself? What actions would this require in your life as a university student?

3. Rich refers to the "depersonalizing and cheapening pressures of the present-day academic scene." Judging from your own experience of a university campus, what do you think she has in mind?

4. Do you agree with Rich that actively taking control of one's education is especially difficult for women? If so, do you think her explanation for this is accurate?

▼ Writing Assignments

1. Observe your friends and the students in your classes. Present portraits of the ones who are, in your view, "claiming" their education.
2. Write on what you take to be the special difficulties for women in claiming an education.

▼ Journal Entry

1. Are you claiming your education? If so, what are the evidences of this? If not, what actions would you have to take in order to do this?

▼ Vocabulary

aspirations	dispersal	extraneous	intrinsically
dilettante	exhilarating	rife	

23

▼

Unlearning to Not Speak

Marge Piercy

Born in Detroit in 1936, Marge Piercy is a political radical, poet, and novelist. One of her avowed purposes in writing poetry is to raise the consciousness of women.

Blizzards of paper
in slow motion
sift through her.
In nightmares she suddenly recalls
a class she signed up for   5
but forgot to attend.
Now it is too late.
Now it is time for finals:
losers will be shot.
Phrases of men who lectured her   10
drift and rustle in piles:
Why don't you speak up?
Why are you shouting?
You have the wrong answer,
wrong line, wrong face.   15
They tell her she is womb-man,
babymachine, mirror image, toy,
earth mother and penis-poor,
a dish of synthetic strawberry ice cream
rapidly melting.   20
She grunts to a halt.
She must learn again to speak
starting with I
starting with We
starting as the infant does   25
with her own true hunger
and pleasure
and rage.

▼ Questions for Reflection

1. "Now it is time for finals: / losers will be shot." What is the poet trying to convey with the words "losers will be shot"? Have you had nightmares like this? Is there any reason to think women would be more likely to have such nightmares than men?

2. "Why don't you speak up? / Why are you shouting?" What does the poet convey by following the first question with the second?

3. "She must learn again to speak. / Starting with I / starting with We." What do you think she means by "starting with We"?

4. What is the point of the comparison to the infant in the last four lines? What would be examples of this way of speaking? Do you think this kind of speech is part of what Adrienne Rich (Reading 22) has in mind by "taking responsibility toward yourself," or are these very different ideas?

5. What is the poet revolting against in the poem? Why? How does she propose to resolve her frustrations?

▼ Journal Entries

1. Do you think you speak in your present college environment in the way that Piercy is urging you to speak? What evidence do you have for answering as you do?

2. Are there aspects of college or aspects of your response to college that you would like to revolt against? How would you conduct this revolt?

24

▼

Learning and Growing Up

Jacob Neusner

A professor of religious studies at Brown University, Jacob Neusner came to na-tional attention in 1981 with the publication of a scathing commencement address in which he recites a **litany** *of failures of both students and their teachers. En-couraged to expand upon his ideas in the form of cautionary advice to incoming freshmen, he wrote* How to Grade Your Professors and Other Unexpected Advice *(1984), from which two selections in this text have been drawn. In the first of these selections, Neusner discusses the relationship between university study and the young student's primary task: growing up.*

"I just can't take hold, Mom. I can't take hold of some kind of a life." That is what Biff says to his mother in Arthur Miller's play *Death of a Salesman,* and that, I believe, expresses a fundamental concern of our students. Students come to college not only to learn but also to grow up. They leave their homes, or if they continue to live there, they assert their independence in other ways. At the same time they do not take up the tasks of the workaday world. They rarely support themselves but depend in some measure upon others, whether parents or univer-sities. Students come to us, in the main, at the last stage of childhood, toward the end of adolescence, and they leave us, in the main, as mature men and women. During the four swift years between, they have to solve the last problem of their earlier life and the first of the life beyond: Who am I? During this time, they declare a **moratorium** on making firm decisions and begin a period of subdued inner searching. They play many roles in this period, experimenting with each of them in search of a place in society, a **niche**, as Erik Erikson says in *Identity: Youth and Crisis,* "which is firmly defined and yet seems to be uniquely made" for them.

The time of college education marks a way station between the complete dependence of a child and the total independence of an adult. What do people do during this interim period? They study various subjects. How does what they study relate to the process of maturing? This is a crucial question for professors. If we cannot relate the encounter with learning in college to the student's experiment in defining an identity, we ignore what is truly essential. If I can show that what we do—that is, learning a subject in a particular way—is critical to what the students want to become, mature and independent women and men, then I will realize the ideal of the college experience.

Students arrive in college thinking they know the answers to certain basic questions—What am I doing here? Why now? Why me? Then they find out they do not know the answers. They have the difficult task of shaping an adult identity. But where should they do this? Why in college in particular? Simple logic demands that if you are in college, you study subjects of higher education. But if these subjects do not relate to that other important task—growing up—then there will be tension between what the student is learning and what the student has to ac-complish in personal growth.

Since much is asked of each student, and much is expected by those who send young people to college, a student's inability to find answers to those questions

litany: an incantation
moratorium: suspension of action
niche: place where you fit perfectly

151

of purposes will lead to a sense of betrayal and shame. The students will feel they have betrayed those who helped them go to college—parents and high school teachers. They will feel ashamed of themselves. Rather than endure either of these feelings, they may retreat within, to the protected world of their peer group, avoiding a confrontation with the disturbing and distressing issues of a larger world. They will move **insensately** from classroom to dormitory, from dining hall to the movies (rarely to the library), in the company of others like themselves.

I do not exaggerate the consequences of the inability to find a bridge between learning and maturing. If anything, I understate them. Many students find exceedingly difficult the discovery of what relates their personal problems and concerns—the problems of growth and the discovery of identity—to the questions they ask themselves as university students.

It is easy to pretend the issue is an illusion. Many students are able to give a clear-cut answer to the questions, Why are you at college? What do you seek in this classroom? Those students who have (for the moment) declared themselves premedical, prelegal, or preprofessional solve the problem without ever facing it during the college years. But the solution will not serve. The problem is only postponed to a less **propitious** time. And identity is not the same thing as knowing how one plans to make a living five, ten, or twenty years from now. A preprofessional commitment in the liberal arts setting is an evasion, not an answer, to the question, Why here? Why now? Why me? These questions add up to a single one: Who am I?

Questions are addressed to their teachers as well. Why are you telling us these things? What is important for us? What is relevant to us in your lessons? If few students know the answers, still fewer professors are able to help. For between professors and students there is a conflict not only of interest but also of orientation. A teacher's work is to criticize, to rethink established knowledge. The goal is to come to a finer and more critical perception of learning and, inevitably, to a carefully **circumscribed** segment of knowledge. In part, the faculty member has to communicate what he or she is learning; that communication is central to the teacher's work within the university. But a university is what it is because men and women work through what others accept as truth; they make their own, through the power of the intellect, what others may take at face value. Unfortunately, this sometimes gives us the appearance of learning more and more about less and less.

The conflict between professor and student actually revolves around very specific issues. Secure in an identity formed through the years, the professor strives to solve an external problem, alert to his or her and to others' ignorance.

Further, the work is conducted as part of a life that includes a distinguished personal history, including relationships of love and of responsibility to a larger world. To this, students offer only a contrast. Their problems are **subjective** and are resolved as their identity becomes clear. As they struggle with their problems they are barely aware of their ignorance. Students enjoy little past and almost no personal history; most are not married and do not make a living for themselves.

What brings men and women whose problems are those of maturity together with adolescents who are not yet certain about what problems they are going to confront? Why do professors with answers seek students who are unsure of the questions?

For the student, confronting and taking seriously a person well along the path of life can stimulate a greater maturity. Certainly, meeting men and women who sincerely hold that what is important in life need bear no relationship to material comfort, who earn less than they might in other callings, who work much harder than they would in other professions and yet do not think they "work" at all—to meet such people is apt to have **salutary** benefits, to offer a vivid example of how life may be lived. For the teacher, the student's fundamental question about the worth and use of knowledge is necessary, for such questions lead back to the

insensately: without feeling
propitious: presenting favorable circumstances
circumscribed: confined
subjective: personal
salutary: wholesome

basics of a subject: and it is there that true insight is found. The student, if open to the answers to his or her questions, will **vivify** the life of the teacher.

The primary goal of the student is to reach out toward an adult identity. What does the student actually do? A student's everyday life consists of attending lectures and participating in discussions, reading books, writing papers, working in laboratories—of devoting most of the day to the disciplines of the mind. One may do these things in form, and many students do. One can go through the motions of learning; indeed one may well learn a great many things. Yet if learning is irrelevant to one's personal situation, then the forms are formalities; the center, the spirit, will be lacking. And nothing that is learned will matter.

What is the relationship between learning and maturing, between study and the formation of a strong and **autonomous** personality? Through learning—mastery of that part of human experience **accessible** in books and laboratories—we both prepare for life and engage in living. Learning is liberating, not merely by relieving us of ignorance, but by supplying us with understanding and insight, with knowledge of the reality in which, and against which, we form our sense of self. There can be no purpose in the discovery of the self without the exploration of the context in which the self takes shape. Liberal learning brings the person out of the self and leads to an encounter with other people, their yearnings and complexities.

Through the record of civilization—that is, through the part of human life preserved in books and **enshrined** in permanent sources of knowledge—we confront the collective and accumulated experience of vast numbers of people. Repeatedly in these materials, in the legal documents or in the tales for pleasure, we find a record of earlier men and women grappling with the same problems. L. Joseph Stone and Joseph Church, in *Childhood and Adolescence: A Psychology of the Growing Person,* write, "It is, after all, in literature, with its power of enlisting strong identifications, that we learn the **profoundest** lessons about human relationships and the nature of social institutions. The scientist and the philosopher have been grappling for years with exactly the cosmic problems that intrigue and frighten the adolescent." In college the student finds new avenues to explore in the search for answers and new minds struggling with the same issues.

Behind all that we do as students and scholars are the three great components of reality: humanity, society, and nature. These are the center of our curriculum in the humanities, social sciences, and natural sciences. For all our impersonal devotion to our several subjects, good teachers do not forget the central issue of study: the understanding of humankind, of the complex structures formed by men and women, and of the natural setting of our brief life together on earth.

I cannot think of a more promising opportunity than that presented by this curious conflict between the subjectivity of the student and the objectivity of the teacher, between the excessive self-obsession of the young and the equally excessive submergence of self by the mature person. Neither is wholly true; each must correct the other. The teacher must draw the student out of his or her personal preoccupation in part by demonstrating the shared nature of that experience among many men and women, alive and dead; but in greater part by introducing concerns and questions, interests and commitments, currently lacking yet important and relevant to self-identification.

Let us look specifically at what this relationship between teacher and student can mean. Let us consider as an example the subject I teach, which is the history of Judaism, an old and honored religious tradition. I teach both Christian and Jewish students. The Christian students want to know about that old religion, some because of their correct belief that Christianity emerged from Judaism, many simply because it is an interesting religion. The Jewish students have a different motive. They are part of a minority, and they wonder why they should not join the majority. Their religious tradition makes demands on them, makes them different, limits their choice, for instance, of a marriage partner and restricts their diet. The Jewish stu-

vivify: animate
autonomous: self-directed
accessible: easily obtained
enshrined: preserved as sacred
profoundest: deepest

dents want to know why they should be Jewish. When they come to me, they perceive that I teach not *about Judaism* but Judaism, and conflict arises. They want to be told why they should be Jewish. I want to tell them what makes Judaism a complex and interesting religion, within the context of a larger study of religion. They have a deeply personal problem to work out, and I have a profoundly objective inquiry to carry on. This is a conflict of interests, a conflict between my interests and those of my students. The students introduce issues of self-identification. They rightly insist that I teach, not impersonally, but personally to Peter and Jennifer and Steve, who are deeply concerned. And they remind me that this "interesting thing" is a religion that real people live by and die for. And yet, if students only want to know what is relevant to themselves, it is hard to see what role learning and teaching can play in their growth. We are intellectuals. We insist upon analysis and interpretation, not solely upon feeling and commitment.

In this conflict of interests is the resolution. The student must draw the teacher back from the pretense of objectivity and the claim to indifference to the human meaning of his or her learning. The student serves the teacher well by asking, What does this mean to me? or What ought this to mean? And in attempting to answer, despite the frailty and impermanence of the answer, the teacher will serve the student too.

At the very center of things is this: The scholar and the adolescent have in common the capacity to look with fresh eyes on the stale world. The student is full of idealism, can see the future ahead, is not tired or jaded, and has high hopes for himself or herself and for the world. Professors also take a fresh look at old perceptions, an idealism that says that things not of this world are important. We take on the task of rethinking what everyone takes for granted, just as the student does.

We ask ourselves the most fundamental questions about the part of the world or of human experience that forms our study, just as the student asks basic questions about world, experience, and self. We too have high hopes, both for learning and for the people who learn what we think through. For the scholar is loyal to a vision, and youth is the time of vision and dreaming. And the scholar is, in the nature of things, granted the blessing of a continuing encounter with youth. No profession enjoys a greater privilege than ours, for our work is with and for students, who are our future.

The themes of our curriculum must pertain to the issues of the student's unfolding consciousness. But even more; the very method and substance of our work, the persistent, **tenacious** asking of basic questions, correspond in a close and direct way to the very substance and method of the student's task. The scholar's mode of thought is congruent with the adolescent's personal search. The search for relevance to one's own concerns, pursued self-consciously with a measure of restraint, must lead to the scholar's mode of study.

tenacious: persistent

▼ Questions to Focus Reading

1. In his second paragraph, Neusner defines "the ideal of the college experience." How does he characterize this ideal?

2. Why does Neusner think it is so important that students see the relation between what they are learning in college and their own maturation?

3. "But a university is what it is because men and women work through what others accept as truth; they make their own, through the power of the intellect, what others may take at face value." In this sentence Neusner is calling attention to a key defining characteristic of a university. What do you think he has in mind?

4. Whereas "the professor strives to solve an external problem," the students' problems are "subjective." What does Neusner mean?

5. What can the student gain from the professor? What can the professor gain from the student? What are Neusner's answers to these questions?

6. What is the relation between liberal education and the discovery of the self, according to Neusner?

7. Neusner develops the idea that professor and student correct each other's "excesses." In what way? Explain how the example of his own course in the history of Judaism illustrates his point.

8. Both professor and student see the world with fresh eyes, says Neusner. In what sense(s)?

9. There is an intimate connection, Neusner writes in his last paragraph, between the scholar's work and the student's primary task: growing up. What connection does Neusner have in mind?

▼ Questions for Reflection

1. "Identity is not the same thing as knowing how one plans to make a living five, ten, or twenty years from now." Why not? What is involved in making an identity?

2. "But a university is what it is because men and women work through what others accept as truth; they make their own, through the power of the intellect, what others may take at face value." Think of examples of this process in your classes this semester.

3. In what ways do you expect your university education to help you shape your identity?

▼ Discussion

1. "Identity is not the same thing as knowing how one plans to make a living five, ten, or twenty years from now." Why not? What is involved in making an identity?

2. "But a university is what it is because men and women work through what others accept as truth; they make their own, through the power of the intellect, what others may take at face value." Think of examples of this process in your classes this semester.

3. In what ways do you expect your university education to help you shape your identity?

4. What, in Neusner's view, does the student gain from his or her involvement with professors? What does the professor gain from his or her involvement with students? Does your experience this semester seem to bear out Neusner's views?

5. Neusner believes that the student and the professor correct each other's excesses. What excesses does he have in mind?

▼ Writing Assignments

1. Write an essay about what it means to form an identity and how you expect your college education to help you do this.

2. Write an essay in which you set forth Neusner's ideas about what the student gains from the professor and what the professor gains from the student. Based on your experience this semester, would you want to amend his views?

▼ Journal Entry

1. "There can be no purpose in the discovery of the self without the exploration of the context in which the self takes shape." Liberal learning, Neusner tells us, is the study of that context. What have you been learning

155

this semester that is giving you insight into yourself and into the context for this self-discovery?

▼ Vocabulary

accessible	insensately	profoundest	tenacious
autonomous	litany	propitious	vivify
circumscribed	moratorium	salutary	
enshrined	niche	subjective	

25

▼

Why I Teach

Richard Feynman

Richard Feynman (FINE-man) was a renowned and deeply respected professor of theoretical physics at Caltech from 1951 to his death in 1988. A co-winner of the Nobel Prize for physics in 1965, he wrote two best-selling personal memoirs, from one of which this excerpt has been drawn.

I don't believe I can really do without teaching. The reason is, I have to have something so that when I don't have any ideas and I'm not getting anywhere I can say to myself, "At least I'm living; at least I'm *doing* something; I'm making *some* contribution"—it's just psychological.

When I was at Princeton in the 1940s I could see what happened to those great minds at the Institute for Advanced Study, who had been specially selected for their tremendous brains and were now given this opportunity to sit in this lovely house by the woods there, with no classes to teach, with no obligations whatsoever. These poor bastards could now sit and think clearly all by themselves, OK? So they don't get an idea for a while: They have every opportunity to do something, and they're not getting any ideas. I believe that in a situation like this a kind of guilt or depression worms inside of you, and you begin to worry about not getting any ideas. And nothing happens. Still no ideas come.

Nothing happens because there's not enough *real* activity and challenge: You're not in contact with the experimental guys. You don't have to think how to answer questions from the students. Nothing!

In any thinking process there are moments when everything is going good and you've got wonderful ideas. Teaching is an interruption, and so it's the greatest pain in the neck in the world. And then there are the *longer* periods of time when not much is coming to you. You're not getting any ideas, and if you're doing nothing at all, it drives you nuts! You can't even say "I'm teaching my class."

If you're teaching a class, you can think about the elementary things that you know very well. These things are kind of fun and delightful. It doesn't do any harm to think them over again. Is there a better way to present them? Are there any new problems associated with them? Are there any new thoughts you can make about them? The elementary things are *easy* to think about; if you can't think of a new thought, no harm done; what you thought about it before is good enough for the class. If you *do* think of something new, you're rather pleased that you have a new way of looking at it.

The questions of the students are often the source of new research. They often ask profound questions that I've thought about at times and then given up on, so to speak, for a while. It wouldn't do me any harm to think about them again and see if I can go any further now. The students may not be able to see the thing I want to answer, or the subtleties I want to think about, but they *remind* me of a problem by asking questions in the neighborhood of that problem. It's not so easy to remind *yourself of* these things.

So I find that teaching and the students keep life going, and I would *never* accept any position in which somebody has invented a happy situation for me where I don't have to teach. Never.

▼ **Questions for Reflection**

1. As a Nobel Prize–winning physicist, Richard Feynman could specify the terms of his university appointments. He could have done pure research. But for the several reasons he gives here, he always insisted that teaching be a part of his job. Why?

2. Given what you know of your professors this semester, why do you think they teach?

3. Have you observed any instances in your classes so far where your professor's thinking seemed to be advanced by his or her students? If so, what were those instances?

26

▼

Migrations of the Heart

Marita Golden

Novelist and journalist Marita Golden reminisces here about the upheavals in her identity as she entered college.

When the knowledge came, its taste was sweet, bitter, eye-opening. A drug pulsing hot lead fire and ice through our veins. As clenched fists became the stars giving light to our night, the sound of "brother," "sister," our anthem, tumbled through full, determined lips. Turned the curse into a sacrament. Brow-beating, insistent, unforgiving, we took the offensive and for a moment turned white hatred into fear that drained blood from the face.

The tremors from the riots that convulsed the city had shuddered outward, piercing the solid certainty of the surrounding white world with bulging veins of doubt. Washington's private colleges hastily inaugurated scholarship programs for black high school students. A **salve** that absorbed the sting of the burn but left the wound startlingly clear.

I entered American University [A.U.] in the fall of 1968 as a Frederick Douglass Scholarship student, one of twenty-five from the inner city. The school sat nestled, almost hidden, in the comfortable upper reaches of northwest Washington, surrounded by embassies, cathedrals and the manicured, sprawling lawns of the city's upper class. To enter this world I caught the bus downtown and boarded it with black women domestic workers who rode to the end of the line to clean house for young and middle-aged white matrons. They gazed proudly at me, nodding at the books in my lap, slapping me on the back with a smile. In answer to the concern arching my brow, they told me with pursed, silent lips, "It's all right. It really is. I'd a done something else if I could've. Maybe been a teacher or something like that. But that was so long ago it don't even matter no more. So now you do it for me. But mostly do it for you." I accepted their encouragement and hated America for never allowing them to be selfish or greedy, to feel the steel-hard bite of ambition that could snatch their sleep at night or straighten their spines into a dare. They had **parlayed** their anger, brilliantly shaped it into a soft armor of survival. . . .

But my teachers, I almost forgave them for being white. I learned from all of them. The best ones combined intelligence with wit and polished it to gleaming with caring and concern. I was curious, and impatient with dullness and stupidity, so the reading lists that brought tears of frustration to the eyes of some comforted me. For it was books that, one **luminous** summer I shall always remember, made me want to be Harriet Tubman instead of Tuesday Weld.

The summer before entering American University I had joined the fold of a group of Howard University students. Their uniforms were **dashikis** and blue jeans, and wildly unkempt, brazen Afros. Charter members of SNCC [Student Nonviolent Coordinating Committee], they had conceived and carried out the week-long shutdown of Howard that spring. With their anger turned into calloused hands, they brusquely stripped the lady of her white gloves and formal speech. Teeth now cut, they took on the South, where they registered black voters. One of them slapped a white sheriff and lived to weave that act into the epic poem he saw his life to be.

salve: a medicinal ointment for relieving wounds

parlayed: transformed into something of much greater value

luminous: enlightening

dashikis: brightly colored tunics

159

I went to their parties, held in crumbling, once glorious apartments that surrounded the Howard campus. The infrared darkness hid the copies of *Liberator, Soulbrook,* and *Black World* stacked in piles underfoot. Malcolm X's eyes were spears aimed at us from posters peeling from the wall. When the throb of Sly's *Stand!* or James Brown's "Say It Loud (I'm Black and I'm Proud)" was only a memory frosting the air, we formed a circle and snake danced around the room, hands clapping, feet stomping, singing, "Beep Beep Bang Bang Umgawah Black Power." They taught me the new language, how to roll the words on my tongue. How to drain meanings from the sound of each syllable that no one would ever forget. Power. Revolution. We were prepared for war but would witness only skirmishes that left us bloodied nevertheless.

I fell in love with one of them. He was a twenty-two-year-old guerrilla/singer/songwriter/black poet/revolutionary. Beneath the dingy, wrinkled sheets of his hardly-ever-slept-in bed, tongue sticky wet promising in my ear, he called me his African queen. He bought a .22 caliber handgun the day he discovered his phone was tapped and handled it like a water pistol. Quieting my demands for time with him, he reminded me that dates were what white girls wanted and, anyway, there was no place for socializing in the midst of a revolution.

"Is there a place for love?" I asked, watching him hurriedly pull on his shorts, wondering why his body turned corpse cold when I cradled him in the moments after his frantic release.

"Only of black people as a whole. Not as individuals," he answered in the voice a man uses with a woman he secretly hates. Then he smiled sadly, cupping my chin as though the realization awakened an ache within him. At eighteen I could not suspect how **wantonly** cruel his answer was. So I reached onto the platter for it. Swallowed it whole without tasting. It landed, heavy and rebellious, in the pit of my stomach.

Since there would be no love in our revolution, I turned to hate. It was easy enough to do. The Drum and Spear Bookstore was opened that summer by several members of the group. Its shelves stocked a whole range of books on black and African studies, and they finished the stories my father had begun. I learned of slave revolts, W. E. B. DuBois, black inventors, Carter G. Woodson, Reconstruction, Jean Toomer, Timbuktu, the **precarious** existence of freed slaves, Duke Ellington, Nat Turner, Bessie Smith. Page after page put flesh and blood on the bones of the past my father had kindled for me in spurts, which was our own carefully guarded secret. This was all mine. This wealth. This panorama of genius and endurance. And *they* had kept it from me. Now I knew why. **Invincibility** swelled my mind into a hard, gleaming muscle. And for an uneasy, tortured time I surrendered to hate. Because of two thousand lynchings and four little girls bombed in a Birmingham church. Because they told me I was a slave but never said that once I'd been a king. I became a true believer. I wrote a biweekly column for the *Eagle,* the campus newspaper, in which I spread the gospel of black consciousness, sat on a committee to implement a black studies program at A.U., tutored black high school students and wrote bristling black poetry that sizzled on the page. I was simultaneously driven and inspired. Dizzy with a confidence I'd grown up believing brown girls never knew.

And we never suffered a moment of doubt, **bludgeoning** critics into silence with our smug lack of humility. We knew, for example, that what's *on* your head is as important as what's *in* it.

The natural was sprouting everywhere—dark sunflowers filling a vacant field. No one could see my anger. But they could see my hair. See that I was no longer a Negro girl. That I had chosen to become a black woman.

My mother, nursed in the folds of a town that once christened its black babies Lee, after Robert E., and Jackson, after Stonewall, raised me on a dangerous generation's old belief. Because of my dark brown complexion, she warned me against

wantonly: unjustifiably or maliciously

precarious: uncertain; insecure

invincibility: the condition of being unconquerable

bludgeoning: beating

wearing browns or yellows and reds, assuring me they would turn on me like an ugly secret revealed. And every summer I was admonished not to play in the sun, "'cause you gonna have to get a light husband anyway, for the sake of your children."

My mother would never acknowledge or even suspect her self-denial. It gripped her all the tighter for the carelessness of her vision. Ground into my pores, this was the same skin through which I breathed. The eye through which I saw myself.

Up until I was eighteen, however, every other Saturday I had entered a state of grace. Holding down a rugged corner of 14th and T, on a block given over to funeral parlors, ragged, **unpretentious** barber shops and fried chicken carry-outs, the La Femme Beauty Salon was part haven, part refuge for the women who packed its small rooms on Saturday mornings. Over the click of steaming curlers, they testified, embellishing the fabric of their lives, stretching it into a more agreeable form and shape. When it was full, the shop sheltered, holding the smoky odor of straightening combs thrust into jars of grease and applied with unflinching belief to coarse hair. Special attention was paid to "the kitchen," the hairline at the nape of the neck that harbored the most stubborn patches of hair curled into tiny balls of opposition. Pushing my ear back, the beautician would warn, "Now you gonna have to hold still 'cause I can't be responsible for what this hot comb might do."

Between customers, twirling in her chair, white-stockinged legs crossed, my beautician lamented to the hairdresser in the next stall, "I sure hope that Gloria Johnson don't come in here asking for me today. I swear 'fore God her hair is this long." She snapped her fingers to indicate the length. Contempt riding her words, she lit a cigarette and finished, "Barely enough to wash, let alone press and curl."

Despite those years—perhaps because of them—the day I looked in the mirror at my natural was the first day I ever liked what I saw. "There is everything," I thought. Nappy, defiant, my hair was a small cap tapering around my head. Without apology, my nose claimed the center of my face. Because of the bangs I'd always worn, I'd never noticed my brows, thick and velvety. My eyes were small diamonds. Perfectly cut. This was not the face I had always known. It was the face I refused to believe I had.

I did not **sojourn** alone. My best friend, Wanda, was there. Two dark girls seeing themselves in the other. Don't explain. Had always been there. Waiting. Even before our minds wove together, strong-fingered hands clasped. Amidst the intellectual din, the emotional clutter ringing in the halls of Western High School, we had found one another. Imagination bound us stronger than love. Within its limitless borders we launched ships and love affairs, discovered lost worlds, made buildings and babies, found husbands, wrote letters and Broadway plays. We made ourselves up every day. And because we dreamed of everything, we vowed to rule no possibility out of our lives.

In high school we read Sartre. In college we tossed him aside and reached for Mao and Che Guevara. Summer afternoons were spent stretched on her bed reading Don Lee and Gwendolyn Brooks. Together. Silent. We could read each other's minds. Spellbound listening to Coltrane's "My Favorite Things" over and over, each time a sacrament. Sweating, groaning, we raised the banner of blackness and, after the staff was firmly planted, became part of the women we would always be. And uh-huh, she would be an actress. I, a writer. A hundred loves, it seemed, unreturned, misunderstood.

Me: Jive nigguhs, all they do is rap. What's wrong with the brothers?

Wanda: Askin, "Sistuh, can you *love* a black man?"

unpretentious: modest
sojourn: travel

161

Me: Hey, brother, can you *understand* a black woman?

Us: Laughter so close to tears it hurt.

I lay in the debris of a ruined love affair. Her voice, indignant, terrified in the face of my passion, my tears, charged, "Marita, you give too much."

"And you don't give at all," I slap back, hard. "You take them into your *bed* but never into your *heart.*" She, the small bird chirping, afraid no one listens. Cautious. Fevered. The squirrel storing nuts of doubt. Love floods the rooms of her mind and she fills buckets with it, tossing the treasure out open windows. I am a stranger to half measures. With life I am on the attack, restlessly ferreting out each pleasure, foraging for answers, wringing from it even the pain. I ransack life, hunt it down. I am the hungry peasants storming the palace gates. I will have my share. No matter how it tastes.

*   *   *

My parents watched my transformation, stung by its ferocity and the fierceness of my allegiance to gods they had never known. My mother retreated into befuddled silence, watching me from the corner of her eyes, as though I were a stranger following her down a dark alley. My father said nothing for many months. Then, one afternoon, he waylaid me. He had stalked my moves, waited for my confidence to blossom before breaking it at the root. "I don't like what I see when I look at you now." His face was granite and my uneasy smile chipped away not one particle.
"What's wrong?"
"I want you to take off that makeup. I hate that lipstick, the mascara." His lips curled in disgust as he threw the words like sharpened darts.
"But, Daddy, there's nothing wrong—"
"And I want you to get rid of that natural."
"But why? You always taught me to be proud."
"Sure, I taught you to be proud. But you're still my little girl. My daughter." He said the words almost kindly, asserting his still pivotal role in a life I was wrestling out of his hands. "You're not a woman yet, Marita. You have to do what I say."

His voice was stretched taut with a threat I was afraid to name. I had never even received a spanking from my father. Yet now, as I sat facing him in the front seat of his taxi, my heart was cringing, my hand reaching for the door. I tried to imagine what he would do if I refused. But the bitterness in his eyes, which accused me of betrayal because my lurching journey into womanhood, left no room for denial. He searched my face for assent, for a request for forgiveness. I clenched my teeth and turned away from him, the window witnessing the tears sliding down my cheeks in thin ribbons that he could not see.

I obeyed him and the next day walked into the Soul Corner of A.U.'s cafeteria to stares and questions that peeled the skin from my cheeks. A few months later I got a work-study job at school. No longer financially dependent on my father, I willfully disobeyed him and Afroed my hair once again. I was my own woman, I reasoned, forgetting, with a carelessness for which I would later pay, that I would always be his child.

▼ Questions to Focus Reading

1. The young Marita Golden "hated America" for never allowing black female domestic workers with whom she rode the bus "to be selfish or greedy." What do you think she means by this?
2. One "luminous summer," certain books made her "want to be Harriet Tubman instead of Tuesday Weld." Who were Harriet Tubman and Tuesday Weld? What is the significance of this shift for Golden?
3. The summer before she entered American University, Golden devoted herself to hatred, and this, she writes, was "easy enough to do." Why did she do this? What made it so easy?
4. Why does she dwell on the La Femme Beauty Salon? What does this description help us to understand?
5. She clarifies her understanding of herself by contrasting herself with her best friend, Wanda. What does she learn?
6. How would you explain her father's strong reaction to her new identity?

▼ Questions for Reflection

1. The summer before she entered college was a "luminous" one for Marita Golden. What was illuminated for her?
2. Her impatience "with dullness and stupidity" and her experience of the impact of books on her identity made her greet her professors' reading lists with excited anticipation. Have your values or goals or conception of yourself been affected by books? If so, what books? How?
3. Golden gives us a clear picture of the conception of blackness she was taught, the conception she rebelled against in her college years. Is there some aspect of your identity that you view radically differently from the way it is viewed in your community or in your family?

▼ Discussion

1. Have you had any experiences in college so far in which you've been able to observe personal development or growth? Do any of these involve your roommate? If so, what have these experiences been? What personal growth have you observed in them?

▼ Writing Assignments

1. The beauty parlor conveyed important messages to the young Marita that strongly affected her conception of herself, her values, and her goals. If there is some place in your background, some analogous locus of ritual, that served a similar role in the shaping of yourself, describe that place, trying to capture the feeling of the place and the authentic voices of the people involved.
2. Like Marita Golden, college students typically learn a great deal about themselves in their interaction with close friends and roommates. Describe an incident or conversation involving your roommate this semester that has taught you something important about yourself.
3. Golden describes her father's intense anger at her new identity. Does this scene bring back a similar experience in your recent life? If so, describe a scene from your life that points up a parent's difficulty in accepting some aspect of your changing identity.

▼ Journal Entries

1. Is anything in your reading this semester changing the way you see your-self or the way you want to be? If so, explain.
2. Marita Golden gives us a snippet of conversation between herself and her best friend, Wanda, to help capture the quality of their relationship. Write out a typical piece of dialogue between yourself and a close friend in an attempt to capture the quality of that friendship.

▼ Vocabulary

bludgeoning	luminous	salve	wantonly
dashikis	parlayed	sojourn	
invincibility	precarious	unpretentious	

27

▼

Grading Your Professors

Jacob Neusner

In the second of our two selections from Jacob Neusner's How to Grade Your Professors and Other Unexpected Advice, *the Brown University professor describes the attributes of the A, B, and C professor.*

Since professors stand at the center of the student's encounter with college learning, students ought to ask what marks a good professor, what indicates a bad one. The one who sets high standards and persists in demanding that students try to meet them provides the right experiences. The professor who gives praise cheaply or who pretends to a relationship that does not and cannot exist teaches the wrong lessons. True, the demanding and the critical teacher does not trade in the currency students possess, which is their power to praise or reject teachers. The demanding professor knows that students will stumble. But the ones who pick themselves up and try again—whether in politics or music or art or sport—have learned a lesson that will save them for a lifetime: A single failure is not the measure of any person, and success comes hard. A **banal** truth, but a truth all the same.

The only teacher who taught me something beyond information, who gave me something to guide my life, was the only teacher who read my work carefully and criticized it in detail. To that point everyone had given me A's. After that I learned to criticize myself and not to believe in the A's. The teacher who read my writing and corrected not so much the phrasing as the mode of thought—line by line, paragraph by paragraph, beginning to end—and who composed paragraphs as models for what I should be saying is the sole true teacher I ever had. But I did not need more than one, and neither do you.

I do not mean to suggest that for each one of us there is one perfect teacher who changes our lives and is the only teacher we need. We must learn from many teachers as we grow up and grow old; and we must learn to recognize the good ones. The impressive teacher of one's youth may want to continue to dominate—as teachers do—and may not want to let go. The great teacher is the one who wants to become obsolete in the life of the student. The good teacher is the one who teaches lessons and moves on, celebrating the student's growth. The Talmud relates the story of a disciple in an academy who won an argument over the position held by God in the academy on high. The question is asked, "What happened in heaven that day?" The answer: "God clapped hands in joy, saying, 'My children have **vanquished** me, my children have vanquished me.' " That is a model for the teacher—to enjoy losing an argument to a student, to recognize his or her contribution, to let the student surpass the teacher.

In the encounter with the teacher who takes you seriously, you learn to take yourself seriously. In the eyes of the one who sees what you can accomplish, you gain a vision of yourself as more than you thought you were. The ideal professor is the one who inspires you to dream of what you can be, to try for more than you ever have accomplished before. Everyone who succeeds in life can point to such a teacher, whether in the classroom or on the sports field. It may be a parent, a coach, employer, grade school or high school or art or music teacher. It is always the one who cared enough to criticize, and stayed around to praise.

banal: unoriginal
vanquished: overcome; defeated

But what about college professors? To define an ideal for their work, let me offer guidelines on how to treat professors the way we treat students: to give grades.

Professors grade students' work. The conscientious ones spend time reading and thinking about student papers, inscribing their comments and even discussing with students the strengths and weaknesses of their work. But no professor spends as much time on grading students' work as students spend on grading their professors as teachers and as people. For from the beginning of a course ("Shall I register?") through the middle ("It's boring . . . shall I stick it out?") to the very end ("This was a waste of time"), the students invest time and intellectual energy in deciding what they think, both about how the subject is studied and about the person who presents it. Since effective teaching requires capturing the students' imagination, and since sharp edges and colorful ways excite imagination, the professor who is a "character" is apt, whether liked or disliked, to make a profound impression and perhaps also to leave a mark on the students' minds. The drab professors, not gossiped about and not remembered except for what they taught, may find that even what they taught is forgotten. People in advertising and public relations, politics and merchandising, know that. A generation raised on television expects to be manipulated and entertained.

Yet the emphasis on striking characteristics is irrelevant. Many students have no more sophistication in evaluating professors than they do in evaluating deodorants. This should not be surprising, since they approach them both in the same manner. The one who is "new, different, improved," whether a professor or a bar of soap, wins attention. In this context people have no way of determining good from bad. I once asked an airline pilot, "What is the difference between a good landing and a bad one?" He replied, "A good landing is any landing you can pick yourself up and walk away from." To this pilot, the landing is judged solely by its ultimate goal—safely delivering the plane's passengers. Can we tell when a teacher has safely delivered the student for the next stage of the journey? Can we define the differences between a good teacher and a bad one?

Students have their own definitions of *good* and *bad,* and professors generally have a notion of the meaning of students' grades. Let us consider how students evaluate their teachers, examining in turn the A, B, and C of professors. We will begin at the bottom of the scale and work our way up. Let us at the same time consider what kind of student seeks which grade.

Grade C Professors

The first type is the C professor. This is the professor who registers minimum expectations and adheres to the warm-body theory of grading. If a warm body fills a seat regularly and exhibits vital signs, such as breathing at regular intervals, occasionally reading, and turning in some legible writing on paper, then cosmic justice demands, and the professor must supply, the grade of C or *Satisfactory*. The effort needed to achieve F or *No Credit* is considerably greater. One must do no reading, attend few class sessions, and appear to the world to be something very like a corpse.

The professor who, by the present criteria, earns a C respects the students' rights and gives them their money's worth. He or she sells them a used car, so to speak, that they at least can drive off the lot. At the very least the professor does the following:

1. Attends all class sessions, reaches class on time and ends class at the scheduled hour.

166

2. Prepares a syllabus for the course and either follows it or revises it, so that students always know what topic is under (even totally confused) discussion.

3. Announces and observes scheduled office hours, so that students have access to the professor without **groveling** or special pleading, heroic efforts at bird-dogging, or mounting week-long treasure hunts.

4. Makes certain that books assigned for a course are on reserve in the library and sees to it that the bookstore has ample time in which to order enough copies of the textbooks and **ancillary** reading for a course.

5. Comes to class with a clear educational plan, a well-prepared presentation, a concrete and specific intellectual agenda.

6. Reads examinations with the care invested in them (certainly no more, but also no less) and supplies **intelligible** grades and at least minimal comments; or keeps office hours for the discussion of the substance of the examination (but not the grade); and supplies course performance reports—all these as duty, not acts of grace.

These things constitute student rights. No student has to thank a professor for doing what he or she is paid to do, and these six items, at a minimum, are the prerequisites of professional behavior. They are matters of form, to be sure, but the grade C is deemed by (some) students to be a matter of good form alone; the warm-body theory of this grade applies to professors and students alike.

"Tell me my duty and I shall do it" are the words of the minimally prepared. Just as students of mediocre quality want to know the requirements and assume that if they meet them, they have fulfilled their whole obligation to the subject, so mediocre professors do what they are supposed to do. The subject is in hand; there are no problems. The C professor need not be entirely bored with the subject, but he or she is not apt to be deeply engaged by it.

Grade C professors may be entertaining, warm, loving. Indeed, many of them must succeed on the basis of personality, because all they have to offer is the studied technology of attractive personalities. They may achieve huge followings among the students, keep students at the edge of their seats with jokes and **banter**, badger students to retain their interest, but in the end what they have sold, conveyed, or imparted to the students' minds is themselves, not their mode of thinking or analyzing. Why? Because C professors do not think much; they rely on the analysis of others.

Above all, the grade C professor has made no effort to take over and reshape the subject. This person is satisfied with the mere repetition, accurate and competent repetition to be sure, of what others have discovered and declared to be true. If this sort of professor sparks any vitality and interest in students, then he or she will remind students of their better high school teachers, the people who, at the very least, knew what they were talking about and wanted the students to know. At the end of a course, students should ask themselves, Have I learned facts, or have I grasped how the subject works, its inner dynamic, its logic and structure? If at the end students know merely one fact after another, students should be grateful—at least they have learned that much—but award the professor a polite C. For the professor has done little more than what is necessary.

Grade B Professors

A course constitutes a large and detailed statement on the nature of a small part of a larger subject, a practical judgment upon a particular field of study and how it is to be organized and interpreted. The grade of B is accorded to the student who has mastered the basic and fundamental modes of thought about, and facts contained within, the subject of a course.

groveling: begging
ancillary: auxiliary
intelligible: understandable
banter: good-humored ridicule

The grade B professor is one who can present **coherently** the larger theory and logic of the subject, who will do more than is required to convey his or her ideas to the students, and who will sincerely hope he or she is inspiring the minds of the students. B professors, as they continue to grow as scholars, are not very different from A professors; they might be described as teachers striving to become A professors. But they are definitely very different from C professors. Let us, then, move on to consider A professors, keeping in mind that B professors will probably become A professors.

Grade A Professors

Grade A professors are the scholar-teachers, a university's prized treasures among a faculty full of **intangible** riches. America has many faculties of excellence, groups of men and women who with exceptional intelligence take over a subject and make it their own, reshape it and hand it on, wholly changed but essentially **unimpaired** in tradition, to another generation.

The grade of A goes to student work that attends in some interesting way and with utmost seriousness to the center and whole of the subject of the course. Notice, I did not say that an A goes to the student who says something new and original. That is too much to hope, especially in studying a subject that for hundreds or thousands of years has appeared to the best minds as an intricate and difficult problem.

The grade A professors may have odd ideas about subjects, but they are asking old-new questions, seeking fresh insight, trying to enter into the way in which the subject works, to uncover its logic and inner structure. What makes an effective high school teacher is confidence, even **glibness**. What makes an effective university teacher is doubt and **dismay**. The scholarly mind is marked by self-criticism and thirsty search; it is guided by an awareness of its own limitations and those of knowledge. The scholar-teacher, of whatever subject or discipline, teaches one thing: Knowledge is not sure but uncertain, scholarship is search, and to teach is to impart the lessons of doubt. What is taught is what we do not know.

On whom do you bestow a grade A? It is given to the professor who, stumbling and falling, yet again rising up and walking on, seeks both knowledge and the meaning of knowledge. It is to the one who always asks, Why am I telling you these things? Why should you know them? It is to the professor who demands ultimate seriousness for his or her subject because the subject must be known, who not only teaches but professes, stands for, represents, the thing taught. The grade A professor lives for the subject, needs to tell you about it, wants to share it. The Nobel Prize scientist who so loved biology that she gave her life to it even without encouragement and recognition for a half a century of work, the literary critic who thinks getting inside a poem is entering Paradise, the historian who assumes the human issues of the thirteenth century live today—these exemplify the ones who are ultimately serious about a subject.

One who has made this commitment to a field of scholarship can be readily identified. This is the one full of concern, the one who commits upon the facts the act of **advocacy**, who deems compelling what others find merely interesting. The scholar-teacher is such because he or she conveys the self-evident, the obvious fact that facts bear meaning, constituting a whole that transcends the sum of the parts. True, to the world this sense of ultimate engagement with what is merely interesting or useful information marks the professor as **demented**, as are all those who march to a different drummer. What I mean to say is simple. Anybody who cares so much about what to the rest of the world is so little must be a bit **daft**. Why should such things matter so much—why, above all, things of the mind or the soul or the heart, things of nature and mathematics, things of structure and weight and stress, things of technology and science, society and mind? Professors

coherently: clearly; in a logically connected way

intangible: not material; elusive of grasp

unimpaired: not worsened or weakened

glibness: superficial fluency

dismay: agitation

advocacy: the act of supporting or pleading for a cause

demented: insane

daft: crazy

168

often remember lonely childhoods (for my part, I don't). As adults, too, professors have to spend long hours by themselves in their offices, reading books, or in their laboratories or at their computers, or just thinking all by themselves. That is not ordinary and commonplace behavior. This is what it means to march to a different drummer. A student earns an A when he or she has mastered the larger theory of the course, entered into its logic and meaning, discovered a different way of seeing. Like a professor, the student who through accurate facts and careful, critical thought seeks meaning, the core and center of the subject, earns the grade A.

Yet matters cannot be left here. I do not mean to promote advocacy for its own sake. Students have rights too, and one of these is the right to be left alone, to grow and mature in their own distinctive ways. They have the right to seek their way, just as we professors find ours. The **imperial** intellect, the one that cannot allow **autonomy**, is a missionary, not a teacher. Many compare the imperial teacher with the A professor, but if you look closely at their different ways of teaching, you will see that this is an error. The teacher leads, says, "Follow me," without looking backward. The missionary pushes, imposes self upon another autonomous self. This is the opposite of teaching, and bears no relevance to learning or to scholarship. The teacher persuades; the missionary preaches. The teacher argues; the missionary shouts others to silence. The teacher wants the student to discover; the missionary decides what the student must discover. The teacher enters class with fear and trembling, not knowing where the discussion will lead. The missionary knows at the start of a class exactly what the student must cover by the end of the class.

Grade A professors teach, never indoctrinate. They educate rather than train. There is a fine line to be drawn, an invisible boundary, between great teaching and **self-aggrandizing** indoctrination.

Knowledge and even understanding do not bring salvation and therefore do not have to be, and should not be, forced upon another. And this brings me back to the earlier emphasis upon scholarship as the recognition of ignorance, the awareness not of what we know but of how we know and of what we do not know. The true scholar, who also is the true teacher, is drawn by self-criticism, compelled by doubting, skeptical curiosity, knows the limits of knowing. He or she cannot be confused with the imperial, the arrogant, and the **proselytizing**. By definition, we stand for humility before the unknown. A good professor wants to answer the question, Why am I telling you these things? A good student wants to answer the question, Why am I taking these courses? What do I hope to get out of them? Why are they important to me? I have not put before you any unattainable ideals in these questions. Some of us realize them every day, and nearly all of us realize them on some days. Just as students' transcripts rarely present only A's or *No Credits,* so professors rarely succeed all of the time. No one bears the indelible grade of A.

imperial: characteristic of an emperor

autonomy: self-direction

self-aggrandizing: self-serving; tending to increase one's power or heighten one's stature

proselytizing: converting

▼ Questions to Focus Reading

1. Why, in Neusner's view, was the teacher he describes in his second paragraph the "sole true teacher (he) ever had"?
2. In his third paragraph (page 165), Neusner pinpoints one quality of "the great teacher." What is that quality?
3. In the fourth paragraph (page 165), Neusner points out another characteristic of the teacher who makes a difference. What is that characteristic?
4. Many of the grade C professors, Neusner writes, must succeed on the basis of personality, "because all they have to offer is the studied technology of attractive personalities." What do you think he means by this phrase?
5. What, in Neusner's view, is the key trait of the grade C professor?
6. How does Neusner characterize the grade B professor?

7. What is the mark of the grade A student, in Neusner's view?

8. What are the characteristics of the grade A professor according to Neusner?

9. "The scholar-teacher is such because he or she conveys the self-evident, the obvious fact that facts bear meaning, constituting a whole that transcends the sum of the parts." What do you think this sentence means?

10. The grade A professor "marches to a different drummer." In what sense?

11. Contrast the "imperial teacher" or "missionary" with Neusner's ideal teacher.

▼ Questions for Reflection

1. What are Neusner's criteria for a grade A professor? How are these different from the criteria you would have used to grade your high school teachers?

2. "What makes an effective high school teacher is confidence, even glibness. What makes an effective university teacher is doubt and dismay." What does Neusner mean here? Given your experience to date, does this seem true to you?

3. What are his criteria·for a grade A student? How are these different from the standards you would have used to evaluate high school students?

4. "A good student wants to answer the question, Why am I taking these courses? What do I hope to get out of them? Why are they important to me?" the author writes. How would you answer these questions with regard to the courses you have taken this semester?

5. Neusner praises one of his own teachers for correcting "not so much the phrasing as the mode of thought" in the young Neusner's writing. What do you think he has in mind in this contrast?

6. "Have I learned facts, or have I grasped how the subject works, its inner dynamic, its logic and structure?" Use your courses this semester to illustrate the contrast Neusner has in mind here.

▼ Discussion

1. What are Neusner's criteria for a grade A professor? How are these different from the criteria you would have used to grade your high school teachers?

2. "What makes an effective high school teacher is confidence, even glibness. What makes an effective university teacher is doubt and dismay." What does Neusner mean here? Given your experience to date, does this seem true to you?

3. What are his criteria for a grade A student? How are these different from the standards you would have used to evaluate high school students?

4. "A good student wants to answer the question, Why am I taking these courses? What do I hope to get out of them? Why are they important to me?" the author writes. How would you answer these questions with regard to the courses you have taken this semester?

5. Are there, in your view, important measures of a grade A professor that Neusner omits?

6. It is possible to infer from this essay the author's vision of the highest purposes of a university (since the grade A professor will be the one who does most to advance these purposes). What do you suppose this vision is?

▼ Writing Assignments

1. Write an essay in which you grade your present professors according to Neusner's criteria.

2. Write an essay in which you criticize, develop, and/or supplement Neusner's grading criteria for professors.

▼ Journal Entry

1. Which of your instructors this semester comes closest to your conception of the ideal professor? Why he or she?

▼ Vocabulary

advocacy	coherently	groveling	self-aggrandizing
ancillary	daft	imperial	unimpaired
autonomy	demented	intangible	vanquished
banal	dismay	intelligible	
banter	glibness	proselytizing	

The Badlands and the School

Loren Eiseley

Loren Eiseley, distinguished paleontologist and widely read author, remembers a favorite professor, whose ways of teaching were as unorthodox as they were deeply affecting.

I will never forget my first day of registration at the University of Pennsylvania. I had come directly from the *Mauvaises Terres,* the Tertiary badlands of western Nebraska, into a great city of banging, jangling trolleys, out of a silence as dreadful as that of the moon. As a fossil collector for the Nebraska State Museum, bones, not people, had been my primary concern. Field parties in those days were not equipped with portable radios and television sets. . . .

With some small savings from a bone hunter's salary, plus a certain faith and assistance on the part of my uncle, who had been swept into state office in the Roosevelt landslide of 1932, I found myself before College Hall on the University of Pennsylvania campus in Philadelphia. In an ever-increasing racket, I made my way from one office to another, receiving approvals and obtaining signatures on cards. Suddenly the noise, the **cacophony** of horns, became nerve-shattering. After all, I had spent a long summer in the silences of vanished geological eras. The urban world was, for the moment, unendurable to me. . . .

I climbed then, slowly, up the four flights of stairs to Dr. Frank Speck's office, under the old tower that has since vanished. A pleasant, attractive Indian girl occupied the desk by the door. I was fully enrolled now. Dr. Speck was seated at the little desk I was to come to know so well. His office was large, a former classroom, well lighted, high, and airy. All the wall space was lined with books and folders filled with off-prints. Speck, I was to discover later, disliked the central library. If he had to consult a file of journals, he preferred to send an emissary, which in my later graduate years turned out to be myself.

Mostly he labored in his own office amidst distractions which personally I have never been able to endure. Students lingered between seminars which he conducted usually at a huge table in the center of the room. He wrote letters or papers in a big bold hand at his desk while people murmured about him or plied "Doc" with questions. I find difficulty in describing him now, even though a faded informal winter photograph sits before me as I write. He is clothed in the garments of a trapper of the Canadian forests, part Indian, part of white manufacture. Snowshoes are gripped in one mittened hand. The picture was probably taken in Maine or Labrador in the prime of Frank's life.

Under the muffled fur across his forehead one can detect the outlines of a bold, **formidable countenance** that would have been acceptable among the mountain men who long preceded the rush of white settlement into the high plains. He was a stocky man, slightly below the average in height of this generation. The mouth in the photograph is firm, with a little cigar of the brand known as Between the Acts firmly gripped in a corner of his mouth. The head is massive; a total, lone-wolf independence shows in the stance of the body. The face is in no sense **aquiline** or Emersonian in the old New England sense. It is that of a belated sea captain, decisive, capable of the use of a **belaying pin** in an emergency. Or the

cacophony: harsh, discordant mixture of sounds

formidable: intimidating

countenance: appearance

aquiline: resembling an eagle

belaying pin: a short bar inserted in the rail of a ship for fastening a rope

face of one of those explorers trudging on relentlessly through the waterless seabed of the Great Basin. A man, in short, definitely not of the age he inhabited.

Used to another environment, I, and several other new students, departed promptly at the end of each class hour. "Doc," or "the old man," as we variously called him, appeared surly, or at the very least sulky. I had come to share confidences with another student, Ricky, whose father, then president of a Southern college, had previously taught in an American school in Tokyo. Ricky had grown up in Japan and could speak the language like a native. For an American this was an extraordinary achievement. We became fast friends but worried over our seeming inability to make much human contact with our departmental chairman. To make it worse, one day in class a little heap of square-cut flints had been poured upon the table—one of the surprises with which Speck amused himself.

"What are these?" he barked. "Any of you know?" He looked at me. I was supposed to be the **archaeologist** in the group.

I examined them, and a western memory with an absolute surety came back. "They are not Indian at all. They are eighteenth-century gun flints for **flintlock** rifles."

A titter ran about among the students at the table. They were sure the old man had tripped me.

"What makes you so sure?" he said menacingly, trying to make me back down. "Sir," I said, "I just know. They're square-cut European flint. I've seen them on the guns themselves. I am sure I'm not mistaken."

"You are right," he growled reluctantly. The tittering ceased. "Class is dismissed."

"Jeez," whispered my companion. "The old man will make you pay for that. He likes to win those games. Why didn't you shut up?"

"I couldn't," I said logically. "He asked me directly. I had to answer." Ricky shook his head.

A few days later, a dark, broad-shouldered man a bit older than Ricky and myself hailed us on the street. He had not been a member of that class at the table but had been browsing in Frank's library. I had noted before that he had seemed a particular favorite. Rumors had reached me that he had been a noted athlete who still occasionally refereed games. Now he was an advanced graduate student in the department. He introduced himself as Lou Korn. I did not know it then, but he was destined to become a lifelong friend and stand up at my wedding.

"Look, you fellows," he said. "You're not getting anywhere with the old man. I'll tell you why, if you don't mind."

"Why?" we chorused. "We don't skip class. We study. What's the trouble?"

The athlete with the shoulders of a running back and a dark, ruggedly handsome face grinned quietly. "Because," he said, "you leave directly after class. The old man doesn't like it. He thinks if you're a true **anthropologist**, not just a student, you should stick around. It's part of his way of judging people. You," he poked me good-naturedly, "both pleased and put him out by solving that old gunflint trick of his. But he liked it. Proved you're from the West, you know. Boy, are you going to get an education! Now, remember, when you see him on the campus, 'sing out,' that's his phrase for it."

"Honest?" we said. "You wouldn't kid us?" He shook his head. "Just remember the old man hates formalities and he's spent time in the north woods. Most of what you learn from him, you'll learn across the street at the Greek's. He generally goes over there for coffee and a dish of ice cream at three. His favorites," here he paused, "generally traipse along. Stick around a little more and read in the office. Wait till I give you the nod."

I learned a lot about Lou Korn in those few moments. Secure, himself a favorite, he had gone out of his way to inform two helplessly floundering newcomers who had not grown up as undergraduates under the old man's **tutelage**. Frank, in a strange way which I was never totally to understand, was lonely. His

archaeologist: one who studies artifacts and other remains of past human life and culture

flintlock: a gunlock in which the action of flint striking steel ignites the powder

anthropologist: one who scientifically studies the origin, biological characteristics, and the physical, cultural, and social development of humankind

tutelage: instruction

173

initial growl, which I had not anticipated from my correspondence before coming to Penn, was an assertion of his own independence. He expected perception. If you saw through the gruffness, if you liked books, snakes, the life of the hunting peoples, if you were a good companion, he would do anything to help you.

In return he wanted very little, an exclamation over a rare fern, something in the way of beliefs shared as though by two men who sat before a brush shelter in the flickering dark of a campfire—a fire and a dark that had not changed since man entered the world, a **totemic** dark in which animals spoke and skins were easily shifted.

Once, the Anthropological Association met in Philadelphia during my time there. Distinguished scholars, some from abroad, drifted into the office and were pleasantly received. But they came to Frank Speck. To my knowledge he never attended the meetings. "Loren," he said, "stay with me. Everybody's over there," he gestured. "There're more brains in Philadelphia this week than there is sewage in the Delaware River." His voice had lowered to a growl in which I detected the uncertain tone of a waif.

"Okay, Doc," I said, though I had intended to join the others. "Where shall we go, the pine barrens? The zoo?"

"I know a quick way over by train to the barrens," he answered. "We can tramp and canoe a bit and come back in the late afternoon."

The details of that day are long forgotten, but two men alone exchange confidences. His grandfather had been a sea captain. "These Pineys," Frank swept a hand over the woods through which we tramped, and I knew he was referring to the illiterate inbred woodsmen who inhabited the place, "were wreckers two generations ago. My grandfather's ship was lured onto the shoals by false lights during a storm. Grandfather's body was cast up along with the cargo and some of the crew. In those days that was the Atlantic, with its false lights, and the piratical people of the shore."

He paused and took a quick breath and went on. "My father had to drive down in a wagon and take the body home. It's odd, you know. I've sat around fires with Pineys whose grandfathers did the job. They would half admit it."

I thought silently of the **brakeman** long ago in the desert. I wondered if a wire flickered somewhere in the old man's brain. "My father," Speck continued, "became a broker in New York. I was sent to Columbia. I was intended for the ministry."

There was a gap in his history I was never to fill, except in fragments. Out of the **reticence** of long road experience I never asked questions. I only listened to what people were willing to volunteer. Though Frank's mother was still living when I knew him, there had been a time in childhood when, in ill health, he had been entrusted to the care of an old Mohegan woman. Why this was I never completely understood, save that this foster mother was a family friend. Had his real mother been ill? Or had his parents thought that this would be a valuable experience for the youth? I was never to know. One thing I did know, however: this episode indirectly brought about Speck's eventual meeting with Franz Boas, then the dean of American anthropologists.

In the first decade of this century American anthropologists of distinction could almost be counted on one's fingers, and the places where anthropology was taught as a separate subject were few. Many of these men had actually emerged from different disciplines, drawn, perhaps, by the wild and uncontained boundaries of the subject. Boas, himself the teacher of several anthropologists who later attained great **eminence**, was a **maverick** physicist who had written his doctoral dissertation on the color of seawater.

The sudden rise of the subject was phenomenal. The question of relevance was never raised. In fact, if relevance, as recently defined, had been used as a criterion, I sometimes wonder if the science of anthropology would have survived.

totemic: full of symbolic significance

brakeman: in a train, an assistant to the conductor

reticence: disposition to silence

eminence: high stature or repute

maverick: characteristic of a person who stands outside the group

174

Yet by some paradox it became remarkably popular in the fifties and sixties. Perhaps by then it had come to represent to the young the abolition of ancient taboos and the rationalization of their own life style. Furthermore, it had contributed to the elimination of much ingrained racial prejudice and to a better understanding of the movement of cultural traits around the globe. These are merely observations made in passing and must be so taken. As in the case of any science, not all its practitioners need be regarded as reasonable or without self-interest.

Of Frank Speck I know this much: that because of knowledge of a dying tongue, Mohegan, derived from his Indian foster mother, who taught it and much else to the impressionable boy, he was finally brought to the attention of Franz Boas and turned aside from the ministry into anthropology. The change in professions did not, I have come to believe, effect a total transformation of personality. I base this upon two observations.

Once, strolling in the Philadelphia Zoo, we came upon a wood duck paddling quietly in a little pond. These birds are most beautifully patterned. We stood watching the ducks. "Loren," Speck finally said, quite softly and uncertainly for him, "tell me honestly. Do you believe unaided natural selection produced that pattern? Do you believe it has that much significance to the bird's survival?"

I turned in surprise, because unbeknownst to my distinguished teacher, the same thought had been oppressing me. "I know," he said hastily, "what all my colleagues would say, but they are specialists on man. You have wandered to us out of another field. I'd like to hear what you think."

I tried to choose my words very carefully, not to satisfy a man or promote my own interests, but because, like Frank in his northern forests and amongst the wood people, I had been much alone. "Frank," I said, "I have always had a doubt every time I came out of a laboratory, even every time I have had occasion to look inside a dead human being on a slab. I don't doubt that duck was once something else, just as you and I have sprung from something older and more primitive.

"It isn't that which troubles me. It's the method, the way. Sometimes it seems very clear, and I satisfy myself in modern genetic terms. Then, as perhaps with your duck, something seems to go out of focus, as though we are trying too hard, trying, it would seem, to believe the unbelievable. I honestly don't know how to answer. I just look at things and others like them and end by mystifying myself. I can't answer in any other way. I guess I'm not a very good scientist; I'm not sufficiently proud, nor confident of my powers, nor of any human powers. Neither was Darwin, for that matter. Only his followers. There were times when Charles Darwin wobbled as we are wobbling here. Remember what he said once about the eye?"

"A cold shudder," quoted Speck promptly.

"Well," I added, as the duck paddled along slowly, displaying its intricately patterned feathers, "that's just the way I feel right now, as though the universe were too frighteningly queer to be understood by minds like ours. It's not a popular view. One is supposed to flourish Occam's razor and reduce hypotheses about a complex world to human proportions. Certainly I try. Mostly I come out feeling that whatever else the universe may be, its so-called simplicity is a trick, perhaps like that bird out there. I know we have learned a lot, but the scope is too vast for us. Every now and then if we look behind us, everything has changed. It isn't precisely that nature tricks us. We trick ourselves with our own ingenuity. I don't believe in simplicity."

I subsided, feeling I had merely befogged everything with my confused ignorance. We stood in silence a little while and then went to a cage where Speck let a parrot gnaw his hat. Speck's hats always quickly took on the appearance of those I had seen on the road—even the one he had left hanging on my office wall before he had gone away to die. But that act lay years beyond us.

"Loren," Speck said as we made our way toward the gate. "I feel as you do, maybe even more, because I really live far back with the simpler peoples. You have seen a few come to the office. They trust me and bring things to trade."

"Yes, I know," I answered, "and neither of us can quite speak to our contemporaries. Certainly I don't. But I'll tell you something. A man named Algernon Blackwood, an English writer, once wrote a story about a man in Egypt whose soul was stolen by the past, by all those giant millennia heaped in a little space along the Nile. Oh, he remained here in the flesh, and walked upon his errands, but his mind had otherwise been taken. He had vanished into another age. Perhaps if we go on this way it will happen to both of us."

As a matter of fact it did. I was unknowingly prophetic and I was the last to go. For Frank, perhaps the process was either slower or had unconsciously been effected by his childhood Mohegan experience. Perhaps he was a true **changeling**, a substitute child in everything but appearance. The Indians of the Northeast, long supposed to have vanished or been ethnically absorbed, were always his primary interest. The girl I had met acting as his secretary was one. He had an uncanny way of locating remnants that were already supposed to have disappeared in Thoreau's time.

A later generation of **ethnologists** will have to rely in large part upon Frank's records. He found and recorded customs still **extant** that other workers had assumed were extinct. He lovingly gathered up the broken bits of Algonkian tongues from speakers upon whose lips they were dying. He recorded the last details of their material culture. He worked mostly alone, before the day of the big foundation grants.

It was just as well. What he was seeking was as **elusive** as a beautiful night moth. One found it by oneself or not at all. Students of primitive religion have always utilized his studies of the game lords, of **scapulimancy** as a **circumpolar** trait. Stuart Neitzel, an excavator as far down as the Bayou country, writes to me about him still.

I said earlier that I based my comments upon Speck's essential retreat to the primitive upon two observations. No doubt others could be added from the intervening years, but long after his death I happened to be speaking to Roy Nichols, Penn's nationally known historian and Pulitzer Prize winner. "Frank," he allowed, "was a pioneer in **ethnohistory**." Then, pausing, this cultivated scholar, in some ways the utter **antithesis** of Frank, ventured a comment upon Frank's difficult last days, his pride, his unwillingness to confide his distress even to lifelong colleagues, his pathetic **subterfuges**, his secretive disposal of his valuable library. Nichols closed the chapter. "Frank," he said, "was basically an Indian. He died one. Mentally he went back to the forest. You couldn't help. Don't blame yourself. He wanted no sympathy."

changeling: a child exchanged secretly for another

ethnologists: those who study the branch of anthropology that deals with the origin and distinguishing characteristics of the races of humankind

extant: still in existence

elusive: escaping firm mental grasp

scapulimancy: the practice of divining by observing a shoulder blade cracked from fire

circumpolar: around a pole

ethnohistory: in anthropology, the study of cultures without a native written history

antithesis: the direct opposite

subterfuges: strategies to conceal something

▼ Questions to Focus Reading

1. What does Eiseley's description of Frank Speck's office tell you about this professor?
2. Eiseley summarizes his description of Speck with these words: "a man . . . definitely not of the age he inhabited." What reasons has he given us for believing this about Speck?
3. Why does Speck dismiss class when Eiseley answers his question correctly?
4. What does Eiseley learn about Speck from Lou Korn? What does he learn about Korn from this advice?
5. What did Frank Speck want from students?
6. What does Eiseley learn about Frank Speck's background when they canoe in the pine barrens?

7. Originally headed in the direction of the ministry, Speck turned instead to anthropology. "The change in professions did not, I have come to believe, effect a total transformation of personality." What explanation does Eiseley provide for this statement?

8. What is the focus of the discussion they have about the wood duck? What puzzles Frank Speck about it? What conclusion does Eiseley arrive at?

▼ Questions for Reflection

1. What picture has Loren Eiseley created in your mind of Frank Speck? Which of the details he provides stand out for you? How do you imagine he would teach his classes?

2. What picture do you get of Loren Eiseley?

3. What do you think draws these men to each other as companions?

4. "What he was seeking was as elusive as a beautiful night moth. One found it by oneself or not at all," Eiseley writes of Speck. What do you think he means? Do you know from your own experience of any knowledge that you must find by yourself or not at all?

5. Do you sense that some of your professors are actually restricted in their capacity for teaching by the classroom setting? What about him or her or that setting leads you to think this?

▼ Discussion

1. Interview one of your professors about his or her commitment to the life of an academic. Prepare questions in advance that would elicit his or her deepest reasons for choosing this life, his or her conception of its greatest rewards, the ideal student, the "A" professor. Note details of manner, speech, and appearance that seem to you to disclose something important about this man or woman. Note what you take to be telling details of his or her office. What did you learn from your interview with your professor? What do you know now about his or her motivations, interests, expectations of students, reasons for continuing to teach?

2. Do you know from your own experience of any knowledge that you must find by yourself or not at all?

▼ Writing Assignments

1. Using Eiseley's essay as a model, present a vivid portrait of a professor or teacher who has affected you in some important way. Note how much of Eiseley's portrait of Frank Speck is conveyed in careful descriptions of concrete incidents (the gunflint story, the conversation at the Philadelphia Zoo), quotations that capture the man's voice, and telling personal details (the long description of the photograph, the voice). Try to emulate this concreteness in your reminiscence.

2. Interview one of your professors about his or her commitment to the life of an academic. Prepare questions in advance that would elicit his or her deepest reasons for choosing this life, his or her conception of its greatest rewards, the ideal student, the "A" professor. Note details of manner, speech, and appearance that seem to you to disclose something important about this man or woman. Note what you take to be telling details of his or her office. After the interview, write a portrait of the professor that utilizes all this detail to bring him or her to life for the reader.

▼ **Journal Entry**

1. Have you had a valuable relationship with a teacher or professor? What was valuable about it?

▼ **Vocabulary**

anthropologist	cacophony	ethnohistory	reticence
antithesis	changeling	ethnologist	scapulimancy
aquiline	circumpolar	extant	subterfuge
archaeologist	countenance	flintlock	totemic
belaying pin	elusive	formidable	tutelage
brakeman	eminence	maverick	

29

▼

Remembering Charles

Houston Baker

Houston A. Baker Jr., a leading scholar of African American literature, presents a vivid portrait of a professor who challenged and changed him.

He was a tobacco brown, soft-eyed, angular man. He had transformed himself from a poor, Bluefield, West Virginia, mountain boy into an American intellectual. He had crafted an **Oxonian** mask behind which one could only surmise black beginnings. I caught glimpses of that ethnic past in the twinkle—the almost break-loose and "signifying" laughter—of his eyes when he told us of his **dissertation**. The title of that work in progress, according to him, was: "Some **Ontological** and **Eschatological** Aspects of the Petrarchan Conceit." He never dreamed of writing such a work, but he enjoyed using philosophical words that he knew would send the curious among us scurrying to the dictionary. I believe he actually wrote on the *Canterbury Tales*. He intrigued us. Slowly puffing on the obligatory pipe, he would chide us for the routineness of our analyses of revered works in the British and American literary **canons**. He wore—always—a tie and tweed of Ivy **provenance**, and at the end of the first session of his "World Literature" course at Howard University in the fall of 1963, I had but one response—I wanted to be exactly like him.

The task was to prove myself worthy. I labored furiously at the beginning assignment—an effort devoted to Marvellian Coy mistresses and pounding **parodies** thereof. The result was a D and the comment: "This is a **perfunctory** effort. You have refused to be creative. There are worlds on worlds rolling ever. Try to make contact with them." I was more than annoyed; I was livid. Who did he think he was? I'd show him. My next essay would reveal (cleverly, of course) that I didn't give a tinker's dam for his grade or his comments. "Creative"—Indeed!

At the conclusion of his initial class, he said: "I want you to take these texts home and have intercourse with them and derive a satisfying orgasm." The sharp and shocked intake of breath from all of us surely kept us from seeing the merriment playing over his face. I had scant wisdom vis-à-vis orgasm, and I didn't have a clue what he considered creative. So I followed the general American procedure for such cases: I winged it.

My second essay might properly have been entitled: Love's labor loosed on William Blake. I strained to see every **nuance** of the *Songs of Innocence*. I combed the poems for every mad hint that would help forward my own mad argument. I never turned my eyes from the text as I sought to construct the most infuriating (yet plausible) analysis imaginable. I felt my feet dancing to Muhammed Ali rhythms as I slaved away, darting logical jabs at Professor C. Watkins who would (I was certain) be utterly undone when I threw my **irreverent** straight right. The paper came back with the comment: "This is a **maverick** argument, but stubbornly logical—'A-'." Bingo! The grade in itself gave me almost enough courage to seek him out during office hours—but not quite. I corralled a friend to make the pilgrimage with me.

He was extraordinarily gracious on the mid-autumn afternoon when we had our first long talk. "Come in, Mr. Baker—Miss Pierce. How are you?" His tie was

Oxonian: pertaining to Oxford University

dissertation: the book-length thesis required for the doctoral degree (Ph.D.)

ontological: pertaining to the nature of being

eschatological: in theology, pertaining to final matters: death, judgment, afterlife

canons: bodies of work of particular importance

provenance: place of origin

parodies: satirical imitations

perfunctory: performed as a routine duty

nuance: subtle detail

irreverent: lacking reverence or respect

maverick: characteristic of a person who stands outside the group

loose; he was reared back in his desk chair. There was a clutter of papers and blue books, and they provided a friendly setting for a two-hour conversation. (Apparently no one else had sufficiently overcome the effects of his intimidating **intellectualism** to brave office hours.) He talked easily, describing his **odyssey** from Ohio State to a first teaching position at San Francisco State University and then to Howard. He was currently a doctoral candidate for an Ohio State Ph.D. in English. He was serving time, so to speak, at Howard until his dissertation was completed and his degree conferred. His real love was philosophy, and the New World **metaphysics** of Emerson set his blood warming and brought out his best **polemical** instincts. He held his Howard colleagues in low esteem because they were wedded to an old, old literary history while he was an enlightened devotee of the New Criticism. They were rattling Model Ts of a socio-historical approach, while he occupied a smoothly non-referential world of the Cleanth Brooks and Robert Penn Warren Mercedes. We were thrilled that he considered us (potentially) enough like him to invite us to visit him and his wife two weeks hence—for dessert.

There was far more than dessert. His wife was hospitable, witty, attractive—and white. She was the first such person I had met. For partners in interracial marriages were not common in my hometown of Louisville, Kentucky. The evening surprisingly took on (in my youthful imagination) the cast of Greenwich Village "Beats" and *verboten* revelations. The greatest stimulation, however, came when he played the Library of Congress recording of T. S. Eliot reading "The Waste Land." In that moment, I became, willy-nilly, a party to "modernism" in its **prototypical** form. I was surprised and delighted. I had heard nothing like it before. The Eliotian reading initiated my habit of "listening" for poems rather than "looking" for them. (I spent hours thereafter in the library listening to the sounds of English, French, and American poets. And later in the term when we were assigned "The Waste Land" for analysis, the echoes of that evening were constant.) I stepped into a late fall evening with an entirely new sense of myself and of "worlds on worlds" rolling ever.

I began self-consciously to craft a critical vocabulary. (An instructor commented at the end of one of my assignments: "Are 'ontological' and 'eschatological' the only words you know?") I talked in an American literature class about the dynamics of speech and silence—with the raven as representative of the "ontological foundations" of silence—in Poe's famous poem. I felt I had **acquitted** myself with verve. The Model T in charge said: "Mr. Baker, that's a lot of gobbledygook." When I told Professor Watkins of the incident, he simply said: "Mr. Baker, there are people here who have not read a book or had an original idea for years." (Then, I didn't know he meant not simply Howard but the entire academic world.)

I was reassured. I began to wear ties to class and abandoned my old satchel for a green bookbag. I was happy that I could appear in such attire when he called one day for my assistance. He had suffered the indignity of *two* flat tires, and his call brought me like a shot. Ironically, though, as we kneeled in the late-November snow, I noticed how threadbare *he* was. A frayed collar belied his intellectual elegance. His down-at-the-heels shoes were closer to West Virginia than Oxford. His face was prematurely kneaded and lined. I began to glean then (but only comprehended much, much later) the enormous price he had paid (and continued to pay) for his intellectual being in the world. I felt sorry for him at that instant, but also **prodigiously** attracted to such **ascetic** brilliance.

The semester rolled to a wintry climax, and I received an A for "World Literature." By the end of the term, I had made up my mind that I not only wanted to remain an English major, but also wanted to become a Ph.D.—a university professor. The project seems abundantly feasible in today's world where graduate fellowships for Afro-Americans go begging. But in 1963, it was a rare occurrence

intellectualism: devotion to the life of the mind

odyssey: a long journey marked by adventure and hardship

metaphysics: the study of the nature of ultimate reality

polemical: taking a controversial stand

verboten: forbidden

prototypical: pertaining to the original or model

acquitted (oneself): performed the task

prodigiously: extraordinarily

ascetic: austere; self-denying

for a black person to set his sights on a traditional Ph.D.—not a doctorate in education, or social work, or physical education—but a traditional Ph.D. in arts and sciences. The person most influential in the decisions I made over the next several years was Charles Watkins. He encouraged my ambitions, guided me to fellowships, quieted my doubts, wrote letters of recommendation, and sketched vistas of intellectual work that glowed in my imagination.

I was overjoyed to see him at the Columbus, Ohio, airport in the spring of 1966. He had returned to Ohio State, where he completed his dissertation and took a position as assistant professor in English. We had a wonderful time during my visit. We conversed on every topic of which I was capable, including Emersonian essays. He read my **fledgling** poetry, and the twinkle in his eye told me I had many rivers to cross. He was generously complimentary of my scholarly progress, and I knew, on leaving, that I loved this West Virginia man who, by dint of main force, had shaped himself into an American Scholar.

News of his death came quite unexpectedly. I received it, quite indirectly, while attending a black writers conference. He died of heart trouble. He and I lost touch during the years he was in Seattle. He had taken a post at the University of Washington. I felt that he had little sympathy for my recently acquired interests in black literature and black studies. (A lack of sympathy that was, perhaps, justified since he had received threats and ugly harassment from black power advocates at San Francisco State who were displeased with his interracial marriage and insisted that he either join them or suffer.) He was a man of the New Criticism, and I was moving under gloriously socio-historical and polemical banners of The Black Aesthetic, where **referentiality** was of the utmost importance. I had joyfully allied myself with black critics who were **repudiating** traditional, Oxonian masks—making, so we thought, the world all "new"—redefining it in BLACK terms. I felt that I had outgrown Charles. But the wisdom of hindsight allows me to see that "growth" is merely a sign for "moving things around"—outrageous posturing designed to convince those we love that we are still worthy of consideration, to solicit from them an acknowledgment of our changing sameness. I felt profoundly lonely. I also felt guilty and helpless because Charles and I had lost touch. The only thing I could offer as a gesture of **appeasement** and love was the dedication of my book *Singers of Daybreak.* I sent a copy to his wife with a feeling that someone I cared for had virtually vanished, leaving no tangible trace.

In the fall of 1985, however, I received a telephone call that began: "Hello, Houston, this is Rita Watkins." Charles and Rita's son Jonathan is currently employed as a Senate aide in the District of Columbia, and his mother wondered if I would mind calling him on one of my trips to Washington. She hoped I would tell him about his father because he was only nine when Charles died. I assured her that I would be happy to call. As soon as I hung up, I began to think of what I would say to Charles' firstborn. I will tell him, I believe, that Charles was a courageous black man who carved from the granite of racism and impoverishment a role for himself as master of the best that has been thought and said in the world.

He was a teacher par excellence. He knew, better than anyone I have encountered since, how to convey the worth and excitement of a demanding intellectual enterprise to a country boy from Louisville, Kentucky. I am certain I will tell Jonathan that his father knew **consummately** well how to bless, inspire, and encourage the threadbare thinkers among us.

fledgling: marked by inexperience
referentiality: the thing a symbol stands for
repudiating: disowning
appeasement: conciliation
consummately: in a manner expressing the highest degree

▼ Questions to Focus Reading

1. Baker's first paper comes back with a grade of D and this comment: "This is a perfunctory effort. You have refused to be creative. There are worlds on worlds rolling ever. Try to make contact with them." What does this

mean? What do we learn about Charles Watkins, Baker's professor, from this comment?

2. How does Baker win the respect of Professor Watkins?

3. When Baker leaves Watkins's house the night he'd been invited for dessert, he "stepped into a late fall evening with an entirely new sense of [himself] and of 'worlds on worlds' rolling ever." Judging from the context of this statement, what do you think this new sense was?

4. What does Baker learn from the close look he gets at his professor when he helps the older man fix his tires?

5. Why does the young Houston Baker come to believe he had outgrown his old professor?

▼ Questions for Reflection

1. For what qualities especially did Baker respect and love his professor?

2. What portrait of Charles Watkins emerges in your mind as a result of Baker's reminiscence? What details about Watkins seem most revealing to you? How would you describe him?

3. What picture do you get of Houston Baker from this essay?

4. At the end of the first class meeting of Watkins's World Literature course, Baker "wanted to be exactly like him." Have you had a similar response to a professor or teacher? If so, what was it about that person that prompted that reaction? To what extent have you incorporated that person within your own identity?

5. Reflecting on his sense as a young man that he had "outgrown" Charles Watkins, Baker says he now sees that growth "is merely a sign for 'moving things around'—outrageous posturing designed to convince those we love that we are still worthy of consideration, to solicit from them an acknowledgment of our changing sameness." What do you take him to mean by this? Do you think this is what has happened when we take ourselves to have "grown"? Is it true of *any* case of supposed "growth"?

▼ Discussion

1. Interview one of your professors about his or her commitment to the life of an academic. Prepare questions in advance that would elicit his or her deepest reasons for choosing this life, his or her conception of its greatest rewards, the ideal student, the "A" professor. Note details of manner, speech, and appearance that seem to you to disclose something important about this man or woman. Note what you take to be telling details of his or her office. What did you learn from your interview with your professor? What do you know now about his or her motivations, interests, expectations of students, reasons for continuing to teach?

▼ Writing Assignments

1. Using Baker's essay as a model, present a vivid portrait of a professor or teacher who has affected you in some important way. Note how much of Baker's portrait of Charles Watkins is conveyed in careful descriptions of concrete incidents (the first class session, the meeting in his office, the evening at his house), quotations that capture the man's authentic voice, and telling personal details (the "tie and tweed of Ivy provenance," the "merriment playing over his face" when he shocks his students with his words, the frayed collar that "belied his intellectual elegance"). Try to emulate this concreteness in your reminiscence.

2. Interview one of your professors about his or her commitment to the life of an academic. Prepare questions in advance that would elicit his or her deepest reasons for choosing this life, his or her conception of its

greatest rewards, the ideal student, the "A" professor. Note details of manner, speech, and appearance that seem to you to disclose something important about this man or woman. Note what you take to be telling details of his or her office. After the interview, write a portrait of the professor that utilizes all this detail to bring him or her to life for the reader.

▼ Journal Entries

1. Has any of your instructors this semester interested or even intrigued you as a person? What about this person has interested you?
2. Have you ever felt that you had "outgrown" someone? If so, what about you or this person leads you to feel this way?

▼ Vocabulary

acquitted (oneself)	fledgling	ontological	provenance
appeasement	intellectualism	Oxonian	referentiality
ascetic	irreverent	parody	repudiating
canon	maverick	perfunctory	verboten
consummately	metaphysics	polemical	
dissertation	nuance	prodigiously	
eschatological	odyssey	prototypical	

▼

30

Backpack Almanac

Education

Percentage of Chinese teenagers who can correctly identify the size of the world's population: 85
[J. Mayone Stycos, Cornell University (Ithaca, N.Y.), 1989]
Percentage of American adults who can: 35
[Louis Harris and Associates (New York City)—Planned Parenthood (New York City), 1989]

Percentage of college students who say "the higher the tuition, the better the quality of the education": 27
[Gallup Organization (Princeton, N.J.), 1989]

Percentage of Americans who can correctly name the Chief Justice of the Supreme Court: 9
Percentage who can correctly name the judge on *The People's Court:* 54
[*Washington Post* Poll, 1989]

Percentage of American twenty-one-year-olds who can read a bus schedule: 20
[Educational Testing Service (Princeton, N.J.), 1989]

Portion of all MBAs ever awarded by U.S. universities that were awarded during the 1980s: 1/2
[U.S. Dept. of Education, 1989]

Average number of words added to the English language every day since 1966: 6.5
[Random House (New York City), 1988]

Number of states that claim test scores in their elementary schools are above the national average: 50
[Friends for Education (Daniels, W. Va.), 1988]

Average ratio of students to teachers in an American public school classroom in 1955: 27:1
Average ratio in 1989: 18:1
[U.S. Dept. of Education, 1989]

Percentage of high school students who say the telephone was invented after 1950: 10
[National Endowment for the Humanities (Washington, D.C.), 1987]

Number of Japanese children who have died since 1985 as a result of disciplinary beatings by
school personnel: 5
[Susan Chira, *New York Times* (Tokyo), 1988]

Average number of words in the written vocabulary of a 6- to 14-year-old American child in 1945: 25,000
[*A Basic Vocabulary of Elementary School Children,* by H. D. Rinsland (Macmillan, New York City), 1990]
Average number in 1990: 10,000
[Gary Ingersoll, University of Indiana (Indianapolis), 1990]

Number of the 6 best-selling extracurricular books in college bookstores that are collections of cartoons: 4
[*Chronicle of Higher Education* (Washington, D.C.), 1990]

Percentage of Americans under the age of 30 who say they read a daily newspaper: 40
Percentage of Americans over the age of 50 who say they do: 65
[Times Mirror Center for the People & the Press (Washington, D.C.), 1990]

Number of American universities that have instituted restrictions on public speech since 1988: 137
[American Civil Liberties Union (New York City), 1990]

Percentage increase, since 1989, in the number of alcohol-related hospitalizations of Boston College students: 100
[Debra Rosenberg, *Newsweek* (Boston), 1991]

Rank of Washington, D.C., high school students, among students with the lowest mathematics scores
nationwide: 1
Rank of Washington, D.C., high school students, among those most likely to say they are "good in math": 1
[U.S. Dept. of Education, 1991]

Percentage of business students at American universities who admit to having cheated on an exam: 57
[Don McCabe, Rutgers University (Newark, N.J.), 1991]

Percentage of American households in which no books were bought in 1991: 60
[Book Industry Study Group (New York City), 1992]

Chances that a member of an American public school's staff is a classroom teacher: 1 in 2
[U.S. Dept. of Education, 1992]

What Is a University?

Chances that an American does not know that the Bill of Rights is the first ten amendments to the Constitution: 2 in 3
[Research USA (Chicago), 1992]

Percentage of male college students who believe that life is "a meaningless existential hell": 27
Percentage of female college students who say this: 13
[*Esquire's* College Survey (New York City), 1992]

Ratio of the average alcohol consumption of a college fraternity-house resident to that of a male college student: 3:1
[Cheryl Presley, Southern Illinois University (Carbondale), 1993]

Chances that a job created in the United States in 1994 will require a college degree: 1:3
[National Center on Education and the Economy (Washington, D.C.), 1994]

▼

What Is the Case for Broad Learning? A Symposium: The Challenges of the Twenty-First Century

Why does your school want you to be conversant with the languages of natural science and social science, literature, philosophy, history, and art? Because educators believe that these knowledges will be required of the citizen of the twenty-first century who chooses to be fully alive. The purpose of the collection of readings in this symposium is to give you a vivid demonstration of why we believe this.

31

▼

The Ones Who Walk Away from Omelas

Ursula Le Guin

*A writer of fiction can stimulate our thinking about the future by presenting a utopia or a **dystopia** with recognizable roots in our own world. Ursula Le Guin's haunting story does exactly this. But the portrait is ambiguous, for Omelas is simultaneously utopia and dystopia. Those who walk away have a different vision.*

With a clamor of bells that set the swallows soaring, the Festival of Summer came to the city Omelas, bright-towered by the sea. The rigging of the boats in harbor sparkled with flags. In the streets between houses with red roofs and painted walls, between old moss-grown gardens and under avenues of trees, past great parks and public buildings, processions moved. Some were **decorous**: old people in long stiff robes of mauve and grey, grave master workmen, quiet, merry women carrying their babies and chatting as they walked. In other streets the music beat faster, a shimmering of gong and tambourine, and the people went dancing, the procession was a dance. Children dodged in and out, their high calls rising like the swallows' crossing flights over the music and the singing. All the processions wound towards the north side of the city, where on the great water-meadow called the Green Fields boys and girls, naked in the bright air, with mud-stained feet and ankles and long, **lithe** arms, exercised their **restive** horses before the race. The horses wore no gear at all but a halter without bit. Their manes were braided with streamers of silver, gold, and green. They flared their nostrils and pranced and boasted to one another; they were vastly excited, the horse being the only animal who has adopted our ceremonies as his own. Far off to the north and west the mountains stood up half encircling Omelas on her bay. The air of morning was so clear that the snow still crowning the Eighteen Peaks burned with white-gold fire across the miles of sunlit air, under the dark blue of the sky. There was just enough wind to make the banners that marked the racecourse snap and flutter now and then. In the silence of the broad green meadows one could hear the music winding through the city streets, farther and nearer and ever approaching, a cheerful faint sweetness of the air that from time to time trembled and gathered together and broke out into the great joyous clanging of the bells.

Joyous! How is one to tell about joy? How to describe the citizens of Omelas?

They were not simple folk, you see, though they were happy. But we do not say the words of cheer much any more. All smiles have become archaic. Given a description such as this one tends to make certain assumptions. Given a description such as this one tends to look next for the King, mounted on a splendid stallion and surrounded by his noble knights, or perhaps in a golden litter borne by great-muscled slaves. But there was no king. They did not use swords, or keep slaves. They were not barbarians. I do not know the rules and laws of their society, but I suspect that they were singularly few. As they did without monarchy and slavery, so they also got on without the stock exchange, the advertisement, the secret police, and the bomb. Yet I repeat that these were not simple folk, not **dulcet** shepherds, noble savages, bland utopians. They were not less complex than us. The trouble is that we have a bad habit, encouraged by **pedants** and sophisticates, of considering happiness as something rather stupid. Only pain is intellectual, only

dystopia: an imaginary place in which people live fearful and dehumanized lives

decorous: exhibiting decorum or proper behavior

lithe: marked by effortless grace

restive: impatient or nervous under pressure, restriction, or delay

dulcet: having a soothing and agreeable quality

pedants: persons who make an excessive display of their learning

evil interesting. This is the treason of the artist: a refusal to admit the **banality** of evil and the terrible boredom of pain. If you can't lick 'em, join 'em. If it hurts, repeat it. But to praise despair is to condemn delight, to embrace violence is to lose hold of everything else. We have almost lost hold, we can no longer describe a happy man, nor make any celebration of joy. How can I tell you about the people of Omelas? They were not naive and happy children—though their children were, in fact, happy. They were mature, intelligent, passionate adults whose lives were not wretched. O miracle! but I wish I could describe it better. I wish I could convince you. Omelas sounds in my words like a city in a fairy tale, long ago and far away, once upon a time. Perhaps it would be best if you imagined it as your own fancy bids, assuming it will rise to the occasion, for certainly I cannot suit you all. For instance, how about technology? I think that there would be no cars or helicopters in and above the streets; this follows from the fact that people of Omelas are happy people. Happiness is based on a just discrimination of what is necessary, what is neither necessary nor destructive, and what is destructive. In the middle category, however—that of the unnecessary but undestructive, that of comfort, luxury, exuberance, etc.—they could perfectly well have central heating, subway trains, washing machines, and all kinds of marvelous devices not yet invented here, floating light-sources, fuelless power, a cure for the common cold. Or they could have none of that: it doesn't matter. As you like it. I incline to think that people from towns up and down the coast have been coming in to Omelas during the last days before the Festival on very fast little trains and double-decked trams, and that the train station of Omelas is actually the handsomest building in town, though plainer than the magnificent Farmers' market. But even granted trains, I fear that Omelas so far strikes some of you as goody-goody. Smiles, bells, parades, horses, bleh. If so, please add an orgy. If an orgy would help, don't hesitate. Let us not, however, have temples from which issue beautiful nude priests and priestesses already half in ecstasy and ready to copulate with any man or woman, lover or stranger, who desires union with the deep godhead of the blood, although that was my first idea. But really it would be better not to have any temples in Omelas— at least, not manned temples. Religion yes, clergy no. Surely the beautiful nudes can just wander about, offering themselves like divine **soufflés** to the hunger of the needy and the rapture of the flesh. Let them join the processions. Let tambourines be struck above the copulations, and the glory of desire be proclaimed upon the gongs, and (a not unimportant point) let the offspring of these delightful rituals be beloved and looked after by all. One thing I know there is none of in Omelas is guilt. But what else should there be? I thought at first there were no drugs, but that is puritanical. For those who like it, the faint insistent sweetness of *drooz* may perfume the ways of the city, *drooz* which first brings a great lightness and brilliance to the mind and limbs, and then after some hours a dreamy **languor**, and wonderful visions at last of the very **arcana** and inmost secrets of the Universe, as well as exciting the pleasure of sex beyond all belief; and it is not habit-forming. For more modest tastes I think there ought to be beer. What else, what else belongs in the joyous city? The sense of victory, surely, the celebration of courage. But as we did without clergy, let us do without soldiers. The joy built upon successful slaughter is not the right kind of joy; it will not do; it is fearful and it is trivial. A boundless and generous contentment, a **magnanimous** triumph felt not against some outer enemy but in communion with the finest and fairest in the souls of all men everywhere and the splendor of the world's summer: this is what swells the hearts of the people of Omelas, and the victory they celebrate is that of life. I really don't think many of them need to take *drooz*.

Most of the processions have reached the Green Fields by now. A marvelous smell of cooking goes forth from the red and blue tents of the provisioners. The faces of small children are **amiably** sticky; in the benign grey beard of a man a couple of crumbs of rich pastry are entangled. The youths and girls have mounted

banality: lack of freshness or originality

soufflés: light, fluffy baked dishes

languor: listlessness or stillness

arcana: mysteries

magnanimous: noble; large and generous in spirit

amiably: pleasantly

their horses and are beginning to group around the starting line of the course. An old woman, small, fat, and laughing, is passing out flowers from a basket, and tall young men wear her flowers in their shining hair. A child of nine or ten sits at the edge of the crowd, alone, playing on a wooden flute. People pause to listen, and they smile, but they do not speak to him, for he never ceases playing and never sees them, his dark eyes wholly **rapt** in the sweet, thin magic of the tune.

He finishes, and slowly lowers his hands holding the wooden flute.

As if that little private silence were the signal, all at once a trumpet sounds from the pavilion near the starting line: **imperious**, melancholy, piercing. The horses rear on their slender legs, and some of them neigh in answer. Sober-faced, the young riders stroke the horses' necks and soothe them, whispering, "Quiet, quiet, there my beauty, my hope. . . ." They begin to form in rank along the starting line. The crowds along the racecourse are like a field of grass and flowers in the wind. The Festival of Summer has begun.

Do you believe? Do you accept the festival, the city, the joy? No? Then let me describe one more thing.

In a basement under one of the beautiful public buildings of Omelas, or perhaps in the cellar of one of its spacious private homes, there is a room. It has one locked door, and no window. A little light seeps in dustily between cracks in the boards, secondhand from a cobwebbed window somewhere across the cellar. In one corner of the little room a couple of mops, with stiff, clotted, foul-smelling heads, stand near a rusty bucket. The floor is dirt, a little damp to the touch, as cellar dirt usually is. The room is about three paces long and two wide: a mere broom closet or disused tool room. In the room a child is sitting. It could be a boy or a girl. It looks about six, but actually is nearly ten. It is feeble-minded. Perhaps it was born defective, or perhaps it has become imbecile through fear, malnutrition, and neglect. It picks its nose and occasionally fumbles vaguely with its toes or genitals, as it sits hunched in the corner farthest from the bucket and the two mops. It is afraid of the mops. It finds them horrible. It shuts its eyes, but it knows the mops are still standing there; and the door is locked; and nobody will come. The door is always locked; and nobody ever comes, except that sometimes—the child has no understanding of time or interval—sometimes the door rattles terribly and opens, and a person, or several people, are there. One of them may come in and kick the child to make it stand up. The others never come close, but peer in at it with frightened, disgusted eyes. The food bowl and water jug are hastily filled, the door is locked, the eyes disappear. The people at the door never say anything, but the child who has not always lived in the tool room, and can remember sunlight and its mother's voice, sometimes speaks. "I will be good," it says. "Please let me out. I will be good!" They never answer. The child used to scream for help at night, and cry a good deal, but now it only makes a kind of whining, "eh-haa, eh-haa," and it speaks less and less often. It is so thin there are no calves to its legs; its belly protrudes; it lives on a half-bowl of corn meal and grease a day. It is naked. Its buttocks and thighs are a mass of festered sores, as it sits in its own excrement continually.

They all know it is there, all the people of Omelas. Some of them have come to see it, others are content merely to know it is there. They all know that it has to be there. Some of them understand why, and some do not, but they all understand that their happiness, the beauty of their city, the tenderness of their friendships, the health of their children, the wisdom of their scholars, the skill of their makers, even the abundance of their harvest and the kindly weathers of their skies, depend wholly on this child's **abominable** misery.

This is usually explained to children when they are between eight and twelve, whenever they seem capable of understanding; and most of those who come to see the child are young people, though often enough an adult comes, or comes back, to see the child. No matter how well the matter has been explained to them,

rapt: absorbed
imperious: arrogantly domineering
abominable: loathsome

190

these young spectators are always shocked and sickened at the sight. They feel disgust, which they had thought themselves superior to. They feel anger, outrage, impotence, despite all the explanations. They would like to do something for the child. But there is nothing they can do. If the child were brought up into the sunlight out of the vile place, if it were cleaned and fed and comforted, that would be a good thing, indeed; but if it were done, in that day and hour all the prosperity and beauty and delight of Omelas would wither and be destroyed. Those are the terms. To exchange all the goodness and grace of every life in Omelas for that single, small improvement: to throw away the happiness of thousands for the chance of the happiness of one: that would be to let guilt within the walls indeed.

The terms are strict and absolute; there may not even be a kind word spoken to the child.

Often the young people go home in tears, or in a tearless rage, when they have seen the child and faced this terrible **paradox**. They may brood over it for weeks or years. But as time goes on they begin to realize that even if the child could be released, it would not get much good of its freedom: a little vague pleasure of warmth and food, no doubt, but little more. It is too degraded and imbecile to know any real joy. It has been afraid too long ever to be free of fear. Its habits are too **uncouth** for it to respond to humane treatment. Indeed, after so long it would probably be wretched without walls about it to protect it, and darkness for its eyes, and its own excrement to sit in. Their tears at the bitter injustice dry when they begin to perceive the terrible justice of reality, and to accept it. Yet it is their tears and anger, the trying of their generosity and the acceptance of their helplessness, which are perhaps the true source of the splendor of their lives. Theirs is no **vapid**, irresponsible happiness. They know that they, like the child, are not free. They know compassion. It is the existence of the child, and their knowledge of its existence, that makes possible the nobility of their architecture, the poignancy of their music, the profundity of their science. It is because of the child that they are so gentle with children. They know that if the wretched one were not there snivelling in the dark, the other one, the flute-player, could make no joyful music as the young riders line up in their beauty for the race in the sunlight of the first morning of summer.

Now do you believe in them? Are they not more credible? But there is one more thing to tell, and this is quite incredible.

At times one of the adolescent girls or boys who go to see the child does not go home to weep or rage, does not, in fact, go home at all. Sometimes also a man or woman much older falls silent for a day or two, and then leaves home. These people go out into the street, and walk down the street alone. They keep walking, and walk straight out of the city of Omelas, through the beautiful gates. They keep walking across the farmlands of Omelas. Each one goes alone, youth or girl, man or woman. Night falls; the traveler must pass down village streets, between the houses with yellow-lit windows, and on out into the darkness of the fields. Each alone, they go west or north, towards the mountains. They go on. They leave Omelas, they walk ahead into the darkness, and they do not come back. The place they go towards is a place even less imaginable to most of us than the city of happiness. I cannot describe it at all. It is possible that it does not exist. But they seem to know where they are going, the ones who walk away from Omelas.

paradox: seeming contradiction
uncouth: crude
vapid: flat; dull

▼ Questions for Reflection

1. "We have a bad habit," says the narrator, "of considering happiness as something rather stupid. Only pain is intellectual, only evil interesting. . . . we can no longer describe a happy man, nor make any celebration of joy." Do you think this is true? If so, why has this come to be so?

2. The narrator says, "Happiness is based on a just discrimination of what is necessary, what is neither necessary nor destructive, and what is destructive." Do you agree? What, in your opinion, are the necessary ingredients of happiness?

3. The narrator invites us to add to the description of the joyous city. What is your conception of the joyous city? What belongs in the joyous city?

4. The description of the wretched child and the citizens' attitude toward it is introduced with these lines: "Do you believe? Do you accept the festival, the city, the joy? No? Then let me describe one more thing." Why does the narrator think this description will make Omelas more believable?

5. Upon the child's misery rests all the goodness and grace in the joyous city of Omelas. Are there analogues to this arrangement in our world?

6. The narrator describes at length two very distinct reactions to the child. What are these reactions?

7. Are there analogues in our world to the reactions of the first group, the majority?

8. The narrator comments, "The place they [the others] go towards is a place even less imaginable to most of us than the city of happiness." What might this place be? Why does the author highlight those who leave in her title?

9. What unique contribution does the fiction writer make to our discussion of the challenges of the future?

▼ Discussion

1. What do you think this story is about?

2. The narrator says, "Happiness is based on a just discrimination of what is necessary, what is neither necessary nor destructive, and what is destructive." Do you agree? What, in your opinion, are the necessary ingredients of happiness?

3. Upon the child's misery rests all the goodness and grace in the joyous city of Omelas. Are there analogues to this arrangement in our world?

4. The narrator describes at length two very distinct reactions to the child. What are these reactions?

5. Are there analogues in our world to the reactions of the first group, the majority?

6. The narrator comments, "The place they [the others] go towards is a place even less imaginable to most of us than the city of happiness." What might this place be? Why does the author highlight those who leave in her title?

7. What unique contribution does the fiction writer make to our discussion of the challenges of the future?

▼ Writing Assignments

1. "The Joyous City in the Year 2050" Present your vision of the perfect city of 2050.

2. Present a fictional account of "The Destination of Those Who Walk Away from Omelas."

3. Take a problem confronting our own world and extrapolate it into the future. Write a short piece of fiction in which you describe the effects of this problem in an imaginary society of the future.

4. Consider a problem confronting our society. Describe the problem and work out a program for your personal action in helping to remedy it.

5. "Our Omelas" Describe contemporary analogues to the society depicted by Le Guin.

▼ Journal Entry

1. You are a citizen of the beautiful city of Omelas. You have just seen the child. You know the terms of the city's happiness. What is your reaction to the child?

▼ Vocabulary

abominable	dulcet	magnanimous	soufflés
amiably	dystopia	paradox	uncouth
arcana	imperious	pedants	vapid
banality	languor	rapt	
decorous	lithe	restive	

32

▼

On the Subway

Sharon Olds

Poets as well as fiction writers often use their craft to reflect on problems in society. In this short poem, San Francisco poet Sharon Olds (b. 1942) focuses with insight and dramatic power on racial inequity in America. She is the author of three books of poetry.

The boy and I face each other.
His feet are huge, in black sneakers
laced with white in a complex pattern like a
set of intentional scars. We are stuck on
opposite sides of the car, a couple of   5
molecules stuck in a rod of light
rapidly moving through darkness. He has the
casual cold look of a mugger,
alert under hooded lids. He is wearing
red, like the inside of the body   10
exposed. I am wearing dark fur, the
whole skin of an animal taken and
used. I look at his raw face,
he looks at my fur coat, and I don't
know if I am in his power—   15
he could take my coat so easily, my
briefcase, my life—
or if he is in my power, the way I am
living off his life, eating the steak
he does not eat, as if I am taking   20
the food from his mouth. And he is black
and I am white, and without meaning or
trying to I must profit from his darkness,
the way he absorbs the murderous beams of the
nation's heart, as black cotton   25
absorbs the heat of the sun and holds it. There is
no way to know how easy this
white skin makes my life, this
life he could take so easily and
break across his knee like a stick the way his   30
own back is being broken, the
rod of his soul that at birth was dark and
fluid and rich as the heart of a seedling
ready to thrust up into any available light.

▼ Questions for Reflection

1. "He is wearing / red, like the inside of the body / exposed. I am wearing dark fur, the / whole skin of an animal taken and / used." What do we learn about these two people from these descriptions? What do we learn from these lines about the poet's attitude toward the contrast between herself and the boy?

2. "I am / living off his life," the poet writes. And "I must profit from his darkness, / the way he absorbs the murderous beams of the / nation's heart." What do you think she means by these lines?

3. The poem ends with the image of "the rod of his soul that at birth was dark and / fluid and rich as the heart of a seedling / ready to thrust up into any available light." When you read these lines in the context of the final sentence of the poem, what thoughts occur to you? What feelings does this final image provoke in you?

4. Do you agree with the poet that whether or not she intends or tries to, she "must profit from his darkness"?

5. Relate this poem to Le Guin's story, "The Ones Who Walk Away from Omelas" (Reading 31). Are there thematic similarities? Explain.

6. Imagine the key passage of an essay devoted to expressing the main theme of this poem. Would anything be gained by using the prose form? Would anything be lost?

▼ Journal Entry

1. "I am / living off his life." Do you believe this captures the truth of the relation between poor black and affluent white in America?

33

▼

The Paradox of Perfection

Arlene Skolnick

Arlene Skolnick, a research psychologist at the University of California at Berkeley, writes that the family, a once-cherished value, is now a troubled institution. She argues that the relationship between value and trouble is that of cause and effect.

The American Family, as even readers of *Popular Mechanics* must know by now, is in what Sean O'Casey would have called "a terrible state of chassis." Yet, there are certain ironies about the much-publicized crisis that give one pause.

True, the statistics seem alarming. The U.S. divorce rate, though it has reached something of a plateau in recent years, remains the highest in American history. The number of births out-of-wedlock among all races and ethnic groups continues to climb. The plight of many elderly Americans subsisting on low fixed incomes is well known.

What puzzles me is an ambiguity, not in the facts, but in what we are asked to make of them. A series of opinion polls conducted in 1978 by Yankelovich, Skelley, and White, for example, found that 38 percent of those surveyed had recently witnessed one or more "destructive activities" (for example, a divorce, a separation, a custody battle) within their own families or those of their parents or siblings. At the same time, 92 percent of the respondents said the family was highly important to them as a "personal value."

Can the family be at once a cherished "value" and a troubled institution? I am inclined to think, in fact, that they go hand in hand. A recent "Talk of the Town" report in *The New Yorker* illustrates what I mean:

> A few months ago word was heard from Billy Gray, who used to play brother Bud in "Father Knows Best," the 1950s television show about the nice Anderson family who lived in the white frame house on a side street in some mythical Springfield—the house at which the father arrived each night swinging open the front door and singing out, "Margaret, I'm home!" Gray said he felt "ashamed" that he had ever had anything to do with the show. It was all "totally false," he said, and had caused many Americans to feel inadequate, because they thought that was the way life was supposed to be and that their own lives failed to measure up.

As Susan Sontag has noted in *On Photography,* mass-produced images have "extraordinary powers to determine our demands upon reality." The family is especially **vulnerable** to confusion between truth and illusion. What, after all, is "normal"? All of us have a backstairs view of our own families, but we know The Family, in the **aggregate**, only **vicariously**.

Like politics or athletics, the family has become a media event. Television offers nightly portrayals of lump-in-the-throat family "normalcy" ("The Waltons," "Little House on the Prairie") and, nowadays, even humorous "deviance" ("One Day at a Time," "The Odd Couple"). Family advisers sally forth in syndicated newspaper columns to uphold standards, mend relationships, suggest counseling,

vulnerable: susceptible to being weakened or hurt

aggregate: groups that come together to make a whole unit

vicariously: only through other people's viewpoints

196

and otherwise lead their readers back to the True Path. For commercial purposes, advertisers spend millions of dollars to create stirring **vignettes** of glamorous-but-ordinary families, the kind of family most 11-year-olds wish they had.

All Americans do not, of course, live in such a family, but most share an intuitive sense of what the "ideal" family should be—reflected in the **precepts** of religion, the conventions of etiquette, and the assumptions of law. And, characteristically, Americans tend to project the ideal back into the past, the time when virtues of all sorts are thought to have flourished.

We do not come off well by comparison with that golden age, nor could we, for it is as elusive and mythical as Brigadoon. If Billy Gray shames too easily, he has a valid point: While Americans view the family as the proper context for their own lives—9 out of 10 people live in one—they have no realistic context in which to view the family. Family history, until recently, was as neglected in academe as it still is in the press. The familiar, depressing charts of "leading family indicators"—marriage, divorce, illegitimacy—in newspapers and newsmagazines rarely survey the trends before World War II. The discussion, in short, lacks **ballast**.

Let us go back to before the American Revolution.

Perhaps what distinguishes the modern family most from its colonial counterpart is its newfound privacy. Throughout the seventeenth and eighteenth centuries, well over 90 percent of the American population lived in small rural communities. Unusual behavior rarely went unnoticed, and neighbors often intervened directly in a family's affairs, to help or to **chastise**.

The most dramatic example was the rural "charivari," prevalent in both Europe and the United States until the early nineteenth century. The purpose of these noisy gatherings was to **censure** community members for familial **transgressions**—unusual sexual behavior, marriages between persons of grossly **discrepant** ages, or "household disorder," to name but a few. As historian Edward Shorter describes it in *The Making of the Modern Family:*

> Sometimes the demonstration would consist of masked individuals circling somebody's house at night, screaming, beating on pans, and blowing cow horns . . . on other occasions, the offender would be seized and marched through the streets, seated perhaps backwards on a donkey or forced to wear a placard describing his sins.

The state itself had no qualms about intruding into a family's affairs by statute, if necessary. Consider seventeenth-century New England's "stubborn child" laws that, though never actually enforced, sanctioned the death penalty for chronic disobedience to one's parents.

If the boundaries between home and society seem blurred during the colonial era, it is because they were. People were neither very emotional nor very self-conscious about family life, and, as historian John Demos points out, family and community were "joined in a relation of profound **reciprocity**." In his *Of Domesticall Duties,* William Gouge, a seventeenth-century Puritan preacher, called the family "a little community." The home, like the larger community, was as much an economic as a social unit; all members of the family worked, be it on the farm, or in a shop, or in the home.

There was not much to idealize. Love was not considered the basis for marriage but one possible result of it. According to historian Carl Degler, it was easier to obtain a divorce in colonial New England than anywhere else in the Western world, and the divorce rate climbed steadily throughout the eighteenth century, though it remained low by contemporary standards. Romantic images to the contrary, it was rare for more than two generations (parents and children) to share a household, for the simple reason that very few people lived beyond the age of 60. It is ironic that our nostalgia for the extended family—including grandparents and

vignettes: scenes

precepts: a principle prescribing conduct

ballast: something that gives stability

chastise: punish

censure: to express disapproval strongly

transgressions: violations

discrepant: different

reciprocity: mutual exchange

grandchildren—comes at a time when, thanks to improvements in health care, its existence is less threatened than ever before.

Infant mortality was high in colonial days, though not as high as we are accustomed to believe, since food was plentiful and epidemics, owing to generally low population density, were few. In the mid-1700s, the average age of marriage was about 24 for men, 21 for women—not much different from what it is now. Households, on average, were larger, but not startlingly so: A typical household in 1790 included about 5.6 members, versus about 3.5 today. Illegitimacy was widespread. Premarital pregnancies reached a high in eighteenth-century America (10 percent of all first births) that was not equaled until the 1950s.

In simple **demographic** terms, then, the differences between the American family in colonial times and today are not all that stark; the similarities are sometimes striking.

The chief contrast is psychological. While Western societies have always idealized the family to some degree, the *most vivid* literary portrayals of family life before the nineteenth century were negative or, at best, ambivalent. In what might be called the "high tragic" tradition—including Sophocles, Shakespeare, and the Bible, as well as fairy tales and novels—the family was portrayed as a high-voltage emotional setting, laden with dark passions, sibling rivalries, and violence. There was also the "low comic" tradition—the world of hen-pecked husbands and tyrannical mothers-in-law.

It is unlikely that our eighteenth-century ancestors ever left the book of Genesis or *Tom Jones* with the feeling that their own family lives were seriously flawed.

By the time of the Civil War, however, American attitudes toward the family had changed profoundly. The early decades of the nineteenth century marked the beginnings of America's gradual transformation into an urban, industrial society. In 1820, less than 8 percent of the U.S. population lived in cities; by 1860, the urban concentration approached 20 percent, and by 1900 that proportion had doubled.

Structurally, the American family did not immediately undergo a comparable transformation. Despite the large families of many immigrants and farmers, the size of the *average* family declined—slowly but steadily—as it had been doing since the seventeenth century. Infant mortality remained about the same, and may even have increased somewhat, owing to poor sanitation in crowded cities. Legal divorces were easier to obtain than they had been in colonial times. Indeed, the rise in the divorce rate was a matter of some concern during the nineteenth century, though death, not divorce, was the prime cause of one-parent families, as it was up to 1965.

Functionally, however, America's industrial revolution had a lasting effect on the family. No longer was the household typically a group of interdependent workers. Now, men went to offices and factories and became breadwinners; wives stayed home to mind the hearth; children went off to the new public schools. The home was set apart from the dog-eat-dog arena of economic life; it came to be viewed as a utopian retreat or, in historian Christopher Lasch's phrase, a "haven in a heartless world." Marriage was now valued primarily for its emotional attractions. Above all, the family became something to worry about.

The earliest and most saccharine "sentimental model" of the family appeared in the new mass media that proliferated during the second quarter of the nineteenth century. Novels, tracts, newspaper articles, and ladies' magazines—there were variations for each class of society—elaborated a "Cult of True Womanhood" in which piety, submissiveness, and domesticity dominated the **pantheon** of desirable feminine qualities. This quotation from *The Ladies Book* (1830) is typical:

demographic: relating to the statistical study of populations

pantheon: a temple

See, she sits, she walks, she speaks, she looks—unutterable things!
Inspiration springs up in her very paths—it follows her footsteps. A

198

halo of glory encircles her, and illuminates her whole orbit. With her, man not only feels safe, but actually renovated.

In the late 1800s, science came into the picture. The "professionalization" of the housewife took two different forms. One involved motherhood and childrearing, according to the latest scientific understanding of children's special physical and emotional needs. (It is no accident that the publishing of children's books became a major industry during this period.) The other was the domestic science movement—"home economics," basically—which focused on the woman as full-time homemaker, applying "scientific" and "industrial" rationality to shopping, making meals, and housework.

The new ideal of the family prompted a cultural split that has endured, one that Tocqueville had glimpsed (and rather liked) in 1835. Society was divided more sharply into man's sphere and woman's sphere. Toughness, competition, and practicality were the masculine values that ruled the outside world. The softer values—affection, tranquility, piety—were worshiped in the home and the church. In contrast to the colonial view, the ideology of the "modern" family implied a **critique** of everything beyond the front door.

What is striking as one looks at the writings of the nineteenth-century "experts"—the physicians, clergymen, **phrenologists**, and "scribbling ladies"—is how little their essential message differs from that of the sociologists, psychiatrists, pediatricians, and women's magazine writers of the twentieth century, particularly since World War II.

Instead of men's and women's spheres, of course, sociologists speak of "instrumental" and "expressive" roles. The notion of the family as a retreat from the harsh realities of the outside world crops up as "functional differentiation." And, like the nineteenth-century utopians who believed society could be regenerated through the perfection of family life, twentieth-century social scientists have looked at the failed family as the source of most American social problems.

None of those who promoted the sentimental model of the family—neither the popular writers nor the academics—considered the paradox of perfectionism: the ironic possibility that it would lead to trouble. Yet it has. The image of the perfect, happy family makes ordinary families seem like failures. Small problems loom as big problems if the "normal" family is thought to be one where there are no real problems at all.

One sees this phenomenon at work on the generation of Americans born and reared during the late nineteenth century, the first generation reared on the mother's milk of sentimental imagery. Between 1900 and 1920, the U.S. divorce rate doubled, from four to eight divorces annually per 1,000 married couples. The jump—comparable to the 100 percent increase in the divorce rate between 1960 and 1980—is not attributable to changes in divorce laws, which were not greatly **liberalized**. Rather, it would appear that, as historian Thomas O'Neill believes, Americans were simply more willing to dissolve marriages that did not conform to their ideal of domestic bliss—and perhaps try again.

If anything, family standards became even more demanding as the twentieth century progressed. The new fields of psychology and sociology opened up whole new definitions of familial perfection. "Feelings"—fun, love, warmth, good orgasm—acquired heightened popular significance as the invisible glue of successful families.

Psychologist Martha Wolfenstein, in an analysis of several decades of government-sponsored infant care manuals, has documented the emergence of a "fun morality." In former days, being a good parent meant carrying out certain tasks with **punctilio**; if your child was clean and reasonably obedient, you had no cause to probe his **psyche**. Now, we are told, parents must **commune** with their own feelings and those of their children—an **edict** which has seeped into the **ethos** of

critique: criticism

phrenologists: people who attempt to analyze character by examining the characteristics of the skull

liberalized: made to favor individual freedom

punctilio: precise observance of amenities or formalities

psyche: mind

commune: to communicate with intensity

edict: order or proclamation

ethos: belief system

education as well. The distinction is rather like that between religions of deed and religions of faith. It is one thing to make your child brush his teeth; it is quite another to transform the whole process into a joyous "learning experience."

The task of twentieth-century parents has been further complicated by the advice offered them. The experts disagree with each other and often contradict themselves. The kindly Dr. Benjamin Spock, for example, is full of contradictions. In a detailed analysis of *Baby and Child Care,* historian Michael Zuckerman observes that Spock tells mothers to relax ("trust yourself") yet warns them that they have an "**ominous** power" to destroy their children's innocence and make them discontented "for years" or even "forever."

Since the mid-1960s, there has been a youth rebellion of sorts, a new "sexual revolution," a revival of feminism, and the emergence of the two-worker family. The huge postwar Baby-Boom generation is pairing off, accounting in part for the upsurge in the divorce rate (half of all divorces occur within seven years of a first marriage). Media images of the family have become more "realistic," reflecting new patterns of family life that are emerging (and old patterns that are re-emerging).

Among social scientists, "realism" is becoming something of an ideal in itself. For some of them, realism translates as **pluralism**: All forms of the family, by virtue of the fact that they happen to exist, are equally acceptable—from communes and cohabitation to one-parent households, homosexual marriages, and, come to think of it, the nuclear family. What was once labeled "deviant" is now merely "variant." In some college texts, "the family" has been replaced by "family systems." Yet, this new approach does not seem to have squelched perfectionist standards. Indeed, a palpable strain of perfectionism runs through the pop literature on "alternative" family lifestyles.

ominous: dreaded

pluralism: the idea that no one belief system can explain all the phenomena encountered in life

resilient: recovering speedily from adversity; buoyant

For the majority of scholars, realism means a more down-to-earth view of the American household. Rather than seeing the family as a haven of peace and tranquility, they have begun to recognize that even "normal" families are less than ideal, that intimate relations of any sort inevitably involve antagonism as well as love. Conflict and change are inherent in social life. If the family is now in a state of flux, such is the nature of **resilient** institutions; if it is beset by problems, so is life. The family will survive.

▼ Questions to Focus Reading

1. What reasons does Skolnick give for saying that the family is especially vulnerable to confusion between truth and illusion?

2. What in Skolnick's view was the valid point the actor Billy Gray was making?

3. What evidence does she give for saying the "boundaries between home and society seem blurred during the colonial era"?

4. What does she find ironic in our nostalgia for the extended family, including grandparents and grandchildren?

5. Skolnick tells us that the differences between the American family in colonial times and today are not very great, that demographically, the similarities are quite striking. With what facts does she support this?

6. America's transformation from a rural agrarian to an urban industrial society brought significant changes in people's conception of the key function of the family and in their attitude toward it. What were these changes in function and attitude?

7. What was the "Cult of True Womanhood"?

8. What contribution did science make in the late 1800s to the popular conception of the woman's role?

9. What is the "paradox of perfectionism"? What evidence does she present for the claim that perfectionism has led to trouble?

10. "Family standards became even more demanding as the twentieth century progressed," Skolnick writes. In what way?
11. Skolnick cites some reactions against perfectionist standards for the family. What are the reactions?
12. What justification does she offer for her prediction, "The family will survive"?

▼ Questions for Reflection

1. When you think about your own family, do you find yourself referring to some ideal standard for comparison? If so, what is that standard? From what sources did you derive it? How much of your conception of the ideal family did you derive from the media?
2. What are the ingredients of a good family life in your own view? What characteristics of personality, habits of thought, and habits of behavior are required for the heads of such a family? Do you have these characteristics and habits? If not, do you think you can develop them? How?
3. Why does Arlene Skolnick think it is so important that we get some historical perspective on the family? What does she think that will accomplish?
4. "Among social scientists," she writes, " 'realism' is becoming something of an ideal in itself." Do you think this describes Pepper Schwartz? (See "The Family as a Changed Institution" Reading 34.)
5. Do you share Skolnick's optimism about the future of the family? Why or why not?

▼ Discussion

1. In preparation for class discussion, watch some television programs and commercials that portray family life. Look, too, for some advertisements in magazines that do this. Bring the ads to class. How is the family being depicted on television and in the ads? Do we have in these instances the dangers of perfectionism, or are these cases of the realistic reaction to perfectionism?
2. What are the key characteristics of a good family life? What in the best case would the family accomplish for its members? What personality traits and habits of thinking and acting are required for the heads of the kind of family you have in mind? How would these traits and habits be developed by a person who didn't have them?
3. What is the "paradox of perfectionism"? How did it develop? How has it intensified in the twentieth century? Do you think it continues to intensify, or have the realistic reactions Skolnick alludes to replaced the ideal of perfection? What evidences do you have for your answer?
4. Why does Arlene Skolnick think it is so important that we get some historical perspective on the family? What does she think that will accomplish?

▼ Writing Assignments

1. Write about your own conception of the ideal family. What are its functions? What are the characteristics of the heads of this household?
2. Examine a set of advertisements in magazines and commercials on television. Describe the commercials and, perhaps, cut out the ads. What conception of family life is conveyed in them?
3. Describe an important experience (or experiences) that showed you what a family can be in the best case.

4. In a fictional study report, describe the condition of the American family in 2050.

▼ Journal Entry

1. Is having a family one of your goals in life? If so, why especially is this so important to you? If not, why do you reject the idea?

▼ Vocabulary

aggregate	demographic	pantheon	reciprocity
ballast	discrepant	phrenologists	resilient
censure	edict	pluralism	transgressions
chastise	ethos	precepts	vicariously
commune	liberalized	psyche	vignettes
critique	ominous	punctilio	vulnerable

34

▼

The Family as a Changed Institution

Pepper Schwartz

"In all honesty, we should just take 'for worse' out of the marriage ceremony."
Sociologist Pepper Schwartz (University of Washington) predicts the shape of a
deeply changed American institution.

The American family, as an institution, has been slowly **metamorphosing** for the
past 100 years, and now I think the transformation is quite complete. . . .

The contemporary family is composed of voluntary associations, each person
having limited power over the other. Spouses can leave if necessary, children have
outside resources to draw on if the family has ruptured, and thus all interaction
has an invisible alternative that is weighed in as costs and benefits are assessed.
While love and loyalty and the dream of lifetime commitment are still strong
cultural themes, the fact is that when spouses are unhappy or feel deprived, they
will end their marriages, and when rewards between parents and children diminish,
they may carry out their responsibilities (as they see them) but they will not sacrifice their own life plans for one another.

Most commentators dislike the new individualist and utilitarian ethic and
blame its emergence on a generation (baby boomers), or on women (for leaving
the home and wanting equality), or on capitalism (for evaluating relationships according to goods and services distributed), or even psychiatry (for concentrating
on the self as opposed to the community). This seems like a lot of tree counting
to me when the obvious fact is we are now in a forest. All these arguments have
merit (but for their moral overtones)—except they imply that if people were a little
less selfish, or women a little less interested in personal choice, or we turned from
the material to the spiritual or collective conscience, we could reclaim our familial
bonds. Would that life were so able to be conquered by sheer force of will!

If sociology is useful at all, it is to show us that there have been historical,
social, cultural, and economic forces to put us exactly where we are today and
that at some point enough change occurs so that the institution itself is a new form.
One might hypothesize that the traditional family was **undermined** with the founding of this country on the principle of enlightened self-interest. And when that
principle actually came to be extended to all citizens in practice, not just theory,
it was inevitable that the family, a group that must necessarily compromise some
members' interests for the good of the whole, would change dramatically. And this
has happened. **Individualist utilitarianism** is not only **operational**, it is **normative**. We no longer **laud** a woman who stays with a man who beats her because
she agreed to stay married for better or for worse (in all honesty, we should just
take "for worse" out of the marriage ceremony), nor do we feel that parents should
deprive themselves of all worldly pleasures so that their children can live a little
better. . . .

I think we are in a new evolutionary stage. Individual self-interest will create
three major family types. The single head of household family will proliferate
among the poor and economically unstable unless the partnership can provide benefits that single status cannot. Right now, with the combination of government support for children, the ability of a poor woman to exist financially without a husband

metamorphosing: changing completely in character or circumstances

undermined: seriously weakened
by removing underlying support

individualist utilitarianism: acting to promote one's own happiness

operational: reflecting what is
practiced

normative: reflecting what is assumed as a norm

laud: praise

203

(indeed, finding it difficult to incorporate a low-earning husband into the household), and not enough incentive for a low-earning man to stay married, the family composition of this class seems destined to be reorganized around women and children.

The "blended family" (a misnomer if ever there was one) is the model for the middle class. This class is increasingly composed of two earners, both of whom earn decent salaries, but neither of whom alone can earn enough to provide the desired lifestyle. Thus there is a strong incentive to marry and remarry if the match proves unsatisfactory. There are high financial costs for leaving, so divorce will remain undesirable but still unavoidable for some, given the search for self-fulfillment and/or "a good life." Because marriage is beneficial to both parties, families from previous relationships will be combined, which exacts a high cost. Recent research indicates that the high divorce rates of remarriage are at least partly attributable to the pressures of combining families. Thus divorce in this class will still be high, pushing some people into remarriage and some into single head of household status.

The third type of family will be the executive family, with high enough income so that the woman can decide not to work, or, if they are a dual-career couple, they will have even more money and discretionary income to contribute to home and family. Economic self-interest will be enhanced by either mutual contribution or such high income that the nonearner, anxious to maximize class position, will try to make the other partner feel benefited enough to remain in the marriage. Divorce should be common here too, however, as the level of independence of the individuals in this group is so high that reassessment of the value of one's circumstances, from time to time, is inevitable.

All of these scenarios have this in common: Both individuals are doing the best they can—for themselves first, for their children a far second, and for extended ties, family and peers, least of all. This is not to say there is an absence of generosity or love. This is not the case now, nor do I expect it to be the case in the future. It is *relative* emphasis that is important here, and the point is that the individual will not only come first, he or she will have a social structure that will allow individual **agendas** to be accomplished.

I do not see this as a moral emergency. This is not any worse to me than a system where the family good was to a great extent determined by only one player, the father and husband. The corporate marriage was hard on women, because when individual interest was to be sacrificed, it was the woman who was asked to give more than her fair share. To pine, as Christopher Lasch and other conservative observers do, for the family of yesteryear is to do a whitewash of gigantic proportion—no one who has even modest aspirations as a feminist would **eulogize** the way the traditional family worked as a **collective** enterprise.

But neither nostalgia nor anger at the past should confuse us about the exact nature of the future. The future will be one where compromise will not necessarily be made by women or for children. Then the issues become: What are the long-term effects of the destabilized family on society? How well do individuals fare who pursue their own self-interest (as they see it) rather than attempt to do well within the constrictions and protections of the family?

One understudied and overdescribed place to look is the literature on **cohabitors**. Cohabitors are the Orwellian vision of the family—a place we have not come to yet, but which is certainly a possibility. Under the **amorphous** rules of most cohabitation, each person is basically on his or her own. Not counting those cohabitors who live together for cynical reasons or for convenience, cohabitors stay together for so long as they are in love or until they marry. In the meantime, they do not let their love or sexual attraction undermine each partner's best interests. They are frank about what they will and will not do for one another, the limits of their commitment, and their need to be able to survive without the other person.

agendas: lists or plans of matters to be attended to

eulogize: praise highly

collective: pertaining to a group functioning as a team

cohabitors: unmarried couples who live together

amorphous: without pattern or structure

It is not clear to me that modern marriage will reach this extreme. Children do modify most people's absolute devotion to the self, and many coupled people believe they are highly benefited and wish to stabilize their bargain as much as they possibly can. I am saying that utilitarian individualism is the mentality that emerges out of our present and probable social circumstances, and it is time it was acknowledged and used as part of the way we now analyze family formation and functioning.

▼ Questions to Focus Reading

1. How has the American family been transformed in the last 100 years, according to Schwartz? She calls the new ethic of family life "individualist" and "utilitarian." In what senses is it this?
2. "Individual self-interest will create three major family types." What are these types? What characteristics, according to Schwartz, do they all have in common?
3. Schwartz does not see the transformation of the family as a "moral emergency." Why not?

▼ Questions for Reflection and Discussion

1. Do you agree with Schwartz that the transformation of the family is not a moral emergency? Explain.
2. What effect do you think the "destabilized" family has had on society? What effects do you think it will have in the long term?
3. What is your conception of the key features of a good family?

▼ Writing Assignments

1. Write an essay on the effect on your generation of the high divorce rate in your parents' generation.
2. Project your imagination ahead to the year 2050. Present a fictional account of the state of the American family in that time.

▼ Journal Entry

1. Does Schwartz's prognosis for the American family disturb you? Why or why not?

▼ Vocabulary

agendas	eulogize	metamorphosing
amorphous	individualist	normative
cohabitors	utilitarianism	operational
collective	laud	undermined

35

▼

The Legacy of Raizel Kaidish: A Story

Rebecca Goldstein

Rebecca Goldstein combines in her career two passions: one for fiction, one for philosophy. A professor of philosophy, she is also the author of two novels. This story demonstrates both her passions. It is about a strong woman's moral training of her daughter and her college daughter's very mixed reaction to it.

In 1945 the following incident took place in the death camp of Buchenwald. There were two young Jewish girls who had become very devoted to one another during the few months of their imprisonment. Each was the last survivor of her family. One morning one of them awoke too weak to work. Her name was put on the death list. The other, Raizel Kaidish, argued with her friend that she, Raizel, should go instead. She would tell the Germans there had been a mistake, and when they saw how strong and fit for work she was, it would be all right. Someone informed on the girls and they were both gassed. The informer was rewarded with Raizel's kitchen job.

I am named after Raizel Kaidish. My mother knew her from the camp. It is noteworthy that although the war took all her relatives from her, my mother chose to name her first child, her only child, after someone outside the family, after the heroine of block eight, Buchenwald.

My mother's moral framework was formed in the camp. Forged in the fires, it was strong and inflexible. One of her central concerns was that I, without myself suffering, would come to know all that she had learned there.

My moral education began at an early age. It consisted at first of tales from the camp. People in my real life were nice or mean, usually a little of both. But in the tales there were only saints and sinners, heroes and villains. I remember questioning my mother about this, and her answer to me: "When times are normal, Rose, then normal people are a little nice and a little mean together. But when there are hard times, when there is not enough to eat or drink, when there is war, then you don't find a little nice and a little mean mixed together. You find only greatness. Very great badness and very great goodness."

The people in my life did not seem so real to me as the people in the tales. When I closed my eyes I couldn't picture the faces of my friends or family. All that I could make out of my father was a vaguely sad face around the glinting rimless glasses. (It seemed, in my child's mind, that the light bouncing off from those polished lenses gave the wrong impression, suggesting something hard and resistant, whereas I knew that everything in my father yielded to the touch.) Even my mother's features wouldn't come into focus, only her outline: tall and always erect, in the grey or dark blue suit and the white blouse, her light brown hair in a low bun at the nape of her neck.

But my images of the camp were vivid and detailed. The pink rosebuds on my wallpaper were not as real to me as the grey and drab green of the barracks, the brown of the mud. It seemed to me that I knew the feel through decaying shoes of the sharp stones in the main square, the sight, twice daily, of the terrifying roll-call. It seemed I too had quickly glanced up at the open sky and wondered that others outside saw the same sky.

206

My father, a doctor like my mother, did not approve of the tales:

"She's too young. You'll give her nightmares, traumas. A child this age shouldn't know."

"A child this age. Don't be a hypocrite, Saul. You know you would never consider her old enough to know."

"And why should she know? Can't we forget already? Can't we live like others?"

"No. We can't. I wouldn't even want to. Would you really want it, Saul, to think and live like the others? To join the sleepwalkers, with the glazed eyes and the smug smiles? Is that why we lived when the others didn't? Is that what we want for our daughter?"

And at this point I can hear my father's sigh, the deep drawn-out sigh so characteristic of him, which had always seemed to me, when I was young, to have the slight tremor of a sob. My father's sadness was something I felt I could almost reach out and touch, like my mother's goodness.

The arguments between my parents continued throughout my childhood. And my father, so gentle, was a man who hated to fight. In the quiet of the night, awake in my bed, I would catch the **cadences** of their voices, my father's sad and low, so that I missed much of what he said, my mother's burning with her quiet blue fury.

But the lessons continued, the simple stark tales of cruelty and sacrifice, cowardice and courage. And always she came back to the story of my namesake. She would tell me that she had honored both Raizel and me in choosing my name. (She called me Raizel or even Raizele sometimes, in rare moments of tenderness, stroking back my hair.) She hoped that I too would be capable of real courage, of giving another's life just as much importance as my own.

*   *   *

When I reached fourteen, my mother, deeming me to have arrived at least at the age of reason (and also the age at which Raizel had sacrificed herself), began to instruct me in the moral theory she had worked out in Buchenwald. The theory is elaborate and detailed, **reminiscent** of the German my parents spoke to one another: complications nesting within complications. The brief account I give here is necessarily inadequate, and perhaps not **intrinsically** interesting. But the picture of my mother is incomplete without a description of her moral viewpoint.

My mother believed that the ethical outlook is the impersonal outlook. One is morally obliged to look at a situation without regard for one's own identity in it and to act in the way which is dictated by this impersonal view; to act in the way one believes will minimize the sum of suffering. My mother's emphasis was always on minimizing pain and suffering, never maximizing happiness or well-being. She explained this to me once when, much older, I questioned her: "I know what is evil. To know suffering is to know evil. None of the attempts to identify the good have this same certainty."

So far there is nothing, except for its pessimistic cast, to distinguish my mother's view from the great bulk of **utilitarian** theories. The special twist comes in the foundations she claimed, and it is a twist that mirrors her personality: her uncompromising **rationality**. The expression of this came in her denial of the "separateness" of the ethical realm. Ethics for her was nothing but a species of logic. The moral obligation is nothing over and above the obligation to be logically consistent, and virtue reduces to rationality.

Why is this so? Because to deny the obligation of acting on the impersonal viewpoint, one would have to maintain that one's self has some special **metaphysical** significance, that it makes a difference that one is who one is. And how can this consistency be maintained once one has recognized the existence of other

cadences: rhythmic flow of a series of sounds or words

reminiscent: suggestive (of)

intrinsically: innately

utilitarian: taking as the standard of morality the promotion of the greatest happiness for the greatest number of people

rationality: the habit of governing one's thinking by reason

metaphysical: pertaining to the nature of the ultimate scheme of things

207

selves, each of whom is who he is? (Only the **solipsist** can consistently be unethical.) To use one of her favorite analogies: the person who acts only in his own interest is like a person who says there is always something special about his location, because he can always say "I am here," whereas everyone else is merely there. Once one has granted that there are other subjects of experience, other selves which suffer, then one can maintain that one's own pain matters (and who would deny this?) only if one grants that the pain of everyone else matters in exactly the same way.

*   *   *

Raizel Kaidish's behavior was **paradigmatically** ethical. Viewing the situation impersonally, this fourteen-year-old saw that the stronger child would have a better, though slim, chance to survive. She acted on this view, undeterred by the fact that it was she who was the stronger, she who was unnecessarily risking her life.

After the liberation my mother returned to Berlin to continue her formal training in medicine. She also began her lifelong study of philosophy. She was curious to see who among the philosophically great had shared her discovery. Kant she considered to be the most worthwhile **ethicist**. Socrates she loved for his devotion to the ethical questions, for his conviction that nothing ought to concern us more than the questions of how to live our lives. (Hanging over my bed, the only piece of embroidery I've ever known her to do, was the Socratic quotation: "The unexamined life is not worth living.") But for the most part my mother found the great philosophers of the past a disappointment. The truth, so simple, had eluded them, because they had assumed the separateness of the ethical realm. Some had grasped pieces of it, but few had seen the unseamed whole.

It was contemporary philosophers, however, particularly the **positivists** and their "fellow travelers," who aroused her wrath. For here were philosophers who dismissed the possibility of all ethical reason, who denied the very subject matter of the field. Instead of conducting inquiries into the nature of our moral obligations, they have offered analyses of the grammar of ethical propositions. She would look up from some contemporary philosophical book or journal, her eyes blazing their blue fury:

"Positivists." The intonation she gave the word was similar to that she gave "Nazi." "They don't see because their eyes aren't turned outward but inward, into the blackness of their own minds. To forsake the important questions for this dribble! To spend your life examining quibbles!"

And I? How did I feel about my extensive moral training? The object of so much attention, of all the **pedagogical** theorizing, the fights in the night, I felt ignored, unloved, of no significance. And, especially as I grew older, I felt angry—a dumb, unacknowledged outrage. It was not just a matter of the rigidity of my upbringing, the lack of laughter in a home where one could reach out and touch one's father's sadness and mother's goodness. It was not just the fact that I was always made to feel so different from my friends, so that I often, though always with a great sense of guilt, fantasized myself in another family with parents who were **frivolous** and happy and had no numbers burned into their arms. But it was something else that infuriated me. There is, of course, nothing unusual in a child's resentment of a mother. My friends, from early adolescence onward, were always annoyed with one or another of their parents. But theirs was the pure clean **indignation** which is unashamed of itself. Mine was an anger also angry at itself. Hadn't she suffered enough? Shouldn't I try to do everything to make it up to her? By hating her I joined the ranks of her enemies. I allied myself with the murderers.

And so the resentment, folded back on itself again and again, thickened and darkened. Never once did I ever say, not even to myself, "I am angry at this

solipsist: one who believes that only he or she exists

paradigmatically: serving as a model

ethicist: philosopher who deals with the question about the rightness and wrongness of human actions

positivists: members of a school of philosophy that maintains that sense perception is the basis of all admissible knowledge

pedagogical: pertaining to the art or science of teaching

frivolous: marked by a lack of seriousness

indignation: righteous anger

woman." This acknowledgment came years later, after she was dead, during the time in which I deliberated over having a child of my own. (The mental delivery of this decision was so much more painful than the actual physical delivery.) In debating the reasons for having a child, I asked myself whether any reasons could be right, whether one was ever justified in bringing a person into being for some reason of one's own? But if not for one's own reason, then whose?

It seemed a moral inconsistency woven into the very fabric of human existence. And then I realized that the *act* of parenting need not bear any of this moral compromise: it is possible for the reason one had for creating a child to recede in significance in the face of the fact of that child's existence. The ends for which one bore the child lose themselves in the knowledge of the child itself. This is the essence of good parenting; and it was exactly what I felt to be missing from the relationship between my mother and me. I knew what no child should ever know: that my mother had had me for some definite reason and that she would always see me in terms of this reason. I sensed this in my mother, and I hated her for it.

I said that my anger never showed itself. Actually there was a brief rebellion whose form was so typical of the oddity of my family that now, years later, even I can see its comic aspects and smile. My first semester of college, while my friends developed their own conventional modes of rebellion, I worked out mine. I became a positivist. I took Introduction to Philosophy with a self-intoxicated young professor, a new Ph.D. from Harvard, and, although this would not be his own description, a neopositivist. He told us during the first lecture that he was going to show us, over the course of the semester, why we were lucky, insofar as we were philosophy students, to have been born now; that it was now possible to see that previous generations had devoted themselves to pseudoquestions concerning the nature of Reality, Truth, and The Good; and that such questions were expressions of logical confusion. These fine big words don't name anything, and thus there is nothing there whose nature is to be explored.

I sat there drinking in his words, thinking, "This is it. This is why I came to college." All through that term, Monday, Wednesday, and Friday, from ten to eleven, while others dozed and doodled, I listened in a state of **delirium**, following the arguments with a concentration I have never attained since. My mind bubbled over with the excitement of this **illicit** doctrine, this forbidden philosophy. And the most forbidden, and therefore delicious, view offered in the course was that devoted to ethics, or rather the dismissal of ethics.

I memorized whole passages out of my favorite book, A. J. Ayer's *Language, Truth and Logic:* "We can now see why it is impossible to find a criterion for determining the validity of ethical judgments. It is not because they have an 'absolute' validity which is mysteriously independent of ordinary sense-experience, but because they have no objective validity whatsoever. If a sentence makes no statement at all, there is obviously no sense in asking whether what it says is true or false. And we have seen that sentences which simply express moral judgments do not say anything. They are pure expressions of feeling and as such do not come under the category of truth and falsehood." I was moved by the sparse beauty and elegance of the arguments. How had I never seen if before, never seen that my mother's unshakable theory was nothing but a floating airy **fabrication** of pseudostatements?

*   *   *

My preparations for final exams were trivial compared to my cramming for the visit home during intercession. I arrived back about eleven at night, too late for philosophical debate. But my mind was so teeming with positivist arguments that when my mother wished me "good night" I almost challenged her: "What do you mean by that? What do you mean by 'good'?"

delirium: state of violent emotion or excitement
illicit: unlawful; not permitted
fabrication: something made up

The next evening, after my mother and father arrived home from the hospital, we all sat in the living room while Bertha, our housekeeper, finished dinner. I was waiting for the right moment for launching my attack, any comment which was mildly **speculative**. But my perverse mother was all practicality that night. She asked me about the food at school, about my roommate, even told a funny story about her own roommate, in Berlin before the war. Then finally:

"You were always so brief on the phone when I asked you about your classes. Tell me more about them. You seemed to have enjoyed them very much."

"Yes, they were wonderful. Especially philosophy. I'm going to major in it."

"Really? I've always thought it a rather funny kind of profession. Every person should of course think about philosophy, but it seems an odd way to earn one's living."

"But what about teaching, Marta?" my father, the eternal peacemaker, asked. "Don't you think it's important to have people teaching philosophy?"

"Well yes, that's true. But I suspect that most of them don't think of themselves primarily as teachers, but as thinkers, professional thinkers, however strange that sounds. Well, we can ask Rose here. What do you fancy yourself, a teacher or a philosopher?"

"A philosopher of course. The need for professional training in philosophy is no different than anywhere else, no different than in medicine. People think they can just jump in and start philosophizing and that they'll make sense. They rarely do. It takes technical training."

"Oh? I disagree very much, as you know, with this emphasis on technical training. Instead of humanizing the mathematical sciences they try to mathematize the humanities. Translating into a lot of complicated symbols doesn't show the truth of what you're saying."

"But it does often show its meaninglessness."

"Oh really? Yes, I can see how that might often be true."

Impossible woman! What was wrong with her? Her kindling point was usually so frighteningly low, but tonight she would not burn. She wouldn't even flicker. (The explanation would have been obvious to anyone not occupying my vantage point. She was, quite simply, very happy to see me.)

I had no more patience. I abandoned my hopes for a smooth transition.

"Mother, there's a question about ethics that has been bothering me."

There. I had opened the door. Now I had to walk through.

"Yes? Tell me about it. Perhaps I can help."

"You've always said that the moral obligation is nothing but the obligation to be logically consistent. But why do we have to be logically consistent?"

"I must say you surprise me. Such an antirationalist question. And after a semester of college. The answer is, of course, that the truth is important. And logical inconsistencies can't be true. If you ask me why the truth is important I can't give you a noncircular answer. Anything I say is going to presuppose the importance of truth, as all rational **discourse** presupposes it. And this impossibility of a noncircular answer is itself the answer.

"I don't understand a word you're saying!" I exploded. "The Truth! The sacred lofty Truth! What's the Truth? Where's the Truth? Let me see you point to it. What does it mean to say 'The Truth is important'? What **cognitive** content can it possibly have? It's nonsense. And the same with all the other so-called truths of your so-called theory. You claim to be so rational, but you're only emoting. Eternally emoting. And I'm sick to death of it!"

My speech was not delivered in that cool voice of detached reason I had so **diligently** rehearsed. Instead it tore out of me with a force that amazed me, sweeping me along.

The effect was immediate. My mother's face had the same capacity for instantaneous transformation I have observed in my infant daughter. (I often find

speculative: theoretic

discourse: conversation

cognitive: pertaining to knowledge

diligently: attentively and persistently

210

myself wondering whether this is a trait characteristic of infancy, or whether it is something my Marta has inherited from her grandmother, along with her name.) My mother had never raised her voice to me, and she did not do so now. As always her eyes did all the screaming.

"Positivist." Her introduction was not the usual one. There was outrage and contempt, but it was muffled by sadness.

"After all that I have taught you, you speak that way? You lose everything in one semester of college? Have you so little substance that at your first exposure to the **jargon** of these antithinkers you disintegrate?"

I had no answer. The brilliant arguments cramming my head only the night before were all gone. My head was so hollow it felt like it was floating away from the rest of me. The numbing fog of shame and guilt was settling back over everything. I dimly saw my father sitting there, staring out at us over the wall of his sadness. My mother's voice burned through the haze.

"You disappoint me. You disappoint us all. You are not worthy to be named after Raizel Kaidish."

*   *   *

Soon after my wedding, when my mother was fifty-six, she learned that she had cancer of the uterus and had no more than six months to live. She reacted to her impending death as if she had been preparing for it her whole life, as indeed she had been. She looked at it with her customary objectivity: Yes, she was relatively young, and there were still many things that she would have liked to experience, particularly grandparenthood. But that she, a Jew from Berlin, had been given these past thirty years was a fact whose response was gratitude, not the greedy demand for yet more years.

She never complained. Her greatest worry was the mental pain her illness was causing my father and me. She died as I had always known her to live: with superhuman discipline and courage.

A week before she died she told me that it had been she who had informed on Raizel Kaidish. She asked my forgiveness.

jargon: technical or specialized language

▼ Questions about the Story

1. Rose's mother and father have very different attitudes toward the focus in Rose's moral education on the death camps. How do they defend their conflicting attitudes?

2. What picture do you get from the opening of the story of Rose's mother, her father?

3. What is the mother's moral philosophy? How in her view does virtue reduce to rationality?

4. Why is Raizel Kaidish's action regarded by the mother as a model of ethical behavior?

5. Why does the mother so despise contemporary philosophers?

6. What was Rose's reaction to her moral training?

7. Debating with herself over whether she should have a child, the adult Rose, who is telling the story, concludes, "The ends for which one bore the child lose themselves in the knowledge of the child itself. This is the essence of good parenting." What did she mean by this? What in her own experience made this clear to her?

8. What is it about Rose's philosophy class that so excites her?

9. How is Rose's anger at her mother finally expressed? What is her mother's reaction?

10. What was your reaction to the ending? Does it cast light on the mother's beliefs and teachings? On her treatment of her daughter?

▼ Questions for Reflection

1. Does the ending make you think or feel differently about the mother? Explain.

2. The mother's emphasis in her ethical philosophy was on minimizing pain and suffering, not maximizing happiness or well-being. Her reason for this emphasis was her belief that evil could be identified unmistakably, whereas good could not. Do you agree with her about this?

3. A key event of this story is the confrontation between mother and daughter when Rose unleashes against her mother her new philosophical leanings. Are you experiencing a growing independence of mind as a result of your college life and learning? If so, what effect is your new independence having on your relationships with family members?

4. What were the main influences in your moral training? Has anything in your college study and/or experience so far had an effect on your moral outlook? Explain.

5. Do you expect your college education to have an effect on your moral development? Is moral growth something you think you should be experiencing in college? Why do you answer as you do?

6. Central to the mother's ethical stance was the idea that the ethical outlook is impersonal. If she were to deny this, she argued, she would have to maintain that she was special just because she is herself. But "I am myself" is something anyone can say, so no one is special in the sphere of ethics. Who one is, is irrelevant to moral rules; they apply to anyone and everyone impersonally. Do you understand her argument? Is she right in her view that "one can maintain that one's own pain matters . . . only if one grants that the pain of everyone else matters in exactly the same way?"

▼ Discussion

1. Are you sympathetic with Rose's mother? Explain. Does the ending change your feelings toward her? If so, how?

2. Are there certain ethical principles that are of great importance to you in the way you live your life and deal with others? If so, what are they? How did you arrive at them? Did you develop them as the result of certain teachings, certain experiences, both?

3. Are any aspects of your university experience (in class or outside it) affecting your thinking about morals? What, if any, aspects of university education should provide a basis for moral development?

▼ Writing Assignments

1. Do any of your experiences in college so far illustrate a development in your moral thinking? If so, describe that experience or those experiences and explain how your handling of it (them) represents development in your moral outlook.

2. Has anything you are learning in your classes been affecting your moral outlook? If so, write about these issues and how they are figuring in your examination of moral questions.

3. Is personal moral development something you expect to experience during your college years? If so, what aspects of college learning and life do you expect to be contributing to your moral development?

4. Write about Rose's mother's ethical outlook. What is her ethical philosophy? Do you agree with her? Why or why not?

5. Describe an incident in your life that helped establish one of the mainstays of your personal morality.

▼ Journal Entry

1. Do you feel you have been growing morally since you've been at the university? Why or why not? How do you measure this?

▼ Vocabulary

cadences	fabrication	metaphysical	solipsist
cognitive	frivolous	paradigmatically	speculative
delirium	illicit	pedagogical	utilitarian
diligently	indignation	positivists	
discourse	intrinsically	rationality	
ethicist	jargon	reminiscent	

36

▼

The Lost Cottage

David Leavitt

David Leavitt, novelist, essayist, and short story writer, introduces us to the Dempson family on their last vacation at their summer home.

The Dempson family had spent the last half of June in a little rented cottage called "Under the Weather," near Hyannis, every summer for twenty-six years, and this year, Lydia Dempson told her son, Mark, was to be no exception. "No matter what's happened," she insisted over two thousand miles of telephone wire, "we're a family. We've always gone, and we'll continue to go." Mark knew from her voice that the matter was closed. They would go again. He called an airline and made a plane reservation. He arranged for someone to take care of his apartment. He purged the four pages of his *Week-at-a-Glance* which covered those two weeks of all appointments and commitment.

A few days later he was there. The cottage still needed a coat of paint. His parents, Lydia and Alex, sat at the kitchen table and shucked ears of corn. Alex had on a white polo shirt and a sun visor, and talked about fishing. Lydia wore a new yellow dress, and over it a fuzzy white sweater. She picked loose hairs from the ears Alex had shucked, which were pearl-white, and would taste sweet. Tomorrow Mark's brother and sister, Douglas and Ellen, and Douglas's girlfriend, Julie, would arrive from the West Coast. It seemed like the opening scene from a play which tells the family's history by zeroing in on a few choice summer reunions, presumably culled from a long and happy series; to give the critical information. Mark had once imagined writing such a play, and casting Colleen Dewhurst as his mother, and Jason Robards as his father. The curtain rises. The lights come up to reveal a couple shucking corn. . . .

Six months before, Alex and Lydia had gathered their children around another kitchen table and announced that they were getting a divorce. "For a long time, your mother and I have been caught up in providing a stable home for you kids," Alex had said. "But since you've been out on your own, we've had to confront certain things about our relationship, certain facts. And we have just decided we'd be happier if we went on from here separately." His words were memorized, as Mark's had been when he told his parents he was gay; hearing them, Mark felt what he imagined they must have felt then: not the shock of surprise, but of the unspoken being spoken, the long-dreaded breaking of a silence. Eight words, four and a half seconds: a life changed, a marriage over, three hearts stopped cold. "I can't believe you're saying this," Ellen said, and Mark knew she was speaking literally.

"For several years now," Alex said, "I've been involved with someone else. There's no point in hiding this. It's Marian Hollister, whom you all know. Your mother has been aware of this. I'm not going to pretend that this fact has nothing to do with why she and I are divorcing, but I will say that with or without Marian, I think this would have been necessary, and I think your mother would agree with me on that."

Lydia said nothing. It was two days before Christmas, and the tree had yet to be decorated. She held in her hand a small gold bulb which she played with, slipping it up her sleeve and opening her fist to reveal an empty palm.

"Years," Ellen said. "You said years."

"We need you to be adults now," said Lydia. "I know this will be hard for you to adjust to, but I've gotten used to the idea, and as hard as it may be to believe, you will, too. Now a lot of work has to be done in a very short time. A lot has to be gone through. You can help by sorting through your closets, picking out what you want to save from what can be thrown away."

"You mean you're selling the house?" Mark said. His voice just barely cracked.

"The sale's already been made," Alex said. "Both your mother and I have decided we'd be happier starting off in new places."

"But how can you just sell it?" Ellen said. "You've lived here all our lives—I mean, all your lives."

"Ellen," Alex said, "you're here two weeks a year at best. I'm sorry, honey. We have to think of ourselves."

As a point of information, Douglas said, "Don't think we haven't seen what's been going on all along. We saw."

"I never thought so," Alex said.

Then Ellen asked, "And what about the cottage?"

*   *   *

Three months later, Alex was living with Marian in a condominium on Nob Hill, where they worked at twin oak desks by the picture window. Lydia had moved into a tiny house in Menlo Park, twenty miles down the peninsula, and had a tan, and was taking classes in pottery design. The house in which Douglas, Mark, and Ellen grew up was emptied and sold, everything that belonged to the children packed neatly in boxes and put in storage at a warehouse somewhere—the stuffed animals, the old school notebooks. But none of them were around for any of that. They had gone back to Los Angeles, Hawaii, New York—their own lives. Mark visited his mother only once, in the spring, and she took him on a tour of her new house, showing him the old dining room table, the familiar pots and pans in the kitchen, the same television set on which he had watched "Speed Racer" after school. But there was also a new wicker sofa, and everywhere the little jars she made in her pottery class. "It's a beautiful house," Mark said. "Harmonious." "That's because only one person lives here," Lydia said, and laughed. "No one to argue about the color of the drapes." She looked out the window at the vegetable garden and said, "I'm trying to become the kind of person who can live in a house like this." Mark imagined it, then; Alex and Lydia in their work clothes, sorting through twenty-six years of accumulated possessions, utility drawers, and packed closets. They had had no choice but to work through this final housecleaning together. And how had it felt? They had been married more years than he has lived.

"Under the Weather" is not the strangest name of a Cape Cod cottage, nor the most depressing. On Nantucket, for instance, there is a house called "Beyond Hope"; another called "Weak Moment"; another called "Seldom Inn." "Under the Weather" is small for such a large group, has lumpy beds and leaky faucets, but stands on a bluff, directly over a shoal where lobstermen pull up their traps. Alex and Lydia spent their honeymoon in the cottage one weekend twenty-six years ago, and loved it so much they vowed to return with their children, should they survive the war. A couple of years later, right after Lydia had Douglas, they persuaded the old woman who owned it to rent it to them for two weeks a year on a regular basis, and since then they have come every summer without fail. They hold onto the cottage as a principle, something which persists even when marriages fail, and other houses crumble. Perhaps for this reason, they have never bothered to ask anyone how it got its name. Such a question of origin interests only Mark, for whom the cottage has always been a tainted place. He remembers, as a child, coming upon his parents before dinner piercing live, writhing sea urchins with their forks, drawing them out and eating them raw. He remembers hearing them knocking about in the room next to his while he lay in bed, trying to guess if they were making love or fighting. And he remembers his own first sexual encounters, which took place near the cottage—**assignations** with a fisherman's son in a docked rowboat puddled with stagnant seawater. The way he figures it now, those assignations were the closest thing he has known to being in love, and his parents must have been fighting. No noise comes out of their bedroom now. Alex sleeps in the living room. What keeps Mark awake is the humming of his own brain, as he makes up new names for the place: "Desperate Efforts," perhaps, or simply, "The Lost Cottage." And what of "Under the Weather"? Who gave the cottage that name, and why? He has asked some of the lobstermen, and none of them seem to remember.

Since their arrival, Mark's parents have been distant and civil with each other, but Mark knows that no one is happy with the situation. A few weeks after he got back from his visit with his mother, Alex called him. He was in New York on business, with Marian, and they wanted Mark to have dinner with them. Mark met them at an Indian restaurant on the top of a building on Central Park South where there were gold urinals in the men's room. Marian looked fine, welcoming, and Mark remembered that before she was his father's lover, she had been his friend. That was the summer he worked as her research assistant. He also remembered that Alex almost never took Lydia with him on business trips.

"Well," Alex said, halfway through the meal, "I'll be on Cape Cod this June, as usual. Will you?"

"Dad," Mark said. "Of course."

"Of course. But Marian won't be coming, I'm afraid."

"Oh?"

"I wish she could, but your mother won't allow it."

"Really," Mark said, looking sideways at Marian for some hint as to how he should go on. She looked resolute, so he decided to be honest. "Are you really surprised?" he said.

"Nothing surprises me where your mother is concerned," Alex said. Mark supposed Alex had tried to test how far he could trespass the carefully guarded borders of Lydia's tolerance, how much he could get away with, and found he could not get away with that much. Apparently Lydia had panicked, overcome by thoughts of bedroom arrangements, and insisted the children wouldn't be able to bear Marian's presence. "And is that true?" he asked Mark, leaning toward him. "Would the children not be able to bear it?"

Mark felt as if he were being prosecuted. "I don't think Mom could bear it," he said at last—fudging, for the moment, the question of his siblings' feelings, and his own. Still, that remark was brutal enough. "Don't push it, Alex," Marian said, lighting a cigarette. "Anyway, I'm supposed to visit Kerry in Arizona that week. Kerry's living on a ranch." She smiled, retreating into the haven of her own children.

Once, Mark had been very intimate with Marian. He trusted her so much, in fact, that he came out to her before anyone else, and she responded kindly, coaxing him and giving him the strength to tell his parents he was gay. He admires her, and understands easily why his father has fallen in love with her. But since the divorce, he will not talk to Marian, for his mother's sake. Marian is the one obstacle Lydia cannot get around. Lydia never uses Marian's name because it sticks in her throat like a shard of glass and makes her cry out in pain. "Certain loyalties need to be respected" was all she could say to Alex when he suggested bringing

assignations: trysts

216

Marian to the Cape. And Alex relented, because he agreed with her, and because he realized that two weeks in June was a small enough sacrifice, considering how far she'd stretched, how much she'd given. "Marian and I can survive," he told Mark at the Indian restaurant. "We've survived longer separations." That intimacy scalded him. As if for emphasis, Alex took Marian's hand on top of the table and held it there. "We'll survive this one," he said.

Marian laughed nervously. "Your father and I have been waiting ten years to be together," she said. "What's two weeks?"

*   *   *

Little about the cottage has changed since the Dempson children were children. Though Alex and Lydia talked every year about renovating, the same rotting porch still hangs off the front, the same door creaks on its hinges. The children sleep in the bedrooms they've always slept in, do the chores they've always done. "You may be adults out there," Lydia jokes, "but here you're my kids, and you do what I tell you." Ellen is a lawyer, unmarried. Two days before her scheduled departure she was asked to postpone her vacation in order to help out with an important case which was about to go to trial. She refused, and this (she thinks) might affect her chances to become a partner next year. "Ellen, why?" Mark asked her when she told him. "The family is more important," she said. "Mother is more important." Douglas has brought with him Julie, the woman he's lived with for the past five years. They do oceanographical research in a remote village on Kauai, and hold impressive fellowships. Only Mark has no career and no aspirations. He works at temporary jobs in New York and moves every few months from sublet to sublet, devoting most of his time to exploring the city's homosexual night life. For the last few months he's been working as a word processor at a bank. It was easy for him to get away. He simply quit.

Now, a week into the vacation, things aren't going well. Lydia is angry most of the time, and whenever anyone asks her why, she mentions some triviality: an unwashed pot, an unmade bed. Here is an **exemplary** afternoon: Douglas, Julie, Mark, and Ellen arrive back from the beach, where they've been swimming and riding waves. Lydia doesn't say hello to them. She sits, knitting, at the kitchen table. She is dressed in a fisherman's sweater and a kilt fastened with a safety pin—an outfit she saves and wears only these few weeks on the Cape. "Are we late?" Douglas asks, bewildered by her silence, out of breath.

"No," Lydia says.

"We had fun at the beach," Julie says, and smiles, unsure of herself, still a stranger in this family. "How was your day?"

"Fine," Lydia says.

Ellen rubs her eyes. "Well, Mom," she says, "would you like me to tell you I nearly drowned today? I wish I had. One less person to make a mess. Too bad Mark saved me."

Lydia puts down her knitting and cradles her face in her hands. "I don't deserve that," she says. "You don't know what it's like trying to keep ahead of the mess in this house. You have no right to make fun of me when all I'm trying to do is keep us from drowning in dirty dishes and dirty clothes."

"Didn't we do the dishes after lunch?" Douglas asks. "We must have done the dishes after lunch."

"If you can call that doing them," Lydia says. "They were soapy *and* greasy."

"I'm sorry, Lydia," says Julie. "We were in such a hurry—"

"It's just that if anything's going to get done right around here, I have to do it, and I'm sick of it. I'm sick of it." She reaches for a pack of sugarless chewing gum, unwraps a stick, and goes to work on it.

exemplary: serving to illustrate; typical

"This is ridiculous, Mom," Ellen says. "Dishes are nothing. Dishes are trivial."

"It's that attitude that gets me so riled up," Lydia says. "They're trivial to people like you, so people like me get stuck with them."

"I'm not people. I'm your daughter, Ellen, in case you've forgotten. Excuse me, I have to change."

She storms out of the kitchen, colliding with Alex, whose face and clothes are smeared with mud and sand.

"What are you in such a hurry for?" he asks.

"Ask *her,*" Ellen says, and slams the door of her bedroom.

Lydia is rubbing her eyes. "What was that about?" Alex asks.

"Nothing, nothing," she says, in a weary singsong. "Just the usual. Did you fix that pipe yet?"

"No, almost. I need some help. I hoped Doug and Mark might crawl under there with me." All day he's been trying to fix a faulty pipe which has made the bathtub faucet leak for twenty-five years, and created a bluish tail of rust near the spigot. The angrier Lydia gets, the more Alex throws himself into repair work, into tending to the old **anachronisms** of the house which he has seen fit to ignore in other years. It gives him an excuse to spend most of his days alone, away from Lydia.

"So can you help me?" Alex asks.

"Well," Mark says, "I suppose so. When?"

"I was thinking right now. We have to get out and pick up the lobsters in an hour or so. Henry said we could ride out on the boat with him. I want to get this job done."

"Fine," Douglas says. "I'm game."

Mark hesitates. "Yes," he says. "I'll help you with it. Just let me change first."

He walks out of the kitchen and into his bedroom. It is the smallest in the house, with a tiny child-sized bed, because even though Mark is the tallest member of the family by three inches, he is still the youngest. The bed was fine when he was five, but now most of the springs have broken, and Mark's legs stick a full four inches over the edge. He takes off his bathing suit, dries himself with a towel, and—as he dresses—catches a glimpse of himself in the mirror. It is the same face, as always.

He heads out the door to the hallway, where Alex and Douglas are waiting for him. "All right," he says. "I'm ready."

*   *   *

Of course, it was not this way at first. The day they arrived at the cottage, Lydia seemed **exuberant**. "Just breathe the air," she said to Mark, her eyes fiery with excitement. "Air doesn't smell like this anywhere else in the world." They had spaghetti with clams for dinner—a huge, **decadent**, drunken meal. Halfway through Mark fell to the floor in a fit of laughter so severe it almost made him sick. They went to bed at three, slept dreamlessly late into the morning. By the time Mark woke up, Lydia was irritated, and Alex had disappeared, alone, to go fishing. That evening, Ellen and Julie baked a cake, and Lydia got furious at them for not cleaning up immediately afterward. Douglas and Julie rose to the occasion, eager to appease her, and immediately started scrubbing. Douglas was even more intent than his parents on keeping up a pretense of normality over the vacation, partially for Julie's sake, but also because he cherished these two weeks at the cottage even more than his mother did. Ellen chided him for giving in to her whim so readily. "She'll just get angrier if you take away her only outlet," she said.

anachronisms: things out of another time

exuberant: overflowing with joy

decadent: self-indulgent

"Leave the dirty dishes. If this house were clean, believe me, we'd get it a lot worse from her than we are now."

"I want to keep things pleasant," Douglas said. He kowtowed to his mother, he claimed, because he pitied her, but Mark knew it was because he feared more than anything seeing her lose control. When he and Douglas were children, he remembers, Lydia had been hit on the head by a softball one afternoon in the park. She had fallen to her knees and burst into tears, and Douglas had shrunk back, terrified, and refused to go near her. Now Douglas seemed determined to make sure his mother never did that to him again, even if it meant she had to suffer in silence.

Lydia is still in the kitchen, leaning against the counter, when Mark emerges from under the cottage. She is not drinking coffee, not reading a recipe; just leaning there. "Dad and Doug told me to pack up and come inside," Mark says. "I was more trouble than help."

"Oh?" Lydia says.

"Yes," Mark says, and sits down at the table. "I have no mechanical aptitude. I can hold things and hand things to other people—sometimes. They knew my heart wasn't in it."

"You never did like that sort of thing," Lydia says.

Mark sits silent for a few seconds. "Daddy's just repairing everything this vacation, isn't he?" he says. "For next summer this place'll be tiptop."

"We won't be here next summer," Lydia says. "I'm sure of it, though it's hard to imagine this is the last time."

"I'm sorry it's such an unhappy time for you," Mark says.

Lydia smiles. "Well," she says, "it's no one's fault but my own. You know, when your father first told me he wanted a divorce, he said things could be hard, or they could be very hard. The choice was up to me. I thought I chose the former of those two. Then again, I also thought, if I go along with him and don't make trouble, at least he'll be fair."

"Mom," Mark says, "give yourself a break. What did you expect?"

"I expected people to act like adults," she says. "I expected people to play fair." She turns to look out the window, her face grim. The table is strewn with gum wrappers.

"Can I help you?" Mark asks.

She laughs. "Your father would be happy to hear you say that," she says. "He told me from the beginning, I'll let them hate me, I'll turn the kids against me. Then they'll be there for you. He was so damn sacrificial. But no. You can't help me because I still have some pride."

There is a clattering of doors in the hallway. Male voices invade the house. Alex and Douglas walk into the kitchen, their clothes even more smeared with mud, their eyes triumphant. "Looks like we fixed that pipe," Alex says. "Now we've got to wash up; Henry's expecting us to pick up those lobsters ten minutes ago."

He and Douglas stand at the kitchen sink and wash their hands and faces. From her room, Julie calls, "You fixed the pipe? That's fantastic!"

"Yes," Douglas says, "we have repaired the evil leak which has plagued this house for centuries."

"We'd better get going, Doug," Alex says. "Does Julie want to come hunt lobsters?"

"Lobsters?" Julie says, entering the room. Her smile is bright, eager. Then she looks at Lydia. "No, you men go," she says. "We womenfolk will stay here and guard the hearth."

Lydia looks at her, and raises her eyebrows.

"O.K., let's go," Alex says. "Mark, you ready?"

He looks questioningly at Lydia. But she is gathering together steel wool and Clorox, preparing to attack the stain on the bathtub.

"Yes, I'm ready," Mark says.

*   *   *

At first, when he was very young, Mark imagined the lobstermen to be literal lobster-men, with big pink pincers and claws. Later, as he was entering puberty, he found that all his early sexual feelings focused on them—the red-faced men and boys with their bellies encased in dirty T-shirts. Here, in a docked boat, Mark made love for the first time with a local boy who had propositioned him in the bathroom of what was then the town's only pizza parlor. "I seen you look at me," said the boy, whose name was Erroll. Mark had wanted to run away, but instead made a date to meet Erroll later that night. Outside, in the pizza parlor, his family was arguing about whether to get anchovies. Mark still feels a wave of nausea run through him when he eats with them at any pizza parlor, remembering Erroll's warm breath on his neck, and the smell of fish which seemed to cling to him for days afterward.

Alex is friends with the local lobstermen, one of whom is his landlord's cousin. Most years, he and Douglas and Mark ride out on a little boat with Henry Traylor and his son, Henry Traylor, and play at being lobstermen themselves, at hauling pots and grabbing the writhing creatures and snapping shut their jaws. The lobsters only turn pink when boiled; live, they're sometimes a bluish color which reminds Mark of the stain on the bathtub. Mark has never much liked these expeditions, nor the inflated caricature of machismo which his father and brother put on for them. He looks at them and sees plump men with pale skin, men no man would ever want. Yet they are loved, fiercely loved by women.

Today Henry Traylor is a year older than the last time they saw him, as is his son. "Graduated from high school last week," he tells Alex.

"That's terrific," Alex says. "What's next?"

"Fixing to get married, I suppose," Henry Traylor says. "Go to work, have kids." He is a round-faced, red-cheeked boy with ratty, bright blond hair. As he talks, he manipulates without effort the outboard rudder of the little boat which is carrying them out into the sound, toward the marked buoys of the planted pots. Out on the ocean, Alex seems to relax considerably. "Your mother seems unhappy," he says to Mark. "I try to talk to her, to help her, but it doesn't do any good. Well, maybe Julie and Ellen can do something." He puts his arm around Mark's shoulder—an uncomplicated, fatherly gesture which seems to say, this love is simple. The love of men is simple. Leave the women behind in the kitchen, in the steam of the cooking pot, the fog of their jealousies and compulsions. We will go hunt.

Henry Traylor has hauled up the ancient lobster trap. Lobster limbs stick out of the barnacle-encrusted woodwork, occasionally moving. "Now you just grab the little bugger like this," Henry Traylor instructs Douglas. "Then you take your rubber band and snap him closed. It's simple."

"O.K.," Douglas says. "Here goes." He stands back and cranes his arm over the trap, holding himself at a distance, then withdraws a single, flailing lobster.

"Oh, God," he says, and nearly drops it.

"Don't do that!" shouts Henry Traylor. "You got him. Now just take the rubber band and fix him tight. Shut him up like he's a woman who's sassing you. That's right. Good. See? It wasn't so hard."

"Do that to your wife," says Henry Traylor the elder, "she'll bite your head off quicker than that lobster."

Out of politeness, all three of the Dempson men laugh. Douglas looks at his handiwork—a single lobster, bound and gagged—and smiles. "I did it," he says. Mark wonders if young Henry Traylor has ever thought of making love to other boys, thinks rudely of propositioning him, having him beneath the boat. "I seen you look at me," he'd say. He thinks of it—little swirls of semen coagulating in the puddles, white as the eddies of foam which are gathering now on the sea in which they float, helpless, five men wrestling with lobsters.

220

They go back to shore. The Traylors have asked Alex and Douglas to walk up the hill with them and take a look at their new well, so Mark carries the bag of lobsters back to the house. But when he gets to the screen door to the kitchen, he stops in his tracks; Ellen, Lydia, and Julie are sitting at the table, talking in hushed voices, and he steps back, fearful of interrupting them. "It would be all right," Ellen is saying. "Really, it's not that outrageous these days. I met a lot of really decent guys when I did it."

"What could I say?" Lydia asks.

"Just be simple and straightforward. Attractive woman, divorced, mid-fifties, seeks whatever—handsome, mature man for companionship. Who knows? Whatever you want."

"I could never put that down!" Lydia says, her inflection rising. "Besides, it wouldn't be fair. They'd be disappointed when they met me."

"Of course they wouldn't!" Julie says. "You're very attractive."

"I'm an old woman," Lydia says. "There's no need to flatter me. I know that."

"Mom, you don't look half your age," Ellen says. "You're beautiful."

Mark knocks and walks through the door, his arms full of lobsters. "Here I am," he says, "back with the loot. I'm sorry for eavesdropping, but I agree with everything Ellen says."

"Oh, it doesn't matter, Mark," Lydia says. "Alex wouldn't care anyway if he found out."

"Mom, will you stop that?" Ellen says. "Will you just stop that? Don't worry about him anymore, for Christ's sake, he isn't worth it."

"Don't talk about your father that way," Lydia says. "You can tell me whatever you think I need to know, but you're not to speak of your father like that. He's still your father, even if he's not my husband."

"Jesus," Ellen says.

"What did you say?"

"Nothing," Ellen says, more loudly.

Lydia looks her over once, then walks over to the stove, where the water for the lobsters is boiling. "How many did you get, Mark?" she asks.

"Six. Daddy and Douglas went to look at the Traylors' well. They'll be back any minute."

"Good," Lydia says. "Let's put these things in the water." She lifts the top off the huge pot, and steam pours out of it, fogging her reading glasses. . . .

*   *   *

Dinner passes quietly. Alex is in a questioning mood, and his children answer him obediently. Douglas and Julie talk about the strange sleeping habits of sharks, Ellen about her firm, Mark about a play he saw recently off Broadway. Lydia sits at the head of the table, and occasionally makes a comment or asks a question—just enough to keep them from panicking, or staring at her all through the meal. Mark notices that her eyes keep wandering to Alex.

After dinner is finished, Julie and Lydia carry the dishes into the kitchen, and Douglas says, "O.K., are we getting ice cream tonight, or what?" Every night since their arrival, they have gone to get ice cream after dinner, primarily at the insistence of Douglas and Julie, who thrive on ice cream, but thrive more on ritual. Ellen, who has visited them in Hawaii, revealed to Mark that they feed their cat tea every morning, in bed. "They're daffy," she said, describing to him the way Douglas held the cat and Julie the saucer of tea it licked from. Over the five years they've been together, Mark has noticed, Douglas and Julie have become almost completely absorbed in one another, at the expense of most everything around them, probably as a result of the fact that they've spent so much of that time in remote places, in virtual isolation. They even share a secret language of code words and **euphemisms**. When Julie asked Douglas, one night, to give her a "floogie," Mark burst out laughing, and then they explained that "floogie" was their private word for backrub.

Tonight, Ellen is peculiarly agreeable. Usually she resists these ice cream expeditions, but now she says, "Oh, what a great idea. Let's go." Mark wonders what led her and Lydia to the conversation he overheard, then decides he'd prefer not to know. "Let's go, let's go," Douglas says. "Mom, are you game?"

But Lydia has her face buried in the steam rising from the sink of dishes, which she has insisted on doing herself. "No," she says. "You go ahead."

Douglas backs away from the sorrow in her voice—sorrow which might at any moment turn into irritation, if he pushes her harder. He knows not to. "How about you, Dad?" he asks Alex.

"No," Alex says, "I'm pooped. But bring me back some chocolate chip."

"Give me money?" Douglas says.

Alex hands him a twenty, and the kids barrel into the car and head off to the ice cream parlor in town. They sit down at a pink booth with high-backed, patent-leather seats which remind Mark of pink flamingos on people's lawns, and a waitress in a pink uniform brings them their menus. The waitress is a local girl with bad teeth, and Mark wonders if she's the one Henry Traylor's going to marry someday. He wouldn't be surprised. She's got a lusty look about her which even he can recognize, and which he imagines Henry Traylor would find attractive. And Douglas is watching her. Julie is watching Douglas watch, but she does not look jealous. She looks fascinated.

Ellen looks jealous.

They order several sundaes, and eat them with a kind of labored dedication. Halfway through the blueberry sundae he is sharing with Ellen, Mark realizes he stopped enjoying this sundae, and this ritual, four days before. Julie looks tired, too—tired of being cheerful and shrieking about fixed faucets. And Mark imagines a time when his brother and Julie will feed their cat tea for no other reason than that they always have, and with no pleasure. He remembers one weekend when Julie and Douglas came to visit him in New York. They had taken the train down from Boston, where they were in school, and they were flying to California the next afternoon. All that day on the train Douglas had been looking forward to eating at a Southern Indian restaurant he had read about, but the train arrived several hours late, and by the time he and Julie had gotten their baggage the restaurant was closed. Douglas fumed like a child until tears came to his eyes. "All that day on the train, looking forward to that dinner," he said on the subway ride back to Mark's apartment. Julie put her arms around him, and kissed him on the forehead, but he turned away. Mark wanted to shake her, then, ask her why she was indulging him this way, but he knew that Douglas had indulged her just as often. That was the basis of their love—mutual self-indulgence so excessive that Mark couldn't live with them for more than a few days without thinking he would go crazy. It wasn't that he wasn't welcome. His presence or absence seemed irrelevant to them; as far as they were concerned, he might as well not have existed. And this was coupledom, the revered state of marriage? For Mark, the amorous maneuverings of the heterosexual world are deserving of the same bewilderment and distrust that he hears in his sister's voice when she says, "But how can you just go to bed with someone you've hardly met? *I* could never do that." He wants to respond by saying, I would never pretend that I could pledge eternal allegiance to one person, but this isn't really true. What is true is that he's terrified of what he might turn into once he'd made such a pledge.

"So when's the summit conference taking place?" Ellen says now, dropping her blueberry-stained spoon onto the pink table. Everyone looks at her. "What do you mean?" Julie asks.

euphemisms: substitutions of in-offensive terms for offensive terms

222

"I mean I think we should have a talk about what's happening with Mom and Dad. I mean I think we should stop pretending everything's normal when it isn't."

"I'm not pretending," Douglas says.

"Neither am I," says Julie. "We're aware of what's going on."

Mark watches Ellen's blueberry ice cream melt down the sides of her parfait glass. "What has Mama said to you?" he asks.

"Everything and nothing," Ellen says. "I hear her when she's angry and when she wants to cry she does it in my room. One day she's cheerful, the next miserable. I don't know why she decided to make me her confidante, but she did." Ellen pushes the sundae dish away. "Why don't we just face the fact that this is a failure?" she says. "Daddy doesn't want to be here, that's for sure, and I think Mom's beginning to think that she doesn't want to be here. And I, for one, am not so sure I want to be here."

"Mom believes in tradition," Douglas says softly, repeating a phrase they've heard from her a thousand times.

"Tradition can become repetition," Ellen says, "when you end up holding onto something just because you're afraid to let it go." She shakes her head. "I am ready to let it go."

"Let what go?" Douglas says. "The family?"

Ellen is silent.

"Well, I don't think that's fair," Douglas says. "Sure, things are stressful. A lot has happened. But that doesn't mean we should give up. We have to work hard at this. Just because things are different doesn't mean they necessarily have to be bad. I, for one, am determined to make the best of this vacation—for my sake, but also for Mom's. Except for this, without this—"

"She already has nothing," Ellen says.

Douglas stares at her.

"You can face it," Ellen says. "She has. She's said as much. Her whole life went down the tubes when Daddy left her, Cape Cod or no Cape Cod. This vacation doesn't matter a damn. But that's not the end. She could start a new life for herself. Mark, remember the first time Douglas didn't come home for Christmas? I'll bet you never guessed how upset everyone was, Douglas. Christmas just wasn't going to be Christmas without the whole family being there, I said, so why bother having it at all? But then Christmas came, and we did it without you. It wasn't the same. But it was still Christmas. We survived. And maybe we were a little relieved to find we weren't as dependent on your presence as we thought we'd be, relieved to be able to give up some of those old rituals, some of that nostalgia. It was like a rehearsal for other losses we probably all knew we'd have to face someday—for this, maybe."

Douglas has his arm around Julie, his fingers gripping her shoulder. "No one ever told me that," he says. "I figured no one cared."

Ellen laughs. "That's never been a problem in this family," she says. "The problem in this family is that everybody cares."

*   *   *

They get back to the cottage around eleven to find that the lights are still on. "I'm surprised she's still up," Ellen says to Mark as they clamber out of the car.

"It's not so surprising," Mark says. "She's probably having a snack." The gravel of the driveway crunches beneath his feet as he moves toward the screen door to the kitchen. "Hi, Mom," Mark says as he walks through the door, then stops abruptly, the other three behind him.

"What's going on?" Mark asks.

Alex is standing by the ironing board, in his coat, his face red and puffy. He is looking down at Lydia, who sits in her pink bathrobe at the kitchen table, her head resting on her forearms, weeping. In front of her is half a grapefruit on a plate, and a small spoon with serrated edges.

"What happened?" Ellen asks.

"It's nothing, kids," Alex says. "Your mother and I were just having a discussion."

"Oh, shut up," Lydia says, raising her head slightly. Her eyes are red, swollen with tears. "Why don't you just tell them if you're so big on honesty all of a sudden? Your father's girlfriend has arrived. She's at a motel in town. They planned this all along, and your father never saw fit to tell any of us about it, except I happened to see her this morning when I was doing the grocery shopping."

"Oh, God," Mark says, and leans back against the wall of the kitchen. Across from him, his father also draws back.

"All right, let's not get hysterical," Ellen says. "Let's try to talk this through. Daddy, is this true?"

"Yes," Alex says. "I'm sorry I didn't tell any of you but I was afraid of how you'd react. Marian's just here for the weekend, she'll be gone Monday. I thought I could see her during the day, and no one would know. But now that everything's out, I can see that more deception was just a bad idea to begin with. And anyway, am I asking so much? All I'm asking is to spend some time in town with Marian. I'll be home for meals, and during the day, everything for the family. None of you ever has to see her."

"Do you think all this is fair to Marian?" Ellen asks.

"It was her idea."

"I see."

"Fair to Marian, fair to Marian," Lydia mumbles. "All of this has been fair to Marian. These two weeks you were supposed to be fair to me." She takes a Kleenex and rubs at her nose and eyes. Mark's fingers grip the moldings on the walls, while Julie buttons and unbuttons the collar of her sweater.

"Lydia, look," Alex says. "Something isn't clear here. When I agreed to come these weeks, it was as your friend and as a father. Nothing more."

"So go then!" Lydia shouts, standing up and facing him. "You've brought me lower than I ever thought you would, don't stand there and rub it in. Just go." Shaking, she walks over to the counter, picks up a coffee cup, and takes a sip out of it. Coffee splashes over the rim, falls in hot drops on the floor.

"Now I think we have to talk about this," Ellen says. "We can deal with this if we just work on it."

"There's no point," Douglas says, and sits down at the table. "There's nothing left to say." He looks at the table, and Julie reaches for his hand.

"What do you mean there's nothing left to say? There's everything to be said here. The one thing we haven't done is talk about all of this as a family."

"Oh, be quiet, both of you," Lydia says, putting down her cup. "You don't know anything about this. The whole business is so simple it's embarrassing." She puts her hand on her chest and takes a deep, shaky breath. "There is only one thing to be said here, and I'm the one who has to say it. And that is the simple fact that I love your father, and I will always love your father. And he doesn't love me. And never will."

No one answers her. She is right. None of them know anything about *this,* not even Ellen. Lydia's children are as speechless as spectators watching a woman on a high ledge: unable to do any good, they can only stare, waiting to see what she'll do next.

What she does is turn to Alex. "Did you hear me?" she says. "I love you. You can escape me, but you can never escape that."

He keeps his eyes focused on the window above her head, making sure never to look at her. The expression on his face is almost simple, almost sweet: the lips pressed together, though not tightly, the eyes averted. In his mind, he's already left.

▼ Relating the Story to Yourself

1. Does any aspect of this story provoke memories of your own family life?

2. Has there been a similarly tense and anguishing situation in your own family life? If so, how did you react to it? How would you react if the circumstances were to recur now?

3. Imagine that it is your family in this situation. How would you deal with it?

4. When Douglas expresses surprise that anyone cared when he did not come home for Christmas, Ellen says, "That's never been a problem in this family. The problem in this family is that everyone cares." Can that be said of your family? Why do you answer as you do?

5. Has anyone ever "come out" to you, as Mark does to Marian? If so, how did you react? Why do you think you reacted in that way? If a brother, sister, or friend were to come out to you now, how do you think you would react?

▼ Questions for Reflection

1. When Alex announces to his family that he and Lydia are divorcing, Mark felt "not the shock of surprise, but of the unspoken being spoken, the long-dreaded breaking of a silence." What do you make of this? Why had there been this "silence"?

2. What does the title of the story mean?

3. What impression do you get of Marian? Why? What details is your impression based on?

4. How would you describe the members of the family? What details and events of the story are giving you these impressions?

5. How would you describe the way Ellen, Doug, Mark, Alex, and Lydia are dealing with the divorce?

6. "I expected people to act like adults," Lydia says to her son Mark, speaking of the divorce, "I expected people to play fair (page 219)." What do you think she means?

7. "For Mark, the amorous maneuverings of the heterosexual world are deserving of the same bewilderment and distrust that he hears in his sister's voice when she says, 'But how can you just go to bed with someone you hardly met? I could never do that.' He wants to respond by saying, I would never pretend that I could pledge eternal allegiance to one person, but this isn't really true. What is true is that he's terrified of what he might turn into once he'd made such a pledge (page 222)." What do you think he means by this? What in his fearful imaginings would he "turn into"?

8. How do you react to Alex's announcement that Marian will be in town for the weekend? Why do you react that way?

9. Do you find yourself being more sympathetic with Lydia than with Alex? Explain why you answer as you do. Do you think the narrator of the story is more sympathetic with Lydia? Explain your answer.

▼ Discussion

1. What are the strengths of the Dempson family, as you observe them in this crisis? Is there anything about this family that seems to "work"? Is there anything in their interaction that does not seem healthful to you?

2. How well do you think the various members of the family—Mark, Doug, Ellen, Alex, and Lydia—are handling the divorce? Is there any advice you would want to offer any of them?

3. Toward which, if either, of the two parents do you feel more sympathetic? Why?

4. Do you share Ellen's "bewilderment and distrust" of Mark's homosexual encounters? If so, why? If Mark were your own brother, would his homosexuality affect the way you felt or acted toward him? Explain.

5. Do you believe there are marriages that are best ended in divorce? If so, under what circumstances should this happen? When, in your view, is a marriage still worth working at, even during its darkest passages?

6. Do you think this story portrays the contemporary American family realistically? Why or why not?

▼ Writing Assignments

1. Reflect on your own conception of the ideal family. What are its functions? What are the key characteristics of the heads of such a family? Upon what specific experiences, of either your own family or others, are your views of the ideal family based?

2. Do you think of the present high rate of divorce as a problem, a cause for concern? Why do you answer as you do?

▼ Journal Entry

1. If any aspect or scene of this story moved you emotionally, write about it in your journal.

▼ Vocabulary

anachronism	decadent	exemplary
assignations	euphemism	exuberant

37

▼

The Metaphysics of Oppression

Jorge Valadez

Jorge Valadez, who teaches philosophy at Marquette University, argues here that unexamined philosophical assumptions lie at the foundation of the oppression of the Third World. He identifies those assumptions and argues for a new perspective toward oppression and its alleviation, a perspective fully aware of its own philosophical underpinnings.

Consuelo had been living at a frantic pace for months. She was deeply involved in an organization of mothers who were demanding that the Guatemalan government account for their sons and daughters who had disappeared. Many of the mothers believed that their sons or daughters had probably already been killed by the government security forces, but they continued to hope that perhaps they might be alive and jailed with other political prisoners. The crimes of their loved ones consisted of their having protested and opposed the policies of the militarily controlled government. In Guatemala the degree of poverty and human suffering is staggering and many of the people from the poor and **disfranchised** classes had finally decided that it was necessary to speak up against the government, even if it meant placing themselves in danger.

Consuelo knew all of this, and she also knew that the bloated bodies of some of the disappeared were sometimes found floating in a river or buried in shallow graves. But despite it all she felt that it was preferable for her to know what had happened to her twenty-year-old son. Even the knowledge that he was dead was better than the insufferable uncertainty that haunted her dreams. At least the body could then receive a proper burial.

Early on in her life Consuelo had learned about responsibility and about hardship, and the latter she had come to accept as an inevitable aspect of her existence. She was the eldest child, and by age twelve she had assumed the duties of an adult. She had married while still an adolescent. Later, in her tenth year of marriage her husband left to seek work in the United States. Whether he actually ever made it across the border she never knew, since she had not heard from him since. Through the years, she had convinced herself that it was best to think of him only as part of those joyful scenes that she stored in her memory like precious jewels.

Nothing in her life, however, had prepared her for what occurred that warm Sunday evening when the four armed men broke into her house. The organization of mothers which she headed had been particularly vocal during the last few months and the government wanted to set an example. While two of the men held her, the others grabbed her six-year-old child. One of them took out a pointed pair of pliers and in a savagely methodical motion pulled out the fingernail from one of the horrified child's fingers. The image of her son's contorted face and the sound of his uncontrolled screams pierced and bored into her brain. The child kicked and twisted his whole body in a crazed effort to get free, but the butchers had had practice. One of them put his knee on the boy's chest and pinned him against the floor, while holding down the other small flailing arm. His partner then completed the gruesome task.

disfranchised: those deprived of rights of citizenship

The event just described actually occurred, and incidents of this degree of brutality are not rare in Guatemala and other Central American countries. During the 1980s the United States provided tens of millions of dollars in military aid to the Guatemalan government. Even though Guatemala has an elected civilian president, the military wields a great deal of power. Death squads and special security forces play a crucial role in the maintenance of power by the military and wealthy elites. In Guatemala approximately 2 percent of the population own about 75 percent of the country's land and resources. It is a country where great inequalities of wealth exist between the privileged few and the mostly poor Indian population. About 73 percent of all children under the age of five are malnourished and, for every 1,000 births, 270 will die before reaching the age of five. The national illiteracy rate is 65 percent. Government violence has been responsible for more than 100,000 deaths in the last 30 years.[1]

The problems faced by the Guatemalan people are not unique; they are shared by people in many other Third World countries. These problems could no doubt be analyzed from a variety of perspectives, including the sociological, political, **anthropological**, etcetera. A question that I want to consider here is whether there are certain insights that a distinctively philosophical perspective could give us into the problem of oppression. Are there some elements of this problem that could be **elucidated** by taking the peculiarly general and abstract position of the philosopher? I believe the answer is yes. In what follows, I will try to show that some philosophical orientations dominant in our culture limit our understanding of Third World oppression and contribute to the acceptance of oppressive policies.

In my analyses I will distinguish between two forms of oppression, namely, the economic and the political. I will identify the philosophical orientations that underpin each of these forms of oppression, and will articulate the interconnections that exist between them. I begin by analyzing political forms of oppression.

Metaphysical Imperialism and Political Oppression

One of the most important assumptions of our cultural worldview is that Americans have the right to interfere with and determine the internal politics of Latin American countries. The last century provides us with numerous examples of such interference, including the overthrow of established, elected governments (for example, Chile under Allende) and the invasion of countries like Nicaragua and Mexico. What is important to note here is that this assumption of the right of interference is an expression of our supposed right to impose our visions of reality on Latin America. It is our perception of the world that counts. It is Americans who should determine how other people are to live, how they are to organize their governments, and how they are to choose their values and priorities. This perspective is in effect a kind of **metaphysical imperialism** that involves the forced **imposition** of a dominant culture's vision of reality on another culture.

Most Americans are so convinced of the metaphysical imperialist perspective that it is almost impossible for us to question the basis of this perspective or to think of entering into a real and equal dialogue with the people of Latin America. Instead of engaging in an **egalitarian** effort to understand the world from their point of view, our attitude is that we have the right to impose our own visions of reality (through armed invasion if necessary). When dealing with underdeveloped countries, the notion that political truth is something that emerges as the result of a negotiated, open interchange of perspectives and ideas is foreign to most of us. And the belief that we have the right to impose our way of looking at the world on others is based on an even more deeply rooted philosophical view, namely, that those who are economically, technologically, and militarily superior, and are assumed to be intellectually and morally superior, have the right to control those who are deemed inferior in these same respects. The history of Latin America can

anthropological: pertaining to science dealing with the origins and physical and cultural development of humankind

elucidated: made clear

metaphysical: pertaining to theories about the ultimate nature of reality

imperialism: the policy of extending a nation's authority by territorial acquisition

imposition: the act of laying on (as a burden)

egalitarian: promoting equality

be seen as an example of the concrete implementation of this philosophical principle, first at the hands of Western European countries and then at the hands of the United States.

It is difficult to overemphasize the importance and influence of this last philosophical principle for understanding the historical relationships between Latin America and Western Europe, and in contemporary times, between Latin America and the United States. America has, to a large extent, inherited its intellectual and philosophical traditions from Western Europe, including its attitudes toward underdeveloped or Third World nations. A common thread running through these attempts is not only the metaphysical imperialist **appropriation** of the "truth" but also the above mentioned principle that those who are in possession of this "truth" have the moral right, and in some cases (like that of Christianity), even the moral obligation to impose their vision of reality on others. This principle works by assigning an inferior status to those who fail to meet our criteria of intellectual and moral worth. And once they have been categorized as inferior, it is an easy step toward the attitude that it is the task of their "superiors" either to subjugate them or to transform their perspectives of reality to conform with the ideals of their "superiors."

Examples of the oppression of other cultures, and of the forced imposition of a view of reality on them, can be readily acknowledged: the conquest of Mexico, which involved not only a military conquest, but also the destruction of an **indigenous** metaphysical and religious worldview; the long and well-documented history of racial subjugation of blacks and Native Americans in the United States; the oppression of women and their categorization as secondary and marginal beings, etc. We can elaborate briefly on one of these cases. The refusal to recognize that women have a status equal to that of men is a phenomenon that is deeply entrenched within our historical and cultural traditions. Aristotle, one of the most influential philosophers in Western intellectual history, thought that slaves completely lacked deliberative faculties, while women had such faculties but in an incomplete or imperfect sense. He believed that women's rational capacity was not equal to that of men, that is, that it lacked full legitimacy or authority.

It can be said without fear of exaggeration that understanding the phenomenon of oppression is crucial for an adequate understanding of Western history and civilization. Unfortunately, such an analysis is usually neglected especially at the metaphysical level. A philosophical approach to the phenomenon of oppression helps us to see its scope as well as its deep roots within our intellectual traditions.

Probably all cultures are, to some degree, **ethnocentric** and even predisposed to believe that others see the world as they do. But what makes the Western European culture distinctive is its excessive emphasis on control and its systematic attempts to prove the alleged inferiority of various oppressed groups. Even though in most of these attempts to prove inferiority there may have been no conscious intention to justify oppression, nevertheless the actual impact of several prominent Western theoretical traditions has been to reinforce attitudes which make oppressive behavior toward these groups appear reasonable and justifiable. The above mentioned Aristotelian view of women, the early views of some Spanish conquistadores that Indians did not possess souls, and the pseudo-scientific attempts throughout history to establish the "natural" inferiority of blacks are all examples of theories which have complemented and sometimes justified the control, subjugation, and/or indoctrination of these groups.

The set of philosophical assumptions we have discussed has been used to justify our foreign policies in Latin America. The position taken by the United States during the Cold War years was that we had to keep the armies of the presumably "democratically" elected governments of Latin America strong so that they could repel externally **instigated** Communist threats.

The idea was that the demands that the people of El Salvador or Guatemala, for example, made of their governments for better living conditions and respect of

appropriation: the act of seizing for oneself

indigenous: native

ethnocentric: believing in the inherent superiority of one's own culture

instigated: provoked or incited

their human rights were the result of external Communist interference and not the result of the poverty and oppression that they suffered. Democracy is so far superior to a Communist system of government, so the argument went, that no price was too high to pay to keep Communism away from this hemisphere. Thus we supported elected leaders of Latin American countries even when they reached office through electoral fraud and even when they were controlled by military and wealthy elites. This foreign policy position was bolstered by the alleged threat posed by Communism to our own national security. Further, our continued support of these military regimes was justified by either denying or de-emphasizing the human rights abuses which these governments perpetrated.

In the current post–Cold War era, the emphasis has shifted from fighting Communist infiltration to supporting democratic reforms. The United States supports these democratic reforms, however, only when they are done on our own terms. Time and again the United States has interfered with the rights of Latin American countries for democratic self-determination by giving money to parties that support U.S. political and economic policies. A case in point involves the ten million dollars that the U.S. gave in 1988 to Guillermo Endara's campaign fund to assist his candidacy for president of Panama.[2] Endara was the "U.S. candidate" because he upheld U.S. economic and political interests in Panama. Endara was leading in the presidential elections and appeared to be the certain winner when Manuel Noriega **forfeited** the elections. This action by Noriega was later used by the United States as a **rationale** for invading Panama and installing Endara as the "legitimate" president of Panama. Endara was sworn in as president in a U.S. military base.

Imagine for a moment a scenario in which a foreign country gave a U.S. candidate for president one hundred million dollars for his or her campaign (the latter figure is the approximate realistic equivalent of the ten million given to Endara). Suppose further that this candidate won the election. Without a doubt, such an "election" would be universally condemned in the United States as fraudulent and would be declared invalid. Yet we believe that it is acceptable for us to meddle in the internal democratic processes of Latin America and expect U.S.-influenced elections to be recognized as legitimate by the international community and the people of Latin America. More often than not, which elections are recognized as legitimate is determined by whether the successful party or candidate supports our financial and political interests in the region. Similarly, the United States tends to overlook human rights abuses (such as the widespread abuses in Guatemala and El Salvador) of regimes that are friendly to the United States. In the post–Cold War era, freedom and democracy have become code words for democratization that is conditioned on U.S. concerns.

The International Economic System and Economic Oppression

In order to understand economic oppression, we must see how the international economic system contributes to the economic oppression of Latin American and other Third World countries. Countries like Guatemala, Mexico, Brazil, Peru, and Argentina have collective foreign debts that total in the hundreds of billions of dollars. These foreign debts are primarily the result of an **inequitable** system of international trade. During the colonial period, Third World countries were forced to use their most fertile land to grow export crops for the colonial powers like England and Spain and to mine their minerals for export to these same countries. Thus, many Third World countries are now largely dependent on export crops and minerals for their income. But the industrialized countries have implemented a system of import duties that are higher for manufactured or processed goods and lower for raw materials and unprocessed goods. The manufactured/raw goods

forfeited: gave up
rationale: justification
inequitable: unfair

exchange created conditions of trade that put Third World countries at an economic disadvantage. In addition, the industrialized countries give large subsidies to their domestic agriculture and as a result poor farmers in Third World countries cannot compete with the large-scale subsidized agriculture of the Western countries.[3]

In order to buy the needed manufactured goods (such as tractors, factory machinery, etcetera) that they need to attain a higher level of technological and industrial development, Third World countries have had to borrow from the industrialized countries and from organizations like the International Monetary Fund. They had to pay interest on these loans, but the inequitable terms of international trade made it practically impossible for them to keep up the interest payments without borrowing more to do so. In the last fifteen years the foreign debt of Third World countries has been steadily rising. In 1990 it was well over four hundred billion for Latin American countries alone.[4]

The result of this degree of **indebtedness** is that much needed resources that could be used for health care, education, etcetera, are channeled into the payment of the foreign debt. This in turn creates more misery and poverty for the majority of the population, who remain undernourished, illiterate, and with inadequate medical care. And it gets worse. The dire conditions under which the people are forced to live create an atmosphere of political instability which is **exacerbated** by the realization that the wealth in their countries is concentrated in a few hands. The wealthy classes and the high-ranking military and government officials who benefit from the unjust distribution of resources want to maintain the **status quo**. In order to suppress the demands of the populace for better wages, improved working conditions, etc., the governments of many of these countries use a significant portion of their economic resources to strengthen the military and to create specialized security forces trained in intelligence and internal security operations (intimidation techniques, torture, etcetera). Thus more of these countries' funds are used in areas that do not improve the living conditions of the people. The vicious cycle of poverty and oppression is reinforced—the demands of the poor for the alleviation of their misery lead to their political oppression, and the mechanisms that implement this oppression in turn increase their poverty.

What are the philosophical assumptions of our worldview that underpin the policies of economic oppression that are imposed on Latin American and other Third World countries? The answer to this question emerges from an analysis of the neoliberal economic policies that have been proposed as solutions to the economic dilemmas of these underdeveloped countries. The conventional proposals are another indication of the **ontocentrism**[5] that is so characteristic of our cultural worldview. The neoliberal solution involves greater foreign investment and ownership of businesses in Latin America, privatization of public services, the lifting of trade restrictions, greater reliance on export-based economic systems, and structural economic adjustments that involve reductions in government services to the people. No mention is made of encouraging economic self-sufficiency for Third World countries, of dismantling the military units that help perpetuate corruption and oppression, of a more equitable distribution of resources, of the need to provide better health care, or of the importance of respecting human rights.

In suggesting solutions to the problems of poverty and oppression, these proposals ignore the need of Latin Americans to live in a manner that respects their values and traditions; instead, these solutions call for their greater integration and dependence on the international economic system that has undermined their traditional ways of life. Adopting the industrialized **technocratic** ways of life and the consumption patterns of Western countries will invariably entail a weakening of their cultural heritage and values. To be sure, there are some technological advances that all Third World countries would benefit from, especially regarding medical care and education, but Third World nations can enjoy these advances without having to transform their value system into one which prizes materialism,

indebtedness: obligation

exacerbated: made more severe; irritated or aggravated

status quo: the existing state

ontocentrism: the conviction held by a group that its conception of reality is superior to all others

technocratic: pertaining to a re-ordering of society based on the findings of engineers and technologists

depersonalization, **hierarchical** rigidity, abuse of nature, and individualism over community relationships, rootedness in history and cultural tradition, economic decentralization and self-sufficiency, and an integrated approach to life. The assumption that people of a different culture can deal with the problems of poverty and economic development only by adopting our values and way of life once again betrays the ontocentrism of our conceptual framework.

Oppression in the Homeland

Thus far I have discussed oppression as a phenomenon between industrialized and Third World countries. However, oppression is by no means confined to this level. Before making a tentative proposal for dealing with the problem of oppression, it is important to recognize that intercultural oppression also exists within our own country.

There are widespread misconceptions regarding discrimination and oppression of minority groups. One of the most disturbing experiences I have had teaching college students has dealt with the dogmatic refusal of white students to recognize that racism exists in American society. There is a commonly held perception that racism and discrimination are problems that were resolved in the 1960s. In fact, some students feel that too much is being done for minorities, that is, that minorities are getting a "free ride" and that they "have it made." There is resentment that whites are being treated unfairly when minorities are given preferential consideration. What is so ironic about this situation is that most of these white students are almost totally uninformed of the mass of statistical facts that show that economically, socially, and educationally things are worse for minorities, in relation to whites, than they were ten years ago. A larger percentage of black women and children are living in poverty today than a decade ago. Between 1969 and 1979 the expected lifetime earnings of black men was about 57 percent that of white men, and in 1984 that percentage had actually decreased to 56 percent. Also, a proportionately lower number of black men are attending college today than ten years ago. The high school dropout rate is almost 50 percent for Latinos in some parts of the country and more Latinos are living in poverty than ever before.[6] Recent studies have shown that blacks and Latinos were widely discriminated against when applying for housing loans.

It is an interesting fact that when discussing racism some of those white students who do recognize that racism is a significant factor in society quickly exempt themselves by saying or implying "some whites are racist, but not me." Even though there are surely some white students who can truthfully say this about themselves, I suspect that for some others this statement simply represents a refusal to reflect on racist attitudes which they might have. Students usually get very defensive when issues of racism are discussed. Perhaps this is because feelings of resentment or guilt emerge during such discussions. It is unfortunate that most students do not realize that recognizing prejudiced attitudes that one may have is not a sign of weakness or moral deficiency, but is rather a sign of an emerging intellectual and emotional maturity. It is the first step toward dealing with and eliminating such attitudes. By refusing to reflect openly and honestly on their own prejudices students miss an important opportunity to grow and develop as human beings.

Multiculturalism—A Chance for Renewal

Just as the philosophical point of view has deepened our understanding of oppression, can it now offer us some insights that can serve as a starting point for resolving the problem of oppression in Latin America and the Third World? Even though philosophical reflection by itself will certainly not resolve this problem, philosophy can nevertheless help us to formulate a useful approach to deal with

hierarchical: ordered according to a rank

232

this issue. The approach I want to propose can be called the multicultural **perspective**. According to this perspective, an adequate understanding of reality is one which emerges as the result of an open, mutually liberated dialogue between the participants of the different cultural traditions making up a society. This multicultural context of dialogue and interaction would make possible the recognition and removal of the cultural blinders of each of the participants. Thus, one of the first goals of this dialogue would be for the participants to understand and appreciate the perspectives from which the others perceive reality. The articulation and negotiation of their different needs and interests would be based on this prior understanding. None of the perspectives would have an initial or *a priori* privileged status, nor would there be an initial hierarchical differentiation between perspectives or between the elements of the perspectives.

It is important to note that there would be certain **normative** principles implicit in the adoption of this multicultural perspective. The liberated dialogue would in essence be free from **ideological** distortions; its participants would have an equal access to information (and would have developed the critical thinking skills necessary for evaluating that information); and there would be a lack of hierarchical controls in the exchange of information. The practical and political implications of these principles are profound and wide-ranging. Consider the second of the conditions just mentioned. If the participants in the dialogue are to have equal access to as well as a critical understanding of any information that may be relevant for the negotiation of a case at hand, then this implies at least an approximate **parity** in the educational preparation of the participants, as well as the elimination of economic restrictions that would impose **arbitrary** limitations on the use of available information. Furthermore, a critical understanding of this information presupposes an awareness of sexist, racist, classist, and other ideological factors that may distort its meaning and interpretation. It is important to note that putting these normative principles into practice will take work and effort, and that we should not be discouraged by the realization that these principles will not be implemented simply by adopting the multicultural perspective. Attaining educational parity, for example, or developing modes of communication that are free of ideological distortions and biases, will take strong political efforts to achieve.

The satisfaction of these conditions for liberated dialogue implies the elimination of substantial differences in the economic and educational status of the participants. In the multicultural perspective the connection between the socioeconomic position of the participants of a political community and their capacity to participate meaningfully in the decision-making processes of that community are emphasized. This perspective thus avoids the naive viewpoint of classical liberal political theory that severs the connection between political power and economic power and the capacity to equally exercise one's civil rights in real political settings.

Finally, I want to clarify the multicultural perspective by indicating what it is not. It is not a **relativistic** or perspectival approach according to which all cultural perspectives are "equally valid." It is entirely possible that the participants in the open liberated dialogue may determine that certain cultural practices are oppressive or unethical (traditional views of women are a case in point). Thus we do not naively idealize or romanticize other cultures. This perspective does not tell us ahead of time which practices of what culture are oppressive or not. Instead, what it does is to give us a **methodology** by which the identification of such practices is to be achieved. Also, the multicultural perspective is not a Marxist perspective, because, although it recognizes the important role of economic factors in oppression, it leaves it as an open question whether it is in the best interests of the members of a community (either local, national, or global) to adopt a capitalist, socialist, Communist, or mixed economic system. It is certainly logically possible that one or another of these systems may be more effective and desirable to different communities at different points in time.

perspective: point of view

a priori: known to be certain without need of validation by experience

normative: prescribing a norm or standard

ideological: pertaining to the body of doctrine of a social movement or large group

parity: equivalence

arbitrary: without justification

relativistic: pertaining to the theory that truth is determined by what is believed to be true

methodology: a system of rules and principles

233

It is unlikely that we will be able to deal adequately with the issues of poverty and oppression in the Third World until we recognize the philosophical assumptions which shape the way in which we understand these issues. In our dealings with the Third World and in our own domestic policies we should have the moral courage to strive for economic and social justice, for this is the ethically correct thing to do. But in addition to this compelling moral reason, we have strong practical reasons to do so. We can no longer afford not to do so. The facts that the population of the United States is becoming increasingly multicultural and that we live in an increasingly interdependent world, make it necessary for us to adopt the multicultural perspective in order to function effectively, at a political and economic level, in the future. We must reevaluate the philosophy of egoism and ontocentrism that is so central to our conceptual orientations. And, most importantly, we must realize that refusing to deal with oppression involves an alienation from our own humanity and compassion. The struggle with the problem of oppression is not to be taken lightly, for ultimately the battle is to reclaim our own souls.

Endnotes

1. Guatemala Health Rights Support Project, *Guatemala Health Rights Support Project* (Washington, D.C.: Guatemala Health Rights Support Project, 1987).
2. The Independent Commission of Inquiry on the U.S. Invasion of Panama, *The U.S. Invasion of Panama: The Truth Behind Operation 'Just Cause'* (Boston: South End Press, 1991), p. 132.
3. Paul Vallely, *Bad Samaritans* (Maryknoll, New York: Orbis Books, 1990), pp. 105–108.
4. Scott B. MacDonald, Jane Hughes, and Uwe Bott, *Latin American Debt in the 1990s* (New York: Praeger, 1991), p. 4.
5. "Ontocentrism" is the belief that the vision of reality of one's culture or society is superior to all others.
6. National Academy Press, *A Common Destiny: Blacks and American Society* (Washington, D.C.: National Academy Press, 1989).

▼ Questions to Focus Reading

1. After relating Consuelo's terrible story, Valadez tells us what he will attempt to do in this essay. What is his objective?
2. Metaphysics is the branch of philosophy that deals with theories about the nature of reality. What does Valadez mean by "metaphysical imperialism"?
3. What, according to Valadez, is the philosophical assumption underlying metaphysical imperialism?
4. What is a philosophical approach to the phenomenon of oppression? The author tries to show us how such an approach helps us to see both the roots and the wide-reaching prevalence of oppression. How does he make his case?
5. What, according to the author, distinguishes Western European ethnocentricism from the usual kind?
6. How, according to Valadez, did the United States justify its politically oppressive policies toward Latin America during the cold war? With the end of the cold war, how has that justification changed?
7. Valadez explains the origin of the enormous foreign debt of Third World countries. What is his explanation?
8. What are the social consequences of the indebtedness?

9. Proposed American solutions to the economic dilemmas of underdeveloped countries once again demonstrate ontocentrism, Valadez argues. What is his case for this?

10. What are some of the "widespread misconceptions" about discrimination and oppression at home that the author details?

11. Valadez proposes the multicultural perspective as the basis for resolving the problem of oppression in Latin America and the Third World. What is this perspective? What "normative principles" does it entail?

12. Valadez is concerned to distinguish the multicultural perspective from other approaches with which it may be confused. How is it different from relativism? From Marxism?

13. We in the United States must take the problem of oppression seriously, Valadez says, "for ultimately the battle is to reclaim our own souls." What do you think he means by this?

▼ Questions for Reflection

1. What is Valadez's key objective in this essay?

2. Valadez distinguishes between two forms of oppression, political and economic, and identifies the philosophical orientation that underlies each. To get an overview of his essay, describe these two forms of oppression. What are the philosophical assumptions underlying each?

3. Explain the concept of "metaphysical imperialism." What, according to the author, is the philosophical assumption on which it rests?

4. Valadez argues that American policies toward Latin America have illustrated metaphysical imperialism. What is his case for this? How might U.S. administrations defend their policies against this attack? Would their defense be successful?

5. Has the author presented an accurate account of the origin of Third World debt? Research the subject in order to determine whether he has.

6. The author describes a "vicious cycle of poverty and oppression." Explain. Research the topic to substantiate or dispute his account.

7. In the section entitled "Oppression in the Homeland," Valadez reports "widespread misconceptions" among college students regarding racism in America. What, according to the author, are these misconceptions? Judging from your own experience, would you say his description is accurate?

8. American proposals to solve the problems of poverty in Latin America demonstrate "ontocentrism," the author writes. What does he mean? What reason does he give for saying so? How might the authors of these proposals defend themselves? Would their defense be successful?

9. In the last part of his essay Valadez offers the philosophical groundwork for a resolution of the problems of poverty and oppression in the Third World. Describe the groundwork he lays down. In what respects, if any, do you think his proposals are vulnerable to criticism?

10. What is a philosophical perspective? What contribution has the philosophical perspective made here to the study of oppression?

▼ Discussion

1. What does Valadez mean by "metaphysical imperialism"? What is the deep philosophical connection in which, in his view, it is rooted? What examples does he provide of actions motivated by metaphysical imperialism? Do you think the concept of metaphysical imperialism helps to cast light on these historical events?

2. What is Valadez's account of the origin of Third World debt? Given your own reading on this matter, do you think he has presented an accurate explanation?

3. Valadez notes the defensiveness students often show in discussions of racism. What is his explanation for this? Do you think his observation of defensiveness is accurate? Has he rightly understood the source of this discomfort?
4. What does Valadez mean by the "multicultural perspective"? How could the conditions for the "liberated dialogue" he proposes be established?
5. Valadez claims at the end of his essay that our stake in the battle against oppression is the reclaiming of our own souls. What do you think he means by this? Do you think he is right?

▼ Writing Assignments

1. "American Policy toward the Third World: A Case of Metaphysical Imperialism" or "American Policy Defended." With research of your own, support Valadez's view of American policy, or make a case against his view.
2. Write an essay on Third World debt. You may choose to dwell on its causes, its scope, its relation to oppression, possible solutions, or some combination of these.
3. "Is There Racism on Our Campus?"
4. "The Relevance of Metaphysics to Oppression" How has Valadez made use of a philosophical perspective to illuminate the problem of oppression?

▼ Journal Entries

1. Have you had experience learning to appreciate a perspective at first quite foreign to you? How did you come to appreciate it?
2. Valadez believes racist attitudes to be more common among college students than the students are likely to admit. Judging from your own campus, do you think he is right about this?

▼ Vocabulary

a priori	ethnocentric	indebtedness	ontocentrism
anthropological	exacerbated	indigenous	parity
appropriation	forfeited	inequitable	perspective
arbitrary	hierarchical	instigated	rationale
disfranchised	ideological	metaphysical	relativistic
egalitarian	imperialism	methodology	status quo
elucidated	imposition	normative	technocratic

38

▼

Man and Nature:
The Future of the Global Environment

Jessica Tuchman Mathews

Saving the global environment from catastrophe will require a radical change in our thinking about our relationship to nature. Environmental scientist Jessica Tuchman Mathews is vice president of the World Resources Institute, Washington, D.C., an organization monitoring global ecology. Here she presents both reasons to fear and bases for hope for the future of the earth.

The great French biologist and Nobel laureate Jacques Monod concluded not long ago, that "Mankind was mother nature's only serious mistake." A newspaper reader attentive to the health of the global environment in the 1980s, might almost have been tempted to agree.

Consider for a moment a few of the events of this past decade: the oil price rise and widespread shortages at its beginning; the chemical accident at Bhopal; the **decimation** of European and high altitude U.S. forests from acid rain and other air pollutants; the explosion at Chernobyl;[1] **ozone depletion** and the discovery of a "hole" in the ozone layer over Antarctica; drought and famine in Africa; the Rhine River chemical spill; the homeless freighter that sailed the world for two years without finding a place to unload its toxic cargo; steadily rising rates of tropical **deforestation** and of species extinction; closed beaches from Western Europe to the Baltic to New Jersey; the Exxon *Valdez* oil spill; and, as the decade closed, an outbreak of freakish weather—drought and record-breaking heat in the United States, devastating floods in Bangladesh, the most powerful hurricane ever measured, and the warmest winter in Moscow in more than a century—all bring intense new concern to the possibilities of global warming.

There were more hungry people on the planet as the 1980s drew to a close than ever before. Seven hundred to eight hundred million people, outside of China, eat fewer calories than are necessary for an active life. Malnutrition is a major factor in the deaths of twenty-five thousand infants and children under five each day. Even where adequate calories are available, clean water, which is equally essential, often is not. Waterborne disease, whose solutions are environmental, rather than medical, remains a scourge. Two hundred million people are sick with **schistosomiasis**, 175 million with malaria, 450 million with hookworm, river blindness and sleeping sickness affect 20 million each.

The 1980s also brought rich new scientific insights. As scientists studied the chemical elements essential to life—carbon, nitrogen, phosphorus and sulfur—they quickly found that their natural cycles through earth, air, water and living things were being affected on a global scale by human activities. Non-chemical changes are equally massive. On land, soil erosion and deforestation are accelerating the flow of sediments and nutrients to the ocean in some places, while dams built for irrigation and electricity interrupt the natural flow in others. The permanent loss of species—now estimated to stand at four per hour—utterly disrupts the natural balance between **speciation** and extinction.

decimation: destruction of a great portion

ozone: a form of oxygen

depletion: a serious decrease in the supply

deforestation: clearing of forests

schistosomiasis: organ infection and chronic anemia caused by parasites in feces-contaminated water

speciation: the forming of new species

The more closely scientists looked at the planet's structure and **metabolism**, from the top of the **stratosphere** to the ocean canyons, the more the evidence of rapid change accumulated. A sense of urgency gradually filtered through to governments that man is now the principal agent of environmental change on the planet, and that if humanity is to live successfully with its ability to alter natural systems it must first understand those systems and the ways in which human society depends on their normal functioning. Unless policies change, some scientists warn, man's impacts on the planet are so profound and are accumulated so rapidly that irreversible damage could occur—to put it bluntly—before we have any idea of what we are doing. Since man's ability to tinker inadvertently with the basic physiology of the planet is new in history, it is worth spending a few minutes to look at these changes in more detail.

At the core of all environmental trends lies population growth. It took 130 years for world population to grow from 1 to 2 billion; it will take just this decade to climb from 5 billion to 6 billion. Though the *rate* of growth is slowing, the human family grows by 93 million each year, a larger increment than ever before. Africa, already mired in poverty and struggling against a falling per capita GNP [Gross National Product], will add more than the present population of the United States between 1980 and 2000. If fertility continues to decline at its present slow rate, **demographers** predict that the human population will level off at a staggering 14 billion, almost triple today's population, not at the 9 or 10 billion that seemed most likely just a few years ago.

No simple relationship links population levels and the resource base. Policies, technologies, and institutions intervene between population growth and its impacts and can spell the difference between a highly stressed, degraded environment and one that could sustainably provide for many more people. Sometimes absolute numbers are crucial. Most often, though, the *rate* of growth is most important. Whereas a government might be fully capable of providing food, housing, jobs, and health care for a population growing at one percent per year (and therefore doubling in 72 years), it might be completely overwhelmed by an annual growth rate of three percent, which would double the population in 24 years.

While the United States and the [former] Soviet Union are each growing at just under one percent per year, and Europe only half that fast, Africa is expanding by about three percent annually and Asia and Latin America by about three percent. By 2025 the working age population in the developing countries alone will be larger than the world's current population. Clearly these countries face an urgent choice. For many of them, current rates of growth mean that available capital will be swallowed up in meeting the needs of today's populations rather than invested in the job creation and resource conservation that will be needed to sustain their children. And of course, there are global impacts as well.

The most serious form of renewable resource decline is tropical deforestation. Globally, ten trees are being cut down for every one that is replanted, and an area twice the size of Austria is deforested each year. These luxuriant forests are deceptively fragile. Once disturbed, the entire **ecosystem** can unravel. The loss of the trees interrupts nutrient cycling; the soil loses fertility; plant and animal species lose their habitat and disappear; acute fuelwood shortages arise (especially in the dry tropical forests); without groundcover the soil erodes, and downstream rivers suffer siltation, causing both flooding and droughts, and damage to expensive irrigation and hydroelectric systems on which hopes for economic growth are pinned. Planned to last for 50 to 100 years, the dams can silt up almost overnight, leaving only foreign debt as a legacy. The record is probably held by a large dam in China which silted up completely in 4 years.

Traced through its effects on agriculture, energy supply, and water resources, deforestation impoverishes about a billion people, and often leaves political as well as economic chaos in its wake. In Haiti, many of the boat people who fled to the

metabolism: the totality of physical and chemical processes in an organism by which energy is made available for its functioning

stratosphere: the upper atmosphere

demographers: practitioners of the science of vital and social statistics of population

ecosystem: a system formed by the interaction between a community of organisms and their environment

United States left because of the brutality of the Duvaliers. But many were forced into the boats by the impossible task of farming the bare rock left behind by near total deforestation and soil erosion. Haitians are by no means the only environmental refugees. No one knows the true numbers, but in Indonesia, Central America, and sub-Saharan Africa, millions have been forced to leave their homes in part because the loss of plant cover and the consequent disappearance of soil have made it impossible to grow food. Where the refugees settle, they add to the local demand for food and put new burdens on the land, spreading the environmental stress that forced them from their homes like a disease. Resource mismanagement is not the only cause of these mass movements, of course. Religious and ethnic conflicts, political repression, and other forces are at work. The environmental causes are simply the most often ignored.

The tropical forests also harbor most of the planet's genetic wealth, the heritage of 3.5 billion years of evolution. This diversity is therefore vanishing on a scale not seen since the disappearance of the dinosaurs. Extinction is a normal part of nature, but today's rate is 1,000 to 10,000 times greater than the natural rate. With the loss at already 100 species per day, one-fifth of all the species living in 1980 may be gone by the end of this decade.

The loss will be felt **aesthetically**, scientifically, and economically. Its costs are impossible even to estimate. A few years ago, a Mexican graduate student stumbled upon a primitive form of **perennial** corn which appears to exist nowhere else in the world but on the single hilltop, and which would have been quickly wiped out but for his alertness. If the perennial character can be bred into commercial corn its environmental and economic value will be enormous.

Genetic diversity is a virtually untapped resource. Man currently makes use of less than one percent of what is available. Among the vast numbers of unused types of edible plants, for example, are a great many with equal or greater potential than the few that now form the basis of the human diet. The bitter irony is that genetic diversity is being lost on a grand scale at the very moment when biotechnology makes it possible to fully exploit the resource for the first time.

The most truly global and potentially threatening of environmental trends is greenhouse warming. The greenhouse effect results from the fact that the planet's atmosphere is largely transparent to incoming radiation from the sun but absorbs much of the lower energy radiation re-emitted by the earth. The effect is a natural phenomenon that makes the earth warm enough to support life. But as emissions of greenhouse gases increase, the planet warms *un*naturally. Carbon dioxide, the product of all combustion and therefore of all fossil fuel use, is the principal greenhouse gas.

There are many uncertainties about greenhouse climate change, but a scientific consensus exists on its central features: the soundness of the theory; the identity of the greenhouse gases; the rate at which their concentrations are growing, and in most cases, the reasons for that increase. There is also agreement that global average temperature has risen by slightly more than half a degree centigrade since the industrial revolution began, at the low end of the range the theory predicts. The uncertainties arise over how much warming will result from added greenhouse gases, and how fast it will occur. The questions, in short, are not whether, but when, and how much.

Hotter temperatures are only one of the expected results. Precipitation patterns would shift, perhaps causing Dust Bowl-like conditions in key grain producing areas. Ocean currents may also shift, dramatically altering climate. A diversion of the Gulf Stream, for example, would make Western Europe far colder than it is today. Sea level would rise due to thermal expansion of the oceans and the melting of land-based ice. The predicted rise would inundate large coastal regions, erode shorelines, destroy coastal marshes and swamps (both areas of very high biological productivity), affect water supplies through the intrusion of salt water, and put at

aesthetically: pertaining to the appreciation of beauty

perennial: in botany, having a life cycle longer than two years

239

high risk the vastly disproportionate share of the world's economic infrastructure that is packed along the coastlines. The great low-lying river deltas, from the Mississippi to the Nile and Ganges, would likely be flooded. Some island nations would disappear altogether.

There would be positive consequences as well. Some plants would grow more quickly (though many, alas, will be weeds), fertilized by the additional carbon dioxide. Rainfall may rise in what are now arid but potentially fertile regions. Conditions for agriculture may also improve in some northern regions. The net effect, however, is almost certain to prove costly to all countries because all depend so heavily on the normal, predictable functioning of the climate system. Adapting to a changing climate, where that is possible, and when the impacts can be predicted in time, will be very expensive. Developing countries, with small reserves of capital, few scientists and engineers, and weak central governments, will be especially hard hit. Many needed adaptations will be prohibitively costly, and some of the most severe impacts, such as those on wildlife and ecosystems, will be beyond the reach of human correction.

Greenhouse warming is closely linked to stratospheric ozone depletion, which is caused by a group of man-made compounds known as chlorofluorocarbons, or CFCs. These, it turns out, are also potent greenhouse gases. The increased ultraviolet radiation caused by ozone loss will produce an increase in skin cancers, eye damage, crop loss, and other as yet unknown impacts on plants and animals, including perhaps the suppression of immune systems.

Ozone depletion is a valuable object lesson in environmental humility. Chlorofluorocarbons were thoroughly tested when first introduced and found to be completely **benign**. Their possible effect on the remote stratosphere was simply never considered. More than a decade after the effect was discovered, a related phenomenon came to light that led to a continent-sized "hole" in the layer over Antarctica. This history reminds us that our present knowledge of planetary mechanisms is scanty. The possibility of surprise, possibly a quite nasty surprise, must be placed rather high on the list of likely outcomes. The greatest risk may well come from a completely unanticipated direction, for we lack both crucial knowledge and early warning signals.

Do all these trends mean that the human prospect is bleak? Certainly, we—the human species—cannot go on as we are without fundamental change. Without it there is no way the planet can accommodate a doubling or more of population, at least a fivefold rise in economic output, and a tripling of energy use all by the middle of the next century. We will need to redesign our technologies from the inside out, rather than continue to fiddle with what comes out the end of the pipe. The new designs must follow nature's example in which there are few if any wastes, materials are used with high efficiency, and every byproduct is used as the starting point in other processes. Look in a biochemistry text and you will see that all of nature's systems are circular designs. Nothing is **linear**, as most man-made processes are.

Such change is well within our technological capacity. With only a modest effort many of our present practices could be made to look primitive. The United States could cut its energy use in half with presently available technologies, and there is no telling what could be achieved through a determined research effort. We use a billion pounds of pesticide each year, less than one percent of which reaches a target pest. It should not be beyond us to increase that number three-, five-, or tenfold. Our transportation system uses marginal improvements on fifty- and one hundred-year-old technologies. The hottest thing in mass transit right now is so-called "light rail," which is just another name for the trolley car, a technology that was introduced in the 1880s. We have not begun to use the revolutionary power of information and communication technologies to transform transportation just as they have transformed banking, publishing, retailing, and just about every-

benign: healthful, beneficial; not malignant

linear: resembling a straight line

thing else. In short, we have not yet really tried to make technology serve nature instead of letting nature serve technology as a source of resources and repository for wastes.

Yet even with that ambitious goal, technological change will be the easiest part of the challenge that lies ahead. The difficult part will be understanding what we are doing to the planet before it is too late, summoning the will to choose a different future, and developing the new rules and institutions that will enable us to travel that different path. That is a tall order, I know, but notice what is not included. I do not believe that we need to change human values. We will have to change how we think—especially about the future—and how we behave, especially as a global community. But change in thought and behavior, even in deeply ingrained habit, is well within what history tells us is possible. Indeed, thought and behavior can change quickly and profoundly as conditions and institutions change. Human slavery once seemed essential to economic success, morally acceptable, even ordinary. Now it is unthinkable.

How we act is a function of what we see in the world around us, and what we see is a function of what we understand. Thus science is a powerful shaper of human behavior. From Newton to Einstein our concept of the physical universe changed our way of thinking. Darwin certainly did too. Perhaps now it is Lovelock's turn. Lovelock proposes a theory he calls Gaia after the Greek earth goddess. Gaia sees the earth as a living organism in which the nonliving realm is continuously shaped by the presence of life. Not just species evolve in the Gaian view, but species and their living and nonliving environment together. Thus, the apparent planning and sense of purpose that natural selection produces—and which has always been so hard to grasp—is broadened to include the entire planet. It is far too early to say that Lovelock is correct, but the theory has generated exciting research, which is always suggestive. If Gaia is correct, it will force us to shift our focus from an overriding concern for the welfare of our own species to that of the planet as a whole.

Science regularly makes a fool of anyone who tries to predict its future. Darwin himself wrote in his *Autobiography,* "I rejoice that I have avoided controversies." But I will take the risk and hazard a guess that the revolutionary sciences of our time (just as astronomy and physics have been in the past) will be ecology and the study of earth as a living whole.

From that science will come the realization that despite technology, and what our major religions have taught, beginning with Genesis, man does *not* exercise dominion over nature. The reverse may well be closer to the truth: nature rules man, both because it shapes our minds, bodies, and spirit and because we are and will always remain, so economically dependent upon it. Our worldview now is that man is not only above, but separate from nature, which exists solely to serve his purposes. We do not need to go to the other extreme as some suggest, and see ourselves as no different from nor better than a chimpanzee or a guppy. We can continue to view ourselves as the peak of creation, but we must discard our misguided sense of separateness. In that endeavor lies a great task for organized religion.

Those whose work keeps them closest to nature understand this best. They learn that, except in a narrow sense, or over a short term, it is hard to do better than nature. Let me give you a very simple example. When foresters first began to plant trees where old forests had been cut, they had a terrible time. The new forests looked nice, full of young, healthy trees with clean trunks and without crumbling dead trees in the way, but they didn't grow well. Slowly the foresters learned that everything in the natural forest served a purpose: without the dead hollow trees for owls and woodpeckers to nest in, insect populations got out of control; without the lichen that coats the trunks of old trees, forests could not fix enough nitrogen from the air to fertilize themselves.

Usually, the connections are harder to trace. The human system appears to outperform nature, but only till we count the cost in some other place or at some later time. This is a lesson that will have to be learned again and again. As human demands on the planet accelerate, we will learn the lesson on a larger and larger scale, until eventually we learn to incorporate it into how we think and behave.

The influence of nature on man's spirit should also be a positive force for change. It is the source of man's creativity. Probably the original inspiration for stained glass, like the magnificence that surrounds us, came from someone who had seen how sunlight filters through the leaves of a high tree canopy. Each of us has experienced the force with which a beautiful day lifts the spirit even in the middle of a city. We know the strength of our connection to certain species: witness all the fuss over the three trapped whales a few years ago. And we need wilderness, not just for recreation, but as Wallace Stegner wrote, "for spiritual renewal, the recognition of identity, and the birth of awe." I maybe too optimistic here, because of course these connections have always been with us and in recent centuries haven't been notably influential. But perhaps as nature grows ever more threatened, its value will seem more obvious and urgent. Or perhaps as we see less of nature, it will be the easier to lose.

If science, religion, and man's emotional connections to nature can reshape how we perceive our role on the planet, then institutional changes can pave the way to new policies and economic behavior. Prosaic and rather simple changes will have a sweeping impact. For example, economic indicators currently ignore environmental costs. When countries calculate their national income accounts— their GNP—they value and depreciate everything man-made, even intangibles like knowledge. But the accounts completely ignore environmental resources. The result is policies that cannot distinguish between using income—say, the sustainable yield of lumber or fish—and using up a capital asset, namely the forest or fishery itself. In the private sector, we have indicators that measure how efficiently labor and capital are used, but nothing that measures environmental productivity—how much resources are used and emissions produced per unit of economic output. Changing these and other signals, to which policymakers are exquisitely tuned, will automatically and effortlessly go a long way toward turning bad policies into good ones.

Global environmental trends all pose potentially serious losses to national economies, are immune to solution by one or a few countries, and render geographic borders irrelevant. The internationalization of finance and industry and the boundary-erasing effects of remote sensing technology and linked computers have the same effect. Even the amount we travel makes health policy, once solely a domestic **prerogative**, into an international issue. These invasions of national **sovereignty** make governments less central than they once were. I don't mean to suggest that nation-states will disappear, but some of the powers they have held will be inherited by other actors: by individuals, the business sector, and international organizations.

Individuals have a particularly important role to play. First, because changes in thought and understanding come from people, not institutions. Individuals will also provide much of the impetus toward a functioning global community in place of today's collection of nations. Working through their own international communities—science, business, labor, citizen activism, and so on—people offset the **centrifugal** forces that govern relations among states. Jean Monnet, the father of the European Community, knew this when he described his intention as "not to form coalitions between states, but union among people." That Monnet's wild dream is now a reality, and that Europe is in the longest period of peace in its history, is to me another hopeful **portent**.

Whether each of our individual preferences is for scholarship or business, civic action or research, the nudge of a petition or the slap of a lawsuit, all of us must believe and behave as if, to paraphrase another famous Frenchman, the fate

prerogative: a right or privilege limited to persons of a specific category

sovereignty: supreme and independent authority in government

centrifugal: directed outward from the center

portent: sign

of the planet is too important to be left to governments. Individual efforts in the face of problems which have a global dimension may seem inadequate, even futile. But, in aggregate, they are not. "Your actions may seem insignificant," Gandhi said, "but it's crucial that you do them."

For all that can be achieved outside of government, changes in national policy are also absolutely vital. Looking at the United States today and over the past decade, one cannot be very hopeful about the prospects for leadership in the executive or the congressional branch. Despite the manifest flaws in our political system as it functions today, I cannot put all of the blame on politicians, because leadership is a two-way street.

Leaders need followers who are willing to be led. We Americans have given no sign that we would reward leadership no matter how enlightened or beneficial. We need to care a lot more about our federal government and demand a lot more of it. We should insist that it provide what we want, while being more honest in matching those expectations with our willingness to pay. We must stop being diverted by phony debates over manufactured symbols and images. We need to care more about the budget and less about flag burning. Let's get rid of those who are content to do nothing more than nurse along a manifestly inadequate status quo, and seek out those who are determined to do better. And when we find leaders like that let's do what's necessary to elect them and then hold them accountable.

You will have gathered by this time that I am optimistic about our ability as a species to develop a permanent *modus vivendi* with the earth. Being an intensely practical person I have no other option. But I do not underestimate the challenge. Indeed it is in part because present policies are so bad that I see so much room for improvement. I also believe that a positive outlook is an essential ingredient of success. If our aim is merely to make a bad thing marginally better, we will never unleash the necessary energy and motivation. We need to believe in something bigger than fear of the consequences of inaction.

The historian Barbara Tuchman wrote that "We cannot reckon on the better impulses predominating in the world, only that they will always appear." They are appearing now, in thousands of gatherings that would not have taken place even a few years ago. Our job is to seize this fleeting opportunity and to blow the scattered sparks into a bonfire for change.

modus vivendi: way of living

Endnote

1. The city in the Ukraine that was, in 1986, the scene of the largest nuclear plant accident to date.

▼ Questions to Focus Reading

1. "Mankind was mother nature's only serious mistake," said biologist Jacques Monod. Mathews cites many events of the 1980s that seem to support the Nobel laureate's dark judgment. What are some of these events?

2. Humankind's power to change the global environment is something new in history. Mathews develops this topic in detail. She discusses population growth, tropical deforestation, the diminishing of genetic diversity, greenhouse warming, and ozone depletion. What is the impact on the global environment of each of these phenomena?

3. Mathews calls greenhouse warming the "most threatening of the present environmental trends." Why?

4. Ozone depletion is an example of the kind of "nasty surprise" that may greet us when we "tinker . . . with the physiology of the planet." In what sense was it a "nasty surprise"?

5. Surveying the trends she describes, Mathews does not conclude that the prospect for us human beings must be dismal. But deep changes will be necessary, in our technologies, in our understanding, and in our rules and institutions. What changes does she have in mind?

6. Mathews argues that "science is a powerful shaper of human behavior." On what grounds? How would confirmation of Lovelock's Gaia theory change the way we see?

7. "Science, religion, and man's emotional connection to nature can reshape how we perceive our role on the planet," Mathews writes. What does she think will be the contribution of science? What can be the contribution of organized religion? What may be the part played by our emotional connection to nature?

8. Mathews envisions increasingly important roles for individuals, the business sector, and international organizations in dealing with the problems of our global environment. Why? Can you explain especially the emphasis on the individual?

▼ Questions for Reflection

1. We will have to learn, Mathews insists, that "man does not exercise dominion over nature." Why does she say so?

2. How would a person who took seriously Mathews's challenge to individuals change his or her life?

3. Do you share Mathews's optimism about humankind's stewardship of this earth? Why or why not?

4. What do you believe to be the most serious problems that will confront us in the twenty-first century? In the solution of which of these do you see a role for the natural sciences (astronomy, biology, chemistry, physics)? What would that role be?

▼ Discussion

1. Does Mathews's lecture prompt in you more hope than fear about the global environment, or does it prompt more fear than hope? Explain.

2. Which of the conditions of the global environment that Mathews describes seem to you most troubling? Why?

3. Mathews emphasizes the importance of the individual in changing the prospects for our global environment. Is there anything you can do toward resolving threats to the environment? What specific options for action are available to the individual?

4. Do you believe the individual has a responsibility to take such action? (See above question.) Is he or she morally blameworthy for *not* taking such action? Defend your answer.

5. What is your understanding of Lovelock's Gaia theory? If it is true, how does it change your view of the earth?

▼ Writing Assignments

1. "Nature as Teacher: What We Need to Learn"

2. Prepare a fictional report for a television broadcast on the condition of the global environment. The year is 2050. Include in your report the causes of the condition you describe.

3. "Our Global Environment: Reasons for Hope"

4. "In Despair of the Future of Our Earth"

5. "The Importance of the Individual in the Future of Our Global Environment"

6. "The Population Explosion and the Environment"

7. "___: A Key Threat to the Environment" Research a key threat to the environment. Describe the problem and discuss possible solutions.

8. "___: A Serious Threat to Our Local Environment." Consider the threats to your local environment (specific cases of air or water pollution, destruction of wilderness areas, and so on). Choose one of these to research. Describe the problem. What solutions are possible?

▼ Journal Entry

1. Mathews quotes novelist Wallace Stegner, who writes that our need for wilderness is not just for recreation, but "for spiritual renewal, the recognition of identity, and the birth of awe." What is your own relationship to nature? Does wilderness fulfill your special needs?

▼ Vocabulary

aesthetically	demographers	*modus vivendi*	schistosomiasis
benign	depletion	ozone	sovereignty
centrifugal	ecosystem	perennial	speciation
decimation	linear	portent	stratosphere
deforestation	metabolism	prerogative	

39

▼

Backpack Almanac

The Environment

Number of years it takes the average American car to produce its own weight in carbon: 1
[Rocky Mountain Institute (Old Snowmass, Colo.), 1988]

Portion of all garbage discarded by Americans that is packaging: ⅓
[Franklin Associates (Prairie Village, Kans.), 1988]

Average number of times a beer bottle in Japan is reused: 20
[Glass Bottle Association (Tokyo), 1988]

Portion of all land in downtown Los Angeles that is used for driving, parking, or servicing cars: ⅔
[*New Perspectives in Transportation Research,* edited by Anthony J. Catanese (Lexington Books, Lexington,
Mass.), 1988]

Gallons of water required to produce a pair of cotton pajamas: 500
[National Cotton Council (Memphis, Tenn.), 1988]

Number of countries that had an environmental protection agency in 1972: 26
[World Environment Center (New York City), 1990]

Number that have one today (1990): 161
[United Nations Environment Program (New York City), 1990]

Pounds of pesticide produced in America each year (per capita): 11
[U.S. Environmental Protection Agency, 1988]

Percentage of the cargo shipped from the Port of New York that is wastepaper: 45
[Port Authority of New York–New Jersey, 1988]

Percentage of Africa that is wilderness: 30
Percentage of North America that is: 36
[The Sierra Club (Washington, D.C.), 1988]

Portion of the U.S. land area inhabited by two or fewer people per square mile: ¼
[Prof. Frank Popper, Rutgers University (New Brunswick, N.J.), 1987]

Pounds of industrial chemicals legally released into U.S. waters each year, according to the EPA: 9,700 million
[U.S. Environmental Protection Agency, 1989]

Percentage change, since 1945, in the portion of U.S. crops lost to insects: +86
Percentage change, since 1945, in the amount of insecticide used on U.S. crops: +900
[David Pimentel, Cornell University (Ithaca, N.Y.), 1989]

Percentage of the U.S. hazardous waste shipped abroad that goes to Canada: 90
[U.S. Environmental Protection Agency, 1989]

Portion of all U.S. coastal waters that are too polluted for commercial shellfishing: 1/3
[National Oceanic and Atmospheric Administration (Silver Spring, Md.), 1989]

Estimated increase, since 1982, in the temperature of the world's oceans: 1/2 degree F
[Alan E. Strong, National Oceanic and Atmospheric Administration (Silver Spring, Md.), 1989]

Number of abandoned nuclear reactors in the world's oceans: 9
[Institute for Policy Studies (Washington, D.C.), Greenpeace USA (Washington, D.C.), 1989]

Pounds of toxic chemicals released during each space-shuttle launch: 77,000
[Kennedy Space Center (Fla.), 1989]

Percentage of Americans who consider themselves environmentalists: 76
[Gallup Organization (New York City), 1989]

Percentage of Americans who live in an area where the air does not meet the standards of the 1970
Clean Air Act: 58
[Natural Resources Defense Council, Clean Air Coalition (Washington, D.C.), 1989]

Percentage of the insecticide used in the United States each year that actually reaches a targeted insect: .003
[David Pimentel, Cornell University (Ithaca, N.Y.), 1989]

Estimated number of plant and animal species that have become extinct since 1980, worldwide: 100,000
[Edward O. Wilson, Harvard University (Cambridge, Mass.), 1989]

Number of new plants and animals that have been patented since then: 2,632
[U.S. Patent Office, 1989]

Average number of acres of rain forest cut down each day since 1980, worldwide: 20,000
[Trees for the Future (Silver Spring, Md.), 1989]

Number of the 6 hottest years in this century that have occurred since 1980: 6
[Jim Hansen and Sergej Lebedeff (New York City), 1989]

Barrels of oil that would be saved each day if U.S. auto-efficiency standards were raised
by 1 mile per gallon: 420,000
[Greenpeace USA (Washington, D.C.), 1989]

Acres of Alaska's temperate rain forest cut down each day: 90
[South-East Alaska Conservation Council (Washington, D.C.), 1989]

Rank of Poland, Czechoslovakia, and Japan, among countries with the most industrial waste per square mile: 1, 2, 3
[World Resources Institute (Washington, D.C.), 1989]

Percentage change, since 1980, in federal research and development spending on solar energy: −90
[U.S. Congressional Research Service (Washington, D.C.), 1990]

Percentage change, since 1980, in the cost of generating solar power: −73
[Solar Energy Industry Association (Washington, D.C.), 1990]

Ratio of hazardous waste produced by the Pentagon to that produced by the top 3 industrial-waste producers: 2:1
[U.S. Dept. of Defense/U.S. Environmental Protection Agency–Citizen Action (Washington, D.C.), 1990]

Number of U.S. states that dispose of hazardous waste in another state: 50
[U.S. Environmental Protection Agency (Washington, D.C.), 1990]

Amount the U.S. government lent Brazil in 1989 to build a highway through the Amazon rain forest: $20 million
[Inter-American Development Bank (Washington, D.C.), 1990]

Acres of solar panels it would take to fulfill all human energy needs: 83 million
Percentage of the earth's land mass this represents: 0.2
[Michael Oppenheimer, Environment Defense Fund (New York City), 1990]

Chances that the level of pollution in a U.S. river has gotten worse or not improved since 1970: 9 in 10
[Barry Commoner, Center for the Biology of Natural Systems, Queens College (New York City), 1990]

Barrels of oil that could be saved by raising U.S. auto-efficiency standards by 2.75 miles per gallon: 290 million
[Safe Energy Communication Council (Washington, D.C.), 1990]

Number of car manufacturers worldwide that have built and tested models that get more than 67 miles per gallon: 7
Number of these cars that are currently on the market: 0
[Deborah Bleviss, International Institute for Energy Conservation (Washington, D.C.), 1991]

Percentage of the electricity consumed in the United States that is used for air-conditioning: 13
[Edison Electric Institute (Washington, D.C.), 1991]

Rank of nuclear power, among energy sources, that Americans believe the country should rely on more in the future: 1
Percentage of Americans who say that a nuclear power plant in their own community would be "unacceptable": 60
[Yankelovich Clancy Shulman (Westport, Conn.), 1991]

Ratio of the average amount of pesticide used on U.S. lawns to the amount used on U.S. cropland, per acre: 5:1
[David Pimentel and Lori McLaughlin, Cornell University (Ithaca, N.Y.), 1991]

Tons of garbage generated in the United States in 1992 by CD (compact disc) packaging: 16,700
[Recording Industry Association of America (Washington, D.C.)/*Harper's* Research, 1993]

Chances that a Russian lives in an area in which air pollution exceeds official safety standards by five times: 3 in 4
[Mike Shuster, National Public Radio (Moscow)/Russian Ministry of the Environment (Moscow), 1993]

40

▼

Revolutions Gone Bad

Stanley Kober

Stanley Kober, political analyst at the Cato Institute, presses his knowledge of history to the service of two ends: He tries to understand why the revolutions in Eastern Europe, so promising at their inception, have turned so ugly, and he tries to predict the course they are likely to pursue.

With the end of the Cold War and the threat of nuclear war receding, the prospects for settling regional conflicts seemed to improve for a time. When Iraq invaded Kuwait, the United States and the Soviet Union chose cooperation over their previous confrontation. President George Bush went so far as to talk about the emergence of "a new world order. . . . A world where the strong respect the rights of the weak." During the election campaign he was even more euphoric. "Today," he proclaimed triumphantly on September 15, 1992, "the 'dominoes' all fall in democracy's way."

Such **euphoria** was understandable a few years ago—and was shared by this author. It can no longer be justified. Like the French Revolution, the democratic revolutions of our own era are being transformed into something ugly and dangerous. Bush may have believed the nationalist upheavals sweeping the former Soviet empire were merely "growing pains," but the trends are more **ominous**. "Nationalists and pseudopatriots and Communists, who are now becoming united, represent a great threat to our country," warns General Dmitri Volkogonov, military adviser to Russian president Boris Yeltsin. "I don't exclude the possibility of a reign of terror."

Because the overthrow of communism occurred with so few casualties, the danger of violence for a time seemed permanently averted. The 1917 Bolshevik **coup d'etat** in Russia also produced few casualties at first. Nevertheless, an extremely bloody civil war soon developed. It may be that, an initial calm notwithstanding, the shock of rapid and dramatic change has an inherent tendency to produce violence, and it is the absence of bloodshed in such conditions that should be regarded as remarkable. That, in fact, was the observation of George Washington when he was informed of the beginning of the French Revolution. He was both exhilarated and cautious. He wrote to Gouverneur Morris, who later became the U.S. envoy in Paris, "The revolution which has been effected in France is of so wonderful a nature, that the mind can hardly recognize the fact. If it ends as our last accounts to 1 August [1789] predict, that nation will be the most powerful and happy in Europe."

But Washington harbored a sense of **foreboding**, which in retrospect appears remarkably **prescient**. "Though it has gone triumphantly through the first **paroxysm**, it is not the last it has to encounter before matters are finally settled," he cautioned.

The revolution is of too great a magnitude to be effected in so short a space, and with the loss of so little blood. . . . To forbear running from one extreme to another is no easy matter, and should this be the

euphoria: a feeling of overwhelming well-being

ominous: forbidding

coup d'etat: overthrow of the government

foreboding: inner certainty of coming misfortune

prescient: exhibiting foreknowledge or foresight

paroxysm: spasm

249

case, rocks and shelves, not visible at present, may wreck the vessel, and give a higher-toned despotism than the one which existed before.

Washington's warning echoes today. "One lesson that the history of revolutions teaches us is that attempts to radically and rapidly replace the old system are unavoidably accompanied by a danger that the means will be unintentionally substituted for the end," Mikhail Gorbachev's close associate, Alexander Yakovlev, emphasized in a speech commemorating the two hundredth anniversary of the French Revolution in 1989. "Impatience risks being replaced by intolerance." That intolerance is now evident throughout Europe even in the most stable democracies. "The unification process has been compressed into too short a time," observes a German youth services director. "Kids feel disoriented and overwhelmed. They develop feelings of hatred. In moments of social crisis, people look for someone to blame. Foreigners are the most convenient target."

It was not supposed to be that way. "None of the great thinkers of the nineteenth century predicted this," points out philosopher Isaiah Berlin in the *New York Review of Books.*

> Liberals, democrats, republicans thought that the great European imperial regimes were perhaps the central problem of their [twentieth] century. Once these tyrannical **conglomerations**—the British Empire, the Austro-Hungarian Empire, the Russian Empire—were, together with colonialism, destroyed, the peoples under their heels would live peacefully together and realize their destiny in a productive and creative manner.

Instead, the collapse of empires has led to an upsurge of hatred and conflict. "Nationalism, at least in the West, is created by wounds inflicted by stress," Berlin explains. "As for Eastern Europe and the former Soviet Empire, they seem today to be one vast, open wound." Nowhere is that wound more visible than in Yugoslavia, where historical grievances are cited as justification for war. The atrocities committed today will in turn become the grievances of tomorrow. In the blunt words of Bosnian Serb leader Radovan Karadzic, "We are enemies, and we will be enemies for a long time."

Abraham Lincoln's first inaugural address defines the problem confronting the world today: The national majority in a nation-state cannot change, but must be permanent, for otherwise the character of the nation would be undermined. But in such a world, who would want to be in the minority? The answer, of course, is Lincoln's formulation: "A majority, held in restraint by constitutional checks, and limitations, and always changing easily, with deliberate changes of popular opinions and sentiments, is the only true sovereign of a free people." Now with the breakup of empires, people accustomed to minority status want to be in the majority. But since it is impossible to have a state in which there are no minorities, "the ultimate consequence," as Vladimir Gligorov of the Institute of Economic Sciences in Belgrade has put it, "is not to have a state at all."

The anarchy in many former communist countries today recalls the anarchy that followed the French Revolution two hundred years ago. In 1792 the French Revolution, then three years old, was in trouble. The most acute problem was the collapse of the currency, which threatened economic ruin. "The results of this rapid **depreciation** of the **assignats** were immediate," notes historian Olivier Bernier.

conglomerations: unions; assemblages

depreciation: decline in value

assignats: paper currency issued in France by the revolutionary government and backed by confiscated lands

> The peasants stopped bringing their crops to the market and stocked them, instead; that, in turn, provoked severe shortages and a rapid rise in the price of bread. In January riots occurred in Paris and several other cities, motivated not by politics but by need.... Now the times

250

were harder than ever and the people were all the angrier since their hopes had been so high.

Political turmoil aggravated the financial collapse. Soon France was at war with all of Europe and the Reign of Terror had begun.

To be sure, the current situation in Russia is not identical to that of the French Revolution, but there are uncomfortable similarities, notably the collapse of the currency. "Farmers are refusing to sell," reported a Western correspondent in Moscow in July 1992. "This in turn will lead to huge increases in the price of bread—the most politically sensitive of all prices—and to further inflation." His account went on to note "a warning from Mr. Sergei Stepanshin, the city's security chief, of disturbances 'in the wake of a worsening economic and political situation.' "

Nor do the similarities between 1792 and today end there. In 1792 the National Assembly, originally the embodiment of the revolution, came under attack as an obstacle to it. "The Assembly is your most dangerous enemy," wrote Jean-Paul Marat in his pamphlet, *The Friend of the People to the French Patriots*. "As long as it keeps meeting, it will try to fight you." Today, some in Russia and elsewhere view the legislature in the same manner: originally the instrument by which the Soviet Union would transform itself into a democracy, now an obstacle to change. Accordingly, they would give Yeltsin virtually unrestricted power to undertake economic reforms, but that entails the same Faustian bargain the Marxists offered. "In the West there has been a tendency to stress the *political* aspect of democracy rather than its *economic* aspect," R. N. Carew Hunt noted in *The Theory and Practice of Communism*.

> Although at times this may have been carried too far, the fault is on the right side, seeing that a people which surrenders its political rights in return for promises of economic security will soon discover that it has made a bad bargain, as it is helpless if the promises are not kept.

Democracy, it must be emphasized, is rooted in institutions, not intentions. That distinction defines the difference between the American and French Revolutions. It explains their different outcomes.

"Each of us puts his person and all his powers under the supreme direction of the general will," Jean-Jacques Rousseau wrote in *The Social Contract*. "Anyone who refuses to obey the general will shall be constrained to do so by the whole body. This means nothing else than that he be forced to be free."

The American conception, of course, was entirely different. Madison completely rejected Rousseau's concept of democracy as an effort to fulfill an idealized general will. "As long as the reason of man continues **fallible**, and he is at liberty to exercise it, different opinions will be formed," he wrote in the *Federalist* No. 10. "It is in vain to say that enlightened statesmen will be able to adjust these clashing interests and render them all **subservient** to the public good." Instead, the government should be constructed so that it is "unable to concert and carry into effect schemes of oppression." Thus, whereas Rousseau insisted on concentrating sovereignty, Madison dispersed it. "Ambition must be made to counteract ambition," he emphasized in No. 51. "The constant aim is to divide and arrange the several offices in such a manner as that each may be a check on the other."

As Gorbachev developed **perestroika**, his approach increasingly held the promise that it would be more American than French in conception. Indeed, Rousseau's model was criticized as the philosophy that led the 1917 Russian Revolution astray. As Yakovlev's colleague Alexander Tsipko argued, "the more our society, especially the youth, had been educated in romantic conceptions of the human being (which were, by the way, in harmony with Rousseau's ideas) . . . the easier it was to justify violence to this underdeveloped and still 'impure' people." Re-

fallible: capable of erring

subservient: subordinate

perestroika: sweeping political reform in the former Soviet Union

jecting Rousseau, Gorbachev seemed to be aiming for the Madisonian model. "We must prevent excessive power from being concentrated in the hands of a small group of people," he told *Der Spiegel* in 1988. "We have started dividing responsibility up strictly and consistently between the Party and legislative, executive and judicial authorities. . . . We call it a reform of the political system, although it could be described as a legal revolution."

Unfortunately, Gorbachev was not able to realize his vision. Just as the ideals of the French Revolution were undermined by the political ambitions of those who came to lead it, so the postcommunist revolutions have suffered from rivalries among their leading personalities.

Whose Sovereignty?

"We the People of the United States . . . do ordain and establish this Constitution." Those famous words, as Alexander Hamilton emphasized in the *Federalist* No. 15, were not accidental, but an intentional departure from the earlier Articles of Confederation. "The great and radical vice in the construction of the existing Confederation is in the principle of LEGISLATION for STATES or GOVERNMENTS, in their CORPORATE or COLLECTIVE CAPACITIES, and as **contradistinguished** from the INDIVIDUALS of whom they consist." In contrast to the Articles in which the sovereign states formed the United States, it was the sovereign people who created the United States under the Constitution. And the people were sovereign in their individual, not collective, capacities. "Legislation for communities, as contradistinguished from individuals," Hamilton wrote with Madison in No. 20, "is subversive of the order and ends of civil **polity**."

The Constitution was the fulfillment of the promise of the Declaration of Independence: In place of the sovereign (divine) right of kings, the Declaration affirmed the sovereign (divine) rights of the individual. In so doing, it completely overturned previous notions of the social contract and the purpose of the state.

On the surface, it might appear the French Revolution accomplished the same radical effect as the American. There were two important differences, however, owing to the influence of the Abbé Sieyès. First, Sieyès rejected the American model of dividing authority, which was unacceptable to a "people resuming its full sovereignty. . . . There is only *one* power, only *one* authority." Second, Sieyès placed sovereignty not in the individual, but in the nation. "The nation exists before all, it is the origin of everything," he declared in his influential pamphlet *What is the Third Estate?* "Its will is always legal, it is the law itself." As the Irish writer Conor Cruise O'Brien has put it, "Under the influence of Sieyès and Rousseau, the Rights of Man were turning into the Rights of **Leviathan**."

By placing the rights of the nation before all, the French Revolution gave a mighty push to the sense of nationality that was beginning to emerge in Europe. Increasingly, the state and the nation became identified with one another. In O'Brien's opinion, it was that idea, and not democracy, that was the central contribution of the French Revolution. "The liberal part of the French Declaration was the part that was of American origin," he insists. "The French Revolution's contribution to militant nationalism on the other hand is enormous—much the greatest contribution made by the Revolution to anything in the world."

Ironically, just as that militant nationalism arose from the democratic sentiments of the Enlightenment, so the militant nationalism of our own day is emerging in the more democratic climate that the fall of communism has created. As he was sworn in as president of Russia, Yeltsin proclaimed his loyalty to democratic values,

contradistinguished: distinguished by contrasting opposite qualities

polity: a particular form of government

Leviathan: a monstrous entity

but he also declared that "Great Russia is rising from its knees!" Such sentiments of democracy and nationalism can coexist uneasily for a time, but if pressed they are fundamentally incompatible. "Nationalism is not the idea of freedom for the individual, it is the idea of a national state: Russia for the Russians, Poland for the Poles," Polish historian Adam Michnik has observed. "Nationalism means an exclusive conception of the nation, because the enemy is first of all the other nation, and then the cosmopolitans within one's own."

Democracy assumes that what unites us as human beings is more important than what divides us. In a democracy (at least in one worthy of the name), people of any creed, religion, or nationality have equal rights of citizenship so long as they, in George Washington's words, "demean themselves as good citizens, in giving [the government] on all occasions their effectual support." In a world of true democracies, there would be no need for national self-determination, since every human being's inalienable rights would be protected equally everywhere. Thus Washington, a patriotic American, could harbor a dream of "one great family, in fraternal ties," in which he would be "a citizen of the great republic of humanity at large."

Nationalism, on the other hand, operates on the notion that what divides us is more important than what unites us; otherwise, why is it necessary to have different states to protect different groups? And if national differences are so important that they require different states, they must lead to sentiments of national superiority, for it is impossible to believe that people are equal while at the same time insisting they are so fundamentally different they must be separated from each other. Anyone who doubts that fact should reflect on the American experience. For decades segregation was legal in the United States because the Supreme Court, in *Plessy v. Ferguson,* rejected the "assumption that the enforced separation of the two races stamps the colored race with a badge of inferiority." It was not until 1954 that the Court, in *Brown v. Board of Education,* ended that fraud by acknowledging that "separate educational facilities are inherently unequal."

What holds true for the United States is also true for the international community. As the tragedy of Yugoslavia demonstrates, the belief in "separate but equal" nation-states can lead to the most horrible **abominations**. "Once the concept of 'otherness' takes root, the unimaginable becomes possible," explains a Croatian journalist.

> Nothing but this sense of "otherness" killed Jews [in World War II]. It began with naming them, by reducing them to the "other." Then everything became possible, even the worst atrocities, like concentration camps. Today it is the slaughtering of civilians in Croatia and Bosnia.

And events in Yugoslavia are just a foretaste of the era of irrationality unfolding.

The Rationalist Delusion

As the deadline for Iraqi compliance with United Nations resolutions approached, Bush said he felt Saddam Hussein would withdraw his forces from Kuwait rather than risk war. Acknowledging that "Arab leaders tell me . . . [Hussein] cannot get out," Bush nonetheless felt "he cannot do in Kuwait what he did in Iran . . . any person who has fought a war, once he understands what he is up against in terms of power, is going to have to find a way to see that he does not fight another one."

abominations: abhorrent situations

Bush was wrong, of course. His critical error was in believing that Saddam Hussein would behave in a way Americans would consider rational. That is the underlying assumption in the realist approach to international relations, and it was generally borne out during the Cold War. When the Soviets miscalculated—for example, during the Cuban missile crisis—they retreated when confronted by superior American power. Americans accustomed to such behavior thought Iraq, far inferior to the Soviet military, would similarly retreat when faced with overwhelmingly superior military power, and were genuinely baffled when it did not.

Americans, in that sense, may have been spoiled by the behavior of the Soviets during the Cold War. Soviet rationality may prove to be the exception rather than the rule. Indeed, the assumption that other peoples will behave in a manner Americans would consider rational contributed to the United States defeat in Vietnam. "I underestimated the tenacity of the North Vietnamese," former Secretary of State Dean Rusk has admitted. "They took frightful casualties . . . roughly equivalent to ten million American casualties. I thought North Vietnam would reach a point . . . when it would be unwilling to continue making those terrible sacrifices . . . I was wrong."

The fundamental error implicit in Rusk's statement is that he attempts to understand the North Vietnamese through an American prism. But when North Vietnamese military commander Vo Nguyen Giap was asked whether he experienced any pity for sending people to their deaths, he replied, "Never. Not a single moment." Giap's indifference, shocking to American sensibilities, is explained by his bitter personal experiences. As CBS journalist Morley Safer reports, "Any doubts about his commitment to rid his country of foreigners were swept away in 1941, when his wife and infant daughter died in a French prison and his sister-in-law was guillotined by the French."

There are many causes of what would appear to Americans to be irrational behavior. Perhaps the most obvious is the **megalomania** of a dictator, especially if he views himself as the agent of God or History. For example, even though Adolf Hitler was not religious, he saw himself as the instrument of divine Providence. "When I look back only on the five years which lie behind us," he told a German audience in 1937, "then I feel that I am justified in saying: That has not been the work of man alone." What appears to the outsider as extraordinarily reckless behavior was seen by Hitler as divine inspiration. "I go the way that Providence dictates with the assurance of a sleepwalker," he said a year earlier.

A second cause is the isolation of the leader, especially a dictator, from a variety of information. According to one of his aides, Hitler "let people tell him the things he wanted to hear, everything else he rejected. . . . Hitler refused to let himself be informed.

Another source of irrational behavior is the stupidity of foreign leaders. In explaining the failure of the Bush administration to anticipate Saddam Hussein's invasion of Kuwait, Ambassador April Glaspie admitted "we foolishly did not realize he was stupid." That comment might be self-serving, but what appears to be irrational behavior to foreign observers may be a product of ignorance of the outside world.

Probably the greatest cause of irrational behavior, however, is simply a difference in value systems. That, more than anything else, appears to have led British prime minister Neville Chamberlain astray when he sought to avoid war. "Do not forget that we are all members of the human race and subject to the like passions and affections and fears and desires," he argued. "There must be something in common between us if only we can find it." Hitler's passions and desires were clearly beyond Chamberlain's comprehension. "If men wish to live, then they are forced to kill others," Hitler declared in 1929.

megalomania: a pathological obsession with power

254

There are two differences in values that are particularly important. The first revolves around the belief that all people are created equal. "To the precepts of equality of all men and basic unrestricted freedom of the individual vis-a-vis the State, National Socialism opposes here the harsh but necessary recognition of the natural inequality and differences between men," states the 1936 text *Commentaries to the German Race Laws.* Hitler, accordingly, saw no problem with master races dominating, and even murdering, inferior ones: "If I can send the flower of the German nation into the hell of war without the smallest pity for the spilling of precious German blood, then surely I have the right to remove millions of an inferior race that breeds like vermin."

The second difference concerns the certainty with which one holds one's convictions. As Judge Learned Hand put it, "the spirit of liberty is the spirit which is not too sure that it is right." The worst crimes against humanity are conducted by those who are entirely without doubt, justifying their actions by historical necessity or divine will. "When people believe that they have absolute knowledge, with no test in reality, this is how they behave," scientist and author Jacob Bronowski explained while standing at the death camp at Auschwitz. "This is what men do when they aspire to the knowledge of gods."

Foreign policy realists, like the late Hans Morgenthau, maintain that statesmen choose from "rational alternatives." As we have seen, however, rationality cannot be assumed as a universal condition. World War II was a consequence of the irrationality of the dictators, most notably Hitler. And now, once again, our world is engulfed in irrationality. "This is the Balkans—rationality isn't a reliable compass," notes a Western diplomat in Belgrade. "All through this conflict, we've seen people who have recognized the disaster ahead and plunged forward anyway."

Two kinds of irrational belief are now especially important as successors to the earlier **totalitarianism**. One is religious fanaticism. "The affair of *The Satanic Verses* is a frightening warning," writes Karen Armstrong in her recent book, *Holy War.* "We must not take these religious passions lightly or dismiss them as the crazed fantasies of an **eccentric** minority that cannot long survive in our enlightened world. There is no purely rational explanation or solution to this problem." Islam is not the only religion affected by such extremism. In Israel, some orthodox rabbis argue that the lands seized in the 1967 war are Jerusalem's by divine right. And Americans horrified by ethnic cleansing in Bosnia should recognize that it has been justified, in part, on religious grounds. "Our army surrounds Muslim villages," reports a Serb journal. "If the Muslims do not raise the white flag on the **minarets**, we raze the villages to the ground."

The other new danger is national exclusivity. Unfortunately, just as the French Revolution saw the ideals of democracy transformed into their exact opposite, so the message of our own day from the political systems replacing communism is not the triumph of democracy, but the victory of nationalism. In the words of Czech president Václav Havel:

The sudden outburst of freedom has not only untied the straitjacket made by Communism, it has also unveiled the centuries-old, often thorny history of nations. Peoples are now remembering their past kings and emperors, the states they had formed far back in their past and the borders of those states. . . . It is entirely understandable that such a situation becomes a breeding ground for nationalist fanaticism, **xenophobia** and intolerance, as well as for all kinds of **demagogues**, **authoritarians** and **populists** to whom people, overcome by a deep feeling of uncertainty, may well be inclined to turn for salvation.

totalitarianism: a form of government in which most aspects of life are controlled by the central dictatorial power

eccentric: peculiar; unconventional

minarets: mosques with projecting balconies where townspeople are summoned to hear a supreme or divine ruler

xenophobia: an irrational fear of strangers or foreigners

demagogues: leaders who obtain power by appealing to the emotions and prejudices of the people

authoritarians: people who are driven to have absolute power over others

populists: those who advocate the needs of the common people

255

The consequences are affecting not only the weak states of the former Soviet empire but also the previously stable states of Western Europe. "The collapse of the Soviet Union and the secessionist movements in Yugoslavia [are] helping arouse political stirrings in the far corners of Europe," reported Britain's *Financial Times* in September 1991. "Ripples from the east are prompting leaders of [Spain's] 17 autonomous regions to hammer ever more loudly on the door of the central government in Madrid . . . in some cases calling into question the country's very unity." A Spanish parliamentary leader from Catalonia makes the point bluntly: "The August revolution [in the Soviet Union] affects everyone. We are in attendance at the burial of centralism. It is dead. . . . The issue may be philosophical at the moment but in a few years it will become practical."

Nor is the problem confined to Europe. Following **sectarian** riots in Bombay that left at least 500 dead in January 1993, Prime Minister P. V. Narasimha Rao warned that "if this country forsakes secularism it will break." Even China might not be immune. "The very future of China as a unitary state is in question as the only other great nineteenth-century empire, the Russian one, crumbles," argues W. J. F. Jenner, head of the China Center at the Australian National University.

"(A)nd Cauldron Bubble"

Those problems by themselves would be bad enough. Unfortunately, they coincide with a very dangerous period for the world economy. According to Alan Greenspan, the chairman of the Federal Reserve Board, the recession from which the United States is emerging has been unlike any in the postwar period because of the decline in asset prices. Robin Leigh-Pemberton, Greenspan's outgoing counterpart at the Bank of England, agreed, warning that "the risk of a further world downturn resulting from debt deflation is real."

The problems confronting the United States, notably the accumulation of government debt, are well known. More important in the near future, however, is the economic condition of the other industrialized democracies. In the European Community (EC), unemployment is climbing to 11 percent this year. Germany, in particular, is suffering from the costs of integrating its eastern sector with the west. "We face the total collapse of the social and economic system in eastern Germany," the former economics minister, Jürgen Mölleman has noted somberly. "It is impossible to overcome this in two or even five years. We will need a whole decade." When German chancellor Helmut Kohl came to meet President Bill Clinton recently, he carried the message that "Europe is in a dismal state economically."

The situation in Japan is also worrisome. Japan's economy is in "dire straits," [former] Prime Minister Kiichi Miyazawa admitted last October. The collapse of the "bubble economy" has led to massive asset deflation. All told, Japan has lost about one-third of its financial wealth, approximately $8 trillion, since the bubble burst in 1989. It is also apparent that Japanese employees accustomed to lifetime employment can no longer rest assured: Indeed, one financial analyst in Tokyo has estimated that Japan has at least 2 million excess workers. "Japan's problems," concludes *Business Week,* "are both cyclical and structural and may take longer to cure than Europe's."

Economic recession added to nationalism was the witches' brew of the 1930s that led to totalitarianism and war. Already there is a notable resurgence of right-wing sentiment in Europe. When asked what Hitler had provided that was good, **neo-Nazi** youth today reply in unison: work. An economic collapse combined with rising unemployment and increased refugee flows could destabilize democracy even in countries where it seems to be firmly established. "Nationalism is rising, even in the West, and could still undermine our present assumption that West European

sectarian: partisan

neo-Nazi: referring to a member of a political group that embraces the ideas of Adolf Hitler

256

wars ended in 1945," warns Sir Michael Butler, Britain's former permanent representative to the EC.

Economic weakness in Germany and Japan (as well as in the rest of Europe) places a tremendous responsibility on the United States only now emerging from its own recession. . . .

The end of the Cold War at first was seen as the beginning of a new Age of Enlightenment. Aggression and human suffering were viewed as inappropriate in such an era, and consequently the United States led international efforts to liberate Kuwait and relieve human misery in Somalia.

Regrettably, Kuwait will not be the last victim of aggression, and the crisis in Somalia will not be the last instance of misery. Conflict and hunger exist around the world. In Southeast Asia, the Khmer Rouge are engaging in their own ethnic cleansing against the Vietnamese. In South Asia, India and Pakistan, both with some nuclear capability and both confronting religious fanaticism, eye each other **warily**, having barely avoided war in 1990. In Africa, disease, famine, and violence are endangering an entire generation. "The hopes of the continent will be frustrated well into the next century," warns a report by the United Nations Children's Fund (UNICEF). "Unless urgent action is taken . . . the human foundations for Africa's progress in the twenty-first century will not exist."

The world situation that faces us is similar to the Thirty Years' War, which convulsed Europe in the early seventeenth century. An especially brutal war rooted in religious **animosity**, it endured until parties were too exhausted to continue. Unfortunately, we are still a long way from the point of exhaustion. "We will fight for eternity," proclaims a Serb soldier. "Our destiny is war." And in a heartbreaking interview, a Bosnian woman who was raped wonders if she should have told her story. "If I tell, if other women like me tell, the revenge will never stop, it will go on for generations."

The hopes generated by the success of the coalition against Saddam Hussein, it is now clear, were misplaced. Even if the United Nations is converted into an effective instrument of collective security, the conflicts now engulfing the world are so numerous that they overwhelm any capability to deal with them militarily. Put bluntly, U.N. military forces are entirely dependent on U.S. support in order to be credible and effective, and the United States cannot possibly intervene everywhere there is human suffering. Our primary obligation, in a world obsessed with national rights, is to show how a country can flourish with people of different nationalities living peacefully side by side, secure in the protection of their individual rights. Even if the United States is the only remaining superpower, Americans should not delude themselves that their power is limitless. As Thomas Jefferson wrote, "I hope our wisdom will grow with our power, and teach us, that the less we use our power, the greater it will be."

The next few years will severely test our sensibilities, as television images of unimaginable horror confront us night after night. The twentieth century has been one of breathtaking achievement, but it has also been, as Isaiah Berlin reminds us, "the worst century that Europe has ever had. . . . One can only hope that after the various peoples get exhausted from fighting, the bloody tide will subside." It is not much to hope for, admittedly, but it may have to do. "I've seen hate in my life," Elie Wiesel, a survivor of the Nazi death camps, has acknowledged, "but the hate that exists in Yugoslavia is incomparable." Incredible as it may seem, the worst part of the worst century in history might still be ahead of us.

warily: with extreme caution
animosity: hostility; mistrust

▼ Questions to Focus Reading

1. Euphoria about a "new world order" was understandable a few years ago, Kober writes. Now, however, it cannot be justified. Why was it understandable then? Why is it no longer justified, according to Kober?

2. Kober notes that George Washington's warning about the French Revolution "echoes today." How so?

3. "The anarchy in many former communist countries today recalls the anarchy that followed the French Revolution 200 years ago." In what respects?

4. The main point of contrast between the American and French Revolutions was the different value they placed on the general will. What was the difference, according to Kober? Which of these paths did Gorbachev seem to be following?

5. According to Conor Cruise O'Brien, the central contribution of the French Revolution was not the idea of democracy, but the identification of the state with the nation. What does this mean? What parallel does Kober see between the origin of nationalism in the French Revolution and its emergence today in Eastern Europe?

6. What key distinction does Kober draw between nationalism and democracy?

7. A Croatian journalist writes, "Once the concept of 'otherness' takes root, the unimaginable becomes possible." What does this mean?

8. The "rationalist delusion" is the assumption that other peoples will act in a manner consistent with American standards of rationality. Kober presents two recent examples of American leaders falling prey to this delusion. What are the examples?

9. Kober presents four explanations for the irrationality of foreign leaders. What are his explanations?

10. "Two kinds of irrational belief are now especially important as successors to the earlier totalitarianism" [of Nazi Germany and the Soviet Union] (page 255). What are the two?

11. Kober is concerned about current worldwide economic recession because recession and nationalism were "the witches' brew of the 1930s that led to totalitarianism and war." He summarizes the economic troubles of several countries. What countries does he discuss? What are their troubles?

12. "The hopes generated by the success of the coalition against Saddam Hussein, it is now clear, were misplaced." Why so, according to Kober?

13. In the present climate of rabid nationalism, what does Kober see as the "primary obligation" of the United States to the rest of the world?

▼ Questions for Reflection

1. What are the several parallels Kober is drawing between the French Revolution and recent revolutions in Eastern Europe? What does he hope to learn from these comparisons?

2. Can you cite instances of the "rationalist delusion" through American history (other than the ones Kober mentions)?

3. Reducing a group to the classification "other" becomes a justification for atrocities against them, a Croatian journalist has written. Do you think this is a good explanation of inhumanity against other human beings? Are there alternative explanations?

4. Cite instances in recent news of the dangers of religious fanaticism and national exclusivity.

5. Kober gives four reasons for the irrationality of foreign leaders. Can you think of other possible explanations?

6. What is Czech president Václav Havel's explanation for "nationalist fanaticism" that has afflicted newly liberated Eastern European countries? Is this a plausible explanation?

7. There is some evidence, Kober reports, that nationalist fanaticism is affecting not only the states of the former Soviet Union, but also the "previously stable states of Western Europe," India, and China. Research current newsmagazines to see if there is evidence for this.

8. The combination of nationalist fanaticism and economic depression has had disastrous consequences in the twentieth century, Kober tells us. Research the current economic downturn in Europe, Japan, and Russia.

9. Kober alludes to the Thirty Years' War, "which convulsed Europe" in the first part of the seventeenth century. In the library, see what you can learn about this war. In what respects is the present situation similar to that which precipitated and sustained this war? In what respects is it different?

10. Kober argues that the optimism generated by the success of the international coalition against Iraq was unfounded. Why? Do you think he is right in this assessment?

11. Are you more optimistic than Kober is about the prospects for world peace? Why do you answer as you do?

12. How has Kober used his knowledge of history to gain perspective on the present situation in Eastern Europe?

▼ Discussion

1. Read current newsmagazines for evidences of the dangers of religious fanaticism and national exclusivity in the present world, and be prepared to report what you learn to the rest of the class.

2. What in your view is the importance of a knowledge of history? Suppose no one in the society had such knowledge. What would be the possible consequences of this ignorance?

3. What role do you think the United States should take in regard to the conflicts now engulfing the world?

4. Reducing a group to the classification "other" becomes a justification for atrocities against them, a Croatian journalist has written. Do you think this is a good explanation of inhumanity against other human beings? Are there alternative explanations?

5. There is some evidence, Kober reports, that nationalist fanaticism is affecting not only the states of the former Soviet Union, but also the "previously stable states of Western Europe," India, and China. Research current newsmagazines to see if there is evidence for this.

6. Are you more optimistic than Kober is about the prospects for world peace? Why do you answer as you do?

▼ Writing Assignments

1. Research current developments in the revolutions that have swept Eastern Europe, and use the data you find to attack or defend one of Kober's key themes.

2. What case can you make for optimism about the prospects for world peace? What case can you make for pessimism?

3. Write an essay on the possible explanations of the irrationalism of foreign leaders.

4. Write an essay examining the effects of nationalist fanaticism in Eastern Europe today.

5. "The Proper Role of the United States in the Post–Cold War World"

▼ Journal Entry

1. Does the world situation affect your thinking about your own future? If so, how?

▼ Vocabulary

abominations	demagogues	megalomania	populists
animosity	depreciation	minarets	prescient
assignats	eccentric	neo-Nazi	sectarian
authoritarians	euphoria	ominous	subservient
conglomerations	fallible	paroxysm	totalitarianism
contradistinguished	foreboding	perestroika	warily
coup d'etat	Leviathan	polity	xenophobia

41

▼

Now Everybody (for R. W. Fassbinder), I

Robert Longo

American artist Robert Longo first came to public attention in the mid-1970s and has since received international recognition. The work pictured on the next two pages is typical of his art, both in its disturbing theme and in its monumental scale. The piece on this page is a further example of Longo's art.

Strong in Love, 1983
Acrylic and graphite on canvas
165 × 395 cm
Galerie Bernd Klüser, Munich, Germany

Many thanks to Francine Carraro for her valuable help with this selection—J. G.

▼ Questions for Reflection and Discussion

1. Robert Longo titled his 1982 work *Now Everybody (for R. W. Fassbinder), I.* Who was Fassinder? What do you think the title means?
2. Describe the action in the scene. How is it like a film?
3. Describe the location. Where is this place? Is the locale important?
4. Describe the figure. Why do you suppose Longo chose to combine painting and sculpture into one artwork?
5. How does the scale of the work affect its impact?
6. The four panels are painted in black and white. How does the use of black and white affect the meaning of the image?
7. Why did Longo divide the painting into four panels?

Now Everybody (for R. W. Fassbinder), I. 1982–1983
Charcoal, graphite, and ink on paper; cast bronze
Four panels, overall 243 × 487 cm
bronze 200 × 71 × 114 cm
Ludwig Museum, Budapest, Hungary

8. "My art forces interpretation," Longo has said. "It poses certain questions about living and the pressures of living today." Do you think this work poses questions about the pressures of living today? Explain.
9. Consider several of your own concerns about the world now and in the next fifty years. How might you express these concerns in an artwork so as to provoke similar feelings about them in your viewers?

▼ Writing Assignments

1. "The Meaning of *Now Everybody*"

2. Research other works of Longo's and write an essay on "Longo's Vision of the Future."

3. Choose a contemporary artist to research, and write an essay on the vision of the future portrayed in his or her work.

4. Go to an art museum. Select one or more paintings to discuss under the heading "Reflections of Our Time" or "An Artist's Concerns about the Future."

5. Make a drawing that expresses in a striking and affecting way your concerns about the future, and write an essay explaining the drawing.

6. Go to a concert of contemporary serious music, a production of a recently written play, an exhibit of recent photographic art, or a recent film, and write an essay on the relation of this work to concerns about the world's future.

42

▼

Backpack Almanac

Contemporary Life

Average number of waking hours a two-income American couple spends together each weekday: 3.2
[*American Sociological Review* (Washington, D.C.), 1987]

Average cost of successfully treating a drug addict: $3,850
[New York State Division of Substance Abuse Services (Albany), 1988]

Estimated annual expense incurred by an untreated addict, in health, welfare, and law enforcement costs: $14,000
[Ethan Nadelmann, Woodrow Wilson School of Public and International Affairs at Princeton University
(Princeton, N.J.), 1988]

Number of minutes each day that a working couple spend in "meaningful conversation" with each other: 4
[Michael Fortino, Priority Management (Pittsburgh, Pa.), 1988]

Number of seconds each day that they spend in "meaningful conversation" with their children: 30
[Hasbro (Pawtucket, R.I.)/U.S. Dept. of Defense, 1988]

Percentage of American Southerners who say they support *Roe v. Wade*: 53
[*Atlanta Journal and Atlanta Constitution* Southern Poll (Atlanta), 1989]

Chances that an American woman will have an abortion in her lifetime: 1 in 2
[Alan Guttmacher Institute (New York City), 1989]

Percentage of American fathers who say that they should share child care equally with their wives: 74
Percentage who say that they do: 13
[*Parenting* (San Francisco), 1989]

Estimated number of women worldwide who die each year as a result of illegal abortions: 200,000
[World Health Organization (Geneva), 1989]

Chances that a pregnant American woman will choose to have an abortion: 1 in 4
[Centers for Disease Control (Atlanta), 1989]

Percentage of Americans who watch television during dinner: 50
[Roper Organization (New York City), 1989]

Percentage increase, since 1986, in the number of boys under 13 arrested for rape in New York City: 333
[State Division of Criminal Justice Services (New York City), 1989]

Chances that an American woman will be the victim of a rape or an attempted rape in New York City: 1 in 12
[U.S. Dept. of Justice, 1989]

Ratio of the number of divorces filed by women to the number filed by men: 2:1
[National Center for Health Statistics
(Hyattsville, Md.), 1989]

Percentage of state and local district attorneys who say that marijuana should be decriminalized: 25
[*National Law Journal* (New York City), 1988]

Estimated chances that a couple married in 1988 will get divorced: 2 in 3
[Larry Bumpass, University of Wisconsin (Madison), 1988]

Percentage of Americans who say they approve of searching homes without a warrant in order to combat drugs: 52
[ABC News–*Washington Post* poll (New York City), 1989]

Percentage of American men who say they deal with depression by trying to figure out their problems: 23
Percentage who say they deal with depression by watching television: 35
[Roper Organization (New York City), 1989]

Chances that a first-time cigarette smoker will become addicted: 9 in 10
Chances that a first-time user of cocaine will become addicted: 1 in 6
[Jack Henningfield, National Institute on Drug Abuse (Baltimore), 1989]

Percentage of American college students who say that some races are "more evolved" than others: 45
[*Current Anthropology* (Oxbridge, England), 1989]

Percentage change, since 1979, in the number of harvest combines sold in the United States: –80
[Farm and Industrial Equipment Institute (Chicago), 1989]

Average increase, since 1980, in the amount of garbage an American discards each year, in pounds: 69
[U.S. Environmental Protection Agency, 1989]

Average increase, since 1980, in the amount of junk mail an American receives each year, in pounds: 17
[U.S. Postal Service/U.S. Census Bureau, 1989]

Chances that a black American man was in state or federal prison in 1980: 1 in 56
In 1989: 1 in 36
[U.S. Dept. of Justice, 1989]

Percentage of men living in Bangladesh who live past the age of 65: 55
Percentage of men living in Harlem who do: 40
[Harold Freeman and Colin McCord, Harlem Hospital (New York City), 1990]

Percentage of all billboards in white neighborhoods in Baltimore that advertise alcohol and tobacco: 20
Percentage of all billboards in black neighborhoods that do: 76
[Scenic America (Washington, D.C.), 1990]

Percentage of American gun owners who are white: 88
Percentage who are black: 6
[*Time*–CNN poll, Yankelovich Clancy Shulman (Westport, Conn.), 1990]

Percentage increase, since 1980, in the number of anti-Semitic incidents reported in the United States: 193
[Anti-Defamation League (New York City), 1990]

Percentage change, since 1979, in the average number of hours of television devoted to public affairs: −50
[Essential Information (Washington, D.C.), 1989]

Portion of all oil produced worldwide that is used for transportation in the United States: ⅕
[U.S. Dept. of Energy, 1989]

Portion of all illegal drugs produced worldwide that are consumed in the United States: ⅗
[Senate Foreign Relations Subcommittee on Terrorism, Narcotics, and International Operations, 1989]

Chances that a victim of a violent crime is under the age of 20: 4 in 5
[U.S. Dept. of Justice, 1989]

Chances that an illegal drug user is white: 4 in 5
[National Institute on Drug Abuse (Rockville, Md.), 1989]

Percentage of job applicants to the Houston Police Department who say they have used marijuana: 50
[Houston Police Dept., 1989]

Percentage of male college students who say that "some women look as though they're asking to be raped": 84
[Dorm Byrne, State University of New York (Albany), 1991]

Number of international terrorist organizations in 1969: 13
Number in 1990: 74
[RAND Corp. (Santa Monica, Calif.), 1990]

Chances that the death of a 10- to 14-year-old American in 1968 was a suicide: 1 in 69
Chances in 1990: 1 in 17
[American Medical Association (Chicago)/U.S. Census Bureau/National Center for Health Statistics (Hyattsville, Md.), 1990]

Estimated percentage of AIDS carriers, worldwide, who contracted the virus through heterosexual sex: 60
[World Health Organization Global Program on AIDS (Geneva), 1990]

Percentage of American women who said in 1970 that men were "basically kind, gentle, and thoughtful": 67
Percentage who said this in 1990: 51
[Virginia Slims–Roper Organization poll (New York City), 1990]

Percentage of 8- to 12-year-old boys who agree that "a cool haircut makes a kid cool": 50
[*Sports Illustrated for Kids* (New York City), 1990]

Rank of TV viewing, eating, and shopping, among activities Americans spend the most leisure time
engaged in: 1, 2, 3
[University of Maryland Survey Research Center (College Park), 1990]

Percentage of Americans who thought in 1975 that men had a better life than women: 32
Percentage who thought this in 1990: 49
[Gallup Organization (Princeton, N.J.), 1990]

Estimated portion of all pregnancies ending in abortion that are the result of contraceptive failure: ½
Average number of months an American teenage girl is sexually active before using birth control: 12
[Alan Guttmacher Institute (New York City), 1991]

Rank of white, Hispanic, and black girls, among those who lose the most self-esteem during puberty: 1, 2, 3
[Greenberg-Lake: The Analysis Group (Washington, D.C.), 1991]

Chances that an American child born in 1991 will spend at least one year on welfare before reaching adulthood: 1 in 3
[Senator Daniel Patrick Moynihan (Washington, D.C.), 1991]

Chances that a black American child will be born to a single mother: 2 in 3
[National Center for Health Statistics (Hyattsville, Md.), 1991]

Portion of the world's countries to which the United States has sold arms: ⅚
[Center for Defense Information (Washington, D.C.), 1991]

Chances that an American child is on welfare: 1 in 8
[U.S. Dept. of Health and Human Services/U.S. Census Bureau, 1992]

Percentage of all employed black American men with a college degree who earned poverty-level
wages in 1979: 9.5
Percentage in 1991: 14.8.
[Urban Institute (Washington, D.C.), 1992]

Number of the five most segregated U.S. cities that are in the South: 1
[Dan Gillmor and Stephen K. Doig, Knight-Ridder (Miami), 1992]

Chances that an unmarried American is in love: 1 in 2
[Yankelovich Clancy Shulman (Westport, Conn.), 1992]

Median age of a new mother in 1940: 23.2
Median age today (1992): 23.7
[National Center for Health Statistics (Hyattsville, Md.), 1992]

Chances that a child in New York City lives in a household headed by neither parent: 1 in 7
[New York City Dept. of City Planning, 1992]

Estimated number of bills restricting abortion that have been introduced in state legislatures since 1989: 600
[National Abortion Rights Action League (Washington, D.C.), 1992]

Percentage of Americans in their 20s who say that corruption is "an important factor in getting ahead": 37
[Roper Organization (New York City) and Shearson Lehman Brothers (New York City), 1992]

Percentage of arms-transfer agreements signed by Third World countries in 1986 that involved the United States: 8
Percentage of arms-transfer agreements signed by Third World countries in 1991 that involved the United States: 57
[U.S. Congressional Research Service, 1992]

Chances that an American under the age of 19 participated in a political demonstration in 1991: 2 in 5
Chances that an American under the age of 19 in 1968 participated in a political demonstration that year: 1 in 6
[Higher Education Research Institute, University of California (Los Angeles), 1992]

Percentage of Americans who favor prenatal genetic manipulation to improve intelligence: 42
[March of Dimes Birth Defect Foundation (White Plains, N.Y.), 1993]

Percentage change, since 1982, in the number of juveniles arrested for homicide in the United States: +93
[U.S. Federal Bureau of Investigation, 1993]

Portion of all war fatalities in the last 500 years that took place in this century: ¾
[Ruth Sivard, *World Military and Social Expenditures* (Washington, D.C.), 1993]

Chances that an American teenager believes he or she will be shot to death before reaching old age: 1 in 3
[LH Research (New York City), 1994]

43

Pretend Not to Know What You Know

Adrian Piper

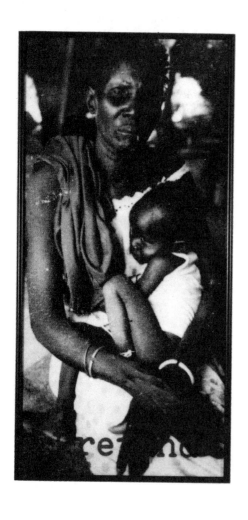

Pretend #2, 1990
3 enlarged newspaper photos, silkscreened text
43⅞" × 96"
Courtesy John Weber Gallery

▼ **Journal Entry**

   1. Describe your reaction to this artwork.

Robert Arneson, *Eye on Mrak (Fatal Laff)*, from the Egghead Series, UC Davis Campus, © UC Regents and Nelson Gallery, all rights reserved.

PART THREE

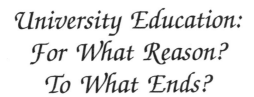

*University Education:
For What Reason?
To What Ends?*

The first several essays in this unit provide many answers to the question, What are the highest aims of a university education? Several others deal with various aspects of the present crisis in American higher education—the decline in the quality of education that U.S. colleges have been delivering, the manifestations of the crisis at some schools, and expressions of racial hostilities on American college campuses. All these essays should help you to think through you own purposes for being at a university. Perhaps one or two of these writers will clarify reasons you already had, but hadn't quite thought out. Others may give you reasons wholly new.

44

The Autobiography of an Uneducated Man

Robert Maynard Hutchins

Robert Maynard Hutchins (1899–1977), for many years the president of the University of Chicago and one of the most influential educators of our time, recounts the failures of his formal education and the circumstances under which his true education commenced. His reflections are guided by a strong sense of the necessary ingredients of a genuine education—an education for freedom.

I was born in the usual way forty-three years ago and brought up in a way that was not unusual for persons born at that time. We had morning prayers with a Bible reading every day. We went to church twice on Sunday. The result of the first is that I was amazed three weeks ago when in a class I was teaching I found a senior at the University of Chicago who had never heard of Joshua. The result of the second is that it is very hard for me to go to church now and that I find myself singing, humming, or moaning third-rate hymns like "Blest Be the Tie That Binds" while shaving, while waiting on the platform to make a speech, or in other moments of abstraction or crisis.

We had at that time many advantages that have been denied to college students in recent years, but that may be restored to their successors. We had no radios, and for all practical purposes no automobiles, no movies, and no slick-paper magazines. We had to entertain ourselves. We could not by turning a small knob or paying a small fee get somebody else to do it for us. It never occurred to us that unless we could go somewhere or do something our lives were empty. We had nowhere to go, and no way to get there. Our recreations were limited to two: reading and physical exercise. The first meant reading anything you could lay your hands on. The second meant playing tennis.

You will notice that the circumstances under which I was brought up gave me some knowledge of one great book, the Bible, and the habit of reading. The habit of physical exercise I was fortunately forced to abandon at an early date. You will notice, too, that the educational system had nothing to do with any of these accomplishments or habits. I do not remember that I ever thought about being educated at all. I thought of getting through school. This, as I recall it, was a business of passing examinations and meeting requirements, all of which were meaningless to me but presumably had some meaning to those who had me in their power. I have no doubt that the Latin and Greek I studied did me good. All I can say is that I was not aware of it at the time. Nor did I have any idea of the particular kind of good it was intended to do me. Since I had got the habit of reading at home, I was perfectly willing to read anything anybody gave me. Apart from a few plays of Shakespeare nobody gave me anything good to read until I was a sophomore in college. Then I was allowed to examine the grammar and **philology** of the *Apology* of Socrates in a Greek course. And since I had had an unusual amount of German, I was permitted to study *Faust*.

My father once happened to remark to me that he had never liked mathematics. Since I admired my father very much, it became a point of honor with me

philology: the study of the original form of a text and the determination of its meaning

not to like mathematics either. I finally squeezed through Solid Geometry. But when, at the age of sixteen, I entered Oberlin College, I found that the authorities felt that one hard course was all anybody ought to be asked to carry. You could take either mathematics or Greek. Of course if you took Greek you were allowed to drop Latin. I did not hesitate a moment. Languages were pie for me. It would have been **unfilial** to take mathematics. I took Greek, and have never seen a mathematics book since. I have been permitted to glory in the possession of an unmathematical mind.

My scientific attainments were of the same order. I had a course in physics in prep school. Every Oberlin student had to take one course in science, because every Oberlin student had to take one course in everything—in everything, that is, except Greek and mathematics. After I had blown up all the retorts in the chemistry laboratory doing the Marsh test for arsenic, the chemistry teacher was glad to give me a passing grade and let me go.

My philosophical attainments were such as may be derived from a ten weeks' course in the History of Philosophy. I do not remember anything about the course except that the book was green and that it contained pictures of Plato and Aristotle. I learned later that the pictures were wholly imaginary representations of these writers. I have some reason to believe that the contents of the book bore the same relation to their doctrines.

So I arrived at the age of eighteen and the end of my sophomore year. My formal education had given me no understanding of science, mathematics, or philosophy. It had added almost nothing to my knowledge of literature. I had some facility with languages, but today I cannot read Greek or Latin except by guess-work. What is perhaps more important, I had no idea what I was doing or why. My father was a minister and a professor. The sons of ministers and the sons of professors were supposed to go to college. College was a lot of courses. You toiled your way through those which were required and for the rest wandered around taking those that seemed most entertaining. The days of the week and the hours of the day at which courses were offered were perhaps the most important factor in determining the student's course of study.

I spent the next two years in the Army. Here I developed some knowledge of French and Italian. I learned to roll cigarettes, to blow rings, and to swear. I discovered that there was a world far from Oberlin, Ohio, devoted to wine, women, and song; but I was too well brought up even to sing.

The horrors of war are all that they are supposed to be. They are even worse; for the worst horror can never be written about or communicated. It is the frightful monotony and boredom which is the lot of the private with nothing to think about. Since my education had given me nothing to think about, I devoted myself, as the alternative to suicide, to the mastery of all the arts implied in the verb "to soldier." I learned to **protract** the performance of any task so that I would not be asked to do another. By the end of the war I could give the impression that I was busy digging a ditch without putting my pick into the ground all day. I have found this training very useful in my present capacity. But on the whole, aside from the physiological benefits conferred upon me by a regular, outdoor life, I write off my years in the Army as a complete blank. The arts of soldiering, at least at the buck-private level, are not liberal arts. The manual of arms is not a great book.

When the war was over, I went to Yale. I thought I would study history, because I could not study mathematics, science, or philosophy; and history was about all there was left. I found that the Yale history department was on **sabbatical** leave. But I found, too, that you could take your senior year in the Law School with credit for the bachelor's degree. So I decided to stay two years in Yale College doing all of my last year's work in the Law School.

Yale was dissatisfied with my year of blowing up retorts in the Oberlin chemistry laboratory. Yale said I had to take another science; any science would do.

unfilial: disloyal to one's parent

protract: prolong

sabbatical: a year's leave extended to a college professor, usually every seventh year

Discussion with my friends revealed the fact that the elementary course in biology was not considered difficult even for people like me. I took that and spent a good deal of time in the laboratory cutting up frogs. I don't know why. I can tell you nothing now about the inside of a frog. In addition to the laboratory we had lectures. All I remember about them is that the lecturer lectured with his eyes closed. He was the leading expert in the country on the **paramecium**. We all believed that he lectured with his eyes closed because he had to stay up all night watching the paramecia reproduce. Beyond this experience Yale imposed no requirements of me, and I wandered aimlessly round until senior year.

In that year I did all my work in the Law School, except that I had to obey a regulation of **obscure** origin and purpose which compelled every Yale College student working in the Law School to take one two-hour course in the College. I took a two-hour course in American Literature because it was the only two-hour course in the College which came at twelve o'clock. A special advantage of this course was that the instructor, who was much in demand as a lecturer to popular audiences, often had to leave at 12:20 to make the 12:29 for New York.

I see now that my formal education began in the Law School. My formal education began, that is, at the age of twenty-one. I do not mean to say that I knew then that I was getting an education. I am sure the professors did not know they were giving me one. They would have been shocked at such an insinuation. They thought they were teaching me law. They did not teach me any law. But they did something far more important: they introduced me to the liberal arts.

It is sad but true that the only place in an American university where the student is taught to read, write, and speak is the law school. The principal, if not the sole, merit of the case method of instruction is that the student is compelled to read accurately and carefully, to state accurately and carefully the meaning of what he has read, to criticize the reasoning of opposing cases, and to write very extended examinations in which the same standards of accuracy, care, and criticism are imposed. It is too bad that this experience is limited to very few students and that those few arrive at the stage where they may avail themselves of it only at about age twenty-two. It is unfortunate that the teachers have no training in the liberal arts as such. The whole thing is on a rough and ready basis, but it is grammar, rhetoric, and logic[1] just the same, and a good deal better than none at all.

One may regret, too, that the materials upon which these disciplines are employed are no more significant than they are. No case book is a great book. Not more than two or three judges in the history of Anglo-American law have been great writers. One who is immersed long enough in the **turgidities** of some of the masters of the split infinitive who have graced the American bench may eventually come to write like them.

One may regret as well that no serious attempt is made in the law schools to have the student learn anything about the intellectual history or the intellectual content of the law. At only one law school that I know of is it thought important to connect the law with ethics and politics. In most law schools there is a course in Jurisprudence. At Yale in my day it was an elective one-semester course in the last year, and was ordinarily taken by about ten students. Still, the Yale Law School did begin my formal education. Though it was too little and too late, it was something, and I shall always be grateful for it.

After I graduated from college and ended my first year of law I took a year and a half off and taught English and History in a preparatory school. This continued my education in the liberal arts. I did not learn any history, because the school was solely interested in getting boys through the College Board examinations. We taught from textbooks, usually the most compact we could find, for we were reasonably sure that if the boys had memorized what was in the textbook

paramecium: a fresh-water one-celled organism
obscure: uncertain
turgidities: excessive complexities

276

they could pass the examinations. We did not allow them to read anything except the textbook for fear of confusing their minds.

But in teaching, and especially in teaching English Composition, I discovered that there were rules of reading, writing, and speaking, and that it was worthwhile to learn them, and even to try to teach them. I came to suspect, for the first time, that my teachers in school had had something in mind. I began to fall into a dangerous **heresy**, the heresy that since the best way to learn something is to teach it, the only way to learn anything is to teach it. I am sure that in what is called "the curriculum" of the conventional school, college, or university, the only people who are getting an education are the teachers. They work in more or less **coherent**, if somewhat narrow, fields, and they work in more or less **intelligible** ways. The student, on the other hand, works through a **multifarious** collection of disconnected courses in such a way that the realms of knowledge are likely to become less and less intelligible as he proceeds. In such an institution the only way to learn anything is to teach it. The difficulty with this procedure is that in the teacher's early years, at least, it is likely to make the education of his students even worse than it would otherwise have been.

After continuing my educating in the liberal arts in this rather unpleasant and inefficient way, I returned to Yale at the age of twenty-three, became an officer of the University, and finished my law work out of hours. Just before I was about to graduate from the Law School at the age of twenty-six, a man who was scheduled to teach in the School that summer got appendicitis, and a substitute had to be found. Since I was on the payroll and everybody else was out of town, I became a member of the faculty of the Law School.

Here I continued my education in the liberal arts, this time unconsciously, for I was no more aware than the rest of the faculty that the liberal arts were what we were teaching. At the end of my first year of this the man who was teaching the law of Evidence resigned, and, because of my unusual qualifications, I was put in his place. My qualifications were that I had never studied the subject, in or out of law school, and that I knew nothing of the disciplines on which the law of Evidence is founded, namely psychology and logic.

The law of Evidence bothered me. I couldn't understand what made it go. There is a rule, for example, that evidence of flight from the scene of a crime is admissible as tending to show guilt. After painful research the only foundation I could find for this was the statement, emanating, I grant, from the very highest source, that the wicked flee when no man pursueth, but the righteous are as bold as a lion.

There is a rule which admits, as worthy the attention of the jury, utterances made immediately after a blow on the head, or after any sudden shock, such as having somebody say "boo" to you. As far as I could discover, this doctrine rested on the psychological principle, long held **incontrovertible**, that a blow on the head or having somebody say "boo" to him prevents even the habitual liar, momentarily but effectually, from indulging in the practice of his art. Since I was supposed to lead my students to the knowledge of what rules ought to be, and not merely of what they were, I wanted to find out whether the wicked really do flee when no man pursueth, whether the righteous really are as bold as a lion, and whether you really can startle a liar out of his disregard for the truth.

It was obviously impossible to conduct controlled experiments on these interesting questions. I could not think about them, because I had had no education. The psychologists and logicians I met could not think about them, because they had had no education either. I could think about legal problems as legal. They could think about psychological problems as psychological. I didn't know how to think about legal problems as psychological; they didn't know how to think about psychological problems as legal. Finally I heard that there was a young psychologist, logician, and philosopher at Columbia by the name of Adler who was actually

heresy: a belief at variance with religious teaching

coherent: logically connected

intelligible: capable of being understood

multifarious: numerous and varied

incontrovertible: not disputable; unquestionable

277

examining the bible of all Evidence teachers, the seven volumes of *Wigmore on Evidence.* A man who was willing to make such sacrifices deserved investigation, and I got in touch with Mr. Adler right away.

I found that Mr. Adler was just as uneducated as I was, but that he had begun to get over it, and to do so in a way that struck me as very odd. He had been teaching for several years in John Erskine's Honors Course in the Great Books at Columbia. I paid no attention and went on trying to find out how I could put a stopwatch on the return of the power to lie after a blow on the head.

I now transport you forward four years, from 1925 to 1929. I am President of the University of Chicago. Mr. Adler is a member of the faculty of the University of Chicago. We had fled from New Haven and New York, and we must have been guilty, for we had fled when I assure you no man had any idea of pursuing us. By this time Mr. Adler had had four more years with the Great Books at Columbia. He looked on me, my work, my education, and my prospects and found us not good. He had discovered that merely reading was not enough. He had found out that the usefulness of reading was some way related to the excellence of what was read and the plan for reading it. I knew that reading was a good thing, but had hitherto been under the impression that it didn't make any difference what you read or how it was related to anything else you read. I had arrived at the age of thirty, you will remember, with some knowledge of the Bible, of Shakespeare, of *Faust,* of one dialogue of Plato, and of the opinions of many semi-literate and a few literate judges, and that was about all. Mr. Adler further represented to me that the sole reading matter of university presidents was the telephone book. He **intimated** that unless I did something drastic I would close my educational career a wholly uneducated man. He broadly hinted that the president of an educational institution ought to have some education. For two years we discussed these matters, and then, at the age of thirty-two, my education began in earnest.

For eleven years we have taught the Great Books[2] in various parts of the University: in University High School, in the College, in the Humanities Division, in the Law School, in the Department of Education, in University College the extension division, four hours a week three-quarters of the year. All this and the preparation for it has had to be carried on between board meetings, faculty meetings, committee meetings, conferences, trips, speeches, money-raising efforts, and attempts to abolish football,[3] to award the B.A. at the end of the sophomore year, and otherwise to wreck the educational system. Thanks to the kind co-operation of the students, I have made some progress with my education. In my more optimistic moments I flatter myself that I have arrived at about the stage which I think the American sophomore should have reached. But this is an exaggeration. The American sophomore, to qualify for the bachelor's degree, should not be ignorant of mathematics and science.

Now what I want to know is why I should have had to wait until the age forty-three to get an education somewhat worse than that which any sophomore ought to have. The liberal arts are the arts of freedom. To be free a man must understand the tradition in which he lives. A great book is one which yields up through the liberal arts a clear and important understanding of our tradition. An education which consisted of the liberal arts as understood through great books and of great books understood through the liberal arts would be one and the only one which would enable us to comprehend the tradition in which we live. It must follow that if we want to educate our students for freedom, we must educate them in the liberal arts and in the great books. And this education we must give them, not by the age of forty-three, but by the time they are eighteen, or at the latest twenty.

We have been so preoccupied with trying to find out how to teach everybody to read anything that we have forgotten the importance of what is read. Yet it is obvious that if we succeeded in teaching everybody to read, and everybody read nothing but pulp magazines, obscene literature, and *Mein Kampf,* the last state of the nation would be worse than the first. Literacy is not enough.

The common answer is that the great books are too difficult for the modern pupil. All I can say is that it is amazing how the number of too difficult books has increased in recent years. The books that are now too difficult for candidates for the doctorate were the regular fare of grammar-school boys in the Middle Ages and the Renaissance. Most of the great books of the world were written for ordinary people, not for professors alone. Mr. Adler and I have found that the books are more rather than less effective the younger the students are. Students in University High School have never heard that these books are too hard for them. They have not had time to get as miseducated as their elders. They read the books and like them because they think they are good books about important matters. The experience at St. John's College, in the Humanities General Course at Columbia, in the General Courses of the College of the University of Chicago, and the University of Chicago College course known as Reading, Writing, and Criticism is the same.

Ask any foreign scholar you meet what he thinks about American students. He will tell you that they are eager and able to learn, that they will respond to the best that is offered them, but that they are miserably trained and dreadfully unenlightened. If you put these two statements together you can come to only one conclusion, and that is that it is not the inadequacy of the students but the inadequacy of the environment and the **irresolution** of teachers that is responsible for the shortcomings of American education.

So Quintilian said: "For there is absolutely no foundation for the complaint that but few men have the power to take in the knowledge that is imparted to them, and that the majority are so slow of understanding that education is a waste of time and labor. On the contrary you will find that most are quick to reason and ready to learn. Reasoning comes as naturally to man as flying to birds, speed to horses and ferocity to beasts of prey: our minds are endowed by nature with such activity and **sagacity** that the soul is believed to proceed from heaven. Those who are dull and unteachable are as abnormal as **prodigious** births and monstrosities, and are but few in number. A proof of what I say is to be found in the fact that boys commonly show promise of many accomplishments, and when such promise dies away as they grow up, this is plainly due not to the failure of natural gifts, but to lack of the requisite care. But, it will be urged, there are degrees of talent. Undoubtedly, I reply, and there will be a corresponding variation in actual accomplishment but that there are any who gain nothing from education, I absolutely deny."

When we remember that only a little more than 1,500 years ago the ancestors of most of us, many of them painted blue, were roaming the trackless forests of Caledonia, Britain, Germany, and trans-Alpine Gaul, despised by the civilized citizens of Rome and Antioch, interested, in the intervals of **rapine**, only in deep drinking and high gaming; savage, barbarous, cruel, and illiterate, we may reflect with awe and expectation on the potentialities of our race. When we remember, too, that it is only a little more than fifty years ago that the "average man" began to have the chance to get an education, we must recognize that it is too early to despair of him.

The President of Dalhousie has correctly said, "Over most of Europe the books and monuments have been destroyed and bombed. To destroy European civilization in America you do not need to burn its records in a single fire. Leave those records unread for a few generations and the effect will be the same."

The alternatives before us are clear. Either we must abandon the ideal of freedom or we must educate our people for freedom. If an education in the liberal arts and in the great books is the education for freedom, then we must make the attempt to give this education to all our citizens. And since it is a long job, and one upon which the fate of our country in war and peace may depend, we shall have to start now.

irresolution: indecisiveness
sagacity: wisdom
prodigious: abnormal; monstrous
rapine: the act of plunder

279

Endnotes

1. The curriculum in the medieval university was composed of the *trivium* (grammar, rhetoric, logic) and *quadrivium* (arithmetic, music, geometry, astronomy). Together they composed the "seven liberal arts."

2. Edited by Hutchins and Adler, the *Great Books* is a 53-volume set of the books, beginning with Plato and ending with Freud, which the editors considered important enough to be studied by anyone, regardless of specialization or major, as the core of an introduction to the enduring ideas and concepts of Western civilization.

3. Under Hutchins's leadership, the University of Chicago—at that time a member of the Big Eight Conference—actually did abolish its participation in intercollegiate football competition.

▼ Questions to Focus Reading

1. Notice the tone of Hutchins's first paragraph. How would you describe it? By what means does he establish this tone?

2. In his second paragraph, Hutchins refers to certain "advantages" of his youth, now denied college students. What were these advantages?

3. What is Hutchins's assessment of his college education?

4. What is Hutchins's evaluation of the learning he gained in the army?

5. Hutchins tells us that his formal education actually began in the Yale Law School, when he was twenty-one. In what sense?

6. Hutchins points out the shortcomings of his law school education. What were these?

7. Why does Hutchins believe that in the conventional school, only the teachers are getting an education?

8. What point is Hutchins trying to make in his discussion of his puzzlement over the law of Evidence (page 277)?

9. Hutchins makes a case for the study of the liberal arts and the great books as essential to freedom. What is his case?

10. How does Hutchins deal with the objection that the great books are too difficult for the modern student?

▼ Questions for Reflection

1. If he could relive his "uneducated" youth, how do you suppose Hutchins would approach his education? What, in his view, would be the ingredients of a genuine education?

2. The student, as opposed to his professor, "works through a multifarious collection of disconnected courses in such a way that the realms of knowledge are likely to become less and less intelligible as he proceeds." Does this characterize your own experience so far in college? How do you suppose Hutchins would correct this? What can you do to keep the realms of knowledge from becoming less and less intelligible as you proceed?

3. "Either we must abandon the ideal of freedom or we must educate our people for freedom." What would it be to educate our people for freedom? Is there evidence today that our people are not being educated for freedom? Explain your answer.

4. "The liberal arts are the arts of freedom. To be free a man must understand the tradition in which he lives." What case could be made for these statements? How is the content of that tradition to be determined?

▼ Discussion

1. If he could relive his "uneducated" youth, how do you suppose Hutchins would approach his education? What, in his view, would be the ingredients of a genuine education?

2. The student, as opposed to his professor, "works through a multifarious collection of disconnected courses in such a way that the realms of knowledge are likely to become less and less intelligible as he proceeds." Does this characterize your own experience so far in college? How do you suppose Hutchins would correct this? What can you do to keep the realms of knowledge from becoming less and less intelligible as you proceed?

3. "Either we must abandon the ideal of freedom or we must educate our people for freedom." What would it be to educate our people for freedom? Is there evidence today that our people are not being educated for freedom? Explain your answer.

4. "The liberal arts are the arts of freedom. To be free a man must understand the tradition in which he lives." What case could be made for these statements? How is the content of that tradition to be determined?

▼ Writing Assignments

1. Write an essay in which you address the question, What are the necessary ingredients in an education for freedom? As part of this essay, evaluate your own public school education in light of your answer to this question and specify the ways in which your college education can be geared to this end.

2. "To be free a man must understand the tradition in which he lives" Write an essay in which you defend or dispute this statement.

3. Suppose a law were passed in Congress prohibiting the teaching of reading to young Americans, so that in a few generations, there was no one left in America who could read. Write an essay in the form of an imaginary news report in which you spell out the consequences of such a law.

4. Suppose a law were passed in Congress prohibiting the teaching of any aspect of history prior to the previous twenty years. (People older than the age of twenty would be prohibited from discussing their experience prior to the past two decades.) What would be lost if we lost our collective knowledge of the past? Write an essay in the form of a news report in which you spell out the consequences of such a law.

▼ Journal Entry

1. What have been the most valuable aspects of your education so far?

▼ Vocabulary

coherent	irresolution	prodigious	turgidities
heresy	multifarious	protract	unfilial
incontrovertible	obscure	rapine	
intelligible	paramecium	sabbatical	
intimated	philology	sagacity	

45

▼

Teaching the Fish the Meaning of Water

Charles Frankel

Charles Frankel, a professor of philosophy at Swarthmore College, traces the idea of a liberal education from its beginnings in the Middle Ages to our own day. The question that concerns him is, What is the ideal purpose of a liberal education today? His answer: To intensify life.

Let me turn to the question of the future of liberal education as I see it....

... When any man discusses education, he should first confess his prejudices. To begin, with, I suspect there is less than meets the eye in much of the educational theory which, for our sins, is visited upon us week by week. I note that when my colleagues stand up at faculty meetings looking **pious** and proud and reciting their educational theories and philosophies, what they usually provide is a recital of their own educational autobiographies. Either the individual enjoyed his own education, in which case *that's* the model, or he hated it, in which case he or she opts for something 180 degrees opposed. In my own case, for example, a central experience when I was in college—one that undoubtedly still affects my outlook—was that there were no jobs. In April of the year in which I was graduating, rumor spread through my class that one man in the class had a job. It was the news of the month. I went to school at a time when one man didn't expect to get a job—not, at any rate, as a result of having gone to school. I hoped there was something available I would be able to do and not be a burden upon my parents any longer. But what I wanted—what all of us wanted—was simply a job. It wasn't self-fulfillment we were thinking of. Then the war came and settled that for us. We all got jobs.

Yet, from an educational point of view, it was a marvelous time to go to school. For in our minds it didn't make any difference what you studied, you were going to take any job that came along, and maybe you were going to be unemployed anyway; so we studied what we liked. And it turned out that the practice was a pretty good preparation for all sorts of things. To be sure, we didn't study just what we liked. At most good schools at that time, faculties tended to think they knew more than students did, and we students tended to think that faculties were right in this belief. There's nothing like self-confidence in an adult to produce proper respect in the young. We didn't think our teachers were **infallible**, by any means; in fact, we thought many of them were stuffed shirts. But the stuffing was good. At any rate, the stuffing was worth serious study to see whether it was only that and nothing more.

Thus my prejudices rest on two elementary ideas forced on me by my early experiences. First, it is good for faculties to have faith in the importance of what they are doing. Second, it is good to study without worrying about the practical payoff. I think a liberal education is an education which is designed to raise an individual to the highest level of civic responsibility and personal culture of which he or she is capable. And if you ask, "Yes, but what is a liberal education for?", *that's* what it's for—that's its end in itself.

So I would not say that liberal education is justified because it's useful, though I don't think it's useless. Nor will I say that if you receive a liberal education

pious: devout
infallible: incapable of error

282

here at Swarthmore you will be happier or more virtuous. Unfortunately, many people who have had excellent liberal educations are neither. However, if you have a liberal education you *will* live more intensely. You will be more aware of the meaning of what is happening to you, of its place in the story of your society and in the sweep of human history. You will live at more than one level. You won't simply respond passively to events, and you won't be concerned about them *only* personally. At least sometimes you will see your fate, whatever it is, as an illustration of the human condition and the destiny of man.

Now, that's not going to make you happy necessarily, but it is what used to be called, at least by the more temperate, a form of salvation. You will be, to some extent, liberated—from your own foolishness, your own narrow passions, and your own impulses. You will be less involved in self. One of the most awful of the current fallacies in the discussion of liberal education is the idea that it is for self-fulfillment. It *is,* but the worst way to achieve self-fulfillment is to seek it. The worst way to find yourself is to go around looking for yourself, as though you had rolled into a forgotten corner or slipped through a crack in the stairs.

You discover yourself by discovering *other* things—things outside you, things that formed you, things that you have obligations toward. *That* is what you can discover from a liberal education, and it offers no promise of happiness; in fact, it is probably a promise of lifelong discontent. If any of you are seeking **bovine** contentment, leave Swarthmore immediately. You will not get your money's worth. It is an exercise in consciousness and intensity of critical awareness that you are seeking, whether you know it or not, when you seek a liberal education.

But what is the content of that liberal education? What should it be? Well, let me look at this question historically for a moment. In the Middle Ages, people knew clearly what a liberal education was—it was the kind of education that members of the society received who did not have to work with their hands for a living. They were members of the privileged classes; they were liberated from the more demeaning and undignified necessities of human life.

These people received an education that was divided into two parts: the trivium and the quadrivium. The trivium—the three roads—consisted of grammar, logic, and rhetoric—the verbal skills. The quadrivium—the four roads—consisted of arithmetic, geometry, music and astronomy. What held these four together? Mathematics. Mathematics, it was believed, opened ultimate secrets of the universe. God in his purest rationality, God at his most clear-sighted, spoke in mathematical terms, sang a mathematical music. Philosophy and theology were outside the trivium and quadrivium. They were subjects you moved to in due time if you did these other subjects well.

Now, what lies behind this concept of education? It was the idea that there were certain things that human beings ought to know simply because they were human beings. Above all else, human beings should know their destiny before God, the nature of His creation. Within that creation, human beings had certain duties—to speak, to think rationally, to understand God's language. And liberal education has, of course, been in trouble ever since the Middle Ages. It has been in trouble because that unifying concept broke down. The notion emerged, indeed, that the world wasn't unified. Maybe there wasn't any great plan behind it after all. Diderot said in the eighteenth century—I offer a free paraphrase—If there is a God, he's at best an experimenter. Moreover, if you look at his experiments they are untidy, and he doesn't really seem to know exactly what he's up to. The notion arose of a **pluralistic** world, of a world that encompassed incompatible plans or designs—or none.

Secondly, the rise of science challenged received ideas about what and how free men should study. Science isn't a purely verbal performance, nor is it a purely mathematical performance. You go out of the classroom. You look at nature. You experiment. You put questions to nature. You use hands as well as brain, you

bovine: cowlike

pluralistic: referring to a condition of society in which groups subscribing to different belief systems coexist

manipulate and do not merely contemplate. This upset the traditions of liberal education as it was understood in the Middle Ages.

Thirdly, in a more democratic world, a form of education had to be developed for people who might, every once in a while, have to get their hands dirty, who might need a form of preparation for a life that could not be charted or defined in advance, and who would be citizens of commonwealths where, sometimes in theory and always in practice, they would have to make peace with the **incommensurability**, the **idiosyncrasy**, the **sanctity** of individual judgment.

Finally, the medieval world erupted into an adventuring world, an enterprising world. When I read things that are said nowadays about capitalism, I can hardly believe my eyes. Some of what is said may be true of current conditions, but it has almost no relationship to the way in which the emergence of capitalism struck most people actively involved in it. It meant the democratization of the chance for an adventure. It meant the **secularization** of the idea of the quest for Holy Grail. In the medieval world the idea of a quest had been reserved for a few privileged people—either the mystical quest or the warrior's quest. Suddenly this idea became open to everybody—in the church or in the marketplace. You could seek your encounter with God for yourself; you could pull up stakes and go to the New World; you could open a business; you could start like Julien Sorel as a peasant's son and move up to become a count or a baron; you could make your own name, literally make it up; you could make your own destiny.

Think of novels of the modern era. They have as a central theme a character who gives himself a name and then lives up to it. *Don Quixote*—a man who decided who he would be and how he would behave, and who sought to see the world in such a form that it was a fitting place for this personage he had created. Read *Tom Jones* and *The Red and the Black* and *Great Expectations* and *The Great Gatsby*—other novels of people who made their own destinies. They speak for a disordered world, an exciting and adventuring world, where knowledge isn't fixed and morality isn't fixed, and no one can be sure just who is really who or who is up or down. In such a world, the object of education can no longer be a celebration of God's unity and the transmission of settled values. This is one among many reasons why I have long thought that Mortimer Adler's and Robert Hutchins's ideas for liberal education had about as much relationship to the modern world as, say, the **stock** as an instrument of punishment.

But does this condemn the idea of liberal education? Not at all. But it is an idea that has had to be readapted. In the eighteenth and nineteenth centuries, particularly in England and America, the older idea developed into an idea of education in piety and civic virtue. It also became a belief in the intrinsic merits of educating a selected group of people in liberal learning because from that group the officers of the society—its central group of leaders—were soon to be recruited.

But what about today? Can we still give some meaning to the idea of liberal education? I think we can, and I would take my own cue from two fundamental suggestions, both present in the old trivium and quadrivium.

The first is that in liberal education you're concerned with "crossroads subjects," subjects that are of use in a wide variety of situations, in a wide variety of disciplines, in unpredictable circumstances. Somehow, in such circumstances, you suddenly recall, "This is what I learned in such-and-such course, and it's pertinent here."

Secondly, these subjects are intended to enable people to step outside whatever it is they are studying or doing and to take an external view of it. They have an intellectual quality. Albert Camus, in one of his brilliant, concise maxims, once defined an intellectual as a person who watches himself while he works. In that sense, very few of us, thank God, are intellectuals all the time. It would be utterly impossible. But four or five hours a day isn't a bad diet of intellectuality, and it has a quality that adds intensity and double and triple meanings to one's life.

incommensurability: having no common standard of comparison

idiosyncrasy: peculiarity

sanctity: sacredness

secularization: the process of removing religious orientation

stock: a framework with holes for securing an offender's ankles or wrists in order to expose him or her to public derision

284

Now, liberal education consists of those subjects which are crossroads subjects and which will give you intellectual perspective. Thus, when you are thinking of yourself as a working person, you will think of work and of the history of work and of the relation of work to play. If you are thinking of yourself as a citizen, you will think of family, the nature of solitude, man's dream of utopia, etcetera. You will have alternatives; you will make ironical comparisons; you will be able to generalize out of your experience and use generalizations to interpret your experience.

That idea of perspective, of intellectual sympathy with many points of view, of moral charity towards and clarity about a variety of human concerns, is what I think is involved in liberal education. Its purpose is large-mindedness, tolerance and the cultivation of a capacity of looking at yourself with humor and irony as others might look at you and of seeing the possibility that others might be right. All of this has the great value of piercing the veil of the commonplace, of getting out of the confines of habit and familiarity which pull us all down every day. We live by the force of gravity, and we easily sink into conventionality day by day. But if you have had a liberal education, you've received a minor kind of preventive medicine which may help you to escape the commonplace. The Germans have a saying that the fish is the last creature in the world to discover the existence of water. Of course, the fish discovers the existence of water only when it is on dry land, and I believe the function of a liberal education is to get you, at least intellectually and emotionally, out of your own element and into another so that you will discover your element and how odd it is. Once having discovered how odd it is, presumably then you may also discover that it's quite natural to be odd.

Let me now turn to the place of the humanities in all this. As I have described a liberal education, the sciences and social sciences are clearly intrinsic to a liberal education. Geology does give you some idea of how foolish and minor are the issues over which we kill one another in human life. This planet is young as solar systems go. Take its fascinating history, and then take the history of mankind and the history of the United States. If you were to put a postage stamp on top of the Empire State Building, you would not have an idea of the relationship of your life to the length of this earth's evolution. Just that thin postage stamp, in relation to the Empire State Building, would be larger in thickness. This may suggest the thought to some of you—a not entirely useless one—that there are forces in the world larger than your ego, a liberalizing if somewhat humbling idea. The social sciences, which study the unintended consequences of human actions and, at times, the woefully mischief-making consequences of good intentions, are similarly liberalizing—or can be when they are not marks for **ideological preachments**.

How about the humanities? The humanities seem to me to come out of a special inclination of human beings for reflexivity, for thinking about ourselves. As you are listening to me, you're not only listening. There's a commentator saying, "Don't get in the way; listen, listen! Don't jump to conclusions; maybe, maybe he'll say something." We are each companies of selves. When we are at our most lively, we have dialogues, trialogues with ourselves. This is a curious capacity we have, to think a second thought even while we are thinking a first one. I don't know that others of the higher animals don't have this capacity, but surely it is extremely highly developed in human beings. And a civilized society is masked by an elaborate, intricate dialogue of the society with itself—its own critical commentary on its **artifacts** and products. That commentary is the humanities and to study them is to become more aware of human consciousness and of the received human commentary on the human condition.

The humanities give us one perspective on a liberal education, and in an age when we have many different faiths and when the search for intellectual unity is probably impossible, we nevertheless can bring into a college or university, with the help of the humanities, a certain integrating focus of interest, a consistent angle

ideological preachments: obtrusive or tedious sermons from a doctrinaire point of view

artifacts: man-made objects

of vision. I don't say the only angle of vision; I think you can study most subject matters also from the point of view of the sciences or the social sciences. But what most students want, and what all of us as human beings want, in the end, is a human judgment somewhere, an answer to the question, "What does this mean to me and the choices I must make as a moral being?" That kind of question can be asked in a course in physics or in a course on Shakespeare. And if you have, throughout a college curriculum, that humanistic perspective, you are bringing back, I think, the heart of liberal education. . . .

[For what purposes do the humanities exist?] They exist as ways of amplifying man's pleasure, his excitement at the human experience, his sense of its complexity and his own sense of commitment and engagement in his society and in the intellectual life. When properly taught, the humanities give you what a liberal education should give you—a sense of the variety of human possibilities and of rational human options, a sense of the costs and difficulty of choosing among these options, and, then, finally and most important, the inescapability of choice. Good things do compete. You have to choose, and you have to pay the price of your choice. The logic, the drama, the tragedy, comedy, and **vicissitudes** of that story are the subject matter of the humanities.

vicissitudes: ups and downs

▼ Questions to Focus Reading

1. Why does Frankel say that from "an educational point of view" his was "a marvelous time to go to school" (page 282)?
2. What are Frankel's "prejudices" about education (page 282)?
3. What, in Frankel's view, is a liberal education for (page 283)?
4. Frankel says that a liberal education can't promise greater happiness or virtue (page 283). What *can* it offer, then, according to Frankel?
5. "It is an exercise in consciousness and intensity of critical awareness that you are seeking, whether you know it or not, when you seek a liberal education" (page 283). What do you think Frankel means by this?
6. What, in the author's view, is the way to discover oneself (page 283)?
7. What was the content of a liberal education in the Middle Ages (page 283)?
8. Why, according to the author, has liberal education been in trouble ever since the Middle Ages (page 283)?
9. In what way did the rise of science upset the traditional idea of liberal education (page 283)?
10. How did the advent of democracy upset the medieval conception of liberal education (page 284)?
11. How did the emergence of an "adventuring world" upset the medieval conception of liberal education (page 284)?
12. What were the chief purposes of liberal education in eighteenth- and nineteenth-century England and America (page 284)?
13. "Now, liberal education consists of those subjects which are crossroads subjects and which will give you intellectual perspective" (page 285). What does he mean by "crossroads subjects"? What does he mean by "intellectual perspective"? Try to give examples other than those Frankel provides of what he has in mind here.
14. What characteristics of personality ought a liberal education to build, according to the author (page 285)?
15. By what means does a liberal education help a person "pierce the veil of the commonplace" (page 285)?
16. How is the study of science "liberalizing," according to Frankel (page 285)?
17. From what well-developed human inclination do the humanities emerge, according to Frankel? What is the nature of the humanities as he conceives it (page 285)?

18. In what sense do the humanities give one a "consistent angle of vision" (page 285)?
19. What about human life is amplified by the study of the humanities? What aspects of human life are clarified (page 286)?

▼ Questions for Reflection

1. When Frankel went to college, almost no one was able to get a job. Why did this turn out to be an advantage in Frankel's view?
2. "I think a liberal education is an education which is designed to raise an individual to the highest level of civic responsibility and personal culture of which he or she is capable." What does this mean?
3. Frankel denies that liberal education will make you happy. But he thinks it will make you live more intensely. Why does he say this?
4. Frankel agrees that liberal education is for self-fulfillment, but argues that this cannot be sought directly. Why not? How *can* we discover ourselves, in his view? Do you think he is right about this?
5. What was the conception of liberal education in the Middle Ages? Frankel presents four reasons for the undermining of this conception in the Western world. What are these reasons?
6. Today, Frankel says, liberal education "consists of those subjects which are crossroads subjects and which will give you intellectual perspective." What does he mean? Do these descriptions apply to your courses this semester?
7. "The fish is the last creature in the world to discover the existence of water." What is the point of this saying? How does Frankel connect it to liberal education?
8. How, in Frankel's view, can the sciences contribute to the "liberalizing" of our perspective?
9. What, in Frankel's view, is the role of the humanities in a liberal education?
10. "When properly taught, the humanities give you what a liberal education should give you—a sense of the variety of human possibilities and of rational human options, a sense of the costs and difficulty of choosing among these options, and then, finally and most important, the inescapability of choice." Try to relate this statement of Frankel's to your courses this semester. Does this describe the direction of the education you are getting? Explain.

▼ Discussion

1. When Frankel went to college, almost no one was able to get a job. Why did this turn out to be an advantage in Frankel's view?
2. Frankel agrees that liberal education is for self-fulfillment, but argues that this cannot be sought directly. Why not? How *can* we discover ourselves, in his view? Do you think he is right about this?
3. What was the conception of liberal education in the Middle Ages? Frankel presents four reasons for the undermining of this conception in the Western world. What are these reasons?
4. Today, Frankel says, liberal education "consists of those subjects which are crossroads subjects and which will give you intellectual perspective." What does he mean? Do these descriptions apply to your courses this semester?
5. "The fish is the last creature in the world to discover the existence of water." What is the point of this saying? How does Frankel connect it to liberal education?

287

6. How, in Frankel's view, can the sciences contribute to the "liberalizing" of our perspective?

7. What, in Frankel's view, is the role of the humanities in a liberal education?

8. "When properly taught, the humanities give you what a liberal education should give you—a sense of the variety of human possibilities and of rational human options, a sense of the costs and difficulty of choosing among these options, and then, finally and most important, the inescapability of choice." Try to relate this statement of Frankel's to your courses this semester. Does this describe the direction of the education you are getting? Explain.

9. Reflect on all aspects of your first semester in college. Which aspects, if any, have contributed to the intensification of your life? Explain.

10. Compare and contrast Frankel's views about the purposes of liberal learning with the views of Hutchins, Peterson, and Rorty. (Note that Frankel derides Hutchins's "Great Books" approach as being out of touch with the modern world (page 282). Why does he think so?)

▼ Writing Assignments

1. "Liberal Education: What More than Job Preparation?"

2. "University Education and Self-Discovery" What relation does Frankel propose between liberal education and self-discovery? Using your experience this semester, what connections have you been finding between university education and the discovery of self?

3. "The Undermining of the Medieval Ideal of Liberal Education" Discuss the aims of liberal education in medieval Europe and the reasons those aims have changed in modern times.

4. "What is the Point of a Liberal Education?" Present Frankel's view of this, then present your own.

5. "Liberal Education and the Intensification of Life" Given your experience this semester, what light can you cast on Frankel's idea that liberal education should intensify your life?

▼ Journal Entry

1. "You discover yourself by discovering *other* things—things outside you, things that formed you, things that you have obligations towards. *That* is what you can discover from a liberal education." Is what you are learning in your classes teaching you in any way about yourself?

▼ Vocabulary

artifacts	idiosyncrasy	pious	stock
bovine	incommensur-	pluralistic	vicissitudes
ideological	ability	sanctity	
preachments	infallible	secularization	

46

▼

The Recoloring of Campus Life

Shelby Steele

A university education should foster, among other qualities, tolerance in a person, Charles Frankel asserted in the previous essay. But in recent years, the institution that had long been a haven of tolerance has itself been marred by racial hostility. The next two essays examine this new issue in campus life. Shelby Steele, a professor of English at San Jose State College, has written widely on problems related to race in America. In this excerpt from The Content of Our Character *(St. Martin's Press, 1990), he tries to uncover the sources of racial tensions on American college campuses.*

In the past few years, we have witnessed what the National Institute Against Prejudice and Violence calls a "**proliferation**" of racial incidents on college campuses around the country. Incidents of on-campus "intergroup-conflict" have occurred at more than 160 colleges in the last two years, according to the institute. The nature of these incidents has ranged from open racial violence—most notoriously, the October 1986 beating of a black student at the University of Massachusetts at Amherst after an argument about the World Series turned into a racial bashing, with a crowd of up to three thousand whites chasing twenty blacks—to the harassment of minority students and acts of racial or ethnic insensitivity, with by far the greatest number of episodes falling in the last two categories. At Yale last year, a swastika and the words "white power" were painted on the university's Afro-American cultural center. Racist jokes were aired not long ago on a campus radio station at the University of Michigan. And at the University of Wisconsin at Madison, members of the Zeta Beta Tau fraternity held a mock slave auction in which pledges painted their faces black and wore Afro wigs. Two weeks after the president of Stanford University informed the incoming freshman class last fall that "bigotry is out, and I mean it," two freshmen defaced a poster of Beethoven—gave the image thick lips—and hung it on a black student's door.

In response, black students around the country have rediscovered the militant protest strategies of the sixties. At the University of Massachusetts at Amherst, Williams College, Penn State University, University of California–Berkeley, UCLA, Stanford University, and countless other campuses, black students have sat in, marched, and rallied. But much of what they were marching and rallying about seemed less a response to specific racial incidents than a call for broader action on the part of the colleges and universities they were attending. Black students have demanded everything from more black faculty members and new courses on racism to the addition of "ethnic" foods in the cafeteria. There is the sense in these demands that racism runs deep. Is the campus becoming the battleground for a renewed war between the races? I don't think so, not really. But if it is not a war, the problem of campus racism does represent a new and surprising hardening of racial lines within the most traditionally liberal and tolerant of America's institutions—its universities.

As a black who has spent his entire adult life on predominantly white campuses, I found it hard to believe that the problem of campus racism was as dramatic as some of the incidents seemed to make it. The incidents I read or heard about

proliferation: rapid spread

289

often seemed prankish and adolescent, though not necessarily harmless. There is a meanness in them but not much menace; no one is proposing to reinstitute Jim Crow on campus. On the California campus where I now teach, there have been few signs of racial tension.

And, of course, universities are not where racial problems tend to arise. When I went to college in the mid-sixties, colleges were oases of calm and understanding in a racially tense society; campus life—with its traditions of tolerance and fairness, its very distance from the "real" world—imposed a degree of broad-mindedness on even the most **provincial** students. If I met whites who were not anxious to be friends with blacks, most were at least vaguely friendly to the cause of our freedom. In any case, there was no guerrilla activity against our presence, no "mine field of racism" (as one black student at Berkeley recently put it to me) to negotiate. I wouldn't say that the phrase "campus racism" is a contradiction in terms, but until recently it certainly seemed an **incongruence**.

But a greater incongruence is the generational timing of this new problem on the campuses. Today's undergraduates were born after the passage of the 1964 Civil Rights Act. They grew up in an age when racial equality was for the first time enforceable by law. This too was a time when blacks suddenly appeared on television, as mayors of big cities, as icons of popular culture, as teachers, and in some cases even as neighbors. Today's black and white college students, veterans of "Sesame Street" and often of integrated grammar and high schools, have had more opportunities to know each other than any previous generation in American history. Not enough opportunities, perhaps, but enough to make the notion of racial tension on campus something of a mystery, at least to me.

To look at this mystery, I left my own campus with its burden of familiarity and talked with black and white students at California schools where racial incidents had occurred: Stanford, UCLA, and Berkeley. I spoke with black and white students—not with Asians and Hispanics—because, as always, blacks and whites represent the deepest lines of division, and because I hesitate to wander onto the complex territory of other minority groups. A phrase by William H. Gass—"the hidden internality of things"— describes, with maybe a little too much grandeur, what I hoped to find. But it is what I wanted to find, for this is the kind of problem that makes a black person nervous, which is not to say that it doesn't unnerve whites as well. Once every six months or so someone yells "nigger" at me from a passing car. I don't like to think that these solo artists might soon make up a chorus, or worse, that this chorus might one day soon sing to me from the paths of my own campus.

I have long believed that the trouble between the races is seldom what it appears to be. It was not hard to see after my first talks with students that racial tension on campus is a problem that misrepresents itself. It has the same look, the **archetypal** pattern, of America's timeless racial conflict—white racism and black protest. And I think part of our concern over it comes from the fact that it has the feel of a relapse, illness gone and come again. But if we are seeing the same symptoms, I don't believe we are dealing with the same illness. For one thing, I think racial tension on campus is more the result of racial equality than inequality.

How to live with racial difference has been America's profound social problem. For the first hundred years or so following emancipation it was controlled by a legally sanctioned inequality that kept the races from each other. No longer is this the case. On campuses today, as throughout society, blacks enjoy equality under the law—a profound social advancement. No student may be kept out of a class or a dormitory or an extracurricular activity because of his or her race. But there is a **paradox** here: on a campus where members of all races are gathered, mixed together in the classroom as well as socially, differences are more exposed than ever. And this is where the trouble starts. For members of each race—young adults coming into their own, often away from home for the first time—bring to

provincial: unsophisticated

incongruence: here, a phrase consisting of incompatible parts

archetypal: pertaining to the original model or pattern; prototypical

paradox: an apparent contradiction

290

this site of freedom, exploration, and (now, today) equality, very deep fears, anxieties, **inchoate** feelings of racial shame, anger, and guilt. These feelings could lie dormant in the home, in familiar neighborhoods, in simpler days of childhood. But the college campus, with its structures of interaction and adult level competition— the big exam, the dorm, the mixer—is another matter. I think campus racism is born of the rub between racial difference and a setting, the campus itself, devoted to interaction and equality. On our campuses, such concentrated micro-societies, all that remains unresolved between blacks and whites, all the old wounds and shames that have never been addressed, present themselves for attention—and present our youth with pressures they cannot always handle.

I have mentioned one paradox: racial fears and anxieties among blacks and whites, bubbling up in an era of racial equality under the law, in settings that are among the freest and fairest in society. But there is another, related paradox, stemming from the notion of—and practice of—affirmative action. Under the provisions of the Equal Employment Opportunity Act of 1972, all state governments and institutions (including universities) were forced to initiate plans to increase the proportion of minority and women employees and, in the case of universities, of students too. Affirmative action plans that establish racial quotas were ruled unconstitutional more than ten years ago in *University of California v. Bakke,* but such plans are still thought by some to secretly exist, and lawsuits having to do with alleged quotas are still very much with us. But quotas are only the most controversial aspect of affirmative action; the principle of affirmative action is reflected in various university programs aimed at redressing and overcoming past patterns of discrimination. Of course, to be conscious of past patterns of discriminations—the fact, say, that public schools in the black inner cities are more crowded and employ fewer top-notch teachers than a white suburban public school, and that this is a factor in student performance—is only reasonable. But in doing this we also call attention quite obviously to difference: in the case of blacks and whites, racial difference. What emerged on campus in recent years—as a result of the new equality and of affirmative action and, in a sense, as a result of progress—is a *politics of difference,* a troubling, volatile politics in which each group justifies itself, its sense of worth and its pursuit of power, through difference alone.

In this context, racial, ethnic, and gender differences become forms of **sovereignty**, campuses become **balkanized**, and each group fights with whatever means are available. No doubt there are many factors that have contributed to the rise of racial tension on campus: What has been the role of fraternities, which have returned to campus with their inclusions and exclusions? What role has the heightened notion of college as some first step to personal, financial success played in increasing competition, and thus tension? But mostly, what I sense is that in interactive settings, fighting the fights of "difference," old ghosts are stirred and haunt again. Black and white Americans simply have the power to make each other feel shame and guilt. In most situations, we may be able to deny these feelings, keep them at bay. But these feelings are likely to surface on college campuses, where young people are groping for identity and power, and where difference is made to matter so greatly. In a way, racial tension on campus in the eighties might have been inevitable.

I would like, first, to discuss black students, their anxieties and vulnerabilities. The accusation black Americans have always lived with is that they are inferior— inferior simply because they are black. And this accusation has been too uniform, too ingrained in cultural imagery, too enforced by law, custom, and every form of power not to have left a mark. Black inferiority was a precept accepted by the founders of this nation; it was a principle of social organization that relegated blacks to the sidelines of American life. So when young black students find themselves on white campuses surrounded by those who have historically claimed superiority, they are also surrounded by the myth of their inferiority.

inchoate: not fully formed
sovereignty: supreme and independent power claimed by a community
balkanized: divided into small states mired in ineffectual conflict

Of course, it is true that many young people come to college with some anxiety about not being good enough. But only blacks come wearing a color that is still, in the minds of some, a sign of inferiority. Poles, Jews, Hispanics, and other groups also endure degrading stereotypes. But two things make the myth of black inferiority a far heavier burden—the broadness of its scope and its incarnation in color. There are not only more stereotypes of blacks than of other groups, but these stereotypes are also more dehumanizing, more focused on the most despised human traits: stupidity, laziness, sexual immorality, dirtiness, and so on. In America's racial and ethnic hierarchy, blacks have clearly been relegated to the lowest level—have been burdened with an ambiguous, animalistic humanity. Moreover, this is made unavoidable for blacks by sheer visibility of black skin, a skin that evokes the myth of inferiority on sight. Today this myth is sadly reinforced for many black students by affirmative action programs, under which blacks may often enter college with lower test scores and high school grade point averages than whites. "They see me as an affirmative action case," one black student told me at UCLA. This reinforces the myth of inferiority by implying that blacks are not good enough to make it into college on their own.

So when a black student enters college, the myth of inferiority compounds the normal anxiousness over whether he or she will be good enough. This anxiety is not only personal but also racial. The families of these students will have pounded into them the fact that blacks are not inferior. And probably more than anything it is this pounding that finally leaves the mark. If I am not inferior, why the need to say so?

This myth of inferiority constitutes a very sharp and ongoing anxiety for young blacks, the nature of which is very precise: it is the terror that somehow, through one's actions or by virtue of some "proof" (a poor grade, a flubbed response in class), one's fear of inferiority—inculcated in ways large and small by society—will be confirmed as real. On a university campus where intelligence itself is the ultimate measure, this anxiety is bound to be triggered.

A black student I met at UCLA was disturbed a little when I asked him if he ever felt vulnerable—anxious about "black inferiority"—as a black student. But after a long pause, he finally said, "I think I do." The example he gave was of a large lecture class he'd taken with over three hundred students. Fifty or so black students sat in the back of the lecture hall and "acted out every stereotype in the book." They were loud, ate food, came in late—and generally got lower grades than whites in the class. "I knew I would be seen like them, and I didn't like it. I never sat by them." Seen like what, I asked, though we both knew the answer. "As lazy, ignorant, and stupid," he said sadly.

Had the group at the back been white fraternity brothers, they would not have been seen as dumb whites, of course. And a frat brother who worried about his grades would not worry that he be seen "like them." The terror in this situation for the black student I spoke with was that his own deeply buried anxiety would be given credence, that the myth would be verified, and that he would feel shame and humiliation not because of who he was but simply because he was black. In this lecture hall his race, quite apart from his performance, might subject him to four unendurable feelings—diminishment, accountability to the preconceptions of whites, a powerlessness to change those preconceptions, and finally, shame. These are the feelings that make up his racial anxiety, and that of all blacks on any campus. On a white campus a black is never far from these feelings, and even his unconscious knowledge that he is subject to them can undermine his self-esteem. There are blacks on any campus who are not up to doing good college-level work. Certain black students may not be happy or motivated or in the appropriate field of study—*just like whites.* (Let us not forget that many white students get poor grades, fail, drop out.) Moreover, many more blacks than whites are not quite prepared for college, may have to catch up, owing to factors beyond their control:

poor previous schooling, for example. But the white who has to catch up will not be anxious that his being behind is a matter of his whiteness, of his being racially inferior. The black student may well have such a fear.

This, I believe, is one reason why black colleges in America turn out 37 percent of all black college graduates though they enroll only 16 percent of all black college students. Without whites around on campus, the myth of inferiority is in **abeyance** and, along with it, a great reservoir of culturally imposed self-doubt. On black campuses, feelings of inferiority are personal; on campuses with a white majority, a black's problems have a way of becoming a "black" problem.

But this feeling of vulnerability a black may feel, in itself, is not as serious a problem as what he or she does with it. To admit that one is made anxious in integrated situations about the myth of racial inferiority is difficult for young blacks. It seems like admitting that one is racially inferior. And so, most often, the student will deny harboring the feelings. This is where some of the pangs of racial tension begin, because denial always involves distortion.

In order to deny a problem we must tell ourselves that the problem is something different from what it really is. A black student at Berkeley told me that he felt defensive every time he walked into a classroom of white faces. When I asked why, he said, "Because I know they're all racists. They think blacks are stupid." Of course it may be true that some whites feel this way, but the singular focus on white racism allows this student to obscure his own underlying racial anxiety. He can now say that his problem—facing a classroom of white faces, *fearing* that they think he is dumb—is entirely the result of certifiable white racism and has nothing to do with his own anxieties, or even that this particular academic subject may not be his best. Now all the terror of his anxiety, its powerful energy, is devoted to simply *seeing* racism. Whatever evidence of racism he finds—and looking this hard, he will no doubt find some—can be brought in to buttress his distorted view of the problem while his actual deep-seated anxiety goes unseen.

Denial, and the distortion that results, places the problem *outside* the self and in the world. It is not that I have any inferiority anxiety because of my race; it is that I am going to school with people who don't like blacks. This is the shift in thinking that allows black students to reenact the protest pattern of the sixties. *Denied racial anxiety-distortion-reenactment* is the process by which feelings of inferiority are transformed into an exaggerated white menace—which is then protested against with the techniques of the past. Under the sway of this process, black students believe that history is repeating itself, that it's just like the sixties, or fifties. In fact, it is not-yet-healed wounds from the past, rather than the inequality that created the wounds, that is the real problem.

This process generates an unconscious need to exaggerate the level of racism on campus—to make it a matter of the system, not just a handful of students. Racism is the avenue away from the true inner anxiety. How many students demonstrating for black theme dorms—demonstrating in the style of the sixties, when the battle was to win for blacks a place on campus—might be better off spending their time reading and studying? Black students have the highest dropout rate and the lowest grade point average of any group in American universities. This need not be so. And it is not the result of not having black theme dorms.

It was my very good fortune to go to college in 1964, when the question of black "inferiority" was openly talked about among blacks. The summer before I left for college, I heard Martin Luther King speak in Chicago, and he laid it on the line for black students everywhere: "When you are behind in a footrace, the only way to get ahead is to run faster than the man in front of you. So when your white roommate says he's tired and goes to sleep, you stay up and burn the midnight oil." His statement that we were "behind in a footrace" acknowledged that, because of history, of few opportunities, of racism, we were, in a sense, "inferior." But this had to do with what had been done to our parents and their parents, not with

abeyance: temporary suspension

inherent inferiority. And because it was acknowledged, it was presented to us as a challenge rather than a mark of shame.

Of the eighteen black students (in a student body of one thousand) who were on campus in my freshman year, all graduated, though a number of us were not from the middle class. At the university where I currently teach, the dropout rate for black students is 72 percent, despite the presence of several academic support programs, a counseling center with black counselors, an Afro-American studies department, black faculty, administrators, and staff, a general education curriculum that emphasizes "cultural pluralism," an Educational Opportunities Program, a mentor program, a black faculty and staff association, and an administration and faculty that often announce the need to do more for black students.

It may be unfair to compare my generation with the current one. Parents do this compulsively and to little end but self-congratulation. But I don't congratulate my generation. I think we were advantaged. We came along at a time when racial integration was held in high esteem. And integration was a very challenging social concept for both blacks and whites. We were remaking ourselves—that's what one did at college—and making history. We had something to prove. This was a profound advantage; it gave us clarity and a challenge. Achievement in the American mainstream was the goal of integration, and the best thing about this challenge was its secondary message—that we *could* achieve.

There is much irony in the fact that black power would come along in the late sixties and change all this. Black power was a movement of uplift and pride, and yet it also delivered the weight of pride—a weight that would burden black students from then on. Black power "nationalized" the black identity, made blackness itself an object of celebration, an allegiance. But if it transformed a mark of shame into a mark of pride, it also, in the name of pride, required the denial of racial anxiety. Without a frank account of one's anxieties, there is no clear direction, no concrete challenge. Black students today do not get as clear a message from their racial identity as my generation got. They are not filled with the same urgency to prove themselves because black pride has said, *You're already proven, already equal, as good as anybody.*

The "black identity" shaped by black power most forcefully contributes to racial tensions on campuses by basing entitlement more on race than on constitutional rights and standards of merit. With integration, black entitlement derived from constitutional principles of fairness. Black power changed this by **skewing** the formula from rights to color—if you were black, you were entitled. Thus the United Coalition Against Racism (UCAR) at the University of Michigan could "demand" two years ago that all black professors be given immediate **tenure**, that there be a special pay incentive for black professors, and that money be provided for an all-black student union. In this formula, black becomes the very color of entitlement, an extra right in itself, and a very dangerous **grandiosity** is promoted in which blackness amounts to specialness.

Race is, by any standard, an unprincipled source of power. And on campuses the use of racial power by one group makes racial, ethnic, or gender difference a currency of power for all groups. When I make my *difference* into power, other groups must seize upon their difference to contain my power and maintain their position relative to me. Very quickly a kind of politics of difference emerges in which racial, ethnic, and gender groups are forced to assert their entitlement and vie for power based on the single quality that makes them different from one another.

On many campuses today academic departments and programs are established on the basis of difference—black studies, women's studies, Asian studies, and so on—despite the fact that there is nothing in these "difference" departments that cannot be studied within traditional academic disciplines. If their **rationale** is truly past exclusion from the mainstream curriculum, shouldn't the goal now be complete

skewing: distorting

tenure: the status of permanence in an academic position

grandiosity: the state of being marked by grandeur

rationale: fundamental justification

294

inclusion rather than separateness? I think this logic is overlooked because those groups are too interested in the power their difference can bring, and they insist on separate departments and programs as tribute to that power.

This politics of difference makes everyone on campus a member of a minority group. It also makes racial tension inevitable. To highlight one's difference as a source of advantage is also, indirectly, to inspire the enemies of that difference. When blackness (and femaleness) become power, then white maleness is also sanctioned as power. A white male student I spoke with at Stanford said, "One of my friends said the other day that we should get together and start up a white student union and come up with a list of demands."

It is certainly true that white maleness has long been an unfair source of power. But the sin of white male power is precisely its use of race and gender as a source of entitlement. When minorities and women use their race, ethnicity, and gender in the same way, they not only commit the same sin but also, indirectly, sanction the very form of power that oppressed them in the first place. The politics of difference is based on a tit-for-tat sort of logic in which every victory only calls one's enemies to arms.

This elevation of difference undermines the communal impulse by making each group foreign and inaccessible to others. When difference is celebrated rather than remarked, people must think in terms of difference, they must find meaning in difference, and this meaning comes from an endless process of contrasting one's group with other groups. Blacks use whites to define themselves as different, women use men, Hispanics use whites and blacks, and on it goes. And in the process each group mythologizes and mystifies its difference, puts it beyond the full comprehension of outsiders. Difference becomes inaccessible preciousness toward which outsiders are expected to be simply and uncomprehendingly reverential. But beware: in this world, even the insulated world of the college campus, preciousness is a balloon asking for a needle. At Smith College graffiti appears: "Niggers, spics, and chinks. Quit complaining or get out."

I think that those who run our colleges and universities are every bit as responsible for the politics of difference as are minority students. To correct the exclusions once caused by race and gender, universities—under the banner of affirmative action—have relied too heavily on race and gender as criteria. So rather than break the link between difference and power, they have reinforced it. On most campuses today, a well-to-do black student with two professional parents is qualified by his race for scholarship monies that are not available to a lower-middle-class white student. A white female with a private school education and every form of cultural advantage comes under the affirmative action umbrella. This kind of inequity is an invitation to backlash.

What universities are quite rightly trying to do is compensate people for past discrimination and the deprivations that followed from it. But race and gender alone offer only the grossest measure of this. And the failure of universities has been their backing away from the challenge of identifying principles of fairness and merit that make finer and more **equitable** distinctions. The real challenge is not simply to include a certain number of blacks, but to end discrimination against all blacks and to offer special help to those with talent who have also been economically deprived.

With regard to black students, affirmative action has led universities to correlate color with poverty and disadvantage in so absolute a way as to encourage the politics of difference. But why have they gone along with this? My belief is that it is due to the specific form of racial anxiety to which whites are most subject.

Most of the white students I talked with spoke as if from under a faint cloud of accusation. There was always a ring of defensiveness in their complaints about blacks. A white student I spoke to at UCLA told me: "Most white students on this campus think the black student leadership here is made up of oversensitive cryba-

equitable: fair and impartial

bies who spend all their time looking for things to kick up a ruckus about." A white student at Stanford said, "Blacks do nothing but complain and ask for sympathy when everyone really knows that they don't do well because they don't try. If they worked harder, they could do as well as everyone else."

That these students felt accused was most obvious in their compulsion to assure me that they were not racist. Oblique versions of some-of-my-best-friends-are stories came ritualistically before or after critiques of black students. Some said flatly, "I am not racist, but . . ." Of course, we all deny being racist, but we only do this compulsively, I think, when we are working against an accusation of bias. I think it was the color of my skin itself that accused them.

This was the **meta-message** that surrounded these conversations like an aura, and it is, I believe, the core of white American racial anxiety. My skin not only accused them; it judged them. And this judgment was a sad gift of history that brought them to account whether they deserve such accountability or not. It said that wherever and whenever blacks were concerned, they had reason to feel guilt. And whether it was earned or unearned, I think it was guilt that set off the compulsion in these students to disclaim. I believe it is true that, in America, black people make white people feel guilty.

Guilt is the essence of white anxiety just as inferiority is the essence of black anxiety. And the terror that it carries for whites is the terror of discovering that one has reason to feel guilt where blacks are concerned—not so much because of what blacks might think but because of what guilt can say about oneself. If the darkest fear of blacks is inferiority, the darkest fear of whites is that their better lot in life is at least partially the result of their capacity for evil—their capacity to dehumanize an entire people for their own benefit and then to be indifferent to the **devastation** their dehumanization has wrought on successive generations of their victims. This is the terror that whites are vulnerable to regarding blacks. And the mere fact of being white is sufficient to feel it, since even whites with hearts clean of racism benefit from being white—benefit at the expense of blacks. This is a conditional guilt having nothing to do with individual intentions or actions. And it makes for a very powerful anxiety because it threatens whites with a view of themselves as inhuman, just as inferiority threatens blacks with a similar view of themselves. At the dark core of both anxieties is a suspicion of incomplete humanity.

So, the white students I met were not just meeting me; they were also meeting the possibility of their own inhumanity. And this, I think, is what explains how some young white college students in the late eighties could so frankly take part in racially insensitive and outright racist acts. They were expected to be cleaner of racism than any previous generation—they were born in the Great Society. But this expectation overlooks the fact that, for them, color is still an accusation and judgment. In black faces there is a discomforting reflection of white collective shame. Blacks remind them that their racial innocence is questionable, that they are the beneficiaries of past and present racism, and the sins of the father may well have been visited on the children.

And yet young whites tell themselves that they had nothing to do with the oppression of black people. They have a stronger belief in their racial innocence than any previous generation of whites and a natural hostility toward anyone who would challenge that innocence. So (with a great deal of individual variation) they can end up in the paradoxical position of being hostile to blacks as a way of defending their own racial innocence.

I think this is what the young white editors of the *Dartmouth Review* were doing when they harassed black music professor William Cole. Weren't they saying, in effect, I am so free of racial guilt that I can afford to attack blacks ruthlessly and still be racially innocent? The ruthlessness of these attacks was a form of denial, a badge of innocence. The more they were charged with racism, the more

meta-message: an unspoken communication that accompanies a spoken one
devastation: utter destruction

296

ugly and confrontational their harassment became (an escalation unexplained even by the serious charges against Professor Cole). Racism became a means of rejecting racial guilt, a way of showing that they were not, ultimately, racists.

The politics of difference sets up a struggle for innocence among all groups. When difference is the currency of power, each group must fight for the innocence that entitles it to power. To gain this innocence, blacks sting whites with guilt, remind them of their racial past, accuse them of new and more subtle forms of racism. One way whites retrieve their innocence is to discredit blacks and deny their difficulties, for in this denial is the denial of their own guilt. To blacks this denial looks like racism, a racism that feeds black innocence and encourages them to throw more guilt at whites. And so the cycle continues. The politics of difference leads each group to pick at the vulnerabilities of the other.

Men and women who run universities—whites, mostly—participate in the politics of difference because they handle their guilt differently than do many of their students. They don't deny it, but still they don't want to *feel* it. And to avoid this feeling of guilt they have tended to go along with whatever blacks put on table rather than work with them to assess their real needs. University administrators have too often been afraid of guilt and have relied on negotiation and **lation** more to appease their own guilt than to help blacks and other ... Administrators would never give white students a racial theme dorm ... could be "more comfortable with people of their own kind," yet m... ...ry universities are doing this for black students, thus fostering a ki... ...ary segregation. To avoid the anxieties of integrated situations bla... ...eme dorms; to avoid guilt, white administrators give theme dorms...

When everyone is on the run from their anxieties abo... ...relations on campus can be reduced to the negotiation of avoidance... ...of demand and concession develops in which both sides use the of... ...themselves. Black studies departments, black deans of student af... ...ounseling programs, Afro houses, black theme dorms, black home... ...es and graduation ceremonies—black students and white administr... ...owly engineered a machinery of separatism that, in the name of s... ...ce, redraws the ugly lines of segregation.

Black students have not sufficiently he... ...ves, and universities, despite all their concessions, have not reall... ...n for blacks. If both faced their anxieties, I think they would see t... ...ng: Academic **parity** with all other groups should be the overriding... ...ack students, and it should also be the first goal that universities h... ...black students. Blacks can only *know* they are as good as others wh... , in fact, as good—when their grades are higher and their dropout rate... ...ning under the sun will substitute for this, and no amount of conces... ...ring it about.

Universities can never be ... guilt until they truly help black students, which means leading and challenging them rather than negotiating and capitulating. It means inspiring them to achieve academic parity, nothing less, and helping them to see their own weaknesses as their greatest challenge. It also means dismantling the machinery of separatism, breaking the link between difference and power, and skewing the formula for entitlement away from race and gender and back to constitutional rights.

As for the young white students who have rediscovered swastikas and the word "nigger," I think that they suffer from an exaggerated sense of their own innocence, as if they were incapable of evil and beyond the reach of guilt. But it is also true that the politics of difference creates an environment that threatens their innocence and makes them defensive. White students are not invited to the negotiating table from which they see blacks and others walk away with concessions. The presumption is that they do not deserve to be there because they are white. So they can only be defensive, and the less mature among them will be

capitulation: the act of yielding or surrendering

parity: equality in standing

297

aggressive. Guerrilla activity will ensue. Of course this is wrong, but it is also a reflection of an environment where difference carries power and where whites have the wrong "difference."

I think universities should emphasize commonality as a higher value than "diversity" and "pluralism"—buzzwords for the politics of difference. Difference that does not rest on a clearly **delineated** foundation of commonality is not only inaccessible to those who are not part of the ethnic or racial group, but also antagonistic to them. Difference can enrich only the common ground.

Integration has become an abstract term today, having to do with little more than numbers and racial balances. But it once stood for a high and admirable set of values. It made difference second to commonality, and it asked members of all races to face whatever fears they inspired in each other. I doubt the word will have a new vogue, but the values, under whatever name, are worth working for.

delineated: described precisely

▼ Questions to Focus Reading

1. Steele remarks on the incongruity of the "generational timing" of the problem of racism on campus. Why is this generational timing so surprising?
2. Although the problem of campus racism has the feeling of relapse, Steele says, it is not in fact the same illness. Why does he think so?
3. What does Steele mean by the phrase "politics of difference"?
4. Why does he think feelings of shame and guilt are likely to surface on a present-day college campus? What is it about a college campus that would make it rife for such an emergence?
5. What is Steele's analysis of the anxiety black students feel? What are its sources, according to Steele?
6. Why and how, according to Steele, are the anxieties of black students distorted?
7. How, according to Steele, did the black power movement of the sixties contribute to today's racial tensions on campus?
8. What does Steele have to say about the nature of white anxiety?
9. "The politics of difference sets up a struggle for innocence among all groups." What does this mean? How, in Steele's view, does the politics of difference do this?
10. How does Steele account for the racial separatism present on most campuses today?
11. What, in Steele's view, must be done to resolve the problem of racial tension on American college campuses?

▼ Questions for Reflection

1. Much of this essay is devoted to analyzing the sources of the anxieties white students and black students feel in regard to race. Leafing through the essay again, call to mind the key points of his analyses. Do you think Steele has gotten to the heart of these anxieties? What evidence are you drawing on to make your judgment?
2. Do you think Steele is right about his claim that whites feel accused by blacks, even where no actual accusation has been made? Why do you answer as you do? What evidence did he present?
3. Steele argues that administrative capitulation to black students' demands is best explained as a reaction to white guilt. Are alternative explanations possible? Which one seems to you most plausible?

4. Do you agree with Steele that blacks exaggerate the extent and intensity of white racism on your campus? Why do you answer as you do? Steele thinks black students focus on racism to avoid their anxieties. What are some possible alternative explanations for this focus? Which one seems to you the most plausible?

5. Is Steele right in thinking that an exaggerated sense of their own innocence enables many whites to adopt racist views?

6. Is the social (and to some extent, academic) separation of the races a fact of life on your campus? If so, how do you feel about it? Do you think Steele has correctly explained why it happens on most American campuses today?

7. What in your opinion should be the goal of a university in regard to race relations on campus?

8. If you were a university administrator, how would you handle a public incidence of racial hostility—the posting of racial slurs on a student's dorm room, for example, or hazing by a group against an individual?

▼ Discussion

1. Are there racial tensions on your campus? If so, what are the evidences of it? What do you think is the best explanation for it? Does Steele's account shed light on its sources?

2. Is the social (and to some extent, academic) separation of the races a fact of life on your campus? If so, how do you feel about it? Do you think Steele has correctly explained why it happens on most American campuses today?

3. What in your opinion should be the goal of a university in regard to race relations on campus?

4. If you were a university administrator, how would you handle a public incidence of racial hostility—the posting of racial slurs on a student's dorm room, for example, or hazing by a group against an individual?

▼ Writing Assignments

1. If there are problems related to race on your campus, describe them. Why in your view do they exist?

2. Has Steele gotten to the heart of the problem of racial tensions on campus? If so, what evidences are to be found for his view on your campus? If not, where does he go wrong? What would be a better explanation than his?

3. Draw on the news, Steele's opening paragraphs, an occurrence on your campus, or your imagination for an example of a racial incident on campus. If you were a university administrator, how would you deal with the incident? Why would you take this approach? Would you endorse a university code for speech and conduct pertaining to racism? Why or why not?

▼ Journal Entries

1. What are your feelings about the presence of races other than your own on your campus? What in your experience and thinking has led you to have these feelings?
2. How do you feel about the social separation of the races on campus? Is this a problem from your point of view? Why do you answer as you do? If as you see it, it is a problem, what if anything should be done about it?

▼ Vocabulary

abeyance	devastation	meta-message	rationale
archetypal	equitable	paradox	skewing
balkanized	grandiosity	parity	sovereignty
capitulation	inchoate	proliferation	tenure
delineated	incongruence	provincial	

47

▼

Loving Blackness as Political Resistance

bell hooks

bell hooks, black studies professor and feminist cultural critic, argues in this excerpt from Black Looks *(South End Press, 1992) that Shelby Steele's goal of integration is wholly misguided in present-day America. Black people, she insists, should be focusing on "decolonizing" their minds by loving their blackness.*

> *We have to change our own mind. . . . We've got to change our own minds about each other. We have to see each other with new eyes. We have to come together with warmth.*
>
> —Malcolm X

The course I teach on black women writers is a consistent favorite among students. The last semester that I taught this course we had the usual passionate discussion of Nella Larsen's novel *Passing*. When I suggested to the class (which had been more eager to discuss the desire of black folks to be white) that Clare, the black woman who has passed for white all her adult life and married a wealthy white businessman with whom she has a child, is the only character in the novel who truly desires "blackness" and that it is this desire that leads to her murder, no one responded. Clare boldly declares that she would rather live for the rest of her life as a poor black woman in Harlem than as a rich white matron downtown. I asked the class to consider the possibility that to love blackness is dangerous in a white supremacist culture—so threatening, so serious a breach in the fabric of social order, that death is the punishment. It became painfully obvious by the lack of response that this group of diverse students (many of them black people) were more interested in discussing the desire of black folks to be white, indeed were fixated on this issue. So much so, that they could not even take seriously a critical discussion about "loving blackness."

They wanted to talk about black self-hatred, to hear one another confess (especially students of color) in eloquent narratives about the **myriad** ways they had tried to attain whiteness, if only symbolically. They gave graphic details about the ways they attempted to appear "white" by talking a certain way, wearing certain clothing, and even choosing specific groups of white friends. Blonde white students seized the opportunity to testify that they had never realized racism had this impact upon the psyches of people of color until they started hanging out with black friends, taking courses in Black Studies, or reading Toni Morrison's *The Bluest Eye*. And better yet, they never realized there was such a thing as "white privilege" until they developed nonwhite connections.

I left this class of more than forty students, most of whom see themselves as radical and progressive, feeling as though I had witnessed a ritualistic demonstration of the impact white supremacy has on our collective psyches, shaping the nature of everyday life, how we talk, walk, eat, dream, and look at one another. The most frightening aspect of this ritual was the extent to which their fascination with the topic of black self-hatred was so intense that it silenced any constructive discussion about loving blackness. Most folks in this society do not want to openly admit that "blackness" as sign primarily evokes in the public imagination of whites

myriad: innumerable

301

(and all the other groups who learn that one of the quickest ways to demonstrate one's kinship within a white supremacist order is by sharing racist assumptions) hatred and fear. In a white supremacist context "loving blackness" is rarely a political stance that is reflected in everyday life. When present it is deemed suspect, dangerous, and threatening.

The oppositional black culture that emerged in the context of **apartheid** and segregation has been one of the few locations that has provided a space for the kind of **decolonization** that makes loving blackness possible. Racial integration in a social context where white supremacist systems are intact undermines marginal spaces of resistance by promoting the assumption that social equality can be attained without changes in the culture's attitudes about blackness and black people. . . .

A vision of cultural **homogeneity** that seeks to deflect attention away from or even excuse the oppressive, dehumanizing impact of white supremacy on the lives of black people by suggesting black people are racist too indicates that the culture remains ignorant of what racism really is and how it works. It shows that people are in denial. Why is it so difficult for many white folks to understand that racism is oppressive not because white folks have prejudicial feelings about blacks (they could have such feelings and leave us alone) but because it is a system that promotes domination and subjugation? The prejudicial feelings some blacks may express about whites are in no way linked to a system of domination that affords us any power to coercively control the lives and well-being of white folks. That needs to be understood.

Concurrently, all social manifestations of black separatism are often seen by whites as a sign of antiwhite racism, when they usually represent an attempt by black people to construct places of political sanctuary where we can escape, if only for a time, white domination. The ideas of conservative black thinkers who buy into the notion that blacks are racist are often evoked by whites who see them as native informants confirming this fact. Shelby Steele is a fine example of this tendency. I believe that his essays were the most xeroxed pieces of writing by white folks in the academy who wanted to share with black colleagues that they have been right all along when they suggested that black folks were racist. Steele suggests that any time black people choose to congregate solely with one another we are either supporting racial separatism because of deeply ingrained feelings of inferiority or a refusal to see racial differences as unimportant (that is, to accept the notion that we are all the same). Commenting on the issue of self-segregation in *The Content of Our Character,* he declares: "There is a **geopolitics** involved in this activity, where race is tied to territory in a way that mimics the whites only/colored only designations of the past." At no point in his analysis does Steele suggest that blacks might want to be away from whites to have a space where we will not be the object of racist assaults.

Every aware black person who has been the "only" in an all white setting knows that in such a position we are often called upon to lend an ear to racist narratives, to laugh at corny jokes, to undergo various forms of racist harassment. And that self-segregation seems to be particularly intense among those black college students who were often raised in material privilege in predominately white settings where they were socialized to believe racism did not exist, that we are all "just human beings," and then suddenly leave home and enter institutions and experience racist attacks. To a great extent they are unprepared to confront and challenge white racism, and often seek the comfort of just being with other blacks.

Steele's refusal to acknowledge this pain—this way that white supremacy manifests itself in daily social interaction—makes it appear that black individuals simply do not like socializing with whites. The reality is that many black people fear they will be hurt if they let down their guard, that they will be the targets of racist assault since most white people have not unlearned racism. In classroom

apartheid: in South Africa, a policy of rigid segregation that was practiced until 1994 against nonwhites

decolonization: release from the status of a colony

homogeneity: sameness, uniformity

geopolitics: combination of geographic and political factors influencing a region or country

settings, I hear so many narratives of black students who accepted the notion that racism did not exist, who felt there was nothing wrong with being with white friends and sharing similar interests, only to find themselves in circumstances where they had to confront the racism of these people. The last story I heard was from a young black woman talking about always being with white buddies in high school. One day they were all joy-riding in someone's car, and they came across a group of young black males crossing the street. Someone in the car suggests they should "just run those niggers down." She talked about her disbelief that this comment had been made, her hurt. She said nothing, but she felt that it was the beginning of an estrangement from white peers that has persisted. Steele's writing assumes that white people who desire to socialize with black people are not actively racist, are coming from a position of goodwill. He does not consider the reality that goodwill can coexist with racist thinking and white supremacist attitudes.

Throughout my tenure as a Yale professor, I was often confronted with white students who would raise the issue of why it is black students sit together in the cafeteria, usually at one table. They saw this as some expression of racial separatism, exclusion, et cetera. When I asked them why did they never raise the issue of why the majority of tables are white students self-segregating, they invariably said things like, "We sit together with folks with whom we share common interests and concerns." They were rarely at the point where they could interrogate whether or not shared "whiteness" allowed them to bond with one another with ease.

While it has become "cool" for white folks to hang out with black people and express pleasure in black culture, most white people do not feel that this pleasure should be linked to unlearning racism. Indeed there is often the desire to enhance one's status in the context of "whiteness" even as one appropriates black culture. In his essay "A Place Called Home: Identity and Cultural Politics of Difference," Jonathan Rutherford comments:

> Paradoxically, capital has fallen in love with difference: advertising thrives on selling us things that will enhance our uniqueness and individuality. It's no longer about keeping up with the Joneses, it's about being different from them. From World Music to exotic holidays in Third World locations, ethnicity dinners to Peruvian hats, cultural difference *sells*.

It makes perfect sense that black people/people of color often self-segregate to protect themselves from this kind of objectifying interaction.

Steele never sees the desire to create a context where one can "love blackness" as a worthy standpoint for bonding, even if such bonding must take the form of self-segregation. Luckily, there are individual nonblack people who have **divested** of their racism in ways that enable them to establish bonds of intimacy based on their ability to love blackness without assuming the role of cultural tourists. We have yet to have a significant body of writing from these individuals that gives expression to how they have shifted attitudes and daily vigilantly resist becoming reinvested in white supremacy. Concurrently, black folks who "love blackness," that is, who have decolonized our minds and broken with the kind of white supremacist thinking that suggests we are inferior, inadequate, marked by victimization, etcetera, often find that we are punished by society for daring to break with the *status quo*. On our jobs, when we express ourselves from a decolonized standpoint, we risk being seen as unfriendly or dangerous.

Those black folks who are more willing to pretend that "difference" does not exist even as they self-consciously labor to be as much like their white peers as possible, will receive greater material rewards in white supremacist society. White supremacist logic is thus advanced. Rather than using coercive tactics of domination to colonize, it seduces black folks with the promise of mainstream

divested: ridded oneself of

success if only we are willing to negate the value of blackness. Contrary to James Cone's hope that whites divest of racism and be born again in the spirit of empathy and unity with black folks, we are collectively asked to show our solidarity with white supremacist *status quo* by overvaluing whiteness, by seeing blackness solely as a marker of powerlessness and victimization. To the degree that black folks embody by our actions and behavior familiar racist stereotypes, we will find greater support and/or affirmation in our culture. A prime example of this is white consumer support of **misogynist** rap which reproduces the idea that black males are violent beasts and brutes.

In Nella Larsen's *Passing,* Clare chooses to assume a white identity because she only sees blackness as a sign of victimization and powerlessness. As long as she thinks this, she has a sustained bond with the black bourgeoisie who often self-segregate even as they maintain contempt for blackness, especially for the black underclass. Clare's bond with Irene, her black bourgeois friend, is broken when she seeks to define blackness positively. In *Passing* it is this bourgeois class and the world of whiteness Clare's husband embodies that turns against her when she attempts to reclaim the black identity she has previously denied. When the novel ends we do not know who has murdered her, the black bourgeois friend or the white husband. She represents a "threat" to the conservative hierarchical social order based on race, class, and gender that they both seek to maintain.

Despite civil rights struggle, the 1960s black power movement, and the power of slogans like "black is beautiful," masses of black people continue to be socialized *via* mass media and nonprogressive educational systems to **internalize** white supremacist thoughts and values. Without ongoing resistance struggle and progressive black liberation movements for self-determination, masses of black people (and everyone else) have no alternative worldview that affirms and celebrates blackness. Rituals of affirmation (celebrating black history, holidays, etcetera) do not intervene on white supremacist socialization if they exist apart from active antiracist struggle that seeks to transform society.

Since so many black folks have succumbed to the post-1960s notion that material success is more important than personal integrity, struggles for black self-determination that emphasize decolonization, loving blackness, have had little impact. As long as black folks are taught that the only way we can gain any degree of economic self-sufficiency or be materially privileged is by first rejecting blackness, our history and culture, then there will always be a crisis in black identity. Internalized racism will continue to erode collective struggle for self-determination. Masses of black children will continue to suffer from low self-esteem. And even though they may be motivated to strive harder to achieve success because they want to overcome feelings of inadequacy and lack, those successes will be undermined by the persistence of low self-esteem.

One of the tragic ironies of contemporary black life is that individuals succeed in acquiring material privilege often by sacrificing their positive connection to black culture and black experience. Paule Marshall's novel *Praisesong for the Widow* is a fictional portrayal of such tragedy. A young black couple, Avey and Jay, start their family life together empowered by their celebration and affirmation of black culture, but this connection is eroded as Jay strives for material success. Along the way, he adopts many mainstream white supremacist ways of thinking about black folks, expressing **disdain** for the very culture that had been a source of joy and spiritual fulfillment. Widowed, her children grown, Avey begins a process of critical remembering where she interrogates their past, asking herself:

misogynist: a person who hates women

internalize: to make a part of one's beliefs or attitudes

disdain: scorn

> Would it have been possible to have done both? That is, to have wrested, as they had done over all those years, the means needed to rescue them from Halsey Street and to see the children through, while preserving, safeguarding, treasuring those things that had come down

304

to them over generations, which had defined them in a particular way? The most vivid, the most valuable part of themselves!

To recover herself and reclaim the love of blackness, Avey must be born again. In that state of rebirth and reawakening, she is able to understand what they could have done, what it would have called for: "Awareness. It would have called for an awareness of the worth of what they possessed. Vigilance. The vigilance needed to safeguard it. To hold it like a jewel high out of the envious reach of those who would either destroy it or claim it as their own." To recover herself, Avey has to relearn the past, understand her culture and history, affirm her ancestors, and assume responsibility for helping other black folks to decolonize their minds.

▼ Questions to Focus Reading

1. What conclusion does hooks draw from the fact that the students in her course on black women writers refused to engage the issue of loving blackness?
2. In response to the charge of racism against blacks, some whites reply, "We are all racist. Blacks are just as racist against whites." But hooks thinks the situations are far from symmetrical, arguing that such a reply demonstrates "denial." What does she think is being denied?
3. hooks insists that black separatism need not be a sign of antiwhite racism. Nor need it be a response to deeply ingrained feelings of inferiority, the view Shelby Steele puts forward in the previous essay. If it is not to be explained in these ways, what is the correct explanation of black self-segregation, as hooks sees it?
4. hooks reports a recent trend among some whites to associate with blacks as a way of being "cool." She rejects this as "objectifying interaction" and finds in it another justification of black self-segregation. What does she mean by "objectifying interaction"?
5. By what means, in hooks's view, does white supremacist culture co-opt blacks?
6. If the rejection of blackness continues to be the price of socioeconomic success for a black person in America, hooks argues, then there will remain a crisis in black identity. What is the alternative she is proposing? How is this alternative exemplified in the novel she cites, *Praisesong for the Widow?*

▼ Questions for Reflection

1. hooks and Shelby Steele have very different views of racial integration as a goal in present-day America. Contrast their views on this subject. Who do you think is right? Why do you think so?
2. Contrast hooks's and Steele's analyses of the sources of black self-segregation on campus. Do you think either has seen to the heart of it? Can they both be right on this score? Explain.
3. hooks thinks that the single black in an all-white milieu is subject to various forms of subtle harassment. Does this square with your experience?
4. hooks charges that Steele "does not consider the reality that goodwill can coexist with racist thinking and white supremacist attitudes." What do you think she has in mind by such coexistence? Do you think this is indeed possible?

5. hooks remarks that it is rarely noted that white students, too, self-segregate. She suggests that it may well be their shared whiteness that leads them to do so. Is this the correct explanation of this phenomenon, as you see it?

6. Blacks are required to show their "solidarity with the status quo by overvaluing whiteness, by seeing blackness solely as a marker of powerlessness and victimization." What evidence does she present for this? Is she right? Is the internalization of white supremacist values a prerequisite for success for a black person in America?

7. As you understand her, just what would it mean for a black person to "love blackness"? What actions would he or she take? What would he or she *not* do?

▼ Discussion

1. hooks and Steele disagree radically on the value of the goal of integration in present-day America. What are their views on this? Is the integration of the races a worthy goal in your opinion? Explain.

2. What as you see it is the explanation for racial self-segregation on campus? Have hooks and/or Steele cast light on this phenomenon for you?

3. Should the university try to do anything about the self-segregation of the races? Why or why not?

4. In response to the charge of racism against blacks, some whites reply, "We are all racist. Blacks are just as racist against whites." But hooks thinks the situations are far from symmetrical, arguing that such a reply demonstrates "denial." What does she think is being denied?

5. hooks charges that Steele "does not consider the reality that goodwill can coexist with racist thinking and white supremacist attitudes." What do you think she has in mind by such coexistence? Do you think this is indeed possible?

6. hooks remarks that it is rarely noted that white students, too, self-segregate. She suggests that it may well be their shared whiteness that leads them to do so. Is this the correct explanation of this phenomenon, as you see it?

7. Blacks are required to show their "solidarity with the status quo by overvaluing whiteness, by seeing blackness solely as a marker of powerlessness and victimization." What evidence does she present for this? Is she right? Is the internalization of white supremacist values a prerequisite for success for a black person in America?

▼ Writing Assignment

1. What do you think of the self-segregation of black and white students? Why do you feel this way about it? Whose account of this—hooks's or Steele's—are you more inclined to accept? Or do you think there is a better explanation than either has offered? If so, what is it?

▼ Journal Entry

1. What do you make of the concept of "loving blackness"? What does it mean to you?

▼ Vocabulary

apartheid	divested	internalize
decolonization	geopolitics	misogynist
disdain	homogeneity	myriad

48

▼

An Apprenticeship in Good and Evil

Wendell Berry

Wendell Berry, novelist, poet, essayist, and English professor at the University of Kentucky, argues here that a university education must provide a broad, basic foundation for learning and for the living of one's life. "The thing being made at a university," he has written, "is humanity." He argues strenuously against the much more narrow focus on career preparation.

Beside every effort of making, which is necessarily narrow, there must be an effort of judgment, of criticism, which must be as broad as possible. That is, every made thing must be submitted to these questions: What is the quality of this thing as a human **artifact**, as an addition to the world of made and of created things? How suitable is it to the needs of human and natural neighborhoods?

It must, of course, sooner or later be submitted as well to the special question: How good is this poem or this farm or this hospital as such? For it to have a human value, it obviously must be well made; it must meet the specialized, technical criteria; it must be *good* as such. But the question of its quality as such is not interesting—in the long run it is probably not even askable—unless we ask it under the rule of the more general questions. If we are disposed to judge apart from the larger questions, if we judge, as well as make, as specialists, then a good forger has as valid a claim to our respect as a good artist.

These two problems, how to make and how to judge, are the business of education. But education has tended increasingly to ignore the doubleness of its obligation. It has concerned itself more and more exclusively with the problem of how to make, narrowing the issue of judgment virtually to the terms of the made thing itself. But the thing made by education now is not a fully developed human being; it is a specialist, a careerist, a graduate. In industrial education, the thing *finally* made is of no concern to the makers.

In some instances, this is because the specialized "fields" have grown so complicated within themselves that the curriculum leaves no time for the broad and basic studies that would inform judgment. In other instances, one feels that there is a potentially embarrassing conflict between judgment broadly informed and the specialized career for which the student is being prepared; teachers of advertising techniques, for example, could ill afford for their students to realize that they are learning the arts of lying and seduction. In all instances, this narrowing is justified by the improbable assumption that young students, before they know anything else, know what they need to learn.

If the disintegration of the university begins in its specialist **ideology**, it is enforced by a commercial compulsion to satisfy the customer. Since the student is now so much a free agent in determining his or her education, the department administrators and the faculty members must necessarily be preoccupied with the problem of how to keep enrollments up. Something obviously must be done to keep the classes filled; otherwise, the students will wander off to more attractive courses or to courses more directly useful to their proposed careers. Under such circumstances it is inevitable that requirements will be lightened, standards lowered,

artifact: a product of human craft

ideology: a set of beliefs that comprises a system

308

grades inflated, and instruction narrowed to the supposed requirements of some supposed career opportunity.

Dr. Johnson told Mrs. Thrale that his cousin, Cornelius Ford, "advised him to study the Principles of every thing, that a general Acquaintance with Life might be the Consequence of his Enquiries—Learn said he the leading **Precognita** of all things . . . grasp the Trunk hard only, and you will shake all the Branches."[1] The soundness of this advice seems indisputable, and the **metaphor** entirely apt. From the trunk it is possible to "branch out." One can begin with a trunk and develop a single branch or any number of branches; although it may be possible to begin with a branch and develop a trunk, that is neither so probable nor so promising. The modern university, at any rate, more and more resembles a loose collection of lopped branches waving about randomly in the air. "Modern knowledge is departmentalized," H. J. Massingham wrote in 1943, "while the essence of culture is initiation into wholeness, so that all the divisions of knowledge are considered as the branches of one tree, the Tree of Life whose roots went deep into earth and whose top was in heaven."[2]

This Tree, for many hundreds of years, seems to have come almost naturally to mind when we have sought to describe the form of knowledge. In Western tradition, it is at least as old as Genesis, and the form it gives us for all that we know is organic, unified, comprehensive, connective—and moral. The tree, at the beginning, was two trees: the tree of life and the tree of the knowledge of good and evil. Later, in our understanding of them, the two trees seem to have become one, or each seems to stand for the other—for in the world after the Fall, how can the two be separated? To know life is to know good and evil; to prepare young people for life is to prepare them to know the difference between good and evil. If we represent knowledge as a tree, we know that things that are divided are yet connected. We know that to observe the divisions and ignore the connections is to destroy the tree. The history of modern education may be the history of the loss of this image, and of its replacement by the pattern of the industrial machine, which subsists upon division—and by industrial economics ("publish or perish"), which is meaningless apart from division.

The need for broadly informed human judgment nevertheless remains, and this need requires inescapably an education that is broad and basic. In the face of this need, which is *both* private and public, "career preparation" is an improper use of public money, since "career preparation" serves merely private ends; it is also a waste of the student's time, since "career preparation" is best and most properly acquired in **apprenticeships** under the supervision of employers. The proper subject for a school, for example, is how to speak and write well, not how to be a "public speaker" or a "broadcaster" or a "creative writer" or a "technical writer" or a journalist or a practitioner of "business English." If one can speak and write well, then, given the need, one can make a speech or write an article or a story or a business letter. If one cannot speak or write well, then the tricks of a trade will be no help.

The work that should, and that can, unify a university is that of deciding what a student should be required to learn—what studies, that is, constitute the trunk of the tree of a person's education. "Career preparation," which has given so much practical support to academic specialization (and so many rewards to academic specialists) seems to have destroyed interest in this question. But the question exists and the failure to answer it (or even to ask it) imposes severe penalties on teachers, students, and the public alike. The penalties imposed on students and graduates by their failure to get a broad, basic education are, I think, obvious enough. The public penalties are also obvious if we consider, for instance, the number of certified expert speakers and writers who do not speak or write well, who do not know that they speak or write poorly, and who apparently do not care whether or not they speak or write honestly. . . .

precognita: the knowledge that composes the base of a discipline; the fundamental facts

metaphor: figure of speech in which a word or phrase designating one thing is applied to something else in an implicit comparison

apprenticeships: positions of apprentices, that is, persons who work for another in order to learn a trade

Teachers, moreover, are not providing "career preparation" so much as they are "preparing young people for life." This statement is not the result of educational doctrine; it is simply the fact of the matter. To prepare young people for life, teachers must dispense knowledge and enlighten ignorance, just as supposed. But ignorance is not only the **affliction** that teaching seeks to cure; it is also the condition, the predicament, in which teaching is done, for teachers do not know the life or the lives for which their students are being prepared.

This condition gives the lie to the claims for "career preparation," since students may not *have* the careers for which they have been prepared: The "job market" may be overfilled; the requirements for this or that career may change; the student may change, or the world may. The teacher, preparing the student for a life necessarily unknown to them both, has no excusable choice but to help the student to "grasp the Trunk. . . ."

This question of what all young people should be expected to learn is now little discussed. The reason, apparently, is the **tacit** belief that now, with the demands of specialization so numerous and varied, such a question would be extremely hard, if not impossible, to answer. And yet this question appears to be as much within the reach of reason and common sense as any other. It cannot be denied, to begin with, that all the disciplines rest upon the knowledge of letters and the knowledge of numbers. Some rest more on letters than numbers, some more on numbers than letters, but it is surely true to say that people without knowledge of both letters and numbers are not prepared to learn much else. From there, one can proceed confidently to say that history, literature, philosophy, and foreign languages rest principally on the knowledge of letters and carry it forward, and that biology, chemistry, and physics rest on the knowledge of numbers and carry it forward. This provides us with a description of a probably adequate "core curriculum"—one that would prepare a student well both to choose a direction of further study and to go in that direction. An equally obvious need, then, is to eliminate from the curriculum all courses without content—that is, all courses in methodologies and technologies that could, and should, be learned in apprenticeships.

Besides the innate human imperfections already mentioned, other painful problems are involved in expecting and requiring students to choose the course of their own education. These problems have to do mainly with the diversity of gifts and abilities: that is, some people are not talented in some kinds of work or study; some, moreover, who are poor in one discipline may be excellent in another. Why should such people be forced into situations in which they must see themselves as poor workers or as failures?

The question is not a comfortable one, and I do not believe that it can or should be comfortably answered. There is pain in the requirement to risk failure and pain in the failure that may result from that requirement. But failure is a possibility; in varying degrees for all of us, it is inescapable. The argument for removing the possibility of failure from schoolwork is therefore necessarily **specious**. The wrong is not in subjecting students to the possibility of failure or in calling their failures failures; the wrong is in the teacher's inability to see that failure in school is not necessarily synonymous with and does not necessarily lead to failure in the world. The wrong is in the failure to see or respect the boundaries between the school and the world. When those are not understood and respected, then the school, the school career, the diploma are all surrounded by such a **spurious** and **modish** dignity that failure in school *is* failure in the world. It is for this reason that it is so easy to give education a money value and to sell it to consumers in job lots.

It is a fact that some people with able minds do not fit well into schools and are not properly valued by schoolish standards and tests. If such people fail in a school, their failure should be so called; a school's worth and integrity depend

affliction: condition of suffering or distress

tacit: unspoken

specious: apparently true or plausible but actually fallacious

spurious: not genuine

modish: stylish

upon its willingness to call things by their right names. But, by the same token, a failure in school is no more than that; it does not necessarily imply or cause failure in the world, any more than it implies or causes stupidity. It is not rare for the judgment of the world to overturn the judgment of schools. There are other tests for human abilities than those given in schools, and there are some that cannot be given in schools. My own life has happened to acquaint me with several people who did not attend high school but who have been more knowledgeable in their "field" and who have had better things to say about matters of general importance than most of the doctors of philosophy I have known. This is not an "anti-intellectual" statement; it is a statement of what I take to be fact, and it means only that the uses of schools are limited—another fact, which schools prepare us to learn by surprise.

Another necessary consideration is that low expectations and standards in universities encourage the lowering of expectations and standards in the high schools and elementary schools. If the universities raise their expectations and standards, the high schools and elementary schools will raise theirs; they will have to. On the other hand, if the universities teach high school courses because the students are not prepared for university courses, then they simply relieve the high schools of their duty and in the process make themselves unable to do their own duty. Once the school stoops to meet the student, the standards of judgment begin to topple at all levels. As standards are lowered—as they cease to be the measure of the students and come to be measured by them—it becomes manifestly less possible for students to fail. But for the same reason it becomes less possible for them to learn and for teachers to teach.

The question, then, is what is to determine the pattern of education. Shall we shape a university education according to the previous schooling of the students, which we suppose has made them unfit to meet high expectations and standards, and to the supposed needs of students in some future still dark to us all? Or shall we shape it according to the nature and demands of the "leading Precognita of all things"—that is, according to the essential subjects of study? If we shape education to fit the students, then we clearly can maintain no standards; we will lose the subjects and eventually will lose the students as well. If we shape it to the subjects, then we will save both the subjects and the students. The inescapable purpose of education must be to preserve and pass on the essential human means—the thoughts and words and works and ways and standards and hopes without which we are not human. To preserve these things and to pass them on is to prepare students for life.

That such work cannot be done without high standards ought not to have to be said. There are necessarily increasing degrees of complexity in the studies as students rise through the grades and the years, and yet the standards remain the same. The first-graders, that is, must read and write in simple sentences, but they read and write, even so, in the language of the King James Bible, of Shakespeare and Johnson, of Thoreau, Whitman, Dickinson, and Twain. The grade-schooler and the graduate student must study the same American history, and there is no excuse for falsifying it in order to make it elementary.

Moreover, if standards are to be upheld, they cannot be specialized, professionalized, or departmented. Only common standards can be upheld—standards that are held and upheld in common by the whole community. When, in a university, for instance, English composition is made the responsibility exclusively of the English department, or of the subdepartment of freshman English, then the quality of the work in composition courses declines and the standards decline. This happens necessarily and for an obvious reason: If students' writing is graded according to form and quality in composition class but according only to "content" in, say, history class and if in other classes students are not required to write at all, then the message to the students is clear: namely, that the form and quality of their writing matters only in composition class, which is to say that it matters very little indeed. High standards of composition can be upheld only if they are upheld everywhere in the university.

Not only must the standards be held and upheld in common but they must also be applied fairly—that is, there must be no conditions with respect to persons or groups. There must be no discrimination for or against any person for any reason. The quality of the individual performer is the issue, not the category of the performer. The aim is to recognize, reward, and promote good work. Special pleading for "disadvantaged" groups—whether disadvantaged by history, economics, or education—can only make it increasingly difficult for members of that group to do good work and have it recognized.

Endnotes

1. W. Jackson Bate, *Samuel Johnson* (New York: Harcourt Brace Jovanovich, 1977), p. 51.
2. H. J. Massingham, *The Tree of Life* (London: Chapman & Hall, 1943).

▼ Questions to Focus Reading

1. Berry writes, "If we are disposed to judge apart from the larger questions, if we judge, as well as make, as specialists, then a good forger has as valid a claim to our respect as a good artist" (page 308). What "larger questions" is he talking about? What do you think he means by this statement?

2. How to make and how to judge are what education must teach us, Berry says, but he regrets that the second of these has come to be ignored. What explanation does he offer for why the cultivation of judgment has come to be ignored (page 308)?

3. The disintegration of the university begins with specialization and the ignoring of judgment, Berry claims. And the disintegration is "enforced by a commercial compulsion to satisfy the customer" (page 308). What does he mean by this latter?

4. "Grasp the Trunk hard only, and you will shake all the Branches," Berry quotes (page 309). He returns to this metaphor throughout his essay. What does it mean as applied to education? What is the trunk? What are the branches?

5. Berry charges that career preparation is "an improper use of public money" and a "waste of the student's time"(page 309). What reasons does he give for this judgment?

6. The public suffers, Berry claims, when universities fail to provide broad, basic education (page 309). How?

7. The life for which the teacher is preparing the student is "necessarily unknown to them both" (page 310). Why does Berry think this, too, argues against career preparation as the focus of a university education? What alternative focus is he proposing?

8. By what process of reasoning does he arrive at his suggested "core curriculum"? What would he eliminate? Why (page 310)?

9. What connection is Berry making between low standards in universities and low standards in high schools and elementary schools (page 311)?

10. "Shall we shape a university education according to the previous schooling of the students, which we suppose has made them unfit to meet high expectations and standards, and to the supposed needs of students in some future still dark to us all?" Berry asks (page 311). Clearly, this is not what he thinks should be done. What is the alternative he is proposing?

11. Berry sketches the means for "preparing students for life" (page 311). What are the means he proposes?

12. Berry argues that the only way to maintain high standards of written expression is by upholding those standards not only in the English department but everywhere in the university (page 311). How does he defend this claim?

▼ Questions for Reflection

1. Do you agree with Berry that your university education should be improving your judgment? Do you think that is happening?

2. Alluding to his "trunk and branches" metaphor, Berry complains that the modern university is a "loose collection of lopped branches waving about randomly in the air" (page 309). What do you think he means by this? Does this image capture your experience of your university courses?

3. "To prepare young people for life is to prepare them to know the difference between good and evil" (page 309). Does it seem to you that your professors are preparing you for life? Explain why you answer as you do. Are they preparing you to know the difference between good and evil? Do you think this should be part of their task?

4. Berry thinks university students and graduates pay an "obvious" price when they do not get a "broad, basic education" (page 309). What do you think he has in mind? Do you agree that there are such "penalties"?

5. What do you think of Berry's arguments against the use of the university for career preparation? What are his arguments? Are they convincing to you, or is his thinking faulty here in some respect(s)?

6. Has Berry convinced you that there must be a core curriculum at a university? Why or why not? If you were to be responsible for creating the core, how would you arrive at it?

7. Do you think your professors in courses other than English should not be concerned with the form and quality of your writing? Should how you write matter only to the English department's faculty?

8. Do you agree with Berry that no allowances should be made for disadvantages when it comes to the application of standards (page 312)?

9. "The inescapable purpose of education must be to preserve and pass on the essential human means—the thoughts and words and works and ways and standards and hopes without which we are not human. To preserve these things and to pass them on is to prepare students for life" (page 311). What do you make of the words "without which we are not human"? In what sense "not human"? What kinds of things would you include among the essential ingredients of humanity (of being human)? Do you think this statement of Berry's describes the process of education in which you are now involved?

▼ Discussion

1. Should preparing students to distinguish between good and evil be any part of the aim of university education?

2. Should the university be preparing you for a career—or for life? Or should it be preparing you for both? Are Berry's arguments against career preparation at the university good arguments? If not, what are their weaknesses? What does it mean to be prepared for life? If preparing you for life is any part of its proper task, as you see it, how can the university do this? Are there courses that can help prepare you for life? If so, are you taking any of these now? Are there other aspects of your university experience that can help prepare you for life?

3. Should it be any part of a university's aim to make you a better human being (not simply a better thinker or a better reader or a better technician, but a better person)? If so, how can it go about doing this? Do you think your experience and education at the university this semester are making you a better human being? Explain.

4. Do you agree with Berry that a university must have a core curriculum? Why or why not? By what reasoning would you establish that core? What would be included in the core curriculum you would design? Why? What would not be included? Why?

5. Do you think your professors in courses other than English should not be concerned with the form and quality of your writing? Should how you write matter only to the English department's faculty?

6. Do you agree with Berry that no allowances should be made for disadvantages when it comes to the application of standards (page 312)?

▼ Writing Assignments

1. Summarize Berry's arguments against career preparation as a focus for university education. Is he right? If you think he is, put yourself in the position of a person who disagrees with him, and criticize his arguments from that person's point of view, then show how Berry can respond to the criticisms. If you think he is wrong, explain where his arguments go wrong. If, in addition, you think there are relevant points he fails to consider, explain what those points are.

2. Should the university have a core curriculum (a set of specific courses required for all graduates)? Explain how Berry answers this question, then evaluate the case he makes. Are there good reasons for not having a core curriculum? Are there reasons for having one that Berry doesn't consider?

3. If it were up to you to create a core curriculum for a university, how would you go about doing this? What would be your starting point for this task? (On what basis would you make your choices?) What would you include in the core? Why? What would you eliminate from the present core? Why?

4. Is it reasonable to expect a university to help make you a better human being? If so, in just what sense(s)? What resources has it for doing this? (How is this to be accomplished?) If certain of your ideas and/or experiences this semester illustrate the way this can happen, present those ideas and/or describe those experiences.

▼ Journal Entry

1. Do you think you are becoming a better person as a result of your university experience and education? If so, in what respects?

▼ Vocabulary

affliction	ideology	precognita	tacit
apprenticeships	metaphor	specious	
artifact	modish	spurious	

49

▼

The Training of the Third Pig

Norman Peterson

Norman Peterson was a professor of English at Southwest Texas State University from 1963 to the time of his death in 1992. A pioneer in Southwest Texas's Freshman Seminar course, he was too cantankerous and iconoclastic to adopt the standard text, so he wrote one of his own. In 1989, the editor of this book persuaded him to distill his philosophy of university education into a single essay. The present chapter was the result. His own text called the educated the "aristocrats" of the society. When this prompted criticism for its apparent elitism, he protested that it was of no importance what one called university graduates: "I'll call them pigs if you like!" Hence, the title of the essay before you, an essay bristling with Norman Peterson's characteristically wicked wit—and filled with his characteristic solicitude. His theme is the purpose of higher education: its purpose, he argues, is the survival of the society.

I am about to give a lecture on the American university, and it seems to me properly **eccentric** to begin with a fairy tale, "The Three Little Pigs." I was fed this old English folktale in the middle 1930s, and I remember vividly the full page horror picture of the pig-chomping beast, his fangs all red and frothy. I liked the book well enough to open it often, but you can bet that I also knew precisely where that wolf was and never looked on him again. Didn't have to. I still see him vividly on the silvering screen of my mind. In the 1930s we still had "The Three Little Pigs" in unsoftened **Teutonic** form. My pig in my straw house did not "scamper away into the woods." He was *eaten*—raw. Thus the bloody fangs in the picture I had only to observe once to have gained sufficient effect. The pig in the stick house, who also ignored the tough, real struggle for survival, was likewise slurped, *a jus cru*. The smart pig labored to build his bricky protection. Not only did he repulse the **primal** force at his door, but he became the *eater* of it. Big bro ate the *wolf,* though remaining suave enough to cook it first. He was a civilized creature, after all.

I just looked at a 1988 version, along with another made into a small play for kindergarten enlightenment. The first two pigs, neglecting proper attention to life's labor, did *not* get eaten. They did not even get very scared. They ran to find Big Brother, who sheltered them in a kind of familial welfare center. Big Brother provided them fun, family, feast. They danced. (Later, maybe, the first two pigs write a vastly acclaimed **libretto** in which two dancers save a village from a wolf. Culture is born.)

Isn't that happy?

My wife (for better human interest, I refer to her as the woman I am currently living with), who first got the tale in the 1940s, says that the happy version is what she got. Typically, this woman I have been currently living with for thirty-one years accused my sainted mother, who got me the book, of unspeakable acts. Without researching it further, I can date the advent of modern child psychology, as well as the propagandizing of an attitude that makes our times so different from earlier ones. *Du bist was du ißt*, and kiddies have for fifty years been eating three quite different pigs than I did, or, for that matter, than did our founding fathers.

eccentric: odd; unusual
Teutonic: Germanic
a jus cru: with raw juice
primal: primeval; primitive
libretto: the text of a dramatic musical work
Du bist was du ißt: a German pun on "You are what you eat"

What if we imagine a nation of pigs, all taught from pigletry that however little they think, know, or try makes no serious difference in the end? Oh, it might get kind of breezy and exciting, but Big Brother will take care of them down the line. Fun, family, feast become **inalienable** Porcine **rights**. I like the notion. I find it very pretty until I wonder what propaganda is going to form the third pig? Would such an odd pig have failed kindergarten, day-dreamed at the wrong time, remained undeluded by his own culture's "Three Little People"?

Maybe none of the above, as they say in Scantron.

Maybe at some point this queer hog would choose the protector's laborious task over the more playful one of his classmates. As I recall, even in elementary school some nutty kid preferred arithmetic class to recess, the little wimp. Maybe he *liked* the burdens of math! Maybe he was seriously withdrawn, much in need of therapy, though such was not yet available at that level. Or maybe he simply craved the protector's peer-status, if indeed a protector is peer to the protectees.

Regrettably, I find I've moved over into the species Man. I say regrettably not because I am not a lover of the guy, but because there is too much of us to make sense from. The tall haystack of our development blinds us to the underpinnings, the holder-uppers, that we find ourselves so high on top of. I remember that in the 1960s many wanted to destroy these underpinnings and begin anew, but fortunately nobody could find where they were.

The pigs' story is, after all, really about humans. Even as a five-year-old I didn't confuse those three English-speaking pink bipeds with my breakfast bacon. We recognize, I hope, that the first two fellows were put into need of protection by their own flighty, stupid ignorance. Wait a minute. Let me take that back. Because they did not know how solid a place to build is not reason to call them flighty or stupid. They got into need for protection, O.K., but their not-knowing (which is what ignorance means) is plenty to lay on them. They simply didn't know what was needed. It looks to me like there's every reason to believe, too, that if the straw house had proved to be the **bastion**, the first guy would have taken in his brothers just as lovingly as the third one. Ignorance or incapacity doesn't lessen brotherly affection and mutual concern. See any movie on the subject.

So the third member of the family, no better or worse in his humanity than the rest, ends up the protector simply because he knows what kind of a house to build.

How did he find that out?

Let's play a game. Pretend (plyke, we used to say), plyke our group has been appointed to defend the university student body. Weird? I don't know why *our* group was so lucky, but there it is. This sudden need for defense, I hear, is that the Verde Faction in the city of Kyle is going to attack us in great force. We must be the protectors against this. What do we do?

I'll confess I've played this game several times before, so I can tell you what you'll probably do upon this announcement. You will sit there patiently, awaiting orders from the Old Man. This, in fact, is exactly what I did through my four years in the armed forces. You will sit there until it gets embarrassing to observe the unlikely spectacle of a silent professor.

Even weirder, when one of you eventually asks what kind of weapons we are supposed to have, I say, by golly by gum by gee, I don't have a clue.

Every class has its gutsy aggressor who eventually says to me, "Well, what *do* you know? Sir."

To which I answer that, shoot, all I know is that we have been appointed protectors of the student body from an attack supposedly coming from the Verde Faction in Kyle.

"Are you real sure?" asks a decent looking young woman, anxious to help. I find out later that she is from Kyle and has not heard of the Verde Faction. This information coming right out of the mouth of a pro*fes*sor distresses her, and she's probably anxious to call home.

inalienable rights: rights that no one can take away from you

bastion: prominent portion of a fortification or rampart

317

"Uh uh," I say. "Except everybody seems real scared."

"I'm calling Daddy," she whispers to the wall.

O.K. In a college classroom you'd hoped to have been informed of things, not to be the source of information. I will deserve the nervous call from the Dean who wants me to explain all this to an angry father from Kyle. What I'm up to here, I tell the Dean, is to orient people to what a college education is all about, not to give the details taught in it. The university is actually *a training ground for the Third Pig,* get it?

If the title is indecorous, I'll find a nicer one.

Let's say instead that the university is the training ground for the American Natural Aristocracy. The adjectives look to be advertising for a health food **elitism**. But also, the Natural Aristocracy is Thomas Jefferson's term for those like himself, whose father walked out of the woods, but who nonetheless came to know sufficient about the Wolf and the Brick House.

If the man from Kyle happens to be your daddy, don't think I blame him. I'm a daddy, too, and I too have turned savage about little snots of teacher perverts bullying around my daughter. Sure, I guess I wanted her to be informed about the world, but can't teachers be nice about it? What is this, goodbye goodbye Miss American Pie? One thing we fathers love about our little girls is the very fact that they sorely need protection. Daughters are cherished protectees. If the university is a training ground for the *opposite,* maybe Dad has made a major mistake here.

Well, sure, I know better. In this sterilized world we like to raise them in, brute reality is what otherwise bright young people need to know about most. Miss American Pie tends to be worthless on those several days without a major beauty pageant.

Daddies, please listen to this confession of mine. When I was getting married, my father-in-law said to me, "I just want you to cherish my little girl." *Cherish?* I swore to him that I would, of course. That was a traumatic moment, considering what I actually had in mind. I actually had things far more—real—in mind.

Among other things, I wanted a love partner to help me bash out a trail through the wilderness. Fight the savages off. You *cherish* babies, dolls, puppies, petunias. I wanted a *woman.*

In my hazy notion of why the devil I was marrying anyhow, there was the image of the two of us, back to back, holding off an attack of circling Cheyenne. She was Patricia Neal, and I, of course, John Wayne. Cherish? No, no. Cherish is what both of us Indian fighters did with *our* daughter. And so it goes, like a big ole wheel each of us keeps trying to stop. Or at least slow down, huh, Dad?

If you think all this is a digression off the point, you're wrong. My confession about not cherishing my own Patricia Neal is exactly to the point of this lecture. It's not some new-fangled idea that a woman must be as capable of Wolf-protection as a man, and she's (or he's) not going to learn that by remaining piggy numbers one and two, who may imagine the primal wolf to be some kind of stuffed toy.

The wolf has frothy, bloody jaws, and the two little pigs are eaten. If the little cherished girl expects to be a woman, she must find out what the third pig knows about wolfish reality.

And so back to class, where our group is discovering how bright we are. Or aren't.

We are the designated protectors of our university populace against some force or another from somewhere or another. Kyle, they say, but where is that in terms of footsteps and dirt? I mean, even knowing quite well about Hong Kong, we still don't know exactly how one gets there. Is this feared attack real, or only a squawk from the beak of Little Red Hen? What weapons do we have? If any, does anybody know how to work one? Who *is* the student body—my God, are there more than we see on the mall? Why does one person want to attack another one, anyhow? Jimminy, has anything like this happened before? Who knows? How do we *go about* knowing?

elitism: allegiance to or membership in a select group

318

What's happening here is just another version of what happens in any colony of people. Somebody, some group has to find out these ridiculously basic things— 1) Where are things? 2) How do things work? 3) Why do people, or any creatures, take action? 4) What has been learned in the past?

Do you think that "higher education"—the training of the third pig—is to build intellect? Well, that's not right. We might indicate various ways to use it, but intellect is what God gave you, not entirely unlike some super-computer put out by IBM, all completely useless until sufficient facts are fed into it. "Higher Education" feeds out these four dirt-basic bunches of facts—1) Where things are, 2) How things work, 3) Why creatures do things, and 4) What has been learned in the past. If sufficient data from these groups get lodged in your memory banks, your intellect is delighted. All this assumes, of course, that your set is plugged in. Intellect is simply a prerequisite, just like 20/20 vision is a prerequisite for flight training. But even to prove 20/20, you have to open your eyes.

Where is Kyle? Maybe we could ask around. The girl with the frantic dad tells us it's seven miles from here. Yeah, but in what direction? So we look at a map (provided we know where to locate one), the *map* being a thing learned from the past. If we pinpoint it, maybe some of us should mosey over there and find out if there really is a Verde Faction, and if so, why are they doing this? O.K. But what if once we get there a bunch of people come fuming out and beat us up? Well, why would they do that, or, for that matter, why wouldn't they come out with lemonade, shaking hands? In any case, maybe we can begin to learn enough to protect somebody, not to mention us.

Maybe we'd find out that the Verde Faction is a horde of green grasshoppers migrating south.

Wow! What a relief. But I'll bet you five bucks that a clot of scared **hawks** at our own Dairy Queen won't believe that green grasshopper crud. Why do people insist on disbelieving the simplest answers? Why, indeed. So now we have to find out why our own protectees act the way they do. Holy Moley, maybe we'd better look at why we are doing all this.

Man, this gets out of hand. Maybe what you hoped from all this training was to end up flashing gold credit cards in New Orleans. The fact is that gold credit cards go only to people who can answer the where, how, why, and what of quite basic things. And as soon as such elite, knowledgeable people neglect to do that, the mass of folk jerk back the gold cards, and if they have to bash in heads to redeem them, they will certainly do that. Right on Bourbon Street.

I doubt that you know this, being probably distracted by your folks mumbling rightfully about what it costs to send you to college, but that cost is *less than a third the expense of your personal training.* Where does the rest of it, the most of it, come from?

I'll tell you where all that money comes from. It is given to you by the mass of plain ole country tax-paying folks who have lack of time, inclination, or desire to go through all the hassle of third pig training. They give these bucks to you in hopes of getting an adequate corps of protectors out of it. You.

If you think they give it to allow you a life of rich-baby ease, you'd better rethink this deal before bashing time comes to N'awlins. Think about it over your party-keg the night before a major exam.

It is because of their effective protective activities that any aristocracy gains prestige and reward from the people. When the elite does not serve this function, it becomes despised and removed. . . . historical knowledge can provide numerous examples of this often bloody phenomenon, such as the American, French, and Russian revolutions.

hawks: people who take a militant attitude and support a war or warlike policy

University Education: For What Reasons?

What the writer of that expects you to know already are the historical causes of common people getting teed off enough to jerk back the gold credit cards from those they'd expected to protect their well-being, but screwed off instead. In the last two events above, they jerked not only the card, but the whole arm holding it. Of course, you wouldn't have anything but a pretty historical-fiction movie for information on such stuff unless you seriously studied the What of the real happenings in the past. The first two piggies see the fun-movie; the third pig gets at reality in some musty place, which can be more labor than love, believe me. So it goes.

Here's a piece of advice. Unless you are determined to labor and sweat here for at least four years out of your young life, and then keep doing it all your life, go home and be cherished. Tell Daddy that one. He will call the Dean. The Dean will ask me why I am determined to get that button on your grafittied desk pushed. The one that says, "Press here, and your professor will disappear."

On the happier hand, let me tell you my sincerest opinion of you people. You devils are the cream of American youth. You are the brightest, most decent, courteous, patient bunch one is going to find—anywhere, anytime. If anybody is going to get reward and prestige, it ought to be you. If I could give all the needed data to you by transfusion or electricity or with a sparkly wand, I would. But that ain't the way it comes. If you are going to get reward and prestige, you'll have to grub it out over a long time. The university doesn't shove it up your nose; the university merely offers data on 1) Where things are, 2) How things work, 3) Why creatures do things, and 4) What happened in the past. If you get at these offerings effectively, nobody in America is going to begrudge you the title of aristocrat, elite, or whatever you want, so long as it all adds up to Third Pig protection. Jefferson, as democratic as any of his peers, never shied away from "**aristocracy**." He was against the stupid notion that people should get such status from simply being born in a privileged family. But anybody of sufficient intelligence, time, and inclination can become a natural aristocrat, no matter if he crawled out of a **bayou** trailing slime. How? Through the university. Of all the extraordinary things that guy did, Jefferson asked only three things to go on his tombstone, and the third was "Founder of the University of Virginia."

Final game. Open the University Catalog to "Contents." You'll see a heading termed "Schools and Departments." Under that are listed seven "schools," each including several "departments." Each department teaches a certain field of knowledge necessary for the running of our civilization. What I ought to say is that *all* these fields of knowledge are necessary for the running of our civilization. Obviously, no single person can know them all, much less teach them, and so that's the reason it's necessary to have specializations for the professors who make up each department.

The first five schools include technical specialties. The last two, Liberal Arts and Science, are dedicated to the essentials that the protectorate-aristocracy must know something about. I want you to arrange each of these Liberal Arts and Science departments under the categories of Where things are, How things work, Why creatures act, and What the lessons of the past are. You'll find, surely, that some of the departments overlap these protector-categories.

It's obvious that Geography belongs under Where, that Physics goes under How, that History fits What we have learned in the past. It is less obvious on the surface of it that English (literature) is a display of why human creatures act as they do, or that Mathematics deals with how things work. Without getting too picky about it, arrange all the departments of Liberal Arts and Science in the four groups.

If you're the ordinary, healthy kind of young person, there will be some of these departments that you never heard of before. One of them, Anthropology, reminds me of my freshman year when I suffered an ignorance that at least some of you may share. I had no idea of what I wanted to major in, and certainly I was

aristocracy: nobility

bayou: an outlet or arm of a river or lake in the southern United States

320

completely blanko on a minor. But the advisor bullied me into "declaring major and minor." Why must they do that? How can you be sure of something you absolutely don't know yet?

(When I turned fifty, I was blitzed by the funeral homes about declaring where I'd be buried. I hadn't yet decided on dying!)

I saw on the list "Anthropology." No, I had no idea of what Anthropology meant. Still, it sounded like something I'd like to announce back home as I sipped a cherry-coke in the drugstore. "Oh, yeah," I'd say lazily, "I'm studying Anthropology, you know."

So that's what I declared as a major. It occurs to me that if I'd picked Aerospace Physics or something, I might not be writing this lecture. I'd be in New Orleans with my Gold Card.

Anyway, the exercise on the catalog, obviously, is to display the university's function as I have explained it. It's pretty complicated. In more primitive situations, such as the problem with the Kyle Verde Faction, the complexity would not be needed. But, as I've said before, we live on top of a gigantic stack of interlocking parts. There is so much necessarily found out by the modern protector-aristocracy that it takes many teaching units to cover even at minimum effectiveness.

As you can tell, it worries me that we, unlike the Princess who could feel a pea under fifty mattresses, will lose sense of the peas at the bottom of it all—our protector responsibilities. Our civilization is so complex that almost all of us must eventually narrow down our individual work inside it. However complex we get, and how much sheltered from the base of things, it still remains the burden of aristocracy to grasp the broadest knowledge, right across the bottom line of Where things are, How things work, Why creatures (especially people) act, and What we have learned in the past. This is why a college degree is not given without "General Education," which at least can acquaint each of us with the four protective categories. We can't know the answers to everything, but we can darn sure know what must be searched out to find the answers. Like the Princess, we are aware of the pea(s). Thus her aristocratic title.

The question that ought to come up in your mind is how the devil you are going to be a protector unless you go into politics or become some chief-of-staff. Most Americans leave such stuff to the Army, the Governor, the President, and expect one of them to take care of all that. But in any mass of people, and not just in a democracy like ours, protective knowledge is exerted in almost every group in every town, whistle-stop, and armadillo hunt. In each group, the educated person is always listened to, no matter what you might otherwise imagine. Elementary school teachers, for instance, have innocent, captive audiences, and thereby a lot of protector influence right at the beginning. Why they keep teaching "The Three Little Pigs" in degutted form is beyond my acceptance. Should there be a law against it? Well, not if we want to maintain freedom, which includes freedom to self-destruct (No, it's not against the law to self-destruct in America.)

The news and entertainment media are extremely effective at protector influence, but they do what their aristocrats tell them. Of course politicians finally put in the protective laws; however, they do precisely what the tiny groups out there tell them to do. And who tells the tiny group?

The Third Pig.

▼ Questions to Focus Reading

1. Peterson begins his essay with some bloody details of "The Three Little Pigs" in "unsoftened Teutonic form." He then presents a recent version. What is the difference in the two versions of the pigs' story?

2. What is Peterson's attitude toward the modern changes in the story of the three pigs? Why does he have this attitude?

3. "The tall haystack of our development blinds us to the underpinnings, the holder-uppers, that we find ourselves so high on top of." What do you think the author means by this sentence?

4. What is the point of Peterson's confession to the "daddies" (page 318)?

5. Peterson rejects the idea that the purpose of higher education is to build intellect. Why?

6. What is the point of the discussion of the attack by the Verde Faction (pages 317–319)? What are the four questions a university education answers, according to Peterson?

7. Peterson is speaking to students at a state university, where the tuition is only a small portion of the expense of their education. Why does he emphasize this fact? What does he do with it?

8. What is the point of his "final game," involving the university catalog (page 320)?

9. Why does the author think we are in danger of losing the sense of "the peas at the bottom of it all" (page 321)?

10. Isn't the role of protector reserved for the politician or the military officer? The last two paragraphs address this question. How does Peterson answer it?

▼ Questions for Reflection

1. What key question is the author trying to answer in this essay? What is his answer? What does his title mean?

2. "What if we imagine a nation of pigs, all taught from pigletry that however little they think, know, or try makes no serious difference in the end?" What, in Peterson's view, will be the problem with this "very pretty" arrangement? Do you think he is right?

3. "In this sterilized world we like to raise them in, brute reality is what otherwise bright young people need to know about most." What do you think the author has in mind by the "sterilized world we like to raise them in"?

4. What does the third pig know about "wolfish reality"? What reality does Peterson have in mind by this metaphor?

5. Play the author's "final game" (page 320). Research the areas unfamiliar to you, either through the reference library or through brief interviews with professors in the relevant fields.

6. "General Education"—Who Needs It? Explain how Peterson would answer. Do you think he is right?

7. Peterson sees a strong connection between the university as an institution and the survival of a society. What case does he make for this connection?

▼ Discussion

1. What key question is the author trying to answer in this essay? What is his answer? What does his title mean?

2. What does the third pig know about "wolfish reality"? What reality does Peterson have in mind by this metaphor?

3. Play the author's "final game" (page 320). Research the areas unfamiliar to you, either through the reference library or through brief interviews with professors in the relevant fields.

4. "General Education"—Who Needs It? Explain how Peterson would answer. Do you think he is right?

5. Peterson sees a strong connection between the university as an institution and the survival of a society. What case does he make for this connection?

6. The author is concerned that we will "lose sense of the peas at the bottom of it all—our protector responsibilities" (page 321). What is the basis of his concern?

▼ Writing Assignments

1. "Education and the Survival of a Society" Write an essay in which you present Peterson's conception of the relation between these. Do you think he is right about the primary mission of a university? You might consider how Hutchins or Rorty would reply.

2. Say members of the local community band together to protest use of a certain textbook in the biology department of your school. They argue that the text offends in several sections against their religious beliefs and insist that it be removed. What "protector knowledge" would be necessary in dealing with this threat?

3. Assume you are one of the survivors of a great catastrophe affecting the entire country. It is necessary to build society anew. What would you and your compatriots have to know in order to do this? You might write this in the form of a fictional diary.

▼ Journal Entry

1. Peterson argues here that you are being trained to fill a certain role in society—the role of "protector." Is that how you see the purpose of your being here?

▼ Vocabulary

a jus cru	bayou	elitism	libretto
aristocracy	Du bist was du ißt	hawks	primal
bastion	eccentric	inalienable rights	Teutonic

50

▼

Impersonal Interests

Bertrand Russell

This is an essay about the emancipation of personal interests from the anxious grip of immediate practical concerns, and it is about the relation of this emancipation to the attainment of happiness. It has been excerpted from The Conquest of Happiness, *a 1930 work of Nobel Prize–winning author Bertrand Russell (1872–1970), one of the most important philosophers of the century.*

I wish to consider not those major interests about which a man's life is built, but those minor interests which fill his leisure and afford relaxation from the tenseness of his more serious preoccupations. In the life of the average man his wife and children, his work and his financial position occupy the main part of his anxious and serious thought. Even if he has extra-matrimonial love affairs, they probably do not concern him as profoundly in themselves as in their possible effects upon his home life. The interests which are bound up with his work I am not for the present regarding as impersonal interests. A man of science, for example, must keep abreast of research in his own line. Towards such research his feelings have the warmth and vividness belonging to something intimately concerned with his career, but if he reads about research in some quite other science with which he is not professionally concerned he reads in quite a different spirit, not professionally, less critically, more disinterestedly. Even if he has to use his mind in order to follow what is said, his reading is nevertheless a relaxation, because it is not connected with his responsibilities. If the book interests him, his interest is impersonal in a sense which cannot be applied to the books upon his own subject. It is such interests lying outside the main activities of a man's life that I wish to speak about.

One of the sources of unhappiness, fatigue and nervous strain is inability to be interested in anything that is not of practical importance in one's own life. The result of this is that the conscious mind gets no rest from a certain small number of matters, each of which probably involves some anxiety and some element of worry. Except in sleep the conscious mind is never allowed to lie **fallow** while subconscious thought matures its gradual wisdom. The result is excitability, lack of **sagacity**, irritability, and a loss of sense of proportion. All these are both causes and effects of fatigue. As a man gets more tired his external interests fade, and as they fade he loses the relief which they afford him and becomes still more tired. This vicious circle is only too apt to end in a breakdown. What is restful about external interests is the fact that they do not call for any action. Making decisions and exercising **volition** are very fatiguing, especially if they have to be done hurriedly and without the help of the subconscious. Men who feel that they must "sleep on it" before coming to an important decision are profoundly right. But it is not only in sleep that the subconscious mental processes can work. They can work also while a man's conscious mind is occupied elsewhere. The man who can forget his work when it is over and not remember it until it begins again next day is likely to do his work far better than the man who worries about it throughout the intervening hours. And it is very much easier to forget work at the times when it ought to be forgotten if a man has many interests other than his work than it is

fallow: (of land) plowed and left unseeded for a season; uncultivated

sagacity: wisdom

volition: conscious choices

if he has not. It is, however, essential that these interests should not exercise those very faculties which have been exhausted by his day's work. They should not involve will and quick decision, they should not, like gambling, involve any financial element, and they should as a rule not be so exciting as to produce emotional fatigue and preoccupy the subconscious as well as the conscious mind.

A great many amusements fulfill all these conditions. Watching games, going to the theater, playing golf, are all **irreproachable** from this point of view. For a man of a bookish turn of mind reading unconnected with his professional activities is very satisfactory. However important a worry may be, it should not be thought about throughout the whole of the waking hours.

All impersonal interests, apart from their importance as relaxation, have various other uses. To begin with, they help a man to retain his sense of proportion. It is very easy to become so absorbed in our own pursuits, our own circle, our own type of work, that we forget how small a part this is of the total of human activity and how many things in the world are entirely unaffected by what we do. Why should one remember this? you may ask. There are several answers. In the first place, it is good to have as true a picture of the world as is compatible with necessary activities. Each of us is in the world for no very long time, and within the few years of his life has to acquire whatever he is to know of this strange planet and its place in the universe. To ignore our opportunities for knowledge, imperfect as they are, is like going to the theater and not listening to the play. The world is full of things that are tragic or comic, heroic or bizarre or surprising, and those who fail to be interested in the spectacle that it offers are forgoing one of the privileges that life has to offer.

Then again a sense of proportion is very valuable and at times very consoling. We are all inclined to get unduly excited, unduly strained, unduly impressed with the importance of the little corner of the world in which we live, and of the little moment of time comprised between our birth and death. In this excitement and overestimation of our own importance there is nothing desirable. True, it may make us work harder, but it will not make us work better. A little work directed to a good end is better than a great deal of work directed to a bad end, though the apostles of the strenuous life seem to think otherwise. Those who care much for their work are always in danger of falling into fanaticism, which consists essentially in remembering one or two desirable things while forgetting all the rest, and in supposing that in the pursuit of these one or two any incidental harm of other sorts is of little account. Against this fanatical temper there is no better **prophylactic** than a large conception of the life of man and his place in the universe. This may seem a very big thing to invoke in such a connection, but apart from this particular use, it is in itself a thing of great value.

It is one of the defects of modern higher education that it has become too much a training in the acquisition of certain kinds of skill, and too little an enlargement of the mind and heart by an impartial survey of the world. You become absorbed, let us say, in a political contest, and work hard for the victory of your own party. So far, so good. But it may happen in the course of the contest that some opportunity of victory presents itself which involves the use of methods calculated to increase hatred, violence and suspicion in the world. For example, you may find that the best road to victory is to insult some foreign nation. If your mental **purview** is limited to the present, or if you have imbibed the doctrine that what is called efficiency is the only thing that matters, you will adopt such **dubious** means. Through them you will be victorious in your immediate purpose, while the more distant consequences may be disastrous. If, on the other hand, you have as part of the habitual furniture of your mind the past ages of man, his slow and partial emergence out of barbarism, and the brevity of his total existence in comparison with **astronomical epochs**—if, I say, such thoughts have molded your habitual feelings, you will realize that the momentary battle upon which you are

irreproachable: above blame

prophylactic: protection

purview: range of understanding or vision

dubious: doubtful

astronomical epoch: an arbitrary fixed date, usually the beginning of a century, used as a reference in giving the elements of a planetary orbit

engaged cannot be of such importance as to risk a backward step towards the darkness out of which we have been slowly emerging. Nay, more, if you suffer defeat in your immediate objective, you will be sustained by the same sense of its momentariness that made you unwilling to adopt degrading weapons. You will have, beyond your activities, purposes that are distant and slowly unfolding, in which you are not an isolated individual but one of the great army of those who have led mankind towards a civilized existence. If you have attained to this outlook, a certain deep happiness will never leave you, whatever your personal fate may be. Life will become a communion with the great of all ages, and personal death no more than a negligible incident. . . .

If I had the power to organize higher education as I should wish it to be, I should seek to substitute for the old orthodox religions—which appeal to few among the young, and those as a rule the least intelligent and the most **obscurantist**—something which is perhaps hardly to be called religion, since it is merely a focusing of attention upon **well-ascertained** facts. I should seek to make young people vividly aware of the past, vividly realizing that the future of man will in all likelihood be immeasurably longer than his past, profoundly conscious of the minuteness of the planet upon which we live and of the fact that life on this planet is only a temporary incident; and at the same time with these facts which tend to emphasize the insignificance of the individual, I should present quite another set of facts designed to impress upon the mind of the young the greatness of which the individual is capable, and the knowledge that throughout all the depths of stellar space nothing of equal value is known to us. Spinoza long ago wrote of human bondage and human freedom; his form and his language make his thought difficult of access to all students of philosophy, but the essence of what I wish to convey differs little from what he has said.

A man who has once perceived, however temporarily and however briefly, what makes greatness of soul, can no longer be happy if he allows himself to be petty, self-seeking, troubled by trivial misfortunes, dreading what fate may have in store for him. The man capable of greatness of soul will open wide the windows of his mind, letting the winds blow freely upon it from every portion of the universe. He will see himself and life and the world as truly as our human limitations will permit; realizing the brevity and minuteness of human life, he will realize also that in individual minds is concentrated whatever of value the known universe contains. And he will see that the man whose mind mirrors the world becomes in a sense as great as the world. In emancipation from the fears that beset the slave of circumstance he will experience a profound joy, and through all the **vicissitudes** of his outward life he will remain in the depths of his being a happy man.

Leaving these large speculations and returning to our more immediate subject, namely the value of impersonal interests, there is another consideration which makes them a great help towards happiness. Even in the most fortunate lives there are times when things go wrong. Few men except bachelors have never quarreled with their wives; few parents have not endured grave anxiety owing to the illnesses of their children; few business men have avoided times of financial stress; few professional men have not known periods when failure stared them in the face. At such times a capacity to become interested in something outside the cause of anxiety is an immense boon. At such times when in spite of anxiety there is nothing to be done at the moment, one man will play chess, another will read detective stories, a third will become absorbed in popular astronomy, a fourth will console himself by reading about the excavations at Ur of the Chaldees. Any one of these four is acting wisely, whereas the man who does nothing to distract his mind and allows his trouble to acquire a complete empire over him is acting unwisely and making himself less fit to cope with his troubles when the moment for action arrives. Very similar considerations apply to irreparable sorrows such as the death of some person deeply loved. No good is done to any one by allowing oneself to

obscurantist: obscuring; tending to prevent human progress and enlightenment

well-ascertained: determined with certainty

vicissitudes: ups and downs

326

become sunk in grief on such an occasion. Grief is unavoidable and must be expected, but everything that can be done should be done to minimize it. It is mere sentimentality to aim, as some do, at extracting the very uttermost drop of misery from misfortune. I do not of course deny that a man may be broken by sorrow, but I do say that every man should do his utmost to escape this fate, and should seek any distraction, however trivial, provided it is not in itself harmful or degrading. Among those that I regard as harmful and degrading I include such things as drunkenness and drugs, of which the purpose is to destroy thought, at least for the time being. The proper course is not to destroy thought but to turn it into new channels, or at any rate into channels remote from the present misfortune. It is difficult to do this if life has hitherto been concentrated upon a very few interests and those few have now become suffused with sorrow. To bear misfortune well when it comes, it is wise to have cultivated in happier times a certain width of interests, so that the mind may find prepared for it some undisturbed place suggesting other associations and other emotions than those which are making the present difficult to bear.

A man of adequate vitality and zest will surmount all misfortunes by the emergence after each blow of an interest in life and the world which cannot be narrowed down so much as to make one loss fatal. To be defeated by one loss or even by several is not something to be admired as a proof of sensibility, but something to be **deplored** as a failure in vitality. All our affections are at the mercy of death, which may strike down those whom we love at any moment. It is therefore necessary that our lives should not have that narrow intensity which puts the whole meaning and purpose of our life at the mercy of accident.

For all these reasons the man who pursues happiness wisely will aim at the possession of a number of **subsidiary** interests in addition to those central ones upon which his life is built.

deplored: regretted strongly
subsidiary: subordinate or secondary

▼ Questions to Focus Reading

1. What does Russell mean by "impersonal interests"?
2. In the second paragraph, Russell is making a practical argument for having interests unrelated to one's work (page 324). What is that argument?
3. Why should we bear in mind the fact that our own pursuits are but a small part of the total of human activity? How does Russell answer this question in the fourth paragraph (page 325)?
4. Russell argues that "a large conception of the life of man and his place in the universe" is a prophylactic against fanaticism. What does he mean by "a large conception of the life of man and his place in the universe"? Why is the large conception an antidote to fanaticism?
5. Russell is critical of the emphasis in higher education on the acquisition of skills, as opposed to the "enlargement of mind and heart." He makes his call for the superiority of the latter emphasis by means of an extended example (page 325). He asks you to imagine that you are involved in a political contest. How does he develop the example? What is his point?
6. The person with a large conception of the life of humankind will have purposes that are "distant and slowly unfolding" (page 326). What does this mean? How will such purposes affect his or her action, according to Russell? What is the connection according to Russell, between this outlook and personal happiness?
7. If he were organizing higher education according to his own lights, Russell would focus students' attention on two sets of facts (page 326). What facts? Why would these be his focus?
8. "The man capable of greatness of soul will open wide the windows of his mind, letting the winds blow freely upon it from every portion of the universe." Explain what Russell means by this metaphor.

9. "[T]he man whose mind mirrors the world becomes in a sense as great as the world." Explain.
10. What is the relation between greatness of soul and personal happiness, according to Russell?
11. Cultivating impersonal interests enables us to bear misfortune well, Russell argues. Explain.
12. "To be defeated by one loss or even by several is not something to be admired as a proof of sensibility, but something to be deplored as a failure in vitality" (page 327). How does Russell argue for this?

▼ Questions for Reflection

1. Periods of relaxation provided by impersonal interests are necessary to effective decision making, Russell says. What case does he make for this? Is the truth of this borne out in your own experience?
2. What, in Russell's view, is the relation between the cultivation of impersonal interests and the development of a sense of proportion?
3. "It is one of the defects of modern higher education that it has become too much a training in the acquisition of certain kinds of skill, and too little an enlargement of the mind and heart by an impartial survey of the world." What do you think Russell means by "an impartial survey of the world"? What is Russell's case for the value of this "enlargement of the mind and heart"? Do you think his case is persuasive?
4. "A sense of proportion is very valuable and at times very consoling." What do you think Russell has in mind when he says it is very consoling?
5. An education that enlarges the mind and heart will produce people who will act with a view to the betterment of mankind and people for whom personal misfortune and even death will seem "no more than a negligible incident." Why should we believe this? What is the connection, as Russell sees it, between such an education and these results? Do you think this proposition is right?
6. If Russell could remake higher education, his primary aim would be to produce in students "greatness of soul." What do you think Russell means by this phrase? Specifically, what would his ideal higher education emphasize?
7. Russell believes higher education should get us out of ourselves and the narrow orbit of our career concerns and out into the world. It should induce in us a desire to "open wide the windows of [our] mind, letting the winds blow freely upon it from every portion of the universe." The person in whom this occurs will remain, he says, "in the depths of his being a happy man." Why? What is the connection, according to Russell, between the enlargement of the domain of one's interests and personal happiness?
8. Russell argues that the cultivation of a wide range of interests helps us to deal with misfortune. What reason does he give for saying this? Is he right?

▼ Discussion

1. "It is one of the defects of modern higher education that it has become too much a training in the acquisition of certain kinds of skill, and too little an enlargement of the mind and heart by an impartial survey of the world." What do you think Russell means by "an impartial survey of the world"? What is Russell's case for the value of this "enlargement of the mind and heart"? Do you think his case is persuasive?
2. An education that enlarges the mind and heart will produce people who will act with a view to the betterment of mankind and people for whom personal misfortune and even death will seem "no more than a negligible

incident." Why should we believe this? What is the connection, as Russell sees it, between such an education and these results? Do you think this proposition is right?

3. If Russell could remake higher education, his primary aim would be to produce in students "greatness of soul." What do you think Russell means by this phrase? Specifically, what would his ideal higher education emphasize?

4. Russell believes higher education should get us out of ourselves and the narrow orbit of our career concerns and out into the world. It should induce in us a desire to "open wide the windows of [our] mind, letting the winds blow freely upon it from every portion of the universe." The person in whom this occurs will remain, he says, "in the depths of his being a happy man." Why? What is the connection, according to Russell, between the enlargement of the domain of one's interests and personal happiness?

5. In your opinion, what are the characteristics of a person with "greatness of soul"? Can higher education help produce such people? If so, how? If not, why not?

6. You can imagine someone reading this essay and thinking that Russell's prescription for deep joy requires too much of a renunciation of passion and engagement. Is there anything to such a criticism? In your opinion, is Russell's deep happiness purchased at the price of disengagement from life?

7. What relation does Russell see between higher education and happiness? What relation do you see between them?

▼ Writing Assignments

1. "The Importance of Impersonal Interests"
2. "What is Greatness of Soul?" What are the characteristics of a "great soul"? How do you think these characteristics are developed?
3. "Greatness of Soul: A Way to Abiding Happiness" or "Russell's Key to Deep Happiness: An Invitation to Quietism and Coldness"
4. "Can Higher Education Build Great Souls?"
5. "Higher Education and Happiness" What is the relation between these in Russell's view? In your view?
6. "On the Meaning of Happiness" What conception of happiness emerges in Russell's essay? What is your own conception of happiness?

▼ Journal Entries

1. Russell believes that the deeply happy person cannot be a slave to circumstance, so he tries to situate happiness in relations invulnerable to accident. *Are* such relations the locus of deep happiness?

2. Russell believes a wide range of "impersonal interests" protects us from the potential devastation of misfortune. Is this borne out in your own experience?

▼ Vocabulary

astronomical	fallow	purview	volition
epoch	irreproachable	sagacity	well-ascertained
deplored	obscurantist	subsidiary	
dubious	prophylactic	vicissitudes	

51

▼

The Opening of American Minds

Richard Rorty

What should American colleges and universities aim to achieve? Richard Rorty, professor of humanities at the University of Virginia, argues here that ideally, the key function of American colleges would be to offer "provocations to self-creation." The essay was adapted from a speech given by Rorty to the American Association of Colleges in January, 1989.

When people on the political right talk about education, they immediately start talking about truth. Typically, they **enumerate** what they take to be familiar and self-evident truths and regret that these are no longer being **inculcated** in the young. When people on the political left talk about education, they talk first about freedom. The left typically views the old familiar truths cherished by the right as a crust to be broken through, **vestiges** of old-fashioned modes of thought from which the new generation should be freed.

When this opposition between truth and freedom becomes explicit, both sides wax philosophical and produce theories about the nature of truth and freedom. The right usually offers a theory according to which if you have truth, freedom will follow automatically. Human beings, says this theory, have within them a truth-tracking faculty called "reason," an instrument capable of uncovering the **intrinsic** nature of things. Once such obstacles as sin or the passions are overcome, the natural light of reason will guide us to the truth. Deep within our souls there is a spark that the right sort of education can fan into flame. Once the soul is afire with love of truth, freedom will follow—for freedom consists of realizing one's *true* self, that is, in the **actualization** of one's capacity to be rational. So, the right concludes, only the truth can make us free.

This Platonic picture of education as the awakening of the true self can easily be adapted to the needs of the left. The left dismisses Platonic **asceticism** and exalts Socratic social criticism. It identifies the obstacles to freedom that education must overcome not with sin or the passions but with convention and prejudice. What the right calls "overcoming the passions," the left calls "stifling healthy animal instincts." What the right thinks of as the triumph of reason, the left describes as the triumph of **acculturation**—acculturation engineered by the powers that be. What the right describes as civilizing the young, the left describes as **alienating** them from their true selves. So, for the left, the proper function of education is to make the young realize that they should not consent to this alienating process of socialization. In the leftist's inverted version of Plato, if you take care of freedom—truth will take care of itself. For truth is what will be believed once the alienating and repressive forces of society are removed.

In both the original, rightist, and the inverted, leftist, accounts of the matter, there is a natural connection between truth and freedom. Both argue for this connection on the basis of a distinction between nature and convention. Both accept the identification of truth and freedom with the essentially human. The difference between them is simply over the question: Is the present socioeconomic setup in accordance, more or less, with nature? Is it, on the whole, a realization of human

enumerate: to name or count off one by one

inculcated: instilled

vestiges: remainders or surviving evidences of some condition or practice

intrinsic: inherent; essential

actualization: the process of making actual one's potential

asceticism: self-denial

acculturation: the process of instilling culture in an individual

alienating: dissociating or estranging from the self

potentialities? Will acculturation to the norms of our society produce freedom or alienation?

On abstract philosophical topics, therefore, the right and the left are largely in agreement. The interesting differences between right and left about education are concretely political. Conservatives think that the present setup is, if not exactly good, at least better than any alternative suggested by the radical left. They think that at least some of the traditional slogans of our society, some pieces of its conventional wisdom, are the deliverances of "reason." That is why they think education should concentrate on resurrecting and re-establishing what they call "fundamental truths which are now neglected or despised." Radicals, in contrast, think that the society in which we live needs to be freed from the grip of those who now control it. So they consider the conservatives' "fundamental truths" to be what Michel Foucault called "the discourse of power." They think that continuing to inculcate the conventional wisdom amounts to betraying the students.

In the liberal democracies of recent times, the tension between these two attitudes has been resolved by a fairly simple, fairly satisfactory compromise. The right has pretty much kept control of primary and secondary education, and the left has gradually gotten control of nonvocational higher education. Thus, education up to the age of eighteen or nineteen is mostly a matter of socialization—of getting the students to take over the moral and political common sense of the society as it is. For any society has a right to expect that whatever else happens in the course of adolescence, the schools will inculcate most of what is generally believed.

Around the age of eighteen or nineteen, however, American students whose parents are **affluent** enough to send them to reasonably good colleges find themselves in the hands of teachers well to the left of the teachers they met in high school. These teachers do their best to nudge each successive college generation a little more to the left, to make them a little more conscious of the cruelty built into our institutions, of the need for reform, of the need to be skeptical about the current **consensus**.

This division means that most of the skirmishing about education between left and right occurs on the borders between secondary and higher education. Even ardent radicals, for all their talk of "education for freedom," secretly hope that elementary schools will teach the kids to wait their turn in line, to obey the cop on the corner, and to spell, punctuate, multiply, and divide. Conversely, only the most resentful and **blinkered** conservatives want to ensure that colleges hire only teachers who will endorse the status quo. Things get difficult only when one tries to figure out where socialization should stop and criticism begin.

The difficulty is aggravated by the fact that conservatives as well as radicals have trouble realizing that education is not a continuous process from age five to twenty-two. Both tend to ignore the fact that the word "education" covers two entirely distinct and equally necessary processes—socialization and **individuation**. Both conservatives and radicals fall into the trap of thinking that a single set of ideas will work for high school and college education. That is why both have had trouble noticing the differences between Allan Bloom's *The Closing of the American Mind* and E. D. Hirsch Jr.'s *Cultural Literacy*. The cultural left in America sees Bloom and Hirsch as examples of the same assault on freedom, twin symptoms of a **fatuous** Reaganite complacency. The conservatives overlook the difference between Bloom's Straussian doubts about democracy and Hirsch's Deweyan hopes for a better-educated democratic electorate: They think of both books as urging us to educate for truth and to worry less about freedom.

Let me now put some of my own cards on the table. I believe that Hirsch is largely right about the high schools and Bloom largely wrong about the colleges. I think that the conservatives are wrong in thinking that we have a truth-tracking faculty called "reason" or a true self that education brings to consciousness. I think that the radicals are right in saying that if you take care of political, economic,

affluent: rich or prosperous
consensus: general agreement; majority opinion
blinkered: blinded
individuation: the process of becoming an individual, a self
fatuous: silly or inane, especially in an unconscious manner

331

cultural, and academic freedom, then truth will take care of itself. But I think the radicals are wrong in believing that there is a true self that will emerge once the repressive influence of society is removed. There is no such thing as human nature, in the deep sense in which Plato and Leo Strauss use this term. Nor is there such a thing as alienation from one's essential humanity as a result of societal repression, in the deep sense of Rousseau and the Marxists. There is only the shaping of an animal into a human being by a process of socialization, followed (with luck) by the self-individualization and self-creation of that human being through his or her own later revolt against that very process.

The point of nonvocational higher education is to help students realize that they can reshape themselves—that they can rework the self-image foisted on them by their past, the self-image that makes them competent citizens, into a new self-image, one that they themselves have helped to create.

I take myself, in holding these opinions, to be a fairly faithful follower of John Dewey. Dewey put a new twist on the idea that if you take care of freedom, truth will take care of itself. For both the original Platonism of the right and the inverted Platonism of the left, that claim means that if you free the true self from various constraints it will automatically see truth.

Dewey showed us how to drop the notion of "the true self" and how to drop the distinction between nature and convention. He taught us to call "true" whatever belief results from a free and open encounter of opinions, without asking whether this result agrees with something beyond that encounter. For Dewey, the sort of freedom that guarantees truth is not freedom from sin or the passions. Nor is it freedom from tradition or from what Foucault called "power." It is simply sociopolitical freedom, the sort of freedom found in bourgeois democracies. Instead of justifying democratic freedoms by reference to an account of human nature and the nature of reason, Dewey takes the desire to preserve and expand such freedoms as a starting point—something we need not look behind.

Let me now turn to the topic of how a Deweyan conceives of the relation between precollege and college education, between the need for socialization and the need to remove the barriers that socialization inevitably imposes. Dewey hoped that the socialization of American children would consist of acquiring an image of themselves as heirs to a tradition of increasing liberty and rising hope. Updating Dewey a bit, we can think of him as wanting the children to come to think of themselves as proud and loyal citizens of a country that, slowly and painfully, threw off a foreign yoke, freed its slaves, enfranchised its women, restrained its robber barons and licensed its trade unions, liberalized its religious practices and broadened its religious and moral tolerance, and built colleges in which 50 percent of its population could enroll—a country that numbered Ralph Waldo Emerson, Eugene V. Debs, Susan B. Anthony, and James Baldwin among its citizens. Dewey wanted the inculcation of this narrative of freedom and hope to be the core of the socializing process.

As Hirsch quite rightly says, that narrative will not be **intelligible** unless a lot of information gets piled up in our children's heads. That is why I maintain Hirsch is right about the high schools. Now suppose that someday the high schools succeed not only in inculcating this narrative of national hope in most of our students but in setting it in the larger context of a narrative of world history and literature, all this against the background of the world picture offered by the natural sciences. What, in such a utopia, would be the educational function of American colleges? I would argue that it would be to offer **provocations** to self-creation.

Socially, the most important provocations will be offered by teachers who make vivid and concrete the failure of the country of which we remain loyal citizens to live up to its own ideals—the failure of America to be what it knows it ought to become. This is the traditional function of the reformist liberal left, as opposed to the revolutionary radical left. Carrying out this function, however, cannot be

intelligible: capable of being understood

provocations: instigations; things that incite

332

made a matter of explicit institutional policy. For if it is being done right, it is too complicated, controversial, and **tendentious** to be the subject of agreement in a faculty meeting. It is a matter that has to be left up to individual college teachers to do or not do as they think fit, as their sense of responsibility to their students and their society inspires them.

In short, if the high schools were doing the job that lots of money and determination might make them able to do, the colleges would not have to worry about Great Books or general education or overcoming fragmentation. The faculty could simply teach whatever seemed good to them to teach, and the administrators could get along nicely without much knowledge of what was being taught.

We Deweyans think that the social function of American colleges is to help the students see that the national narrative around which their socialization has centered is an open-ended one. It is to tempt the students to make themselves into people who can stand to their own pasts as Emerson and Anthony, Debs and Baldwin, stood to their pasts. This is done by helping the students realize that despite the progress that the present has made over the past, the good has once again become the enemy of the better. With a bit of help, the students will start noticing everything that is paltry and mean and unfree in their surroundings. With luck, the best of them will succeed in altering the conventional wisdom, so that the next generation is socialized in a somewhat different way than they themselves were socialized. To hope that this way will be only somewhat different is to hope that the society will remain reformist and democratic, rather than be convulsed by revolution. To hope that it will nevertheless be **perceptibly** different is to hope that our country never becomes satisfied with itself.

tendentious: promoting a particular point of view
perceptibly: observably

▼ Questions to Focus Reading

1. In regard to education what, according to Rorty, is the main concern of the right? Of the left?

2. What, according to the political right, is the relation between truth and freedom, as Rorty sees it?

3. What is the proper function of education according to the political left? What is the relation between truth and freedom in Rorty's depiction of their view?

4. What does Rorty suggest are the points of similarity between the right and the left in regard to truth and freedom? On what key point are they in disagreement?

5. What compromise, according to Rorty, has resolved the tensions in the educational philosophies of right and left?

6. What, in Rorty's view, is the common error of right and left regarding the word "education"?

7. "I think that the radicals are right in saying that if you take care of political, economic, cultural, and academic freedom, then truth will take care of itself." What do you think this means?

8. On what key points is Rorty in disagreement with both the conservatives and the radicals?
9. What, according to Rorty, is the purpose of nonvocational higher education?
10. What were Dewey's teachings about truth and about freedom?
11. What was Dewey's view of what should be inculcated in young Americans in their socialization?
12. What is the proper task of the high schools, in Rorty's view?
13. If the high school were performing their proper task as Rorty conceives it, what in his view would be the educational function of the colleges?
14. What "provocations" will be the most important socially, according to Rorty (page 332)?
15. Why, in Rorty's view, would the improvement of the high schools make it unnecessary for American colleges to concern themselves with Great Books or general education or fragmentation?
16. "We Deweyans think that the social function of American colleges is to help the students see that the national narrative around which their socialization has centered is an open-ended one." What do you think Rorty means by this?

▼ Questions for Reflection

1. In their philosophies of education, Rorty asserts, both leftist and rightist are concerned with the relation between truth and freedom. How does the rightist understand this connection? How does the leftist understand it?
2. What are the key obstacles to freedom, as understood by the rightist? By the leftist? Who do you think is right about this? Explain.
3. What, according to Rorty, is the key point of dispute between the right and the left in regard to education? How has this tension been resolved in America?
4. "Both conservatives and radicals fall into the trap of thinking that a single set of ideas will work for high school and college education," Rorty writes. Why is this a "trap," in Rorty's view? Do you think he is right in believing this thinking is a mistake? Explain.
5. Rorty disagrees with both left and right in regard to the nature of the self. Explain the disagreement. Do you think Rorty is right about this? Explain.
6. What is Rorty's view of the proper task of the high schools? As you understood it, how did your high school conceive of its task? If faculty and administration at your high school had adopted Rorty's view, how would your high school education have been different? Would this have been better or worse? Explain.
7. What is Rorty's view of the point of nonvocational higher education? What do you suppose this would mean in practice; for example, what courses would be taught? How would they be taught? Do any of your present courses seem to be following this plan? What is your own opinion of this conception of higher education?
8. Explain Rorty's title.
9. Imagine a dialogue between Richard Rorty, Norman Peterson, and Robert Maynard Hutchins on the purpose of higher education.

▼ Discussion

1. If Rorty is right, those on the political right and those on the political left in America are equally concerned about freedom. But each has a different conception of what freedom is, what we must become free from. What are these different conceptions? What, in your view, is freedom? What are the characteristics of the free person?
2. What seemed to be the philosophy—the overall conception of purpose guiding your high school? Consider Rorty's ideas about what the high schools should do. If your high school education would have been guided by Rorty's ideas, how would it have been different? Would that have been an improvement?
3. Rorty disputes both left and right in regard to the concept of the self. What is Rorty's conception? Is there any reason to believe he is right? What arguments might be made against this conception? For which side can the stronger case be made?
4. "In short, if the high schools were doing the job that lots of money and determination might make them able to do, the colleges would not have to worry about Great Books or general education or overcoming fragmentation." What do you think Rorty means by this sentence? What reasons might he have for believing this? Is he right?
5. What is Rorty's conception of the highest purpose of American higher education? What, in your view, should the high schools aim to achieve? What should be the aim of the colleges?
6. Imagine Rorty, Hutchins, and Peterson discussing the aims of higher education. On what points would they be in agreement? Where would they differ?

▼ Writing Assignments

1. What are Rorty's conceptions of the proper tasks of high schools and colleges? If you were responsible for establishing the basic missions for American high schools and colleges, what would be the focus of each?
2. "What Is 'the True Self'?" Present Rorty's view on this, and then present your reaction to his views.
3. "The Purpose of a University Education: A Dialogue between Hutchins, Peterson, and Rorty"
4. "What Colleges and Universities Should Aim for"

▼ Journal Entries

1. How would you evaluate your college education to date using Rorty's ideal of "provocations to self-creation"?
2. Rorty thinks that a college student in the ideal case becomes sensitive to the ways in which America has failed "to be what it knows it ought to become." Do you think this is a proper expectation of a college education? Is it happening to you?

▼ **Vocabulary**

acculturation	blinkered	individuation	tendentious
actualization	consensus	intelligible	vestiges
affluent	enumerate	intrinsic	
alienating	fatuous	perceptibly	
asceticism	inculcated	provocations	

Originally printed in <u>The University in Your Life</u>. McGraw Hill, 1996.

Reprint Permission Granted via Copyright Clearance Center.

52

Going Home Again

Richard Rodriguez

In the previous essay, Richard Rorty focused on the opportunity that the university provides for self-creation. In this essay, Richard Rodriguez discusses a problem that arose for him in relation to this opportunity. For the identity he found himself creating at the university put him at a painful distance from his own family.

At each step, with every graduation from one level of education to the next, the refrain from bystanders was strangely the same: "Your parents must be so proud of you." I suppose that my parents were proud, although I suspect, too, that they felt more than pride alone as they watched me advance through my education. They seemed to know that my education was separating us from one another, making it difficult to resume familiar intimacies. Mixed with the instincts of parental pride, a certain hurt also communicated itself—too private ever to be adequately expressed in words, but real nonetheless.

The autobiographical facts pertinent to this essay are simply stated in two sentences, though they exist in somewhat awkward **juxtaposition** to each other. I am the son of Mexican-American parents, who speak a blend of Spanish and English, but who read neither language easily. I am about to receive a Ph.D. in English Renaissance literature. What sort of life—what tensions, feelings, conflicts—connects these two sentences? I look back and remember my life from the time I was seven or eight years old as one of constant movement away from a Spanish-speaking folk culture toward the world of the English language classroom. As the years passed, I felt myself becoming less like my parents and less comfortable with the assumption of visiting relatives that I was still the Spanish-speaking child they remembered. By the time I began college, visits home became **suffused** with silent embarrassment: there seemed so little to share, however strong the ties of our affection. My parents would tell me what happened in their lives or in the lives of relatives; I would respond with news of my own. Polite questions would follow. Our conversations came to seem more like interviews.

A few months ago, my **dissertation** nearly complete, I came upon my father looking through my bookcase. He quietly fingered the volumes of Milton's tracts and Augustine's theology with that combination of reverence and distrust those who are not literate sometimes show for the written word. Silently, I watched him from the door of the room. However much he would have insisted that he was "proud" of his son for being able to master the texts, I knew, if pressed further, he would have admitted to complicated feelings about my success. When he looked across the room and suddenly saw me, his body tightened slightly with surprise, then we both smiled.

For many years I kept my uneasiness about becoming a success in education to myself. I did so in part because I wanted to avoid vague feelings that, if considered carefully, I would have no way of dealing with; and in part because I felt that no one else shared my reaction to the opportunity provided by education. When I began to rehearse my story of cultural dislocation publicly, however, I found many listeners willing to admit to similar feelings from their own pasts. Equally impressive was the fact that many among those I spoke with were *not*

juxtaposition: placing side by side

suffused: pervaded (by)

dissertation: a book-length work written by a candidate for a doctoral degree

from nonwhite racial groups, which made me realize that one can grow up to enter the culture of the academy and find it a "foreign" culture for a variety of reasons, ranging from economic status to religious heritage. But why, I next wondered, was it that, though there were so many of us who came from childhood cultures alien to the academy's, we voiced our uneasiness to one another and to ourselves so infrequently? Why did it take *me* so long to acknowledge publicly the cultural costs I had paid to earn a Ph.D. in Renaissance English literature? Why, more precisely, am I writing these words only now when my connection to my past barely survives except as nostalgic memory?

Looking back, a person risks losing hold of the present while being confounded by the past. For the child who moves to an academic culture from a culture that dramatically lacks academic traditions, looking back can jeopardize the certainty he has about the desirability of this new academic culture. Richard Hoggart's description, in *The Uses of Literacy,* of the cultural pressures on such a student, whom Hoggart calls the "scholarship boy," helps make the point. The scholarship boy must give nearly unquestioning allegiance to academic culture, Hoggart argues, if he is to succeed at all, so different is the **milieu** of the classroom from the culture he leaves behind. For a time, the scholarship boy may try to balance his loyalty between his concretely experienced family life and the more abstract mental life of the classroom. In the end, though, he must choose between the two worlds: if he intends to succeed as a student, he must, literally and **figuratively**, separate himself from his family, with its **gregarious** life, and find a quiet place to be alone with his thoughts.

After a while, the kind of allegiance the young student might once have given his parents is transferred to the teacher, the new parent. Now without the support of the old ties and certainties of the family, he almost mechanically acquires the assumptions, practices, and style of the classroom milieu. For the loss he might otherwise feel, the scholarship boy substitutes an enormous enthusiasm for nearly everything having to do with school.

How readily I read my own past into the portrait of Hoggart's scholarship boy. Coming from a home in which mostly Spanish was spoken, for example, I had to decide to forget Spanish when I began my education. To succeed in the classroom, I needed psychologically to sever my ties with Spanish. Spanish represented an alternate culture as well as another language—and the basis of my deepest sense of relationship to my family. Although I recently taught myself to read Spanish, the language that I see on the printed page is not quite the language I heard in my youth. That other Spanish, the spoken Spanish of my family, I remember with nostalgia and guilt: guilt because I cannot explain to aunts and uncles why I do not answer their questions any longer in their own **idiomatic** language. Nor was I able to explain to teachers in graduate school, who regularly expected me to read and speak Spanish with ease, why my very ability to reach graduate school as a student of English literature in the first place required me to loosen my attachments to a language I spoke years earlier. Yet, having lost the ability to speak Spanish, I never forgot it so totally that I could not understand it. Hearing Spanish spoken on the street reminded me of the community I once felt a part of, and still cared deeply about. I never forgot Spanish so thoroughly, in other words, as to move outside the range of its nostalgic pull.

Such moments of guilt and nostalgia were, however, just that—momentary. They punctuated the history of my otherwise successful progress from *barrio* to classroom. Perhaps they even encouraged it. Whenever I felt my determination to succeed wavering, I tightened my hold on the **conventions** of academic life.

Spanish was one aspect of the problem, my parents another. They could raise deeper, more persistent doubts. They offered encouragement to my brothers and me in our work, but they also spoke, only half jokingly, about the way education was putting "big ideas" into our heads. When we would come home, for example,

milieu: environment

figuratively: in the manner of a figure of speech; symbolically

gregarious: enjoying others' company

idiomatic: pertaining to a dialect or style of speaking peculiar to a people

barrio: an Hispanic ghetto in an American city

conventions: widely observed practices

and challenge assumptions we earlier believed, they would be forced to defend their beliefs (which, given our new verbal skills, they did increasingly less well) or, more frequently, to submit to our logic with the **disclaimer**, "It's what we were taught in our time to believe...." More important, after we began to leave home for college, they voiced regret about how "changed" we had become, how much further away from one another we had grown. They partly yearned for a return to the time before education assumed their children's primary loyalty. This yearning was renewed each time they saw their nieces and nephews (none of whom continued their education beyond high school, all of whom continued to speak fluent Spanish) living according to the conventions and assumptions of their parents' culture. If I was already troubled by the time I graduated from high school by that refrain of congratulations ("Your parents must be so proud...."), I realize now how much more difficult and complicated was my progress into academic life for my parents, as they saw the cultural foundation of their family erode, than it was for me.

Yet my parents were willing to pay the price of **alienation** and continued to encourage me to become a scholarship boy because they perceived, as others of the lower class had before them, the relation between education and social mobility. Lacking the former themselves made them acutely aware of its necessity as prerequisite for the latter. They sent their children off to school in hopes of their acquiring something "better" beyond education. Notice the assumption here that education is something of a tool or license—a means to an end, which has been the traditional way the lower or working classes have viewed the value of education in the past. That education might alter children in more basic ways than providing them with skills, certificates of proficiency, and even upward mobility, may come as a surprise for some, but the financial cost is usually tolerated....

Too often in the last ten years one heard minority group students repeat the joke, never very funny in the first place, about the racial minority academic who ended up sounding more "white" than white academics. Behind the scorn for such a figure was the belief that the new generation of minority group students would be able to avoid having to make similar kinds of cultural concessions. The pressures that might have led to such conformity went unexamined.

For the last few years my annoyance at hearing such jokes was doubtless related to the fact that I was increasingly beginning to sense that I was the "bleached" academic the minority group students found so laughable. I suppose I had always sensed that my cultural allegiance was undergoing subtle alterations as I was being educated. Only when I finished my course work in graduate school and went off to England for my dissertation year did I grasp how far I had traveled from my cultural origins. My year in England was actually my first opportunity to write and reflect upon the kind of material that I would spend my life producing. It was my first chance, too, to be free simultaneously of the distractions of course work and of the insecurities of trying to find my niche in academic life. Sitting in the reading room of the British Museum, I no longer doubted that I had joined academic society. Ironically, this feeling of having finally arrived allowed me to look back to the community whence I came. That I was geographically farther away from my home than I had ever been lent a **metaphorical resonance** to the cultural distance I suddenly felt.

But that feeling was not pleasing. The reward of feeling a part of the world of the British Museum was an odd one. Each morning I would arrive at the reading room and grow increasingly depressed by the silence and what the silence implied—that my life as a scholar would require self-absorption. Who, I wondered, would find my work helpful enough to want to read it? Was not my dissertation— whose title alone would puzzle my relatives—only my grandest exercise thus far in self-enclosure? The sight of the heads around me bent over their texts and papers, many so thoroughly engrossed that they wouldn't look up at the silent

disclaimer: a denial of responsibility; disavowal
alienation: dissociation; estrangement
metaphorical: symbolic
resonance: echoing

339

clock overhead for hours at a stretch, made me recall the remarkable noises of life in my family home. The tedious prose I was writing, a prose constantly qualified by footnotes, reminded me of the capacity for passionate statement those of the culture I was born into commanded—and which, could it be, I had now lost.

As I remembered it during those gray English afternoons, the past rushed forward to define more precisely my present condition. Remembering my youth, a time when I was not restricted to a chair but ran barefoot under a summer sun that tightened my skin with its white heat, made the fact that it was only my mind that "moved" each hour in the library painfully obvious.

I did need to figure out where I had lost touch with my past. I started to become alien to my family culture the day I became a scholarship boy. In the British Museum the realization seemed obvious. But later, returning to America, I returned to minority group students who were still speaking of their cultural ties to their past. How was I to tell them what I had learned about myself in England? . . .

There is a danger of being misunderstood here. I am not suggesting that an academic cannot re-establish ties of any kind with his old culture. Indeed, he can have an impact on the culture of his childhood. But as an academic, one exists by definition in a culture separate from one's nonacademic roots and, therefore, any future ties one has with those who remain "behind" are complicated by one's new cultural perspective.

Paradoxically, the distance separating the academic from his nonacademic past can make his past seem, if not closer, then clearer. It is possible for the academic to understand the culture from which he came "better" than those who still live within it. In my own experience, it has only been as I have come to appraise my past through categories and notions derived from the social sciences that I have been able to think of Chicano life in cultural terms at all. Characteristics I took for granted or noticed only in passing—the spontaneity, the passionate speech, the trust in concrete experience, the willingness to think communally rather than individually—these are all significant phenomena to me now as aspects of a total culture. (My parents have neither the time nor the inclination to think about their culture as a culture.) Able to **conceptualize** a sense of Chicano culture, I am now also more attracted to that culture than I was before. The temptation now is to try to preserve those traits of my old culture that have not yet, in effect, **atrophied**.

The racial self-consciousness of minority group students during the last few years evident in the ethnic costumes, the stylized gestures, and the idiomatic though often evasive devices for insisting on one's continuing membership in the community of the past, are also indications that the minority group student has gained a new appreciation of the culture of his origin precisely because of his earlier alienation from it. As a result, Chicano students sometimes become more Chicano than most Chicanos. I remember, for example, my father's surprise when, walking across my college campus one afternoon, we came upon two Chicano academics wearing **serapes**. He and my mother were also surprised—indeed offended—when they earlier heard student activists use the word "Chicano." For them the term was a private one, primarily descriptive of persons they knew. It suggested intimacy. Hearing the word shouted into a microphone by a stranger left them bewildered. What they could not understand was that the student activist finds it easier than they to use "Chicano" in a more public way, for his distance from their culture and his membership in academic culture permit a wider and more abstract view.

The Mexican-Americans who begin to call themselves Chicanos in this new way are actually forming a new version of what it means to be a Chicano. The culture that didn't see itself as a culture is suddenly prized and identified for being one. The price one pays for this new self-consciousness is the knowledge of just that—it is *new*—and this knowledge is not available to those who remain at home. So it is knowledge that separates as well as unites people. Wanting more desperately than ever to assert his ties with the newly visible culture, the minority group student

paradoxically: in a seemingly contradictory manner

conceptualize: form a concept of

atrophied: wasted away

serapes: blanket-like shawls worn especially in Mexico

is tempted to exploit those characteristics of that culture that might yet survive in him. But the self-consciousness never allows one to feel completely at ease with the old culture. Worse, the knowledge of the culture of the past often leaves one feeling strangely solitary. At home, I hear relatives speak and find myself analyzing too much of what they say. It is embarrassing being a cultural anthropologist in one's own family kitchen. I keep feeling myself little more than a cultural **voyeur**. I often come away from family gatherings suspecting, in fact, that what conventions of my culture I carry with me are no more than illusions. Because they were never there before, because no one back home shares them, I grow less and less to trust their reliability; too often they seem no more than mental bubbles floating before an academic's eye.

Many who have taught minority group students in the last decade testify to sensing characteristics of a childhood culture still very much alive in these students. Should the teacher make these students aware of these characteristics? Initially, most of us would probably answer negatively. Better to trust the unconscious survival of the past than the always problematical, sometimes even clownish, re-creations of it. But the cultural past cannot be assured of survival; perhaps many of its characteristics are lost simply because the student is never encouraged to look for them. Even those that do survive do so **tenuously**. As a teacher, one can only hope that the best qualities in his minority group students' cultural legacy aren't altogether snuffed out by academic education.

More easy to live with and distinguishable from self-conscious awareness of the past are the ways the past unconsciously survives—perhaps even yet survives in me. As it turns out, the issue becomes less acute with time. With each year, the chance that the student is unaware of his cultural legacy is diminished as the habit of academic reflectiveness grows stronger. Although the culture of the academy makes innocence about one's cultural past less likely, this same culture, and the conceptual tools it provides, increases the desire to want to write and speak about the past. The paradox persists.

Awaiting the scholarship boy who finally acknowledges the fact that his perceptions of reality have changed is the **dilemma** of action. The sentimental reaction to this knowledge entails merely a refusal to renew contact with one's nonacademic culture lest one contaminate it. The problem, however, with this sentimental solution is that it overlooks the way academic culture renders one capable of dealing with the transactions of mass society. Academic culture, with its habits of conceptualization and abstraction, allows those of us from other cultures to deal with each other in a mass society. In this sense academic culture does have a profound political impact. Although people intent upon social mobility think of education as a means to an end, education does become an end: its culture allows one to exist more easily in a society increasingly anonymous and impersonal. The truth is, the academic's distance from his own experience brings the capacity for communicating with bureaucracies and understanding one's position in society—a prerequisite for political action.

If the sentimental reaction to nonacademic culture is to fear changing it, the political response, typical especially of working-class and lately minority group leaders, is to see higher education solely in terms of its political and social possibilities. Its cultural consequences, in this view, are disregarded. At this time when we are so keenly aware of social and economic inequality, it might seem beside the point to warn those who are working to bring about equality that education alters culture as well as economic status. And yet, if there is one main criticism that I, as a minority group student, must make of minority group leaders in their past attacks on the "racism" of the academy, it is that they never distinguished between my right to higher education and the desirability of my actually entering the academy—which is another way of saying again that they never recognized that there were things I could lose by becoming a scholarship boy.

voyeur: one who derives sexual gratification by secretly observing sexual acts
tenuously: weakly
dilemma: perplexing situation

Certainly, the academy changes those from alien cultures more than it is changed by them. While minority groups had an impact on higher education, largely because of their advantage in coming as a group, within the last few years students such as myself, who finally ended up certified as academics, also ended up sounding very much like the academics we found when we came to the campus. I do not enjoy making such admissions. But perhaps now the time has come when questions about the cultural costs of education ought to be delayed no longer. Those of us who have been scholarship boys know in our bones that our education has exacted a large price in exchange for the large benefits it has conferred upon us. And what is sadder to consider, after we have paid that price, we go home and casually change the cultures that nurtured us. My parents today understand how they are "Chicanos" in a large and impersonal sense. The gains from such knowledge are clear. But so, too, are the reasons for regret.

▼ Questions to Focus Reading

1. Why was it so hard for Rodriguez to acknowledge publicly the cultural dislocation that had been the cost of his membership in academe?
2. Why did he feel he needed to sever his ties with Spanish?
3. In what ways did his parents raise persistent doubts about his pursuit of higher education?
4. While writing his doctoral dissertation in England, Rodriguez has his clearest perceptions of the contrasts between the academic culture he has chosen and the culture of his upbringing. What were these contrasts? How did his being in England facilitate these reflections?
5. "It is possible for the academic to understand the culture from which he came 'better' than those who still live within it." Why is this?
6. The Mexican American students who become conscious of their culture find a new basis for connection with it, Rodriguez tells us, but they are also irremediably separated from it. In what sense are they separated?
7. As a result of his cultural awareness, his parents, too, now understand "how they are 'Chicanos' in a large and impersonal sense." What new understanding do his parents have? Rodriguez writes, "The gains from such knowledge are clear. But so, too, are the reasons for regret." What are the gains? What are the reasons for regret?

▼ Questions for Reflection

1. Mixed with their pride, Rodriguez writes of his parents, was a certain hurt at the way his education was separating him from them. Is your own experience with your parents in any way comparable to this? Later in the essay, he speaks of his embarrassment at being a "cultural anthropologist" in his own family kitchen, at being a "cultural voyeur" in his family's house. Have you experienced anything like this since being away at college?
2. Rodriguez sees this separation as inevitable for the "scholarship boy." Is it inevitable in your view?
3. For a surprising number of his fellow students, including many whites, the culture of the academy was felt as something "foreign." Is that how the academic environment feels to you? If so, in what respects?
4. How would you describe your own cultural background? Would that background present you with difficulties comparable to those experienced by Rodriguez if you were to pursue a life in academe? Explain.

▼ Discussion

1. How would you describe Rodriguez's problem as a "scholarship boy"?
2. Was the alienation he experienced from his own culture indeed inevitable?
3. When you go home, do you find yourself becoming a "cultural anthropologist" in your own family living room? If so, what are the characteristics of the culture you are now observing?

▼ Writing Assignments

1. Has your identity within your family been changing since you've been in college? If so, in what respects?
2. Rodriguez describes the ambivalence his parents felt toward his success in college: simultaneous pride and regret. Is there anything comparable in your own parents' reactions to your developing identity? If so, depict incidents that illustrate their complex feelings.

▼ Journal Entry

1. Characterize the culture of your background. In what respects is your own identity indebted to this culture?

▼ Vocabulary

alienation	dilemma	idiomatic	resonance
atrophied	disclaimer	juxtaposition	serapes
barrio	dissertation	metaphorical	suffused
conceptualize	figuratively	milieu	tenuously
conventions	gregarious	paradoxically	voyeur

53

▼

Living in Two Worlds

Marcus Mabry

Marcus Mabry, a student at Stanford when he wrote this article in 1988, describes the harsh contrast between his world at the university and his world at home, a contrast that arouses embarrassment, guilt, and a sense of helplessness.

A round, green cardboard sign hangs from a string proclaiming, "We built a proud new feeling," the slogan of a local supermarket. It is a souvenir from one of my brother's last jobs. In addition to being a bagger, he's worked at a fast-food restaurant, a gas station, a garage and a textile factory. Now, in the icy clutches of the Northeastern winter, he is unemployed. He will soon be a father. He is 19 years old.

In mid-December I was at Stanford, among the palm trees and weighty chores of **academe**. And all I wanted to do was get out. I joined the rest of the undergrads in a chorus of excitement, singing the praises of Christmas break. No classes, no midterms, no finals . . . and no freshmen! (I'm a resident assistant.) Awesome! I was looking forward to escaping. I never gave a thought to what I was escaping to.

Once I got home to New Jersey, reality returned. My dreaded freshmen had been replaced by unemployed relatives; **badgering** professors had been replaced by hard-working single mothers, and cold classrooms by **dilapidated** bedrooms and kitchens. The room in which the "proud new feeling" sign hung contained the belongings of myself, my mom and my brother. But for these two weeks it was mine. They slept downstairs on couches.

Most students who travel between the universes of poverty and **affluence** during breaks experience similar conditions, as well as the guilt, the helplessness and, sometimes, the embarrassment associated with them. Our friends are willing to listen, but most of them are unable to imagine the pain of the impoverished lives that we see every six months. Each time I return home I feel further away from the realities of poverty in America and more ashamed that they are allowed to persist. What frightens me most is not that the American socioeconomic system permits poverty to continue, but that by participating in that system I share some of the blame.

Last year I lived in an on-campus apartment, with a (relatively) modern bathroom, kitchen and two bedrooms. Using summer earnings, I added some expensive prints, a potted palm and some other plants, making the place look like the more-than-humble **abode** of a New York City Yuppie. I gave dinner parties, even a *soirée française*.

For my roommate, a doctor's son, this kind of life was nothing extraordinary. But my mom was struggling to provide a life for herself and my brother. In addition to working 24-hour-a-day cases as a practical nurse, she was trying to ensure that my brother would graduate from high school and have a decent life. She knew that she had to compete for his attention with drugs and other potentially dangerous things that can look attractive to a young man when he sees no better future.

Living in my grandmother's house this Christmas break restored all the forgotten, and the never acknowledged, guilt. I had gone to boarding school on a full

academe: the world of the university

badgering: pestering; nagging

dilapidated: reduced to decay or ruin

affluence: wealth

abode: dwelling

soirée française: an elegant party in the French style

scholarship since the ninth grade, so being away from poverty was not new. But my own growing affluence has increased my distance. My friends say that I should not feel guilty: what could I do substantially for my family at this age, they ask. Even though I know that education is the right thing to do, I can't help but feel, sometimes, that I have it too good. There is no reason that I deserve security and warmth, while my brother has to cope with potential unemployment and prejudice. I, too, encounter prejudice, but it is softened by my status as a student in an affluent and intellectual community.

More than my sense of guilt, my sense of helplessness increases each time I return home. As my success leads me further away for longer periods of time, poverty becomes harder to **conceptualize** and feels that much more oppressive when I visit with it. The first night of break, I lay in our bedroom, on a couch that let out into a bed that took up the whole room, except for a space heater. It was a little hard to sleep because the springs from the couch stuck through at inconvenient spots. But it would have been impossible to sleep anyway because of the groans coming from my grandmother's room next door. Only in her early 60s, she suffers from many chronic diseases and couldn't help but moan, then pray aloud, then moan, then pray aloud.

This **wrenching** of my heart was interrupted by the 3 A.M. entry of a relative who had been allowed to stay at the house despite rowdy behavior and threats toward the family in the past. As he came into the house, he slammed the door, and his heavy steps shook the second floor as he stomped into my grandmother's room to take his place, at the foot of her bed. There he slept, without blankets on a bare mattress. This was the first night. Later in the vacation, a Christmas turkey and a Christmas ham were stolen from my aunt's refrigerator on Christmas Eve. We think the thief was a relative. My mom and I decided not to exchange gifts that year because it just didn't seem festive.

A few days after New Year's I returned to California. The Northeast was soon hit by a blizzard. They were there, and I was here. That was the way it had to be, for now. I haven't forgotten; the ache of knowing their suffering is always there. It has to be kept deep down, or I can't find the logic in studying and partying while people, my people, are being killed by poverty. Ironically, success drives me away from those I most want to help by getting an education.

Somewhere in the midst of all that misery, my family has built, within me, "a proud feeling." As I travel between the two worlds it becomes harder to remember just how proud I should be—not just because of where I have come from and where I am going, but because of where they are. The fact that they survive in the world in which they live is something to be very proud of, indeed. It inspires within me a sense of **tenacity** and accomplishment that I hope every college graduate will someday possess.

conceptualize: to form a concept (of)
wrenching: forceful pulling away
tenacity: persistence

▼ Questions to Focus Reading

1. When Mabry returns home during breaks, he experiences guilt, helplessness, and embarrassment. What are the sources of his guilt?
2. What specific experiences lead him to feel helpless?
3. How does he deal with these feelings when he returns to school?
4. The slogan he quotes in his ironic first paragraph reappears in his last. How has his family built within him a "proud feeling"?

▼ Questions for Reflection

1. What do you think he means by the "embarrassment" associated with the abject poverty of his home life?

2. Marcus Mabry and Richard Rodriguez both discuss the contrast between the two main worlds to which they belong, and both describe the feelings that living in these two worlds provokes in them. But there are several significant differences in their focus and in the feelings they describe. What are the differences?

▼ Journal Entries

1. Is there some sense in which your hometown life—whether with your family or with your old high school friends—seems to be a different world from your world at the university? If so, what are the prominent differences and what feelings do they provoke in you?

2. Has being away at college given you a new perspective on your home life? If so, what insights have you had into that home life?

▼ Vocabulary

abode	badgering	*soirée française*
academe	conceptualize	tenacity
affluence	dilapidated	wrenching

54

▼

A Never-Ending Story

Frank Conroy

Sometimes understanding comes with a belated click of resolution. Sometimes it comes in small doses, spread through a lifetime, never achieving resolution. Novelist Frank Conroy illustrates his points about how we learn with vivid portraits from his youth.

When I was sixteen I worked selling hot dogs at a stand in the Fourteenth Street subway station in New York City, one level above the trains and one below the street, where the crowds continually flowed back and forth. I worked with three Puerto Rican men who could not speak English. I had no Spanish, and although we understood each other well with regard to the tasks at hand, sensing and adjusting to each other's body movements in the extremely confined space in which we operated, I felt isolated with no one to talk to. On my break I came out from behind the counter and passed the time with two old black men who ran a shoeshine stand in a dark corner of the corridor. It was a poor location, half hidden by columns, and they didn't have much business. I would sit with my back against the wall while they stood or moved around their ancient elevated stand, talking to each other or to me, but always staring into the distance as they did so.

As the weeks went by I realized that they never looked at anything in their immediate vicinity—not me or their stand or anybody who might come within ten or fifteen feet. They did not look at approaching customers once they were inside the perimeter. Save for the instant it took to discern the color of the shoes, they did not even look at what they were doing while they worked, but rubbed in polish, brushed, and buffed by feel while looking over their shoulders, into the distance, as if awaiting the arrival of an important person. Of course there wasn't all that much distance in the underground station, but their behavior was so focused and consistent they seemed somehow to **transcend** the physical. A powerful mood was created, and I came almost to believe that these men could see through walls, through girders, and around corners to whatever **hyperspace** it was where whoever it was they were waiting and watching for would finally emerge. Their scattered talk was hip, **elliptical**, and hinted at mysteries beyond my white boy's **ken**, but it was the staring off, the long, steady staring off, that had me hypnotized. I left for a better job, with handshakes from both of them, without understanding what I had seen.

Perhaps ten years later, after playing jazz with black musicians in various Harlem clubs, hanging out uptown with a few young artists and intellectuals, I began to learn from them something of the extraordinarily varied and complex **riffs** and rituals embraced by different people to help themselves get through life in the ghetto. Fantasy of all kinds—from playful to dangerous—was in the very air of Harlem. It was the spice of uptown life.

Only then did I understand the two shoeshine men. They were trapped in a demeaning situation in a dark corner in an underground corridor in a filthy subway system. Their continuous staring off was a kind of statement, a kind of dance. Our bodies are here, went the statement, but our souls are receiving nourishment from

transcend: to go beyond

hyperspace: a mathematical term used here metaphorically to mean mysterious space

elliptical: not fully elaborated

ken: range or vision

riffs: constantly repeated melodic phrases that form an accompaniment to a jazz soloist

distant sources only we can see. They were powerful magic dancers, sorcerers almost, and thirty-five years later I can still feel the pressure of their spell.

The light bulb may appear over your head, is what I'm saying, but it may be a while before it actually goes on. Early in my attempts to learn jazz piano, I used to listen to recordings of a fine player named Red Garland, whose music I admired. I couldn't quite figure out what he was doing with his left hand, however; the chords **eluded** me. I went uptown to an obscure club where he was playing with his trio, caught him on his break, and simply asked him. "Sixths," he said cheerfully. And then he went away.

I didn't know what to make of it. The basic jazz chord is the seventh, which comes in various **configurations**, but it is what it is. I was a self-taught pianist, pretty shaky on theory and harmony, and when he said sixths I kept trying to fit the information into what I already knew, and it didn't fit. But it stuck in my mind—a **tantalizing** mystery.

A couple of years later, when I began playing with a bass player, I discovered more or less by accident that if the bass played the root and I played a sixth based on the fifth note of the scale, a very interesting chord involving both instruments emerged. Ordinarily, I suppose I would have skipped over the matter and not paid much attention, but I remembered Garland's remark and so I stopped and spent a week or two working out the **voicings**, and greatly strengthened my foundations as a player. I had remembered what I hadn't understood, you might say, until my life caught up with the information and the light bulb went on.

I remember another, more complicated example from my sophomore year at a small liberal arts college outside Philadelphia. I seemed never to be able to get up in time for breakfast in the dining hall. I would get coffee and a doughnut in the Coop instead—a basement area with about a dozen small tables where students could get something to eat at odd hours. Several mornings in a row I noticed a strange man sitting by himself with a cup of coffee. He was in his sixties, perhaps, and sat straight in his chair with very little **extraneous** movement. I guessed he was some sort of distinguished visitor to the college who had decided to put in some time at a student hangout. But no one ever sat with him. One morning I approached his table and asked if I could join him.

"Certainly," he said. "Please do." He had perhaps the clearest eyes I had ever seen, like blue ice, and to be held in their steady gaze was not, at first, an entirely comfortable experience. His eyes gave nothing away about himself while at the same time creating in me the eerie impression that he was looking directly into my soul. He asked a few quick questions, as if to put me at my ease, and we fell into conversation. He was William O. Douglas from the Supreme Court, and when he saw how startled I was he said, "Call me Bill. Now tell me what you're studying and why you get up so late in the morning." Thus began a series of talks that stretched over many weeks. The fact that I was an ignorant sophomore with literary **pretensions** who knew nothing about the law didn't seem to bother him. We talked about everything from Shakespeare to the possibility of life on other planets. One day I mentioned that I was going to have dinner with Judge Learned Hand. I explained that Hand was my girlfriend's grandfather. Douglas nodded, but I could tell he was surprised at the coincidence of my knowing the chief judge of the most important court in the country save the Supreme Court itself. After fifty years on the bench Judge Hand had become a famous man, both in and out of legal circles—a living legend, to his own dismay. "Tell him hello and give him my best regards," Douglas said.

Learned Hand, in his eighties, was a short, barrel-chested man with a large, square head, huge, thick, bristling eyebrows, and soft brown eyes. He radiated energy and would sometimes bark out remarks or questions in the living room as if he were in court. His humor was sharp, but often **leavened** with a touch of self-mockery. When something caught his funny bone he would burst out with

eluded: escaped

configurations: arrangements

tantalizing: provoking interest or desire but remaining out of reach

voicings: fine tunings

extraneous: extra

pretensions: laying of a claim to something

leavened: permeated with a transforming influence

explosive laughter—the laughter of a man who enjoyed laughing. He had a large **repertoire** of dramatic expressions involving the use of his eyebrows—very useful, he told me conspiratorially, when looking down on things from behind the bench. (The court stenographer could not record the movement of his eyebrows.) When I told him I'd been talking to William O. Douglas, they first shot up in exaggerated surprise, and then lowered and moved forward in a glower.

"Justice William O. Douglas, young man," he admonished. "Justice Douglas, if you please." About the Supreme Court in general, Hand insisted on a tone of profound respect. Little did I know that in private correspondence he had referred to the Court as "The Blessed Saints, Cherubim and Seraphim," "The Jolly Boys," "The Nine Tin Jesuses," "The Nine Blameless Ethiopians," and my particular favorite, "The Nine Blessed **Chalices** of the Sacred **Effluvium**."

Hand was badly stooped and had a lot of pain in his lower back. Martinis helped, but his strict Yankee wife approved of only one before dinner. It was my job to make the second and somehow slip it to him. If the pain was particularly acute he would get out of his chair and lie flat on the rug, still talking, and finish his point without missing a beat. He flattered me by asking for my impression of Justice Douglas, instructed me to convey his warmest regards, and then began talking about the Dennis case, which he described as a particularly tricky and difficult case involving the prosecution of eleven leaders of the Communist party. He had just started in on the First Amendment and free speech when we were called into dinner.

William O. Douglas loved the outdoors with a passion, and we fell into the habit of having coffee in the Coop and then strolling under the trees down toward the duck pond. About the Dennis case, he said something to this effect: "Eleven Communists arrested by the government. Up to no good, said the government; dangerous people, violent overthrow, etc., First Amendment, said the defense, freedom of speech, etc." Douglas stopped walking. "Clear and present danger."

"What?" I asked. He often talked in a **telegraphic** manner, and one was expected to keep up with him. It was sometimes like listening to a man thinking out loud.

"Clear and present danger," he said. "That was the issue. Did they constitute a clear and present danger? I don't think so. I think everybody took the language pretty far in Dennis." He began walking, striding along quickly. Again, one was expected to keep up with him. "The F.B.I. was all over them. Phones tapped, constant **surveillance**. How could it be clear and present danger with the F.B.I. watching every move they made? That's a ginkgo," he said suddenly, pointing at a tree. "A beauty. You don't see those every day. Ask Hand about clear and present danger."

I was in fact reluctant to do so. Douglas's argument seemed to me to be crushing—the last word, really—and I didn't want to embarrass Judge Hand. But back in the living room, on the second martini, the old man asked about Douglas. I sort of scratched my nose and **recapitulated** the conversation by the ginkgo tree.

"What?" Hand shouted. "Speak up, sir, for heaven's sake."

"He said the F.B.I. was watching them all the time so there couldn't be a clear and present danger," I blurted out, blushing as I said it.

A terrible silence filled the room. Hand's eyebrows writhed on his face like two huge caterpillars. He leaned forward in the wing chair, his face settling, finally, into a grim expression. "I am astonished," he said softly, his eyes holding mine, "at Justice Douglas's newfound faith in the Federal Bureau of Investigation." His big, granite head moved even closer to mine, until I could smell the martini. "I had understood him to consider it a politically corrupt, incompetent organization, directed by a power crazed lunatic." I realized I had been holding my breath throughout all of this, and as I relaxed, I saw the faintest trace of a smile cross Hand's face. Things are sometimes more complicated than they first appear, his

repertoire: the list of pieces one is prepared to perform

chalices: cups for the wine of the mass or Eucharist

effluvium: an invisible vapor or exhalation

telegraphic: in the staccato, abbreviated form of a telegram

surveillance: systematic vigilance

recapitulated: summarized

smile seemed to say. The old man leaned back. "The proximity of the danger is something to think about. Ask him about that. See what he says."

I chewed the matter over as I returned to campus. Hand had pointed out some of Douglas's language about the F.B.I. from other sources that seemed to bear out his point. I thought about the words "clear and present danger," and the fact that if you looked at them closely they might not be as simple as they had first appeared. What degree of danger? Did the word "present" allude to the **proximity** of the danger, or just the fact that the danger was there at all—that it wasn't an **anticipated** danger? Were there other hidden factors these great men were weighing of which I was unaware?

But Douglas was gone, back to Washington. (The writer in me is tempted to create a scene here—to invent one for dramatic purposes—but of course I can't do that.) My brief time as a messenger boy was over, and I felt a certain frustration, as if, with a few more exchanges, the matter of *Dennis v. United States* might have been resolved to my satisfaction. They'd left me high and dry. But, of course, it is precisely because the matter did not resolve that has caused me to think about it, off and on, all these years. "The Constitution," Hand used to say to me flatly, "is a piece of paper. The Bill of Rights is a piece of paper." It was many years before I understood what he meant. Documents alone do not keep democracy alive, nor maintain the state of law. There is no particular safety in them. Living men and women, generation after generation, must continually remake democracy and the law, and that involves an ongoing state of tension between the past and the present which will never completely resolve.

Education doesn't end until life ends, because you never know when you're going to understand something you hadn't understood before. For me, the magic dance of the shoeshine men was the kind of experience in which understanding came with a kind of click, a resolving kind of click. The same with the experience at the piano. What happened with Justice Douglas and Judge Hand was different, and makes the point that understanding does not always mean resolution. Indeed in our intellectual lives, our creative lives, it is perhaps those problems that will never resolve that rightly claim the lion's share of our energies. The physical body exists in a constant state of tension as it maintains **homeostasis**, and so too does the active mind embrace the tension of never being certain, never being absolutely sure, never being done, as it engages the world. That is our special fate, our inexpressibly valuable condition.

proximity: nearness; closeness
anticipated: expected
homeostasis: internal stability

▼ Questions to Focus Reading

1. Conroy realizes ten years after his experience at the shoeshine stand that the continuous staring of the two old black men was "a kind of statement, a kind of dance." How does he mean this? What point is he trying to make with this story?
2. "Sixths," Garland tells him, and he doesn't understand. What is the point of this anecdote (page 348)?
3. What is the point of the story about Justice Douglas and Judge Hand?

▼ Questions for Reflection and Discussion

1. Have you had experiences similar to Conroy's, when you realized the meaning of an event or piece of advice or teaching only after several years? Has this been true of anything you had read?
2. Are there issues for you that keep your interest precisely because they have not reached resolution? If so, what are they? Describe the competing voices that have so far precluded resolution.

3. Have you learned anything in your classes this semester that has either given you the experience of a click of resolution or opened a whole new field of questioning?

▼ Writing Assignments

1. Describe an instance of belated understanding similar to Conroy's.
2. Write about an issue that has not achieved resolution for you. Is it an issue that your college education may help to resolve for you?

▼ Vocabulary

anticipated	extraneous	proximity	telegraphic
chalices	homeostasis	recapitulated	transcend
configurations	hyperspace	repertoire	voicings
effluvium	ken	riffs	
elliptical	leavened	surveillance	
eluded	pretensions	tantalizing	

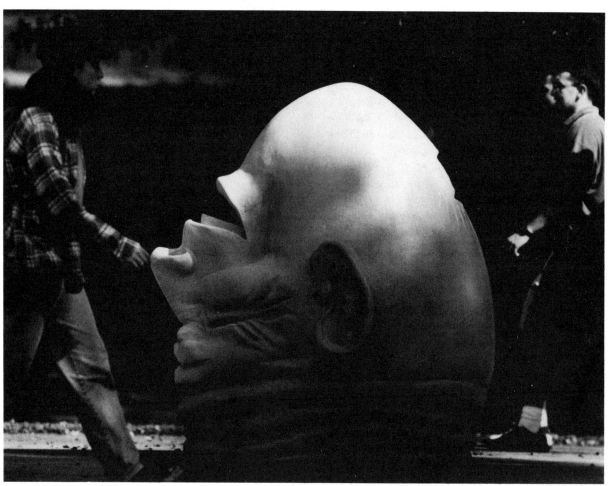

Robert Arneson, *Eye on Mrak (Fatal Laff)*, from the Egghead Series, UC Davis Campus, © UC Regents and Nelson Gallery, all rights reserved.

PART FOUR

Everyday Matters

Like all challenging projects in life, going to college has its logistics, its practical dimension. Mastering these everyday matters can take you a long way toward making this passage a safe and fulfilling one.

De Sellers is a reading specialist and a pioneer in the development of laboratories in which university students provide academic assistance for their peers. For ten years she served at Southwest Texas State University as dean of the College of General Studies, the college responsible for administering the core curriculum there.

In this final section of the book, she turns her attention to the most pressing of the practical matters that have been the shoals on which too many college careers have foundered: What sort of thinking is expected of a college student as opposed to a high school student? How can you take control of your time? How can you use time spent in class most productively? What is the best way to prepare for tests? How can you deal most effectively with the pressures of the actual taking of tests? How can you manage the other stresses of college life? Can you become the master of your own sexuality? De Sellers provides some useful, often unexpected answers.

55

▼

College Thinking

De Sellers

"To be successful in college, you will have to learn how to think," writes De Sellers, dean of the College of General Studies at Southwest Texas State University. She devotes the rest of the article to explaining just what this means.

When you go away to college, it seems as if everyone has some advice for you. From Aunt Sarah to your brother Bob, people relate their own college experiences or what they've heard. They talk of dorms and professors and fraternities and adventures. They talk of competition and money and success. They talk about how different college is from high school. Tests are hard; you are on your own. College is wonderful. College is terrible. Amidst the flurry of packing and goodbyes, the weight of the advice is another kind of luggage.

They forgot to mention one thing—the major academic difference between high school and college. A simple thing. To be successful in college, you will have to learn how to think.

But, you say, you know how to think. After all, haven't you spent endless years in school? True, you didn't read your textbooks in school; it was easy to pass by memorizing and giving your teachers what they wanted. School was hard only in the sense that it was boring. But you are the successful one—the graduate. Doesn't that high school diploma mean that you are smart? You have played the educational game for twelve years and won.

College is a different game. The purpose of the game is different; the rules are different. It is likely that you are entering college so that you can get a degree and a good job. Maybe your thoughts have not even gone that far; you are here simply because there is no place else you want to be and your friends are here. Perhaps you are here because you want to understand more about yourself and your world.

Professors don't really care about whether you get a good job afterward. Oh, they will talk about the economic advantages of a college degree, but that is just to capture your attention and motivation. For them, the purpose of the college game is to make you an educated person. An educated person is an independent thinker—someone who can formulate a question, gather information, establish priorities, use logical thinking, construct an argument, and arrive at a decision within a moral framework.

College is a different game. On the surface, it will seem hauntingly like high school. Classes and teachers and assignments and blackboards. Teachers talking and you listening. But if you play the game as casually as you did in high school—an afterthought to your friends, job, social life, drugs, or whatever—you will fail. Ironically, working hard is not the answer either. A plaintive freshman comment frequently overheard in October is "I studied harder for that test than I have ever studied in my life, and I made a 52 . . . or a 47 . . . or a 58."

As you sit in classes or in front of your textbooks, you may feel overwhelmed by the cascade of facts, names, places, theorems, words, ideas all flowing through your mind. You will try to grasp some as they flow past so that you can regurgitate them on the test. Your instinct is right—grab them, but then understand them.

That's right, the first step in college thinking is to understand those ideas, events, facts, and so on. How do you know if you've understood something? The easiest way is to explain it to someone else. Explain it without looking at your notes or the book. Understanding takes much more effort than remembering. You may have to reread the text, ask questions of your professor, look for other explanations in the library, get help from a tutor. The key is to do whatever is necessary to get the substance of the material. But understanding is only the beginning, the foundation of college thinking.

College is a different game. College professors want you to understand the material, and you will earn points on the test for this. But they will demand that you do something with that understanding. Yes, you have to remember those ideas and pieces of data, and yes, you will have to understand them. Do something with them, do what? Three different types of thinking, that's what.

First, they want you to apply that understanding in a new situation. For example, the problems on the math test will not look exactly like those you did for homework. The test problems will combine various aspects of the homework problems and often be more complicated. In economics, psychology, and other subjects, you will be expected to label (classify) a new example by some sort of system that you have studied. This type of question begins your journey as a college thinker. It is not enough to merely follow the mental paths of others; you must demonstrate your understanding of an idea by using it in an unfamiliar situation.

Second, professors expect you to analyze what you are studying. History professors will demand that you trace cause-effect relationships, that you attempt to determine why certain events occurred. Science classes will also require that you answer why, not just what. Analysis in literature means separating a work into its language, form, structure, and then investigating each part and its relationship to the other parts and to the whole. Analytical questions often ask you to compare (show the similarities) and contrast (show the differences) among several ideas, works, theories. The process frequently leads to differing conclusions. There is usually no one right answer. This type of question enhances your development as a college thinker; stretching beyond simply reflecting the content you begin to use it to explore patterns.

An extension of application and analysis is argumentation—the third type of thinking professors will expect of you. Argumentation lies at the heart of university study. It asks you to propose an idea and defend it. Sounds simple, doesn't it? Yet becoming competent will take years of your effort. Argumentation—the crux of the difference between high school and college—is based on one crucial premise: the premise that questions are more important than answers.

Questions are more important than answers because answers are temporary. Professors believe that we use what we know to try to understand the world, but what we know is constantly increasing and changing, so what we understand is also changing. Answers are temporary. New discoveries, new insights, new creations all have the power to change the answers. As you advance in college, you will study what we know now, but the possibility is always open for change. Professors relish the uncertainty and excitement of the unknown. Sometimes they scorn the comfortable, limited ideas of those outside academics.

If answers to questions are temporary, then what is important? What is important to professors is the quality of your argument. Have you asked a thoughtful question based on the data available? Have you carefully created a theoretical answer to that question? Most importantly, in defending your answer, have you considered all the available data and used logical thinking? Such an argument is the goal of college thinking.

What stands in the way of your becoming competent in argumentation? Laziness and prejudice will, of course. But the most obvious obstacle is the belief that there is only one answer to any thoughtful question. Oh, there may be one way the professor wants you to solve a math problem, one definition to choose on a test, statements that must be labeled true or false. But the true focus of college and college tests is to start you on that journey to independent thinking through application, analysis, and argumentation.

Different academic disciplines lead to different kinds of arguments. Historians, artists, scientists, philosophers, mathematicians, literary critics, and thinkers in any discipline bring different and valid viewpoints to the discussion of any issue. When you study these courses in college, you must learn how these specialists think, not just what they think. Many of your beginning college courses will demonstrate such types of thinking.

A corollary to argumentation is academic honor. An honorable person always credits the ideas (the arguments) of others. Anything else is theft. Theft of ideas is the most heinous crime in academics since ideas are the only products professors have. Since ideas and the ownership of ideas are so important to professors, there are great punishments for plagiarism and cheating. There is little mercy for either crime in academics.

College is a different game. The typical student questions, Did I miss anything important? Is this going to be on the test? and What's *the* answer? anger professors because such questions reveal that those students do not understand the purpose of a college education. A college education is not just the accrual of fifty grades in fifty courses, not just "getting those courses over with" as if one were taking medication, not just being around for four or five years. No; a college education is the result of mental effort. It is the collection of mental abilities and knowledge that hold promise of an exciting future: one that encompasses the intellectual riches of the world. As an educated person, you can use and extend the products of human wisdom. If you will venture down that intellectual road of asking questions and discovering temporary answers, then you are giving yourself a chance of completing college with an education, not with just a degree.

▼ Questions to Focus Reading

1. In the fourth paragraph (page 354), Sellers suggests several reasons you might have for choosing to go to college. What was your reason? Do you have any new reasons now?

2. In her fifth paragraph (page 354), Sellers proposes a definition of the educated person. What is that definition?

3. Professors, Sellers insists, expect you not simply to memorize, but to understand. What does she mean by "understanding"?

4. "Your professors will demand that you do something with that understanding," Sellers writes. Explain what it is they will want you to do.

5. Sellers says argumentation is based on one crucial premise. What is this premise? What are the typical obstacles to the mastery of argumentation?

6. Sellers tells us that college students must learn *how* thinkers from the various disciplines think, not just *what* they think. What differences are there in the ways, for example, that an artist and a scientist think?

7. What is plagiarism? Professors tend to treat cheating and plagiarism with severity. Sellers suggests a reason for this severity. What is it?

8. Why are professors angered by the questions, Did I miss anything important? Is this going to be on the test? What is *the* answer? Why are these questions so offensive to professors?

▼ Questions for Reflection

1. Think of examples from your present classes of assignments that require you to apply what you are learning to new situations, that require you to analyze material, and that require you to create arguments.
2. Sellers suggests that answers are temporary. Why, then, spend four or five years in college studying merely temporary answers?
3. "A college education is not just the accrual of fifty grades in fifty courses," Sellers writes. "It is the collection of mental abilities and knowledge that hold promise of an exciting future: one that encompasses the intellectual riches of the world. As an educated person, you can use and extend the products of human wisdom." What do you think she has in mind? How would such a life be different from a life without a college education?

▼ Discussion

1. Summarize the key differences between the kind of thinking that was expected of you in high school and the kind of thinking that is expected of you in college. What are some examples from your present classes of the new expectation?
2. Different disciplines approach questions in different ways. Have you observed such differences among your classes? What differences in thought processes have you observed?
3. What reasons did you have for going to college? Now that you have been here a while and have been thinking about the point of going to college, have your reasons changed any? If so, what are your new reasons?
4. A recent article on cheating in college reported that 40 percent of today's college students cheat at some time in their university careers, a figure that suggests a kind of epidemic of academic dishonesty. What, in your view, are the causes of this epidemic? What do you think should be done about it?

▼ Writing Assignments

1. Consider a recent assignment a professor has made in one of your classes, an assignment that has required that you stretch your present powers of mind. Describe the assignment and explain how it demands that you stretch your mental powers or think in a new way.
2. Write a "how-to" essay in which you explain to other students what techniques they might use to *comprehend* lectures and reading material, rather than to merely memorize them.
3. List in order of importance five goals you have as a college student. Explain these goals and describe why they are important to you.
4. What, in your view, are the causes of the epidemic of cheating currently sweeping American colleges and universities? What would you propose should be done about it?

▼ Journal Entry

1. Is college affecting your way of thinking—both what you are thinking about and how you are thinking?

56

▼

The Time of Your Life

De Sellers

Why should I learn to manage my time? And how can I do it? De Sellers provides some succinct answers.

Time is the great equalizer. Whether you are smart or dumb, ugly or beautiful, you have the same 168 hours each week that everyone else has. How you spend that valuable commodity determines the quality of your life just as surely as if you walked into a department store and ordered it. Time is more precious than any possession.

You have probably already noticed that time passes more quickly for you than it once did. Those endless hours and days of childhood slip away by adolescence, and adulthood brings an ever increasing acceleration. Most college freshmen fall prey to the conviction that they have enough time to do everything, enough time to forgo planning. A dangerous self-deception. One of the purposes of college is to determine which people can control their time in order to meet their goals. Think about it. Most blue-collar or pink-collar jobs require employees to punch a time clock. The employer structures the time and the tasks. But college graduates who have professional jobs structure their own time and often the tasks as well. *A hidden requirement for success in college and in the professional world is the desire and the ability to use time wisely.* Such a skill is not instantly conferred on graduation, but it is slowly and painfully constructed throughout the college years.

Most students shudder at the thought of controlling their time; they envision a jail of schedules and charts that would not allow them to feel free. The irony of that prejudice is that good time management is a key—a key to achieving goals and enjoying life. The beginning is simple, a promise to yourself to be honest, and the first stage is the willingness to differentiate among fantasies, dreams, and goals.

I may fantasize that I am a rock star, adored by millions, or I may dream that upon graduation from college I will acquire a glamorous job with a large salary. This latter dream usually involves rewards but not the work itself. Fantasies and dreams are alike in that they are always effortless. No work, no struggle, but instantaneous. The magic of Hollywood. Fantasies are impossible; dreams are possible, but unlikely. Fantasies and dreams help us to escape. They serve no other purpose. Escape can be good entertainment, but goals are the markers on the road of accomplishment.

Goals are those accomplishments that we deliberately set out to achieve. They may be small and simple: I'll do the dishes tonight. Or they may be large, complex, and long term: I want to enjoy my work and do it well, or I want to create a family based on love and respect. We may choose goals in every aspect of our lives: personal, social, academic, occupational, athletic, spiritual. A broad goal, such as good health, may spawn many smaller goals, such as maintaining a regular exercise schedule, eating a healthy diet, and getting regular medical checkups. Some goals are behaviors we want to decrease or increase or maintain.

New Year's resolutions—those wild promises we make to ourselves after the indulgences of the holidays—are rarely kept, for we try to change too much too quickly. *The truth of the matter is that if we want to change a behavior permanently we usually have to change it slowly.* Changing a behavior requires some discipline, but not the amount most people imagine. The way to change a behavior slowly is to make a small promise to ourselves, keep it, and reward ourselves. A typical example would be a freshman who has decided to attend his 8 A.M. class the next day. He knows he needs to go to class to pass, so he promises himself that he will go to sleep by midnight. He sets the alarm for 7 A.M. and places it across the room. When it goes off, he reminds himself of his promise and why it is important. As he's getting ready, he compliments himself on his behavior and tells himself that going to class is important.

How we spend the minutes and hours of our days determines what we accomplish. Thinking about studying will not help our grades. Only studying does. Talking about our weight while we are eating pizza does not cause weight loss. Exercise and a sensible diet will control our weight. Those links from behaviors to accomplishments to goals are crucial. Do our behaviors and accomplishments lead us to our goals or away from them?

Most freshmen would like a satisfying collegiate experience that includes good grades and a social life that is fun and emotionally satisfying. They do not enjoy great amounts of stress. Students can often have other goals about work, family, sports. If your current behaviors will not lead you to your goals, try the following three steps for two weeks. This time management system is not a jail.

Write down three goals you want to accomplish this semester. You may want a 3.0, a date with the redhead in your math class, or a better relationship with your roommate. Your goal may be large or small. If your life seems out of control right now, write down one goal for this week. What will you have to do to accomplish that goal?

Isolate the key behaviors for your goals. Key academic behaviors include going to class, paying attention and taking notes, reading the assignments when they are assigned, keeping an academic calendar with all tests noted. Key financial behaviors include writing down every check in the register (and keeping a running balance), planning a weekly budget, paying bills on time. Key personal behaviors include handling business details such as insurance and car inspections promptly, keeping your personal space neat, getting adequate sleep.

We lie to ourselves about key behaviors. They are often boring and mundane, and we want to delay them. Actually, we want someone else to do them. We want them to disappear. So we lie; we say that we will do it later, after the party or the movie. Tomorrow. Those lies usually result in late papers (lower grades), late payments (penalties), lower self-esteem. The more lies, the greater the amount of chaos.

Those lies are part of a larger behavior pattern called procrastination. We may procrastinate in just one area of our life such as studying or that pattern may permeate the entirety of our life. Procrastination occurs when we deliberately choose to delay or omit a behavior that we believe we should do. The reasons are legion. The most common cause of procrastination is our unwillingness to recognize and to pay the "price tag" for an outcome we say we want. An example would be that we want an A on the next history test, but the price tag is that we have to read and study the chapters (15 hours), attend class for those five weeks (15 hours), participate in a study group (10 hours), and study individually (8 hours). Forty-eight hours for one test! How much do we really want that A? And then there is no guarantee that we will make it; that 48 hours just gives us the opportunity to achieve that grade. Any goal can be subjected to that kind of scrutiny. Price tags are usually much higher than we want to admit. We always look for a bargain; witness the current spate of television ads about weight loss without effort or denial.

There are more serious causes of procrastination. We may be so overcommitted that exhaustion engulfs us. We may be so bound to the conviction that what we do should be perfect that we are afraid to start, for whatever we accomplish it will not be perfect. We may be rebellious, even to the extent of rebelling against ourselves and our own goals. We may be afraid to succeed because our families or significant others have told us we are failures and we believe them. We may feel more comfortable with failure than with success. We may be depressed emotionally and feel so "dragged out" that we cannot start any new behavior. We may be lazy and simply unwilling to work.

If procrastination is a characteristic of your life and you dislike the consequences of it, then take some time to reflect on why you do it. The suggestions that follow in this essay will help you overcome a mild case of procrastination, but if your behavior stems from serious causes and is engulfing your life, then seek professional help through your campus counseling center. Procrastination is a learned behavior; you can learn not to do it. You can learn to set your goals, plan your actions, and accomplish those actions in a timely manner.

If you want to change how you manage your own behaviors, then select a goal that is important to you. Write down the key behaviors for that goal. Which ones are you currently doing? Which key behavior would you like to change? Focus on it. What can you do to increase the likelihood you will do that behavior? *Make a plan to make that key behavior a habit.* When a key behavior becomes a habit (a behavior we don't have to think about), we benefit. We are doing the right thing without a struggle.

Imagine a student in a freshman math class. She wants to make at least a B and realizes that a key behavior is completing the homework problems on time. Her class is Tuesday–Thursday, and she often does her homework late on Monday and Wednesday evenings. By that time, she has forgotten what went on in class, and the problems seem overwhelmingly difficult. Two key behaviors for her goal would be to do the homework as soon as it is assigned and then review it before class. Her plan to make those behaviors habits is simple: On Tuesdays and Thursdays after history, she walks to the library and picks a quiet place to study. (She has set the video cassette recorder to record her favorite soap.) It has only been two hours since the math class, so she still remembers what went on in class. She starts working on the homework problems. If she gets confused or stuck, she takes a short break and then attempts the problem again. If she still cannot do it, she leaves it and attempts other problems. After working on several others, she again attempts the confusing one(s). If she's successful, she completes her work and goes home. If there are unsolved problems, she goes to one of the campus learning labs and requests help. Several days later, she takes thirty minutes before math class to look over the problems and quickly work one or two. She's ready for class. After two weeks, it's automatic for her to go to the library after history class. The habit is in place.

Two habits that can transform the quality of your life are simple and powerful. *When something needs to be done, DO IT.* Do it right away. Don't put it off. You will just think about it and feel guilty. The longer you delay, the guiltier you will feel. Whether it is getting out of bed and getting cleaned up or picking up the trash or reading the chapter—just do it.

Give yourself ten minutes. If you get up ten minutes earlier in the morning, you won't have to rush. If you leave for class or an appointment ten minutes earlier, you arrive on time, regardless of traffic or parking. That extra ten minutes reduces stress, and it also reduces the likelihood that you will make a mistake because you are hurrying. That extra ten minutes adds quality to your life.

Being a successful college student is a full-time job. Treat it like a job. If you are going to miss a class, call your professor in advance, just as you would an employer. If you have an assignment, do it; that assignment is your work, as is learning in class. Tests and papers are how you demonstrate whether you have been doing your job. Your professors are your supervisors. They evaluate your performance, and your performance record is your academic transcript. *Your transcript reflects your cumulative performance and is an accurate indicator of how well you have mastered the use of time.* When you master time, then you are a professional.

▼ Exercise: Controlling Procrastination

Check off the areas where you tend to procrastinate:

Household
____ daily chores (dishes, laundry)
____ small repairs and home projects
____ large home projects
____ yard care and gardening
____ phoning a repair service
____ returning merchandise
____ paying bills
____ shopping for groceries
____ running errands for others
____ other _____

Work
____ being on time
____ being on time for appointments
____ making calls
____ decision making
____ paperwork
____ reports
____ confronting someone in regard to a problem
____ paying a compliment
____ implementing new ideas
____ billing
____ requesting a raise or promotion
____ arranging a meeting with your supervisor
____ reading current literature
____ looking for a new job
____ plotting a direction for your career
____ other _____

School
____ going to classes
____ doing daily assignments
____ doing required reading
____ studying for exams
____ writing term papers
____ having a conference with a professor
____ applying to graduate or professional school
____ registering
____ paying tuition and fees
____ attending to degree requirements
____ returning books to library
____ inquiring about classes for next term
____ other _____

Social Relationships
____ phoning friends
____ calling on friends
____ corresponding
____ inviting friends to your home
____ calling, writing relatives
____ visiting relatives
____ asking someone out
____ planning recreational or social activities with others
____ expressing appreciation
____ sending thank-you notes
____ sending cards or gifts
____ having parties
____ being on time for recreational or social activities
____ asking for help
____ confronting a friend with regard to a problem
____ ending a stagnant relationship
____ other _____

Finances

____ filing income tax forms on time

____ organizing bills, receipts

____ keeping tax records

____ consulting with an accountant

____ budgeting

____ phoning the bank about discrepancies

____ paying fines

____ paying back loans

____ collecting money from debtors

____ paying car insurance

____ balancing checkbook

____ paying bills

____ other _____

57

▼

How to Learn in Class

De Sellers

De Sellers offers some straightforward counsel on how to utilize class time.

In four years of college you will spend almost two thousand hours in classrooms listening to lectures and participating in class discussions. If you master the skill of learning in class, not only will you be more successful academically, but your college experience will be much less stressful because studying out of class will be more effective.

It is easy to spot students who do not know how to learn in class. Pretend you are from another century or planet and watch a typical American college freshman class. How many students dash in moments before the professor? wander in ten or fifteen minutes late? head toward the back of the room, the farther from the professor the better? forget their notebooks or have to borrow a pen? sink gratefully into a desk and are immediately asleep? have hangovers so obvious that they could be wearing a sign? read textbooks for other courses? talk with the person sitting next to them? are masters at daydreaming? or create elaborate doodles instead of notes?

Make no mistake. *The purpose of a college class is to advance your learning in that course.* The ideas that are presented, explained, and developed are often not duplicated in the text. When you learn what you should in class, your study time can then focus on the outside readings and exercises instead of on the material you should have already mastered in class.

You may want to examine the following sets of behaviors, which characterize successful students. You will notice that many of these behaviors occur outside of class (before and after) in order that your learning in class be powerful.

The first set of behaviors can be represented by the Boy Scout motto Be Prepared. Preparation begins the day before class. Are any assignments due? If so, do them. Read or at least skim the assigned reading; this strategy is crucial for it will prepare you to take competent class notes. More about this later. Become familiar with the main topics and new vocabulary and at least look at charts and graphs. Be sure to quickly skim chapter summaries.

Organize your life and your schedule to arrive at class five to ten minutes early in a relatively good physical state (enough sleep, breakfast, no speeding tickets, no hangovers). You may have to do serious surgery on your social life to accomplish such a goal, but the rewards are equally serious. If you are hungry, sleepy, or hungover, your chances of learning in class are nil. Your body is there; your mind is elsewhere. Make believe that class is a job; you have to show up ready and able to work.

Whether you use a spiral or a looseleaf binder, your notebook should contain a pocket for handouts and returned tests, a place to insert the syllabus, and enough paper to write on only one side of the page. You may use one notebook for each class or group, Monday–Wednesday–Friday classes in one and Tuesday–Thursday classes in another. You may also want to put enough bluebooks and Scantrons in a notebook pocket for the entire semester. Take several pens (pencil marks fade by semester's end). Some professors lecture from the text; if yours does, take your book to class and make notes directly in it.

The last step in preparedness comes in the five minutes preceding class. Look back over the notes from the last meeting. What were the major ideas? How do they connect to the reading for today? This intellectual warm-up is analogous to the stretching an athlete does before he or she performs. In psychological terms, this rapid review brings to your conscious mind the ideas and facts you learned in the last class and stored in your memory.

Be Active is the motto of the second set of behaviors; it offers a guideline for your approach in the classroom. Class learning is more than simply transcribing the professor's notes into your study book. It is more than remembering the stories and jokes the professor uses as illustrations and forgetting the main ideas. Your learning strategies should vary in lecture, discussion, and problem-solving classes.

In lecture classes, you create study notes that, when combined with your outside readings, should constitute your learning resources. Those notes should not replicate the book, but instead they should comprise a record of the main points of the lecture (there are usually five or six), relevant facts to support those points, and explanations of difficult ideas. Listen for concepts and facts you did not find in the readings.

When you begin to take lecture notes, think about what you are trying to accomplish. What do you want to learn? How will you be tested? How much do you already know about the subject? How easy is it for you to learn in this subject? Search for the main ideas of the lecture by carefully watching your professor. Your professor may write an outline on the board, or make introductory comments during the first moments of class, or repeat an idea several times, or raise her/his voice, or gesture, or use words like *the main point, most importantly, in summary.* Any of these cues can signal a main point.

Usually you will capture a main point in a sentence or phrase. Writing the concepts *in your own words* helps you understand them. If you simply copy the professor's words without understanding them, they will be useless to you later. Putting the key ideas in your own words increases the likelihood that you understand them. When you understand the material, you will better remember it.

Record definitions, facts, opinions that seem relevant. Do not write down everything the professor says; instead carefully select what you write. Here is where reading or skimming the text in the preparation stage helps. Do not spend all your time rewriting material that is in the text but do write down new material.

Leave space between items. Number or organize whenever you can. Put a question mark when you get lost or confused and leave blank space (you can ask the professor for help after class or during office hours). Mark with an asterisk (*) items that you believe will be on the test. Remember that you are creating a study book; recopying takes too long, so create a readable page.

The key to creating a useful set of lecture notes is thinking. Think about what is important in this material; think about what you need to learn; think about whether you are writing down the main points. Leave space for your own thoughts later.

Discussion classes are often great fun, but students frequently leave class without any notes. That behavior is dangerous since we rarely remember concepts unless we write them down and go over them, even if we have been interested in the discussion. In this type of class, the professor usually summarizes a main point when the discussion ends. Listen for those summaries and record them. Discussion notes tend to be shorter, and they usually do not follow any particular structure. Ideas are important here, not details.

The purpose of problem-solving classes is simple: class time is used to solve problems and to discuss the process of doing so. The strategy for taking good notes in such a class is to write down not only the problem but also the verbalization of the steps. The sequence of steps is crucial. Math, accounting, economics, finance, computer programming are all examples of problem-solving classes.

Class is not over when the professor stops talking. The motto Be Thorough represents the behaviors that occur after class. As soon after class as is practical, edit your notes by filling in the blank spaces, numbering or labeling series of items, and marking important ideas. Meet with a friend to compare notes and skim the text quickly for connections to the lecture material. Determine that your notes are complete. If you have any questions, write them down and see the professor. This edit-and-review stage is crucial for powerful and permanent learning because we need several exposures to ideas and facts to learn them.

Remember the two thousand hours. If you spend that time learning effectively, your outside study time can be much more productive.

▼ Exercise: A Checklist for Listening and Notetaking

Best class	Worse class	
		Before Class:
_____	_____	• Buy notebooks that will help you organize your work. (Recommendation: separate looseleaf or spiral notebooks for each course.)
_____	_____	• Quiz yourself over the previous lecture.
_____	_____	• Review reading assignments to bring to mind key ideas.
_____	_____	• Take action to improve physical and mental alertness.
_____	_____	• Quiet your mind to prepare to listen.
		During Class:
_____	_____	• Be attentive to the beginning of the lecture for possible review.
_____	_____	• Listen for the outline or agenda for the day's session.
_____	_____	• Avoid distractions.
_____	_____	• Write enough for notes to be meaningful to you later.
_____	_____	• Try to use a consistent form.
_____	_____	• Listen for verbal cues (for example, "The point I have been making . . . ," "There are three arguments for this view," "The first objection I want to consider . . . ").
_____	_____	• Listen to class discussion.
_____	_____	• Include in notes the instructor's summary of important points in the discussion.
		After Class:
_____	_____	• Clear up points of confusion by talking with lecturer or classmates.
_____	_____	• Use text to fill in missing points or to clarify doubts.
_____	_____	• Edit notes as soon as possible.
_____	_____	• Jot down in margins the notes of your own reflections and ideas.
_____	_____	• Do foreign language and math assignments while the material is still fresh.
		Periodically:
_____	_____	• Review your notes.
_____	_____	• Jot down brief cues for recall, then use them to quiz yourself.
_____	_____	• Be alert to developing themes.
_____	_____	• Create likely test questions and answer them.

58

▼

How to Study

De Sellers

Here De Sellers answers one of the questions most frequently raised by freshmen: "What is the best way to go about studying?"

Most freshmen think about studying often. They talk about it, complain about it, procrastinate about it. They religiously take their books home on the weekend, or to the park, or to a friend's place. They promise themselves that they will study after the party or after the movie. Do they study? Well, sometimes, but rarely is it effective, because most freshmen believe that memorizing is enough. Memorizing at the last minute (or cramming) is the most popular form of freshman studying. No wonder that 40 percent fail.

Understanding, not memory, is the foundation of college learning. The trick is to study to understand, then memorize what is important. The place to begin to understand is the textbook. Studying is different from reading. We read the newspaper, a recipe, a novel. The purpose is usually to acquire information or to be entertained. *To study is to apply the mind so as to acquire understanding and knowledge.*

The first type of study is learning from your textbook. Studying a textbook is a careful and thoughtful process. At the beginning of the semester, examine your text just as you would examine any new tool. How are the chapters organized? Are they grouped into units with introductions? What is the structure of each chapter? Do they contain case studies, summaries, introductory outlines, boxed inserts, graphs and charts, problems, questions? What appendices exist? Is there a glossary (a dictionary of terms used in the book), index, background information (science books often contain an explanation of the scientific method, and government books contain the Constitution, and so on)? If a study guide exists for the text, buy it; it is worth every dollar.

Be sensible about where, when, and how you study. *Study first, then party,* rather than the other way around. Study during the day if possible (the soaps will still be there on holidays). Turn the television off. Sit at a table or desk. Use a good light. Music is okay if the volume is low. Schedule specific times to study, just as if you were going to work. Study at a high energy time because effective studying is hard work and you will need all the energy you can get.

Chapters are the normal units of textbooks. Although you may spend several sittings studying a chapter, it is best to consider each one as a whole. To study a chapter effectively you will have to go through it several times. The first step is to look over the entire chapter. Read the main headings and the summary if there is one. Think about the two or three main ideas that this chapter is about. Say them aloud or write them down. You may want to phrase them as questions. These ideas will form the foundation of what you will learn, and they will be the primary method by which you will remember the information in the chapter.

Most modern textbooks are partitioned into sections and subsections. This deliberate structure helps you to learn, for as you acquire new ideas and information you need to store them in your memory. Research tells us that items stored at random are hard to remember, but ideas and items stored on the basis of their meaning and context are much easier to remember. Thus, understand the material first; then work to remember it.

As you study each section, do the following: read the heading and look for the primary idea about the heading in the first or second paragraph. When you find it, mark it by underlining or highlighting. Then read the first subsection without marking anything. Stop and think. What in that subsection is important about the primary idea? You may find one or two or three items to mark, but be selective, for if you mark too much, the markings are useless. Work your way through each subsection, back and forth, reading . . . thinking . . . marking. As you work, be sure to look over any charts, graphs, or boxed inserts. They can help you understand the ideas. Work for fifteen to twenty minutes and then get up and take a five-minute break. Then back to work.

If text material is especially difficult, make an outline of the section. If there is new vocabulary, make flash cards (à la grade school) with the word on one side and the definition on the other. Flash cards also work for identifications and grouped items (types, characteristics). Carry them in your purse or pocket and practice them several times a day. If you are lucky enough to have a study guide for the text (a call to your college bookstore will tell you if one is in print), use it to organize your efforts by going back and forth between the guide and the text.

The end result of a productive study session is twofold: you have an understanding of the main ideas of the text reading, and you have a marked text that will help you prepare for exams. The markings are yours, your choices; that is why it is useful to buy unmarked texts. Other people's decisions will not help you.

If you have read this far and are fairly intimidated by these suggestions, take heart; you can learn how to study. Most high school students rarely read their texts, and few if any study them. One of the hardest adjustments most college freshmen must make is learning to study their textbooks because it is a new behavior. It will take many false starts and miscalculations, but with practice you can learn. You will not only get better with practice, you will get faster.

If you are a competent reader and simply out of practice, the practical suggestions above should improve your reading effectiveness within 45 days. However, there are three kinds of reading difficulties that are much more serious and require direct intervention. The first is poor concentration (or gifted daydreaming). If your mind wanders each time you pick up a textbook, the cure is ruthless. Study in ten-minute sessions. Read the chapter one subsection at a time. Turn the heading into a question and when you find the answer, write it down. Hold yourself accountable for every minute you are looking at the page. If you have to stand up and hold the book, do so. After each ten-minute session, test yourself on the material. Daydreaming is a habit; so is concentration. Get in the habit of concentrating when you are looking at a text. Each time you realize that you are daydreaming, pull your mind back to the information on the page.

The second kind of reading difficulty is lack of a collegiate vocabulary. If every tenth word in your freshman English reader is unfamiliar, you need to do specific vocabulary development. The fastest method is to go to the campus learning lab and study Greek and Latin roots and prefixes. Another is to keep a dictionary with you at all times *and use it*. Make vocabulary cards, write sentences using new words, and become a wordsmith, a craftsman with language. Reading will greatly aid your vocabulary development. Persistence is the key; if you can truly learn one new word each day, your vocabulary will grow as your intellectual abilities grow.

A third kind of reading difficulty occurs when students have problems with understanding the basic content of the text. If you try to read and seem to miss the main points the professor and other students talk about, then find a campus source that will assess your reading skills. There may be a learning or reading lab, an education department, a counseling center. This is not the time to be shy; reading difficulties can be overcome, but you will need the help of specialists.

As mentioned earlier, the first type of study was learning from your textbook. A second type is solving problems for courses such as math, statistics, accounting, physics. Attempt the homework as soon after class as possible (you will remember more). As you are practicing a procedure for solving a problem, talk aloud about what you are doing and why. Better still, write down what you are doing and why. When you get stuck, take a short break and try again. If you stay stuck, get help from your professor or a classmate or a tutor in one of the learning labs. Persistence is the key to success. A good way to ensure that you understand—rather than just remember—the process is to explain it to someone else. An emergency technique, if math is extremely difficult for you, is to begin by working unassigned problems for which you have the answers, to verify that you understand the procedure.

A third type of study is the study group. Groups can be either opportunities or dangers. The dangers are obvious: you may visit instead of learn; your partners may give you wrong information; you may spend all your time teaching them and not learning anything new; your group may contain a leech who cannot contribute but clings to others. However, the opportunities are equally great. Students in effective groups combine their skills and knowledge as well as motivate each other to greater accomplishments.

If you want to establish an effective study group, choose two other students who share your desire for success (three is the magic number for a group). Set a specific time, place, and topic. A good place is the library. Expect everyone to have completed the initial study of the material and to bring questions to the group. Compare notes from the lecture across the group. Focus the discussion on two points: the unanswered questions about the material from the lecture and the reading and the predicted questions for the next test.

A lively, competitive interaction in a group will help everyone's learning. Debate the issues or quiz each other. Assign topics and let each person "teach" for five minutes. If you have been unwise enough to choose a lazy person or a leech, eject him or her from the group. Older returning students are good additions to a group because they are usually highly motivated and willing to work hard.

Studying is not just reading and memorizing, although it encompasses both. *Studying is the active learning of academic ideas and information. It is the work of a student.* Most study skills books tell students to study two hours for every hour of class. Not a bad average, but it is an average. Some courses will require four hours for every hour of class and some will require thirty minutes. The two-for-one average will usually yield average grades. Yes, unlike high school, it takes effort even to make Cs. As and Bs come much harder.

Studying is like any job. With time and effort and attention, you can learn to do it well. Practice in studying will allow you to master the most powerful skill in the human arsenal: the ability to concentrate.

▼ Exercise: Concentration

1. Complete the attached checklists in order to be aware of distractions.
2. Try this plan for reducing internal distractions and increasing the amount of time you can read productively:
   a. Begin with a relatively easy assignment as a "warm-up." Divide the assignment into three or four segments.
   b. Read the first segment. When your attention starts drifting, stop, turn away from the book, note the number of paragraphs you were able to read with concentration. Briefly review those paragraphs and remind yourself of the key points, then continue reading this first segment. Repeat this process as often as necessary until you complete the segment.

    c. When you finish the first segment, note the average number of paragraphs you were able to read with concentration. If your average was, say, four, set a goal of six for the next segment.

    d. Skim the next segment and mark the end of the passage you hope to read without distraction.

    e. Repeat step (b) until you have worked through the second segment.

    f. Work through the entire assignment using this technique.

3. Describe aloud or write the main content of the assignment you just read.

4. Take a short relaxing break, then turn to a more challenging assignment, using the same technique.

▼ Exercise: Checklist for External Distractions

1. Describe the place where you are studying: _____

_____

_____

Study Area	Description	How to Improve It
Amount of space		
Furniture		
Lighting		
Temperature		
Noise		
Visual distraction		
Other		

▼ Exercise: Checklist for Internal Distractions

1. Describe your present mental state: _____

_____

_____

Internal Distractions	Description	How to Improve/Cope
Reactions to noise		
Fatigue		
Daydreaming		
Lack of interest in subject		
Anxiety about scope of task		
Personal problems		
Other		

59
▼

Center Stage: Performing on College Tests

De Sellers

Tests—the bane of the student's life. Here is some good advice for making them, if not downright enjoyable, at least much less threatening.

Tests are an integral part of American life. Our society uses tests (and contests) to sort and categorize us. Whether it is the SAT or an algebra test, a basic skills test or a history exam, the CPA exam or a kindergarten reading readiness test, tests stand at the gateway of opportunity. Tests should accurately reflect our knowledge of particular subjects or predict our ability to perform in future circumstances, and sometimes they do. Tests designed by teachers vary greatly in quality; some are thorough and fair, others seem capricious and thoughtless.

As students enter each new level of competition, they usually experience the apprehension of the unknown, the shock of higher standards, and the sense of inadequate preparation. Classic examples of this phenomenon occur each fall on American college campuses as freshmen face their first exams. Their frequent frenetic attempts—at preparation by cramming all night and worrying endlessly—testify to their earnestness but rarely help them perform.

Students commonly have ambivalent feelings about tests. Anxiety, avoidance, and anger can occur beforehand, while celebration, remorse, and relief can be the aftermath. All are powerful emotions that can directly affect your sense of well-being and self-esteem. How can you harness these emotional engines to help you accomplish your college goals? The first step is to understand the basic nature of college tests; the second is to master a test preparation method that counteracts avoidance; and the third is to learn how to perform a test to the best of your ability and knowledge.

College tests, especially freshman level, should effectively sample your knowledge of the subject you are studying. Whatever the structure, a test should be balanced along two dimensions. The first is the breadth of content covered in class lecture/discussion and out-of-class study. Your first task is to determine the range of material each professor expects you to master for the test. Three methods may help: ask the professor directly, ask former students, and determine if your teacher puts old tests on file at the library or departmental office. The second dimension is somewhat more difficult to describe. It is the level of performance required of you. Will you simply have to regurgitate facts and definitions or merely recognize something that has been mentioned in lectures or in the text? This level (Memory) is the lowest and resembles most high school learning. Although it occurs in college, it will rapidly decrease after the freshman year. The second level of performance occurs when you understand an idea or the significance of an example. Test questions at this level (Understanding) may be worded differently from the initial presentation of the material. When you are asked to use an idea or a process, especially in a new situation, that level is Use. The fourth level is the most important, and the most difficult, for freshmen. It is the demonstration of your intellectual ability to explain cause/effect relationships or the similarities/differences between two or more ideas/theories/events. This level (Analysis) requires different preparation and performance strategies than the other three levels.

Another performance level (Creation) usually occurs for freshmen only in the original construction of a theme or speech.[1]

There is a reasonable, logical, and effective method of test preparation. The key point is deceptively simple—you must learn to think like a teacher, not a student, and the first step is the recognition of the difference between learning through study and preparation for performance. Learning occurs in repeated practice. Your efforts should focus on understanding the material and remembering key points or definitions. *All initial learning should be completed at least 48 hours before the test.* That revolutionary concept is the foundation of the preparation phase.

Preparation begins with an analysis of the domain of the test. Assemble your class notes, texts, handouts, and so on. List all the topics you believe the professor might use for test questions. It is crucial that your list is complete so take the time needed. Look over your list. Can you group any items together? Is there a logical progression (linking) of topics? What organization of topics did your professor use? Is it the same as in the text? The final result of your reflection should be an exhaustive list of topics. Now look at the topics. Mark with an asterisk the ones that seem most likely to occur on the test. (Most professors give strong clues through repetition and emphasis.) Your predictive abilities will improve with practice.

This stage of preparation is not yet complete. Look at your list of topics, the domain, and beside each one write your estimate of the level (Memory, Understanding, Use, Analysis) at which you will be asked to perform for that topic. Be careful and cautious. How many clues has your professor given? Is he or she concerned with details or ideas, tracing cause/effect relationships, identifying and defining terms? Essay exams are almost always at the Analysis level; problem-solving exams or case studies at the Use level. Multiple-choice exams are deceptive, for students assume they are at the Memory level, and they can be. But they can also test the other three levels.

The foregoing analysis of domain should take 30–45 minutes. Take a break, then return to construct your plan. As you look at each topic and your prediction of performance level, do an inventory. What are the gaps between your learning and your ability to perform at the predicted level? The simplest method is to test yourself. Write a list of terms or events and define them; construct an essay question and answer it. If you have a study guide for the text, answer the practice questions. What is your current performance level?

Once you have ascertained your current level, you will begin to realize what you must do to be ready to perform for the test. This is the "cramming" stage. You must master the material and hold it in your mind in an organized format so that you can access it for the test. There are several basic principles to successful cramming. First, try to practice performing the material *at the level* you predicted. For Memory, practice recitation until your recall is reliable. For Understanding, explain concepts or the significance of examples aloud, as if you were teaching someone else. For Use, especially in math, statistics, accounting, and economics, solve problems. Do not simply review those you have already worked; try to combine problems in new ways. For Analysis, try to predict questions that compare and contrast larger amounts of information. Use organizational tools like charts, graphs, mindmaps, outlines. Create simple matrices that allow you to organize comparative information. One dimension lists the topics; the other lists characteristics (see table, page 373).

As each stage of preparation intensifies, you will find you are condensing the material, picking significant ideas or facts around which you can cluster other information. Each successive practice furthers the selection process; you begin to feel mastery over the material. This condensation process is desirable, for your personal organization of the material will allow you to answer questions even if they are not phrased in the same way you have worded your practice question. One hint: study more than you believe necessary.

Civil War: Battles in Chronological Order

	First Battle of Bull Run	Battle of Shiloh	Battle of Antietam	Battle of Gettysburg
Date				
Location				
Leaders				
Causes				
Winner				
Effects				

There are practical issues to address as the test approaches. Get some sleep, but get up early enough to spend one hour in a final review session. Be sure to take whatever supplies are necessary: blue book, answer sheets, watch, pens, pencils. Go to class about ten minutes early, but do not listen to the anxious conversations among your classmates. Instead, go over your review sheet and practice recalling the key information from your memory.

When the test is distributed, your performance begins. Read the test, paying special attention to the directions, and notice the value of each section. Determine how you will allocate your time. Begin with the section that you feel most confident with. Read each question carefully and try to ascertain what your professor wants to know. If you do not understand a question, approach him or her and ask, "Does this question mean _____ or _____?" Do not ask "What does this question mean?" Work at a calm, measured pace, but keep your eye on the time. Do not hurry.

Some quick tips:

True/false   Be wary of absolute words (all, always, must, and so on). Such terms often make statements false.

Multiple-choice   Read the stem (first part) of the question with each alternative. Read all before choosing. If you are not sure of an answer, but can eliminate one or two choices, guess.

Definition or short answer   Give several sentences and an example.

Essay   Write a thesis statement that acknowledges the *entire* question and shows the main idea and structure of your answer (a brief outline will help you organize your answer). If you run out of time, outline the remainder of your essay.

After you have completed the exam, resist the temptation to turn it in and escape. There are several strategies that may add points to your score. Verify that you have answered all the required questions and, if you are using a machine-scored sheet, that your answers are in the correct rows and columns. Be cautious about changing your answers. Sometimes your performance will improve during the test and changing your answers will garner points. However, last-minute anxieties may persuade you to change a correct answer. If you generally gain points when you change answers, then do so. The opposite is good advice if you frequently lose points. Reread your essay answers and make any necessary grammatical or spelling corrections. Insert additional material.

It can be quite normal to become anxious during a test. If that happens, simply stop and take a deep breath. Remind yourself that you have prepared and then focus on the next question. The most effective stress management technique is to keep your attention on performing, not on the results of your performance. If your thoughts continue to spin away from the test, then sit quietly for a few moments with your eyes closed. Try to physically relax by breathing deeply. Say the same things to yourself that you would say to a friend, for example, "I will answer one question at a time," "I have prepared for this exam," and so on.

A powerful technique to improve your second test scores is a thorough analysis of your first performance. Allow yourself the appropriate emotional response to the results of your first test performance, then settle down to do a thoughtful evaluation of the strategies you used. First, reflect over your preparation. Did you choose the right topics and levels? Did you study enough or in the most productive manner? During your performance, did you use time wisely? Did you follow directions? Did guessing help or hurt your performance? How well did you manage stress? What changes should you make in either preparation or performance?

Two more intensive strategies may be helpful. If you are confused about your performance on the test questions you missed and believe you understood the material but could not show that, make an appointment with your professor to carefully review those questions. Take your class notes and the text with you and describe your preparation process. Your teacher is the best source of help for improving your performance. If stress played a major role in hurting your performance, then a visit to your campus counseling center can help you to learn how to manage stress so that it will not interfere with your performance.

Learning to prepare and perform in the spotlight of college tests is an important skill, which you will carry with you into professional life. A vital part of that process is a decision that you may have already made. That decision is your commitment to a personal code of honor. In other words, is the work that you claim to be your work really yours? Cheating is theft, theft of another's knowledge, and the gravest punishment is the loss of personal honor, not getting caught. If you have already made that decision to be honorable, good. If not, please consider it carefully, for the implications are vast.

Endnote

1. This concept of vertical dimension is based on B. Bloom's *Taxonomy of Educational Objectives.*

▼ Exercise: Test Preparation

1. Date of test: _____ Course: _____
2. Time allowed for this test: _____
3. Complete the chart below:

Material to be covered on exam	Completed/ready to review	Incomplete and time needed to complete
Chapters in text		
Outside reading		
Class notes		
Other		

60

▼

Walking the Tightrope

De Sellers

De Sellers offers some specific pointers on how to keep the stress in your life from exceeding your tolerance for it.

Why does everyone seem so tense and worried? I thought college was supposed to be fun (From a new freshman during the first week of class).

Well, college is supposed to be fun. But the first few weeks of your freshman year can leave you with feelings of exhilaration, terror, and a myriad of other emotions. You may feel tired, homesick, excited, or apprehensive or a combination of all these and more.

If you are entering college (or re-entering it), this first six to eight weeks is a crucial passage time. Even if you are commuting, most of your life is undergoing enormous change. You are in a new environment that makes unfamiliar expectations and demands, and with new people who may or may not be like you. If you have moved away from your family home for the first time, you probably have a roommate, share a common bath, and eat in a cafeteria. You may be in a different town or state or country. Enormous change. Change is wonderful and scary. Times of change are stressful times. Even if you have dreamed of going away to college for years, and now your dreams have come true, this much change is stressful.

Stress has become one of those words in the American language that everyone uses but few people can really define. The only applicable dictionary definition is *mental* or *physical pressure,* but that definition is not helpful. So, let's try to understand why you might be feeling tired, grumpy, unsettled, or nervous in the midst of this most exciting time and what strategies you can use to ameliorate the stress and to enjoy this freshman year.

As humans, we respond to new situations in two ways—physical and mental. Two major physical centers of response are our cardiovascular system (heart, lungs, and so on) and our gastrointestinal system (stomach, colon, and so on). So when we get excited or afraid, our bodies can respond with increased heart rate or respiration, butterflies, headaches, nausea, clammy hands or feet, or many other symptoms. We also respond cognitively to new situations. We may find concentration enhanced or diminished. The internal dialogue (those statements we make to ourselves in the privacy of our own minds) may be helpful or hurtful. We may experience intense emotions of joy or loneliness. We may feel afraid or depressed. Generally, stressful times seem to narrow our focus and exaggerate our reactions.

Here are some basic premises about stress:

1. Stress is the word we use to describe our physical and mental responses to situations. We create our reactions; in other words, outside events do not cause stress, we choose to react to outside events.
2. Stressful situations can be positive or negative. Some situations are stressful but fun—competing, performing, responding to physical or mental challenges.
3. Life without stress would be boring (to most of us).

376

4. Stress is cumulative; that is, if you have just ended a romantic relationship and begun a new job, you will experience combined stress from both circumstances.

5. Individuals desire different levels of stress in their lives, and they also have different tolerances for stress.

As we move into adulthood, a major task is to learn to manage our reactions in order to have a relatively calm and joyful life. The techniques used are often referred to as stress management, and they can be helpful as we construct our lives, especially at juncture points as dramatic as the freshman year.

There are many stress management techniques. Through careful use of some of these strategies, you can maintain the level of stress you desire in your life. What follows is a short description of techniques that former freshmen recommend:

Have realistic goals and expectations. Sit down with or call a good friend or family member and write down the goals and expectations you have of this semester. These should include academic (more than a GPA, what do you want to learn?), social (dating, relationships, friendships) and personal (health, money, beliefs). Are your goals realistic? Achievable? Try to have no more than two goals in any category. Post them where you will see them each day.

Take care of your body. Even if you are 18, you will quickly feel and look 30 or more if you cheat your body of sleep, exercise, and good nutrition. Many freshmen take better care of their cars than of their bodies. Be smart. Sleep. Exercise. Eat right. Remember that alcohol and other drugs cost you double time—the time you are high and the time to recover. Can you afford that?

Take care of your business. Balance your checkbook (the hot check charges can kill you). Don't carry your checkbook with you; carry cash instead and try hard to live on your budget. Call home when you are homesick, but try to talk late at night and talk quickly. Put a clock by the phone and a list of the charges per minute. Do the maintenance on your car and pay your bills on time.

Do your job as a student. Go to class. That's right, every single class. Cutting is the student disease that will lead you straight to probation. Keep a master calendar and post all assignments and tests. Get a campus map and explore. Know the campus policies (not myths) about absences, dropping classes, and so on. In other words, read the student handbook and the catalog; don't rely on fellow students; they often believe the myths. Keep copies of all the papers you complete. Oh yes, study the material when it is assigned. Every time you procrastinate, the bad stress builds, and you usually feel guilty as well. Your work as a student is the most important job you have this semester; it comes first.

Take care of your stuff. Keep your notebooks and handouts organized. Keep your room bearable and your clothes clean (anyone can learn to use a washer and dryer). Living like a slob just increases the pressure because the simplest things become difficult.

Invest in relationships. It helps to have friends—people who truly care about you and your life. Write your friends and call when you can afford it. Spend some time talking with your family and spend at least one or two weekends at home, if you can. As you make new acquaintances on campus, allow some time for those new relationships to evolve into friendships. Friendships can take time to mature, so don't push a new, fragile relationship too hard.

Be thoughtful and honorable in romantic relationships. If you have a significant other in another town and you decide you want to date someone on campus, be honest with both people. If you hide or lie, the stress can be unbearable.

Give yourself room. In other words, you need to learn how to be a freshman—a competent, successful, happy freshman—you do not need to be perfect. Be honest about your feelings, with yourself and others. Try to realize that these are the feelings you have now, but they will probably change within a short time.

Learn to say No. No is the least favorite word for freshmen. Choose two regular activities that you like and participate. Go out two nights a week, preferably on the weekends, and avoid the Thursday night parties. You cannot afford either the money or the time for more.

Talk to yourself as you would to a friend. It's easier to give a friend good advice than to give the same to ourselves. Pretend you are talking with a close friend. What would he or she say to you?

When you feel overwhelmed, take a quick, brisk walk. Look at the physical world and try to attune yourself to its cadence.

Set aside 30 minutes a day just for you. Do something you enjoy (or nothing at all). Listen to music, read, whatever. This is personal time, time when you invest in yourself.

Make your room or apartment your home. Put pictures or posters up and bring some of your favorite things from your parents' home. Your home should be your sanctuary, even if it's half of a small dorm room.

Talk to your teachers. Go by during office hours to introduce yourself and ask a question or two based on the lectures. Most profs will welcome you.

Explore the campus and its offerings. There are always many concerts, movies, lectures, groups, and they are free. Attend one each week.

Make use of small pieces of time. Five minutes here, ten there. Study vocabulary words for a science class, write a letter, pick up your clothes.

Study during the day. Try to finish all studying by 8 P.M.

If you feel your life is spinning out of control, go immediately to the campus counseling center and talk with a counselor. Stress can enhance our lives, but it can also drain all the pleasure from them.

As new freshmen, the changes in your lives are not simply external pressures. You will probably be undergoing significant personal and philosophical changes during this year as you explore new ideas and ways of living. Such rapid and profound changes are challenging, but with a little careful thought, you can walk the tightrope and create a successful college career.

▼ Life Inventory

Write whatever comes to mind. Do not worry if you repeat yourself. Don't censor anything.

1. Peak experiences in my life:

   _____

   _____

   _____

   _____

2. What I do well:

   _____

   _____

   _____

   _____

3. What I do poorly:

_____

_____

_____

_____

4. What I want to stop doing:

_____

_____

_____

_____

5. What I would like to do well:

_____

_____

_____

_____

6. Attitudes, personal characteristics, values I'd like to acquire:

_____

_____

_____

_____

7. Peak experiences I want to have:

_____

_____

_____

_____

8. What I want to start doing now:

_____

_____

_____

_____

LIFELINE

Beginning

End

Draw a line above to indicate the ups and downs in your life: past, present, and future. After you have drawn the line, label the high and low points, then place a check mark along it to indicate where you are right now.

Explain why you drew the line as you did and why you put the check mark where you did.

61

▼

Thoughtfulness and Sexuality

De Sellers

To bring thoughtfulness to sexuality requires a special effort, De Sellers writes, for "thoughtfulness is frequently a small voice trampled by the driving force of passion." Here she offers some suggestions for joining these seemingly alien domains.

What are you doing tonight? Getting drunk and getting laid?

Nice ass, I wish it were mine.

But we love each other; that makes it all right.

Well, yes, we did it, but I was drinking, and he talked me into it.

She won't talk to me. Maybe I wasn't good enough for her.

Everybody gets laid but me.

I just want someone to love me.

Who am I taking home tonight?

We are physical creatures. Mind, heart, and soul incarnated in a physical body. It is not a simple existence for any of us, for our physical natures encompass sexual drives. And those drives alternately promote pleasure and pain. As humans we struggle with physical urges and yearn for their gratification.

All cultures attempt to regulate sexual behavior by establishing rigorous and elaborate rules. American culture is no different. Parents and churches and much of our society say to wait—that sex and love are not children's toys, but adult responsibilities. As Americans, we spend much of our time and energy thinking, talking, focusing on the immediate gratification of sex. When the sexual tidal wave rolls over an adolescent, that American teenager usually has few resources. For the issue is complicated: pleasure, pregnancy, AIDS, sexually transmitted diseases (STDs), not to mention the emotional boomerang of acceptance and rejection or the vulnerability of feelings. A further complication is that movies, advertisements, television all promote the message of immediate gratification as a response to physical beauty.

The typical reaction of many adolescents is to think about sex and sexual relationships most of the time, but not to be thoughtful about those issues. Thoughtfulness, that deliberate mode of thinking that incorporates emotion and ethics as well as logic, is the primary vehicle humans have to make those decisions that lead to the creation of a good life. But thoughtfulness is frequently a small voice trampled by the driving force of our sexual passions. So we avoid thinking, and the easiest way to do that is to deaden our minds through alcohol or other drugs. Another powerful avoidance technique is denial of the future, that is, telling ourselves that tomorrow and consequences will not come. A variant of this technique is the "That can't happen to me" conviction. A third avoidance technique is rationalization, for example, "This one time is okay."

The fact is we can damage our bodies. More importantly, we can damage our minds, hearts, and souls. On the other hand, all of us need to learn how to live (that's different from existing), and sexuality is an important part of life. That conflict between the danger of thoughtless sexual behavior and the opportunity for powerfully pleasurable sexual experiences is at the heart of the difficult decisions we make. The ability to be comfortable with one's own sexual nature, the ability to create a sexual relationship that is loving and ethical as well as physically pleasurable, the ability to accept other people's choices about sexuality—these abilities are not automatically bestowed at the eighteenth birthday. They are not bestowed at all. They must be learned. And there are few good teachers in our culture.

Families, church, or peer groups often dictate divergent sets of behaviors and attitudes about sexuality. The pressure to conform to the group's sexual mores can be intense, and it can be easy to simply accept one set of rules. There's just one catch. The group's rules rarely work for the individual, for the rules come from outside the person. The work of the individual is to build a life, from the inside. Each person should create a personal set of guidelines, including sexual guidelines. Mine may be different from yours. Hers may be different from his. Each set must be uniquely fitted to the individual.

Being thoughtful is difficult because sentimentality and romanticism must play subdued roles. In other words, thoughtfulness requires clarity. If we allow the powerful immediacy of romantic feelings or the nostalgic images of romance to silence the cool voice of reason, then we are likely to make decisions that we will come to regret. However, life without romance is bleak, so the goal is to incorporate those feelings and desires but not let them overwhelm our thinking.

We can begin a journey of thoughtfulness from many different starting points. You may be trying to make an immediate decision. You may be vaguely dissatisfied with the decisions you have been making. You may be miserable. You might begin with a careful examination of the beliefs and values you hold about sexuality. What messages did you get from your parents? from your peers? from your religion? Not only messages about right and wrong, but good and bad. What do you believe about sexual behaviors? What role does sex have in your life? Does your sexual behavior reflect your ethical beliefs?

Our personal histories shape many of our ethical beliefs, either positively or negatively. And those beliefs, in turn, shape our feelings about ourselves and others. When we respect another person, we acknowledge that person's value. When we respect ourselves, we are doing the same. Respect also means we have that person's (as well as our own) welfare in mind. Exploitative sex is not respectful. When we meet our own sexual needs at the expense of another's welfare, we are practicing exploitative sex. The common parlance for such behavior is *using*. Users and useds both suffer from the exchange, but in different ways. Useds often feel unloved and unwanted. They may come to believe they are worthless, meant to be discarded as trash. And this may make it easier to fall victim to the blandishments of the next user, spiraling downward in a torrent of self-hatred. Users believe that they can escape the consequences of their actions, but they rarely do. Their hungers are not satisfied by the consumption of their victims, and their hearts become coarsened by the inevitable conviction that relationships can only be exploitative. Only suckers care. They pursue and pursue, increasingly jaded by their conquests, transforming themselves into grasping creatures who live the shallow material life. The loss they suffer is immense, for they lose the opportunity to give and receive love within the context of an ethical, caring relationship.

Respect is the basis for ethical sexual behavior. But that is only the first step. A necessary corollary is a comfortable acceptance of our physical selves. How hard that is today, with the millions of images promoted by the media. We equate good with beauty, as if a person beautiful on the outside is automatically a good, worthy person. What a dangerous premise! For the myth of physical beauty—that such beauty equals goodness—is a cruel myth. Because so many of us accept that myth as truth, we long to be beautiful and are dissatisfied with the image we see in the mirror. No one measures up to the standard of physical perfection. We are like Goldilocks in her search for the perfect porridge; we want to be perfect. We want to be thinner, stronger, taller, prettier . . . there are myriad ways to find fault with our physical selves. To be healthy, happy, productive, loving: those are the signs of true beauty.

Accepting our physical selves—how we are and how we look and what we feel—is important. Oh, we can groom ourselves, but at the same time we can avoid the obsessive attention to our outward appearance. How and where do we begin the comfortable acceptance of ourselves? Many times we begin that process as children when we are unconditionally loved by our parents. Sometimes we begin it as our bodies mature through adolescence. However, many of us become adults and still have a persistent uneasiness about our bodies. Some of us even despise and abuse our bodies. As adults, what can we do to become more comfortable with our physical natures? Perhaps by listening to those people who love us; they see beauty in us, even when we cannot see it ourselves. Perhaps by something as simple as really looking at our own bodies and paying attention to what feels pleasurable. A professional massage allows us to experience sensuality without sex. Exercise and physical exertion also attune us to our bodies. Masturbation is one practical method many people use to learn about their bodies. Understanding how our bodies respond sexually helps us to become more aware of our needs and the needs of other people. The thoughts and feelings we have about our bodies directly influence what we can give and what we can get from sexual experiences.

It is often difficult to understand how varied the sexual experience is for individuals. Not only do women and men differ, but there is great variance between people of the same gender. In our culture we rarely talk about our experiences truthfully. We brag, or lie, or romanticize. If you can find a mature person who will genuinely describe his or her sexual responses, then you may learn from another person's experience. Understanding the sexual possibilities of ourselves and others helps us decide how we want to live and what we can and should expect in sexual relationships. As pedantic as it sounds to suggest, reading informative texts will help. Taking a psychology course in sexual issues may also increase our knowledge and change our perspective. Sex is like any other powerful part of life; accurate knowledge helps us make good choices.

Sexual relationships are complex and tumultuous. They are the joining together of two people through the multiple connections of physical attraction, intense concern, and emotional bonding. Sexual encounters differ from sexual relationships. A sexual encounter usually results from a tempestuous decision, based on physical needs, with little regard to emotional or physical safety. Such encounters are rarely ethical or caring, and often dangerous. We choose to engage in encounters and deny or dismiss the dangers because our sexual drives run rampant over our minds or because we foolishly believe that a sexual connection can assuage our loneliness for more than a few minutes. Sexual encounters rarely provide a good beginning for a relationship. Too much, too soon, too bad.

A sexual relationship implies a larger relationship with another person. The physical link is a primary factor in the linking of your life with someone else, but there are other connecting points: interests, activities, and friendships. The physical lies within the context of the entire relationship. Creating a loving and ethical sexual relationship requires two people who are willing to do three things—to communicate their desires and responses truthfully, to be sensitive to and accepting of each other's needs and expectations, and to use physical intimacy in a generous and open manner. It is too easy to use the bed as a battleground, to use sex as a punishment or a reward, to be cruel or controlling. It requires restraint and maturity to refrain from these behaviors.

A good sexual relationship takes time and effort. We may quickly learn how to have sex, but we slowly learn to make love. The respect from each partner to each partner engenders trust, and trust allows us to be free. That freedom releases our genuine selves from hiding, and the result is that we know each other in ways no one else knows us. Few occurrences in life are as thrilling.

As we become comfortable with our sexual natures and learn to establish loving relationships with others, it becomes easier to affirm the delightful variability of humans. Not only are we different physically, intellectually, emotionally, spiritually, but we are different sexually. We can accept, even appreciate, those differences without understanding or experiencing them when we no longer feel threatened by someone different from ourselves. We are different genders. We have different sexual orientations. We have different levels of sexual needs, physical and emotional. It is much easier to be tolerant, which is the grudging recognition of difference, than appreciative, which is the loving celebration of difference. To truly appreciate the diversity of others requires the joining of a loving heart and an open mind.

As humans, we have differing ethical systems, and those systems lead us to diverse decisions. Our choice may be celibacy or abstinence until marriage or premarital sex or long-term sexual relationships or casual sex. Each sexual decision we make matters. Through these and other decisions, we create our lives. The transition between adolescence and adulthood is marked by the realization that our decisions are irrevocable. We construct who we are.

Part of being human is our sexual nature. It seems to do little good to deny it or repress it. And it does less good to fall prey to the glittering enticements of sexual exploitation. Instead, let us explore and evaluate thoughtfully. We can ask questions, read, write, and reflect. We have time. We have all of our lives to understand and enjoy this part of life.

Glossary

a jus cru: with raw juice 316

a priori: known to be certain without need of validation by experience 233

abashing: disconcerting 24

abeyance: temporary suspension 293

abode: dwelling 344

abominable: loathsome 190

abominations: abhorrent situations 253

absolution: forgiveness 19

abutting: touching 24

academe: the world of the university 344

accessible: easily obtained 153

acculturation: the process of instilling culture in an individual 330

acquitted (oneself): performed the task 180

actualization: the process of making actual one's potential 330

adjudicate: settle judicially 34

advocacy: the act of supporting or pleading for a cause 168

aesthetic: dealing with the beautiful 79

aesthetically: pertaining to the appreciation of beauty 239

affliction: condition of suffering or distress 310

affluence: wealth 344

affluent: rich or prosperous 331

agendas: lists or plans of matters to be attended to 204

aggrandized: made to appear greater 95

aggregate: groups that come together to make a whole unit 196

alienating: dissociating or estranging from the self 330

alienation: dissociation; estrangement 13, 339

allegiance: loyalty; obligation 116

alleviate: take away 121

altruistic: unselfishly devoted to the welfare of others 95

amalgam: combination 69

ambiguous: uncertain; vague 18

ambivalent: exhibiting conflicting feelings 19, 140

amiably: pleasantly 189

amorphous: without pattern or structure 204

amulets: a charm or talisman used to ward off evil spirits 18

anachronisms: things out of another time 218

anarchism: disorder and confusion 78

ancillary: auxiliary 167

animosity: hostility; mistrust 257

anorectic: marked by prolonged loss of appetite 56

anthropological: pertaining to science dealing with the origins and physical and cultural development of humankind 228

anthropologist: one who scientifically studies the origin, biological characteristics, and the physical, cultural, and social development of humankind 173

anticipated: expected 350

antinomianism: refusal to accept a social moral system 78

antithesis: the direct opposite 176

apartheid: in South Africa, a policy of rigid segregation that was practiced until 1994 against nonwhites 302

apocalypse: cosmic upheaval 56

appeasement: conciliation 181

apprenticeships: positions of apprentices, that is, persons who work for another in order to learn a trade 309

appropriation: the act of seizing for oneself 229

aquiline: resembling an eagle 172

arbitrary: without justification 233

arcana: mysteries 189

archaeologist: one who studies artifacts and other remains of past human life and culture 173

archetypal: pertaining to the original model or pattern; prototypical 290

ardency: passion 69

aristocracy: nobility 320

articulation: the act of expressing interrelated thoughts in a clear and understandable manner 27

artifacts: products of human craft; man-made objects 285, 308

ascetic: self-disciplined, austere; self-denying 116, 180

asceticism: self-denial 330

aspirations: goals 145

assiduously: diligently 79

assignations: trysts, appointments 18, 216

assignats: paper currency issued in France by the revolutionary government and backed by confiscated lands 250

assimilated: to take in and make part of oneself 15

assimilation: absorption; the process of incorporating as one's own 132

astronomical epoch: an arbitrary fixed date, usually the beginning of a century, used as a reference in giving the elements of a planetary orbit 325

atrophied: wasted away 340

attained: achieved 114

attar: fragrance 24

authoritarians: people who are driven to have absolute power over others 255

autonomous: self-directed 153

autonomy: the condition of being independent; self-ruling; self-direction 138, 169

avidly: fervently 73

badgering: pestering; nagging 344

balkanized: divided into small states mired in ineffectual conflict 291

ballast: something that gives stability 197

banal: unoriginal 165

banality: lack of freshness or originality 189

banter: good-humored ridicule 167

baroque: a period of art, from 1550 to 1700, characterized by extravagant, flamboyant, and sometimes grotesque forms and shapes 61

barrio: a Hispanic ghetto in an American city 338

bastion: prominent portion of a fortification or rampart; strongholds 68, 317

bayou: an outlet or arm of a river or lake in the southern United States 320

belaying pin: a short bar inserted in the rail of a ship for fastening a rope 172

beleaguered: troubled 91

belligerent: hostile 63, 131

benign: kind and gracious; healthful; beneficial; not malignant 68, 240

blinkered: blinded 331

bludgeoning: beating 160

bourgeoisie: middle class 73

bovine: cowlike 283

brakeman: in a train, an assistant to the conductor 174

burgeoned: bloomed 24

burnished: lustrous; polished 24

cacophony: harsh, discordant mixture of sounds 172

cadences: rhythmic flow of a series of sounds or words 207

cannily: slyly 62

canons: bodies of work of particular importance 179

capitulation: the act of yielding or surrendering 297

caste system: a social system characterized by a highly ordered class structure 76

castigating: criticizing 95

catechism: belief system forced on you by your environment 6

cathartic: purging 75

celestial: relating to the heavens or sky 28

censure: to express disapproval strongly 197

centrifugal: directed outward from the center 242

chalices: cups for the wine of the Mass or Eucharist 349

chameleon: inconsistent person 137

changeling: a child exchanged secretly for another 176

chasteness: virtuousness 73

chastise: punish 197

circumpolar: around a pole 176

circumscribed: confined 152

clarion: a call to action 78

cognitive: pertaining to knowledge 210

cohabitors: unmarried couples who live together 204

coherent: logically connected 277

coherently: clearly; in a logically connected way 168

collaborate: work together 138

collective: pertaining to a group functioning as a team 204

comely: attractive 24

commiserated: expressed sorrow or compassion 41

commiserative: sympathetic or sorrowful 20

commune: to communicate with intensity 199

conceptualize: to form a concept (of) 340, 345

configurations: arrangements 348

confluence: gathering 67

conformation: physical structure 57

conglomerations: unions; assemblages 250

consensus: general agreement; majority opinion 136, 331

consortium: association 91

consummately: in a manner expressing the highest degree 181

contemptible: despicable 37

contradistinguished: distinguished by contrasting opposite qualities 252

contrived: devised 120

conventions: widely observed practices 338

coquettish: flirting 73

cornucopia: a curved receptacle shaped like a horn of a goat that is usually overstuffed with fruit to symbolize abundance 24

corollary: natural consequence 75

Corybantic: resembling attendants of the Greek nature goddess Cybele, known for their orgiastic processions and rituals. 75

countenance: appearance 172

countervailing: counteracting 76

coup d'etat: overthrow of the government 249

crabbed minutiae: minor details 24

critique: criticism 199

crucible: a test of great magnitude 67

culinary: referring to cookery 23

culmination: climax 75

cultivate: promote 116

cursory: hasty; superficial 69

daft: crazy 168

dashikis: brightly colored tunics 159

dearth: inadequate supply 72

debauchee: the person corrupted by a debaucher 135

debaucher: a corrupter; one who indulges in unrestrained sensuality 135

debauchery: sensual indulgence 38

decadent: self-indulgent 218

decimation: destruction of a great portion 237

decolonization: release from the status of a colony 302

decorous: exhibiting decorum or proper behavior 188

deforestation: clearing of forests 237

delineated: described precisely 298

delirium: state of violent emotion or excitement 209

deluge: an overwhelming flood 27

demagogues: leaders who obtain power by appealing to the emotions and prejudices of the people 255

demented: insane 168

demographers: practitioners of the science of vital and social statistics of population 238

demographic: relating to the statistical study of populations 197

depletion: a serious decrease in the supply 237

deplored: regretted strongly 327

depreciation: decline in value 250

despicable: worthless; contemptible 45

desuetude: discontinued use 72

desultory: random 47

devastation: utter destruction 296

devil's advocate: a person arguing against a position for the sake of argument 135

diametrically: in a manner exactly opposed to 135

dilapidated: reduced to decay or ruin 344

dilemma: perplexing situation 341

dilettante: one who toys with a variety of interests 145

diligently: attentively and persistently 210

disclaimer: a denial of responsibility; disavowal 339

discourse: speech; conversation 136, 210

discrepant: different 197

disdain: scorn 304

disenchanted: unenthralled 68

disenchantment: loss of an illusion about something 14

disfranchised: those deprived of rights of citizenship 227

disinherited: deprived of rights and privileges 68

dismay: agitation 168

dismayed: astonished 63

dismembered: having had one's body taken apart 103

disparagement: belittlement 104

dispersal: breaking up and scattering 146

dispositions: usual temperaments 69

dissertation: the book-length thesis required for the doctoral degree (Ph.D.) 179, 337

diversity: variety 116

divested: ridded oneself of 303

Du bist was du ißt: a German pun on "You are what you eat" 316

dubious: doubtful 325

dulcet: having a soothing and agreeable quality 188

dystopia: an imaginary place in which people live fearful and dehumanized lives 188

ebullience: enthusiasm and liveliness 23

eccentric: peculiar; unconventional; odd; unusual 255, 316

eccentricity: oddity; peculiarity 132

ecosystem: a system formed by the interaction between a community of organisms and their environment 238

edict: order or proclamation 199

effaced: worn away 62

efflorescences: development; blossoming 23

effluvium: an invisible vapor or exhalation 349

egalitarian: promoting equality 228

elated: overjoyed 37

eliciting: bringing out 75

elitism: allegiance to or membership in a select group 318

elliptical: not fully elaborated 347

eloquence: graceful power in verbal expression 136

eloquent: vivid; expressive 119

elucidated: made clear 228

eluded: escaped 348

elusive: escaping firm mental grasp 176

emanations: emissions 75

emblematic: symbolic 40

eminence: high stature or repute 174

emotive: emotional 73

empathize: identify with; understand 138

empirical: based on observation 95

enamored: captivated by 131

encapsulates: epitomizes; puts in capsule form 79

enfeebled: weakened 93

enshrined: preserved as sacred 153

enumerate: to name or count off one by one 330

envisage: conceive a certain picture 140

epitomized: exemplified 78

equitable: fair and impartial 295

eschatological: in theology, pertaining to final matters: death, judgment, afterlife 179

ethicist: philosopher who deals with the question about the rightness and wrongness of human actions 208

ethnocentric: believing in the inherent superiority of one's own culture 229

ethnohistory: in anthropology, the study of cultures without a native written history 176

ethnologists: those who study the branch of anthropology that deals with the origin and distinguishing characteristics of the races of humankind 176

ethos: fundamental value; belief system 88, 199

eulogize: praise highly 204

euphemisms: substitutions of inoffensive terms for offensive terms 222

euphoria: a feeling of overwhelming well-being 249

evanescent: fleeting 88

exacerbated: made more severe, irritated, or aggravated 231

exemplary: serving to illustrate; typical 217

exhilarating: invigorating 146

exhortations: language that is intended to encourage and excite 91

exhorting: urging strongly 69

extant: still in existence 176

extraneous: nonessential; extra 145, 348

extricate: disengage 140

exuberant: overflowing with joy 218

exuded: oozed 67

fabrication: something made up 209

fallible: capable of erring 251

fallow: (of land) plowed and left unseeded for a season; uncultivated 324

fanaticism: excessive, uncritical devotion 116

fatuous: silly or inane, especially in an unconscious manner 331

figuratively: in the manner of a figure of speech; symbolically 338

finical: extremely accurate or exact 23

fledgling: marked by inexperience 181

flintlock: a gunlock in which the action of flint striking steel ignites the powder 173

foreboding: inner certainty of coming misfortune 249

forfeited: gave up 230

formidable: of discouraging difficulty; intimidating 132, 172

frivolous: marked by a lack of seriousness 208

fruition: completion 24

fulcrum: support 76

geopolitics: combination of geographic and political factors influencing a region or country 302

gladiatorial: pertaining to gladiators; characterized by a fight to the death 76

glibness: superficial fluency 168

Gothic: pertaining to a style of architecture popular in Western Europe between the twelfth and sixteenth centuries 67

grandiosity: the state of being marked by grandeur 294

gratuitously: in a manner that is not called for by the circumstances 103

gregarious: enjoying others' company 338

groveling: begging 167

haphazardly: without plan or order 15

hawks: people who take a militant attitude and support a war or warlike policy 319

heady: intoxicating 67

heresy: a belief at variance with religious teaching 277

hierarchical: ordered according to a rank 232

historicity: being situated in history 8

hither: toward; to 121

homeostasis: internal stability 350

homogeneity: sameness; uniformity 302

hyperspace: a mathematical term used here metaphorically to mean mysterious space 347

idealism: commitment to an ideal beyond self-interest 69

ideological: pertaining to the body of doctrine of a social movement or large group 233

ideological preachments: obtrusive or tedious sermons from a doctrinaire point of view 285

ideology: a set of beliefs that makes up a system 308

idiomatic: pertaining to a dialect or style of speaking peculiar to a people 338

idiosyncrasy: peculiarity 284

illicit: unlawful; not permitted 209

imbibing: drinking in 68

imminent: impending 83

impeccably: flawlessly 23

impediment: hindrance 72

imperial: characteristic of an emperor 169

imperialism: the policy of extending a nation's authority by territorial acquisition 228

imperious: arrogantly domineering 190

impetuosity: impulsive vehemence 27

impetus: stimulus 62

imposition: the act of laying on (as a burden) 228

inalienable rights: rights that no one can take away from you 317

inchoate: not fully formed 291

incommensurability: having no common standard of comparison 284

incompetence: being unqualified 120

incongruence: here, a phrase consisting of incompatible parts 290

incontrovertible: not disputable; unquestionable 277

inculcated: instilled 330

indebtedness: obligation 231

indeterminate: not determined 122

indigenous: native 229

indignation: righteous anger 208

individualist utilitarianism: acting to promote one's own happiness 203

individuation: the process of becoming an individual, a self 331

inequitable: unfair 230

inexplicable: unexplainable 28

infallible: incapable of error 282

infinitesimal: incalculably minute 117

inherent: intrinsic 116

insensately: without feeling 152

insidious: operating inconspicuously but with gravely harmful effect 140

instigated: provoked or incited 229

intangible: not material; elusive of grasp; insubstantial or immaterial 19, 168

integuments: links 64

intellectualism: devotion to the life of the mind 180

intelligible: capable of being understood 167, 277, 332

interminable: having no end in sight 18

internalize: to make a part of one's beliefs or attitudes 304

intimated: suggested 278

intrinsic: inherent; essential; inmost 20, 330

intrinsically: by its very nature; innately 146, 207

intuitively: with keen insight 120

invincibility: the condition of being unconquerable 160

ire: intense anger 78

irreproachable: above blame 325

irresolution: indecisiveness 279

irreverent: lacking reverence or respect 179

irrevocably: impossible to alter 19

jargon: technical or specialized language 211

juxtaposition: placing side by side 337

ken: range or vision 347

languor: listlessness or stillness 189

latent: undeveloped 69

laud: praise 203

leavened: permeated with a transforming influence 348

Leviathan: a monstrous entity 252

liaison: relationship 19

liberalized: made to favor individual freedom 199

libretto: the text of a dramatic musical work 316

linear: resembling a straight line 240

litany: an incantation; incantatory recital 5, 151

lithe: marked by effortless grace 188

ludicrous: laughable 20

luminous: enlightening 159

lurid: ghastly pale; gruesome 83, 135

magnanimous: noble; large and generous in spirit 46, 189

malcontents: bitterly dissatisfied people 68

malleable: adaptable 41

manifestation: evidence 83

maverick: characteristic of a person who stands outside the group 174, 179

meditation: reflection 114

megalomania: a pathological obsession with power 254

metabolism: the totality of physical and chemical processes in an organism by which energy is made available for its functioning 238

meta-message: an unspoken communication that accompanies a spoken one 296

metamorphosing: changing completely in character or circumstances 203

metaphor: figure of speech in which a word or phrase designating one thing is applied to something else in an implicit comparison 309

metaphorical: symbolic 339

metaphysical: pertaining to the nature of the ultimate scheme of things 207, 228

metaphysics: the study of the nature of ultimate reality 180

methodology: a system of rules and principles 233

meticulous: done with extreme care 23

mettlesome: thrusting oneself into the affairs of others 24

milieu: environment 338

minarets: mosques with projecting balconies where townspeople are summoned to hear a supreme or divine ruler 255

ministerial: serving as a means or instrument 75

misogynist: a person who hates women 304

miter: match or pair up 24

modish: stylish 310

modus vivendi: way of living 243

monomaniacally: with excessive care given to a single object 23

moratorium: suspension of action 151

multifarious: numerous and varied 277

mundane: commonplace 44

myriad: innumerable 301

mystic: pertaining to an immediate intuition that produces spiritual ecstasy 121

nascent: coming into existence recently 79

neo-Nazi: referring to a member of a political group that embraces the ideas of Adolf Hitler 256

niche: place where you fit perfectly 151

normative: reflecting what is assumed as a norm; prescribing a norm or standard 203, 233

nuance: subtle detail 179

objectified: made into or treated as an object 102

obscurantist: obscuring; tending to prevent human progress and enlightenment 326

obscure: uncertain 276

odyssey: a long journey marked by adventure and hardship 180

ominous: forbidding; dreaded 200, 249

onanism: masturbation 76

ontocentrism: the conviction held by a group that its conception of reality is superior to all others 231

ontological: pertaining to the nature of being 179

operational: reflecting what is practiced 203

opiate: narcotic causing sleep or inaction 78

oppressors: tyrants 121

orators: speakers 67

ostensibly: appearing to be such 14

ostentatious: showy 37

overt: open 36

Oxonian: pertaining to Oxford University 179

ozone: a form of oxygen 237

panache: flamboyant style 23

pantheon: a temple 198

paradigmatically: serving as a model 208

paradox: an apparent contradiction 62, 191, 290

paradoxically: in a seemingly contradictory way 20, 340

paramecium: a fresh-water, one-celled organism 276

parity: equivalence; equality in standing 233, 297

parlayed: transformed into something of much greater value 159

parodies: satirical imitations 179

paroxysm: spasm 249

pedagogical: pertaining to the art or science of teaching 208

pedants: persons who make an excessive display of their learning 188

perceptibly: observably 333

perennial: in botany, having a life cycle longer than two years 239

perestroika: sweeping political reform in the former Soviet Union 251

perfunctory: performed as a routine duty 179

pernicious: insidiously harmful 5

persona non grata: not welcome 39

perspective: point of view 233

philology: the study of the original form of a text and the determination of its meaning 274

phrenologists: people who attempt to analyze character by examining the characteristics of the skull 199

pinafore: a sleeveless apron 61

pious: devout 282

platitudes: clichés 18

pluralism: the idea that no one belief system can explain all the phenomena encountered in life 200

pluralistic: referring to a condition of society in which groups subscribing to different belief systems co-exist 283

polemical: taking a controversial stand 180

polity: a particular form of government 252

polymorphous: occurring in various forms 75

populists: those who advocate the needs of the common people 255

portent: sign 242

positivists: members of a school of philosophy that maintains that sense perception is the basis of all admissible knowledge 208

pragmatic: practical 7, 92

precarious: uncertain; insecure 160

precepts: a principle prescribing conduct 197

precocity: unusually early development 40

precognita: the knowledge that composes the base of a discipline; the fundamental facts 309

predecessor: someone who came before 135

predilection: preference 140

prefiguring: foreshadowing 121

premonitory: warning 74

prerogative: a right or privilege limited to persons of a specific category 242

prescient: exhibiting foreknowledge or foresight 249

pretension: a claim of importance or worth; laying of a claim to something 62, 348

primal: primeval; primitive 316

proclivity: predisposition 137

prodigality: extravagance 24

prodigious: abnormal; monstrous 279

prodigiously: extraordinarily 180

proffered: presented for acceptance 77

profoundest: deepest 153

profusion: abundance 24

proletarian: a member of the lowest economic and social class of a community 78

proliferation: rapid spread 289

promulgate: set forth publicly 7

prophylactic: protection 325

propitious: presenting favorable circumstances 152

prosaic: dull; ordinary 75

proselytizing: converting 169

prototypical: pertaining to the original or model 180

protract: prolong 275

provenance: place of origin 179

provincial: unsophisticated 290

provocations: instigations; things that incite 332

proximity: nearness; closeness 350

prudent: wise 114

psyche: mind 199

pubescent: relating to puberty 76

punctilio: precise observance of amenities or formalities 199

purview: range of understanding or vision 325

putative: supposed 35

Pythagorean: referring to the Greek philosopher and mathematician Pythagoras 121

quagmires: predicaments 24

rapine: the act of plunder 279

rapt: absorbed 190

rationale: fundamental justification 230, 294

rationality: the habit of governing one's thinking by reason 207

reascended: climbed up again 120

recapitulated: summarized 349

reciprocity: mutual exchange 197

referentiality: the thing a symbol stands for 181

regalia: special dress characterized by bright colors, emblems, or symbols 69

reified: regarded as material or concrete things 101

relativism: a view that ethical truths are dependent on the individuals or groups that hold them: what is true is what is believed to be true 77

relativistic: pertaining to the theory that truth is determined by what is believed to be true 233

reminiscent: suggestive (of) 207

remuneration: payment; salary 91

repertoire: the list of pieces one is prepared to perform 349

repressed: restrained 69

repudiating: disowning 181

reputed: considered 121

resilient: recovering speedily from adversity; buoyant 200

resolute: unwavering; committed 115

resoluteness: strong determination 69

resonance: echoing 339

resonates: echoes 62

respective: individual 120

restive: restless; impatient or nervous under pressure, restriction, or delay 73, 188

reticence: disposition to silence 174

reverberate: echo 121

rife: common; frequent 146

riffs: constantly repeated melodic phrases that form an accompaniment to a jazz soloist 347

sabbatical: a year's leave extended to a college professor, usually every seventh year 275

sagacity: wisdom 279, 324

salutary: wholesome 152

salve: a medicinal ointment for relieving wounds 159

sanctity: sacredness 284

sansculottism: radical or violent extremism 73

satyr: a Greek mythological figure that was a cross between a horse or goat and a man with excessive, uncontrollable sexual desire 78

scapulimancy: the practice of divining by observing a shoulder blade cracked from fire 176

schistosomiasis: organ infection and chronic anemia caused by parasites in feces-contaminated water 237

scrupulously: painstakingly 24

sectarian: partisan 256

secularization: the process of removing religious orientation 284

self-aggrandizing: self-serving; tending to increase one's power or heighten one's stature 169

self-trammeled: self-restricting 24

seminal: germinative; original 119

sepia: brownish 61

serapes: blanket-like shawls worn especially in Mexico 340

sicklied: sickened 115

skewing: distorting 294

smarmy: marked by an ingratiating and false earnestness 76

smorgasbord: variety 121

soirée française: an elegant party in the French style 344

sojourn: travel 161

solicitude: concern 8

solidarity: unity 73

solipsist: one who believes that only he or she exists 208

soufflés: light, fluffy baked dishes 189

sovereignty: supreme and independent authority claimed by a government 242, 291

speciation: the forming of new species 237

specious: apparently true or plausible but actually fallacious 310

specter: ghost 20

speculative: theoretic 210

spurious: not genuine 310

stagnate: fail to progress 115

static: going nowhere 139

status quo: the existing state 231

stigma: a sign of shame 90

stock: a framework with holes for securing an offender's ankles or wrists in order to expose him or her to public derision 284

stratosphere: the upper atmosphere 238

strident: grating 68

subjective: personal 152

subservient: subordinate 251

subsidiary: subordinate or secondary 327

subterfuges: strategies to conceal something 176

subversive: disorderly 131

suffragettes: women who advocated extending the right to vote to all women 24

suffused: pervaded (by) 337

sullen: dismal; gloomy 27

surveillance: systematic vigilance 349

tableaux: pictures or representations of a scene 76

tableaux vivants: photographs in which people are in costume as if they are acting 83

tacit: unspoken 310

tacitly: in a manner that is not spoken but implied 5

tangible: real; concrete 117

tantalizing: provoking interest or desire but remaining out of reach 348

technocratic: pertaining to a reordering of society based on the findings of engineers and technologists 231

tedious: tiresome or boring 67

telegraphic: in the staccato, abbreviated form of a telegram 349

tenacious: persistent 154

tenacity: persistence 345

tendentious: promoting a particular point of view 333

tentative: not worked out; provisional 12, 62

tenuously: weakly 341

tenure: the status of permanence in an academic position 294

Teutonic: Germanic 316

thither: away; from 121

thraldom: bondage 117

totalitarianism: a form of government in which most aspects of life are controlled by the central dictatorial power 255

totemic: full of symbolic significance 174

transcend: to go beyond 347

transgressions: violations 197

treatise: systematic account in writing 138

trifles: items of little value 23

trig: extremely precise 38

turgidities: excessive complexities 276

tutelage: instruction 173

ubiquitous: widespread 108

ubiquitously: in an omnipresent way 6

unabashed: not embarrassed 73

unassailable: undeniable 6

uncouth: crude 191

undermined: seriously weakened by removing underlying support 203

unencumbered: unburdened 78

unfathomable: deeply puzzling; incomprehensible 121

unfilial: disloyal to one's parent 275

unimpaired: not worsened or weakened 168

univocal: unambiguous 68

unobtrusively: in a nonaggressive way 14

unpretentious: modest 161

untenable: undefendable 20

utilitarian: taking as the standard of morality the promotion of the greatest happiness for the greatest number of people 207

vacuous: empty 37

vanquished: overcome; defeated 165

vapid: flat; dull 191

variegations: diversifications 5

verboten: forbidden 180

vestibule: a small passage, hall, or room within a building 61

vestiges: remainders or surviving evidences of some condition or practice 330

vicariously: only through other people's viewpoints 196

vicissitudes: ups and downs 286, 326

vigilant: alert; watchful 116

vignettes: scenes 197

vivify: animate 153

voicings: fine tunings 348

volition: conscious choices 324

voracious: insatiable or huge 75

votaries: devoted admirers 72

voyeur: one who derives sexual gratification by secretly observing sexual acts 341

voyeurism: sexual gratification from visual experience 75

vulnerable: susceptible to being weakened or hurt 196

wantonly: unjustifiably or maliciously 160

warily: with extreme caution 257

well-ascertained: determined with certainty 326

whimsicality: unpredictable playfulness 34

wistfully: with yearning desire 48

wrenching: forceful pulling away 345

xenophobia: an irrational fear of strangers or foreigners 255